After The New Testament

After The
New Testament

A Reader In Early Christianity

Bart D. Ehrman

New York   Oxford
Oxford University Press
1999

Oxford University Press

Oxford New York
Athens Auckland Bangkok Bogotá Buenos Aires Calcutta
Cape Town Chennai Dar es Salaam Delhi Florence Hong Kong Istanbul
Karachi Kuala Lumpur Madrid Melbourne Mexico City Mumbai
Nairobi Paris São Paulo Singapore Taipei Tokyo Toronto Warsaw

and associated companies in
Berlin Ibadan

Published by Oxford University Press, Inc.
198 Madison Avenue, New York, New York 10016

Oxford is a registered trademark of Oxford University Press

Library of Congress Cataloging-in-Publication Data

Ehrman, Bart D.
     After the New Testament : a reader in early Christianity / Bart D.
  Ehrman.
          p.   cm.
     Includes bibliographical references.
     ISBN 0–19–512483–9 (alk. paper). — ISBN 0–19–511445–0 (pbk. :
  alk. paper)
     1. Christian literature. Early.   I. Title.
BR63. E37   1998   97–47660
270. 1—dc21   CIP

20 19 18 17 16 15 14 13 12 11 10
Printed in the United States of America
on acid-free paper.

To Mom

Contents

><->-0-<->-<

Preface   xi

1 **General Introduction**   1

2 **The Spread of Christianity: Early Christians and their Converts**   7

  1. The Acts of John   10
  2. The Acts of Thomas   13
  3. Justin: Dialogue with Trypho   18

3 **The Attack on Christianity: Persecution and Martyrdom in the Early Church**   25

  4. The Letter of Ignatius to the Romans   28
  5. The Martyrdom of Polycarp   30
  6. The Letter of the Churches of Vienne and Lyons   35
  7. The Acts of the Scillitan Martyrs   41
  8. The Martyrdom of Perpetua and Felicitas   42

4 **The Defense of Christianity: The Early Christian Apologists**   51

  9. Minucius Felix: Octavius   54
 10. Justin: First Apology   57
 11. Athenagoras: Plea Regarding the Christians   65
 12. The Letter to Diognetus   71
 13. Tertullian: Apology   75
 14. Origen: Against Celsus   82

5 **Anti-Judaic Polemic: The Opposition to Jews in Early Christianity**   95

 15. The Epistle of Barnabas   98

16. Justin: Dialogue with Trypho   106
17. Melito of Sardis: On the Passover   115
18. Tertullian: Answer to the Jews   129

6 The Diversity of Early Christianity: Writings Later Deemed Heretical   131

Jewish-Christian Texts
19. The Gospel According to the Ebionites   134
20. The Letter of Peter to James and Its Reception   136
21. The Homilies of Clement   139

Gnostic-Christian Texts
22. The Secret Book of John   146
23. The First Thought in Three Forms   154
24. The Gospel of Truth   160
25. Ptolemy's Letter to Flora   165
26. On the Origin of the World   170
27. The Wisdom of Jesus Christ   177
28. The Treatise on the Resurrection   182
29. The Hymn of the Pearl   185
30. The Gospel of Philip   187

7 The Internal Conflicts of Christianity: Writings Against the "Heretics"   193

Proto-Orthodox Heresiologists
31. Irenaeus: Against the Heresies   196
32. Tertullian: Prescription of the Heretics   211
33. Tertullian: On the Flesh of Christ   218
34. Tertullian: Against Praxeas   224

Gnostic Heresiologists
35. The Coptic Apocalypse of Peter   227
36. The Second Treatise of the Great Seth   230

8 "Apostolic" Writings Outside the Canon: New Testament Apocrypha/Pseudepigrapha   235

Apocryphal Gospels
37. The Gospel of Thomas   237
38. The Gospel of Peter   244
39. The Proto-Gospel of James   247
40. The Infancy Gospel of Thomas   255
41. The Epistle of the Apostles   259

Apocryphal Acts
42. The Acts of Peter   263
43. The Acts of Paul   275
44. The Acts of Thecla   278
45. The Acts of John   284

Apocryphal Epistles
46. Paul's Third Letter to the Corinthians   290
47. The Correspondence Between Paul and Seneca   292
48. Paul's Letter to the Laodiceans   295

Apocryphal Apocalypses
49. The Apocalypse of Peter   296
50. The Apocalypse of Paul   301

9 The New Scriptures: Canonical Lists in Early Christianity   309

51. The Muratorian Canon   311
52. Irenaeus: Against the Heresies   313
53. Origen of Alexandria   314
54. Eusebius: Ecclesiastical History   315

10 The Structure of Early Christianity: The Development of Church Offices   317

55. First Clement   320
56. The Didache   323
57. The Letters of Ignatius to the Ephesians, Magnesians, and Smyrneans   325
58. Hippolytus: The Apostolic Tradition   328
59. The Didascalia   333
60. Cyprian: On the Unity of the Catholic Church   340

11 The Development of the Liturgy: Ritual Practices in Early Christianity   343

61. The Didache   346
62. Justin: First Apology   347
63. Tertullian: Apology   349
64. Tertullian: On the Crown   352
65. Hippolytus: The Apostolic Tradition   353
66. The Didascalia   356

12 The Proclamation of the Word: Homilies in Early Christianity   361

67. Second Clement   363
68. Origen: Homilies on Luke   369
69. Origen: Homilies on Genesis   375

13 Leading the Upright Life: The Role of Ethics in Early Christianity   383

70. The Didache   385
71. Clement of Alexandria: The Educator   387
72. Tertullian: To His Wife   399

14 The Emergence of Orthodoxy: Theological Writings of Proto-Orthodox Christians   405

73. Tertullian: Against Praxeas   408
74. Origen: On First Principles   413
75. Novatian: On the Trinity   430
76. Dionysius of Rome: Letter to Dionysius of Alexandria   435

Preface
>-+•>••O-•<•+-<

The impetus for this collection of texts arose from my classroom experience. One of the courses I regularly teach, "The Birth of Christianity," deals with developments within the Christian church during the second and third centuries, from, roughly, the period immediately after the New Testament up to, but not including, the writings of the church historian Eusebius. There is no satisfactory sourcebook for this period. The present collection of texts, whose scope and rationale are given in the Introduction, is intended to fill the void. It is meant not only for classroom use but also for anyone curious about the early development of the Christian religion, whether professionals, students, or other generally interesting people.

All of the texts are already available in suitable, if not easily accessible, translations; rather than reinvent wheels by providing yet another English version to clutter the market, here I've simply used translations that are, in my judgment, the most readable and current, with full permission. I have tried to standardize these texts in minor ways to make them cohere better with one another, with occasional modifications involving such matters as capitalization, spelling, punctuation, and (sporadic) modernizations of language (I have changed "thee"s and "thou"s, for example, and altered, wherever easily possible without modifying the sense of the text, the most conspicuous instances of unnecessarily noninclusive language).

My goal throughout has been to provide the reader with access to these intriguing and important ancient texts; it has not been my goal to explain or comment upon them. I have, however, provided a general introduction the collection, brief introductions to each selection (explaining its historical context and overarching theme), and cross-references to explicit references to other literature (mainly the Bible).

First among those whom I would like to acknowledge for this work are my undergraduate classes at the University of North Carolina at Chapel Hill; there are some very bright students in this world, and I seem to get a lot of them. I am particularly appreciative of the work of some very able-bodied graduate students in the Department of Religious Studies at UNC, Scott McGinnis, Frank Judd, and Stephanie Cobb, all of whom proved faithful, reliable, and willing to assume for a time the headache of another.

Above all, I would like to thank three colleagues and friends who have read through my introductions and made useful comments about them: Elizabeth Clark at Duke, Derek Krueger at UNC-Greensboro, and Jeff Siker at Loyola Marymount. If every author could have such readers, this would be a very happy planet.

I have dedicated this collection to my mom, my first and best teacher, who taught me to love the early Christian tradition.

Chapter 1

General Introduction

Over the past century and a half, archaeological discoveries have played a significant role in our understanding of early Christianity. These include (a) the serendipitous discovery of entire libraries of ancient texts, such as the Dead Sea Scrolls, found in the wilderness of Judea, and the library of Gnostic writings uncovered near Nag Hammadi, Egypt; (b) the equally fortuitous unearthing of individual documents, such as a noncanonical Gospel and an Apocalypse, both attributed to the apostle Peter, and of an early church manual called the Didache ("found," actually, in a monastic library); and (c) the uncovery and excavation of buried sites, such as Dura Europas in Syria on the Euphrates, a city that housed the earliest surviving structure known to have served as a Christian church. These findings have enriched our understanding of early Christianity, but, more than that, they have forced scholars to reconceptualize major aspects of the religion, leading to what is perhaps the most significant "discovery" of them all, made not in the sands of Egypt or the dirt of Mesopotamia but in the private libraries of historians—the discovery that Christianity during the first three centuries of the Common Era was remarkably diverse.

Most of our evidence for these early years of Christianity consists of literary texts produced by the Christians themselves. The surviving literature is by no means complete, or even completely representative, even with our newly discovered texts; it is nonetheless a rich testimony to the social history of early Christianity, and to the wide-ranging concerns, values, beliefs, and practices of its adherents. But readers who are interested in earliest Christianity are, as a rule, poorly informed concerning this literature; as a result, very few people, outside the ranks of the professional scholar, realize the diverse character of the religion in its earliest period. Even among church people, it is scarcely realized that early Christians engaged in heated and often acrimonious debates over fundamental issues, such as whether there was one God or two (or twelve or 365), whether the Jews were the chosen people of God or the evil children of the Devil, whether women could serve as ministers of the church or were to remain silent and subservient to men, whether a Christian should seek to be martyred for the faith or avoid persecution at all costs, whether the Scriptures included the Gospels allegedly written by Matthew and John or those by Mary Magdalene and Jesus' own twin brother, Thomas. Each of these positions—and many others on many other issues—had strong and vocal advocates among the Christian faithful of the second and third centuries.

The present book is concerned with such issues and others like them; its purpose is to make the primary materials that are relevant for discussing them more widely available to the general reader.

Probably the one ancient book that most students of the period are already familiar with, or at least have heard of, is the famous *Ecclesiastical History* of Eusebius, commonly known as the "Father of Church History." Eusebius was the first Christian author to provide a full sketch of the history of the church, from the days of Jesus down to his own time (his first edition was published in 311 C.E.). Scholars of early Christianity have naturally turned to this volume for their information. And quite valuable information it is, too, for Eusebius not only narrates what happened over the course of the first three Christian centuries, he also cites primary texts written in the period, many of which no longer survive. But Eusebius cannot be blindly trusted to provide a disinterested account of earliest Christianity, as many researchers now realize. For he, like everyone else, had his own particular slant, his own beliefs and perspectives that affected his retelling of the early days of Christianity, determining both how he told the story and which sources he decided to cite.

In Eusebius's view, Jesus taught his disciples the truth about God and the world, and they passed these views along, after his death, to their own followers. From the outset, Christianity grew by miraculous leaps and bounds, as God's hand guided and directed the mission to nonbelievers. Any setbacks that the Christians experienced at the hands of their opponents—for example, persecutions and martyrdoms—were turned to the good, leading to further growth and strength. Moreover, according to Eusebius, the Christian communities enjoyed internal peace and unity. There were, to be sure, false teachers who occasionally disrupted the tranquility of the church, "heretics" inspired by the Devil to pervert the truth of God, but these stood merely on the margins of the Great Church and were easily overpowered by the truth affirmed by the genuine followers of Christ, the representatives of Christian "orthodoxy" (literally: right doctrine or correct belief). For Eusebius, the vast majority of believers have always subscribed to the orthodox views promulgated by Jesus' disciples, passed along through the powerful bishops of the major churches throughout the known world and embodied in the Christian scriptures, books penned by the apostles themselves. These "orthodox" views, needless to say, were the ones that Eusebius himself happened to embrace.

Historians are no longer able to accept Eusebius's account uncritically. For a careful analysis of his text, along with other documents that survive from the period, shows that Christianity before his time was in fact widely diverse and that many of the issues that he discusses could be, and were, understood differently by other Christians of the time. Whether or not this scholarly opinion is right, it should at least be clear that for those who want to understand the history of the early Christian church, restricting oneself to Eusebius's *Ecclesiastical History* is not the best way to proceed. It is far better, and now more widely possible, to supplement Eusebius's accounts with the primary texts.

That is where the present collection can serve a useful purpose. For in it is presented a broad range of primary texts from the early years of Christianity, roughly between the last book of the "New Testament" (say, 100 or 120 C.E.) and the time Eusebius began writing his church history. For the sake of convenience, we may speak of the second and third Christian centuries, 100–300 C.E. My objective in making the collection has been to provide readers with as full a set of texts as possible, within the restrictions naturally imposed by a work of a single volume.

Other collections of Christian texts already exist, of course, and here I should say a word about how this one is distinct. Among the other anthologies, some present scattered quotations from the writings of early authors like Irenaeus, Tertullian, and Origen,

arranged according to the categories of systematic theology (i.e., brief quotations that illustrate "the" early Christian views of God, Christ, the Holy Spirit, the church); others
are fuller assemblages of proto-orthodox authors artificially grouped together, such as
those labeled the "apostolic fathers" or simply the "early Church fathers" (by which are
meant, again, the early "orthodox" fathers—that is, those who stand within the tradition
embraced by Eusebius); and yet others are translations of important "heterodox" works,
such as those of the Gnostics (e.g., the "Nag Hammadi Library") or of documents forged
in the name of the apostles, collectively known as the New Testament Apocrypha. Each
of these collections is important and valuable in its own right. But none is like the one
presented here, which attempts to provide as broad a spectrum as possible of the surviving early Christian texts, dealing with a range of significant issues, such as the conversion of nonbelievers, persecution and martyrdom, apologetics, antagonism towards Jews
and "heretics," the development of church offices, liturgical practices, ethics, and beliefs.

Moreover, rather than presenting little snippets of texts, I have decided to provide
large chunks—complete texts when possible, lengthy excerpts when not. Readers can thus
get a feel for the literary quality of these works, rather than settle for brief extracts designed to illustrate a simple point. It did not make sense to organize these texts according to the categories of systematic theology, since many of them are unrelated to such
matters. Nor could I give them in simple chronological sequence, since many of them
cannot be dated with any degree of confidence, except to say that they certainly, or very
probably, fall within the chronological parameters I have envisaged. It seemed best, then,
to group these texts according to the topics that they themselves address and to arrange
these topical rubrics in accordance with how one might want to think through various aspects of early Christianity—for example, in a college or seminary level course devoted
to the subject.

It might be useful, then, by way of introduction, to say a word about the nature of
these rubrics and the logic of their sequencing. This need not entail a lengthy discussion.
Each chapter begins with a sketch of the important historical aspects of the topic, and
each individual text is introduced with brief comments concerning its historical context
and significance.

One of the first things to consider about early Christianity is how it spread so far and
wide in its early years. Starting out as a Jewish sect—a handful of followers of Jesus of
Nazareth located in the Jewish homeland of Judea—it somehow managed to convert
masses of people so that in less than three centuries it numbered some three million adherents. But how did this happen? What did the Christians say, and how did they make
their message convincing, especially to audiences that were overwhelmingly non-Jewish,
that is, who were Gentiles following the various polytheistic religions scattered throughout the empire? No complete answers can be found in our surviving texts, but it may at
least be worth seeing what Christians themselves said about their message and the reasons for its success. Several texts that narrate conversions to Christianity—representative
of the few such texts that survive—are given in Chapter 2.

Most non-Christians, of course, completely rejected the Christian message; many
scorned it as ludicrous, and some found it to be socially and religiously dangerous. As a
result, from the earliest of times Christianity met hostile opposition, sometimes resulting
in mob violence or official actions ending in martyrdom. We have numerous accounts of
the social and political antipathy expressed towards Christians from the pens of second-
and third-century Christians themselves, including several firsthand reports of actual le-

gal proceedings and executions. Several such accounts of persecutions and martyrdoms, some of them graphic in their detail, are given in Chapter 3.

In the face of widespread opposition, Christians had a natural tendency to defend themselves against public calumny and/or official charges of wrongdoing. These defenses became a literary artform in the hands of some of the more highly educated Christians who converted to the religion beginning in the middle of the second century, authors who produced literary defenses or "apologies" for the faith, arguing that Christians were completely innocent of all slanders and charges against them and that their faith was in fact morally and theologically superior to every other religion. Selections from some of the most important and best known Greek and Latin apologists, including Justin Martyr, Tertullian, and Origen, are provided in Chapter 4.

Early Christians had to defend themselves not only against angry mobs and powerful state officials but also against Jews who found Christian claims objectionable or even ludicrous—especially the claims that Jesus, a crucified criminal, was the messiah and that his Gentile believers, who did not follow the Jewish Law, were the true people of the God of Israel. The Christian response to this kind of rejection turned aggressive, as Christians claimed for themselves the Scriptures and traditions of the Jews, insisting that the Jewish God had in fact rejected the people of Israel to bestow his favor upon the Christians. Some of the harsh polemic against the Jews and their religion can be found in the anti-Judaic texts excerpted in Chapter 5.

Early Christians were engaged in polemics not only against those on the outside, Gentile and Jewish nonbelievers, but also within, among believers in Christ who took radically different views on matters of practical and theological importance. Fundamental issues were at stake, including such matters as the nature of God (is there only one?), the person of Christ (is he human? divine? both?), the status of the Jewish Scriptures (are they inspired by the true God? by a malevolent deity?), the world (is it good, created by God? evil, created by cruel demons?), and just about everything else. Few writings have survived from Christians who took views *other* than the ones that came to dominate Christianity by the time of Eusebius, although, in the second and third centuries, the questions were harshly debated and the answers were not at all obvious. But some alternative views have turned up, especially from Christians who remained true to their Jewish heritage and from those who accepted forms of Christian Gnosticism (e.g., the writings from the Nag Hammadi library). A range of texts from such groups is introduced and presented in Chapter 6.

Given the importance early Christians ascribed to what a person believes (a unique aspect of the religion, oddly enough, in the ancient world), it is no surprise that the "heterodox" groups whose writings are excerpted in Chapter 6 came under attack by Christians who took opposing points of view. What is somewhat more surprising, perhaps, is that even Christians who embraced "proto-orthodox" positions—that is, the views that eventually came to be dominant, as embodied in such fourth-century productions as the Apostles' and the Nicene Creeds—were condemned by their opponents (e.g., some of the Gnostics) for propagating false religion. Chapter 7 presents selections from two of the most famous proto-orthodox heresiologists (= describers of heresy) of the second and early third centuries, Irenaeus and Tertullian, along with two gnostic treatises, including a book allegedly written by the apostle Peter, that attack views later declared to be orthodox.

Christians of every theological persuasion appear to have supported their views by appealing to books that claimed to be written by Jesus' own apostles. The second and third centuries saw a host of Christian documents forged to provide just such support—as well as other forgeries meant, evidently, simply to exhort or entertain their audiences. Many of these "pseudepigrapha" (= "writings under a false name") were at one time or another accepted as Scripture by various Christian groups. Not surprisingly, they represent the same genres of writing attested in the books that eventually came to be called the New Testament (i.e., Gospels, Acts, Epistles, and Apocalypses)—books that were also allegedly written by Jesus' apostles, even though modern scholars have sometimes called even *their* traditional ascriptions into question. Chapter 8 presents a range of early non-canonical Pseudepigrapha, some of them "orthodox," that have come down to us today.

Given the wide dissemination of forgeries in the names of the apostles, different groups eventually had to decide which "apostolic" books were to be ascribed authority and which were not. The New Testament as we have it today comprises twenty-seven books that were collected and deemed Scripture by the group that won the early struggles for theological dominance. Other groups had other sets of books; even within proto-orthodox circles, there was no complete agreement as to which books should be included and which rejected. This much can be seen from the various "canon" lists that survive from second- and third-century authors, Christians living many years before any final decisions were reached (the first "canon list" that gives exactly our own set of twenty-seven books was written in 367 C.E.–nearly 300 years after most of the books of the NT were actually written!). The most important surviving lists are presented in Chapter 9.

Just as the canon of Scripture came to be discussed and, eventually, settled in order to help define and shape the nature of "orthodox" Christianity, so too there was a movement to solidify and structure the organization of the church, in part to prevent "heretics" from acquiring any kind of foothold within it. Early in the second century, there were calls for a rigid church structure that could bring order out of chaos in the early Christian communities and so guarantee the preservation and perpetuation of the true religion. By the middle of the third century, the leaders of the Christian church could exercise considerable power over their congregations. Developments throughout the period in the matter of church government can be seen in the range of texts provided in Chapter 10.

From the earliest of times, Christians gathered in communities to worship the true God who had called the followers of Jesus to be his people. Already in the first century, important liturgical practices had developed throughout the Christian church, with two in particular holding a special prominence, the ritual of baptism for converts (an initiatory rite) and the periodic celebration of the eucharist for those already among the elect (a sacred meal commemorating Jesus' death). Both aspects of Christian liturgy developed dramatically over the second and third centuries, as can be seen in the descriptions of the services of worship and ritual given by the Christians themselves, excerpted in the selections found in Chapter 11.

A central feature of the early Christian services of worship involved the public exposition of Scripture, one of the chief methods of exhortation and teaching throughout this period. Some early preachers produced written copies of their homilies for a broader audience. Few of these sermons happen now to survive, but those that do can show how various Christian leaders approached their texts of Scripture and used them to guide their congregations in how to live and what to believe. Several representative examples from the second and third centuries are presented in Chapter 12.

Christian leaders exhorted their fellow believers to ethical behavior not only in their homilies but also in literary tractates explicitly devoted to the purpose. This constitutes another distinctive aspect of the religion in its Greco-Roman milieu: although personal ethical behavior, as a rule, was as important to people then as it is now, ethics did not normally play any part in sacred cult; it was instead a matter of social norm and expectation (and of philosophy, for the more highly educated). Christians, however, like Jews before them, tied ethical behavior to religious belief and practice, and so Christian leaders became particularly assiduous in demanding that their readers (or bearers) behave in certain ways, as is seen in the selection of moral tractates included in Chapter 13.

Finally, while Christian doctrines did not encompass the *entire* concern of the early Christians—even though some historians of Christianity continue to think so, portraying Christianity as an intellectual rather than a social movement—theology *was*, nonetheless, a matter of particular importance for Christians, especially those who have left us the texts. Proto-orthodox Christians insisted that the content of what one *believes* matters for one's standing before God. As a result, early Christian intellectuals felt compelled to work out the correct system of Christian doctrine. This doctrinal emphasis can be seen in a number of the selections throughout this volume, but it is the sole concern of the final chapter. Here are presented some of the more sophisticated attempts at theological reflection among Christian scholars who became important forerunners for the doctrinal positions that later came to define fourth-century orthodoxy.

Many more selections of Christian texts from the second and third centuries could have been provided in this collection, and much more could have been said about each one of them. Some scholars would no doubt substitute other texts for the ones I have chosen to include; others would construe the background or significance of this or that text in a different way or provide an entirely different understanding of the early Christian movement. But choices have had to be made, and I have tried to make them judiciously. For all of the chapters, in addition to the introductory remarks, a brief bibliography has been included to guide the reader to further discussions.

In any event, the best way to become familiar with the history of early Christianity is not simply to read *about* it in the works of modern-day scholars but to become immersed in the primary sources themselves. The present collection should, at the very least, provide a useful entree into this venture for anyone choosing to undertake it.

For Further Reading: General
Overviews of Early Christianity
and Basic Reference Works

Chadwick, Henry. *The Early Church.* New York: Penguin, 1967.

Ferguson, Everett, ed. *The Encyclopedia of Early Christianity.* 2nd ed. New York: Garland, 1997.

Frend, W. H. C. *The Rise of Christianity.* Philadelphia: Fortress, 1984.

Livingstone, E. A. and F. L. Cross (eds.) *The Oxford Dictionary of the Christian Church.* 3rd ed. Oxford: Oxford University Press, 1997.

Chapter 2

The Spread of Christianity

Early Christians and Their Converts

Christianity started out as a small band of Jews who had followed Jesus during his ministry and remained faithful to him after his death. According to New Testament sources, the original group consisted of the eleven disciples (after Judas had killed himself), a handful of women, and several other men, all of whom had evidently accompanied Jesus from Galilee to Jerusalem the last week of his life (Acts 1). Having become convinced of Jesus' resurrection, these earliest believers immediately set out to persuade others that Jesus was the Jewish messiah sent from God to die for the sins of others.

Their success was limited at first, especially among their Jewish compatriots. But with the conversion of one of their earliest opponents, Paul, the mission was taken beyond the world of Judaism; Gentiles, who as participants in various so-called "pagan" religions were polytheists rather than followers of the God of Israel, became the chief target of evangelism. The church soon spread throughout much of the Roman empire, with major urban areas the chief foci of the mission.

By the end of the third century, the new religion had become numerically significant. Most experts think that the Roman empire comprised some sixty million persons at this time, nearly 5 percent of them Christian. Soon thereafter, due largely to the conversion of the emperor Constantine in the early part of the fourth century, their numbers rose dramatically; by the end of the century, nearly half the empire called itself Christian.

A range of questions could be asked about the early spread of Christianity. Prior to the conversion mania of the fourth century, what led to the Christians' success? How did a small band of illiterate, lower-class, Jewish peasants transform themselves into a significant world religion, claiming some three million adherents, in less than three centuries? What did Christians tell potential converts to convince them to abandon their worship of the gods and to believe in the one God of Israel and in his Son Jesus, to abandon the socially acceptable and often joyous and festive cultic practices of their families and friends to join a relatively secretive, frequently maligned, and sometimes persecuted group?

Unfortunately, the paucity of our sources restricts what we can know about such things. To be sure, modern scholars who examine these problems have developed some interesting and compelling theories, especially through cross-cultural studies of modern religious movements that accumulate converts through their cultivation of close personal contacts with outsiders. (The Mormons, for example, have grown at a comparable rate to the early Christians, about 40 percent each decade; see Stark). The ancient Christians who tell the stories of conversations, however, were obviously not trained sociologists. They ascribe the success of the mission, ultimately, to the miraculous working of God.

Our earliest source is the apostle Paul, who informed his Gentile listeners that their idols were dead and lifeless and that there was only one true and living God, whose Son had died and been raised and was soon to return from heaven in judgment (1 Thess 1:9–10). It is difficult to say why some of his hearers found this message persuasive, but Paul intimates that it may have been because of the "powerful deeds" (miracles?) that he accomplished in their midst as corroborating proof (2 Cor 12:12). Much clearer on this matter is the book of Acts, which actually narrates the miraculous deeds (and their later retellings) that provided all the evidence people needed (e.g., Acts 2–3).

Accounts of conversions from the second and third centuries continue to emphasize the miraculous. Very few descriptions of large-scale conversions have survived from antiquity, but those that do stress the importance of such spectacular events as the supernatural destruction of idol temples and miraculous public healings, exorcisms, and resuscitations.

Other factors appear to have played a role as well. Christians, for example, were highly distinctive in claiming to have an exclusive right to the "truth." Other religions of antiquity were widely tolerant of one another, with none of them claiming that it alone was "right" and that the others, therefore, were "wrong." That is to say, as polytheistic religions, Greco-Roman cults recognized each other's validity: all the gods deserved to be worshipped, and so a person could (and should) participate in a variety of cultic practices. Christians, however, maintained that there was only one true God, that this God was the only one to be worshipped, and that this true worship could come only through God's son, Jesus. Anyone who rejected this true religion would pay the penalty, if not in this life, then in the next. Those who converted to Christianity, therefore, necessarily gave up their pagan ways; as a result, unlike followers of other religions of the empire (which did not insist on exclusive devotion), Christians automatically destroyed other religions while promoting their own (see Macmullen).

This exclusivity in early Christianity helps explain the willingness of some Christians to suffer persecution and even martyrdom for their faith (see Chapter 3). Christians who wrote about these martyrdoms claimed that in them, God's miraculous hand was again at work, that the supernatural courage Christians displayed in the face of torment and death convinced numerous bystanders of the supreme power of the Christian God. Possibly this is what Tertullian meant when he claimed that the persecution of Christians, rather than devastating their spirit, only swelled their ranks, "the blood of martyrs is seed" (*Apol.* 50).

Moreover, the Christian accounts of martyrdoms (see Chapter 3) invariably stress that God's miraculous power extends beyond this life to the life to come. Martyrs are said to be eager to endure the torments of an hour in exchange for the bliss of eternity. Possibly this was a factor in conversion as well, as Christians proclaimed the rewards of those who worshipped their God but the eternal torments of those who resisted.

Eventually, highly educated persons such as Justin in Rome and Tertullian in Carthage came to be converted to the faith. These literary persons—from whom a good deal of our evidence survives—tended to emphasize the more intellectual aspects of the religion as positive forces of conversion, including the philosophical superiority of Christian views and the convincing evidence of its truth claims in Jesus' own fulfillment of ancient prophecies from the Hebrew Scriptures. It is difficult to know, though, how far these more cerebral aspects of the religion played a role in the conversions of the thousands and thousands of persons who joined the religion in the second and third centuries.

The following texts provide a cross-sample of ancient narrations of conversion to Christianity, as understood and presented, of course, by Christians themselves.

For Further Reading

Dodds, E. R. *Pagan and Christian in an Age of Anxiety: Some Aspects of Religious Experience from Marcus Aurelius to Constantine*. New York: Norton, 1965.

Lane Fox, Robin. *Pagans and Christians*. New York: Knopf, 1987.

Macmullen, Ramsey. *Christianizing the Roman Empire* A.D. 100–400. New Haven, Conn.: Yale University Press, 1984.

Stark, Rodney. *The Rise of Christianity*. Princeton: Princeton University Press, 1996.

von Harnack, Adolph. *The Mission and Expansion of Early Christianity*, tr. J. Moffat, 2 vols. New York: Putnam, 1908.

THE TEXTS

For a related text, see Hippolytus, "The Apostolic Tradition" in Chapter 11.

1. The Acts of John

The "Acts of John" is one of the Apocryphal Acts (see Chapter 8), early legendary accounts of the exploits of Jesus' disciples after his death. Throughout these narratives, the apostles do miraculous deeds that convince the crowds of the superior power of their God, leading then, to massive conversions. In the first excerpt that follows, John is said to heal a paralyzed woman named Cleopatra, leading the entire city of Ephesus to marvel; in the second, he engages in a kind of battle of the gods, overthrowing the pagan idols in Ephesus, killing their priest, and destroying their temple—all by a word of prayer. The crowds who are present are completely convinced and terrified; they convert to worship the God John proclaims and to beg his forgiveness. Such entertaining narratives may not present "history as it actually happened," but they do indicate how Christians from the period *understood* the process of conversion to belief in the God of Jesus.

The Acts of John is preserved only in fragmentary manuscripts and probably dates to the late second century. Additional excerpts can be found in Chapter 8.

19 When we came near the city Lycomedes, the commander-in-chief of the Ephesians, a wealthy man, met us, fell down before John and asked him for help, with these words, "Your name is John; the God whom you preach has sent you to help my wife, who has been paralyzed for seven days and lies past recovery. But glorify your God and treat her out of compassion for us. Whilst I was reflecting what to do, a man came to me and said, 'Desist, Lycomedes, from the evil thought which militates against you. Do not submit. For out of compassion for my servant Cleopatra I have sent you a man from Miletus, named John, who will comfort her and restore her to you cured.' Delay not, therefore, servant of the God who announced you to me, but hasten to the ailing woman." And John went at once from the gate with the brethren who were with him, and followed Lycomedes into his house. And Cleobius said to his servants, "Go to my relative Callippus and make yourselves comfortable in his house—for I am coming there with his son—that we may find everything prepared!"

20 When Lycomedes and John had come into the house in which the woman was lying, he grasped his feet again, and said, "See, Lord, the lost beauty, see the youth, see the much talked of bloom of my unhappy wife, the admiration of all Ephesus! Woe to me, unhappy man! I was envied, humbled, the enemy's eye was fixed on me. I never wronged anyone, although I could harm many. I envisaged this situation and I was always anxious to experience no sorrow or anything like it! Of what use is my care now, Cleopatra? What good

---

was it to me, that I was called godly to this day? I suffer more than a heathen, seeing you, Cleopatra, suffering so. The sun in his circuit shall not see me, if you are no more with me. Cleopatra, I will die before you. I will not spare my life though I am still youthful. I will justify myself before the goddess of right, whom I served in righteousness, though I might indict her for her unrighteous sentence. I will avenge myself on her by coming as a shade. I will say to her, 'You have forced me to leave the light of life, because you tore away Cleopatra. You are the cause of my death, by having prepared for me this fate. You have forced me to blaspheme Providence by destroying my joy.' "

21 And Lycomedes spoke more to Cleopatra, went to her couch, and cried bitterly. But John drew him away and said, "Abandon these tears and unbecoming words! It is not proper for you, who saw the vision, to be disbelieving. Know that your partner for life will be restored to you. Therefore join us, who have come for her sake, and pray to the God whom you saw, when he showed me to you in a vision! What is the matter, Lycomedes? Wake up and open also your soul! Cast from you heavy sleep! Call on the Lord, beseech him for your wife, and he will support her." But he fell to the ground and wept dejectedly. And John said with tears, "Woe to the treachery of the vision, woe to the new temptation prepared for me, woe to the new craft of him who devises cunnings against me! Did the voice from heaven, which came to be the way, intend this for me, predicting to me what should here take place? Will it deliver me up to such a great multitude of citizens, for the sake of Lycomedes? The man lies here lifeless, and I know that I shall not leave this house alive. Why do you delay, Lord? Why have you deprived us of your gracious promise? I beseech you, Lord, let him not rejoice who delights in the sorrow of others. Let him not dance who always laughs at us! But let your holy name and your compassion come quickly! Waken the bodies of the two, who are against me!"

22 While John was crying, the city of Ephesus ran to the house of Lycomedes, supposing him dead. And when John saw the great multitude, he prayed to the Lord, "Now the time of re-freshing and confidence has come with you, O Christ; now is the time for us weary ones to have help from you, physician, who heal freely. Keep my entrance here free from derision! I beseech you, Jesus, help such a great multitude to come to the Lord of the universe. Behold the affliction, behold those who lie here! Even those who came here, make holy instruments for your service, after they have seen your gift. For you have said yourself, O Christ, 'Ask and it shall be given you.'[1] We therefore beseech you, O King, not for gold, not for silver, not for riches, not for possession, nor for any transient, earthly goods, but for two souls through whom you will convert those present to your way, to your knowledge, to your confidence, and to your infallible promise. For many of them shall be saved, after they have known your power through the resurrection of the departed. Give us, therefore, hope in you! I will go to Cleopatra and say, 'Arise, in the name of Jesus Christ.' "

23 And he went, touched her face, and said, "Cleopatra, he whom every ruler fears, and every creature, power, abyss, and darkness and unsmiling death and the heights of heaven and the caverns of the lower world and the resurrection of the dead and the sight of the blind and the whole power of the ruler of the world, and the pride of its prince, says, 'Rise and become not a pretext for many who will not believe, and an affliction for souls who hope and could be saved.' " And Cleopatra cried out at once, "I will rise, master, save your handmaiden!" When she had risen after the seven days, the whole city of Ephesus was stirred by the miraculous sight. . . .

38 After two days the birthday of the idol's temple was celebrated. While everybody was dressed in white garments, John wore black and went to the temple. They laid hold of him and tried to kill him. But John said, "Men, you are mad to lay hold of me, the servant of the only God." And climbing on to the platform he spoke to them:

39 "Men of Ephesus, you are in danger of behaving like the sea. Every discharging river and every precipitating spring, downpours

---

[1]Matt 7:7.

and incessant waves and torrents rushing from the rock, are permeated by the bitter salt which is in the sea. Thus to this day you are unchangeably hostile to true piety, and you perish in your old idolatry. How many miraculous deeds did you see me perform, how many cures! And still you are hardened in the heart and cannot see clearly. What now, men of Ephesus? I have ventured now to come up to this idol's temple, to convince you that you are wholly without God and dead to human reasoning. Behold, here I stand. You all assert that Artemis is powerful. Pray to her, that I alone die! Or if you cannot accomplish this, I alone will call upon my God to kill you all because of your unbelief."

40 Since they already knew him and had seen the dead raised, they cried aloud, "Do not treat us so and kill us, we beseech you, John; we know indeed that you can do it." And John answered them, "If you do not wish to die, let me convince you of your idolatry. Any why? So that you may desist from your old error. Be now converted by my God or I will die at the hands of your goddess. For I will pray in your presence to my God, and ask him to have mercy upon you."

41 After these words he prayed, "God, who are God above all so-called gods, who to this day have been despised at Ephesus, you induced me to come to this place, which I never had in view. You have abrogated every form of worship through conversion to you. In your name every idol, every demon, and every unclean spirit is banished. May the deity of this place, which has deceived so many, now also give way to your name, and thus show your mercy on this place! For they walk in error."

42 And with these words of John the altar of Artemis suddenly split into many parts, and the oblations put up in the temple suddenly fell to the ground, and its glory broke, and so did more than seven of the idols. And half of the temple fell down, so that when the roof came down,

the priest also was killed at one stroke. And the people of the Ephesians cried, "There is only one God, that of John, only one God who has compassion for us; for you alone are God; now we have become converted, since we saw your miraculous deeds. Have mercy upon us, God, according to your will, and deliver us from our great error." And some of them lay on their faces and cried; others bent their knees and prayed; others rent their garments and lamented; still others tried to escape.

43 And John stretched out his hands and prayed with uplifted soul to the Lord, "Glory be to you, my Jesus, the only God of truth, who procure your servants in manifold ways!" And after these words he said to the people, "Rise up from the ground, people of Ephesus, pray to my God, and know how his invisible power was made manifest and his miraculous deeds took place before your eyes! Artemis herself should have helped. Her servant should have received help from her and not have died. Where is the power of the deity? Where are the sacrifices? Where the birthday? Where the festivals? Where the garlands? Where the great enchantment and the poison allied to it?"

44 And the people rose up from the ground and made haste to destroy the remainder of the temple, crying, "We know that the God of John is the only one, and henceforth we worship him, since we have obtained mercy from him." And as John came down, many of the people touched him, saying, "Help us, John, help us who die in vain! You see our intention; you see how the multitude following you cleaves to hope in your God. We have seen the way in which we have gone astray when we were lost. We have seen that our gods were erected in vain. We have seen their great and disgraceful derision. But give us, we beseech you, help without hindrance, when we have come to your house! Receive us, who are desperate!"

2. Acts of Thomas

The Acts of Thomas recounts the missionary trip to India made by the apostle Jude (Judas), also called Thomas (Aramaic for "twin"). According to traditions circulated in Syria, Judas Thomas was Jesus' own twin brother. Among the legendary accounts of these Acts are two fascinating episodes that show how belief in the afterlife played a central role in the Christian evangelization of pagans. The first story—the heavenly palace of King Gundaphorus—emphasizes the heavenly rewards for those who renounce pleasure in this life for the sake of doing good to others; the second—a description of the terrors of hell by a woman raised from the dead—stresses the horrific punishments reserved for those who continue in lives of sin. Both the prospect of heavenly reward and the fear of hellish torments are said to lead unbelievers to repent in this life, while there is still time.

The Acts of Thomas was probably written sometime in the early third century.

17 When the apostle came into the cities of India with Abban the merchant, Abban went away to greet King Gundaphorus and told him about the carpenter whom he had brought with him. And the king was glad and ordered him to appear before him. When he had come in the king said to him, "What trade do you know?" The apostle said to him, "That of the carpenter and the housebuilder." The king said to him, "What work in wood do you know and what in stone?" The apostle said, "In wood, plows, yokes, balances, pulleys, and ships and oars and masts; in stone, monuments, temples, and royal palace." And the king said, "Will you build be a palace?" And he answered, "Yes, I shall build it and finish it; for because of this I have come, to build and to do carpenter's work."

18 And the king, having accepted him, took him out of the gates of the city, and on the way began to discuss with him the building of the palace, and how the foundations should be laid, till they came to the place where the work was to be carried out. And he said, "Here is where I wish the building to be!" And the apostle said, "Yes, this place is suitable for the building." For the place was wooded and there was water there. And the king said, "Begin at once!" And he answered, "I cannot commence now." The king said, "When can you?" He said, "I shall begin in November and finish in April." And the king was surprised, and said, "Every building is built in the summer, but can you build and finish a palace in the winter?" And the apostle replied "Thus it must be done; it is impossible any other way." And the king said, "If you have resolved upon this, draw a plan for me how the work is to be done, since I shall come here after some time." And the apostle took a reed, measured the place, and marked it out: the doors to be set towards the rising of the sun, to face the light; the windows toward the west, to the winds; the bakehouse he made toward the south; and the water-pipes necessary for the supply toward the north. When the king saw this, he said to the apostle, "You are truly a craftsman, and it is fitting that you should serve kings." And having left a lot of money with him, he went away.

19 And at the appointed times the king sent coined silver and the necessities for his and the workmen's living. And the apostle took everything and divided it, going about in the cities and surrounding villages, distributing to the poor and needy, and bestowing alms, and gave them relief, saying, "The king knows that he will receive royal recompense, but the poor must be refreshed, as their condition requires it." After this the king sent a messenger to the apostle, having written the following: "Let me know what you have done or what I should send to you or what you need." The apostle sent word to him saying, "The palace is built, and only the roof remains to be done." Upon hearing this the king sent him again gold and uncoined silver and wrote, "If the palace is built, let it be roofed." And the apostle said to the Lord, "I thank you, Lord, in every respect, that you died for a short time, that I may live in you for ever, and that you have sold me, to deliver many through me." And he did not cease to teach and refresh the afflicted, saying, "The Lord has dispensed this to you and he gives to each his food. For he is the support of the orphans and the nourisher of the widows, and rest and repose to all who are afflicted."

20 When the king came to the city he inquired of his friends concerning the palace with Judas, surnamed Thomas, had built for him. And they said to him, "He has neither built a palace, nor did he do anything of that which he promised to do, but he goes about in the cities and villages, and if he has anything he gives it to the poor, and teaches a new God, heals the sick, drives out demons, and performs many miracles. And we believe that he is a magician. But his acts of compassion and the cures done by him as a free gift, still more his simplicity and gentleness and fidelity, show that he is a just man, or an apostle of the new God, whom he preaches. For he continually fasts and prays and eats only bread with salt, and his drink is water, and he wears one coat, whether in warm weather or in cold, and he takes nothing from anyone but gives to others what he has." Upon hearing this the king hit his face with his hands, shaking his head for a long time.

21 And he sent for the merchant who had brought him, and for the apostle, and said to him, "Have you built the palace?" And he said, "Yes, I have built it." The king said, "When shall we go to inspect it?" And he answered and said, "Now you cannot see it, but you shall see it when you depart this life." And the kind was very angry and ordered both the merchant and Judas Thomas to be bound and cast into prison, until he should find out to whom the property of the king had been given, and so destroy him and the merchant. And the apostle went to prison rejoicing and said to the merchant, "Fear nothing, believe only in the God who is preached by me, and you shall be freed from this world, and obtain life in the world to come."

And the king considered by what death he should kill them. He decided to flog them and burn them with fire. On that very night Gad, the king's brother, fell ill; and through the grief and disappointment which the king had suffered he was grievously depressed. And having sent for the king he said to him, "Brother and king, I commend to you my house and my children. For I have been grieved on account of the insult that has befallen you, and lo, I am dying, and if you do not proceed against the life of that magician you will give my soul no rest in Hades." And the king said to his brother, "I considered the whole night by what death I should kill him, and I have decided to flog him and burn him with fire, together with the merchant who brought him."

22 While they were talking, the soul of Gad, his brother, departed, and the king mourned for Gad exceedingly, because he loved him, and ordered him to be prepared for burial in a royal and costly robe. While this was going on, angels received the soul of Gad, the king's brother, and took it up into heaven, showing him the palaces and mansions there, asking him, "In what place do you wish to dwell?" And when they came near the edifice of the apostle Thomas, which he had erected for the king, Gad, upon beholding it, said to the angels, "I entreat you, my lords, let me dwell in one of these lower chambers." But they said to him, "In this building you cannot dwell." And he said, "Why not?" They answered, "This palace is the one which that Christian has built for your brother." But he said, "I entreat you, my lords, allow me to go to my brother to buy this palace from him. For my brother does not know what it is like, and he will sell it to me."

23 And the angels let the soul of Gad go. And as they were putting on him the burial robe his soul came into him. And he said to those standing round him, "Call my brother to me, that I may beg of him a request." Straightway they sent the good news to their king, saying, "Your brother has become alive again!" And the king arose and with a great multitude went to his brother. And coming in he went to the bed as if stupefied, unable to speak to him. And his brother said, "I know and I am convinced, brother, that if anyone had asked of you the half of your kingdom, you would give it for my sake. Wherefore I entreat you to grant one favor, which I beg of you to do: that you sell to me that which I ask from you." And the king answered and said, "And what is it that you wish me to sell to you?" And he said, "Assure me by an oath that you will grant it to me." And the king swore to him, "Whatever of my possession you ask I will give you." And he said to him, "Sell me the palace which you have in heaven." And the king said, "A palace in heaven—where does this come to me from?" And he said, "It is the one that Christian built for you, the man who is now in prison, whom the merchant brought, having bought him from a certain Jesus. I mean that Hebrew slave whom you wished to punish, having suffered some deception from him, on account of whom I also was grieved and died, and now have come alive again."

24 Then the king heard and understood his words about the eternal benefits that were conferred upon him and destined for him, and said, "That palace I cannot sell you, but I pray to be permitted to enter into it and to dwell there, being deemed worthy to belong to its inhabitants. And if you really wish to buy such a palace, behold, the man is alive, and will build you a better one than that." And immediately he sent and brought the apostle out of prison, and the merchant who had been shut up along with him, saying, "I entreat you, as a man entreating the servant of God, pray for me, and ask him, whose servant you are, to pardon

me and to overlook what I have done to you or intended to do, and that I may become worthy to be an inhabitant of that house for which indeed I have done nothing, but which you, laboring alone, have built for me with the help of the grace of your God, and that I may also become a servant and serve this God, whom you preach." His brother also fell down before the apostle and said, "I entreat you and supplicate before your God that I may become worthy of this service and become partaker of that which was shown to me by his angels. . . ."

51 Now there was a certain young man, who had committed a nefarious deed. He came and partook of the eucharist. And his two hands withered, so that he could no longer put them to his mouth. When those present saw him, they told the apostle what had happened. And the apostle called him and said, "Tell me, my son, and be not afraid of what you have done before you came here. For the eucharist of the Lord has convicted you. For this gift, by entering many, brings healing, especially to those who come in faith and love; but you it has withered away, and what has happened has happened not without some justification." And the young man convicted by the eucharist of the Lord came up, fell at the apostle's feet, and besought him and said, "An evil deed has been done by me, whilst I thought to do something good. I loved a woman who lived in an inn outside the city, and she loved me also. And when I heard about you, believing that you proclaim the living God, I came and received the seal from you along with the others. And you said, 'Whoever shall indulge in impure intercourse, especially in adultery, shall not have life with the God whom I preach.' As I loved her very much, I entreated her and tried to persuade her to live with me in chaste and pure conduct, as you teach. And she would not. Since she would not, I took a sword and killed her. For I could not see her commit adultery with another."

52 When the apostle heard this he said, "O insane intercourse, how you lead to shamelessness! O unrestrained lust, how have you excited this man to do this! O work of the serpent, how you rage in your own!" And the apostle ordered some water to be brought in a dish. And when the water had been brought he said, "Come, waters from the living waters; everlasting, sent to us from the everlasting; rest, sent to us from the one who gives rest; power of salvation, proceeding from that power which overcomes all and subjects it to its will—come and dwell in these waters, that the gift of the Holy Spirit may be completely fulfilled in them!" And to the young man he said, "Go, wash your hands in these waters." And when he had washed them they were restored. And the apostle said to him, "Do you believe in our Lord Jesus Christ, that he can do all things?" And he said, "Though I am the least, yet I believe. But I did this in the hope of doing something good. For I entreated her, as I told you already, but she would not be persuaded by me to keep herself chaste."

53 And the apostle said to him, "Come, let us go to the inn where you committed the deed, and let us see what happened." And the young man went before the apostle on the road. When they had come to the inn they found her lying there. And when the apostle saw her he was sad, for she was a beautiful girl. And he ordered her to be brought into the middle of the inn. And putting her on a couch they carried it out and set it in the midst of the courtyard of the inn. And the apostle laid his hand on her and began to say, "Jesus, who appear to us at all times—for this is your will, that we should always seek you, and you have given us the right to ask and to receive, and have not only permitted us this, but have also taught us how to pray—who are not seen by us with the bodily eyes, but who are never hidden from those of our soul, and who are hidden in form, but manifested to us by your works; by your many deeds we have recognized you as much as we are able, and you have given us your gifts without measure saying, 'Ask, and it shall be given you; seek, and you shall find; knock, and it shall be opened unto you.'[1] We pray, therefore, being afraid of our sins. And we ask you not for riches or gold or silver or possessions or any of those things that come from earth and go into the earth again; but we beg of you and entreat that in your holy name you raise this woman lying here by your power, to your glory and to an awakening of faith in those who stand by."

54 And he said to the young man, after sealing him, "Go and take her hand and say to her, 'With iron I killed you with my hands, and with my hands I raise you because of faith in Jesus.' " And the young man went and stood by her, saying, "I have believed in you, O Christ Jesus." And looking upon Judas Thomas the apostle, he said to him, "Pray for me, that my Lord, upon whom I call, may come to my help." And laying his hand on her hand he said, "Come, Lord Jesus Christ, give her life and me the reality of your faith." And he drew her by the hand, and she sprang up and sat looking at the great multitude standing around. And she also saw the apostle standing opposite her, and leaving her couch she sprang up and fell at his feet and took hold of his garments, saying, "I pray, Lord, where is your companion who has not left me to remain in that fearful and grievous place, but has given me up to you, saying, 'Take this one, that she may be made perfect, and thereafter be brought into her own place'?"

55 And the apostle said to her, "Tell us where you have been." And she answered, "Do you, who were with me, to whom also I was entrusted, wish to hear?" And she commenced thus: "An ugly-looking man, entirely black, received me; and his clothing was exceedingly filthy. And he took me to a place where there were many chasms, and a great stench and most hateful vapor were given forth thence. And he made me look into each chasm, and in the first I saw blazing fire, and fiery wheels running, and souls were hung upon these wheels, dashing against each other. And there was crying and great lamentation and no Savior was there. And that man said to me, 'These souls are akin to you, and in the days of reckoning they were delivered to punishment and destruction. And then others are brought in their stead; in like manner all these are again succeeded by others. These are they who perverted the intercourse of man and wife.' And again I looked down, and saw infants heaped upon each other, struggling and lying upon each other. And he said to me, 'These are their children, and for this they are placed here for a testimony against them.'

---

[1]Matt 7:7.

56 "And he brought me to another chasm, and as I looked into it I saw mud and worms spouting forth, and souls swallowing there; and I heard a great gnashing of teeth come from them. And that man said to me, 'These are the souls of women who left their husbands and committed adultery with others, and they have been brought to this torment.' And he showed me another chasm, and looking into it I saw souls hung up, some by the tongue, some by the hair, some by the hands, others by the feet, head downward, and reeking with smoke and sulphur. Concerning these the man who accompanied me said the following: 'The souls hung up by the tongue are slanderers and such as have spoken false and disgraceful words and are not ashamed. Those hung up by their hair are the shameless, who are not ashamed at all and go about with uncovered heads in the world. Those hung up by the hands are they who took that which did not belong to them and have stolen, and who never gave anything to the poor, nor helped the afflicted; but they did so because they wished to get everything, and cared neither for law nor right. And these hung up by the feet are those who lightly and eagerly walked in wicked ways and disorderly paths, not visiting the sick nor escorting those who depart this life. On this account each soul receives what it has done.'

57 "And again he led me forth and showed me a very dark cavern, exhaling a very bad stench. Many souls were peeping out thence, wishing to get some share of the air. And their keepers would not let them look out. And my companion said to me, 'This is the prison of those souls which you saw. For when they have fully received their punishment for that which each has done, others succeed them. Some are fully consumed, others are given up to other punishments.' And the keepers of the souls in the dark cavern said to the man that had charge of me, 'Give her to us, that we may bring her to the others till the time comes when she is handed over to punishment.' But he said to them, 'I will not give her to you, because I am afraid of him who delivered her to me. For I was not told to leave her here; I shall take her back with me, till I get an injunction about her.' And he took me and brought me to another

place, where there were men who were cruelly tortured. He who is like you took me and gave me up to you, saying to you, 'Take her, for she is one of the sheep which have wandered away.' And received by you, I now stand before you. I beg, therefore, and supplicate you that I may not come to those places of punishment which I have seen."

58 And the apostle said, "You have heard what this woman has recounted. And these are not the only punishments, but there are others worse than these. And you too, unless you turn to the God whom I preach, and abstain from your former works and from the deeds which you did in ignorance, shall find your end in these punishments. Believe, therefore, in Christ Jesus, and he will forgive you the former sins and will cleanse you from all your bodily desires that remain on the earth, and will heal you from the faults that follow after you and go along with you and are found before you. Let every one of you put off the old man and put on the new, and leave your former course of conduct and behavior. Those who steal, let them steal no more, but let them live, laboring and working. The adulterers are no more to commit adultery, lest they give themselves up to everlasting punishment. For with God adultery is an evil exceedingly wicked above all other evils. Put away also covetousness and lying and drunkenness and slandering, and do not return evil for evil! For all these are alien and strange to the God whom I preach. But walk rather in faith and meekness and holiness and hope, in which God rejoices, that you may become this kin, expecting from him those gifts which only a few receive."

59 The whole people therefore believed and presented obedient souls to the living God and Christ Jesus, rejoicing in the blessed works of the Most High and in his holy service. And they brought money for the service of the widows. For he had them gathered together in the cities, and he sent to all of them by his deacons what was necessary, both clothing as well as food. He himself did not cease to preach and to speak to them and to show that this Jesus is the Messiah of whom the Scriptures have spoken that he should be crucified and be raised after three days from the dead. He also showed to them and explained, beginning from the prophets, what was said concerning the Messiah, that it was necessary for him to come, and that everything had to be accomplished which had been prophesied of him. And the fame of him spread over all the cities and villages, and all who had sick persons or such as were troubled by unclean spirits brought them to him; and some they laid on the road by which he was to pass, and he healed all by the power of the Lord. And those who were healed by him said with one accord and one voice, "Glory to you, Jesus, who in like manner has given healing to all through your servant and apostle Thomas! And being in good health and rejoicing, we pray that we may become members of your flock and be counted among your sheep. Receive us, therefore, O Lord, and consider not our trespasses and our former transgressions, which we did while we were in ignorance!"

><+>+O+<+I+<

3. Justin: Dialogue with Trypho

Justin was a Christian philosopher who lived in Rome in the mid-second century. One of the first intellectuals to convert to Christianity, he authored three major works that still survive: two apologies (intellectual defenses of Christianity; see Chapter 4) and the 'Dialogue with Trypho,' an account of a two-day debate with a non-Christian Jewish scholar, Trypho, over whether Jesus could be the Jewish messiah predicted in the Jewish Scriptures. The debate took place around 135 C.E. in the city of Ephesus; Justin's account of the event, written perhaps twenty years later, strives to show the superiority of Christianity over Judaism. He begins by narrating his initial encounter with Trypho and explaining how, as a young man, he experimented with a range of Greek philosophical schools before becoming convinced, largely on the basis of the prophecies of the Hebrew prophets, that Jesus was the savior of the world who alone could teach the true meaning of life.

For further excerpts from the *Dialogue with Trypho*, see Chapter 5.

Chapter 1

One morning as I was walking along a broad avenue, a man, accompanied by some friends, came up to me and said: "Good morning, Philosopher." Whereupon, he and his friends walked along beside me.

After returning his greeting, I asked: "What is the matter? Is there anything special you wish of me?"

He answered: "Corinthus the Socratic taught me in Argos never to slight or ignore those who wear your garb, but to show them every consideration and to converse with them, since from such a conversation some good might be derived by them or myself. It would be to the advantage of both if either should benefit from this meeting. Accordingly, whenever I see anyone wearing such

Justin: 'Dialogue with Trypho,' from *Saint Justin Martyr*, ed. Thomas Falls. Fathers of the Church, 6. Washington, D.C.: Catholic University Press of America, 1977. Used with permission.

a robe, I gladly accost him. So, for this same reason, it has been a pleasure to greet you. These friends of mine share my hope of hearing something profitable from you."

"Who, indeed, are you, most excellent sir?" I asked with a smile.

He did not hesitate to tell me his name and background. "Trypho," he said, "is my name. I am a Hebrew of the circumcision, a refugee from the recent war, and at present a resident of Greece, especially of Corinth."

"How," I asked, "can you gain as much from philosophy as from your own lawgiver and prophets?"

"Why not," he replied, "for do not the philosophers speak always about God? Do they not constantly propose questions about his unity and providence? Is this not the task of philosophy, to inquire about the Divine?"

"Yes, indeed," I said, "we, too, are of the same opinion. But the majority of the philosophers have simply neglected to inquire whether there is one or even several gods, and whether or not a divine providence takes care of us, as if this knowledge were unnecessary to our happiness. Moreover, they try to convince us that God takes care of the universe with its genera and species, but not of me and you and of each individual, for otherwise there would be no need of our praying to him night and day. It is not difficult to see where such reasoning leads them. It imparts a certain immunity and freedom of speech to those who hold these opinions, permitting them to do and to say whatever they please, without any fear of punishment or hope of reward from God. How could it be otherwise, when they claim that things will always be as they are now, and that you and I shall live in the next life just as we are now, neither better nor worse. But there are others who think that the soul is immortal and incorporeal, and therefore conclude that they will not be punished even if they are guilty of sin; for, if the soul is incorporeal, it cannot suffer; if it is immortal, it needs nothing further from God."

Then, smiling politely, he said, "Explain to us just what is your opinion of these matters, and what is your idea of God, and what is your philosophy."

Chapter 2

"I will explain to you," I replied, "my views on this subject. Philosophy is indeed one's greatest possession, and is most precious in the sight of God, to whom it alone leads us and to whom it unites us, and they in truth are holy who have applied themselves to philosophy. But, many have failed to discover the nature of philosophy, and the reason why it was sent down to men; otherwise, there would not be Platonists, or Stoics, or Peripatetics, or Theoretics, or Pythagoreans, since this science of philosophy is always one and the same. Now, let me tell you why it has at length become so diversified. They who first turned to philosophy, and, as a result, were deemed illustrious, were succeeded by others who gave no time to the investigation of truth, but, amazed at the courage and self-control of their teachers as well as with the novelty of their teachings, held that to be the truth which each had learned from his own teacher. And they in turn transmitted to their successors such opinions, and others like them, and so they became known by the name of him who was considered the father of the doctrine. When I first desired to contact one of these philosophers, I placed myself under the tutelage of a certain Stoic. After spending some time with him and learning nothing new about God (for my instructor had no knowledge of God, nor did he consider such knowledge necessary), I left him and turned to a Peripatetic who considered himself an astute teacher. After a few days with him, he demanded that we settle the matter of my tuition fee in such a way that our association would not be unprofitable to him. Accordingly, I left him, because I did not consider him a real philosopher. Since my spirit still yearned to hear the specific and excellent meaning of philosophy, I approached a very famous Pythagorean, who took great pride in his own wisdom. In my interview with him, when I expressed a desire to become his pupil, he asked me, 'What? Do you know music, astronomy, and geometry? How do you expect to comprehend any of those things that are conducive to happiness, if you are not first well acquainted with those studies which draw your mind away from objects of the senses and render it fit for the intellectual, in order that it may contemplate what is good and beautiful?' He continued to speak at great length in praise of those sciences, and of the necessity of knowing them, until I admitted that I knew nothing about them; then he dismissed me. As was to be expected, I was downcast to see my hopes shattered, especially since I respected him as a man of considerable knowledge. But, when I reflected on the length of time that I would have to spend on those sciences, I could not make up my mind to wait such a long time. In this troubled state of mind the thought occurred to me to consult the Platonists, whose reputation was great. Thus it happened that I spent as much time as possible in the company of a wise man who was highly esteemed by the Platonists and who had but recently arrived in our city. Under him I forged ahead in philosophy and day by day I improved. The perception of incorporeal things quite overwhelmed me and the Platonic theory of ideas added wings to my mind, so that in a short time I imagined myself a wise man. So great was my folly that I fully expected immediately to gaze upon God, for this is the goal of Plato's philosophy."

Chapter 3

"As I was in this frame of mind and desired absolute solitude devoid of human distractions, I used to take myself to a certain spot not far from the sea. One day, as I approached that place with the intention of being alone, a respectable old man, of meek and venerable mien, followed me at a short distance. I stopped, turned quickly, and stared sharply at him."

" 'Do you know me?' he asked.

"I replied that I did not."

" 'Why, therefore,' he continued, 'do you stare at me so?'

" 'Because,' I answered, 'I am surprised to find you here. I didn't expect to see anyone here.'

" 'I am worried,' he said, 'about some missing members of my household, and I am therefore looking around with the hope that they may show up somewhere in the vicinity. But what brings you here?'

" 'I take great delight,' I answered, 'in such walks, where I can converse with myself without hindrance because there is nothing to distract my attention. Places like this are most suitable for philology.'

" 'Are you, then, a philologian,' he asked, 'rather than a lover of deeds and of truth? Do you not strive to be a practical man rather than a sophist?'

" 'But what greater deed,' I replied, 'could one perform than to prove that reason rules all, and that one who rules reason and is sustained by it can look down upon the errors and undertakings of others, and see that they do nothing reasonable or pleasing to God. People cannot have prudence without philosophy and straight thinking. Thus, everyone should be devoted to philosophy and should consider it the greatest and most noble pursuit; all other pursuits are only of second- or third-rate value, unless they are connected with philosophy. Then they are of some value and should be approved; if they are devoid of philosophy and are not connected with it in any way, they then become base and coarse pursuits to those who practise them.'

"Interrupting, he asked, 'Does philosophy therefore produce happiness?'

" 'Absolutely,' I replied, 'and it alone.'

" 'Tell me,' he asked, 'what is philosophy and what is the happiness it engenders, if there is nothing which prevents your speaking.'

" 'Philosophy,' I answered, 'is the knowledge of that which exists, and a clear understanding of the truth; and happiness is the reward of such knowledge and understanding.'

" 'But how do you define God?' he asked.

" 'God is the Being who always has the same nature in the same manner, and is the cause of existence to all else,' I replied.

"Pleased with my words, he once again asked, 'Is not knowledge a word applied commonly to different matters? For, whoever is skilled in any of the arts, for example, in the art of military strategy or of navigation or of medicine, is called skillful. But this is not true in divine and human matters. Is there a science which furnishes us with an understanding of human and divine things, and, besides, a higher science of the divinity and virtue in them?'

" 'Certainly,' I replied.

" 'Well, now,' he asked, 'is the knowledge of humanity and God similar to that of music, arithmetic, astronomy, and the like?'

" 'Not at all,' I answered.

" 'Your answer has not been correct, then,' he continued, 'for we acquire the knowledge of some things by study or practice, and of other things by sight. Now, if anyone were to say to you that in India there exists an animal different from all others, of such and such a species, assuming many shapes and colors, you would have no definite knowledge of it unless you saw it, nor could you attempt to give any description of it, unless you had heard of it from one who had seen it.'

" 'Absolutely not,' I agreed.

" 'Then, how,' he reasoned, 'can the philosophers speculate correctly or speak truly of God, when they have no knowledge of him, since they have never seen nor heard him?'

" 'But the Deity, father,' I rejoined, 'cannot be seen by the same eyes as other living beings are. He is to be perceived by the mind alone, as Plato affirms, and I agree with him.'

Chapter 4

" 'Does our mind, then,' he inquired, 'possess such and so great a power? Or does it not perceive that which exists through the senses? Or will the human mind be capable of seeing God, if not aided by the Holy Ghost?'

" 'Plato truly states,' I retorted, 'that the eye of the mind has this special power, which has been given to us in order that we may see with it, when it is pure, the very Being who is the cause of everything the mind perceives, who has neither color, nor form, nor size, nor anything the eye can see, but who is beyond all essence, who is ineffable and indescribable, who alone is beautiful and

good, and who comes at once into those souls which are well disposed because of their affinity to and desire of seeing him.'

" 'What affinity, then,' he asked, 'have we with God? Is the soul also divine and immortal and a part of the Supreme Mind itself? And as this Supreme Mind sees God, are we, in like manner, able to perceive the Deity in our mind, and thus be happy even now?'

" 'Absolutely,' I replied.

" 'Do all the souls," he asked, 'of all the animals perceive Him? Or is a human's soul different from that of a horse or an ass?'

" 'No,' I answered, 'the souls of all creatures are the same.'

" 'Then,' he continued, 'shall horses and asses see God, or have they ever seen God at any time?'

" 'No,' I replied, 'for not even most people see him; only those who are honest in their life, and who have been purified through their justice and every other virtue.'

" 'Then you would say,' he persisted, 'that one does not see God because of an affinity with him, nor because one possesses an intellect, but because one is temperate and just?'

" 'Certainly,' I answered, 'and also because one has the faculty of thinking of God.'

" 'Would you say,' he asked, 'that goats or sheep do an injustice to anyone?'

" 'They do not in any way do an injustice to anyone,' I replied.

" 'So, according to your reasoning,' he said, 'these animals will see God?'

" 'No, they won't,' I answered, 'because they are hindered from doing so by the form of their bodies.'

" 'If these animals had the power of speech,' he retorted, 'you can be sure that they would have more right to revile our bodies. But, for the present let us ignore this topic and I'll concede that what you say is true. Tell me this: Does the soul see God while it is in the body, or after it has been released from it?'

" 'Even while it is in the human body,' I replied, 'it can see God by means of the intellect, but especially after it has been released from the body, and exists of itself, does it perceive God whom it always loved.'

" 'Does it remember,' he asked, 'this vision of God when it is again united to a human body?'

" 'I don't think so,' I answered.

" 'What, then,' he continued, 'is the advantage of having seen God? What advantage has one who has seen God over one who has not, unless one at least remembers the fact that one has seen Him?'

" 'That I cannot answer,' I admitted.

" 'And what,' asked he, 'will be the punishment for those deemed unworthy to see God?'

" 'As a punishment,' I answered, 'they will be imprisoned in the bodies of certain wild beasts.'

" 'Will they be conscious that for this reason they are imprisoned in such bodies and that they have committed some sin?'

" 'I don't think so.'

" 'Then, it would seem that they benefit in no way from such punishment; in fact, I would say that they suffer no punishment at all, unless they are conscious that it is a punishment.'

" 'No, indeed,' I conceded.

" 'Therefore,' he concluded, 'souls do not see God, nor do they transmigrate into other bodies, for they would know that they were being thus punished, and they would be afraid thereafter to commit even the slightest sin. But I do concede that souls can perceive that there is a God, and that justice and piety are admirable.'

" 'You speak the truth,' I agreed.

Chapter 5

" 'Those philosophers, then, know nothing,' he went on, 'about such matters, for they can't even explain the nature of the soul.'

" 'It seems not,' I consented.

" 'Nor should we call the soul immortal, for, if it were, we would certainly have to call it unbegotten.'

" 'Some Platonists,' I answered, 'consider the soul both unbegotten and immortal.'

" 'Do you affirm,' he asked, 'that the universe also is unbegotten?'

" 'There are some who hold that opinion,' I replied, 'but I don't agree with them.'

" 'Right you are,' he continued. 'Why would one think that a body that is so solid, firm, composite, and mutable, a body that deteriorates and is renewed each day, has not originated from some first cause? Now, if the universe has been begotten, souls, too, of necessity, are begotten. Perhaps there is a time when they do not exist, for they were created for the sake of humans and other living creatures, even if you claim that they have been begotten separately by themselves, and not together with their own bodies.'

" 'I think you are right. The souls, then, are not immortal?'

" 'No,' he said, 'since it appears that the world itself was generated.'

" 'On the other hand,' he continued, 'I do not claim that any soul ever perishes, for this would certainly be a benefit to sinners. What happens to them? The souls of the devout dwell in a better place, whereas the souls of the unjust and the evil abide in a worse place, and there they await the judgment day. Those, therefore, who are deemed worthy to see God will never perish, but the others will be subjected to punishment as long as God allows them to exist and as long as he wants them to be punished.'

" 'Does not your assertion agree with what Plato taught in his *Timaeus* concerning the world, namely, that it can be destroyed since it is a created thing, but that it will not be destroyed or be destined for destruction since such is the will of God? Don't you think that the same thing could be said of the soul and, in short, of all other creatures? For, whatever exists or shall exist after God has a nature subject to corruption, and therefore capable of complete annihilation, for only God is unbegotten and incorruptible. For this reason he is God, and all other things after him are created and corruptible. This is also the reason why souls die and are punished, for, if they were unbegotten, they would not have sinned nor have become so foolish; they would not have been so timid at one time, and so daring at another; nor would they, of their own account, ever have entered into swine, serpents, and dogs. Furthermore, if they were unbegotten it would not be right to coerce them, for one who is unbegotten is similar and equal to another unbegotten, nor can he be preferred to the other either in power or in honor. We must conclude, therefore, that there are not many beings that are unbegotten, for, if there were some difference between them, you could not, no matter how you searched, find the cause of such difference; but, after sending your thought always to infinity, you would finally become tired and have to stop before the one Unbegotten and declare that he is the cause of all things. Do you think that these things escaped the notice of Plato and Pythagoras, those wise men who became, so to say, a wall and bulwark of our philosophy?'

Chapter 6

" 'I don't care,' he answered, 'if Plato or Pythagoras or anyone else held such views. What I say is the truth, and here is how you may learn it. The soul itself either is life or it possesses life. If it is life, it would cause something else to exist, not itself, just as motion causes something other than itself to move. Now, no one would deny that the soul lives; and if it lives, it does not live as life itself, but as a partaker of life. But, that which partakes of anything is different from that of which it partakes. Now, the soul partakes of life because God wishes it to live; it will no longer partake of life whenever God doesn't wish it to live. For the power to live is not an attribute of the soul as it is of God. As one does not live forever, and one's body is not forever united to one's soul, since, whenever this union must be discontinued, the soul leaves the body and one no longer exists, so also, whenever the soul must cease to live, the spirit of life is taken from it and it is no more, but it likewise returns to the place of its origin.'

Chapter 7

" 'If these philosophers,' I asked, 'do not know the truth, what teacher or method shall one follow?'

" 'A long time ago,' he replied, 'long before the time of those reputed philosophers, there lived blessed men who were just and loved by God, men who spoke through the inspiration of the Holy Spirit and predicted events that would take place in the future, which events are now taking place. We call these men the Prophets. They alone knew the truth and communicated it to people, whom they neither deferred to nor feared. With no desire for personal glory, they reiterated only what they heard and saw when inspired by the Holy Spirit. Their writings are still extant, and whoever reads them with the proper faith will profit greatly in his knowledge of the origin and end of things, and of any other matter that a philosopher should know. In their writings they gave no proof at that time of their statements, for, as reliable witnesses of the truth, they were beyond proof; but the happenings that have taken place and are now taking place force you to believe their words. They also are worthy of belief because of the miracles which they performed, for they exalted God, the Father and Creator of all things, and made known Christ, his Son, who was sent by him. This the false prophets, who are filled with an erring and unclear spirit, have never done nor even do now, but they undertake to perform certain wonders to astound people and they glorify the demons and spirits of error. Above all, beseech God to open to you the gates of light, for no one can perceive or understand these truths unless he has been enlightened by God and his Christ.'

Chapter 8

"When he said these and many other things which it is not now the fitting time to tell, he went his way, after admonishing me to mediate on what he had told me, and I never saw him again. But my spirit was immediately set on fire, and an affection for the prophets, and for those who are friends of Christ, took hold of me; while pondering on his words, I discovered that his was the only sure and useful philosophy. Thus it is that I am now a philosopher. Furthermore, it is my wish that everyone would be of the same sentiments as I, and never spurn the Savior's words; for they have in themselves such tremendous majesty that they can instil fear into those who have wandered from the path of righteousness, whereas they ever remain a great solace to those who heed them. Thus, if you have any regard for your own welfare and for the salvation of your soul, and if you believe in God, you may have the chance, since I know you are no stranger to this matter, of attaining a knowledge of the Christ of God, and, after becoming a Christian, of enjoying a happy life."

Chapter 3

The Attack on Christianity

Persecution and Martyrdom in the Early Church

Since Christianity began as a group of Jews who saw in Jesus the Jewish messiah sent from the Jewish God in fulfillment of the Jewish Scriptures, they naturally began to propagate their views by trying to convert other Jews (see Chapter 2). The early Jewish mission was not an overwhelming success, however, as most Jews found the Christian claims about Jesus unbelievable and ludicrous, or even blasphemous. First-century Jews who were expecting a messiah anticipated a person of power and grandeur, a great warrior-king who would overthrow Israel's political enemies or a cosmic deliverer who would destroy the evils of this world. Jesus, on the other hand, was a relatively unknown teacher from a remote rural area who was executed for sedition against the state. The Christian claim that he was the messiah seemed nonsensical to most Jews; the corollary claim by some that Gentiles who did not keep the Jewish law were the true heirs of the promises made to the Jewish ancestors simply served to exacerbate the tensions.

Understandably, then, the earliest persecution of Christians was by Jews. This is clear from the oldest historical account of the incipient Christian movement, the books of Acts, and from the writings of Paul, who indicates that as a Jewish Pharisee he had persecuted Christians (Gal 1:13) and that later, as a Christian, he himself was punished by Jewish authorities (2 Cor 11:24).

Even bigger problems were in store for Christians, however, when the movement transcended its original Jewish matrix and entered into the larger Greco-Roman world. To be sure, it is *not* true, as is sometimes believed, that Christianity was immediately outlawed in the Roman empire and that Christians had to go into hiding. But there was considerable and widespread social antipathy toward Christians in the first three centuries, regular threats of mob violence, and occasional instances of governmental persecution.

New Testament sources indicate that, early on, Christians were seen as antisocial and that their refusal to participate in normal cultic and social activities in their communities led to hatred and opposition (e.g., 1 Pet 4:3–5). Throughout non-Christian sources of the second and third centuries, they are written off as ignorant, lower class, obstinant, superstitious, and antisocial (see Wilken). Early in the period, the Roman historian Tacitus indicates that they were widely known for their "hatred of the human race." Sometimes, specific changes were leveled against them. Since they did not worship any of the state or local gods, they were called "atheists" (literally, "without the gods"); since they held secret meetings at night, in which they exchanged a "kiss" of peace and ate the body of the Son of God and drank his blood, they were accused of holding nocturnal orgies that included cannibalistic rites (see Chapter 4).

Widespread suspicion against the Christians may have led to the occasional acts of mob violence against them. Firmly held religious convictions among the non-Christian populace at large may have played a role as well: pagans who believed that their own gods were to be worshipped and that a community that failed to do so could evoke divine wrath were increasingly prone to blame Christian "nonworshippers" when any disaster arose. In the words of Tertullian: "They consider that the Christians are the cause of every public calamity and every misfortune of the people. If the Tiber rises as high as the city walls, if the Nile does not rise to the fields, if the weather will not change, if there is an earthquake, a famine, a plague—straightway the cry is heard: 'Toss the Christians to the lion!'" (*Apol.* 40; see Chapter 4).

In some scattered instances, local governmental officials stepped in, both to prevent uncontrolled riot and to provide a legal outlet for the will of the people. There is some ambiguity in our sources concerning the legal charges against the Christians in such cases, since there were no Roman laws that prescribed the new religion (until the emperor Decius, ca. 250 C.E.). But it should be emphasized that throughout the Roman provinces criminal law *in general* was lax by our modern standards. There were no mandated criminal codes or proceedings; instead, the Romans appointed governors and other administrators to rule the provinces, and these appointed officials were responsible for maintaining the peace and administering justice as the situation demanded. Troublemakers could be tried and punished on the spot, with no possibility of trial by jury or legal appeals.

Why, then, if there were no explicit laws against Christianity, were Christians occasionally put on trial, punished, and even executed? Any ruling official who suspected that Christians engaged in crimes against nature as part of their religion (incestuous orgies, cannibalism) would certainly have grounds to act; in such a case, simply being a Christian would be a criminal offense. Moreover, since Christians were known not to worship the Roman gods, who were widely acknowledged as responsible for the peace and prosperity of the state, and since failing to worship the gods could bring divine retribution on the state itself, the existence of the Christians may have been seen as dangerous to the state, at least by the masses, if not by the more highly educated governors (whose job it was, however, to keep peace among the masses and who may have been willing to sacrifice some Christians in order to do so). In particular, the Roman emperor was widely understood in the provinces to represent the gods and so to be worthy of divine honors.

On only rare occasions did emperors themselves actually engage in active opposition to Christians. The first to do so was Nero in 64 C.E. According to Tacitus, when a large portion of Rome was burned and the populace began to suspect the emperor's involvement (since the destruction of the city would have allowed him to implement his new building plans), Nero found a ready scapegoat in the Christians, many of whom he rounded up and subjected to public tortures and executions. It is important to realize that Nero persecuted Christians only in Rome (not throughout the empire) and that he did so not for their religion per se but for arson (even though the charge was false). Nonetheless, his actions may have set a precedent for future generations. The next recorded imperial involvement occurred some fifty years later, when Trajan approved the actions of his governor of Bythinia-Pontus, Pliny the Younger, for executing Christians when they refused to recant and perform an act of worship toward Trajan's cultic image. Some sixty years after that, the emperor Marcus Aurelius sanctioned the terrible persecution of the Christians in Lyons and Vienne (see reading 6 in this chapter). But it was not until the emperor Decius saw the church as a threat and tried (unevenly and unsuccessfully) to wipe it out by an empire-wide persecution (ca 250 C.E.) that being a Christian was actually deemed "illegal."

Included among our ancient sources of early Christianity are several eyewitness accounts of the trial proceedings against Christians and of their martyrdoms. These are all written by Christians and portray a decidedly Christian perspective on the proceedings. According to these accounts, many Christians found a way to hide or to escape during times of persecution, others could afford to bribe their way out of punishment, and yet others found no problem in recanting their beliefs for a time until the persecution had passed. But there were some who refused to budge and so paid the full price of their convictions. We do not know how many Christians were martyred in the first three centuries; judging from the details provided in the early Christian historian Eusebius, however, they probably numbered in the hundreds (rather than many thousands).

For Further Reading

Bowersock, G. W. *Martyrdom and Rome*. Cambridge: University Press, 1995.

Frend, W. H. C. *Martyrdom and Persecution in the Early Church*. Oxford: Blackwell, 1965.

Ferguson, Everett, ed. *Church and State in the Early Church*. New York: Garland, 1993. (A collection of classic essays; see especially G. E. M. de Ste. Croix, "Why Were the Early Christians Persecuted?" and the subsequent exchange with A. N. Sherwin-White)

Musurillo, H., ed. *The Acts of the Christian Martyrs*. Oxford: Clarendon, 1972.

Perkins, Judith. *The Suffering Self*. New York: Routledge, 1995.

Wilken, Robert. *The Christians as the Romans Saw Them*. New Haven, Conn.: Yale University, 1984.

THE TEXTS

4. The Letter of Ignatius to the Romans

Ignatius, the bishop of Antioch in Syria, was arrested around 110 C.E., evidently for Christian activities. Rather than being tried on the spot, he was sent to Rome under armed guard to face trial and execution (possibly because he was a Roman citizen). Along the way, he was greeted by representatives of various local churches, to which he then wrote letters sending his greetings and warning against false teachers, church dissension, and, especially, lack of reverence for the ruling bishops. Seven of Ignatius's letters survive. The one given here is perhaps the most distinctive of all. It is written to the Christians of Rome, pleading with them not to interfere with the proceedings against him. Ignatius *wants* to be thrown to the wild beasts and so become a martyr for Christ, a true Christian. He urges the Roman Christians to grant him his wish and allow him to imitate the passion of his Lord.

Unfortunately, we do not have a historically reliable account of what happened to Ignatius once he arrived in Rome.

Greetings in Jesus Christ, the Son of the Father, from Ignatius, the "God-inspired," to the church that is in charge of affairs in Roman quarters and that the Most High Father and Jesus Christ, his only Son, have magnificently embraced in mercy and love. You have been granted light both by the will of him who willed all that is, and by virtue of your believing in Jesus Christ, our God, and of loving him. You are a credit to God: you deserve your renown and are to be congratulated. You deserve praise and success and are privileged to be without blemish. Yes, you rank first in love, being true to Christ's law and stamped with the Father's name. To you, then, sincerest greetings in Jesus Christ, our God, for you cleave to his every commandment—observing not only their letter but their spirit—being permanently filled with God's grace and purged of every stain alien to it.

1 Since God has answered my prayer to see you godly people, I have gone on to ask for more. I mean, it is as a prisoner for Christ Jesus that I hope to greet you, if indeed it be [God's] will that I should deserve to meet my end.

2 Things are off to a good start. May I have the good fortune to meet my fate without interference! What I fear is your generosity, which may prove detrimental to me. For you can easily do what you want to, whereas it is hard for me to get to God unless you let me alone.

2 I do not want you to please humans, but to please God, just as you are doing. For I shall

The "Letter of Ignatius to the Romans," reproduced from *Early Christian Fathers*, ed. Cyril C. Richardson (Library of Christian Classics Series), 1970. Used by permission of Westminster John Knox Press.

never again have such a chance to get to God, nor can you, if you keep quiet, get credit for a finer deed. For if you quietly let me alone, people will see in me God's Word. But if you are enamored of my mere body, I shall, on the contrary, be a meaningless noise.

2 Grant me no more than to be a sacrifice for God while there is an altar at hand. Then you can form yourselves into a choir and sing praises to the Father in Jesus Christ that God gave the bishop of Syria the privilege of reaching the sun's setting when he summoned him from its rising. It is a grand thing for my life to set on the world, and for me to be on my way to God, so that I may rise in his presence.

3 You never grudged anyone. You taught others. So I want you to substantiate the lessons that you bid them heed.

2 Just pray that I may have strength of soul and body so that I may not only talk [about martyrdom], but really want it. It is not that I want merely to be called a Christian, but actually to *be* one. Yes, if I prove to be one, then I can have the name. Then, too, I shall be a convincing Christian only when the world sees me no more.

3 Nothing you can see has a real value. Our God Jesus Christ, indeed, has revealed himself more clearly by returning to the Father. The greatness of Christianity lies in its being hated by the world, not in its being convincing to it.

4 I am corresponding with all the churches and bidding them all realize that I am voluntarily dying for God—if, that is, you do not interfere. I plead with you, do not do me an unseasonable kindness. Let me be fodder for wild beasts—that is how I can get to God. I am God's wheat and I am being ground by the teeth of wild beasts to make a pure loaf for Christ.

2 I would rather that you fawn on the beasts so that they may be my tomb and no scrap of my body be left. Thus, when I have fallen asleep, I shall be a burden to no one. Then I shall be a real disciple of Jesus Christ when the world sees my body no more. Pray Christ for me that by these means I may become God's sacrifice.

3 I do not give you orders like Peter and Paul. They were apostles: I am a convict. They were at liberty: I am still a slave. But if I suffer, I shall be emancipated by Jesus Christ; and united to him, I shall rise to freedom.

5 Even now as a prisoner, I am learning to forgo my own wishes. All the way from Syria to Rome I am fighting with wild beasts, by land and sea, night and day, chained as I am to ten leopards (I mean to a detachment of soldiers), who only get worse the better you treat them. But by their injustices I am becoming a better disciple, though not for that reason am I acquitted.

2 What a thrill I shall have from the wild beasts that are ready for me! I hope they will make short work of me. I shall coax them on to eat me up at once and not to hold off, as sometimes happens, through fear. And if they are reluctant, I shall force them to it.

3 Forgive me—I know what is good for me. Now is the moment I am beginning to be a disciple. May nothing seen or unseen begrudge me making my way to Jesus Christ. Come fire, cross, battling with wild beasts, wrenching of bones, mangling of limbs, crushing of my whole body, cruel tortures of the devil—only let me get to Jesus Christ!

6 Not the wide bounds of earth nor the kingdoms of this world will avail me anything. I would rather die and get to Jesus Christ than reign over the ends of the earth. That is whom I am looking for—the One who died for us. That is whom I want—the One who rose for us.

2 I am going through the pangs of being born. Sympathize with me, my brothers! Do not stand in the way of my coming to life—do not wish death on me. Do not give back to the world one who wants to be God's; do not trick him with material things. Let me get into the clear light and manhood will be mine.

3 Let me imitate the Passion of my God. If anyone has him in him, let him appreciate what I am longing for, and sympathize with me, realizing what I am going through.

7 The prince of this world wants to kidnap me and pervert my godly purpose. None of you, then, who will be there, must abet him. Rather be

on my side—that is, on God's. Do not talk Jesus Christ and set your heart on the world.

2 Harbor no envy. If, when I arrive, I make a different plea, pay no attention to me. Rather heed what I am now writing to you. For though alive, it is with a passion for death that I am writing to you. My Desire has been crucified and there burns in me no passion for material things. There is living water in me, which speaks and says inside me, "Come to the Father."

3 I take no delight in corruptible food or in the dainties of this life. What I want is God's bread, which is the flesh of Christ, who came from David's line; and for drink I want his blood: an immortal love feast indeed!

8 I do not want to live anymore on a human plane. And so it shall be, if you want it to. Want it to, so that you will be wanted! Despite the brevity of my letter, trust my request.

2 Yes, Jesus Christ will clarify it for you and make you see I am really in earnest. He is the guileless mouth by which the Father has spoken truthfully.

3 Pray for me that I reach my goal. I have written prompted, not by human passion, but by God's will. If I suffer, it will be because you favored me. If I am rejected, it will be because you hated me.

9 Remember the church of Syria in your prayers. In my place they have God for their shepherd. Jesus Christ alone will look after them—he, and your love.

2 I blush to be reckoned among them, for I do not deserve it, being the last of them and an afterthought. Yet by his mercy I shall be something, if, that is, I get to God.

3 With my heart I greet you; and the churches which have welcomed me, not as a chance passerby, but in the name of Jesus Christ, send their love. Indeed, even those that did not naturally lie on my route went ahead to prepare my welcome in the different towns.

10 I am sending this letter to you from Smyrna by those praiseworthy Ephesians. With me, along with many others, is Crocus—a person very dear to me.

2 I trust you have had word about those who went ahead of me from Syria to Rome for God's glory. Tell them I am nearly there. They are all a credit to God and to you; so you should give them every assistance.

3 I am writing this to you on the twenty-fourth of August. Farewell, and hold out to the end with the patience of Jesus Christ.

⊱┈◆┈○┈◆┈⊰

5. The Martyrdom of Polycarp

One of the persons to whom Ignatius addressed a letter was Polycarp, the bishop of Smyrna in Asia Minor. Some forty-five years later, around 155 C.E. Polycarp himself was arrested, tried, and executed for being a Christian. The surviving account is the earliest "martyrology" (= description of a martyrdom) to have survived from early Christianity outside of the New Testament (see Acts 7:56–60). It is based on an eyewitness report and is embedded in a letter written soon thereafter by the church of Smyrna in Philomelium, also in Asia Minor.

The Martyrdom of Polycarp, from *The Apostolic Fathers*, ed. J. B. Lightfoot and J. R. Harmer; 2d ed. by Michael W. Holmes. Grand Rapids, Mich.: Baker Book House, 1992.

The author indicates that Polycarp's death was "conformable to the gospel," and he appears to have modeled this description on familiar traditions of Christ's own death (e.g., the betrayal, the officer named Herod, Polycarp's prayer for God's will to be done, his entry into the city on a donkey). In addition to such legendary accretions as the fragrant aroma arising from Polycarp's pyre, the story is important for showing that a Christian could be condemned simply for refusing to worship the state gods and could escape punishment by reverencing the divine spirit (genius) of the emperor. As typically happens in the martyrologies, Polycarp steadfastly refuses, insisting that the tortures of the moment are far to be preferred to the eternal torments that await those who deny Christ.

The church of God which sojourns at Smyrna to the church of God which sojourns in Philomelium and to all the communities of the holy and catholic church sojourning in every place: may mercy, peace, and love from God the Father and our Lord Jesus Christ be multiplied.

1 We are writing to you, brothers, an account of those who were martyred, especially the blessed Polycarp, who put an end to the persecution as though he were setting his seal upon it by his martyrdom. For nearly all the preceding events happened in order that the Lord might show us once again a martyrdom which is in accord with the gospel.

2 For he waited to be betrayed, just as the Lord did, in order that we too might be imitators of him, not looking only to that which concerns ourselves, but also to that which concerns our neighbors. For it is the mark of true and steadfast love to desire not only that oneself be saved, but all the brothers as well.

2 Blessed and noble, therefore, are all the martyrdoms that have taken place in accordance with the will of God (for we must reverently assign to God the power over all things).

2 For who could fail to admire their nobility and patient endurance and loyalty to the Master? For even when they were so torn by whips that the internal structure of their flesh was visible as far as the inner veins and arteries, they endured so patiently that even the bystanders had pity and wept.

But they themselves reached such a level of bravery that not one of them uttered a cry or a groan, thus showing to us all that at the very hour when they were being tortured the martyrs of Christ were absent from the flesh, or rather that the Lord was standing by and conversing with them.

3 And turning their thoughts to the grace of Christ they despised the tortures of this world, purchasing at the cost of one hour an exemption from eternal punishment. And the fire of their inhuman torturers felt cold to them, for they set before their eyes the escape from that eternal fire which is never extinguished, while with the eyes of their heart they gazed upon the good things which are reserved for those who endure patiently, things which neither ear has heard nor eye has seen, nor has it entered into the human heart, but which were shown to them by the Lord, for they were no longer humans but already angels.

4 And in a similar manner those who were condemned to the wild beasts endured terrible punishments: they were forced to lie on sharp shells and afflicted with various other forms of torture in order that he might, if possible, by means of the unceasing punishment compel them to deny their faith; for the devil tried many things against them.

3 But thanks be to God, for he did not prevail against any of them. For the most noble Germanicus encouraged them, fearful though they were, by his own patient endurance; he also fought with the wild beasts in an outstanding way. For when the proconsul wished to persuade him and asked him to consider his youthfulness, he forcibly dragged the wild beast toward himself, desiring to be released as quickly as possible from their unrighteous and lawless life.

2 So after this all the multitude, marvelling at the bravery of the God-loving and God-fearing race of Christians, began shouting, "Away with the atheists! Find Polycarp!"

4 (Now there was one man, Quintus by name, a Phrygian recently arrived from Phrygia, who, when he saw the wild beasts, turned coward. This was the man who had forced himself and some others to come forward voluntarily. The proconsul, after many appeals, finally persuaded him to swear the oath and to offer the sacrifice. For this reason therefore, brothers, we do not praise those who hand themselves over, since the gospel does not so teach.)

5 Now the most admirable Polycarp, when he first heard the news, was not disturbed. In fact, he wanted to remain in town, but the majority persuaded him to withdraw. So he withdrew to a farm not far distant from the city, and there he stayed with a few companions, doing nothing else night and day except praying for everyone and for the churches throughout the world, for this was his constant habit.

2 And while he was praying he fell into a trance three days before his arrest, and he saw his pillow being consumed by fire. And he turned and said to those who were with him: "It is necessary that I be burned alive."

6 And as those who were searching for him persisted, he moved to another farm. Immediately, those searching for him arrived, and not finding him, they seized two slave boys, one of whom confessed under torture.

2 For it was really impossible for him to remain hidden, since the very persons who betrayed him were people of his own household. And the captain of the police, who just happened to have the same name—Herod, as he was called—was eager to bring him into the stadium, in order that he [Polycarp] might fulfill his appointed destiny of being made a sharer with Christ, while those who betrayed him received the punishment of Judas himself.

7 So, taking the youth slave with them, on Friday about suppertime the mounted police and horsemen set out, armed with their usual weapons as though chasing after an armed rebel. And closing in on him late in the evening, they found him in bed in an upstairs room in a small cottage; and though he still could have escaped from there to another place, he refused, saying, "May God's will be done."

2 So when he heard that they had arrived, he went and talked with them, while those who were present marvelled at his age and his composure, and wondered why there was so much eagerness for the arrest of an old man like him. Then he immediately ordered that a table be set for them to eat and drink as much as they wished at that hour, and he asked them to grant him an hour so that he might pray undisturbed.

3 When they consented, he stood and prayed, so full of the grace of God that for two hours he was unable to stop speaking; those who heard him were amazed, and many regretted that they had come after such a godly old man.

8 Now when at last he finished his prayer, after remembering everyone who had ever come into contact with him, both small and great, known and unknown, and all the universal church throughout the world, it was time to depart, and so they seated him on a donkey and brought him into the city on the day of a great Sabbath.

2 Herod, the police captain, and his father, Nicetes, came out to meet him. After transferring him to their carriage and sitting down at his side, they tried to persuade him, saying, "Why, what harm is there in saying, 'Caesar is Lord,' and offering incense" (and other words to this effect) "and thereby saving yourself?" Now at first he gave them no answer. But when they persisted, he said, "I am not about to do what you are suggesting to me."

3 Thus failing to persuade him, they began to utter threats and made him dismount in such a hurry that he bruised his shin as he got down from the carriage. And without even turning around, he went on his way eagerly and quickly as if nothing had happened to him, and as he was led to the stadium, there was such a tumult in the stadium that no one could even be heard.

9 But as Polycarp entered the stadium, there came a voice from heaven: "Be strong, Polycarp, and act like a man." And no one saw the speaker, but those of our people who were present heard the voice. And then, as he was brought forward, there was a great tumult when they heard that Polycarp had been arrested.

2 Therefore, when he was brought before him, the proconsul asked if he were Polycarp. And when he confessed that he was, the proconsul tried to persuade him to recant, saying, "Have respect for your age," and other such things as they are accustomed to say: "Swear by the Genius of Caesar; repent; say, 'Away with the atheists!'" So Polycarp solemnly looked at the whole crowd of lawless heathen who were in the stadium, motioned toward them with his hand, and then (groaning as he looked up to heaven) said, "Away with the atheists!"

3 But when the magistrate persisted and said, "Swear the oath, and I will release you; revile Christ," Polycarp replied, "For eighty-six years I have been his servant, and he has done me no wrong. How can I blaspheme my King who saved me?"

10 But as he continued to insist, saying, "Swear by the Genius of Caesar," he answered: "If you vainly suppose that I will swear by the Genius of Caesar, as you request, and pretend not to know who I am, listen carefully: I am a Christian. Now if you want to learn the doctrine of Christianity, name a day and given me a hearing."

2 The proconsul said: "Persuade the people." But Polycarp said: "You I might have considered worthy of a reply, for we have been taught to pay proper respect to rulers and authorities appointed by God, as long as it does us no harm; but as for these, I do not think they are worthy, that I should have to defend myself before them."

11 So the proconsul said: "I have wild beasts; I will throw you to them, unless you change your mind." But he said: "Call for them! For the repentance from better to worse is a change impossible for us; but it is a noble thing to change from that which is evil to righteousness."

2 Then he said to him again: "I will have you consumed by fire, since you despise the wild beasts, unless you change your mind." But Polycarp said: "You threaten with a fire that burns only briefly and after just a little while is extinguished, for you are ignorant of the fire of the coming judgment and eternal punishment, which is reserved for the ungodly. But why do you delay? Come, do what you wish."

12 As he spoke these and many other words, he was inspired with courage and joy, and his face was filled with grace, so that not only did he not collapse in fright at the things which were said to him, but on the contrary the proconsul was astonished, and sent his own herald into the midst of the stadium to proclaim three times: "Polycarp has confessed that he is a Christian."

2 When this was proclaimed by the herald, the entire crowd, Gentiles as well as Jews living in Smyrna, cried out with uncontrollable anger and with a loud shout: "This is the teacher of Asia, the father of the Christians, the destroyer of our gods, who teaches many not to sacrifice or worship." Saying these things, they shouted aloud and asked Philip the Asiarch to let a lion loose upon Polycarp. But he said that it was not lawful for him to do so since he had already brought to a close the animal hunts.

3 Then it occurred to them to shout out in unison that Polycarp should be burned alive. For it was necessary that the vision which he received concerning his pillow be fulfilled, when he saw it on fire while praying, and turned and said prophetically to the faithful who were with him, "It is necessary that I be burned alive."

13 These things then happened with such swiftness, quicker than words could tell, the crowd swiftly collecting wood and kindling from the workshops and baths, the Jews being especially eager to assist in this, as is their custom.

2 When the pyre was prepared, he took off all his clothes and removed his belt; he also tried to take off his shoes, though not previously in the habit of doing this, because all the faithful were always eager to be the first to touch his flesh. For he had been treated with all honor on account of his holy life even before his gray hair appeared.

3 Then the materials prepared for the pyre were placed around him; and as they were also about to nail him, he said: "Leave me as I am; for

he who enables me to endure the fire will also enable me to remain on the pyre without moving, even without the sense of security which you get from the nails."

14 So they did not nail him, but tied him instead. Then he, having placed his hands behind him and having been bound, like a splendid ram chosen from a great flock for a sacrifice, a burnt offering prepared and acceptable to God, looked up to heaven and said: "O Lord God Almighty, Father of your beloved and blessed Son Jesus Christ, through whom we have received knowledge of you, the God of angels and powers and of all creation, and of the whole race of the righteous who live in your presence,

2 "I bless you because you have considered me worthy of this day and hour, that I might receive a place among the number of martyrs in the cup of your Christ, to the resurrection to eternal life, both of soul and of body, in the incorruptibility of the Holy Spirit. May I be received among them in your presence today, as a rich and acceptable sacrifice, as you have prepared and revealed beforehand, and I have now accomplished, you who are the undeceiving and true God.

3 "For this reason, indeed for all things, I praise you, I bless you, I glorify you, through the eternal and heavenly High Priest, Jesus Christ, your beloved Son, through whom to you with him and the Holy Spirit be glory both now and for the ages to come. Amen."

15 When he had offered up the "Amen" and finished his prayer, the men in charge of the fire lit the fire. And as a mighty flame blazed up, we saw a miracle (we, that is, to whom it was given to see), and we have been preserved in order that we might tell the rest what happened.

2 For the fire, taking the shape of an arch, like the sail of a ship filled by the wind, completely surrounded the body of the martyr; and it was there in the middle, not like flesh burning but like bread baking or like gold and silver being refined in a furnace. For we also perceived a very fragrant odor, as if it were the scent of incense or some other precious spice.

16 When the lawless men eventually realized that his body could not be consumed by the fire, they ordered an executioner to go up to him and stab him with a dagger. And when he did this, there came out a large quantity of blood, so that it extinguished the fire; and the whole crowd was amazed that there should be so great a difference between the unbelievers and the elect.

2 Among them most certainly was this man, the most remarkable Polycarp, who proved to be an apostolic and prophetic teacher in our own time, bishop of the holy church in Smyrna. For every word which came from his mouth was accomplished and will be accomplished.

17 But the jealous and envious Evil One, the adversary of the race of the righteous, when he observed the greatness of his martyrdom and that his life was irreproachable from the beginning, and that he was now crowned with the crown of immortality and had won a prize which no one could challenge, saw to it that not even his poor body should be taken away by us, even though many desired to do this and to touch his holy flesh.

2 So he incited Nicetes, the father of Herod and brother of Alce, to plead with the magistrate not to give up his body, "or else," he said, "they may abandon the crucified one and begin to worship this man"—all this being done at the instigation and insistence of the Jews, who even watched when we were about to take it from the fire; they did not know that we will never be able to either to abandon the Christ who suffered for the salvation of the whole world of those who are saved, the blameless on behalf of sinners, or to worship anyone else.

3 For this one, who is the Son of God, we worship, but the martyrs we love as disciples and imitators of the Lord, as they deserve, on account of their matchless devotion to their own King and Teacher. May we also become their partners and fellow disciples!

18 The centurion, therefore, seeing the opposition raised by the Jews, set it in the middle and cremated it, as is their custom.

2 And so later on we took up his bones, which are more valuable than precious stones and finer than refined gold, and deposited them in a suitable place.

3 There gathering together, as we are able, with joy and gladness, the Lord will permit us to celebrate the birthday of his martyrdom in commemoration of those who have already fought in the contest, and for the training and preparation of those who will do so in the future.

19 Such is the story of the blessed Polycarp. Although he was martyred in Smyrna along with eleven others from Philadelphia, he alone is especially remembered by everyone, so that he is spoken of everywhere, even by pagans. He proved to be not only a distinguished teacher, but also an outstanding martyr, whose martyrdom all desire to imitate, since it was in accord with the pattern of the gospel of Christ.

2 By his endurance he defeated the unrighteous magistrate and so received the crown of immortality; now he rejoices with the apostles and all the righteous, and glorifies the almighty God and Father, and blesses our Lord Jesus Christ, the Savior of our souls and Helmsman of our bodies and Shepherd of the catholic church throughout the world.

20 You did indeed request that the things which happened be reported to you in some detail, but for the present we have given a summary, as it were, through our brother Marcianus. When you have informed yourselves about these things,

send the letter on to the brothers who are farther away, in order that they too may glorify the Lord, who makes selection from among his own servants.

2 Now to him who is able to bring us all by his grace and bounty into his eternal kingdom, through his only begotten Son, Jesus Christ, be glory, honor, power, and majesty forever. Greet all the saints. Those who are with us greet you, as does Evarestus, who wrote this, and his whole house.

21 Now the blessed Polycarp was martyred on the second day of the first part of the month Xanthicus, seven days before the kalends of March, on a great Sabbath, about two o'clock P.M. He was arrested by Herod, when Philip of Tralles was high priest during the proconsulship of Statius Quadratus, but while Jesus Christ was reigning as King forever. To him be glory, honor, majesty, and the eternal throne, from generation to generation. Amen.

22 We bid you farewell, brothers, as you walk by the word of Jesus Christ which is in accord with the gospel; with whom be glory to God for the salvation of the holy elect; just as the blessed Polycarp was martyred, in whose footsteps may we also be found in the kingdom of Jesus Christ.

>--+->--O--<-+-<

6. The Letter of the Churches of Vienne and Lyons

A major persecution erupted in 177 C.E. in the towns of Vienne and Lyons (Gaul) during the reign of Marcus Aurelius, who sanctioned the proceedings. The surviving account was written by Christians who managed to escape, who saw the hand of the Devil behind the

The Letter of the Churches of Vienne and Lyons, from *Eusebius: The History of the Church from Christ to Constantine*, trans. G. A. Williamson, rev. Andrew Louth (Penguin Classic 965, rev. ed. 1989) copyright © G. A. Williamson 1965. Revisions copyright © Andrew Louth, 1989. Used with permission.

brutalities. The persecution started with widespread social antagonism against the Christians (as they were banned from public places), erupted into mob violence, and ended in governmental intervention and official prosecution. Those confessing to be Christian were imprisoned and subjected to horrific tortures explicitly designed to make them apostatize. Those who did so were then released. Most of those arrested, however, remained true to their convictions, displaying remarkable zeal in their loyalty to one another and to their God, claiming that, despite the rumors of wrongdoing, they had done nothing to deserve punishment and insisting that the torments of the present were not at all to be compared with the fire that burns forever.

The servants of Christ at Vienne and Lyons in Gaul to our brothers in Asia and Phrygia who have the same faith and hope of redemption as we: peace, grace, and glory from God the Father and Christ Jesus our Lord.

The severity of our trials here, the unbridled fury of the heathen against God's people, the untold sufferings of the blessed martyrs, we are incapable of describing in detail: indeed no pen could do them justice. The adversary swooped on us with all his might, giving us now a foretaste of his advent, which undoubtedly is imminent. He left no stone unturned in his efforts to train his adherents and equip them to attack the servants of God, so that not only were we debarred from houses, baths, and the forum: they actually forbade any of us to be seen in any place whatever. But against them the grace of God put itself at our head, rescuing the weak and deploying against our enemies unshakeable pillars, able by their endurance to draw upon themselves the whole onslaught of the evil one. These charged into the fight, standing up to every kind of abuse and punishment, and made light of their heavy load as they hastened to Christ, proving beyond a doubt that the sufferings of the present time are not to be compared with the glory that is in store for us.

To begin with, they heroically endured whatever the surging crowd heaped on them, noisy abuse, blows, dragging along the ground, plundering, stoning, imprisonment, and everything that an infuriated mob normally does to hated enemies. Then they were marched into the forum and interrogated by the tribune and the city authorities before the whole population. When they confessed Christ, they were locked up in jail to await the governor's arrival. Later, when they were taken before him and he treated them with all the cruelty he reserves for Christians, Vettius Epagathus, one of our number, full of love towards God and towards his neighbor, came forward. His life conformed so closely to the Christian ideal that, young as he was, the same tribute might be paid to him as to old Zacharias: he had scrupulously observed all the commandments and ordinances of the Lord, and was untiring in service to his neighbor, utterly devoted to God and fervent in spirit. As such he found the judgment so unreasonably given against us more than he could bear: boiling with indignation, he applied for permission to speak in defence of the Christians, and to prove that there was nothing godless or irreligious in our society. The crowd round the tribunal howled him down, as he was a man of influence, and the governor dismissed his perfectly reasonable application with the curt question: "Are *you* a Christian?" In the clearest possible tones Vettius replied: "I am." And he, too, was admitted to the ranks of the martyrs. He was called the Christians' advocate, but he had in himself the Advocate, the Spirit that filled Zacharias, as he showed by the fullness of his love when he gladly laid down his own life in defence of his brother Christians. For he was and is a true disciple of Christ, following the Lamb wherever he goes.

Then the rest fell into two groups. It was clear that some were ready to be the first Gallic martyrs: they made a full confession of their testimony with the greatest eagerness. It was equally clear that others were not ready, that they had not trained and were still flabby, in no fit condition to face the strain of a struggle to the death. Of these some ten proved stillborn, causing us great distress and inexpressible grief, and damping the enthusiasm of those not yet arrested. However, in spite of the agonies they were suffering, these people stayed with the martyrs and did not desert them. But at the time we were all tormented by the doubts about their confessing Christ: we were not afraid of the punishments inflicted, but looking to the outcome and dreading lest anyone might fall away. But the arrests went on, and day after day those who were worthy filled up the number of the martyrs, so that from the two dioceses were collected all the active members who had done most to build up our church life. Among those arrested were some of our heathen domestics, as the governor had publicly announced that we were to be hunted out. These were ensnared by Satan, so that fearing the tortures which they saw inflicted on God's people, at the soldiers' instigation they falsely accused us of Thyestean banquets and Oedipean incest, and things we ought never to speak or think about, or even believe that such things ever happened among human beings. When these rumors spread, people all raged like wild beasts against us, so that even those who because of blood-relationship had previously exercised restraint now turned on us, grinding their teeth with fury. So was proved true the saying of our Lord: "The time will come when whoever kills you will think he is doing a service to God."[1] From then on the holy martyrs endured punishments beyond all description, while Satan strove to wring even from them some of the slanders.

The whole fury of crowd, governor, and soldiers fell with crushing force on Sanctus, the deacon from Vienne; on Maturus, very recently baptized but heroic in facing his ordeal; on Attalus, who had always been a pillar and support of the church in his native Pergamum; and on Blandina, through whom Christ proved that things which men regard as mean, unlovely, and comtemptible are by God deemed worthy of great glory, because of her love for him shown in power and not vaunted in appearance. When we were all afraid, and her earthly mistress (who was herself facing the ordeal of martyrdom) was in agony lest she should be unable even to make a bold confession of Christ because of bodily weakness, Blandina was filled with such power that those who took it in turns to subject her to every kind of torture from morning to night were exhausted by their efforts and confessed themselves beaten—they could think of nothing else to do to her. They were amazed that she was still breathing, for her whole body was mangled and her wounds gaped; they declared that torment of any one kind was enough to part soul and body, let alone a succession of torments of such extreme severity. But the blessed woman, wrestling magnificently, grew in strength as she proclaimed her faith, and found refreshment, rest, and insensibility to her sufferings in uttering the words: "I am a Christian: we do nothing to be ashamed of."

Sanctus was another who with magnificent, superhuman courage nobly withstood the entire range of human cruelty. Wicked people hoped that the persistence and severity of his tortures would force him to utter something improper, but with such determination did he stand up to their onslaughts that he would not tell them his own name, race, and birthplace, or whether he was a slave or free; to every question he replied in Latin: "I am a Christian." This he proclaimed over and over again, instead of name, birthplace, nationality, and everything else, and not another word did the heathen hear from him. Consequently, the governor and his torturers strained every nerve against him, so that when they could think of nothing else to do to him they ended by pressing red-hot copper plates against the most sensitive parts of his body. These were burning, but Sanctus remained unbending and unyielding, firm in his confession of faith, bedewed and fortified by the heavenly fountain of the water of life that flows from the depths of Christ's being. But his poor body was a witness to what he had suffered—it was all one wound and bruise, bent up and robbed of outward human shape, but, suffering in that body, Christ accomplished most glorious things, utterly defeat-

---

[1]John 16:2.

ing the adversary and proving as an example to the rest that where the Father's love is nothing can frighten us, where Christ's glory is nothing can hurt us. A few days later wicked people again put the martyr on the rack, thinking that now that his whole body was swollen and inflamed a further application of the same instruments would defeat him, unable as he was to bear even the touch of a hand; or that by dying under torture he would put fear into the rest. However, nothing of the sort happened: to their amazement his body became erect and straight as a result of these new torments, and recovered its former appearance and the use of the limbs; thus through the grace of Christ his second spell on the rack proved to be not punishment but cure.

Biblis again, one of those who had denied Christ, was handed over to punishment by the devil, who imagined that he had already devoured her and hoped to damn her as a slanderer by forcing her to say wicked things about us, being—so he thought—a feeble creature, easily broken. But on the rack she came to her senses, and, so to speak, awoke out of deep sleep, reminded by the brief chastisement of the eternal punishment in hell. She flatly contradicted the slanderers: "How could children be eaten by people who are not even allowed to eat the blood of brute beasts?" From then on she insisted that she was a Christian, and so she joined the ranks of the martyrs.

When the tyrant's instruments of torture had been utterly defeated by Christ through the endurance of the blessed saints, the devil resorted to other devices—confinement in the darkness of a filthy prison; clamping the feet in the stocks, stretched apart to the fifth hole; and other agonies which warders when angry and full of the devil are apt to inflict on helpless prisoners. Thus the majority were suffocated in prison—those whom the Lord wished to depart in this way, so revealing His glory. Some, though tortured so cruelly that even if they received every care it seemed impossible for them to survive, lived on in the prison, deprived of all human attention but strengthened by the Lord and fortified in body and soul, stimulating and encouraging the rest. But the young ones who had been recently arrested and had not previously undergone physical torture could not bear the burden of confinement and died in prison.

Blessed Pothinus, who had been entrusted with the care of the Lyons diocese, was over ninety years of age and physically very weak. He could scarcely breathe because of his chronic physical weakness, but was strengthened by spiritual enthusiasm because of his pressing desire for martyrdom. Even he was dragged before the tribunal, and though his body was feeble from age and disease, his life was preserved in him, that thereby Christ might triumph. He was conveyed to the tribunal by the soldiers, accompanied by the civil authorities and the whole populace, who shouted and jeered at him as though he were Christ himself. But he bore the noble witness. When the governor asked him "Who is the Christians' god?", he replied: "If you are a fit person, you shall know." Thereupon he was mercilessly dragged along beneath a rain of blows, those close by assailing him viciously with hands and feet and showing no respect for his age, and those at a distance hurling at him whatever came to hand, and all thinking it a shocking neglect of their duty to be behind-hand in savagery towards him, for they imagined that in this way they would avenge their gods. Scarcely breathing, he was flung into prison, and two days later he passed away.

Then occurred a great dispensation of God, and the infinite mercy of Jesus was revealed to a degree rarely known in the brotherhood of Christians, but not beyond the skill of Christ. Those who when the first arrests took place had denied him were jailed with the others and shared their sufferings: on this occasion they gained nothing by their denial, for whereas those who declared what they were were jailed as Christians, no other charge being brought against them, the others were further detained as foul murderers and punished twice as much as the rest. For the faithful were relieved of half their burden by the joy of martyrdom and hope of the promises, and by love towards Christ and the Spirit of the Father, but the unfaithful were tormented by their conscience, so that as they passed they could easily be picked out from the rest by the look on their faces. The faithful stepped out with a happy smile, wondrous glory and grace blended on their faces, so that even their fetters hung like beautiful ornaments around them and they resembled a bride adorned with golden lace elaborately wrought; they were perfumed also with the sweet savour of Christ, so that some people thought they had smeared themselves with worldly cosmetics. The unfaithful were dejected, downcast, ill-favoured, and devoid of charm; in addition they were gibed at by the heathen as contemptible cowards; they were accused of homicide, and had lost the honorable, glorious, life-giving name. The sight of this stiffened the resistance of the rest: those who were arrested unhesitatingly declared their faith without one thought for the devil's promptings. . . .

From that time on, their martyrdoms embraced death in all its forms. From flowers of every shape and color they wove a crown to offer to the Father; and so it was fitting that the valiant champions should endure an everchanging conflict, and having triumphed gloriously should win the mighty crown of immortality. Maturus, Sanctus, Blandina, and Attalus were taken into the amphitheater to face the wild beasts, and to furnish open proof of the inhumanity of the heathen, the day of fighting wild beasts being purposely arranged for our people. There, before the eyes of all, Maturus and Sanctus were again taken through the whole series of punishments, as if they had suffered nothing at all before, or rather as if they had already defeated their opponents in bout after bout and were now battling for the victor's crown. Again they ran the gauntlet of whips, in accordance with local custom; they were mauled by the beasts, and endured every torment that the frenzied mob on one side or the other demanded and howled for, culminating in the iron chair which roasted their flesh and suffocated them with the reek. Not even then were their tormentors satisfied: they grew more and more frenzied in their desire to overwhelm the resistance of the martyrs, but do what they might they heard nothing from Sanctus beyond the words he had repeated from the beginning—the declaration of his faith.

In these two, despite their prolonged and terrible ordeal, life still lingered; but in the end they were sacrificed, after being made all day long a spectacle to the world in place of the gladiatorial contest in its many forms. But Blandina was hung on a post and exposed as food for the wild beasts let loose in the arena. She looked as if she were hanging in the form of a cross, and through her ardent prayers she stimulated great enthusiasm in those undergoing their ordeal, who in their agony saw with their outward eyes in the person of their sister the One who was crucified for them, that he might convince those who believe in him that any man who has suffered for the glory of Christ has fellowship forever with the living God. As none of the beasts had yet touched her she was taken down from the post and returned to the jail, to be kept for a second ordeal, that by victory in further contests she might make irrevocable the sentence passed on the crooked serpent, and spur on her brother Christians—a small, weak, despised woman who had put on Christ, the great invincible champion, and in bout after bout had defeated her adversary and through conflict had won the crown of immortality.

Attalus too was loudly demanded by the mob, as he was a man of note. He strode in, ready for the fray, in the strength of a clear conscience, for he had trained hard in the school of Christ and had been one of our constant witnesses to the truth. He was led round the amphitheater preceded by a placard on which was written in Latin "This is Attalus the Christian," while the people were bursting with fury against him. But when the governor was informed that he was a Roman, he ordered him to be put back in jail with the others, about whom he had written to Caesar and was awaiting instructions.

Their time of respite was not idle or unfruitful: through their endurance the infinite mercy of Christ was revealed; for through the living the dead were being brought back to life; and martyrs were bestowing grace on those who had failed to be martyrs, and there was great joy in the heart of the Virgin Mother, who was receiving her stillborn children back alive; for by their means most of those who had denied their Master travelled once more the same road, conceived and quickened a second time, and learned to confess Christ. Alive now and braced up, their ordeal sweetened by God, who does not desire the death of the sinner but is gracious towards repentance, they advanced to the tribunal to be again interrogated by the governor. For Caesar had issued a command that they should be tortured to death, but any who still denied Christ should be released; so at the inauguration of the local festival, at which all the heathen congregate in vast numbers, the governor summoned them to his tribunal, making a theatrical show of the blessed ones and displaying them to the crowds. After re-examination, all who seemed to possess Roman citizenship were beheaded and the rest sent to the beasts. Christ was greatly glorified in those who had previously denied him but now confounded heathen expectation by confessing him. They were individually examined with the intention that they should be released, but they confessed him and so joined the ranks of the martyrs. Left outside were those who had never had any vestige of faith or notion of the wedding-garment or thought of the fear of God, but by their very conduct brought the Way into disrepute—truly the sons of perdition. But the rest were all added to the Church. . . .

To crown all this, on the last day of the sports Blandina was again brought in, and with her Ponticus, a lad of about fifteen. Day after day they had been taken in to watch the rest being punished, and attempts were made to make them swear by the heathen idols. When they stood firm and treated these efforts with contempt, the mob was infuriated with them, so that the boy's tender age called forth no pity and the woman no respect. They subjected them to every horror and inflicted every punishment in turn, attempting again and again to make them swear, but to no purpose. Ponticus was encouraged by his sister in Christ, so that the heathen saw that she was urging him on and stiffening his resistance, and he bravely endured every punishment till he gave back his spirit to God. Last of all, like a noble mother who had encouraged her children and sent them before her in triumph to the King, blessed Blandina herself passed through all the ordeals of her children and hastened to rejoin them, rejoicing and exulting at her departure as if invited to a wedding supper,

not thrown to the beasts. After the whips, after the beasts, after the griddle, she was finally dropped into a basket and thrown to a bull. Time after time the animal tossed her, but she was indifferent now to all that happened to her, because of her hope and sure hold on all that her faith meant, and of her communing with Christ. Then she, too, was sacrificed, while the heathen themselves admitted that never yet had they known a woman suffer so much or so long.

Not even this was enough to satisfy their insane cruelty to God's people. Goaded by a wild beast, wild and barbarous tribes were incapable of stopping, and the dead bodies became the next object of their vindictiveness. Their defeat did not humble them, because they were without human understanding; rather it inflamed their bestial fury, and governor and people vented on us the same inexcusable hatred, so fulfilling the scripture. "Let the wicked man be wicked still, the righteous man righteous still."[2] Those who had been suffocated in jail they threw to the dogs, watching carefully night and day to see that no one received the last offices at our hands. Then they threw out the remains left by the beasts and the fire, some torn to ribbons, some burnt to cinders, and set a military guard to watch for days on end the trunks and severed heads of the rest, denying burial to them also. Some raged and ground their teeth at them, longing to take some further revenge on them; others laughed and jeered, magnifying their idols and giving them credit for the punishment of their enemies; while those who were more reasonable, and seemed to have a little human feeling, exclaimed with the utmost scorn: "Where is their god? and what did they get for their religion, which they preferred to their own lives?" Such were their varied reactions, while we were greatly distressed by our inability to give the bodies burial. Darkness did not make it possible, and they refused all offers of payment and were deaf to entreaty; but they guarded the remains with the greatest care, regarding it as a triumph if they could prevent burial . . .

Thus the martyrs' bodies, after six days' exposure to every kind of insult and to the open sky,

---

[2]Rev 22:11.

were finally burnt to ashes and swept by these wicked men into the Rhône which flows near by, that not even a trace of them might be seen on the earth again. And this they did as if they could defeat God and rob the dead of their rebirth, "in order," they said, "that they may have no hope of resurrection—the belief that has led them to bring into this country a new foreign cult and treat torture with contempt, going willingly and cheerfully to their death. Now let's see if they'll rise again, and if their god can help them and save them from our hands."

⊱━◈━◦━◇━◈━⊰

7. The Acts of the Scillitan Martyrs

The oldest Christian document to survive from North Africa, the Latin account of the Scillitan Martyrs provides an actual trial narrative of twelve Christians in Carthage, under the proconsul Saturninus in the year 180 C.E. The account is remarkable for showing both the firm resolve of the prisoners, who refuse to countenance any form of compromise, and the sincere attempts of the magistrate to convince them of the folly of their ways and to make a simple act of worship of the divine spirit (genius) of the emperor. Refusing to bow under pressure, the twelve are condemned to death and immediately taken out and beheaded.

In the consulship of Praesens (for the second time) and Claudian, on the seventeenth day of July there were arraigned at Carthage in the governor's chambers Speratus, Nartzalus, Cittinus, [Veturius, Felix, Aquilinus, Laetantius, Januaria, Generosa,][1] Donata, Secunda, and Vestia.

The proconsul Saturninus said: "If you return to your senses, you can obtain the pardon of our lord the emperor."

Speratus said: "We have never done wrong; we have never lent ourselves to wickedness. Never have we uttered a curse; but when abused, we have given thanks, for we hold our own emperor in honor."

Saturninus the proconsul said: "We too are a religious people, and our religion is a simple one: we swear by the genius of our lord the emperor and we offer prayers for his health—as you also ought to do."

Speratus said: "If you will give me a calm hearing, I shall tell you the mystery of simplicity."

"If you begin to malign our sacred rites," said Saturninus, "I shall not listen to you. But swear rather by the genius of our lord the emperor."

Speratus said: "I do not recognize the empire of this world. Rather, I serve that God whom no one has seen, nor can see, with these eyes. I have

[1]The list here, which gives only six of the martyrs instead of the twelve who are executed (in § 16), seems to have been accidentally shortened in the manuscripts.

not stolen; and on any purchase I pay the tax, for I acknowledge my lord who is the emperor of kings and of all nations."

The proconsul Saturninus said to the others: "Cease to be of this persuasion."

Speratus said: "It is an evil persuasion to commit murder, to bear false witness."

Saturninus the proconsul said: "Have no part in this folly of his!"

Cittinus said: "We have no one else to fear but our Lord God who is in heaven."

Donata said: "Pay honor to Caesar as Caesar; but it is God we fear."

Vestia said: "I am a Christian."

Secunda said: "I wish to be what I am."

The proconsul Saturninus said to Speratus: "Do you persist in remaining a Christian?"

Speratus said: "I am a Christian." And all agreed with him.

Saturninus the proconsul said: "You wish no time for consideration?"

Speratus said: "In so just a matter there is no need for consideration."

The proconsul Saturninus said: "What have you in your case?"

Speratus said: "Books and letters of a just man named Paul."

The proconsul Saturninus said: "You are granted a reprieve of thirty days: think it over."

Once again Speratus said, "I am a Christian!" And with him all the others agreed.

Saturninus the proconsul read his decision from a tablet: "Whereas Speratus, Nartzalus, Cittinus, Donata, Vestia, Secunda, and the others have confessed that they have been living in accordance with the rites of the Christians, and whereas though given the opportunity to return to the usage of the Romans they have persevered in their obstinacy, they are hereby condemned to be executed by the sword."

Speratus said: "We thank God!"

Nartzalus said: "Today we are martyrs in heaven. Thanks be to God!"

The proconsul Saturninus had the following proclaimed by a herald: "Sperata, Nartzalus, Cittinus, Veturius, Felix, Aquilinus, Laetantius, Januaria, Generosa, Vestia, Donata, Secunda, are to be led forth to execution."

They all said: "Thanks be to God!" And straightway they were beheaded for the name of Christ.

▷—⊷—○—⊶—◁

8. The Martyrdom of Perpetua and Felicitas

An account filled with gripping pathos, "The Martyrdom of Perpetua and Felicitas" records the arrest, imprisonment, trials, and execution of a young Roman matron, Perpetua, and her female slave, Felicitas. Remarkably, the first part of the account reproduces Perpetua's own diary, kept while she was in prison and edited by the anonymous author who provided the concluding story of the martyrdom itself. The action takes place in Carthage in 202–203 C.E., during the reign of the Emperor Septimius Severus. Among the notable features of the report are (a) Perpetua's familial relations, especially with her in-

The Martyrdom of Perpetua and Felicitas, from *The Acts of the Christian Martyrs*, trans. Herbert Musurillo.
© Oxford University Press, 1972. Reprinted by permission of Oxford University Press.

fant child, whom she must relinquish, her anguished (non-Christian) father, who begs her to relent, and her dead brother, whom she sees twice in dreams; (b) her vivid night visions, which she narrates as divine predictions of her fate but which also reveal a good deal about her understanding of the world and her own internal struggles, and (c) the explicit details of her prison life and, especially, of the martyrdom she endures along with her slave, Felicitas, who herself has just recently given birth.

1 The deeds recounted about the faith in ancient times were a proof of God's favor and achieved the spiritual strengthening of people as well; and they were set forth in writing precisely that honor might be rendered to God and comfort to people by the recollection of the past through the written word. Should not then more recent examples be set down that contribute equally to both ends? For indeed these too will one day become ancient and needful for the ages to come, even though in our own day they may enjoy less prestige because of the prior claim of antiquity.

Let those then who would restrict the power of the one Spirit to times and seasons look to this: the more recent events should be considered the greater, being later than those of old, and this is a consequence of the extraordinary graces promised for the last stage of time. For "in the last days, God declares, I will pour out my Spirit upon all flesh and their sons and daughters shall prophesy and on my manservants and my maidservants I will pour my Spirit and the young men shall see visions and the old men shall dream dreams."[1] So too we hold in honor and acknowledge not only new prophecies but new visions as well, according to the promise. And we consider all the other functions of the Holy Spirit as intended for the good of the Church; for the same Spirit has been sent to distribute all his gifts to all, as the Lord apportions to everyone. For this reason we deem it imperative to set them forth and to make them known through the word for the glory of God. Thus no one of weak or despairing faith may think that supernatural grace was present only among men of ancient times, either in the grace of martyrdom or of visions, for God always achieves what he promises, as a witness to the non-believer and a blessing to the faithful.

And so, my brethren and little children, that which we have heard and have touched with our hands we proclaim also to you, so that those of you that were witnesses may recall the glory of the Lord and those that now learn of it through hearing may have fellowship with the holy martyrs and, through them, with the Lord Christ Jesus, to whom belong splendor and honor for all ages. Amen.

2 A number of young catechumens were arrested, Revocatus and his fellow slave Felicitas, Saturninus and Secundulus, and with them Vibia Perpetua, a newly married woman of good family and upbringing. Her mother and father were still alive and one of her two brothers was a catechumen like herself. She was about twenty-two years old and had an infant son at the breast. (Now from this point on the entire account of her ordeal is her own, according to her own ideas and in the way that she herself wrote it down.)

3 While we were still under arrest (she said) my father out of love for me was trying to persuade me and shake my resolution. "Father," said I, "do you see this vase here, for example, or waterpot or whatever?"

"Yes, I do," said he.

And I told him: "Could it be called by any other name than what it is?"

And he said: "No."

"Well, so too I cannot be called anything other than what I am, a Christian."

At this my father was so angered by the word "Christian" that he moved towards me as though he would pluck my eyes out. But he left it at that and departed, vanquished along with his diabolical arguments.

---

[1] Acts 2:17–18.

For a few days afterwards I gave thanks to the Lord that I was separated from my father, and I was comforted by his absence. During these few days I was baptized, and I was inspired by the Spirit not to ask for any other favor after the water but simply the perseverance of the flesh. A few days later we were lodged in the prison; and I was terrified, as I had never before been in such a dark hole. What a difficult time it was! With the crowd the heat was stifling; then there was the extortion of the soldiers; and to crown all, I was tortured with worry for my baby there.

Then Tertius and Pomponius, those blessed deacons who tried to take care of us, bribed the soldiers to allow us to go to a better part of the prison to refresh ourselves for a few hours. Everyone then left that dungeon and shifted for himself. I nursed my baby, who was faint from hunger. In my anxiety I spoke to my mother about the child, I tried to comfort my brother, and I gave the child in their charge. I was in pain because I saw them suffering out of pity for me. These were the trials I had to endure for many days. Then I got permission for my baby to stay with me in prison. At once I recovered my health, relieved as I was of my worry and anxiety over the child. My prison had suddenly become a palace, so that I wanted to be there rather than anywhere else.

4 Then my brother said to me: "Dear sister, you are greatly privileged; surely you might ask for a vision to discover whether you are to be condemned or freed."

Faithfully I promised that I would, for I knew that I could speak with the Lord, whose great blessings I had come to experience. And so I said: "I shall tell you tomorrow." Then I made my request and this was the vision I had.

I saw a ladder of tremendous height made of bronze, reaching all the way to the heavens, but it was so narrow that only one person could climb up at a time. To the sides of the ladder were attached all sorts of metal weapons: there were swords, spears, hooks, daggers, and spikes; so that if anyone tried to climb up carelessly or without paying attention, he would be mangled and his flesh would adhere to the weapons.

At the foot of the ladder lay a dragon of enormous size, and it would attack those who tried to climb up and try to terrify them from doing so. And Saturus was the first to go up, he who was later to give himself up of his own accord. He had been the builder of our strength, although he was not present when we were arrested. And he arrived at the top of the staircase and he looked back and said to me: "Perpetua, I am waiting for you. But take care; do not let the dragon bite you."

"He will not harm me," I said, "in the name of Christ Jesus."

Slowly, as though he were afraid of me, the dragon stuck his head out from underneath the ladder. Then, using it as my first step, I trod on his head and went up.

Then I saw an immense garden, and in it a grey-haired man sat in shepherd's garb; tall he was, and milking sheep. And standing around him were many thousands of people clad in white garments. He raised his head, looked at me, and said: "I am glad you have come, my child."

He called me over to him and gave me, as it were, a mouthful of the milk he was drawing; and I took it into my cupped hands and consumed it. And all those who stood around said: "Amen!" At the sound of this word I came to, with the taste of something sweet still in my mouth. I at once told this to my brother, and we realized that we would have to suffer, and that from now on we would no longer have any hope in this life.

5 A few days later there was a rumor that we were going to be given a hearing. My father also arrived from the city, worn with worry, and he came to see me with the idea of persuading me.

"Daughter," he said, "have pity on my grey head—have pity on me your father, if I deserve to be called your father, if I have favored you above all your brothers, if I have raised you to reach this prime of your life. Do not abandon me to be the reproach of others. Think of your brothers, think of your mother and your aunt, think of your child, who will not be able to live once you are gone. Give up your pride! You will destroy all of us! None of us will ever be able to speak freely again if anything happens to you."

This was the way my father spoke out of love for me, kissing my hands and throwing himself down before me. With tears in his eyes he no longer addressed me as his daughter but as a woman. I was sorry for my father's sake, because he alone of all my kin would be unhappy to see me suffer.

I tried to comfort him saying: "It will all happen in the prisoner's dock as God wills; for you may be sure that we are not left to ourselves but are all in his power."

And he left me in great sorrow.

6 One day while we were eating breakfast we were suddenly hurried off for a hearing. We arrived at the forum, and straight away the story went about the neighborhood near the forum and a huge crowd gathered. We walked up to the prisoner's dock. All the others when questioned admitted their guilt. Then, when it came my turn, my father appeared with my son, dragged me from the step, and said: "Perform the sacrifice—have pity on your baby!"

Hilarianus the governor, who had received his judicial powers as the successor of the late proconsul Minucius Timinianus, said to me: "Have pity on your father's grey head; have pity on your infant son. Offer the sacrifice for the welfare of the emperors."

"I will not," I retorted.

"Are you a Christian?" said Hilarianus.

And I said: "Yes, I am."

When my father persisted in trying to dissuade me, Hilarianus ordered him to be thrown to the ground and beaten with a rod. I felt sorry for father, just as if I myself had been beaten. I felt sorry for his pathetic old age.

Then Hilarianus passed sentence on all of us: we were condemned to the beasts, and we returned to prison in high spirits. But my baby had got used to being nursed at the breast and to staying with me in prison. So I sent the deacon Pomponius straight away to my father to ask for the baby. But father refused to give him over. But as God willed, the baby had no further desire for the breast, nor did I suffer any inflammation; and so I was relieved of any anxiety for my child and of any discomfort in my breasts.

7 Some days later when we were all at prayer, suddenly while praying I spoke out and uttered the name Dinocrates. I was surprised; for the name had never entered my mind until that moment. And I was pained when I recalled what had happened to him. At once I realized that I was privileged to pray for him. I began to pray for him and to sigh deeply for him before the Lord. That very night I had the following vision. I saw Dinocrates come out of a dark hole, where there were many others with him, very hot and thirsty, pale and dirty. On his face was the wound he had when he died.

Now Dinocrates had been my brother according to the flesh; but he had died horribly of cancer of the face when he was seven years old, and his death was a source of loathing to everyone. Thus it was for him that I made my prayer. There was a great abyss between us: neither could approach the other. Where Dinocrates stood there was a pool full of water; and its rim was higher than the child's height, so that Dinocrates had to stretch himself up to drink. I was sorry that, though the pool had water in it, Dinocrates could not drink because of the height of the rim. Then I woke up, realizing that my brother was suffering. But I was confident that I could help him in his trouble; and I prayed for him every day until we were transferred to the military prison. For we were supposed to fight with the beasts at the military games to be held on the occasion of the emperor Geta's birthday. And I prayed for my brother day and night with tears and sighs that this favor might be granted me.

8 On the day we were kept in chains, I had this vision shown to me. I saw the same spot that I had seen before, but there was Dinocrates all clean, well dressed, and refreshed. I saw a scar where the wound had been; and the pool I had seen before now had its rim lowered to the level of the child's waist. And Dinocrates kept drinking water from it, and there above the rim was a golden bowl full of water. And Dinocrates drew close and began to drink from it, and yet the bowl remained full. And when he had drunk enough of the water, he began to play as children do. Then I

awoke, and I realized that he had been delivered from his suffering.

9 Some days later, an adjutant named Pudens, who was in charge of the prison, began to show us great honor, realizing that we possessed some great power within us. And he began to allow many visitors to see us for our mutual comfort.

Now the day of the contest was approaching, and my father came to see me overwhelmed with sorrow. He started tearing the hairs from his beard and threw them on the ground; he then threw himself on the ground and began to curse his old age and to say such words as would move all creation. I felt sorry for his unhappy old age.

10 The day before we were to fight with the beasts I saw the following vision. Pomponius the deacon came to the prison gates and began to knock violently. I went out and opened the gate for him. He was dressed in an unbelted white tunic, wearing elaborate sandals. And he said to me: "Perpetua, come; we are waiting for you."

Then he took my hand and we began to walk through rough and broken country. At last we came to the amphitheater out of breath, and he led me into the center of the arena.

Then he told me: "Do not be afraid. I am here, struggling with you." Then he left.

I looked at the enormous crowd who watched in astonishment. I was surprised that no beasts were let loose on me; for I knew that I was condemned to die by the beasts. Then out came an Egyptian against me, of vicious appearance, together with his seconds, to fight with me. There also came up to me some handsome young men to be my seconds and assistants.

My clothes were stripped off, and suddenly I was a man. My seconds began to rub me down with oil (as they are wont to do before a contest). Then I saw the Egyptian on the other side rolling in the dust. Next there came forth a man of marvellous stature, such that he rose above the top of the amphitheater. He was clad in a beltless purple tunic with two stripes (one on either side) running down the middle of his chest. He wore sandals that were wondrously made of gold and silver,

and he carried a wand like an athletic trainer and a green branch on which there were golden apples.

And he asked for silence and said: "If this Egyptian defeats her he will slay her with the sword. But if she defeats him, she will receive this branch." Then he withdrew.

We drew close to one another and began to let our fists fly. My opponent tried to get hold of my feet, but I kept striking him in the face with the heels of my feet. Then I was raised up into the air and I began to pummel him without as it were touching the ground. Then when I noticed there was a lull, I put my two hands together linking the fingers of one hand with those of the other and thus I got hold of his head. He fell flat on his face and I stepped on his head.

The crowd began to shout and my assistants started to sing psalms. Then I walked up to the trainer and took the branch. He kissed me and said to me: "Peace be with you, my daughter!" I began to walk in triumph towards the Gate of Life. Then I awoke. I realized that it was not with wild animals that I would fight but with the Devil, but I knew that I would win the victory. So much for what I did up until the eve of the contest. About what happened at the contest itself, let him write of it who will.

11 But the blessed Saturus has also made known his own vision and he has written it out with his own hand. We had died, he said, and had put off the flesh, and we began to be carried towards the east by four angels who did not touch us with their hands. But we moved along not on our backs facing upwards but as though we were climbing up a gentle hill. And when we were free of the world, we first saw an intense light. And I said to Perpetua (for she was at my side): "This is what the Lord promised us. We have received his promise."

While we were being carried by these four angels, a great open space appeared, which seemed to be a garden, with rose bushes and all manner of flowers. The trees were as tall as cypresses, and their leaves were constantly falling. In the garden there were four other angels more splendid than the others. When they saw us they paid us homage and said to the other angels in admiration: "Why, they are here! They are here!"

Then the four angels that were carrying us grew fearful and set us down. Then we walked across to an open area by way of a broad road, and there we met Jucundus, Saturninus, and Artaxius, who were burnt alive in the same persecution, together with Quintus who had actually died as a martyr in prison. We asked them where they had been. And the other angels said to us: "First come and enter and greet the Lord."

12 Then we came to a place whose walls seemed to be constructed of light. And in front of the gate stood four angels, who entered in and put on white robes. We also entered and we heard the sound of voices in unison chanting endlessly: "Holy, holy, holy!" In the same place we seemed to see an aged man with white hair and a youthful face, though we did not see his feet. On his right and left were four elders, and behind them stood other aged men. Surprised, we entered and stood before a throne: four angels lifted us up and we kissed the aged man and he touched our faces with his hand. And the elders said to us: "Let us rise." And we rose and gave the kiss of peace. Then the elders said to us: "Go and play."

To Perpetua I said: "Your wish is granted."

She said to me: "Thanks be to God that I am happier here now than I was in the flesh."

13 Then we went out and before the gates we saw the bishop Optatus on the right and Aspasius the presbyter and teacher on the left, each of them far apart and in sorrow. They threw themselves at our feet and said: "Make peace between us. For you have gone away and left us thus."

And we said to them: "Are you not our bishop, and are you not our presbyter? How can you fall at our feet?"

We were very moved and embraced them. Perpetua then began to speak with them in Greek, and we drew them apart into the garden under a rose arbor.

While we were talking with them, the angels said to them: "Allow them to rest. Settle whatever

quarrels you have among yourselves." And they were put to confusion.

Then they said to Optatus: "You must scold your flock. They approach you as though they had come from the games, quarreling about the different teams."

And it seemed as though they wanted to close the gates. And there we began to recognize many of our brethren, martyrs among them. All of us were sustained by a most delicious odor that seemed to satisfy us. And then I woke up happy.

14 Such were the remarkable visions of these martyrs, Saturus and Perpetua, written by themselves. As for Secundulus, God called him from this world earlier than the others while he was still in prison, by a special grace that he might not have to face the animals. Yet his flesh, if not his spirit, knew the sword.

15 As for Felicitas, she too enjoyed the Lord's favor in this wise. She had been pregnant when she was arrested, and was now in her eighth month. As the day of the spectacle drew near she was very distressed that her martyrdom would be postponed because of her pregnancy; for it is against the law for women with child to be executed. Thus she might have to shed her holy, innocent blood afterwards along with others who were common criminals. Her comrades in martyrdom were also saddened; for they were afraid that they would have to leave behind so fine a companion to travel alone on the same road to hope. And so, two days before the contest, they poured forth a prayer to the Lord in one torrent of common grief. And immediately after their prayer the birth pains came upon her. She suffered a good deal in her labor because of the natural difficulty of an eight months' delivery.

Hence one of the assistants of the prison guards said to her: "You suffer so much now—what will you do when you are tossed to the beasts? Little did you think of them when you refused to sacrifice."

"What I am suffering now," she replied, "I suffer by myself. But then another will be inside me who will suffer for me, just as I shall be suffering for him."

And she gave birth to a girl; and one of the sisters brought her up as her own daughter.

16 Therefore, since the Holy Spirit has permitted the story of this contest to be written down and by so permitting has willed it, we shall carry out the command or, indeed, the commission of the most saintly Perpetua, however unworthy I might be to add anything to this glorious story. At the same time I shall add one example of her perseverance and nobility of soul.

The military tribune had treated them with extraordinary severity because on the information of certain very foolish people he became afraid that they would be spirited out of the prison by magical spells.

Perpetua spoke to him directly. "Why can you not even allow us to refresh ourselves properly? For we are the most distinguished of the condemned prisoners, seeing that we belong to the emperor; we are to fight on his very birthday. Would it not be to your credit if we were brought forth on the day in a healthier condition?"

The officer became disturbed and grew red. So it was that he gave the order that they were to be more humanely treated; and he allowed her brothers and other persons to visit, so that the prisoners could dine in their company. By this time the adjutant who was head of the jail was himself a Christian.

17 On the day before, when they had their last meal, which is called the free banquet, they celebrated not a banquet but rather a love feast. They spoke to the mob with the same steadfastness, warned them of God's judgment, stressing the joy they would have in their suffering, and ridiculing the curiosity of those that came to see them. Saturus said: "Will not tomorrow be enough for you? Why are you so eager to see something that you dislike? Our friends today will be our enemies on the morrow. But take careful note of what we look like so that you will recognize us on the day." Thus everyone would depart from the prison in amazement, and many of them began to believe.

18 The day of their victory dawned, and they marched from the prison to the amphithe-

ater joyfully as though they were going to heaven with calm faces, trembling, if at all, with joy rather than fear. Perpetua went along with shining countenance and calm step, as the beloved of God, as a wife of Christ, putting down everyone's stare by her own intense gaze. With them also was Felicitas, glad that she had safely given birth so that now she could fight the beasts, going from one blood bath to another, from the midwife to the gladiator, ready to wash after childbirth in a second baptism.

They were then led up to the gates and the men were forced to put on the robes of priests of Saturn, the women the dress of the priestesses of Ceres. But the noble Perpetua strenuously resisted this to the end.

"We came to this of our own free will, that our freedom should not be violated. We agreed to pledge our lives provided that we would do no such thing. You agreed with us to do this."

Even injustice recognized justice. The military tribune agreed. They were to be brought into the arena just as they were. Perpetua then began to sing a psalm: she was already treading on the head of the Egyptian. Revocatus, Saturninus, and Saturus began to warn the onlooking mob. Then when they came within sight of Hilarianus, they suggested by their notions and gestures: "You have condemned us, but God will condemn you" was what they were saying.

At this the crowds became enraged and demanded that they be scourged before a line of gladiators. And they rejoiced at this that they had obtained a share in the Lord's sufferings.

19 But he who said, "Ask and you shall receive,"[2] answered their prayer by giving each one the death he had asked for. For whenever they would discuss among themselves their desire for martyrdom, Saturninus indeed insisted that he wanted to be exposed to all the different beasts, that his crown might be all the more glorious. And so at the outset of the contest he and Revocatus were matched with a leopard, and then while in the stocks they were attacked by a bear.

---

[2]John 16:24.

As for Saturus, he dreaded nothing more than a bear, and he counted on being killed by one bite of a leopard. Then he was matched with a wild boar; but the gladiator who had tied him to the animal was gored by the boar and died a few days after the contest, whereas Saturus was only dragged along. Then when he was bound in the stocks awaiting the bear, the animal refused to come out of the cages, so that Saturus was called back once more unhurt.

20 For the young women, however, the Devil had prepared a mad heifer. This was an unusual animal, but it was chosen that their sex might be matched with that of the beast. So they were stripped naked, placed in nets, and thus brought out into the arena. Even the crowd was horrified when they saw that one was a delicate young girl and the other was a woman fresh from childbirth with the milk still dripping from her breasts. And so they were brought back again and dressed in unbelted tunics.

First the heifer tossed Perpetua and she fell on her back. Then sitting up she pulled down the tunic that was ripped along the side so that it covered her thighs, thinking more of her modesty than of her pain. Next she asked for a pin to fasten her untidy hair: for it was not right that a martyr should die with her hair in disorder, lest she might seem to be mourning in her hour of triumph.

Then she got up. And seeing that Felicitas had been crushed to the ground, she went over to her, gave her her hand, and lifted her up. Then the two stood side by side. But the cruelty of the mob was by now appeased, and so they were called back through the Gate of Life.

There Perpetua was held up by a man named Rusticus who was at the time a catechumen and kept close to her. She awoke from a kind of sleep (so absorbed had she been in ecstasy in the Spirit) and she began to look about her. Then to the amazement of all she said: "When are we going to be thrown to that heifer or whatever it is?"

When told that this had already happened, she refused to believe it until she noticed the marks of her rough experience on her person and her dress. Then she called for her brother and spoke to him together with the catechumens and said: "You must all stand fast in the faith and love one another, and do not be weakened by what we have gone through."

21 At another gate Saturus was earnestly addressing the soldier Pudens. "It is exactly," he said, "as I foretold and predicted. So far not one animal has touched me. So now you may believe me with all your heart: I am going in there and I shall be finished off with one bite of the leopard." And immediately as the contest was coming to a close a leopard was let loose, and after one bite Saturus was so drenched with blood that as he came away the mob roared in witness to his second baptism: "Well washed! Well washed!" For well washed indeed was one who had been bathed in this manner.

Then he said to the soldier Pudens: "Goodbye. Remember me, and remember the faith. These things should not disturb you but rather strengthen you."

And with this he asked Pudens for a ring from his finger, and dipping it into his wound he gave it back to him again as a pledge and as a record of his bloodshed.

Shortly after he was thrown unconscious with the rest in the usual spot to have his throat cut. But the mob asked that their bodies be brought out into the open that their eyes might be the guilty witnesses of the sword that pierced their flesh. And so the martyrs got up and went to the spot of their own accord as the people wanted them to, and kissing one another they sealed their martyrdom with the ritual kiss of peace. The others took the sword in silence and without moving, especially Saturus, who being the first to climb the stairway was the first to die. For once again he was waiting for Perpetua. Perpetua, however, had yet to taste more pain. She screamed as she was struck on the bone; then she took the trembling hand of the young gladiator and guided it to her throat. It was as though so great a woman, feared as she was by the unclean spirit, could not be dispatched unless she herself were willing.

Ah, most valiant and blessed martyrs! Truly are you called and chosen for the glory of Christ Jesus our Lord! And any one who exalts, honors, and worships his glory should read for the consolation of the Church these new deeds of heroism which are no less significant than the tales of old. For these new manifestations of virtue will bear witness to one and the same Spirit who still operates, and to God the Father almighty, to his Son Jesus Christ our Lord, to whom is splendor and immeasurable power for all the ages. Amen.

Chapter 4

The Defense of Christianity
The Early Christian Apologists

When Christians came under attack by their opponents—whether non-Christian Jews or pagans, whether families, friends, mobs, or governmental officials—they naturally had to defend themselves. In the Greek language spoken throughout the Roman empire, the term for "defense" is "apologia." An "apology," in this context, does not mean "saying I'm sorry"; it means mounting a reasoned defense. An apologist is therefore a defender of a religious or philosophical point of view.

From the earliest times Christians were involved in apologetics: within the New Testament, the book of 1 Peter urges its readers to "be prepared always to make a defense (literally: an apology) to anyone who asks you a reason for the hope that is in you" (3:15), and in the last part of the book of Acts, the apostle Paul is repeatedly put on trial and made to defend his beliefs and actions. Many scholars have suspected that the book of Acts itself is a kind of literary apology, written to a Roman administor named Theophilus (1:1) precisely to show that Christians are socially innocuous and should therefore not be persecuted.

But it was not until the middle of the second century that well-trained and highly educated apologists began to appear among the ranks of the Christians, intellectuals like Justin in Rome, Athenagoras in Athens, Tertullian in Carthage, and Origen in Alexandria. These individuals were scholars of the first rank, who were able to mount intellectual arguments to establish the innocence of Christians and, even more, to assert the superiority of the Christian religion over other Greco-Roman cults, including Judaism. It is difficult to know how much these scholarly defenses represent the views of the common Christian, from whom we have no surviving testimony (except in quotations preserved by the literary elite among them): most Christians, like most other people in the ancient world, could neither read nor write. But these surviving works do give us a sense of how intellectuals beginning to join the Christian movement understood and argued for its religious superiority.

In their defense of Christianity against the standard charges brought against it (see Chapter 3), the early apologists replayed several themes time and again. Against the charge that Christians were "atheists," they insisted that Christians alone worshiped the true creator God who is superior to every other divine being (including the pagan deities, who were alleged to be wicked demons); against the charge that Christians were wildly promiscuous, the apologists pointed to Jesus' teachings in the Sermon on the Mount, where believers are instructed not only to behave morally but to remain pure even in their thoughts; to the charge of ritual cannibalism, they argued that Christians did not even allow abortions or the exposure of infants (common practices throughout the empire); to the charge that they were withdrawn from the social and civic life of their communities, they replied that the Christians' high morality improved society and preserved it from the wrath of God; to the charge that they refused to worship the emperor and to embrace the cause of the empire, they noted that they prayed for the well-being of the state and its ruler.

The apologists were never content, however, simply to mount a defense against charges. They were also determined to prove the absolute superiority of their Christian views. To do so, they sometimes went on the attack, maligning other religions for worshipping gods that were portrayed in the pagan myths themselves as wild, capricious, and sexually immoral, and mocking the wide varieties and (in their Christian eyes) mutually exclusive views of the pagan cults.

In addition, they were quick to adduce proofs for the Christian message. For the most part, these proofs were built on assumptions that were widely held in the ancient world, for example, that for a religion or philosophy to be "true" it had to be ancient (how could something be "true" if no one had believed it before?). On the other hand, this assumption created a problem for Christian apologists, since they (and everyone else) knew that Jesus had lived relatively recently. But the apologists claimed that the religion founded on Jesus was much, much older, that in fact Jesus fulfilled the promises made to Moses and the Jewish prophets centuries before, as evident in everything from Jesus' virgin birth in Bethlehem to his death, resurrection, and ascension. Thus, for them, Christianity was not a new thing; it was quite ancient—older even than the oldest Greek philosophies and cults, since Moses lived 800 years before Plato (the great philosopher) and 400 years before Homer and Hesiod (sources for the Greek stories about the gods). In addition, the apologists claimed, the greater antiquity of Christianity explains why so many of the things Jesus did and experienced (e.g., his supernatural birth, his miracles, his ascent to heaven) were similarly attributed to figures in Greek and Roman myths: ancient pagan writers gleaned stories from Moses and applied them to their own heros!

The constant insistence that Jesus fulfilled ancient prophecy relates to another weapon in the apologists' arsenal, the claim that divine miracles vindicate the truthfulness of the Christian religion. No mere human could have performed the supernatural acts of Jesus, faithfully recorded by his followers; Jesus was clearly the Son of God. And the miracles did not cease with his departure; his apostles also performed wonders in his name. According to some of the apologists, miracles continued to occur down to their own time. On occasion, the apologists challenged their readers to bring forth anyone who was demon-possessed and watch the person be healed in the name of Jesus.

Finally, the Christian apologists appealed on humanitarian grounds to the rulers of the empire to put a halt to their senseless suffering. They maintained that since Christians harm no one, they should be allowed to worship in any way they see fit—in effect, that there should be a separation between the powers of a government and the religious observances of its people. This notion of the separation of church and state never did catch on in the ancient world, where most people believed that matters of the gods *were* concerns of public policy. Eventually, Christians, too, came to share this view, especially after the emperors themselves converted to the faith and became more willing to use their political, economic, and military power to promote the Christian cause.

Even though the apologists addressed their writings to their opponents (especially to the Roman emperors themselves), many scholars believe that their books were principally designed for internal consumption among the Christians, as a way to buttress their faith and strengthen their resolve, and possibly to provide them with the ammunition they needed to fight off the attacks of their public adversaries.

For Further Reading

Chadwick, Henry. *Early Christian Thought and the Classical Tradition: Studies in Justin, Clement and Origen.* New York: Oxford University Press, 1965.

Droge, Arthur J. *Moses of Homer: Early Christian Interpretations of the History of Culture.* Tübingen: Mohr/Siebeck, 1989.

Fiorenza, Elizabeth Schüssler. *Aspects of Religious Propaganda in Judaism and Early Christianity.* Notre Dame: Notre Dame University Press, 1976.

Grant, Robert M. *Greek Apologists of the Second Century.* Philadelphia: Westminster Press, 1988.

THE TEXTS

9. Minucius Felix: Octavius

Even though the "Octavius" was one of the latest of the apologies excerpted here, I have put it first because it expresses so well the accusations made against Christians by their pagan opponents throughout the second and third centuries. The author is Minucius Felix, a Christian intellectual originally from North Africa, who appears to have practiced law in Rome during the early part of the third century. This is his only surviving work.

It is a firsthand account, in Latin, of a day-long discussion beside the sea, in which one of the author's friends, the Christian Octavius, addresses the hostile arguments of another, the pagan Caecilius, and finally convinces him of the superiority of the Christian religion. The portion excerpted here comes from Caecilius's opening statement, in which he (a) praises the Romans for their serious devotion to religion and their respect for ancient sacred practices, and (b) levels the charges commonly made against Christians for their repudiation of the Roman gods, their flagrant immorality, and their senseless adherence to an ineffectual religion.

Chapter 6

1 "Thus [claimed Caecilius] we have either Fortune, whose character we know, or Nature, whose character we do not know. In that case, you [Christians], hierophants of truth, would surely show greater reverence—and hence be better advised—if you embraced the system taught by your ancestors, if you worshipped according to traditional practice, if the gods you adored were those whom your parents trained you as children first to fear—only later might you get to know them more intimately. You would be better advised if you did not pronounce any opinion of your own on deities; you should, rather, trust your forbears who in a still uncultured age at the very infancy of the world were blessed with gods who were propitious—or their kings.

"And this is precisely the explanation why right throughout all empires, provinces, and towns, we observe that individual groups have their native rites and rituals and worship their local gods. For example, the Eleusinians have Ceres, the Phrygians the Great Mother Goddess, the Epidaurians Aesculapius, the Chaldaeans Baal, the Syrians Astarte, the Taurians Diana, the Gauls Mercury, and the Romans have them all.

2 "As a result, the power and sway of the Romans has encompassed the entire circuit of the globe, it has spread its domain beyond the paths of the sun, the very bounds of Ocean. And this is so because they have been plying arms with religious valor, fortifying their city with religious rituals, with the chastity of their virgins, and with the many dignities and titles they grant their

The "Octavius of Minucius Felix," from *The Octavius of Marcus Minucius Felix*, ed. G. W. Clarke. Mahway, N.J.: Paulist Press, 1974. Used by permission of Paulist Press.

priests. When, for example, they had been taken by siege and captured all but for the Capitol, they still worshiped their gods—and gods whom anyone else would by that time have rejected as angered with them; the Romans astounded the Gauls with their intrepid piety—they moved through their battle ranks unprotected by weapons save for the arms of their religious observances.

"Even though the Romans have stood on the enemies' ramparts which they have captured, still flushed with victory, they have persisted in respecting the divinities they conquered; from every quarter they have continued to seek gods to be their guests, to make them their own, to erect altars even to unknown deities and to the shades of the dead.

3 "By adopting the rites of all nations in this way, they have won their empires as well. And to this day there has been no pause in the unending reverence they show; indeed, it has been strengthened rather than impaired with the long passage of time; for, as a general rule, the greater the age that ceremonies and shrines accumulate, the more hallowed these institutions become with their accruing years.

Chapter 7

1 "At this stage I might venture myself to concede a point—and to err in better company. It was not, I would claim, without sound reasons that our forbears zealously strove to watch auguries, consult entrails, establish rituals, and dedicate sanctuaries.

2 "Consider what you read in our chronicles. You readily discover why they introduced every manner of religious ritual; it was to repay divine favor, to avert impending wrath, or to placate the actual rage and fury of the gods.

Chapter 8

1 "And so the conclusion I draw is that while the origin and nature of the immortal gods may still remain obscure, there nevertheless continues to be unhesitating agreement from all nations about their existence. This religious belief is so venerable, so beneficial, and so salutary; and I cannot therefore tolerate that anyone in the arrogance of his irreligious 'enlightenment' should have the effrontery to try to weaken or destroy it. . . .

"In view of this, is it not an absolute scandal—you will allow me, I hope, to be rather forthright about the strong feelings I have for my case—is it not scandalous that the gods should be mobbed by a gang of outlawed and reckless desperadoes?

4 "They have collected from the lowest possible dregs of society the more ignorant fools together with gullible women (readily persuaded, as is their weak sex); they have thus formed a rabble of blasphemous conspirators, who with nocturnal assemblies, periodic fasts, and inhuman feasts seal their pact not with some religious ritual but with desecrating profanation; they are a crowd that furtively lurks in hiding places, shunning the light; they are speechless in public but gabble away in corners.

"They despise our temples as being no more than sepulchres, they spit after our gods, they sneer at our rites, and, fantastic though it is, our priests they pity—pitiable themselves; they scorn the purple robes of public office, though they go about in rags themselves.

5 "How amazingly stupid, unbelievably insolent they are. Tortures of the present they scoff at, but they live in dread of the uncertain tortures of the future; they are afraid to die after they are dead, but meantime they have no fear of death. So effectively are they beguiled of alarm by the comforting expectation of a renewal of life hereafter.

Chapter 9

1 "Evil weeds grow apace and so, day by day, this depraved way of life now creeps further over all the face of the globe and the foul religious shrines of this abominable congregation are getting a stronger hold. This confederacy must be torn out, it must be sworn to perdition.

2 "They recognize each other by secret marks and signs; hardly have they met when they love each other, throughout the world uniting in the

practice of a veritable religion of lusts. Indiscriminately they call each other brother and sister, thus turning even ordinary fornication into incest by the intervention of these hallowed names. Such a pride does this foolish, deranged superstition take in its wickedness.

3 "Unless there were some underlying truth, such a wide variety of charges, and very serious ones, would not be made about them; they can hardly be repeated in polite company. Rumor is a shrewd informant. I hear, for example, that they do reverence to the head of that most degraded of beasts, an ass; I cannot imagine what absurdity has persuaded them to consecrate it, but it is indeed a cult born of such morals and well suited for them.

4 "It is also reported that they worship the genitals of their pontiff and priest, adoring, it appears, the sex of their 'father.' Perhaps this is incorrect but it certainly is a suspicion that befits their clandestine and nocturnal ceremonies. There are also stories about the objects of their veneration: they are said to be a man who was punished with death as a criminal and the fell wood of his cross, thus providing suitable liturgy for the depraved fiends: they worship what they deserve.

5 "To turn to another point. The notoriety of the stories told of the initiation of new recruits is matched by their ghastly horror. A young baby is covered over with flour, the object being to deceive the unwary. It is then served before the person to be admitted into their rites. The recruit is urged to inflict blows onto it—they appear to be harmless because of the covering of flour. Thus the baby is killed with wounds that remain unseen and concealed. It is the blood of this infant—I shudder to mention it—it is this blood that they lick with thirsty lips; these are the limbs they distribute eagerly; this is the victim by which they seal their covenant; it is by complicity in this crime that they are pledged to mutual silence; these are their rites, more foul than all sacrileges combined.

6 "We all know, too, about their banquets; they are on everyone's lips, everywhere as the speech of our Cirtensian testifies. On a special day they gather for a feast with all their children, sisters, mothers—all sexes and all ages. There, flushed with the banquet after such feasting and drinking, they begin to burn with incestuous passions. They provoke a dog tied to the lampstand to leap and bound towards a scrap of food which they have tossed outside the reach of his chain.

7 "By this means the light is overturned and extinguished, and with it common knowledge of their actions; in the shameless dark with unspeakable lust they copulate in random unions, all equally being guilty of incest, some by deed, but everyone by complicity. For whatever may happen in individual cases is the general aspiration and desire of them all.

Chapter 10

1 "I am deliberately passing over a number of points—those that I have already given are more than enough; and that all of them, or practically all, are true is revealed by the very obscurity which shrouds this perverted religion.

2 "Why else should they go to such pains to hide and conceal whatever it is they worship? One is always happy for honorable actions to be made public; crimes are kept secret. Why do they have no altars, no temples, no publicly-known images? Why do they never speak in the open, why do they always assemble in stealth? It must be that whatever it is they worship—and suppress—is deserving either of punishment or of shame.

3 "Furthermore, who is this unique god of theirs, what is his origin, where does he live, so solitary, so totally forlorn that no free nation has knowledge of him, nor any empire—not even the religious fanatics of Rome?

4 "The only other group to have worshipped one god is the wretched tribe of the Jews, but they did so in the open, with temples and altars, with sacrifice and ceremonial. But you can see that this god has neither power nor strength; he and his very own people are captives of the Romans, who are but humans. . . .

Chapter 12

2 "Look: some of you, the greater half (the better half, you say), go in need, suffer from cold, from hunger and toil. And yet your god allows it,

he connives at it; he will not or he cannot assist his own followers. This proves how weak he is—or wicked.

3 "You have dreams of posthumous immortality, but when you quake in the face of danger, when you burn with fever or are racked by pain, are you still unaware of your real condition? Do you still not recognize your human frailty? Poor wretch, whether you like it or not, you have proof of your own infirmity, and still you will not admit it!

4 "But these evils, common to us all, I omit. Look: you Christians are menaced with threats, torments and tortures, with crosses—meant not this time to be adored but endured—and with fire as well, just as you foretell and fear. And where is that god of yours who can help those who come to life again, but cannot help those who are alive?

5 "Is it not true that without the help of your god Rome has her dominions and empire, she has the whole world to enjoy, and she has you as well beneath her sway?

"But in the meantime, in your anxious state of expectation, you refrain from honest pleasures: you do not go to our shows, you take no part in our processions, you are not present at our public banquets, you shrink in horror from our sacred games, from food ritually dedicated by our priests, from drink hallowed by libation poured upon our altars. Such is your dread of the very gods you deny.

6 "You do not bind your head with flowers, you do not honor your body with perfumes; ointments you reserve for funerals, but even to your tombs you deny garlands; you anemic, neurotic creatures, you indeed deserve to be pitied—but by our gods. The result is, you pitiable fools, that you have no enjoyment of life while you wait for the new life which you will never have."

>-+-+>-○-<+-+-<

10. Justin: First Apology

Justin Martyr was the first major Christian apologist. Born and raised in Samaria, he moved to Rome after his conversion (see Chapter 2) and opened a Christian school there. His First Apology was composed around 155 C.E. As became customary for Christian apologists, Justin wrote the book as a kind of open letter to the Roman authorities, in this case, to the emperor Antoninus Pius and his two sons, Marcus Aurelius and Lucius Verus. Many scholars think, though, that the book was actually meant not for the imperial court but for internal consumption among the Christians.

The book sets the tone for many of the subsequent Christian apologists. In the excerpts that follow, Justin demands a fair hearing for Christians rather than summary condemnation; he attacks pagan idolatry and defends Christians against charges of atheism and immorality, and he warns his readers about punishment in the afterlife for those who refuse to believe. Perhaps most important, Justin argues that pagan philosophers who spoke the truth were inspired by the divine "logos" (translated as either "reason" or

Justin: "First Apology," from *St. Justin Martyr: The First and Second Apologies*, ed. Leslie William Barnard. Mahway, N.J.: Paulist Press, 1997. Used by permission of Paulist Press.

"word") and that, since Christ is himself the Logos (Word) become flesh, he embodies what is truest of all religion and philosophy, foreshadowed in the pagan myths and predicted in Moses and the ancient Jewish prophets.

For other extracts from the First Apology, see Chapter 11.

1 To the Emperor Titus Aelius Hadrianus Antoninus Pius Augustus Caesar, and to his philosopher son Verissimus, and to Lucius the philosopher, Caesar's natural son and Pius's adopted son, a lover of culture, and to the Sacred Senate and all the Roman people—on behalf of people of every nation who are unjustly hated and grossly abused, I, Justin, son of Priscus and grandson of Bacchius, from Flavia Neapolis in Syria-Palestine, myself being one of them, have drawn up this address and petition.

2 Reason dictates that those who are truly pious and philosophers should honor and love only the truth, declining to follow the opinions of the ancients, if they are worthless. For not only does sound reason dictate that one should not follow those who do or teach unjust things, but the lover of truth should choose by all means, and even before his own life, even though death should remove him, to speak and do righteous things. So you, then, since you are called pious and philosophers and guardians of justice and lovers of culture, listen in every way; and it will be shown if you are such. For we have come into your company not to flatter you by this writing, nor please you by our address, but to ask that you give judgment, after an exact and searching enquiry, not moved by prejudice or by a wish to please superstitious people, nor by irrational impulse or long prevalent rumors, so as to give a decision which will prove to be against yourselves. For we indeed reckon that no evil can be done to us, unless we are proved to be evildoers, or shown to be wicked. You are able to kill us, but not to hurt us.

3 But that nobody should think that this is an unreasonable and daring utterance, we ask that the charges against us be investigated, and that, if they are substantiated let us be punished as

is fitting. But if nobody can prove anything against us, true reason forbids you, because of an evil rumor, to wrong innocent people, and indeed rather [to wrong] yourselves, who think fit to instigate action, not by judgment, but by passion. Every honorable person will recognize this as the only fair and righteous challenge, namely, that the subjects should give a straightforward account of their own life and teaching; and likewise that the rulers should give their decision as having followed, not violence and tyranny, but piety and philosophy. For thus both rulers and subjects would reap benefit. For even one of the ancients said somewhere, "Unless both rulers and ruled love wisdom it is impossible to make cities prosper." It is then our task to offer to all an opportunity of inspecting our life and teachings, lest, on account of those who do not really know of our affairs, we should incur the penalty due to them for mental blindness. But it is for you, as reason demands, to listen [to us] and to be found good judges. For if, having learned the truth, you fail to do what is righteous, you have no defense before God.

4 By the mere statement of a name, nothing is decided, either good or evil, apart from the actions associated with the name; indeed, as far as the name with which we are accused goes, we are most gentle people. But we do not think it just to ask to be acquitted on account of the name, if we are convicted as evildoers, so, on the other hand, if we are found to have committed no wrong, either in the appellation of the name, or in our citizenship, you must be exceedingly anxious against incurring righteous judgment by unjustly punishing those who are not convicted. For from a name neither approval nor punishment could fairly come, unless something excellent or evil in action could be shown about it. For you do not punish the accused among yourselves before they are convicted;

but in our case you take the name as proof against us, and this although, as far as the name goes, you ought rather to punish our accusers. For we are accused of being Christians, and to hate what is favorable is unjust. Again if one of the accused deny the name, saying that he is not [a Christian], you acquit him, as having no proof that he is an evildoer; but if any one acknowledges that he is one, you punish him on account of this acknowledgement. You ought also to enquire into the life both of the confessor and the denier, that by his deeds it would appear what kind of person each is. For as some who have been taught by the Teacher, Christ, not to deny him encourage others when they are put to the test, so similarly do those who lead evil lives give some excuse to those who, without consideration, like to accuse all the Christians of impiety and wickedness. And this also is improper. For in philosophy, too, some assume the name and the dress who do nothing worthy of their profession; and as you are aware those among the ancients whose opinions and teachings were quite different are yet called by the one name of philosopher. And some of these taught atheism; and those who became poets get a laugh out of the impurity of Zeus with his own children. And those who follow such teaching are unrestrained by you; but, on the contrary, you offer prizes and honors to those who euphoniously insult them.

5 Why, then, should this be? In our case, who pledge ourselves to do nothing wicked, nor to hold these godless opinions, you do not investigate the charges made against us; but, giving in to unreasoning passion, and the instigation of evil demons, you punish us without trial or consideration. For the truth shall be told; since of old these evil demons manifested themselves, both defiled women and corrupted boys, and showed terrifying sights to people, that those who did not use their reason in judging the acts that were done, were filled with terror; and being taken captive by fear, and not knowing that these were demons, they called them gods, and gave to each the name which each of the demons had chosen for himself. And when Socrates tried, by true reasoning and definite evidence, to bring these things to light, and

deliver people from the demons, then the demons themselves, by means of people who rejoiced in wickedness, compassed his death, as an atheist and impious person, on the charge of introducing new divinities, and in our case they show a similar activity. For not only among the Greeks through Socrates were these things revealed by reason [logos], but also among the Barbarians were they revealed by logos personally, when he had taken shape, and become man, and was called Jesus Christ; and in obedience to him, we not only deny that they who did such things as these are gods, but state that they are wicked and impious demons, whose actions will not bear comparison with those even of people who long after virtue.

6 Hence we are called atheists. And we confess that we are atheists with reference to gods such as these, but not with reference to the most true God, the Father of righteousness and temperance and the other virtues, who is unmixed with evil. But we worship and adore both him and the Son who came from him, and taught us these things, and the army of the other good angels, who follow him and are made like him, and the prophetic Spirit, giving honor [to him] in reason and truth, and to everyone who wishes to learn handing over without grudging, what we have been taught. . . .

8 Consider that we have said these things for your sakes, for it is in our power when we are examined to deny [our Christianity]; but we would not live by telling a lie. For, impelled by the desire for the eternal and pure life, we seek to dwell with God, the Father and Demiurge of all things, and hasten to confess [our faith], being persuaded and convinced that those who have shown to God by their works that they follow him, and long to dwell with him where there is no evil to cause disturbance, are able to obtain these things. This, then, to speak briefly, is what we look for and have learned from Christ, and teach. Likewise Plato said that Rhadamanthus and Minos would punish the wicked who came before them; and we say that this is what will happen, but at the hand of Christ, and to the same bodies, reunited with their souls and destined for eternal punishment,

and not for a thousand-year period only, as he said. And if anyone says that this is incredible or impossible, this mistake of ours is one which concerns us only, and no one else, as long as we are not convicted of doing any evil.

9 But neither do we honor with many sacrifices and garlands of flowers the objects that people have formed and set in temples and named gods; since we know that they are lifeless and dead and have not the form of God [for we do not think that God has such a form as some say is fashioned to his honor], but have the names and shapes of those evil demons which have appeared. For why must we tell you who already know, what the craftsmen fashion their material into, by planing and cutting, casting and hammering? And often out of vessels used for dishonorable purposes, by merely changing the form, and making an image of the appropriate shape, they make what they call gods. We consider this not only irrational, but to be even insulting to God, who, though of ineffable glory and form, yet has his name set upon things which are corruptible and need to be cared for. And that the craftsmen of these are impure and, not to enter into details, are given to all kinds of vice, you very well know; they even corrupt their own slave girls who work alongside them. What stupidity, that dissolute people should be said to fashion and make gods for public worship, and that you should appoint such people the guardians of temples where they are set up, not recognizing that it is unlawful even to think or say that people are the guardians of gods. . . .

13 What sober-minded person then will not admit that we are not atheists, since we worship the Maker of this Universe, and declare, as we have been taught, that he has no need of blood and libations and incense, whom we praise to the utmost of our power through the word of prayer and thanksgiving for all things that we receive. We have been taught that the only honor that is worthy of him is not to consume by fire the things he has brought into being for our sustenance, but contribute them for ourselves and those in need, and with thanksgiving to him celebrating our solemnities in hymns and speech, for our cre-

ation, and for all the means of health, and for the qualities of the different kinds of things, and for the changes of the seasons, and presenting before him petitions that we may live again in incorruption through faith in him. Our teacher of these things is Jesus Christ, who was also born for this purpose, and was crucified under Pontius Pilate, procurator of Judaea in the time of Tiberius Caesar; and we will show that we worship Him rationally, having learned that he is the Son of the true God himself, and holding him in the second place, and the prophetic Spirit in the third rank. For they charge our madness to consist in this, that we give to a crucified man second place after the unchangeable and eternal God, begetter of all things, for they do not know the mystery involved in this, to which we ask you to give heed as we expound it to you.

14 For we warn you in advance to be on your guard, lest the demons whom we have previously accused should deceive you and divert you from reading and understanding what we say. For they strive to have you as their slaves and servants, and sometimes by appearances in dreams, sometimes by magical tricks, they subdue all who do not struggle to the utmost for their own salvation, as we do also who, after being persuaded by the Word, renounced them, and follow the only unbegotten God through his Son. Those who formerly delighted in fornication now embrace chastity alone, those who formerly made use of magical arts have dedicated themselves to the good and unbegotten God, we who once valued above everything the gaining of wealth and possessions now bring what we have into a common stock, and share with everyone in need; we who hated and destroyed one another, and would not share the same hearth with people of a different tribe on account of their different customs, now since the coming of Christ, live familiarly with them, and pray for our enemies, and try to persuade those who unjustly hate us to live according to the good advice of Christ, to the end that they may share with us the same joyful hope of a reward from God the Master of all. But lest we should seem to deceive, we consider it right, before embarking on our promised demonstration, to cite a few of the precepts given by Christ himself. It is for you then, as powerful rulers, to find out whether we have been taught and do teach these things truly. Short and concise utterances come from Him, for he was no sophist, but his word was the power of God.

15 Concerning chastity he said this. "Whosoever looks upon a woman to lust after her has already committed adultery with her in his heart before God."[1] And: "If your right eye offends you, cut it out; for it is better for you to enter into the Kingdom of Heaven with one eye, than with two eyes to be cast into eternal fire."[2] And: "Whosoever shall marry her that is divorced from another husband, commits adultery."[3] And: "There are some who have been made eunuchs by men, and some who were born eunuchs, and some who have made themselves eunuchs for the Kingdom of Heaven's sake; but not all can receive this saying."[4] So that all who according to human law make second marriages are sinners in the sight of our Master, as are those who look on a woman to lust after her. For not only the man who in act commits adultery is condemned by him, but also the man who desires to commit adultery; since not only our deeds but also our thoughts are open before God. And many, both men and women, who have been Christ's disciples from childhood, have preserved their purity at the age of sixty or seventy years; and I am proud that I could produce such from every race of men and women. . . .

18 Since consciousness remains for all who have lived, and eternal punishment awaits [the wicked], do not neglect to be convinced and believe that these things are true. For necromancy, and the divinations you practice through innocent children, and the invoking of departed human souls, and those who are called among the magi dream-senders and familiars, and all that is done by those who are skilled in such things—let these persuade you that even after death souls are still conscious; and those who are seized and torn by the spirits of the dead, whom all call demoniacs or madmen; and what you call oracles, both of Amphilochus, Dodona, Pytho, and many others

such as exist; and the teachings of the authors, Empedocles and Pythagoras, Plato and Socrates, and the pit in Homer and the descent of Odysseus to visit the dead, and all that has been spoken of a like kind. Receive us, even if you receive us only on an equality with them, who believe in God not less but more firmly than they do, since we expect to receive again our own bodies, though they be dead and buried in the earth, saying that nothing is impossible with God.

19 And to any thoughtful person what would seem more incredible, than if we were not in the body, and someone should say it was possible that from a small drop of human seed, bones and sinews and flesh were formed into a shape such as we see? For let this now be said by way of supposition: If you were not such as you now are, born of such parents, and one were to show you the human seed and a picture of a man or woman, and were to say confidently that from such a substance such a being could grow, would you believe before you saw it happening? No one would dare to contradict [and to say that you would disbelieve]. In the same way, then, you are now incredulous because you have never seen a dead person rise again. But as at first you would not have believed it possible that from a small drop such persons could be produced, yet now you see them thus produced, so also consider that it is not impossible for the bodies of men and women, dissolved and like seeds resolved into earth, to rise again in God's appointed time and put on incorruption. . . .

21 And when we say also that the Word, who is the First-begotten of God, was born for us without sexual union, Jesus Christ our teacher, and that he was crucified and died and rose again and ascended into heaven, we propound nothing new beyond [what you believe] concerning those whom you call sons of Zeus. For you know of how many sons of Zeus your esteemed writers speak:

[1]Matt 5:28.
[2]Matt 5:29.
[3]Matt 5:32.
[4]Matt 19:12.

Hermes, the interpreting Word and teacher of all; Asclepius, who, though he was a great healer, after being struck by a thunderbolt ascended into heaven; and Dionysus too who was torn in pieces; and Heracles, when he had committed himself to the flames to escape his pains; and the Dioscuri, the sons of Leda; and Perseus, son of Danae; and Bellerophon, who, though of mortal origin, rose to heaven on the horse Pegasus. For what shall I say of Ariadne, and those who, like her, have been said to have been placed among the stars? And what of your deceased emperors, whom you think it right to deify, and on whose behalf you produce someone who swears that he has seen the burning Caesar ascend to heaven from the funeral pyre? And what kind of deeds are related of each of these reputed sons of Zeus, it is needless to tell those who already know. This only shall be said, that they are written for the benefit and instruction of students, for all consider it an honorable thing to imitate the gods. But far be it from every sound mind to entertain such a thought concerning the deities as to believe that Zeus himself, the governor and begetter of all things, was both a parricide and the son of a parricide, and that being overcome by the love of evil and shameful pleasures he came into Ganymede and to those many women whom he seduced, and that his sons did like actions. But, as we have said above, wicked devils perpetrated these things. And we have been taught that only those are deified who have lived near to God in holiness and virtue; and we believe that those who live unjustly and do not change their ways are punished in eternal fire.

22 Now the Son of God, called Jesus, even if only an ordinary man, is on account of his wisdom worthy to be called Son of God; for all writers call God Father of humans and gods. For if we say that the Word of God was begotten of God in a peculiar manner, different from the ordinary method of birth, let this, as said before, be not a strange thing to you, who say that Hermes is the announcing word from God. But if anyone objects that he was crucified, this is in common with those whom you call sons of Zeus, who

suffered as we have now enumerated. For their sufferings at death are recorded as not all alike, but different; so that not even by the strangeness of his passion does he seem to be inferior to them; but, as we promised in the preceding part of this discourse, we will now prove him better—or rather have already proved him to be so—for the better is revealed by his deeds. And even if we say that he was born of a virgin, let this be to you in common with Perseus. And when we say that he healed the lame, the paralytic, and those born blind, and raised the dead, we appear to say things similar to those said to have been done by Asclepius.

23 And that this may now be clear to you [firstly], that whatever things we say as having been learned from Christ, and the prophets who came before him, are alone true, and older than all the writers who have lived, and we ask to be accepted, not because we say the same things as they do, but because we speak the truth; and [secondly] that Jesus Christ alone was really begotten as Son by God, being his Word and First-begotten and Power, and becoming man by his will he taught us these things for the conversion and restoration of the human race; and [thirdly] that before he became a human among humans some, under the influence of the wicked demons already mentioned, related as real occurrences the myths which the demons had devised through the poets, in the same manner as they have caused to be fabricated the scandalous reports against us and impious deeds, of which there is neither witness nor proof—we shall bring forward this proof. . . .

30 But lest anyone should argue against us, what excludes [the reasoning] that he who is called by us Christ, a human born of humans, performed what we call his might works by magical art, and by this appeared to be Son of God?—we will now offer proof, not trusting in mere assertions, but being of necessity persuaded by those who prophesied [these things] before they happened, for with our own eyes we see things that have happened and are happening just as they were predicted; and this will, we think, appear to you the strongest and surest evidence.

31 Then there were certain persons among the Jews, who were prophets of God, through whom the prophetic Spirit announced beforehand things that were to come to pass before they happened. And the successive rulers of the Jews carefully preserved in their possession their prophecies, as they were spoken and when they were uttered, in their own Hebrew language when they had been arranged in books by the prophets themselves. But when Ptolemy, the King of Egypt, formed a library and set out to collect the writings of all people, he heard also about these prophecies, and sent to Herod, who was at that time King of the Jews, asking that the prophetic books be sent to him. And King Herod indeed sent them, writing in the already mentioned Hebrew language. Since their contents were found to be unintelligible to the Egyptians, he again sent and asked that people be sent to translate them into the Greek language. And when this was done the books remained with the Egyptians where they are until now; and they are everywhere with all the Jews; but though they read them they do not understand what is said, but consider us enemies and opponents; and like yourselves they kill and punish us whenever they can, as you can well realize. For in the Jewish war which lately happened, Bar-Cochba, the leader of the revolt of the Jews, gave orders that Christians alone should be led to terrible punishments, unless they would deny Jesus the Christ and blaspheme. In these books, then, of the prophets we have found it predicted that Jesus our Christ would come, born of a virgin, growing up to manhood, and healing every disease and every sickness and raising the dead, and hated and unrecognized and crucified, and dying and rising again and ascending into heaven, and both being and being called Son of God. [We find it also predicted] that certain people should be sent by him into every nation to proclaim these things, and that rather among the Gentiles people should believe on him. And he was predicted before he appeared, first five thousand years before, and again three thousand, and then two thousand, and again one thousand, and yet again eight hundred, for in the succession of generations other prophets again and again arose.

But lest some, reasoning absurdly, with a view to refuting what we teach, should maintain that we say that Christ was born a hundred and fifty years ago under Cyrenius, and somewhat later, under Pontius Pilate, taught what we say he taught, and should object as though all people who were born before him were not accountable—let us anticipate and solve the difficulty. We have been taught that Christ is the First-born of God, and we have suggested above that he is the logos of whom every race of men and women were partakers. And they who lived with the logos are Christians, even though they have been thought atheists; as, among the Greeks, Socrates and Heraclitus, and people like them; and among the barbarians, Abraham, and Ananias, and Asarias, and Misael, and Elias, and many others whose actions and names we now decline to recount, because we know it would be tedious. So that even they who lived before Christ, and lived without logos, were wicked and hostile to Christ, and slew those who lived with the logos. . . .

52 Since then we show that all things that have already happened had been proclaimed through the prophets before they came to pass, it must necessarily be believed also that those things that were similarly predicted, but are yet to come to pass, will certainly take place. For as the things that have already happened came to pass when proclaimed before, and even unrecognized, so will the things that remain, even though unknown and disbelieved, come to pass. For the prophets have proclaimed before two comings of his: one, which has already happened, as that of a dishonored and suffering man; and the second, when, as has been proclaimed, he will come from heaven with glory with his angelic host; when also he will raise the bodies of all the people who have lived, and will cloth the worthy with incorruption, but will send those of the wicked eternally conscious, into eternal fire with the wicked demons. . . .

54 But those who deliver the myths invented by the poets offer no proof to the youths who learn them—and we proceed to prove that they have been told by the power of the wicked demons to deceive and lead astray the human race. For when they heard it proclaimed through the prophets that the Christ was to come, and that the ungodly among men and women would be punished by fire, they caused many to be called sons of Zeus, thinking that they would be able to cause people to believe that the statements about Christ were marvelous tales, like the assertions of poets. And these things were said both among the Greeks and among all nations where they [the demons] heard the prophets proclaiming that Christ would be especially believed in. But that in hearing what was said through the prophets they did not understand it accurately, but imitated, like people in error, what was said concerning our Christ, we will make plain. The prophet Moses, then, was, as we have said before, older than all writers, and through him, as we have also said before, it was thus predicted: "A ruler will not depart from Judah nor the leader from his thighs, until he comes for whom it is reserved; and he will be the expectation of the nations, binding his foal to the vine, washing his robe in the blood of the grape."[5] Therefore when the demons heard these prophetic words they said that Dionysus had been the son of Zeus, and handed down that he was the discoverer of the vine, and they ascribe wine among his mysteries, and taught that, having been torn in pieces, he ascended into heaven. And since through the prophecy of Moses it had not been expressly signified whether he who was to come would be the Son of God, and whether, mounted on a foal, he would remain on earth or ascend into heaven, and because the name "foal" could signify either the foal of an ass or a horse, they, not knowing whether the predicted one would bring the foal of an ass or of a horse as the sign of his coming, nor whether he was the Son of God or of a man, as we said before, said that Bellerophon, a human born of humans, had himself gone up to heaven on the horse Pegasus. And when they heard it said through the other prophet Isaiah, that he would be born of a virgin, and would ascend into heaven by his own [power], they caused Perseus to be spoken of. And when they knew what was said, as has been cited before, in the ancient prophecies, "Strong as a giant to run his course,"[6] they said that Heracles was strong, and had traveled over the whole earth. And, again, when they learned that it had been predicted that he would heal every disease and raise the dead, they brought forwarded Asclepius.

55 But in no instance, not even in the case of those called sons of Zeus, did they imitate the crucifixion; for they did not understand, as had been explained, that all the things said about it were put symbolically. Yet, as the prophet predicted, [this] is the greatest symbol of his power and rule, as also is shown from the things which fall under view. For consider all the things in the cosmos, whether without this form they could be governed or be interrelated. For the sea is not traversed except this token of victory, which is called a sail, remains safe in the ship; and the land is not ploughed without it; likewise diggers and craftsmen do not do their work except with tools which have this form. And the human form differs from that of the irrational animals in nothing else than in its being erect and having the hands stretched out, and having on the face extending from the forehead what is called the nose, through which there is breath for the living creature—and this shows no other form than that of the Cross. And so it was said throughout the prophet, "The breath before our face is Christ the Lord." And the power of this form is shown by your own symbols on what are called standards and trophies to the accompaniment of which all your state processions are made, using these as the

---

[5]Gen 49:10–11.
[6]Ps 19:5.

signs of your rule and power, even though you do so without knowing. And with this form you set up the images of your deceased emperors, and you name them gods by inscriptions. Since, then, we have urged you both by reason and by the visible form, as far as we can, we know that now we are blameless even though you disbelieve; for our part is done and finished.

>—•>—O—<•—<

11. Athenagoras: Plea Regarding the Christians

Although arguably the most eloquent of the Greek apologists, Athenagoras is scarcely mentioned in our ancient sources. Possibly from Athens, he composed his apology in 177 C.E., addressing it to the emperor Marcus Aurelius and his son Commodus. In it he makes an impassioned plea that Christians should not be condemned merely for their name but only for criminal activities. He devotes the bulk of his defense to showing that the charges often leveled against Christians—atheism, cannabalism, and incest—are completely unfounded.

Athenagoras maintains that, far from being atheists (without gods), Christians worship the one true God, along with his Son, the embodiment of God's Logos, and the divine Spirit (three beings, he claims, who are unified in power but distinguished in rank). This true worship, he insists, stands in sharp contrast to the senseless idolatry of the pagans. Moreover, the high moral standards of the Christians, who ban even the *thought* of evil-doing, shows the absurdity of the charges of incest and cannabalism—charges better leveled, Athenagoras wryly observes, against the gods that pagans describe in their own myths. Athenagoras concludes by arguing that the surest incentive for upright behavior is the uniquely Christian belief in the resurrection of the dead to everlasting reward or punishment.

To the Emperors Marcus Aurelius Antoninus and Lucius Aurelius Commodus, conquerors of Armenia and Sarmatia, and—what is more important—philosophers:

1 In your Empire, Your Most Excellent Majesties, different peoples observe different laws and customs; and no one is hindered by law or fear of punishment from devotion to his ancestral ways, even if they are ridiculous. A citizen of Troy calls Hector a god, and worships Helen, taking her for Adrasteia. The Lacedaemonian venerates Agamemnon as Zeus, and Phylonoë, the daughter of Tyndareus, under the name of Enodia.

Athenagoras: "Plea Regarding Christians," reproduced from *Early Christian Fathers*, ed. Cyril C. Richardson (Library of Christian Classics Series), 1970. Used by permission of Westminster John Knox Press.

The Athenian sacrifices to Erechtheus as Poseidon. The Athenians also perform religious rites and celebrate mysteries in honor of Agraulus and Pandrosus, whom they imagine guilty of impiety for opening the box. In brief, among every nation and people, people perform whatever sacrifices and mysteries they wish. The Egyptians reckon among their gods even cats, crocodiles, serpents, asps, and dogs. And to all these cults both you and the laws grant toleration. For you think it impious and wicked to believe in no god at all; and you hold it necessary for everyone to worship the gods he pleases, so that they may be kept from wrongdoing by fear of the divine. [With us, on the contrary, although you yourselves are not, like the crowd, led astray by rumors, our name is the object of hatred. But names do not deserve to be hated. It is wrongdoing which merits penalty and punishment.]

Accordingly, while everyone admires your mildness and gentleness and your peaceful and kindly attitude toward all, they enjoy equal rights under the law. The cities, according to their rank, share in equal honor, and the whole Empire through your wisdom enjoys profound peace.

But you have not cared for us who are called Christians in this way. Although we do no wrong, but, as we shall show, are of all people most religiously and rightly disposed toward God and your Empire, you allow us to be harassed, plundered, and persecuted, the mob making war on us only because of our name. We venture, therefore, to state our case before you. From what we have to say you will gather that we suffer unjustly and contrary to all law and reason. Hence we ask you to devise some measures to prevent our being the victims of false accusers.

The injury we suffer from our persecutors does not concern our property or our civil rights or anything of less importance. For we hold these things in contempt, although they appear weighty to the crowd. We have learned not only not to return blow for blow, nor to sue those who plunder and rob us, but to those who smite us on one cheek to offer the other also, and to those who take away our coat to give our overcoat as well. But when we have given up our property, they plot against our bodies and souls, pouring upon us a multitude of accusations which have not the slightest foundation, but which are the stock in trade of gossips and the like.

2 If, indeed, anyone can convict us of wrongdoing, be it trifling or more serious, we do not beg off punishment, but are prepared to pay the penalty however cruel and unpitying. But if the accusation goes no farther than a name—and it is clear that up to today the tales about us rest only on popular and uncritical rumor, and not a single Christian has been convicted of wrongdoing—it is your duty, illustrious, kind, and most learned Emperors, to relieve us of these calumnies by law. Thus, as the whole world, both individuals and cities, shares your kindness, we too may be grateful to you, rejoicing that we have ceased to be defamed.

It does not befit your sense of justice that others, accused of wrongdoing, are not punished before they have been convicted, while with us the mere name is of more weight than legal proof. Our judges, moreover, do not inquire if the accused has committed any wrong, but let loose against the name as if *it* were a crime. But no name in and of itself is good or bad. It is by reason of the wicked or good actions associated with names that they are bad or good. You know all that better than anyone, seeing you are versed in philosophy and thoroughly cultured.

That is why those who are tried before you, though arraigned on the most serious charges, take courage. For they know that you will examine their life and not be influenced by names if they mean nothing, or by accusations if they are false. Hence they receive a sentence of condemnation on a par with one of acquittal. We claim for ourselves, therefore, the same treatment as others. We should not be hated and punished because we are called Christians, for what has a name to do with our being criminals? Rather should we be tried on charges brought against us, and either acquitted on our disproving them or punished on our being convicted as wicked people, not because of a name (for no Christian is wicked unless he is a hypocrite), but because of a crime.

It is in this way, we know, that philosophers are judged. None of them before the trial is viewed by the judge as good or bad because of his system or profession, but he is punished if he is found guilty. (No stigma attaches to philosophy on that account, for he is a bad person for not being a philosopher lawfully, and philosophy is not responsible.) On the other hand, he is acquitted if he disproves the charges. Let the same procedure be used in our case. Let the life of those who are accused be examined, and let the name be free from all reproach.

I must at the outset of my defense beg you, illustrious Emperors, to hear me impartially. Do not prejudge the case through being influenced by popular and unfounded rumor, but apply your love of learning and of truth to our cause. Thus you will not be led astray through ignorance, and we, disproving the uncritical rumors of the crowd, shall cease to be persecuted.

3 Three charges are brought against us: atheism, Thyestean feasts, and Oedipean intercourse. If these are true, spare no class; proceed against our crimes; destroy us utterly with our wives and children, if anyone lives like a beast. Beasts, indeed, do not attack their own kind. Nor for mere wantonness do they have intercourse, but by nature's law and only at the season of procreation. They recognize, too, those who come to their aid. If, then, anyone is more savage than brutes, what punishment shall we not think it fitting for him to suffer for such crimes?

But if these charges are inventions and unfounded slanders, they arise from the fact that it is natural for vice to oppose virtue and it is in accord with God's law for contraries to war against each other. You yourselves, moreover, are witness to the fact that we are guilty of none of these things, since it is only the confession of a name that you forbid. It remains for you, then, to examine our lives and teachings, our loyalty and obedience to you, to your house, and to the Empire. By doing so you will concede to us no more than you grant to our persecutors. And we shall triumph over them, giving up our very lives for the truth without any hesitation.

4 We are of course not atheists (I will meet the charges one by one)—and I hope it does not sound too silly to answer such an allegation. Rightly, indeed, did the Athenians accuse Diagoras of atheism, since he not only divulged the Orphic doctrine as well as the mysteries of Eleusis and of the Cabiri and chopped up a statue of Heracles to boil his turnips, but he proclaimed outrightly that God simply did not exist. In our case, however, is it not mad to charge us with atheism, when we distinguish God from matter, and show that matter is one thing and God another, and that there is a vast difference between them? For the divine is uncreated and eternal, grasped only by pure mind and intelligence, while matter is created and perishable.

If we shared the views of Diagoras when we have so many good reasons to adore God—the order, harmony, greatness, color, form, and arrangement of the world—we should rightly be charged with impiety and there would be due cause to persecute us. But since our teaching affirms one God who made the universe, being himself uncreated (for what exists does not come into being, only what does not exist), and who made all things through his Word, on two scores, then, we are treated unreasonably—by being slandered and by being persecuted. . . .

10 I have sufficiently shown that we are not atheists since we acknowledge one God, who is uncreated, eternal, invisible, impassible, incomprehensible, illimitable. He is grasped only by mind and intelligence, and surrounded by light, beauty, spirit, and indescribable power. By him the universe was created through his Word, was set in order, and is held together. [I say "his Word"], for we also think that God has a Son.

Let no one think it stupid for me to say that God has a Son. For we do not think of God the Father or of the Son in the way of the poets, who weave their myths by showing that gods are no better than humans. But the Son of God is his Word in idea and in actuality; for by him and through him all things were made, the Father and the Son being one. And since the Son is in the Father and the Father in the Son by the unity and power of the Spirit, the Son of God is the mind and Word of the Father.

But if, owing to your sharp intelligence, it occurs to you to inquire further what is meant by the Son, I shall briefly explain. He is the first offspring of the Father. I do not mean that he was created, for, since God is eternal mind, he had his Word within himself the beginning, being eternally wise. Rather did the Son come forth from God to give form and actuality to all material things, which essentially have a sort of formless nature and inert quality, the heavier particles being mixed up with the lighter. The prophetic Spirit agrees with this opinion when he says, "The Lord created me as the first of his ways, for his works."[1]

Indeed we say that the Holy Spirit himself, who inspires those who utter prophecies, is an effluence from God, flowing from him and returning like a ray of the sun. Who, then, would not be astonished to hear those called atheists who admit God the Father, God the Son, and the Holy Spirit, and who teach their unity in power and their distinction in rank? Nor is our theology confined to these points. We affirm, too, a crowd of angels and ministers, whom God, the maker and creator of the world, appointed to their several tasks through his Word. He gave them charge over the good order of the universe, over the elements, the heavens, the world, and all it contains.

11 Do not be surprised that I go into detail about our teaching. I give a full report to prevent your being carried away by popular and irrational opinion, and so that you may know the truth. Moreover, by showing that the teachings themselves, to which we are attached, are not human, but were declared and taught by God, we can persuade you not to hold us for atheists. What, then, are these teachings in which we are reared? "I say to you, love your enemies, bless those who curse you, pray for those who persecute you, that you may be sons of your Father in heaven, who makes his sun to shine on the evil and on the good, and sends his rain on the just and on the unjust.". . .[2]

13 Since many of those who charge us with atheism do not have the vaguest idea of God, being unversed in, and ignorant of, physics and theology, they measure religion by the observance of sacrifices, and charge us with not having the same gods as the cities. Heed what I have to say, Your Majesties, on both these counts. And first about our not sacrificing.

The creator and Father of the universe does not need blood or the smell of burnt offerings or the fragrance of flowers or incense. He himself is perfect fragrance. He lacks nothing and has need of nothing. But the greatest sacrifice in his eyes is for us to realize who stretched out the heavens in a sphere, who set the earth in the center, who gathered the water into seas and separated the light from darkness, who adorned the sky with the stars and made the earth bring forth all kinds of seed, who made the animals and fashioned humans. When, therefore, we recognize God the creator of the universe, who preserves it and watches over it with the wisdom and skill he does, and lift up holy hands to him, what need has he then of a hecatomb?

> "It is with sacrifices and humble prayer,
> With libation and burnt offering that people
>   implore [the gods]
> And turn [their wrath], when any has offended or sinned."[3]

What need have I of burnt offerings, when God does not need them? Rather is it needful to present a bloodless sacrifice, to offer a spiritual worship.

14 Regarding their other charge, that we neither accept nor venerate the same gods as the cities, it is quite senseless. The very ones who accuse us of atheism for not acknowledging the same gods that they believe in are not agreed among themselves about the gods. The Athenians have set up Celeus and Metanira as gods; the Lacedaemonians, Menelaus—they sacrifice to him and keep his festival; the Trojans cannot bear his

---

[1]Prov 8:22.
[2]Matt 5:44, 45; Luke 6:27, 28.
[3]*Iliad* 9:499–501.

name, and worship Hector; the Ceans adore Aristaeus, imagining he is identical with Zeus and Apollo; the Thasians worship Theagenes, who committed a murder at the Olympian games; the Samians, Lysander for all his slaughter and wickedness! ... The Cilicians worship Niobe; the Sicilians, Philip the son of Boutacides; the Amathusians, Onesilus; the Carthaginians, Hamilcar. The day is too short to enumerate the rest.

When, then, they fail to agree among themselves about their gods, why do they charge us with disagreeing with them?

15 But grant that they worship the same gods. What then? Since the populace cannot distinguish between matter and God or appreciate the chasm that separates them, they have recourse to idols made of matter. Shall we, then, who can distinguish and differentiate between uncreated and created, between being and nonbeing, between the intelligible and the sensible, and who call these things by their proper names—shall we, just because of the populace, come and worship statues? If matter and God are identical, two names for the same thing, we are surely irreligious for not thinking that stones, wood, gold, and silver are gods. But if there is a vast difference between them, as great as separates the craftsman and his materials, why are we called to account?

It is like the potter and the clay. The clay is matter, the potter is an artist. So is God the creator an artist, while matter is subject to him for the sake of his art. But as clay cannot by itself become pottery without art, so matter, which is altogether pliable, cannot receive distinction, form, or beauty apart from God the creator. We do not, moreover, reckon pottery of more value than the potter, or bowls or vessels of gold than the artisan. If they have artistic merit, we praise the artist. It is he who reaps the renown for making them. So it is with matter and God. It is not matter which justly receives praise and honor for the arrangement and beauty of the world, but its creator, God. If, then, we were to worship material forms as gods, we should seem to be insensitive to the true God, identifying what is eternal with what is subject to dissolution and corruption.

For when your subjects come to you, they do not fail to pay their homage to you, their lords and masters, from whom they may obtain what they need. They do not have recourse to the magnificence of your palace. . . .

That, therefore, we are not atheists, since we worship God the creator of this universe, and his Word, I have proved as best I can, even if I have not done the subject justice.

31 Our accusers have made up the further charges against us of impious feasts and intercourse. They do this to convince themselves that they have grounds for hating us. They imagine, moreover, that by fear they will either draw us away from our present mode of life or else, by the enormity of the accusations, render our princes harsh and implacable. But this a foolish approach toward those who realize that of old, and not merely in our time, wickedness has a habit of warring against virtue, in obedience to some divine law and principle. Thus, for instance, Pythagoras with three hundred companions was put to the flames. Heraclitus and Democritus were banished, the one from the city of Ephesus, the other, charged with insanity, from Abdera. Finally, the Athenians condemned Socrates to death. And just as the virtue of these men suffered no whit from the opinions of the mob, so our uprightness of life is in no way obscured by the reckless calumnies of some persons. For we are in good standing with God.

Nonetheless, I will meet these charges too, although I am very confident that I have made my case by what I have already said. You, who are more intelligent than others, know that those who faithfully regulate their lives by reference to God, so that each of us stands before him blameless and irreproachable, will not entertain even the thought of the slightest sin. Were we convinced that this life is the only one, then we might be suspected of sinning, by being enslaved to flesh and blood and by becoming subject to gain and lust. But since we realize that God is a witness day and night of our thoughts and our speech, and that by being pure light he can see into our very hearts, we are convinced that when we depart this present life we shall live another. It will be better than this one, heavenly, not earthly. We shall live close to God and with God, our souls steadfast and free from passion. Even if we have flesh, it will not seem so: we shall be heavenly spirits. Or else, if we fall along with the rest, we shall enter on a worse life and one in flames. For God did not make us like sheep and oxen, a bywork to perish and be done away with. In the light of this it is not likely that we would be purposely wicked, and deliver ourselves up to the great Judge to be punished.

32 It is nothing surprising that our accusers should invent the same tales about us that they tell of their gods. They present their sufferings as mysteries; and, had they wanted to judge shameless and indiscriminate intercourse as a frightful thing, they should have hated Zeus. For he had children from his mother, Rhea, and his daughter Kore, and married his own sister. Or else, they should have detested Orpheus, who invented these tales, because he made Zeus even more unholy and wicked than Thyestes. For the latter had intercourse with his daughter in pursuance of an oracle, and because he wanted to gain a throne and avenge himself.

But we, on the contrary, are so far from viewing such crimes with indifference that we are not even allowed to indulge a lustful glance. For, says the Scripture, "He who looks at a woman lustfully, has already committed adultery in his heart."[4]

We feel it is a matter of great importance that those, whom we thus think of as brothers and sisters and so on, should keep their bodies undefiled and uncorrupted. For the Scripture says again, "If anyone kisses a second time because he found it enjoyable . . ." Thus the kiss, or rather the religious salutation, should be very carefully guarded. For if it is defiled by the slightest evil thought, it excludes us from eternal life.

33 Having, therefore, the hope of eternal life, we despise the enjoyments of the present, even the pleasures of the soul. According to our laws, each of thinks of the woman he has married as his wife only for the purpose of bearing chil-

dren. For as the farmer casts his seed on the soil and awaits the harvest without sowing over it, so we limit the pleasure of intercourse to bearing children.

You would, indeed, find many among us, both men and women, who have grown to old age unmarried, in the hope of being closer to God. If, then, to remain virgins and eunuchs brings us closer to God, while to indulge in wrong thoughts and passions drives us from him, we have all the more reason to avoid those acts, the very thought of which we flee from. For we center our attention not on the skill of making speeches but on the proof and lessons of actions. We hold that a man should either remain as he is born or else marry only once. For a second marriage is a veiled adultery. The Scripture says, "Whoever puts away his wife and marries another, commits adultery."[5]

34 Since we are such (and why should I speak of such degrading things?), our situation resembles that of the proverb, "The harlot reproves the chaste." It is these people who revile us with the very things they are conscious of in themselves and which they attribute to their gods. They boast of them indeed, as noble acts and worthy of gods. Adulterers and corrupters of boys, they insult eunuchs and those once married.

35 Since this is our character, what person of sound judgment would say that we are murderers? For you cannot eat human flesh until you have killed someone. If their first charge against us is a fiction, so is the second. For if anyone were to ask them if they had seen what they affirm, none of them would be so shameless as to say he had.

Moreover, we have slaves: some of us more, some fewer. We cannot hide anything from them; yet not one of them has made up such tall stories against us. Since they know that we cannot endure to see any one being put to death even justly, who of them would charge us with murder or cannibalism? Who among our accusers is not eager to

---

[4]Matt 5:28.
[5]Mark 10:11.

witness contests of gladiators and wild beasts, especially those organized by you? But we see little difference between watching a man being put to death and killing him. So we have given up such spectacles. How can we commit murder when we will not look at it, lest we should contract the stain of guilt? What reason would we have to commit murder when we say that women who induce abortions are murderers, and will have to give account of it to God? For the same person would not regard the fetus in the womb as a living thing and therefore an object of God's care, and at the same time slay it, once it had come to life. Nor would he refuse to expose infants, on the ground that those who expose them are murderers of children, and at the same time do away with the child he has reared. But we are altogether consistent in our conduct. We obey reason and do not override it.

36 What person, moreover, who is convinced of the resurrection would make himself into a tomb for bodies that will rise again? The same persons would surely not believe that our bodies will rise again and then eat them as if there were no resurrection. They would not think that the earth will give back its dead and then imagine that it will fail to demand those entombed in them.

On the contrary, those who deny they will have to give account of the present life, be it wicked or good, who reject the resurrection and who count on the soul's perishing along with the body and, so to say, flickering out, are likely to stop at no outrage. But those who are convinced that God will look into everything and that the body which has aided the soul in its unreasonable lusts and passions will be punished along with it, they have no good reason to commit even the slightest sin.

⌖

12. The Letter to Diognetus

We know very little about the origin of the Letter to Diognetus. It was written anonymously and was addressed to someone who cannot otherwise be identified; nor is it ever mentioned in our ancient sources. Scholars generally date the book to the end of the second century or the beginning of the third.

Like other apologists, the author attacks the folly of both pagan idolatry and Jewish superstition (as seen, he contends, in such customs as kosher food laws and circumcision). Christians are portrayed as good citizens who have done nothing to harm the social order; on the contrary, since their full allegiance is to heaven, they are to the world as the soul is to the body. For this author, Christ was sent from God to convince the world of the error of its ways and to bring all people to God. But, in striking contrast to other apologists, this author explicitly denies that pagan philosophy and myth reflect the divine logos as precursors to Christ; before the coming of the Maker of the universe into the world, all people stood in complete error and darkness.

The "Letter to Diognetus," from *The Apostolic Fathers*, ed. J. B. Lightfoot and J. R. Harmer; 2d ed. by Michael W. Holmes. Grand Rapids, Mich.: Baker Book House, 1992.

1 Since I see, most excellent Diognetus, that you are extremely interested in learning about the religion of the Christians and are asking very clear and careful questions about them—specifically, what God do they believe in and how do they worship him, so that they all disregard the world and despise death, neither recognizing those who are considered to be gods by the Greeks nor observing the superstition of the Jews; what is the nature of the heartfelt love they have for one another; and why has this new race of humans or way of life come into the world we live in now and not before?—I gladly welcome this interest of yours, and I ask God, who empowers us both to speak and to listen, that I may be enabled to speak in such a way that you will derive the greatest possible benefit from listening, and that you may listen in such a way that the speaker will have no regrets.

2 Come, then, clear your mind of all its prejudices and cast aside the custom that deceives you, and become a new man, as it were, from the beginning, as if you were about to hear a new message, even as you yourself admit. See not only with your eyes but also with your intellect what substance or what form those whom you call and regard as gods happens to have.

2 Is not one of them stone, like that which we walk upon, and another bronze, no better than the utensils that have been forged for our use, and another wood, already rotted away, and another silver, which needs a watchman to guard it lest it be stolen, and another iron, corroded by rust, and another pottery, not a bit more attractive than that made for the most unmentionable use?

3 Are not all these made of perishable matter? Are they not forged by iron and fire? Did not the sculptor make one of them, and the coppersmith another, the silversmith another, and the potter yet another? Before they were shaped by the skills of these craftsmen into the form they have, was it not possible—indeed, is it not even now possible—for each of them to have been given a different form? Might not the ordinary utensils now formed out of the same material be made similar to such images as these, if the same craftsmen were available?

4 Again, could not these things which are now worshiped by you be made into utensils like the rest? Are they not all deaf and blind, without souls, without feelings, without movement? Do they no all rot, do they not all decay?

5 These are the things you call gods; you serve them, you worship them, and in the end you become like them.

6 This is why you hate the Christians: because they do not consider these objects to be gods.

7 For do not you yourselves, who now regard and worship them as gods, in fact much more despise them? Are you not mocking and insulting them much more when you leave unguarded the stone or pottery gods you worship but lock up the silver and gold ones at night and post guards by them during the day, lest they be stolen?

8 And as for the honors that you think you are offering them: if they are aware of them, then you are in fact insulting them; but if they are not aware, then you are showing them up by worshiping them with the blood and fat of victims.

9 Let one of you undergo this treatment, let someone allow these things to be done to him! Why, there is not a single individual who would willingly submit to such punishment, for a human being has feelings and reason; but the stone does submit, for it has no feeling. Therefore you disprove its ability to feel.

10 Well, I could say many other things about the fact that Christians are not enslaved to such gods, but if these arguments should seem insufficient to anyone, then I think it is useless to say more.

3 And next I suppose that you are especially anxious to hear why Christians do not worship in the same way as the Jews.

2 The Jews indeed, insofar as they abstain from the kind of worship described above, rightly claim to worship the one God of the universe and to think of him as Master; but insofar as they offer this worship to him in the same way as those already described, they are altogether mistaken.

3 For whereas the Greeks provide an example of their stupidity by offering things to sense-

less and deaf images, the Jews, thinking that they are offering these things to God as if he were in need of them, could rightly consider it folly rather than worship.

4 For he who made the heaven and the earth and all that is in them, and provides us all with what we need, cannot himself need any of the things that he himself provides to those who imagine that they are giving to him.

5 In any case, those who imagine that they are offering sacrifices to him by means of blood and fat and whole burnt offerings and are honoring him with these tokens of respect do not seem to me to be the least bit different from those who show the same respect to deaf images: the latter make offerings to things unable to receive the honor, while the former think they offer it to the One who is in need of nothing.

4 But with regard to their qualms about meats, and superstition concerning the Sabbath, and pride in circumcision, and hypocrisy about fasting and new moons, I doubt that you need to learn from me that they are ridiculous and not worth discussing.

2 For is it not unlawful to accept some of the things created by God for human use as created good but to refuse others as useless and superfluous?

3 And is it not impious to slander God, as though he forbids us to do any good thing on the Sabbath day?

4 And is it not also ridiculous to take pride in the mutilation of the flesh as a sign of election, as though they were especially beloved by God because of this?

5 And as for the way they watch the stars and the moon, so as to observe months and days, and to make distinctions between the changing seasons ordained by God, making some into feasts and others into times of mourning according to their own inclinations, who would regard this as an example of godliness and not much more of a lack of understanding?

6 So then, I think you have been sufficiently instructed to realize that the Christians are right to keep their distance from the thoughtlessness and deception common to both groups and from the fussiness and pride of the Jews. But as for the mystery of the Christian's own religion, do not expect to be able to learn this from a human.

5 For Christians are not distinguished from the rest of humanity by country, language, or custom.

2 For nowhere do they live in cities of their own, nor do they speak some unusual dialect, nor do they practice an eccentric life-style.

3 This teaching of theirs has not been discovered by the thought and reflection of ingenious people, nor do they promote any human doctrine, as some do.

4 But while they live in both Greek and barbarian cities, as each one's lot was cast, and follow the local customs in dress and food and other aspects of life, at the same time they demonstrate the remarkable and admittedly unusual character of their own citizenship.

5 They live in their own countries, but only as aliens; they participate in everything as citizens, and endure everything as foreigners. Every foreign country is their fatherland, and every fatherland is foreign.

6 They marry like everyone else, and have children, but they do not expose their offspring.

7 They share their food but not their wives.

8 They are "in the flesh," but they do not live "according to the flesh."

9 They live on earth, but their citizenship is in heaven.

10 They obey the established laws; indeed in their private lives they transcend the laws.

11 They love everyone, and by everyone they are persecuted.

12 They are unknown, yet they are condemned; they are put to death, yet they are brought to life.

13 They are poor, yet they make many rich; they are in need of everything, yet they abound in everything.

14 They are dishonored, yet they are glorified in their dishonor; they are slandered, yet they are vindicated.

15 They are cursed, yet they bless; they are insulted, yet they offer respect.

16 When they do good, they are punished as evildoers; when they are punished, they rejoice as though brought to life.

17 By the Jews they are assaulted as foreigners, and by the Greeks they are persecuted, yet those who hate them are unable to give a reason for their hostility.

6 In a word, what the soul is to the body, Christians are to the world.

2 The soul is dispersed through all the members of the body, and Christians throughout the cities of the world.

3 The soul dwells in the body, but is not of the body; likewise Christians dwell in the world, but are not of the world.

4 The soul, which is invisible, is confined in the body, which is visible; in the same way, Christians are recognized as being in the world, and yet their religion remains invisible.

5 The flesh hates the soul and wages war against it, even though it has suffered no wrong, because it is hindered from indulging in its pleasures; so also the world hates the Christians, even though it has suffered no wrong, because they set themselves against its pleasures.

6 The soul loves the flesh that hates it, and its members, and Christians love those who hate them.

7 The soul is enclosed in the body, but it holds the body together; and though Christians are detained in the world as if in a prison, they in fact hold the world together.

8 The soul, which is immortal, lives in a mortal dwelling; similarly Christians live as strangers amidst perishable things, while waiting for the imperishable in heaven.

9 The soul, when poorly treated with respect to food and drink, becomes all the better; and so Christians when punished daily increase more and more.

10 Such is the important position to which God has appointed them, and it is not right for them to decline it.

7 For this is, as I said, no earthly discovery that was committed to them, nor some mortal idea that they consider to be worth guarding so carefully, nor have they been entrusted with the administration of merely human mysteries.

2 On the contrary, the omnipotent Creator of all, the invisible God himself, established among humans the truth and the holy, incomprehensible word from heaven and fixed it firmly in their hearts, not, as one might imagine, by sending to people some subordinate, or angel or ruler or one of those who manage earthly matters, or one of those entrusted with the administration of things in heaven, but the Designer and Creator of the universe himself, by whom he created the heavens, by whom he enclosed the sea within its proper bounds, whose mysteries all the elements faithfully observe, from whom the sun has received the measure of the daily courses to keep, whom the moon obeys as he commands it to shine by night, whom the stars obey as they follow the course of the moon, by whom all things have been ordered and determined and placed in subjection, including the heavens and the things in the heavens, the earth and the things in the earth, the sea and the things in the sea, fire, air, abyss, the things in the heights, the things in the depths, the things in between—this one he sent to them!

3 But perhaps he sent him, as a person might suppose, to rule by tyranny, fear, and terror?

4 Certainly not! On the contrary, he sent him in gentleness and meekness, as a king might send his son who is a king; he sent him as God; he sent him as a human to humans. When he sent him, he did so as one who saves by persuasion, not compulsion, for compulsion is no attribute of God.

5 When he sent him, he did so as one calling, not pursuing; when he sent him, he did so as one loving, not judging.

6 For he will send him as Judge, and who will endure his coming? . . .

7 [Do you not see] how they are thrown to wild beasts to make them deny the Lord, and yet are not conquered?

8 Do you not see that as more of them are punished, the more others increase?

9 These things do not look like the works of a human; they are the power of God, they are proofs of his presence.

8 For what person had any knowledge at all of what God was, before he came?

2 Or do you accept the empty and nonsensical statements of those pretentious philosophers, some of whom said that God was fire (the very thing they are headed for, they call God!), and others, water, and still others some other one of the elements created by God.

3 And yet, if any of these statements is worthy of acceptance, then every one of the other created things might just as well be declared to be God.

4 No, these things are merely the illusions and deceit of the magicians.

5 No one has either seen or recognized him, but he has revealed himself.

6 And he revealed himself through faith, which is the only means by which it is permitted to see God.

7 For God, the Master and Creator of the universe, who made all things and arranged them in order, was not only tender-hearted but also very patient.

8 Indeed, so he always was and is and will be, kind, good, without anger, and true, and he alone is good.

9 And after conceiving a great and marvelous plan, he communicated it to his Child alone.

10 Now as long as he kept it a secret and guarded his wise design, he seemed to neglect and be unconcerned about us,

11 but when he revealed it through his beloved Child and made known the things prepared from the beginning, he gave us everything at once, both to share in his benefits and to see and understand things which none of us ever would have expected. . . .

13. Tertullian: Apology

Tertullian was a prolific and enormously influential Christian author from Carthage. Raised as a pagan and thoroughly trained in secular schools of rhetoric, Tertullian converted to Christianity near the end of the second century. He then focused his keen rhetorical sense and acerbic wit on a range of critical issues facing the Christian church, especially in the areas of apologetics, heresy, and ethics. The breadth of his interests can be seen throughout this anthology (see Chapters 5, 7, 11, 13, and 14). In particular, his doctrinal writings became foundational for later thinkers, especially in Western Christendom; he is widely known as the father of Latin theology.

As an apologist, Tertullian dealt with many of the same issues as his Greek predecessors, especially the standard charges against the Christians and the injustice of their condemnation. What makes his work particularly interesting is not so much his perspective as the way he phrases it. His rhetoric is brilliant and biting, and he bars no holds. Using keen (and sometimes dubious) logic and rapier-like (and often sarcastic) wit, he dismantles and ridicules both the serious accusations and the popular sentiment against the Christians.

Tertullian: "Apology," from *Tertullian: Apologetical Works and Minucius Felix: Octavius*, ed. Rudolph Arbesmann. Fathers of the Church, 10; 2d ed. Washington, D.C.: Catholic University Press of America, 1977. Used with permission.

The following excerpts come from Tertullian's earliest and best-known apologetic treatise, the "Apology," written, probably, around 197 C.E.

Chapter 2

1 If, then, it is decided that we are the most wicked of people, why do you treat us so differently from those who are on a par with us, that is, from all other criminals? The same treatment ought to be meted out for the same crime.

2 When others are charged with the same crimes as we, they use their own lips and the hired eloquence of others to prove their innocence. There is full liberty given to answer the charge and to cross-question, since it is unlawful for people to be condemned without defense or without a hearing.

3 Christians alone are permitted to say nothing that would clear their name, vindicate the truth, and aid the judge to come to a fair decision. One thing only is what they wait for; this is the only thing necessary to arouse public hatred: the confession of the name of Christian, not an investigation of the charge.

4 Yet, suppose you are trying any other criminal. If he confesses to the crime of murder, sacrilege, incest, or treason—to particularize the indictments hurled against us—you are not satisfied to pass sentence immediately; you weigh the attendant circumstances, the character of the deed, the number of times it was committed, the time, the place, the witnesses, and the partners-in-crime.

5 In our case there is nothing of this sort. No matter what false charge is made against us, we must be made to confess it; for example, how many murdered babies one has devoured, how many deeds of incest one has committed under cover of darkness, what cooks and what dogs were on hand. Oh, what glory for that governor who should have discovered someone who had already consumed a hundred infants! . . .

Chapter 7

1 We are spoken of as utter reprobates and are accused of having sworn to murder babies and to eat them and of committing adulterous acts af-

ter the repast. Dogs, you say, the pimps of darkness, overturn candles and procure license for our impious lusts.

2 We are always spoken of in this way, yet you take no pains to bring into the light the charges which for so long a time have been made against us. Now, either bring them into the light, if you believe them, or stop believing them, inasmuch as you have not brought them to light! Because of your hypocrisy, the objection is made against you that the evil does not exist which you yourselves dare not bring to light. Far different is the duty you enjoin upon the executioner against the Christians, not to make them state what they do, but to make them deny what they are.

3 The origin of this religion, as we have already said, dates from the time of Tiberius. Truth and hatred came into existence simultaneously. As soon as the former appeared, the latter began its enmity. It has as many foes as there are outsiders, particularly among Jews because of their jealousy, among soldiers because of their blackmailing, and even among the very members of our own household because of corrupt human nature.

4 Day by day we are besieged; day by day we are betrayed; oftentimes, in the very midst of our meetings and gatherings, we are surprised by an assault.

5 Who has ever come upon a baby wailing, as the accusation has it? Who has ever kept for the judge's inspection the jaws of Cyclopes and Sirens, bloodstained as he had found them? Who has every found any traces of impurity upon [Christian] wives? Who has discovered such crimes, yet concealed them or been bribed to keep them secret when dragging these people off to court? If we always keep under cover, whence the betrayal of our crimes?

6 Rather, who could have been the traitors? Certainly not the accused themselves, since the obligation of pledged silence is binding upon all mysteries by their very nature. The mysteries of

Samothrace and of Eleusis are shrouded in silence; how much more such rites as these which, if they were made public, would provoke at once the hatred of all humankind—while God's wrath is reserved for the future?

7 If, then, Christians themselves are not the betrayers, it follows that outsiders are. Whence do outsiders get their knowledge, since even holy initiation rites always ban the uninitiated and are wary of witnesses? Unless you mean that the wicked are less afraid.

8 The nature of rumor is well known to all. It was your own poet who said: "Rumor, an evil surpassing all evils in speed."[1] . . .

Chapter 10

1 "You do not worship the gods," you say, "and you do not offer sacrifice for the emperors." It follows that we do not offer sacrifices for others for the same reason that we do not do it even for ourselves—it follows immediately from our not worshipping the gods. Consequently, we are considered guilty of sacrilege and treason. This is the chief accusation against us—in fact, it is the whole case—and it certainly deserves investigation, unless presumption and injustice dictate that decision, the one despairing of the truth, the other refusing it.

2 We cease worshipping your gods when we find out that they are non-existent. This, then, is what you ought to demand, that we prove that those gods are non-existent and for that reason should not be worshipped, because they ought to be worshipped only if they were actually gods. Then, too, the Christians ought to be punished if the fact were established that those gods do exist whom they will not worship because they consider them non-existent.

3 "But, for us," you say, "the gods do exist." We object and appeal from you to your conscience. Let this pass judgment on us, let this condemn us, if it can deny that all those gods of yours have been mere men.

4 But, if it should deny this, it will be refuted by its own documents of ancient times from which

it has learned of the gods. Testimony is furnished to this very day by the cities in which they were born, and the regions in which they left traces of something they had done and in which it is pointed out that they were buried. . . .

Chapter 17

1 The object of our worship is the one God, who, out of nothing, simply for the glory of his majesty, fashioned this enormous universe with its whole supply of elements, bodies, and spirits, and did so simply by the Word wherewith he bade it, the Reason whereby he ordered it, the Power wherewith he was powerful. Hence it is that even the Greeks apply the appropriate word "cosmos" to the universe.

2 He is invisible, although he may be seen; intangible, although manifested by grace; immeasurable, although he may be measured by human senses. Therefore, he is so true and so great. However, what can be generally seen, touched, and measured is less than the eyes by which it is seen, the hands by which it is touched, and the senses by which it is discovered. But, what is infinite is known only to itself.

3 Thus it is that God can be measured, although he is beyond all measure; thus, the force of his magnitude makes him known to people and yet unknown. And this is the gravest part of the sin of those who are unwilling to recognize him of whom they cannot remain in ignorance. . . .

Chapter 18

1 But, in order that we might more fully and more energetically approach God himself as well as his designs and desires, he has added the assistance of books, in case one wishes to search for God; and after searching, discover him; and after discovering him, believe in him; and after believing in him, serve him.

2 From the beginning he sent into the world people who, because of their innocence and right-

---

[1]Virgil, *Aeneid* 4.174.

eousness, were worthy to know God and to make him known to others. These people he filled with the Holy Spirit that they might teach that there is but one God who made the universe and formed man from the earth. He is the true Prometheus, who has regulated the world with a fixed order and fixed endings for the ages.

3 Furthermore, what signs of his sovereign power to judge has he manifested by means of rain and fire! What regulations has he prescribed for placing people under obligation to himself! What recompense has he determined for those who are ignorant of them, those who neglect them, and those who observe them; for, after the present life is ended, he will direct his faithful followers to the reward of eternal life, but the wicked to everlasting and unending fire. Then, all those who have died from the beginning of time will be revived. Their bodies will be reformed. There will be a general review, and everyone will be examined according to his own merits.

4 These are points at which we, too, laughed in times past. We are from your own ranks: Christians are made, not born!

5 These teachers whom we mentioned are called prophets, because it is their function to foretell the future. Their words, as well as the miracles which they performed to win faith in their divine mission, are preserved in the treasures of literature and these are accessible. . . .

Chapter 19

1 Their great antiquity claims prime authority for these records. Among you, too, it is in accord with your superstitious ideas to make faith depend on times past. . . .

Moses was the first of the Prophets; he wove from the past the account of the foundation of the world and the formation of the human race and afterwards the mighty deluge which took vengeance upon the godlessness of that age; he prophesied events right up to his own day. Then, by means of conditions of his own time, he showed forth an image of times to come; according to him, too, the order of events, arranged from the beginning, supplied the reckoning of the age of the world: Moses

is found to be alive about 300 years before Danaus, your most ancient of men, came over to Argos.

2 He is 1,000 years earlier than the Trojan War and, therefore, the time of Saturn himself. For, according to the history of Thallus, where it is related that Belus, King of the Assyrians, and Saturn, King of the Titans, fought with Jupiter, it is shown that Belus antedated the fall of Troy by 322 years. It was by this same Moses, too, that their own true law was given to the Jews by God. . . .

Chapter 24

1 This whole confession of [the devils], whereby they deny that they are gods and declare that there is no other god but the One whose subjects we are, is quite sufficient to repel the charge of treason to the Roman religion. For, if the existence of the gods is uncertain, then surely the existence of your religion is uncertain, too. If there is no religion, since you have no gods for certain, then it is certain we are not guilty of violating religion.

2 On the contrary, your charge will act as a boomerang upon yourselves. In worshipping falsehood you not only neglect—or, I should say (even more than this), do violence to—the true religion of the true God, you actually commit the crime of positive irreligion.

3 Now, suppose the fact were established that gods exist: do you not acquiesce in the common opinion that some god is more sublime and more powerful, and, as it were, the ruler of this universe, a god of perfect majesty? That is the way most people apportion divine power; they would have the power of supreme command in the hands of one, but its exercise in the hands of many. Thus, Plato describes the mighty Jupiter in heaven attended by a host of both gods and demons; so (they say) the procurators, prefects, and governors ought to be held in equal esteem.

4 Yet, what crime does one commit who, in order to render better service to Caesar, transfers his attention and his hope and declares that the title of God, like that of emperor, belongs to none other than the one sovereign, since it is considered a capital offense to call anyone Caesar but Caesar and to listen to such talk?

5 Let one worship God, and another Jupiter; let one extend his hands in supplication to heaven, and another to the altar of Fides; let one (if you so suppose), count the clouds as he prays, and another the squares of the panelled ceiling; let one offer to his God his own soul, and another the soul of a goat.

6 See to it, rather, that this, too, does not tend to confirm the reproach of irreligion; namely, for you to take away one's freedom of religion and put a ban on one's free choice of a god, with the result that it is not lawful for me to worship whom I will, but I am compelled to worship contrary to my will. No one, not even a human, will be willing to receive the worship of an unwilling client.

7 Even the Egyptians were allowed the right—vain superstition that it was—to deify birds and beasts and to condemn to death anyone who killed a god of this sort.

8 Then, too, every province and city has its own god; for example, there is Atargatis in Syria, Dusares in Arabia, Belenus in Noricum, Caelestis in Africa, and the petty kings in Mauretania. The provinces which I have mentioned are, I believe, Roman, but the gods are not, because they are not worshipped at Rome any more than those gods who are listed on the roster of local deities all through Italy itself: Delventinus of Casinum, Visidianus of Narnia, Ancharia of Asculum, Nortia of Volsinii, Valentia of Ocriculum, and Hostia of Sutrium; Juno, among the Faliscans, even received a surname in honor of Father Curis.

9 We are the only ones kept from having our own religion. We offend the Romans and are not considered Romans because we do not worship the god of the Romans.

10 It is well that there is one God of all, to whom we all belong whether we will or not. But among you it is lawful to worship anything you choose except the true God, as if he were not the God of all to whom we all belong.

Chapter 25

1 It seems to me that I certainly have given sufficient proof of [the difference between] false and true divinity, now that I have pointed out how

the proof depends not merely on discussion and argument, but also on the spoken testimony of those very ones whom you believe to be gods; so that there is no necessity of adding anything further to this topic.

2 However, since we made particular mention of the name of Rome, I will not avoid the issue which is provoked by that presumption on the part of those who say that the Romans, as a result of their painstaking, scrupulous, religious observance, have been exalted to such sublime heights that they have become masters of the world; and that, in consequence, their gods have brought it about that those surpass all others in prosperity who surpass all others in devotion to their deity.

3 You may be sure that the price was paid by the Roman gods to the name of Rome for the favor. . . .

12 But, how senseless it is to attribute the dignity of the Roman name to their scrupulous religious observances, for it was after the institution of imperial, or, call it, still kingly power, that religion made advances. Although it was Numa who begot the superstitious punctiliousness, nevertheless divine service, with statues and temples, was not established among the Romans at that time.

13 Religious services were shabby, the rituals were unpretentious, and there was no Capitol struggling skyward; altars were improvised and built of sod, vessels were still made of clay from Samos, the odor from sacrifice was slight; the god himself had nowhere put in his appearance. At that time the genius of the Greeks and Tuscans for fashioning statues had not deluged the city. Consequently, the Romans' religious attitude did not precede their greatness, and, therefore, it was not for the fact that they were religious that they are great. . . .

14 On the contrary, how could their greatness be attributed to their religious attitude, since their greatness resulted from their indifference to religion? For, unless I am mistaken, every kingdom or empire is acquired by wars and extended by victories. Yet, wars and victories generally consist in the capture and destruction of cities. This business is not without its violence to the gods; there is indiscriminate destruction of city

walls and temples, slaughter of citizens and priests without distinction, pillaging of treasures sacred and profane alike.

15 The sacrileges of the Romans are as numerous as their trophies; their triumphs over the gods as many as those over nations; there is as much plunder as there are statues of the captured gods still on hand.

16 The gods, therefore, endure being adored by their enemies and decree "empire without end" to those whose offences they should have requited, rather than their servile fawning. However, the injury of those who are devoid of feeling is as free from punishment as the worship of them is devoid of significance.

17 Certainly, the assumption cannot harmonize with truth that those people seem to have attained greatness on the merits of their religious service who, as we have pointed out, have either grown by giving offence to religion or have given offence by their growth. Even those whose realms were melted into the sum total of the Roman Empire were not devoid of religious attitudes when they lost their power. . . .

Chapter 37

1 If, as I have said above, we are commanded to love our enemies, who is there for us to hate? Likewise, if we are forbidden to return an injury, lest, through our action, we become wrong-doers like them, who is there for us to injure?

2 Examine yourselves on this point! How often do you rage furiously against the Christians, partly in response to your own feelings, partly out of respect for the laws? How often, too, has a hostile mob, without consulting you, attacked us on their own initiative, with stones and torches in their hands? Why, with the very fury of Bacchanals, they spare not even the corpses of Christians, but drag them from the response of the grave, from that resting place, as it were, of death; although they are already changed and by now rotting in corruption, they cut them into bits and tear them limb from limb.

3 Yet, what fault do you ever find with people who are bound together by such intimate ties,

what retaliation for injury do you ever experience from those who are so disposed even to death, though even a single night, with a few little torches, could produce such rich vengeance, if it were permitted us to requite evil with evil? But, far be it from us that our God-given religion avenge itself with human fire or that it grieve to endure the suffering whereby it is put to the test.

4 If we wanted to act as open enemies and not merely as secret avengers, would we lack the strength of numbers and troops? Take the Moors and Marcomani and the Parthians themselves or any tribes at all who, even if they are numerous, still live in one place and inhabit their own territories—are they really more numerous than the Christians who are scattered over the whole world? We are but of yesterday, yet we have filled every place among you—cities, islands, fortresses, towns, marketplaces, camp, tribes, town councils, the palace, the senate, the forum; we have left nothing to you but the temples of your gods.

5 For what war would we not have been fit and ready, even though unequally matched in military strength, we who are so ready to be slain, were it not that, according to our rule of life, it is granted us to be killed rather than to kill?

6 Even unarmed and without any uprising, merely as malcontents, simply through hatred and withdrawal, we could have fought against you. For, if such a multitude of people as we are had broken loose from you and had gone into some remote corner of the earth, the loss of so many citizens, of whatever kind they might be, would certainly have made your power blush for shame; in fact, it would even have punished you by this very desertion.

7 Without a doubt, you would have been exceedingly frightened at your loneliness, at the silence of your surroundings, and the stupor, as it were, of a dead world. You would have had to look around for people to rule; there would have been more enemies than citizens left to you.

8 For, now, the enemies whom you have are fewer because of the number of Christians, inasmuch as nearly all the citizens you have in nearly all the cities are Christians. But, you have preferred to call them the enemies of the human race rather than of human error.

9 But, who would snatch you away from those secret enemies that are constantly destroying your spiritual and bodily health—I mean, from the attacks of demons which we ward off from you without any reward and without pay? This alone would have been sufficient revenge for us, if from then on you were left open and exposed to the possession of the impure spirits.

10 Furthermore, instead of thinking of any compensation for so great a protection, you have preferred to consider as enemies a class of people, who, far from being a troublesome burden to you, are actually indispensable. To tell the truth, we are enemies, not, however, of the human race, but rather of human error.

Chapter 40

1 On the other hand, those people deserve the name of a secret society who band together in hatred of good and virtuous people, who cry out for the blood of the innocent, at the same time offering as a justification of their hatred the idle plea that they consider that the Christians are the cause of every public calamity and every misfortune of the people.

2 If the Tiber rises as high as the city walls, if the Nile does not rise to the fields, if the weather will not change, if there is an earthquake, a famine, a plague—straightway the cry is heard: "Toss the Christians to the lion!" So many of them for just one beast?

3 I ask you, before the reign of Tiberius, that is, before the coming of Christ, what great misfortunes befell the world and its cities? We read that the islands of Hiera, Anaphe, Delos, Rhodes, and Cos were swallowed up with many thousands of people.

4 Plato, too, relates that a land larger than Asia or Africa was washed away by the Atlantic Ocean. An earthquake emptied the Corinthian Sea, and the might of the waves wrested Lucania away [from Italy] and left it separate under the name of Sicily. Naturally, these happenings could not fail to be attended by injury to the inhabitants.

5 In those days, when the great flood poured its waters over the whole world, or, as Plato thought, merely over the plains, where then were—I shall not say the Christians who scorn your gods—but your gods themselves? . . .

9 It is to be noted, in connection with such misfortune, that if any disaster befell the cities, the same destruction was visited upon temples as upon city walls; hence, I can clearly demonstrate that the gods were not the cause of the misfortunes, inasmuch as similar misfortunes befell them, too.

10 At all times the human race has deserved ill at God's hands. . . .

12 So, the race now must experience the anger of this same God just as [it did] also in times past, before the name of Christian was even mentioned. His were the blessings people enjoyed, bestowed before they fashioned any of their own deities; why do they not realize that the misfortunes as well come from him whose blessings they have failed to recognize? They are guilty before him toward whom they have been ungrateful. . . .

Chapter 47

11 Everything against truth has been constructed from truth itself. The spirits of error effect this rivalry. By them has this kind of corruption of our life-giving doctrine been instigated; by them, too, have certain tales been started, which, by virtue of their resemblance to the truth, would weaken faith in the latter, or rather, would win it over for themselves, so that anyone may consider that Christians must not be believed because poets and philosophers must not be—or he may think that poets and philosophers should be believed all the more because they are not Christians.

12 Hence, we are ridiculed when we proclaim that God will hold a final judgment. Yet, in like manner the poets and philosophers establish a tribunal in the underworld. And, if we threaten hell, which is a subterranean storehouse of punishment consisting of a mysterious fire, we are laughed to scorn for it. Yet, Pyriphlegethon is also called a river among the dead.

13 If we mention paradise, a place of supernatural beauty destined to receive the souls of the blessed, separated from knowledge of the ordi-

nary world by the wall, as it were, of that fiery zone, the Elysian Fields have already won belief.

14 Whence, I ask you, comes such close resemblance with the philosophers and poets? From no place else but from our own doctrines. If from our doctrines as their primary source, then our doctrines are more reliable and more worthy of belief than the copies of them which also find belief. But, if from their own ideas, then our doctrines will be considered copies of things subsequent to themselves—something which the nature of things precludes. For, no shadow ever exists before the body nor does a copy precede the original. . . .

Chapter 50

12 But, carry on, good officials; you will become much better in the eyes of the people if you sacrifice the Christians for them. Crucify us—torture us—condemn us—destroy us! Your iniquity is the proof of our innocence. For this reason God permits us to suffer these things. In fact, by recently condemning a Christian maid to the *pander* rather than to the *panther* [in the arena], you confessed that among us a stain on our virtue is con-

sidered worse than any punishment or any form of death.

13 Yet, your tortures accomplish nothing, though each is more refined than the last; rather, they are an enticement to our religion. We become more numerous every time we are hewn down by you: the blood of Christians is seed.

14 Many among you urge people to endure suffering and death, as Cicero does in his *Tusculans*, Seneca in his essay on chance, Diogenes, Pyrrho, and Callinicus; yet, their words do not discover such disciples as do the Christians who teach by deeds.

15 That very obstinacy which you rebuke is the teacher. For, who is not stirred by the contemplation of it to inquire what is really beneath the surface? And who, when he has inquired, does not approach us? Who, when he has approached, does not desire to suffer so that he may procure the full grace of God, that he may purchase from him full pardon by paying with his own blood?

16 For, by this means, all sins are forgiven. That is why we thank you immediately for your sentences of condemnation. Such is the difference between things divine and human. When we are condemned by you, we are acquitted by God.

14. Origen: Against Celsus

Origen was the most brilliant, prolific, and influential author of the early church. Born in 185 C.E. and raised by Christian parents, he was something of a child prodigy among the Christians of Alexandria, Egypt. While still in his late teens, he was, according to Eusebius, appointed head of the famed Catechetical School, a kind of institution of Christian higher education. Origen soon became the leading proto-orthodox spokesperson of his day. Unfortunately, his sophisticated exegetical and theological works survive only in part, largely because some of his views were pronounced heretical three centuries after

Origen: Against Celsus, from *Origen: Contra Celsum*, ed. H. Chadwick. 2d ed. Cambridge: Cambridge University Press, 1965. Reprinted with the permission of Cambridge University Press.

his death (see Chapter 14).

Unlike the other apologies given here, Origen's *Against Celsus* is directed against a specific opponent, a philosopher named Celsus, who wrote the first known literary attack on the Christians, a book called "The True Word" (ca. 170 C.E.). This treatise evidently made little impact in its own day; it is completely unknown apart from Origen's refutation, which was written some eighty years later.

Celsus had argued that Christianity was composed of simple-minded, uneducated members of the lower classes who had been hoodwinked into abandoning the revered traditions of their ancestors by reports of Jesus, a disreputable magician of dubious character. Celsus' knowledge of Christianity was based on firsthand knowledge of the Gospels and other Christian writings. Origen's detailed refutation, in which he quotes Celsus' work at length, ran to a full eight books. The following are excerpts drawn from Book I, including Origen's dismissal of the arguments of an imaginary character that Celsus had introduced, a Jewish intellectual who attacked the rational basis of Christianity.

1 Celsus' first main point in his desire to attack Christianity is that the Christians secretly make associations with one another contrary to the laws, because *societies which are public are allowed by the laws, but secret societies are illegal.*[1] And wishing to slander the so-called *love (agape) which Christians have for one another,* he says that *it exists because of the common danger and is more powerful than any oath.* As he talks much of *the common law* saying that *the associations of the Christians violate this,* I have to make this reply. Suppose that a person were living among the Scythians whose laws are contrary to the divine law, who had no opportunity to go elsewhere and was compelled to live among them; such a person for the sake of the true law, though illegal among the Scythians, would rightly form associations with like-minded people contrary to the laws of the Scythians. So, at the bar of truth, the laws of the nations such as those about images and the godless polytheism are laws of the Scythians or, if possible, more impious than theirs. Therefore it is not wrong to form associations against the laws for the sake of truth. For just as it would be right for people to form associations secretly to kill a tyrant who had seized control of their city, so too, since the devil, as Christians call him, and falsehood reign as tyrants, Christians form associations against the devil contrary to his laws, in order to save others whom they might be able to persuade to abandon the law which is like that of the Scythians and of a tyrant.

2 Next he says that *the doctrine* (obviously meaning Judaism with which Christianity is connected) *was originally barbarian.* Having an open mind he does not reproach the gospel for its barbarian origin, but praises *the barbarians* for being *capable of discovering doctrines;* but he adds to this that *the Greeks are better able to judge the value of what the barbarians have discovered, and to establish the doctrines and put them into practice by virtue.* Taking up the words he has used this is our reply in respect of the fundamental truths of Christianity. A person coming to the gospel from Greek conceptions and training would not only *judge* that it was true, but would also *put* it *into practice* and so prove it to be correct; and he would complete what seemed to be lacking judged by the criterion of a Greek proof, thus establishing the truth of Christianity. Moreover, we have to say this, that the gospel has a

---

[1]Italics in this document indicate statements that Origen has evidently drawn directly from Celsus' book, *The True Word.*

proof which is peculiar to itself, and which is more divine than a Greek proof based on dialectical argument. This more divine demonstration the apostle calls a "demonstration of the Spirit and of power"—of spirit because of the prophecies and especially those which refer to Christ, which are capable of convincing anyone who reads them; of power because of the prodigious miracles which may be proved to have happened by this argument among many others, that traces of them still remain among those who live according to the will of the Logos.

3 After this he says that *Christians perform their rites and teach their doctrines in secret*, and *they do this with good reason to escape the death penalty that hangs over them*. He compares the *danger* to *the risks encountered for the sake of philosophy as by Socrates*. He could also have added "as by Pythagoras and other philosophers." I reply to this that in Socrates' case the Athenians at once regretted what they had done, and cherished no grievance against him or against Pythagoras; at any rate, the Pythagoreans have for a long time established their schools in the part of Italy which has been called Magna Graecia. But in the case of the Christians the Roman Senate, the contemporary emperors, the army, the people, and the relatives of believers fought against the gospel and would have hindered it; and it would have been defeated by the combined force of so many unless it had overcome and risen above the opposition by divine power, so that it has conquered the whole world that was conspiring against it. . . .

9 After this he urges us to *follow reason and a rational guide in accepting doctrines* on the ground that *anyone who believes people without so doing is certain to be deceived*. And he compares those who believe without rational thought to the *begging priests of Cybele and soothsayers, and to worshippers of Mithras and Sabazius, and whatever else one might meet, apparitions of Hecate or of some daemon or daemons. For just as among them scoundrels frequently take advantage of the lack of education of gullible people and lead them wherever they wish, so also*, he

says, *this happens among the Christians.* He says that *some do not even want to give or to receive a reason for what they believe, and use such expressions as "Do not ask questions; just believe,"* and *"Your faith will save you."* And he affirms that they say: *"The wisdom in the world is an evil, and foolishness a good thing."* My answer to this is that if every one could abandon the business of life and devote his time to philosophy, no other course ought to be followed but this alone. For in Christianity, if I make no vulgar boasting, there will be found to be no less profound study of the writings that are believed; we explain the obscure utterances of the prophets, and the parables in the gospels, and innumerable other events or laws which have a symbolical meaning. However, if this is impossible, since, partly owing to the necessities of life and partly owing to human weakness, very few people are enthusiastic about rational thought, what better way of helping the multitude could be found other than that given to the nations by Jesus?

Moreover, concerning the multitude of believers who have renounced the great flood of evil in which they formerly used to wallow, we ask this question—is it better that those who believe without thought should somehow have been made reformed characters and be helped by the belief that they are punished for sin and rewarded for good works, or that we should not allow them to be converted with simple faith until they might devote themselves to the study of rational arguments? For obviously all but a very few would fail to obtain the help which they have derived from simple belief, but would remain living a very evil life. Therefore whatever other proof there may be that a doctrine so beneficial to mankind could not have come to human life apart from divine providence this consideration must also be enumerated with the rest. A religious person will not suppose that even a physician concerned with bodies, who restores many people to health, comes to live among cities and nations without divine providence, for no benefit comes to humankind without God's action. If a person who has healed the bodies of many or improved their condition does not cure people without divine providence, how much more must that be true of him who cured, converted, and improved the souls of many, and attached them to the supreme God, and taught them to refer every action to the standard of his pleasure, and to avoid anything that is displeasing to him, down to the most insignificant of words or deeds or even of casual thoughts? . . .

27 Anyone who examines the facts will see that Jesus ventured to do things beyond the power of human nature and that what he ventured to do he accomplished. From the beginning every one opposed the spread of his doctrine over the whole world, the emperors in each period, the chief generals under them, and all governors, so to speak, who had been entrusted with any power at all, and furthermore, the rulers in each city, the soldiers, and the people. Yet it conquered, since as the word of God it could not be prevented; and as it was stronger than all those adversaries it overcame all Greece and the most part of the barbarian countries, and converted innumerable souls to follow its worship of God. However, it was inevitable that in the great number of people overcome by the word, because there are many more *vulgar and illiterate* people than those who have been trained in rational thinking, the former class should far outnumber the more intelligent. But as Celsus did not want to recognize this fact, he thinks that the love to humankind shown by the word, which even extends to every soul from the rising of the sun, is *vulgar* and that *it is successful only among the uneducated because of its vulgarity and utter illiteracy.* Yet not even Celsus asserts that only vulgar people have been converted by the gospel to follow the religion of Jesus; for he admits that *among them there are some moderate, reasonable, and intelligent people who readily interpret allegorically.*

28 He also introduces an imaginary character, somehow imitating a child having his first lessons with an orator, and brings in a Jew who addresses childish remarks to Jesus and says nothing worthy of a philosopher's grey hairs. This too let us examine to the best of our ability and prove that he has failed to keep the character entirely consistent with that of a Jew in his remarks.

After this he represents the Jew as having a conversation with Jesus himself and refuting him on many charges, as he thinks: first, because *he fabricated the story of his birth from a virgin*; and he reproaches him because *he came from a Jewish village and from a poor country woman who earned her living by spinning.* He says that *she was driven out by her husband, who was a carpenter by trade, as she was convicted of adultery.* Then he says that *after she had been driven out by her husband and while she was wandering about in a disgraceful way she secretly gave birth to Jesus.* And he says that *because he was poor he hired himself out as a workman in Egypt, and there tried his hand at certain magical powers on which the Egyptians pride themselves; he returned full of conceit because of these powers, and on account of them gave himself the title of God.* In my judgment, however, (and I cannot allow anything said by unbelievers to pass unexamined, but study the fundamental principles), all these things are in harmony with the fact that Jesus was worthy of the proclamation that he is son of God.

29 Among people noble birth, honorable and distinguished parents, an upbringing at the hands of wealthy people who are able to spend money on the education of their child, and a great and famous native country, are things which help to make a person famous and distinguished and get his name well known. But when a man whose circumstances are entirely contrary to this is able to rise above the hindrances to him and to become well known, and to impress those who hear him so that he becomes eminent and famous throughout the whole world so that people alter their tone about him, should we not admire at once such a nature for being noble, for tackling great difficulties, and for possessing remarkable boldness?

If one were also to inquire further into the circumstances of such a man, how could one help trying to find out how a man, brought up in meanness and poverty, who had no general education and had learnt no arguments and doctrines by which he could have become a persuasive speaker to crowds and a popular leader and have won over many hearers, could devote himself to teaching new doctrines and introduce to mankind a doctrine which did away with the customs of the Jews while reverencing their prophets, and which abolished the laws of the Greeks particularly in respect of the worship of God? How could such a man, brought up in this way, who had received no serious instruction from humans (as even those who speak evil of him admit), say such noble utterances about the judgment of God, about the punishment for wickedness, and rewards for goodness, that not only rustic and illiterate people were converted by his words, but also a considerable number of the more intelligent, whose vision could penetrate the veil of apparently quite simple expressions, which conceals within itself, as one might say, a more mysterious interpretation?

The Seriphian in Plato reproached Themistocles after he had become famous for his generalship, saying that he had not won his fame by his own character, but from the good luck to have had the most famous city in all Greece as his home. From Themistocles, who was open-minded and saw that his home had also contributed to his fame, he received the answer: "I would never have been so famous if I had been a Seriphian, nor would you have been a Themistocles if you had had the good luck to be an Athenian." But our Jesus, who is reproached for having *come from a village*, and that not a Greek one, who did not belong to any nation prominent in public opinion, and who is maligned as the son of *a poor woman who earned her living by spinning* and as having left his home country *on account of poverty* and *hired himself out as a workman in Egypt,* was not just a Seriphian, to take the illustration I have quoted, who came from the least and most insignificant island, but was a Seriphian of the very lowest class, if I may say so. Yet he has been able to shake the whole human world, not only more than Themistocles the Athenian, but even more than Pythagoras and Plato and any other wise men or emperors or generals in any part of the world.

30 Who, therefore, that does not give merely a cursory study to the nature of the facts, would not be amazed at a man who overcame and

was able to rise above all the factors that tended to discredit him, and in his reputation to surpass all the distinguished men that have ever lived? It is uncommon for people who are eminent among others to have the ability to acquire fame for several things at once. One has been admired and become famous for wisdom, another for generalship, and some barbarians for miraculous powers in incantations, and some for one talent, some for another; they have not been admired and become eminent for several abilities at the same time. Yet Jesus, in addition to his other abilities, is admired for his wisdom, for his miracles, and for his leadership. For he persuaded some to join him in abandoning the laws, not like a tyrant, nor like a robber who incites his followers against others, nor like a rich person who provides support for those who come over to his side, nor like any who by common consent are regarded as blameworthy. He did this as a teacher of the doctrine about the God of the universe, of the worship offered to him and of every moral action which is able to bring the person whose life follows his teaching into relationship with the supreme God. To Themistocles or any of the other eminent men nothing happened to militate against their fame; but in the case of Jesus, besides the points I have mentioned which have sufficient influence to hide a man's character in ignominy even if he were a most noble person, his death by crucifixion which seems to be disgraceful was enough to take away even such reputation as he had already gained, and to make those who had been deluded (as people who do not agree with his teaching think) abandon their delusion and condemn the man who had deceived them.

31 In addition to this, if, as people who malign Jesus say, his disciples did not see him after he rose from the dead and were not convinced that there was something divine about him, one might wonder how it came about that they were not afraid to suffer the same fate as their master and met danger boldly, and that they left their homes to obey Jesus' will by teaching the doctrines which he gave to them. I think that a person who examines the facts with an open mind would say that these men would not have given themselves up to a precarious existence for the sake of Jesus' teaching unless they had some deep conviction which he implanted in them when he taught them that they should not only live according to his precepts but should also influence others—and should do so in spite of the fact that destruction, as far as human life is concerned, clearly awaited anyone who ventured to introduce new opinions in all places and to all people, and who would not keep up friendship with any one who continued to hold his former opinions and habits. Did the disciples of Jesus fail to see this? They dared not only to show to the Jews from the sayings of the prophets that he was the one to whom the prophets referred, but also showed to the other nations that he who was crucified quite recently accepted this death willingly for the human race, like those who have died for their country to check epidemics of plague, or famines, or stormy seas. For it is probable that in the nature of things there are certain mysterious causes which are hard for the multitude to understand, which are responsible for the fact that one righteous man dying voluntarily for the community may avert the activities of evil daemons by expiation, since it is they who bring about plagues, or famines, or stormy seas, or anything similar.

Let people therefore who do not want to believe that Jesus died on a cross for others, tell us whether they would not accept the many Greek and barbarian stories about some who have died for the community to destroy evils that had taken hold of cities and nations. Or do they think that, while these stories are historically true, yet there is nothing plausible about this man (as people suppose him to be) to suggest that he died to destroy a great daemon, in fact the ruler of daemons, who held in subjection all the souls of humans that have come to earth? As the disciples of Jesus saw this and much more besides, which they probably learnt from Jesus in secret, and as they were also filled with a certain power, since it was not just a virgin imagined by a poet who gave them "strength and courage" but the true understanding and wisdom of God, they sought eagerly that they might become "well-known among all people," not only among all the Argives, but even among all the Greeks and barbarians also, and that "they might carry away a good report."

32 Let us return, however, to the words put into the mouth of the Jew, where *the mother of Jesus* is described as having been *turned out by the carpenter who was betrothed to her, as she had been convicted of adultery and had a child by a certain soldier named Panthera.* Let us consider whether those who fabricated the myth that the virgin and Panthera committed adultery and that the carpenter turned her out, were not blind when they concocted all this to get rid of the miraculous conception by the Holy Spirit. For on account of its highly miraculous character they could have falsified the story in other ways without, as it were, unintentionally admitting that Jesus was not born of an ordinary marriage. It was inevitable that those who did not accept the miraculous birth of Jesus would have invented some lie. But the fact that they did not do this convincingly, but kept as part of the story that the virgin did not conceive Jesus by Joseph, makes the lie obvious to people who can see through fictitious stories and show them up. Is it reasonable that a man who ventured to do such great things for humankind in order that, so far as in him lay, all Greeks and barbarians in expectation of the divine judgment might turn from evil and act in every respect acceptably to the Creator of the universe, should have had, not a miraculous birth, but a birth more illegitimate and disgraceful than any? As addressing Greeks and Celsus in particular who, whether he holds Plato's doctrines or not, nevertheless quotes them, I would ask this question. Would he who sends souls down into human bodies compel a man to undergo a birth more shameful than any, and not even have brought him into human life by legitimate marriage, when he was to do such great deeds and to teach so many people and to convert many from the flood of evil? Or is it more reasonable (and I say this now following Pythagoras, Plato, and Empedocles, whom Celsus often mentions) that there are certain secret principles by which each soul that enters a body does so in accordance with its merits and former character? It is therefore probable that this soul, which lived a more useful life on earth than many others (to avoid appearing to beg the question by saying "all" others), needed a body which was not only distinguished among human bodies, but was also superior to all others.

33 Suppose it is true that a certain soul which in accordance with certain mysterious principles does not deserve to be in the body of a completely irrational being, yet is not worthy to be in that of a purely rational being, puts on a monstrous body so that reason cannot be fully developed in one born in this way, whose head is out of proportion to the rest of the body and is far too small; and suppose that another soul receives a body of such a kind that it is slightly more rational than the former instance, and another still more so, the nature of the body being more or less opposed to the apprehension of reason. Why then should there not be a certain soul that takes a body which is entirely miraculous, which has something in common with others in order to be able to live with them, but which also has something out of the ordinary, in order that the soul may remain uncontaminated by sin? Suppose that the views of the physiognomists are granted, of Zopyrus, Loxus, or Polemon, or anyone else who wrote about these matters and professed to possess some remarkable knowledge, that all bodies conform to the habits of their souls; then for the soul that was to live a miraculous life on earth and to do great things, a body was necessary, not, as Celsus thinks, produced by the adultery of Panthera and a virgin (for the offspring of such impure intercourse must rather have been some stupid man who would harm people by teaching licentiousness, unrighteousness, and other evils, and not a teacher of self-control, righteousness and the other virtues), but, as the prophets foretold, the offspring of a virgin who according to the promised sign should give birth to a child whose name was significant of his work, showing that at his birth God would be with people.

34 It appears to me that it would have been appropriate to the words he has put into the mouth of the Jew to have quoted the prophecy of Isaiah which says that Emmanuel shall be born of a virgin. Celsus, however, did not quote this, either because he did not know it, though he professes to know everything, or if he had read it, because he wilfully said nothing of it to avoid appearing unintentionally to support the doctrine which is opposed to his purpose. The passage reads as follows: "And the Lord spoke again to Ahaz saying, Ask a sign of the Lord your God, either in the depth or in the height. And Ahaz said, I will not ask, neither will I tempt the Lord. And he said, Hear now, oh house of David, is it a small thing to you to strive with people? How also do you strive with the Lord? Therefore shall the Lord give you a sign. Behold a virgin shall conceive in her womb and bring forth a son, and you shall call his name Emmanuel," which is interpreted "God with us." That it was out of wickedness that Celsus did not quote the prophecy is made clear to me from the fact that although he has quoted several things from the gospel according to Matthew, such as *the star that arose at the birth of Jesus* and other miracles, yet he has not even mentioned this at all. But if a Jew should ingeniously explain it away by saying that it is not written "Behold a virgin" but, instead of that, "behold a young woman," we should say to him that the Word Aalma, which the Septuagint translated by "parthenos" (virgin) and others by "neanis" (young woman), also occurs, so they say, in Deuteronomy applied to a virgin. The passage reads as follows: "If a girl that is a virgin is betrothed to a man, and a man finds her in a city and lie with her, you shall bring both out to the gate of the city and stone them with stones that they die, the young woman because she did not cry out in the city, and the man because he disgraced his neighbor's wife." And after that: "If a man finds a girl that is betrothed in the country and the man force her and lie with her, you shall kill only the man that lay with her, and you shall do nothing to the young woman; there is no sin worthy of death in the young woman."[3]

---

[2]Isa 7:10–14; cf. Matt 1:23.
[3]Deut 22:23–26.

35 However, lest we appear to depend on a Hebrew word to explain to people, who do not understand whether to accept it or not, that the prophet said that this man would be born of a virgin (concerning whose birth it was said "God with us"), let us explain the affirmation from the passage itself. The Lord, according to the scripture, said to Ahaz: "Ask a sign from the Lord your God, either in the depth or in the height." And then the sign that is given in this: "Behold a virgin shall conceive and bear a son." What sort of a sign would it be if a young woman not a virgin bore a son? And which would be more appropriate as the mother of Emmanuel, that is "God with us," a woman who had had intercourse with a man and conceived by female passion, or a woman who was still chaste and pure and a virgin? It is surely fitting that the latter should give birth to a child at whose birth it is said "God with us." If, however, he explains this away by saying that Ahaz was addressed in the words "ask a sign of the Lord your God," we will say: Who was born in Ahaz's time whose birth is referred to in the words "Emmanuel, which is God with us"? For if no one is to be found, obviously the words to Ahaz were addressed to the house of David, because according to the scripture our Saviour was "of the seed of David according to the flesh."[4] Furthermore, this sign is said to be "in the depth or in the height," since "this is he who descended and who ascended far above all heavens that he might fill all things."[5] I say these things as speaking to a Jew who believes the prophecy. But perhaps Celsus or any who agree with him will tell us with what kind of mental apprehension the prophet speaks about the future, whether in this instance or in the others recorded in the prophecies. Has he foreknowledge of the future or not? If he has, then the prophets possessed divine inspiration. If he has not, let Celsus account for the mind of a man who ventures to speak about the future and is admired for his prophecy among the Jews. . . .

37 I think that it has been fairly substantiated not only that our Saviour was to be born of a virgin, but also that there were prophets among the Jews who did not merely make general pronouncements about the future, such as those about Christ and about the kingdoms of the world, and the future destiny of Israel, and that the Gentiles would believe in the Saviour, and many other utterances about him. They also made particular predictions, as for instance of the way in which the lost asses of Kish were to be found, and of the illness which the son of the king of Israel suffered, or any other story of this sort.

To Greeks, however, who disbelieve in the virgin birth of Jesus I have to say that the Creator showed in the birth of various animals that what he did in the case of one animal, he could do, if he wished, also with others and even with people themselves. Among the animals there are certain females that have no intercourse with the male, as writers on animals say of vultures; this creature preserves the continuation of the species without any copulation. Why, therefore, is it incredible that if God wished to send some divine teacher to humankind he should have made the organism of him that was to be born come into being in a different way instead of using a generative principle derived from the sexual intercourse of men and women? Moreover, according to the Greeks themselves not all people were born from a man and a woman. For if the world was created as even many Greeks think, the first people must have had come into existence without sexual intercourse, but from the earth instead, generative principles having existed in the earth. But I think this more incredible than that Jesus should have been born half like other people. And in addressing Greeks it is not out of place to quote Greek stories, lest we should appear to be the only people to have related this incredible story. For some have thought fit (not in respect of any ancient stories and heroic tales but of people born quite recently) to record as though it were possible that when Plato was born of Amphictione Ariston was prevented from having sexual intercourse with her until she had brought forth the child which she had by Apollo. But these stories are really myths, which have led people to in-

[4]Rom 1:3.
[5]Eph 4:10.

vent such a tale about a man because they regarded him as having superior wisdom and power to the multitude, and as having received the original composition of his body from better and more divine seed, thinking that this was appropriate for people with superhuman powers. But when Celsus has introduced the Jew as disputing with Jesus and pouring ridicule on the pretence, as he thinks, of his birth from a virgin, and as quoting the Greek myths about *Danae* and *Melanippe* and *Auge* and *Antiope*, I have to reply that these words would be appropriate to a vulgar buffoon and not to a person who takes his professed task seriously.

38 Moreover, although he took the story of Jesus' departure to Egypt from the narrative in the gospel according to Matthew, he did not believe all the miracles connected with it, nor that an angel directed this, nor that Jesus' departure from Judaea and sojourn in Egypt had some hidden meaning. He made up another tale. For although he somehow accepts the incredible miracles which Jesus did, by which he persuaded the multitude to follow him as Christ, yet he wants to attack them as though they were done by magic and not by divine power. He says: *He was brought up in secret and hired himself out as a workman in Egypt, and after having tried his hand at certain magical powers he returned from there, and on account of those powers gave himself the title of God.* I do not know why a magician should have taken the trouble to teach a doctrine which persuades everyone to do every action as before God who judges each one for all his works, and to instill this conviction in his disciples whom he intended to use as the ministers of his teaching. Did they persuade their hearers because they had been taught to do miracles in this way, or did they not do any miracles? It is quite irrational to maintain that they did no miracles at all, but that, although they had believed without any adequate reasons comparable to the dialectical wisdom of the Greeks, they devoted themselves to teaching a new doctrine to any whom they might visit. What inspired them with confidence to teach the doctrine and to put forward new ideas? On the other hand, if they did perform miracles, is it plausible

to suggest that they were magicians, when they risked their lives in great dangers for a teaching which forbids magic?

39 I do not think it worthwhile to combat an argument which he does not put forward seriously, but only as mockery: *Then was the mother of Jesus beautiful? And because she was beautiful did God have sexual intercourse with her, although by nature He cannot love a corruptible body? It is not likely that God would have fallen in love with her since she was neither wealthy nor of royal birth; for nobody knew her, not even her neighbors.* It is just ridicule also when he says: *When she was hated by the carpenter and turned out, neither divine power nor the gift of persuasion saved her. Therefore,* he says, *these things have nothing to do with the kingdom of God.* What is the difference between this and vulgar abuse at street corners, and the talk of people who say nothing worth serious attention?

40 After this he takes the story from the gospel according to Matthew and perhaps also from the other gospels, about the descent of the dove upon the Saviour when he was baptized by John, and wants to attack the story as a fiction. But after he has pulled to pieces, as he thought, the story of our Saviour's birth from a virgin, he does not quote the next events in order. For passion and hatred have no orderly method, and people who are in a rage and have some personal hostility say whatever comes into their heads when they attack those whom they hate, since they are prevented by their passion from stating their accusations carefully and in order. If he had been careful about the order, he would have taken the gospel and, having set out to criticise it, would have brought his objections against the first story first, and then the second, and so on with the rest. But in fact after the birth from the virgin Celsus, who professed to know everything, goes on to criticize our story about the appearance of the Holy Spirit in the form of a dove at the Baptism; then after this he attacks the prophecy about our Saviour's advent, and after that runs back to what is recorded after the birth of Jesus, the story about the star and the magi who came from the east to worship the child. And if you were to look yourself, you would find many muddled statements of Celsus throughout his book; so by this those who know how to preserve and to look for order may prove that he was very arrogant and boastful when he entitled his book *The True Doctrine*, a title used by none of the distinguished philosophers. Plato says that a sensible person will not be confident about such obscure questions. And Chrysippus, who always gave an account of the reasons which influenced him, refers us to people whom we might find to give a better explanation than himself. Celsus, therefore, is wiser than both these men and the other Greeks; it was consistent with his assertion that he knows everything when he entitled his book *The True Doctrine*.

41 Lest we should appear to pass over his points intentionally for lack of an answer, we decided to refute each of his objections to the best of our ability, with a view not to the natural order and sequence of subjects but to the order of the objections written in his book. Let us, then, see what he says when attacking the story of the physical appearance, as it were, of the Holy Spirit seen by the Saviour in the form of a dove. His Jew continues by saying this to him whom we confess to be our Lord Jesus: *When*, he says, *you were bathing near John, you say that you saw what appeared to be a bird fly towards you out of the air.* His Jew then asks: *What trustworthy witness saw this apparition, or who heard a voice from heaven adopting you as son of God? There is no proof except for your word and the evidence which you may produce of one of the men who were punished with you.*

42 Before we begin the defence, we must say that an attempt to substantiate almost any story as historical fact, even if it is true, and to produce complete certainty about it, is one of the most difficult tasks and in some cases is impossible. Suppose, for example, that someone says the Trojan war never happened, in particular because it is bound up with the impossible story about a certain Achilles having had Thetis, a sea-goddess, as his mother, and Peleus, a man, as his

father, or that Sarpedon was son of Zeus, or Ascalaphus and Ialmenus of Ares, or Aeneas of Aphrodite. How could we substantiate this, especially as we are embarrassed by the fictitious stories which for some unknown reason are bound up with the opinion, which everyone believes, that there really was a war in Troy between the Greeks and the Trojans? Suppose also that someone does not believe the story about Oedipus and Jocasta, and Eteocles and Polyneices, the sons of them both, because the half-maiden Sphinx has been mixed up with it. How could we prove the historicity of a story like this? So also in the case of the Epigoni, even if there is nothing incredible involved in the story, or in that of the return of the Heraclidae, or innumerable other instances. Anyone who reads the stories with a fair mind, who wants to keep himself from being deceived by them, will decide what he will accept and what he will interpret allegorically, searching out the meaning of the authors who wrote such fictitious stories, and what he will disbelieve as having been written to gratify certain people. We have said this by way of introduction to the whole question of the narrative about Jesus in the gospels, not in order to invite people with intelligence to mere irrational faith, but with a desire to show that readers need an open mind and considerable study, and, if I may say so, need to enter into the mind of the writers to find out with what spiritual meaning each event was recorded. . . .

46 The law and the prophets are filled with accounts as miraculous as that recorded of Jesus at the baptism about the dove and the voice from heaven. But I think that the miracles performed by Jesus are evidence that the Holy Spirit was seen then in the form of a dove, although Celsus attacks them by saying that he learnt how to do them among the Egyptians. And I will not mention these only, but also, as is reasonable, those which were done by Jesus' apostles. For without miracles and wonders they would not have persuaded those who heard new doctrines and new teachings to leave their traditional religion and to accept the apostles' teachings at the risk of their lives. Traces of that Holy Spirit who appeared in the form of a dove are still preserved among Christians. They charm daemons away and perform many cures and perceive certain things about the future according to the will of the Logos. Even if Celsus, or the Jew that he introduced, ridicule what I am about to say, nevertheless it shall be said that many have come to Christianity as it were in spite of themselves, some spirit having turned their mind suddenly from hating the gospel to dying for it by means of a vision by day or by night. We have known many instances like this. But if we were to commit them to writing, although we were eyewitnesses at the time, we would bring upon ourselves downright mockery from the unbelievers, who would think that we were inventing the stories ourselves like those whom they suspect of having invented such tales. But as God is witness of our good conscience, we want to lend support to the divine teaching not by any false reports, but by definite facts of various kinds.

Since, however, it is a Jew who raises difficulties in the story of the Holy Spirit's descent in the form of a dove to Jesus, I would say to him: My good man, who is the speaker in Isaiah that says "And now the Lord sent me and his spirit"? In this text although it is doubtful whether it means that the Father and the Holy Spirit sent Jesus or that the Father sent Christ and the Holy Spirit, it is the second interpretation which is right. After the Saviour had been sent, then the Holy Spirit was sent, in order that the prophet's saying might be fulfilled; and, as it was necessary that the fulfillment of the prophecy should also be made known to posterity, for this reason the disciples of Jesus recorded what had happened.

47 I would like to have told Celsus, when he represented the Jew as in some way accepting John as a baptist in baptizing Jesus, that a man who lived not long after John and Jesus recorded that John was a baptist who baptized for the remission of sins. For Josephus in the eighteenth book of the Jewish antiquities bears witness that John was a baptist and promised purification to people who were baptized.[6] The same author, although he did not believe in Jesus as

Christ, sought for the cause of the fall of Jerusalem and the destruction of the temple. He ought to have said that the plot against Jesus was the reason why these catastrophes came upon the people, because they had killed the prophesied Christ; however, although unconscious of it, he is not far from the truth when he says that these disasters befell the Jews to avenge James the Just, who was a brother of "Jesus the so-called Christ," since they had killed him who was a very righteous man. This is the James whom Paul, the true disciple of Jesus, says that he saw, describing him as the Lord's brother, not referring so much to their blood-relationship or common upbringing as to his moral life and understanding. If therefore he says that the destruction of Jerusalem happened because of James, would it not be more reasonable to say that this happened on account of Jesus the Christ? His divinity is testified by great numbers of churches, which consist of people converted from the flood of sins and who are dependent on the Creator and refer every decision to his pleasure. . . .

68 After this, suspecting that the great works done by Jesus would be pointed out, of which, although there is much to say, we have only said a little, Celsus pretends to grant that the scriptures may be true when they speak of *cures or resurrection or a few loaves feeding many people, from which many fragments were left over, or any other monstrous tales,* as he thinks, *related by the disciples.* And he goes on to say: *Come, let us believe that these miracles really were done by you.* Then he at once puts them on a level with *the works of sorcerers who profess to do wonderful miracles, and the accomplishments of those who are taught by the Egyptians, who for a few obols make known their sacred lore in the middle of the market-place and drive daemons out of people and blow away diseases and invoke the souls of heroes, displaying expensive banquets and dining-tables and cakes and dishes which are nonexistent, and who make things move as though they were alive although they are not really so,*

---

[6]*Antiquities* 18.5.2.

but only appear as such in the imagination. And he says: *Since these men do these wonders, ought we to think them sons of God? Or ought we to say that they are the practices of wicked men possessed by an evil daemon?*

You see how by these words he gives his assent, as it were, to the reality of magic. I do not know whether he is the same as the man who wrote several books against magic. But because it happens to be to his advantage for his purpose he compares the stories about Jesus with tales of magic. They might have been comparable if Jesus had done his miracles, like magicians, merely to show his own powers. But in fact no sorcerer uses his tricks to call the spectators to moral reformation; nor does he educate by the fear of God people who were astounded by what they saw, nor does he attempt to persuade the onlookers to live as people who will be judged by God. Sorcerers do none of these things, since they have neither

the ability nor even the will to do so. Nor do they even want to have anything to do with reforming people, seeing that they themselves are filled with the most shameful and infamous sins. Is it not likely that one who used the miracles that he performed to call those who saw the happenings to moral reformation, would have shown himself as an example of the best life, not only to his genuine disciples but also to the rest? Jesus did this in order that his disciples might give themselves up to teaching people according to the will of God, and that the others, who have been taught as much by his doctrine as by his moral life and miracles the right way to live, might do every action by referring to the pleasure of the supreme God. If the life of Jesus was of this character, how could anyone reasonably compare him with the behavior of sorcerers and fail to believe that according to God's promise he was God who had appeared in a human body for the benefit of our race?

Chapter 5

Anti-Judaic Polemic

The Opposition to Jews in Early Christianity

Jesus and his followers were Jews who worshipped the Jewish God, followed the Jewish law, interpreted the Jewish Scriptures, and kept Jewish customs. And yet, within a century of Jesus' death, the Christian church had become widely and actively anti-Jewish. How did this happen?

Many scholars locate the roots of the problem, ultimately, in the failure of the Christian mission to the Jews (see Chapter 2). When Jews by and large rejected the Christian message about Jesus, Christians naturally sought to defend this message by appealing to the Jewish Bible itself. Their interpretations of Scripture, however, were not widely accepted outside of Christian circles; a rift resulted, each side arguing that the other was blind both to the obvious sense of the text and to the will of God who inspired it. Battle lines were drawn, and the resultant polemic and counterpolemic grew harsh. Eventually, there emerged two separate religions, one maintaining that Jesus was the messiah who brought salvation for all people, Jews and Gentiles, apart from the Jewish law, the other denying Jesus' messiahship and insisting that Jews alone were God's chosen people, whose special standing before God was shown precisely by the practice of Judaism, as set forth in the law.

This situation naturally presented the followers of Jesus with a range of sociopolitical and theological difficulties. On the sociopolitical level were the questions already mentioned in Chapter 4: how could Christians claim to represent an ancient religion (and thereby justify their existence in a world that respected antiquity but not innovation), when communities that originally embraced that religion were still thriving—especially when the Christians themselves did not observe the religion's best-known practices and customs (circumcision, kosher foods, sabbath)?

Theologically, the problems were no less acute: if the God of the Old Testament had called the people of Israel and given them his law, how could Christians who did not follow that law claim to be his people? And if there was only one God, how could they both—Jews and Christians—be his special people? Moreover, how were Jews who accepted Jesus as messiah to be treated in the church? Should they be required to give up their Jewishness? Ultimately the questions involved the relationship of the New to the

Old, of Christ to Moses, of salvation through Jesus' death and resurrection to the election of the children of Israel.

As with most aspects of early Christianity, an almost endless range of answers emerged. Some Christians who had converted from Judaism maintained that Christianity needed to remain true to its Jewish roots, that, contrary to the general opinion (which was indebted to the persuasive influence of the apostle Paul), anyone who believed in Jesus needed to become Jewish to be a full heir of the promises made to Israel. For these believers, the New fulfilled the Old, but the Old, as rightly interpreted by Jesus, was still true and valid. This was the view advanced by Paul's Christian opponents in Galatia, possibly the community behind the Gospel of Matthew, and by such second-century Jewish-Christian groups as the Ebionites.

Other Christians maintained that the New was foreshadowed by the Old and that when Jesus came in fulfillment of the Old, the earlier foreshadowings were no longer needed. In this view, the Old Testament was a useful pointer to Christ, but Christ alone embodied the reality that it foreshadowed, so the Old necessarily was to pass away. This was the view advanced by the author of the New Testament book of Hebrews and later, in a more extreme form, by the second-century Melito of Sardis.

Other Christians maintained that the Old had been given by God but that the Jews had never understood its true meaning because of the hardness of their hearts. In this view, the Jews had broken God's covenant as soon as it was made with them; as a result, they misunderstood their own law. Jews had always, therefore, propagated a false religion, for in fact the Old Testament was a Christian, not a Jewish book. This was the view advanced by the epistle of Barnabas.

Yet other Christians went so far as to say that Judaism and its Scriptures were and always had been completely false, because the God of Israel is not the true God, the God of Jesus. In this view, the God who created this world, chose Israel, and gave it his law is a secondary and inferior deity; Jesus came to save all people from this God of wrath and justice. Christians therefore are to reject all things Jewish, including the Old Testament. This was a view advanced by the followers of a prominent second-century Christian named Marcion.

From among these views, most of the anti-Judaic writings that happen to survive see Christianity as superior to but in basic continuity with Judaism. The authors of these works attack Jews for their rejection of the Christian message and maintain that the hardness of their hearts has blinded them to the workings of God. A good deal of emphasis is placed on the Jewish rejection of Jesus himself. During this period Jews came to be maligned as "Christ-killers." Moreover, as Christians became increasingly convinced that Christ was himself divine, the charges escalated: Jews came to be implicated in the murder of God.

As a result of the Jews' rejection of God, these Christian authors maintained, God has in turn rejected them. This opinion was thought to be borne out by the course of historical events—in particular, the destruction of Jerusalem by Roman armies in 70 C.E. and the brutal suppression of the second Jewish revolt in 135 C.E. To support these claims, Christians turned to the Hebrew prophets, who had predicted that God would make a "new covenant" since the Jews had broken the old (Jer 31:31–34) and who indicated that

God had declared that "those who were not my people I will call my people" (Rom 9:25–26; see Hos 1:10; 2:23). Some Christian authors maintained, in fact, that God gave his law to the Jews as a punishment for their rejection of him; in particular, he gave Jews the rite of circumcision to mark them off from all other peoples for persecution. Christians, circumcised spiritually in their hearts rather than physically on their foreskins, were the true heirs of the tradition.

This kind of harsh polemic did not have serious political implications at first, during the second and third centuries, when Christians were an insignificant and powerless minority in the empire. But when Christianity acquired political, economic, and military clout after the conversion of Constantine, Christian leaders took the rhetorical claims of their forebears seriously and implemented them socially, leading to the widespread acts of hatred and violence against Jews known to us from the horrific history of Christian anti-Semitism.

For Further Reading

Gager, John. *The Origins of Anti-Semitism: Attitudes Toward Judaism in Pagan and Christian Antiquity.* New York: Oxford University Press, 1983.

Isaac, Jules. *Jesus and Israel*, tr. Sally Gran. New York: Holt, Rinehart & Winston, 1971.

Ruether, Rosemary. *Faith and Fratricide: The Theological Roots of Anti-Semitism.* New York: Seabury, 1974.

Setzer, Claudia. *Jewish Responses to Early Christians: History and Polemics 30–150 C.E.* Minneapolis: Fortress, 1994.

Siker, Jeffrey. *Disinheriting the Jews: Abraham in Early Christian Controversy.* Louisville: Westminster/John Knox, 1991.

Simon, Marcel. *Versus Israel: A Study of the Relations between Christians and Jews in the Roman Empire (135–425)*, tr. H. McKeating. Oxford: Oxford University Press, 1986.

THE TEXTS

15. The Epistle of Barnabas

The Epistle of Barnabas was widely read in churches of the second and third centuries; some Christians thought that it should be included among the books of the New Testament. Although it came to be attributed to Barnabas, the companion of the apostle Paul, the book itself is anonymous. Most scholars think it was written around 130 C.E. possibly in Alexandria, Egypt, where it was especially popular.

The purpose of the book is to show that Christianity is superior to Judaism, that Judaism, in fact, is and always has been a false religion. In this author's opinion, Jews have misunderstood the law given to them by God: because they hardened their hearts and broke God's covenant, they mistakenly assumed that he meant his law to be taken literally. Instead, according to this author, it was all along intended symbolically as a pointer to Christ. Using an allegorical method of interpretation popular among other Alexandrian thinkers—Jew, pagan, and Christian alike—the author thus interprets key passages of the Old Testament as mysterious witnesses to Christ, whose meaning completely escaped the Jews to whom it was originally given. For this author, the Old Testament is a Christian, not a Jewish, book, and it is Christians, not Jews, who are the people of God.

1 Greetings, sons and daughters, in the name of the Lord who has loved us, in peace. . . .

2 Inasmuch as the days are evil and the Worker himself is in power, we ought to be on our guard and seek out the righteous requirements of the Lord.

2 Our faith's helpers, then, are fear and patience, and our allies are endurance and self-control.

3 When these things persist in purity in matters relating to the Lord, wisdom, understanding, insight, and knowledge rejoice with them.

4 For he has made it clear to us through all the prophets that he needs neither sacrifices nor whole burnt offerings nor general offerings, saying on one occasion:

5 " 'What is the multitude of your sacrifices to me?' says the Lord. 'I am full of whole burnt offerings, and I do not want the fat of lambs and blood of bulls and goats, not even if you come to appear before me. For who demanded these things from your hands? Do not continue to trample my court. If you bring fine flour, it is in vain; incense is detestable to me; your new moons and sabbaths I cannot stand.' "[1]

6 Therefore he has abolished these things, in order that the new law of our Lord Jesus Christ, which is free from the yoke of compulsion, might have its offering, one not made by humans.

---

[1]Isa 1:11–13.

The "Epistle of Barnabas," from *The Apostle Fathers*, ed. J. B. Lightfoot and J. R. Harmer; 2d ed. by Michael W. Holmes. Grand Rapids, Mich.: Baker Book House, 1992.

7 And again he says to them: "I did not command your fathers, when they were coming out of the land of Egypt, to bring whole burnt offerings and sacrifices, did I?[2]

8 "On the contrary, this is what I commanded them: 'Let none of you bear a grudge in his heart against his neighbor, and do not love a false oath.' "[3]

9 We ought to perceive, therefore (since we are not without understanding), the gracious intention of our Father, because he is speaking to us; he wants us to seek how we may approach him, rather than go astray like they did.

10 To us, therefore, he says this: "A sacrifice to God is a broken heart; an aroma pleasing to the Lord is a heart that glorifies its Maker." So, brothers, we ought to give very careful attention to our salvation, lest the evil one should cause some error to slip into our midst and thereby hurl us away from our life.

3 Therefore he speaks again to them concerning these things: " 'Why do you fast for me,' says the Lord, 'so that today your voice is heard crying out loudly? This is not the fast I have chosen,' says the Lord, 'not a man humiliating his soul.

2 " 'Not even if you bend your neck into a circle, and put on sackcloth and lie in ashes, not even then will you call a fast that is acceptable.' "[4]

3 But to us he says: " 'Behold, this is the fast I have chosen,' says the Lord: 'Break every unjust bond, untie the knots of forced agreements, set free those who are oppressed, and tear up every unjust contract. Share your bread with the hungry, and if you see someone naked, clothe him; bring the homeless into your house, and if you see someone of lowly status, do not despise him, nor shall the members of your house or family do so.

4 " 'Then your light will break forth early in the morning, and your healing will rise quickly, and righteousness will go before you, and the glory of God will surround you.

5 " 'Then you will cry out, and God will hear you; while you are still speaking he will say, "Here I am"—if you rid yourself of oppression and scornful gestures and words of complaint, and give your bread to the hungry from the heart, and have mercy on a downtrodden soul.' "[5]

6 So for this reason, brothers, he who is very patient, when he foresaw how the people whom he had prepared in his Beloved would believe in all purity, revealed everything to us in advance, in order that we might not shipwreck ourselves by becoming, as it were, "proselytes" to their law.

4 We must, therefore, investigate the present circumstances very carefully and seek out the things that are able to save us. Let us, therefore, avoid absolutely all the works of lawlessness lest the works of lawlessness overpower us, and let us hate the deception of the present age, so that we may be loved in the age to come.

2 Let us give no rest to our soul that results in its being able to associate with sinners and evil persons, lest we become like them.

3 The last stumbling block is at hand, concerning which the Scriptures speak, as Enoch says. For the Master has cut short the times and the days for this reason, that his beloved might make haste and come into his inheritance.

4 And so also speaks the prophet: "Ten kingdoms will reign over the earth, and after them a little king will arise, who will subdue three of the kings with a single blow."[6]

5 Similarly Daniel says, concerning the same one: "And I saw the fourth beast, wicked and powerful and more dangerous than all the beasts of the earth, and how ten horns sprang up from it, and from these a little offshoot of a horn, and how it subdued three of the large horns with a single blow."[7]

6 You ought, therefore, to understand. Moreover, I also ask you this, as one of you and who in a special way loves all of you more than my own soul: be on your guard now, and do not be like certain people; that is, do not continue to pile

---

[2]Jer 7:22–23.
[3]Zech 8:17.
[4]Isa 58:4–5.
[5]Isa 58:6–10.
[6]Dan 7:24.
[7]Dan 7:7–8.

up your sins while claiming that your covenant is irrevocably yours, because in fact those people lost it completely in the following way, when Moses had just received it.

7 For the Scripture says: "And Moses was on the mountain fasting for forty days and forty nights, and he received the covenant from the Lord, stone tablets inscribed by the fingers of the hand of the Lord."[8]

8 But by turning to idols they lost it. For thus says the Lord: "Moses, Moses, go down quickly, because your people, whom you led out of Egypt, have broken the Law."[9] And Moses understood and hurled the two tablets from his hands, and their covenant was broken in pieces, in order that the covenant of the beloved Jesus might be sealed in our heart, in hope inspired by faith in him.

9 (Though I would like to write a great deal more, not as a teacher but as befits one who does not like to leave out anything we possess, nevertheless I hasten to move along—your devoted servant.)

Consequently, let us be on guard in the last days, for the whole time of our faith will do us no good unless now, in the age of lawlessness, we resist as well the coming stumbling blocks, as befits God's children, lest the black one find an opportunity to sneak in.

10 Let us flee from every kind of vanity; let us hate completely the works of the evil way. Do not withdraw within yourselves and live alone, as though you were already justified, but gather together and seek out together the common good.

11 For the Scripture says: "Woe to those who are wise in their own opinion, and clever in their own eyes."[10] Let us become spiritual; let us become a perfect temple for God. To the best of our ability, let us cultivate the fear of God and strive to keep his commandments, that we may rejoice in his ordinances.

12 The Lord will judge the world without partiality. Each person will receive according to what he has done: if he is good, his righteousness will precede him; if he is evil, the wages of doing evil will go before him.

13 Let us never fall asleep in our sins, as if being "called" was an excuse to rest, lest the evil

ruler gain power over us and thrust us out of the kingdom of the Lord.

14 Moreover, consider this as well, my brothers: when you see that after such extraordinary signs and wonders were done in Israel, even then they were abandoned, let us be on guard lest we should be found to be, as it is written, "many called, but few chosen."[11]

5 For it was for this reason that the Lord endured the deliverance of his flesh to corruption, that we might be cleansed by the forgiveness of sins, that is, by his sprinkled blood.

2 For the Scripture concerning him relates partly to Israel and partly to us, and speaks as follows: "He was wounded because of our transgressions, and has been afflicted because of our sins; by his wounds we were healed. Like a sheep he was led to slaughter, and like a lamb he was silent before his shearer."[12]

3 We ought, therefore, to be exceedingly thankful to the Lord, because he has both made known to us the past and given us wisdom in the present circumstance, and with regard to future events we are not without understanding.

4 Now the Scripture says, "Not unjustly are nets spread out for the birds."[13] This means that a person deserves to perish if, having knowledge of the way of righteousness, he ensnares himself in the way of darkness.

5 And furthermore, my brothers: if the Lord submitted to suffer for our souls, even though he is Lord of the whole world, to whom God said at the foundation of the world, "Let us make man according to our image and likeness,"[14] how is it, then, that he submitted to suffer at the hand of others? Learn!

6 The prophets, receiving grace from him, prophesied about him. But he himself submitted, in order that he might destroy death and demon-

---

[8]Exod 34:28; 31:18.
[9]Exod 32:7; Deut 9:12.
[10]Isa 5:21.
[11]Matt 22:14.
[12]Isa 53:5,7.
[13]Prov 1:17.
[14]Gen 1:26.

strate the reality of the resurrection of the dead, because it was necessary that he be manifested in the flesh.

7 Also, he submitted in order that he might redeem the promise to the fathers and—while preparing the new people for himself—prove, while he was still on earth, that after he has brought about the resurrection he will execute judgment.

8 Furthermore, by teaching Israel and performing extraordinary wonders and signs, he preached and loved them intensely.

9 And when he chose his own apostles who were destined to preach his gospel (who were sinful beyond all measure in order that he might demonstrate that he did not come to call the righteous, but sinners), then he revealed himself to be God's Son.

10 For if he had not come in the flesh, people could in no way have been saved by looking at him. For when they look at merely the sun they are not able to gaze at its rays, even though it is the work of his hands and will eventually cease to exist.

11 Therefore the Son of God came in the flesh for this reason, that he might complete the full measure of the sins of those who persecuted his prophets to death.

12 It was for this reason, therefore, that he submitted. For God says that the wounds of his flesh came from them: "When they strike down their own shepherd, then the sheep of the flock will perish."[15]

13 But he himself desired to suffer in this manner, for it was necessary for him to suffer on a tree. For the one who prophesies says concerning him: "Spare my soul from the sword,"[16] and "Pierce my flesh with nails, for bands of evil men have risen up against me."[17]

14 And again he says: "Behold, I have given my back to scourges, and my cheeks to blows, and I set my face like a solid rock."[18] . . .

7 Understand, therefore, children of joy, that the good Lord revealed everything to us beforehand, in order that we might know to whom we ought to give thanks and praise for all things.

2 If, therefore, the Son of God, who is Lord and is destined to judge the living and the dead,

suffered in order that his wounds might give us life, let us believe that the Son of God could not suffer except for our sake.

3 But he also was given vinegar and gall to drink when he was crucified. Hear how the priests of the temple have revealed something about this: when the command that "Whoever does not keep the fast shall surely die"[19] was written, the Lord commanded it because he himself was planning to offer the vessel of his spirit as a sacrifice for our sins, in order that the type established by Isaac, who was offered upon the altar, might be fulfilled.

4 What, therefore, does he say in the prophet? "And let them eat from the goat that is offered at the fast for all their sins"—pay careful attention!— "and let all the priests (but only them) eat the unwashed entrails with vinegar."

5 Why? "Since you are going to give me, when I am about to offer my flesh for the sins of my new people, gall with vinegar to drink, you alone must eat, while the people fast and lament in sackcloth and ashes"—this was to show that he must suffer at their hands.

6 Pay attention to what he commanded: "Take two goats, fine and well-matched, and offer them, and let the priest take one for a whole burnt offering for sins."[20]

7 But what shall they do with the other one? "The other one," he says, "is cursed."[21] Notice how the type of Jesus is revealed!

8 "And all of you shall spit upon it and jab it, and tie scarlet wool around its head, and then let it be driven out into the wilderness." And when these things have been done, the man in charge of the goat leads it into the wilderness, and he removes the wool and places it upon the bush commonly called rachia (the buds of which we are accustomed to eat when we find them in the countryside; only the fruit of the rachia is sweet.)

---

[15]Zech 13:7; Matt 26:31.
[16]Ps 22:20.
[17]Ps 22:16.
[18]Isa 50:6–7.
[19]Lev 23:29.
[20]Lev 16:7, 9.
[21]Lev 16:8.

9 What is the meaning of this? Note well: "the one is for the altar, and the other is cursed," and note that the one cursed is crowned. For they will see him on that day, wearing a long scarlet robe about his body, and they will say, "Is this not the one whom we once crucified and insulted by spitting upon him? Surely this was the man who said then that he was the Son of God!"

10 Now how is he like that goat? The goats are similar, fine and well-matched, for this reason: in order that when they see him coming then, they may be amazed at the similarity of the goat. Observe, therefore, the type of Jesus, who was destined to suffer.

11 And what does it mean when they place the wool in the midst of the thorns? It is a type of Jesus, set forth for the church, because whoever desires to take away the scarlet wool must suffer greatly because the thorns are so terrible, and can only gain possession of it through affliction. Likewise, he says, those who desire to see me and to gain my kingdom must receive me through affliction and suffering.

8 Now what type do you think was intended, when he commanded Israel that the men whose sins are complete should offer a heifer, and slaughter and burn it, and then the children should take the ashes and place them in containers, and tie the scarlet wool around a tree (observe again the type of the cross and the scarlet wool), and the hyssop, and then the children should sprinkle the people one by one, in order that they may be purified from their sins?

2 Grasp how plainly he is speaking to you: the calf is Jesus; the sinful men who offer it are those who brought him to the slaughter. Then the men are no more; no more is the glory of sinners.

3 The children who sprinkle are those who preached to us the good news about the forgiveness of sins and the purification of the heart, those to whom he gave the authority to proclaim the gospel; there were twelve of them as a witness to the tribes, because there are twelve tribes of Israel.

4 And why are there three children who sprinkle? As a witness to Abraham, Isaac, and Ja-

cob, because these men were great in God's sight.

5 And then there is the matter of the wool on the tree: this signifies that the kingdom of Jesus is on the tree, and that those who hope in him will live forever.

6 But why the wool and the hyssop together? Because in his kingdom there will be dark and evil days, in which we will be saved, because the one who suffers in body is healed by means of the dark juice of the hyssop.

7 So, that these things happened for this reason is obvious to us, but to them they were quite obscure, because they did not listen to the voice of the Lord.

9 Furthermore, with respect to the ears he describes how he circumcised our heart. The Lord says in the prophet: "As soon as they heard, they obeyed me."[22] And again he says: "Those who are far off will hear with their ears, and they shall understand what I have done."[23] Also, "Circumcise your hearts," says the Lord.[24] And again, he says: "Hear, Israel, for this is what the Lord your God says."[25] And again the Spirit of the Lord prophesies: "Who is the one who desires to live forever? With the ear let him hear the voice of my servant."[26]

3 And again he says: "Hear, heaven, and give ear, earth, for the Lord has spoken these things as a testimony."[27] And again he says: "Hear the word of the Lord, you rulers of this people."[28] And again he says: "Hear, children, the voice of one crying in the wilderness."[29]

4 In short, he circumcised our ears in order that when we hear the word we might believe.

But the circumcision in which they have trusted has been abolished, for he declared that circumcision was not a matter of the flesh. But they disobeyed, because an evil angel "enlightened" them.

---

[22]Ps 18:44.
[23]Isa 33:13.
[24]Jer 4:4.
[25]Jer 7:2–3.
[26]Ps 34:12.
[27]Isa 1:2.
[28]Isa 1:10; 28:14.
[29]Isa 40:3.

5 He says to them: "This is what the Lord your God says [here I find a commandment]: 'Do not sow among thorns, be circumcised to your Lord.'"[30] And what does he say? "Circumcise your hardheartedness, and stop being stiff-necked."[31] Take this again:[78] "Behold, says the Lord, all the nations have uncircumcised foreskins, but this people has an uncircumcised heart!"[32]

6 But you will say: "But surely the people were circumcised as a seal!" But every Syrian and Arab and all the idol-worshiping priests are also circumcised; does this mean that they, too, belong to their covenant? Why, even the Egyptians practice circumcision!

7 Learn abundantly, therefore, children of love, about everything: Abraham, who first instituted circumcision, looked forward in the spirit to Jesus when he circumcised, having received the teaching of the three letters.

8 For it says: "And Abraham circumcised ten and eight and three hundred men of his household."[33] What, then, is the knowledge that was given to him? Observe that it mentions the "ten and eight" first, and then after an interval the "three hundred." As for the "ten and eight," The I is ten and the H is eight;[34] thus you have "Jesus."[35] And because the cross, which is shaped like the T, was destined to convey grace, it mentions also the "three hundred." So he reveals Jesus in the two letters, and the cross in the other one.

9 He who placed within us the implanted gift of his covenant understands. No one has ever learned from me a more reliable word, but I know that you are worthy of it.

10 Now when Moses said, "You shall not eat swine, or eagle or hawk or crow, or any fish that does not have scales,"[36] he received, according to the correct understanding, three precepts.

2 Furthermore, he says to them in Deuteronomy, "I will set forth as a covenant to this people my commandments." Therefore it is not God's commandment that they should not eat; rather Moses spoke spiritually.

3 Accordingly he mentioned the swine for this reason: you must not associate, he means, with such people, people who are like swine. That is, when they are well off, they forget the Lord, but when they are in need, they acknowledge the Lord, just as the swine ignores its owner when it is feeding, but when it is hungry it starts to squeal and falls silent only after being fed again.

4 "Neither shall you eat the eagle nor the hawk nor the kite nor the crow."[38] You must not, he means, associate with or even resemble such people, people who do not know how to provide food for themselves by labor and sweat but lawlessly plunder other people's property; indeed, though they walk about with the appearance of innocence, they are carefully watching and looking around for someone to rob in their greed, just as these birds alone do not provide food for themselves but sit idle and look for ways to eat the flesh of others—they are nothing more than pests in their wickedness.

5 "And you shall not eat," he says, "sea eel or octopus or cuttlefish."[39] You must not, he means, even resemble such people, people who are utterly wicked and are already condemned to death, just as these fish alone are cursed and swim in the depths, not swimming about like the rest but living in the mud beneath the depths.

6 Furthermore, "You shall not eat the hare."[40] Why? Do not become, he means, one who corrupts boys, or even resemble such people, because the hare grows another opening every year, and thus has as many orifices as it is years old.

---

[30]Jer 4:3–4.
[31]Deut 10:16.
[32]Jer 9:26.
[33]Gen 14:14; 17:23.
[34]In Greek (the author of *Barnabas* was obviously working with the LXX) the letters of the alphabet can have numerical value (A = 1, B = 2, Γ = 3, etc.); here H = 8, I = 10, and T = 300.
[35]I.e., IH are the first two letters (and a not uncommon abbreviation) of the Greek form of "Jesus" (IHΣΟΥΣ), and are understood by the author to represent the whole name.
[36]Lev 11:7–15; Deut 14:8–14.
[37]Deut 4:1, 10, 13.
[38]Lev 11:13–16.
[39]Lev 11:10.
[40]Lev 11:6.

7 Again, "Neither shall you eat the hyena." Do not become, he means, an adulterer or a seducer, or even resemble such people. Why? Because this animal changes its nature from year to year, and becomes male one time and female another.

8 But he also hated the weasel, and with good reason. Do not become, he means, like those people who, we hear, with immoral intent do things with the mouth that are forbidden, nor associate with those immoral women who do things with the mouth that are forbidden. For this animal conceives through its mouth.

9 Concerning food, then, Moses received three precepts to this effect and spoke in a spiritual sense, but because of their fleshly desires the people accepted them as though they referred to actual food.

10 David also received knowledge of the same three precepts, and says: "Blessed is the one who has not followed the counsel of ungodly people"—just as the fish move about in darkness in the depths; "and has not taken the path of sinners"—just as those who pretend to fear the Lord sin like swine; "and has not sat in the seat of pestilent ones"[41]—just as the birds that sit waiting for plunder. You now have the full story concerning food.

11 Again Moses says: "Eat anything that has a divided hoof and chews the cud."[42] Why does he say this? Because when it receives food it knows the one who is feeding it and, relying upon him, appears to rejoice. He spoke well with regard to the commandment. What, then, does he mean? Associate with those who fear the Lord, with those who meditate in their heart on the special significance of the word which they have received with those who proclaim and obey the Lord's commandments, with those who know that meditation is a labor of joy and who ruminate on the word of the Lord. But why does he mention "the divided hoof"? Because the righteous person not only lives in this world but also looks forward to the holy age to come. Observe what a wise lawgiver Moses was!

12 But how could those people grasp or understand these things? But we, however, having rightly understood the commandments, explain them as the Lord intended. He circumcised our ears and hearts for this very purpose, that we might understand these things. . . .

14 Now let us see if [God] has actually given the covenant which he swore to the fathers he would give to the people. He has indeed given it; but they were not worthy to receive it because of their sins.

2 For the prophet says: "And Moses was fasting on Mount Sinai forty days and forty nights, in order to receive the Lord's covenant with the people. And Moses received from the Lord the two tablets which were inscribed by the finger of the hand of the Lord in the spirit."[43] And when Moses received them he began to carry them down to give to the people.

3 And the Lord said to Moses: "Moses, Moses, go down quickly, because your people, whom you led out of the land of Egypt, has broken the Law." And Moses realized that once again they had made cast images for themselves, and he flung the tablets from his hands, and the tablets of the Lord's covenant were shattered.[44]

4 So, Moses received it, but they were not worthy.

But how did we receive it? Learn! Moses received it as a servant, but the Lord himself gave it to us, that we might become the people of inheritance, by suffering for us.

5 And he was made manifest in order that they might fill up the measure of their sins and we might receive the covenant through the Lord Jesus who inherited it, who was prepared for this purpose, in order that by appearing in person and redeeming from darkness our hearts, which had already been paid over to death and given over to the lawlessness of error, he might establish a covenant in us by his word.

6 For it is written how the Father commands him to redeem us from darkness and to prepare a holy people for himself.

7 Therefore the prophet says: "I, the Lord your God, have called you in righteousness, and I

---

[41]Ps 1:1.
[42]Lev 11:3; Deut 14:6.
[43]Exod 24:18; 31:18.
[44]Exod 32:7–8, 19.

will grasp your hand and strengthen you; and I have given you as a covenant to the people, a light to the nations, to open the eyes of the blind, and to release from their shackles those who are bound and from the prisonhouse those who sit in darkness."[45] We understand, therefore, from what we have been redeemed.

8 Again the prophet says: "Behold, I have established you as a light to the nations, that you may be the means of salvation to the ends of the earth; thus says the Lord God who redeemed you."[46]

9 Again the prophet says: "The Spirit of the Lord is upon me, because he has anointed me to preach good news about grace to the humble, he has sent me to heal the broken-hearted, to proclaim freedom for the prisoners and recovery of sight for the blind, to announce the Lord's year of favor and day of recompense, to comfort all who mourn."[47]

15 Furthermore, concerning the Sabbath it is also written, in the "Ten Words" which he spoke to Moses face to face on Mount Sinai: "And sanctify the Lord's Sabbath, with clean hands and clean heart."[48]

2 And in another place he says: "If my sons guard the Sabbath, then I will bestow my mercy upon them."[49]

3 He speaks of the Sabbath at the beginning of the creation: "And God made the works of his hands in six days, and finished on the seventh day, and rested on it, and sanctified it."[50]

4 Observe, children, what "he finished in six days" means. It means this: that in six thousand years the Lord will bring everything to an end, for with him a day signifies a thousand years. And he himself bears me witness when he says "Behold, the day of the Lord will be as a thousand years."[51] Therefore, children, in six days—that is, in six thousand years—everything will be brought to an end.

5 "And he rested on the seventh day." This means: when his Son comes, he will destroy the time of the lawless one and will judge the ungodly and will change the sun and the moon and the stars, and then he will truly rest on the seventh day.

6 Furthermore, he says: "You shall sanctify it with clean hands and a clean heart." If, therefore, anyone now is able, by being clean of heart, to sanctify the day which God sanctified, we have been deceived in every respect.

7 But if that is not the case, accordingly then we will truly rest and sanctify it only when we ourselves will be able to do so, after being justified and receiving the promise; when lawlessness no longer exists, and all things have been made new by the Lord, then we will be able to sanctify it, because we ourselves will have been sanctified first.

8 Finally, he says to them: "I cannot bear your new moons and sabbaths."[52] You see what he means: it is not the present sabbaths that are acceptable to me, but the one that I have made; on that Sabbath, after I have set everything at rest, I will create the beginning of an eighth day, which is the beginning of another world.

9 This is why we spend the eighth day in celebration, the day on which Jesus both arose from the dead and, after appearing again, ascended into heaven.

16 Finally, I will also speak to you about the temple, and how those wretched people went astray and set their hope on the building, as though it were God's house, and not on their God who created them.

2 For they, almost like the heathen, consecrated him by means of the temple. But what does the Lord say in abolishing it? Learn! "Who measured heaven with the span of his hand, or the earth with his palm? Was it not I, says the Lord? Heaven is my throne, and the earth is a footstool for my feet. What kind of house will you build for me, or what place for me to rest?"[53] You now know that their hope was in vain.

3 Furthermore, again he says: "Behold, those who tore down this temple will build it themselves."[54]

---

[45]Isa 42:6–7.

[46]Isa 49:6–7.

[47]Isa 61:1–2.

[48]Exod 20:8; Deut 5:12.

[49]Jer 17:24–25?

[50]Gen 2:2.

[51]Ps 90:4.

[52]Isa 1:13.

[53]Isa 40:12; 66:1.

[54]Isa 49:17.

4 This is happening now. For because they went to war, it was torn down by their enemies, and now the very servants of their enemies will rebuild it.

5 Again, it was revealed that the city and the temple and the people of Israel were destined to be handed over. For the Scripture says: "And it will happen in the last days that the Lord will hand over the sheep of the pasture and the sheep-fold and their watchtower to destruction."[55] And it happened just as the Lord said.

6 But let us inquire whether there is in fact a temple of God. There is—where he himself says he is building and completing it! For it is written: "And it will come to pass that when the week comes to an end God's temple will be built gloriously in the name of the Lord."[56]

7 I discover, therefore, that there is in fact a temple. How, then, will it be built in the name of the Lord? Learn! Before we believed in God, our heart's dwelling-place was corrupt and weak, truly a temple built by human hands, because it was full of idolatry and was the home of demons, for we did whatever was contrary to God.

8 "But it will be built in the name of the Lord." So pay attention, in order that the Lord's temple may be built gloriously. How? Learn! By receiving the forgiveness of sins and setting our hope on the Name, we became new, created again

from the beginning. Consequently God truly dwells in our dwelling-place—that is, in us.

9 How? The word of his faith, the call of his promise, the wisdom of his righteous decrees, the commandments of his teaching, he himself prophesying in us, he himself dwelling in us; opening to us who had been in bondage to death the door of the temple, which is the mouth, and granting to us repentance, he leads us into the incorruptible temple.

10 For the one who longs to be saved looks not to the person but to the One who dwells and speaks in him, and is amazed by the fact that he had never before heard such words from the mouth of the speaker nor for his part ever desired to hear them. This is the spiritual temple that is being built for the Lord.

17 To the extent that it is possible clearly to explain these things to you, I hope, in accordance with my desire, that I have not omitted anything of the matters relating to salvation.

2 For if I should write to you about things present or things to come, you would never understand, because they are found in parables. So much, then, for these things.

---

[55]1 Enoch 89:56.
[56]Dan 9:24–27; 1 Enoch 91:13, Tobit 14:15; 2 Sam 7:13(?)

16. Justin: Dialogue with Trypho

We have already encountered Justin's "Dialogue with Trypho" in Chapter Two (see the introduction here). The excepts given here begin with the opening discussion between Justin and his Jewish interlocutor.

In his attempt to convince Trypho of the superiority of his Christian philosophy, Justin appeals to the Old Testament to show that God has planned from the very begin-

---

Justin: "Dialogue with Trypho," from *Saint Justin Martyr*, ed. Thomas Falls. Fathers of the Church, 6. Washington, D.C.: Catholic University Press of America, 1977. Used with permission.

ning for Judaism to be superseded by Christianity. In his view, God gave the Jewish people his laws (e.g., of circumcision and sabbath observance) not because Jews were special in his eyes but because he wanted to punish them. For Justin, therefore, because Jews have always violated God's will and continue to do so (as is evident in their violent and slanderous opposition to the Christians), they are not God's chosen people; instead, it is the followers of Christ who are the true heirs of the promises made to the Jewish ancestors. Thus, the Jewish Scriptures actually belong to Christians, not Jews, and, when properly understood, Justin repeatedly argues, they point directly to Christ.

It is difficult to know whether this discussion really took place and, if so, how Trypho reacted to Justin's opinions. As with all such dialogues (e.g., those of Plato), we hear only the arguments of the author and the responses he himself placed in the mouth of his opponent. Still, it is hard to imagine a Jew finding Justin's arguments convincing—which makes it all the more interesting that, at the end, Trypho is not said to convert.

Chapter 10

When they had finished their conversation, I once again addressed them in this fashion: "My friends, is there any other accusation you have against us than this, that we do not observe the Law, nor circumcise the flesh as your forefathers, nor keep the sabbaths as you do? Or do you also condemn our customs and morals? This is what I say, lest you, too, believe that we eat human flesh and that after our banquets we extinguish the lights and indulge in unbridled sensuality. Or do you only condemn us for believing in such doctrines and holding opinions which you consider false?"

"This last charge is what surprises us," replied Trypho. "Those other charges which the rabble lodge against you are not worthy of belief, for they are too repulsive to human nature. But the precepts in what you call your Gospel are so marvelous and great that I don't think that anyone could possibly keep them. For I took the trouble to read them. But this is what surprises us most, that you who claim to be pious and believe yourselves to be different from the others do not segregate yourselves from them, nor do you observe a manner of life different from that of the Gentiles, for you do no keep the feasts or sabbaths, nor do you practice the rite of circumcision. You place your hope in a crucified man, and still expect to receive favors from God when you disregard his commandments. Have you not read that

the male who is not circumcised on the eighth day shall be cut off from his people?[1] This precept was for stranger and purchased slave alike. But you, forthwith, scorn this covenant, spurn the commands that come afterwards, and then you try to convince us that you know God, when you fail to do those things that every God-fearing person would do. If, therefore, you can give a satisfactory reply to these charges and can show us on what you place your hopes, even though you refuse to observe the Law, we will listen to you most willingly, and then we can go on and examine in the same manner our other differences."

Chapter 11

"Trypho," I began, "there never will be, nor has there ever been from eternity, any other God except him who created and formed this universe. Furthermore, we do not claim that our God is different from yours, for he is the God who, with a strong hand and outstretched arm, led your ancestors out of the land of Egypt. Nor have we placed our trust in any other (for, indeed, there is no other), but only in him whom you also have trusted, the God of Abraham and of Isaac and of Jacob. But, our hope is not through Moses or through the Law, otherwise our customs would be the same as yours. Now, indeed, for I have read,

---

[1]Gen 17:14.

Trypho, that there should be a definitive law and a covenant, more binding than all others, which now must be respected by all those who aspire to the heritage of God. The law promulgated at Horeb is already obsolete, and was intended for you Jews only, whereas the law of which I speak is simply for all people. Now, a later law in opposition to an older law abrogates the older; so, too, does a later covenant void an earlier one. An everlasting and final law, Christ himself, and a trustworthy covenant has been given to us, after which there shall be no law, or commandment, or precept. Have you not read these words of Isaiah: 'Give ear to me, and listen to me, my people; and you kings, give ear unto me: for a law shall go forth from me, and my judgment shall be a light to the nations. My Just One approaches swiftly, and my Savior shall go forth, and nations shall trust in my arm'?[2] Concerning this new covenant, God thus spoke through Jeremiah: 'Behold the days shall come, says the Lord, and I will make a new covenant with the house of Israel, and with the house of Judah: not according to the covenant which I made with their fathers, in the day that I took them by the hand to bring them out of the land of Egypt.'[3] If, therefore, God predicted that he would make a new covenant, and this for a light to the nations, and we see and are convinced that, through the name of the crucified Jesus Christ, people have turned to God, leaving behind them idolatry and other sinful practices, and have kept the faith and have practiced piety even unto death, then everyone can clearly see from these deeds and the accompanying powerful miracles that he is indeed the new law, the new covenant, and the expectation of those who, from every nation, have awaited the blessings of God. We have been led to God through this crucified Christ, and we are the true spiritual Israel, and the descendants of Judah, Jacob, Isaac, and Abraham, who, though uncircumcised, was approved and blessed by God because of his faith and was called the father of many nations. . . .

God, and the Lord of lords, a great God and mighty and terrible, who regards not persons nor takes bribes.'[4] And in Leviticus it is written: 'Because they have transgressed against me and despised me, and because they have walked contrary to me, I also will walk contrary to them, and I will destroy them in the land of their enemies. Then shall their uncircumcised heart be ashamed.'[5] Indeed the custom of circumcising the flesh, handed down from Abraham, was given to you as a distinguishing mark, to set you off from other nations and from us Christians. The purpose of this was that you and only you might suffer the afflictions that are now justly yours; that only your land be desolate, and your cities ruined by fire; that the fruits of your land be eaten by strangers before your very eyes; that not one of you be permitted to enter your city of Jerusalem. Your circumcision of the flesh is the only mark by which you can certainly be distinguished from other people. Nor do I believe that any of you will attempt to deny that God either had or has foreknowledge of future events, and that he does not prepare beforehand what everyone deserves. Therefore, the above-mentioned tribulations were justly imposed upon you, for you have murdered the Just One, and his prophets before him; now you spurn those who hope in him, and in him who sent him, namely, Almighty God, the Creator of all things; to the utmost of your power you dishonor and curse in your synagogues all those who believe in Christ. Now, indeed, you cannot use violence against us Christians, because of those who are in power, but as often as you could, you did employ force against us. For this reason, God cries out to you through Isaiah, saying: 'Behold how the just perish, and no one lays it to heart. For the just one is taken away from before the face of evil. His burial shall be in peace, he is taken away from among us. But draw near hither, you wicked ones, seed of the adulterers and children of the harlot. Upon whom have you jested,

Chapter 16

"God himself, through Moses, exclaimed: 'Circumcise therefore the hardness of your hearts, and stiffen your neck no more. For the Lord is your

[2]Isa 51:4–5.
[3]Jer 31:31–32.
[4]Deut 10:16–17.
[5]Lev 26:40–41.

and upon whom have you opened your mouth wide, and put out your tongue?' "[6]

Chapter 17

"The other nations have not treated Christ and us, his followers, as unjustly as have you Jews, who, indeed, are the very instigators of that evil opinion they have of the Just One and of us, his disciples. After you had crucified the only sinless and just man (through whose sufferings are healed all those who approach the Father through him), and after you realized that he had risen from the dead and had ascended into heaven (as had been predicted by the prophets), you not only failed to feel remorse for your evil deed, but you even dispatched certain picked men from Jerusalem to every land, to report the outbreak of the godless heresy of the Christians and to spread those ugly rumors against us which are repeated by those who do not know us. As a result, you are to blame not only for your own wickedness, but also for that of all others. With good reason, therefore, does Isaiah cry out: 'Because of you My name is blasphemed among the Gentiles.' And: 'Woe unto their soul, for they have taken evil counsel against themselves, saying, Let us bind the Just One, for he is useless to us. Therefore they eat the fruit of their deeds. Woe unto the wicked: evil shall be rendered to him, in accordance with the works of his hands.'[7] And again, in another passage: 'Woe unto them that draw iniquity as with a long cord, and their injustices as it were with the rope of a cart. That say: Let his speed come near, and let the counsel of the Holy One of Israel come, that we may know it. Woe unto them that call evil good, and good evil; that put light for darkness, and darkness for light; that put bitter for sweet, and sweet for bitter.'[8] Thus have you spared no effort in disseminating in every land bitter, dark, and unjust accusations against the only guiltless and just Light sent to people by God. For he seemed to be inconvenient to you, when he cried out, 'It is written. My house shall be called a house of prayer, but you have made it a den of thieves.'[9] Then he even overturned the money-changers' tables in the temple, and exclaimed, 'Woe to you, Scribes and Pharisees, hypocrites! because you pay tithes on mint and rue, and

never think of the love of God and justice. You are whited sepulchres, which outwardly appear beautiful, but within are full of dead people's bones.'[10] And to the scribes he said, 'Woe unto you, scribes, for you have the keys, and you do not enter in yourselves, and you hinder them that are entering; you blind guides!' "

Chapter 18

"Since you, Trypho, admit that you have read the teachings of him who is our Savior, I do not consider it out of place to have added those few short sayings of his to the quotations from the prophets: 'Wash yourselves, be clean, and take away evil from your souls.'[12] Thus does God order you to be washed in this laver, and to be circumcised with the true circumcision. We, too, would observe your circumcision of the flesh, your sabbath days, and, in a word, all your festivals, if we were not aware of the reason why they were imposed upon you, namely, because of your sins and your hardness of heart. If we patiently bear all the evils thrust upon us by vicious persons and demons, and still, amid indescribable tortures and death, ask mercy even for our persecutors and do not wish that anybody be requited with even a little of them, as our new Lawgiver decreed, why is it, Trypho, that we should not observe those rites which cannot harm us, such as the circumcision of the flesh, the sabbaths, and the festivals?"

Chapter 19

"That," interposed Trypho, "is precisely what we *are* puzzled about—why you endure all sorts of tortures, yet refuse to follow the [Jewish] customs now under discussion."

---

[6]Isa 57:1–4.
[7]Isa 3:9–11.
[8]Isa 5:18–20.
[9]Matt 21:13.
[10]Matt 23:23, 27; Luke 11:43.
[11]Luke 11:52.
[12]Isa 1:16.

"As I already explained," I answered, "it is because circumcision is not essential for all people, but only for you Jews, to mark you off for the suffering you now so deservedly endure. Nor do we approve of your useless baptism of the wells, which has no connection at all with our baptism of life. Thus has God protested that you have forsaken him, 'the fountain of living water, and have digged for yourselves broken cisterns which can hold no water.'[13] You Jews, who have the circumcision of the flesh, are in great need of our circumcision, whereas we, since we have our circumcision, do not need yours. For if, as you claim, circumcision had been necessary for salvation, God would not have created Adam uncircumcised; nor would he have looked with favor upon the sacrifice of the uncircumcised Abel, nor would He have been pleased with the uncircumcised Enoch, who 'was seen no more, because God took him.'[14] The Lord and his angels led Lot out of Sodom; thus was he saved without circumcision. Noah, the uncircumcised father of our race, was safe with his children in the ark. Melchisedech, the priest of the Most High, was not circumcised, yet Abraham, the first to accept circumcision of the flesh, paid tithes to him and was blessed by him; indeed, God, through David, announced that he would make him a priest forever according to the order of Melchisedech. Circumcision, therefore, is necessary only for you Jews, in order that, as Hosea, one of the twelve prophets, says, 'your people should not be a people, and your nation not a nation.'[15] Furthermore, all these men were just and pleasing in the sight of God, yet they kept no sabbaths. The same can be said of Abraham and his descendants down to the time of Moses, when your people showed itself wicked and ungrateful to God by molding a golden calf as an idol in the desert. Wherefore, God, adapting his laws to that weak people, ordered you to offer sacrifices to his name in order to save you from idolatry, but you did not obey even then, for you did not hesitate to sacrifice your children to the demons. Moreover, the observance of the sabbaths was imposed upon you by God so that you would be forced to remember him, as he himself said, 'That you may know that I am God your Savior.' "[16]

Chapter 20

"You were likewise forbidden to eat certain kinds of meat, so that when you ate and drank you would keep God before your eyes, for you have always been disposed to forget him, as Moses himself testifies: 'The people ate and drank, and rose up to play.'[17] And in another passage: 'Jacob ate and was filled, and grew fat; my beloved kicked, he grew fat and thick and broad, and forsook God who made him.' "[18]. . .

Chapter 23

. . . "Is it not evident to you that the elements are not idle, and that they do not observe the sabbaths? Stay as you were at birth. For if circumcision was not required before the time of Abraham, and before Moses there was no need of sabbaths, festivals, and sacrifices, they are not needed now, when in accordance with the will of God, Jesus Christ, his Son, has been born of the Virgin Mary, a descendant of Abraham. Indeed, when Abraham himself was still uncircumcised, he was justified and blessed by God because of his faith in him, as the Scriptures tell us. Furthermore, the Scriptures and the facts of the case force us to admit that Abraham received circumcision for a sign, not for justification itself. Thus was it justly said of your people: 'That soul which shall not be circumcised on the eighth day shall be destroyed out of his people.'[19] Moreover, the fact that females cannot receive circumcision of the flesh shows that circumcision was given as a sign, not as an act of justification. For God also bestowed upon women the capability of performing every good and virtuous act. We see that the physical formation of male and female is different, but it is equally evident that the bodily form is not what makes ei-

---

[13]Jer 2:13.
[14]Gen 5:24.
[15]Hos 1:9.
[16]Ezek 20:20.
[17]Exod 32:6.
[18]Deut 32:15.
[19]Gen 17:14.

ther of them good or evil. Their righteousness is determined by their acts of piety and justice.". . .

Chapter 25

. . ."Do I understand you to say," interposed Trypho, "that none of us Jews will inherit anything on the holy mountain of God?"

Chapter 26

"I didn't say that," I replied, "but I do say that those who have persecuted Christ in the past and still do, and do not repent, shall not inherit anything on the holy mountain, unless they repent. Whereas the Gentiles, who believe in Christ and are sorry for their sins, shall receive the inheritance, along with the Patriarchs, the Prophets, and every just descendant of Jacob, even though they neither practise circumcision nor observe the sabbaths and feasts. . . ."

Chapter 27

. . . "Thus, as your sinfulness was the reason why God first issued those precepts, so now because of your enslavement to sin, or rather your greater inclination to it, by means of the same precepts, he calls you to remember and know him. But you Jews are a ruthless, stupid, blind, and lame people, children in whom there is no faith. As God himself says: 'Honoring him only with your lips, but your hearts are far from him, teaching your own doctrines and not his.' "[20]. . .

Chapter 29

. . . "I am positive that I can persuade by these words even those of weak intellectual faculties, for the words which I use are not my own, nor are they embellished by human rhetoric, but they are the words as David sang them, as Isaiah announced them as good news, as Zachariah proclaimed them, and as Moses wrote them. Aren't you acquainted with them, Trypho? You should be, for they are

contained in your Scriptures, or rather not yours, but ours. For we believe and obey them, whereas you, though you read them, do not grasp their spirit. You should not be angry with us, therefore, nor blame us for the uncircumcision of our body; indeed, God created us that way. Nor should you consider it dreadful if we drink hot water on the Sabbath, for God doesn't stop controlling the movement of the universe on that day, but he continues directing it then as he does on all other days. Besides, your chief priests were commanded by God to offer sacrifices on the Sabbath, as well as on other days. Then, too, there are so many just people who are approved by God himself, yet they never performed any of your legal ceremonies."

Chapter 30

"The fact that God can be falsely accused by the foolish of not having always taught the same truthful doctrines to all, you can blame on your own sinfulness. Indeed, many deemed such doctrines senseless and unworthy of God, for they were not illuminated by grace to understand that these same doctrines have called your people, mired in sin and sick of a spiritual disease, to conversion and spiritual repentance; nor did they understand that prophecy, which was given to mankind after the death of Moses, is eternal. This, my friends, is indeed mentioned in the Psalm. That we, who have been enlightened by these doctrines, consider them to be sweeter than honey and the honey-comb, is evident from the fact that even under the threat of death we do not deny his name. Furthermore, it is equally clear (as the word of the prophecy, speaking in the name of one of his followers, metaphorically affirms) that we believers beseech him to safeguard us from strange, that is, evil and deceitful, spirits. We constantly ask God through Jesus Christ to keep us safe from those demons who, while they are strangers to the worship of God, were once adored by us; we pray, too, that, after our conversion to God through Christ, we may be without blame. We call him our helper and re-

---

[20]Isa 29:13.

deemer, by the power of whose name even the demons shudder; even to this day they are overcome by us when we exorcise them in the name of Jesus Christ, who was crucified under Pontius Pilate, the Governor of Judaea. Thus, it is clear to all that his Father bestowed upon him such a great power that even the demons are subject both to his name and to his preordained manner of suffering.". . .

Chapter 40

"The mystery of the lamb which God ordered you to sacrifice as the Passover was truly a type of Christ, with whose blood the believers, in proportion to the strength of their faith, anoint their homes, that is, themselves. You are all aware that Adam, the result of God's creative act, was the abode of his inspiration. In the following fashion I can show that God's precept concerning the paschal lamb was only temporary. God does not allow the paschal lamb to be sacrificed in any other place than where his name is invoked (that is, in the Temple at Jerusalem), for he knew that there would come a time, after Christ's Passion, when the place in Jerusalem (where you sacrificed the paschal lamb) would be taken from you by your enemies, and then all sacrifices would be stopped. Moreover, that lamb which you were ordered to roast whole was a symbol of Christ's Passion on the Cross. Indeed, the lamb, while being roasted, resembles the figure of the cross, for one spit transfixes it horizontally from the lower parts up to the head, and another pierces it across the back, and holds up its forelegs. Likewise, the two identical goats which had to be offered during the fast (one of which was to be the scapegoat and the other the sacrificial goat) were an announcement of the two advents of Christ: of the first advent, in which your priests and elders sent him away as a scapegoat, seizing him and putting him to death; of the second advent, because in that same place of Jerusalem you shall recognize him whom you had subjected to shame, and who was a sacrificial offering for all sinners who are willing to repent and to comply with that fast which

Isaiah prescribed when he said 'loosing the knot of violent contracts,'[21] and to observe likewise all the other precepts laid down by him (precepts which I have already mentioned and which all Christian believers fulfill). You also know very well that the offering of the two goats, which had to take place during the fast, could not take place anywhere else outside of Jerusalem."

Chapter 41

"Likewise," I continued, "the offering of flour, my friends, which was ordered to be presented for those cleansed from leprosy, was a prototype of the eucharistic bread, which our Lord Jesus Christ commanded us to offer in remembrance of the Passion he endured for all those souls who are cleansed from sin, and that at the same time we should thank God for having created the world, and everything in it, for the sake of mankind, and for having saved us from the sin in which we were born, and for the total destruction of the powers and principalities of evil through him who suffered in accordance with his will.". . .

Chapter 44

"I will be absolutely without blame in my obligations to you, if I endeavor to convince you with every possible proof. But, if you persist in your obstinacy of heart and feebleness of mind, or if you refuse to agree to the truth through fear of the death which awaits every Christian, you will have only yourselves to blame. And you are sadly mistaken if you think that, just because you are descendants of Abraham according to the flesh, you will share in the legacy of benefits which God promised would be distributed by Christ. No one can by any means participate in any of these gifts, except those who have the same ardent faith as Abraham, and who approve of all the mysteries. For I say that some precepts were given for the worship of God and the practice of virtue, whereas

---

[21]Isa 58:6.

other commandments and customs were arranged either in respect to the mystery of Christ [or] the hardness of your people's hearts.". . .

Chapter 47

"But," Trypho again objected, "if a person knows that what you say is true, and, professing Jesus to be the Christ, believes in and obeys him, yet desires also to observe the commandments of the Mosaic Law, shall he be saved?"

"In my opinion," I replied, "I say such a person will be saved, unless he exerts every effort to influence other people (I have in mind the Gentiles whom Christ circumcised from all error) to practice the same rites as himself, informing them that they cannot be saved unless they do so. You yourself did this at the opening of our discussion, when you said that I would not be saved unless I kept the Mosaic precepts."

"But why," pressed Trypho, "did you say, 'In my opinion such a person will be saved?' There must, therefore, be other Christians who hold a different opinion."

"Yes, Trypho," I conceded, "there are some Christians who boldly refuse to have conversation or meals with such persons. I don't agree with such Christians. But if some [Jewish converts], due to their instability of will, desire to observe as many of the Mosaic precepts as possible—precepts which we think were instituted because of your hardness of heart—while at the same time they place their hope in Christ, and if they desire to perform the eternal and natural acts of justice and piety, yet wish to live with us Christians and believers, as I already stated, not persuading them to be circumcised like themselves, or to keep the Sabbath, or to perform any other similar acts, then it is my opinion that we Christians should receive them and associate with them in every way as kinfolk and brethren. But if any of your people, Trypho, profess their belief in Christ, and at the same time force the Christian Gentiles to follow the Law instituted through Moses, or refuse to share in communion with them this same common life, I certainly will also not approve of them. But

I think that those Gentiles who have been induced to follow the practices of the Jewish Law, and at the same time profess their faith in the Christ of God, will probably be saved. Those persons, however, who had once believed and publicly acknowledged Jesus to be the Christ, and then later, for one reason or another, turned to the observance of the Mosaic Law, and denied that Jesus is the Christ, cannot be saved unless they repent before their death. The same can be said of those descendants of Abraham, who follow the Law and refuse to believe in Christ to their very last breath. Especially excluded from eternal salvation are they who in their synagogues have cursed and still do curse those who believe in that very Christ in order that they may attain salvation and escape the avenging fires of hell. God in his goodness, kindness, and infinite richness considers the repentant sinner to be just and innocent, as he declared through the prophet Ezechiel, and the one who turns from the path of piety and justice to follow that of injustice and impiety God judges to be an impious and unjust sinner. Thus has our Lord Jesus Christ warned us: 'In whatsoever things I shall apprehend you, in them also I shall judge you.' ". . .

Chapter 59

Then I continued, "Allow me now to show you from the words of the book of Exodus how this very person who was at the same time Angel and God and Lord and Man, and who was seen by Abraham and Jacob, also appeared and talked to Moses from the flame of the fiery bush." And when I was assured by my audience that they would listen gladly, patiently, and eagerly, I went on, . . .

"Trypho," I said, "I now wish to prove to you that in the apparition under discussion, He who is termed an angel and is God was the only One who talked to and was seen by Moses. Here is the Scriptural proof: 'The angel of the Lord appeared to him in a flame of fire out of the midst of a bush; and he saw that the bush was on fire and was not burnt. And Moses said: I will go and see this great sight, why the bush is not burnt. And when the Lord saw that he went forward to see, he called to him out of the midst of the bush.'[22] Now, as the Scripture refers to him who appeared to Jacob in a dream as an angel, and then states that the same angel said to Jacob in his sleep, 'I am the God who appeared to you when you did flee from the face of your brother Esau,'[23] and as Scripture also affirms that, in the judgment of Sodom in the days of Abraham, the Lord executed the will of the Lord who is in heaven; so when the Scripture here states that an angel of the Lord appeared to Moses, and then announces that he is Lord and God, it refers to the same person who is identified in many of our earlier quotations as the minister to God, who is above the world, and above whom there is no other God."

Chapter 61

"So, my friends," I said, "I shall now show from the Scriptures that God has begotten of himself a certain rational power as a beginning before all other creatures. The Holy Spirit indicates this power by various titles, sometimes the Glory of the Lord, at other times Son, or Wisdom, or Angel, or God, or Lord, or Word. He even called himself Commander-in-chief when he appeared in human guise to Joshua, the son of Nun. Indeed, he can justly lay claim to all these titles from the fact both that he performs the Father's will and that he was begotten by an act of the Father's will. But, does not something similar happen also with us humans? When we utter a word, it can be said that we beget the word, but not by cutting it off, in the sense that our power of uttering words would thereby be diminished. We can observe a similar example in nature when one fire kindles another, without losing anything, but remaining the same; yet the enkindled fire seems to exist of itself and to shine without lessening the brilliancy of the first fire.". . .

Chapter 96

"The words of the Law, 'Cursed is every one who hangs on a tree,'[24] strengthen our hope which is sustained by the crucified Christ, not because the crucified one is cursed by God, but because God predicted what would be done by all of you Jews, and others like you, who are not aware that this is he who was before all things, the eternal priest of God, the King, and Christ. Now, you can clearly see that this has actually happened. For, in your synagogues you curse all those who through him have become Christians, and the Gentiles put into effect your curse by killing all those who merely admit that they are Christians. To all our persecutors we say: 'You are our brothers; apprehend, rather, the truth of God.' But when neither they nor you will listen to us, but you do all in your power to force us to deny Christ, we resist you and prefer to endure death, confident that God will give us all the blessings which he promised us through Christ. Furthermore, we pray for you that you might experience the mercy of Christ; for he instructed us to pray even for our enemies, when he said: 'Be kind and merciful, even as your heavenly Father is merciful.'[25] We can observe that almighty God is kind and merciful, causing his sun to shine on the ungrateful and on the just, and sending rain to both the holy and the evil; but all of them, he has told us, he will judge."

Chapter 97

"Besides, the fact that the prophet Moses remained until evening in the form of the cross, when his hands were held up by Aaron and Hur, happened in the likeness of this sign. For the Lord also remained upon the cross almost until evening when he was buried. Then he arose from the dead on the third day, as David foretold when he said: 'I have cried to the Lord with my voice, and he has heard me from his holy hill. I have slept and have taken my rest; and I have risen up, because the Lord has sustained me.'[26] Isaiah likewise foretold the manner of his death in these words: 'I have spread forth my hands to an unbelieving and contradicting people, who walk in a

---

[22]Exod 3:2–4.
[23]Gen 35:7.
[24]Deut 21:23.
[25]Luke 6:36.
[26]Ps 3:4–5.

way that is not good.'[27] And the same Isaiah also predicted his resurrection: 'His burial has been taken out of the midst,'[28] and: 'I will give the rich for his death.'[29] And again, David, in his twenty-first Psalm, refers to his passion on the cross in mystical parable: 'They have pierced my hands and feet. They have numbered all my bones. And they have looked and stared upon me. They parted my garments amongst them, and upon my vesture they cast lots.'[30] For, when they nailed him to the cross they did indeed pierce his hands and feet, and they who crucified him divided his garments among themselves, each casting lots for the garment he chose. You are indeed blind when you deny that the above-quoted Psalm was spoken of Christ, for you fail to see that no one among your people who was ever called King ever had his hands and feet pierced while alive, and died by this mystery (that is, of the cross), except this Jesus only.". . .

Chapter 108

"Now, you Jews were well acquainted with these facts in the life of Jonah and though Christ proclaimed to you that he would give you the sign of Jonah, and he pleaded with you to repent of your sins at least after His resurrection from the dead, and to lament before God as did the Ninevites that your nation and city might not be seized and destroyed, as it has been; yet you not only refused to repent after you learned that he arose from the dead, but, as I stated, you chose certain men and commissioned them to travel throughout the whole civilized world and announce: 'A godless and lawless sect has been started by an impostor, a certain Jesus of Galilee, whom we nailed to the cross, but whose body, after it was taken from the cross, was stolen at night from the tomb by his disciples, who now try to deceive people by affirming that he has arisen from the dead and has ascended into heaven.' And you accuse him of having taught those irreverent, riotous, and wicked things, of which you everywhere accuse all those who look up to and acknowledge him as their Christ, their teacher, and the Son of God. And, to top your folly, even now, after your city has been seized and your whole country ravaged, you not only refuse to repent, but you defiantly curse him and his followers. But, as far as we Christians are concerned, we do not hate you, nor those who believed the wicked rumors you have spread against us; on the contrary, we pray that even now you may mend your ways and find mercy from God the Father of all, who is most benign and compassionate."

[27]Isa 65:2.
[28]Isa 57:2.
[29]Isa 53:9.
[30]Ps 22:16–18.

17. Melito of Sardis: On the Passover

One of the most eloquent homilies from the early church (see Chapter 12) comes from the pen of Melito, an otherwise little-known bishop of the city of Sardis in Asia Minor. Entitled "On the Passover," the sermon provides a rhetorically powerful and religiously

Melito of Sardis: "On the Passover," from "A New English Translation of Melito's Paschal Homily," by Gerald F. Hawthorne. *Current Issues in Biblical and Patristic Interpretation*, ed. Gerald F. Hawthorne. Grand Rapids, Mich.: Eerdmans, 1975. Used with permission.

polemical exposition of the Old Testament account of the Passover meal instituted under Moses. For Melito, Jesus himself was the true passover lamb whose shed blood brings salvation. As the reality to which the Old Testament pointed, Christ is far superior to the religion of Judaism, which therefore no longer has any independent value (just as a model of a building can be destroyed once construction is completed). Moreover, Jesus' death, for Melito, is not only a message of salvation but also of judgment, especially for the Jews who were responsible for it. In executing Jesus, the Jews killed their own messiah. Indeed, since Melito sees Jesus as divine ("by nature, both God and man"), Jews are guilty of murdering their own God, the God who created the world and called Israel to be his people.

This is the first known instance of a Christian charging Jews with deicide in the death of Jesus. The emotional impact of the charge is significantly heightened by the powerful and gripping rhetoric that Melito uses to put it forth.

Melito is known to have died around 190 C.E.; this sermon would therefore have been preached sometime in the second half of the second century.

1 First of all, the Scripture about the Hebrew
     Exodus has been read
   and the words of the mystery have been ex-
     plained
   as to how the sheep was sacrificed
   and the people were saved.
2 Therefore, understand this, O beloved:
   The mystery of the passover is
   new and old,
   eternal and temporal,
   corruptible and incorruptible,
   mortal and immortal
   in this fashion:
3 It is old insofar as it concerns the law,
   but new insofar as it concerns the gospel;
   temporal insofar as it concerns the type,
   eternal because of grace;
   corruptible because of the sacrifice of the
     sheep,
   incorruptible because of the life of the Lord;
   mortal because of his burial in the earth,
   immortal because of his resurrection from
     the dead.
4 The law is old,
   but the gospel is new;
   the type was for a time,
   but grace is forever.
   The sheep was corruptible,

but the Lord is incorruptible,
who was crushed as a lamb,
but who was resurrected as God.
For although he was led to sacrifice as a
  sheep,
yet he was not a sheep;
and although he was as a lamb without voice,
yet indeed he was not a lamb.
The one was the model;
the other was found to be the finished
  product.
5 For God replaced the lamb,
   and a man the sheep;
   but in the man was Christ,
   who contains all things.
6 Hence, the sacrifice of the sheep,
   and the sending of the lamb to slaughter,
   and the writing of the law—
   each led to and issued in Christ,
   for whose sake everything happened in the
     ancient law,
   and even more so in the new gospel.
7 For indeed the law issued in the gospel—
   the old in the new,
   both coming forth together from Zion and
     Jerusalem;
   and the commandment issued in grace,
   and the type in the finished product,

and the lamb in the Son,
and the sheep in a man,
and the man in God.

8 For the one who was born as Son,
and led to slaughter as a lamb,
and sacrificed as a sheep,
and buried as a man,
rose up from the dead as God,
since he is by nature both God and man.

9 He is everything:
in that he judges he is law,
in that he teaches he is gospel,
in that he saves he is grace,
in that he begets he is Father,
in that he is begotten he is Son,
in that he suffers he is sheep,
in that he is buried he is man,
in that he comes to life again he is God.

10 Such is Jesus Christ,
to whom be the glory forever. Amen.

11 Now comes the mystery of the passover,
even as it stands written in the law,
just as it has been read aloud only moments
ago.[1]
But I will clearly set forth the significance of
the words of this Scripture,
showing how God commanded Moses in
Egypt,
when he had made his decision,
to bind Pharaoh under the lash,
but to release Israel from the lash
through the hand of Moses.

12 For see to it, he says,
that you take a flawless and perfect lamb,
and that you sacrifice it in the evening
with the sons of Israel,
and that you eat it at night, and in haste.
You are not to break any of its bones.

13 You will do it like this, he says:
In a single night
you will eat it by families and by tribes,
your loins girded,
and your staves in your hands.
For this is the Lord's passover,
an eternal reminder for the sons of Israel.

14 Then take the blood of the sheep,
and anoint the front door of your houses
by placing upon the posts of your entrance-
way
the sign of the blood, in order to ward off the
angel.
For behold I will strike Egypt,
and in a single night
she will be made childless from beast to man.

15 Then, when Moses sacrificed the sheep
and completed the mystery at night
together with the sons of Israel,
he sealed the doors of their houses
in order to protect the people
and to ward off the angel.

16 But when the sheep was sacrificed,
and the passover consumed,
and the mystery completed,
and the people made glad,
and Israel sealed,
then the angel arrived to strike Egypt,
who was neither
initiated into the mystery,
participant of the passover,
sealed by the blood,
nor protected by the Spirit,
but who was the enemy and the unbeliever.

17 In a single night the angel struck and made
Egypt childless.
For when the angel had encompassed Israel,
and had seen her sealed with the blood of the
sheep,
he advanced against Egypt,
and by means of grief subdued the stubborn
Pharaoh,
clothing him,
not with a cloak of mourning,
nor with a torn mantle,
but with all of Egypt, torn,
and mourning for her firstborn.

18 For all Egypt,
plunged in troubles and calamities,
in tears and lamentations,
came to Pharaoh in utter sadness,
not in appearance only,

---

[1]Exod 12:11–30.

but also in soul,
having torn not only her garments
but her tender breasts as well.

19 Indeed it was possible to observe an extraor-
     dinary sight:
in one place people beating their breasts,
in another those wailing,
and in the middle of them Pharaoh,
mourning, sitting in sackcloth and cinders,
shrouded in thick darkness
as in a funeral garment,
girded with all Egypt,
as with a tunic of grief.

20 For Egypt clothed Pharaoh
     as a cloak of wailing.
Such was the mantle that had been woven for
     his royal body.
With just such a cloak did the angel of right-
     eousness clothe
the self-willed Pharaoh:
with bitter mournfulness,
and with thick darkness,
and with childlessness.
For that angel warred against the firstborn of
     Egypt.
Indeed, swift and insatiate
was the death of the firstborn.

21 And an unusual monument of defeat,
set up over those who had fallen dead in a
     moment,
could be seen.
For the defeat of those who lay dead
became the provisions of death.

22 If you listen
to the narration of this extraordinary event
you will be astonished.
For these things befell the Egyptians:
a long night,
and darkness which was touchable,
and death which touched,
and an angel who oppressed,
and Hades which devoured
their firstborn.

23 But you must listen to
something still more extraordinary and terri-
     fying:
in the darkness which could be touched

was hidden death which could not be touched.
And the ill-starred Egyptians touched the
     darkness,
while death, on the watch,
touched the firstborn of the Egyptians
as the angel had commanded.

24 Therefore, if anyone touched the darkness
he was led out by death.
Indeed one firstborn,
touching a dark body with his hand,
and utterly frightened in his soul,
cried aloud in misery and in terror:
What has my right hand laid hold of?
At what does my soul tremble?
Who cloaks my whole body with darkness?
If you are my father, help me;
if my mother, feel sympathy for me;
if my brother, speak to me;
if my friend, sit with me;
if my enemy, go away from me
since I am a firstborn son!

25 And before the firstborn was silent,
the long silence held him in its power,
     saying:
You are mine, O firstborn!
I, the silence of death, am your destiny.

26 And another firstborn,
taking note of the capture of the firstborn,
denied his identity,
so that he might not die a bitter death:
I am not a firstborn son;
I was born like a third child.
But he who could not be deceived
touched that firstborn,
and he fell forward in silence.
In a single moment
the firstborn fruit of the Egyptians was de-
     stroyed.
The one first conceived,
the one first born,
the one sought after,
the one chosen
was dashed to the ground;
not only that of men
but that of irrational animals as well.

27 A lowing was heard in the fields of the earth,
of cattle bellowing for their nurslings,

a cow standing over her calf,
and a mare over her colt.
And the rest of the cattle,
having just given birth to their offspring
and swollen with milk,
were lamenting bitterly and piteously
for their firstborn.

28 And there was a wailing and lamentation
because of the destruction of the people,
because of the destruction of the firstborn
    who were dead.
And all Egypt stank,
because of the unburied bodies.

29 Indeed one could see a frightful spectacle:
of the Egyptians
there were mothers with dishevelled hair,
and fathers who had lost their minds,
wailing aloud in terrifying fashion in the
    Egyptian tongue:
O wretched persons that we are!
We have lost our firstborn
in a single moment!
And they were striking their breasts with their
    hands,
beating time in hammerlike fashion to the
    dance for their dead.

30 Such was the misfortune which encompassed
    Egypt.
In an instant it made her childless.
But Israel, all the while, was being protected
by the sacrifices of the sheep
and truly was being illumined
by its blood which was shed;
for the death of the sheep
was found to be a rampart for the people.

31 O inexpressible mystery!
the sacrifice of the sheep
was found to be the salvation of the people,
and the death of the sheep
became the life of the people.
For its blood warded off the angel.

32 Tell me, O angel,
At what were you turned away?
At the sacrifice of the sheep,
or the life of the Lord?
At the death of the sheep,
or the type of the Lord?

At the blood of the sheep,
or the Spirit of the Lord?
Clearly you were turned away

33 because you saw the mystery of the Lord
taking place in the sheep,
the life of the Lord
in the sacrifice of the sheep,
the type of the Lord
in the death of the sheep.
For this reason you did not strike Israel,
but it was Egypt alone that you made
    childless.

34 What was this extraordinary mystery?
It was Egypt struck to destruction
but Israel kept for salvation.
Listen to the meaning of this mystery:

35 Beloved, no speech or event takes place
without a pattern or design;
every event and speech
involves a pattern—
that which is spoken, a pattern,
and that which happens, a prefiguration—
in order that as the event
is disclosed through the prefiguration,
so also the speech
may be brought to expression through its
    outline.

36 Without the model,
no work of art arises.
Is not that which is to come into existence
seen through the model which typifies it?
For this reason a pattern of that which is to
    be is made
either out of wax,
or out of clay,
or out of wood,
in order that by the smallness of the model,
destined to be destroyed,
might be seen that thing which is to arise
    from it—
higher than it in size,
and mightier than it in power,
and more beautiful than it in appearance,
and more elaborate than it in ornamentation.

37 So, whenever the thing arises
for which the model was made,
then that which carried the image of the fu-

ture thing
is destroyed as no longer of use,
since it has transmitted its resemblance to
 that which is
by nature true.
Therefore, that which once was valuable, is
 now without value
because that which is truly valuable has appeared.
38 For each thing has its own time:
there is a distinct time for the type,
there is a distinct time for the material,
and there is a distinct time for the truth.
You construct the model.
You want this,
because you see in it the image of the future
 work.
You procure the material for the model.
You want this,
on account of that which is going to arise because of it.
You complete the work
and cherish it alone,
for only in it do you see both the type and the
 truth.
39 Therefore, if it was like this with models of
 perishable objects,
so indeed will it also be with those of imperishable objects.
If it was like this with earthly things,
so indeed also will it be with heavenly things.
For even the Lord's salvation and his truth
were prefigured in the people,
and the teaching of the gospel
was proclaimed in advance by the law.
40 The people, therefore, became the model for
 the church,
and the law a parabolic sketch.
But the gospel became the explanation of the
 law
and its fulfilment,
while the church became the storehouse of
 truth.
41 Therefore, the type had value
prior to its realization,
and the parable was wonderful
prior to its interpretation.

This is to say that
the people had value
before the church came on the scene,
and the law was wonderful
before the gospel was brought to light.
42 But when the church came on the scene,
and the gospel was set forth,
the type lost its value
by surrendering its significance to the truth,
and the law was fulfilled
by surrendering its significance to the gospel.
Just as the type lost its significance
by surrendering its image to that which is
 true by nature,
and as the parable lost its significance
by being illumined through the interpretation,
43 so indeed also the law was fulfilled
when the gospel was brought to light,
and the people lost their significance
when the church came on the scene,
and the type was destroyed
when the Lord appeared.
Therefore, those things which once had value
are today without value,
because the things which have true value
 have appeared.
44 For at one time the sacrifice of the sheep was
 valuable,
but now it is without value because of the
 life of the Lord.
The death of the sheep once was valuable,
but now it is without value because of the
 salvation of the Lord.
The blood of the sheep once was valuable,
but now it is without value because of the
 Spirit of the Lord.
The silent lamb once was valuable,
but now it has no value because of the blameless Son.
The temple here below once was valuable,
but now it is without value because of the
 Christ from above.
45 The Jerusalem here below once had value,
but now it is without value because of the
 Jerusalem from
above.
The meager inheritance once had value;

now it is without value because of the abundant grace.

For not in one place alone,

nor yet in narrow confines,

has the glory of God been established,

but his grace has been poured out

upon the uttermost parts of the inhabited
world,

and there the almighty God

has taken up his dwelling place

through Jesus Christ,

to whom be the glory for ever. Amen.

46 Now that you have heard the explanation of
the type and of that which corresponds to it,

hear also what goes into making up the
mystery.

What is the passover?

Indeed its name is derived

from that event—

"to celebrate the passover" (to paschein) is
derived from

"to suffer" (tou pathein).

Therefore, learn

who the sufferer is

and who he is who suffers along with the
sufferer.

47 Why indeed was the Lord present upon the
earth?

In order that having clothed himself with the
one who suffers,

he might lift him up to the heights of heaven.

In the beginning, when God made heaven
and earth,

and everything in them through his word,

he himself formed man from the earth

and shared with that form his own breath,

and himself placed him in paradise,

which was eastward in Eden,

and there they lived most luxuriously.[2]

Then by way of command God gave them
this law:

For your food you may eat from any tree,

but you are not to eat

from the tree of the one who knows good and
evil.

For on the day you eat from it,

you most certainly will die.

48 But man,

who is by nature capable of receiving good
and evil

as soil of the earth is capable of receiving
seeds from

both sides,

welcomed the hostile and greedy counsellor,

and by having touched that tree

transgressed the command,

and disobeyed God.

As a consequence, he was cast out into this
world

as a condemned man is cast into prison.

49 And when he had fathered many children,

and had grown very old,

and had returned to the earth

through having tasted of the tree,

an inheritance was left behind by him for his
children.

Indeed, he left his children an inheritance—

not of chastity but of unchastity,

not of immortality but of corruptibility,

not of honor but of dishonor,

not of freedom but of slavery,

not of sovereignty but of tyranny,

not of life but of death,

not of salvation but of destruction.

50 Extraordinary and terrifying indeed

was the destruction of people upon the earth.

For the following things happened to them:

They were carried off as slaves by sin, the
tyrant,

and were led away into the regions of desire

where they were totally engulfed

by insatiable sensual pleasures—

by adultery,

by unchastity,

by debauchery,

by inordinate desires,

by avarice,

by murders,

by bloodshed,

by the tyranny of wickedness,

by the tyranny of lawlessness.

---

[2]Gen 2–3.

51 For even a father of his own accord lifted up
      a dagger against his son;
    and a son used his hands against his father;
    and the impious person smote the breasts that
      nourished him;
    and brother murdered brother;
    and host wronged his guest;
    and friend assassinated friend;
    and one man cut the throat of another
    with his tyrannous right hand.
52 Therefore all people on the earth
    became either murderers,
    or parricides,
    or killers of their children.
    And yet a thing still more dreadful and ex-
      traordinary was
    to be found:
    A mother attacked the flesh which she gave
      birth to,
    a mother attacked those whom her breasts
      had nourished;
    and she buried in her belly
    the fruit of her belly.
    Indeed, the ill-starred mother became a dread-
      ful tomb,
    when she devoured the child which she bore
      in her womb.
53 But in addition to this
    there were to be found among people
    many things still more monstrous and terri-
      fying and brutal:
    father cohabits with his child,
    and son with his mother,
    and brother with sister,
    and male with male,
    and each man lusting after the wife of his
      neighbor.
54 Because of these things sin exulted,
    which, because it was death's collaborator,
    entered first into the souls of people,
    and prepared as food for him the bodies of
      the dead.
    In every soul sin left its mark,
    and those in whom it placed its mark
    were destined to die.
55 Therefore, all flesh fell under the power of
      sin,

and every body under the dominion of death,
for every soul was driven out from its house
  of flesh.
Indeed, that which had been taken from the
  earth
was dissolved again into earth,
and that which had been given from God
was locked up in Hades.
And that beautiful ordered arrangement was
  dissolved,
when the beautiful body was separated (from
  the soul).
56 Yes, the human was divided up into parts by
      death.
    Yes, an extraordinary misfortune and captiv-
      ity enveloped him:
    he was dragged away captive under the
      shadow of death,
    and the image of the Father remained there
      desolate.
    For this reason, therefore,
    the mystery of the passover has been com-
      pleted
    in the body of the Lord.
57 Indeed, the Lord
    prearranged his own sufferings
    in the patriarchs,
    and in the prophets,
    and in the whole people of God,
    giving his sanction to them through the law
      and the prophets.
    For that which was to exist in a new and
      grandiose fashion
    was pre-planned long in advance,
    in order that when it should come into exis-
      tence
    one might attain to faith,
    just because it had been predicted long in
      advance.
58 So indeed also the suffering of the Lord,
    predicted long in advance by means of types,
    but seen today,
    has brought about faith, just because it has
      taken place
    as predicted.
    And yet people have taken it as something
      completely new.

Well, the truth of the matter is
the mystery of the Lord
is both old and new—
old insofar as it involved the type,
but new insofar as it concerns grace.
And what is more, if you pay close attention
 to this type
you will see the real thing through its fulfillment.
59 Accordingly, if you desire to see the mystery
 of the Lord,
pay close attention to Abel who likewise was
 put to death,
to Isaac who likewise was bound hand and
 foot,
to Joseph who likewise was sold,
to Moses who likewise was exposed,
to David who likewise was hunted down,
to the prophets who likewise suffered
because they were the Lord's anointed.
60 Pay close attention also
to the one who was sacrificed as a sheep in
 the land of Egypt,
to the one who smote Egypt
and who saved Israel
by his blood.
61 For it was through the voice of prophecy
that the mystery of the Lord was proclaimed.
Moses, indeed, said to his people:
"Surely you will see your life suspended before your eyes night and day,
but you surely will not believe on your Life."[3]
62 And David said:
"Why were the nations haughty
and the people concerned about nothing?
The kings of the earth presented themselves
and the princess assembled themselves
 together
against the Lord and against his anointed."[4]
63 And Jeremiah:
"I am as an innocent lamb
being led away to be sacrificed.
They plotted evil against me and said:
Come! let us throw him a tree for his food,
and let us exterminate him from the land of
 the living,
so that his name will never be recalled."[5]

64 And Isaiah:
"He was led as a sheep to slaughter,
and, as a lamb is silent
in the presence of the one who shears it,
he did not open his mouth.
Therefore who will tell his offspring?"[6]
65 And indeed there were many other things
proclaimed by numerous prophets
concerning the mystery of the passover,
which is Christ,
to whom be the glory forever. Amen.
66 When this one came from heaven to earth
for the sake of the one who suffers,
and had clothed himself with that very one
through the womb of a virgin,
and having come forth as a man,
he accepted the sufferings of the sufferer
through his body which was capable of
 suffering.
And he destroyed those human sufferings
by his spirit which was incapable of dying.
He killed death which had put humans to
 death.
67 For this one,
who was led away as a lamb,
and who was sacrificed as a sheep
by himself delivered us from servitude to the
 world
as from the land of Egypt,
and released us from bondage to the devil
as from the hand of Pharaoh,
and sealed our souls by his own spirit
and the members of our bodies by his own
 blood.
68 This is
the one who covered death with shame
and who plunged the devil into mourning
as Moses did Pharaoh.
This is the one who smote lawlessness
and deprived injustice of its offspring,
as Moses deprived Egypt.

[3]Deut 28:66.
[4]Ps 2:1–2.
[5]Jer 11:19.
[6]Isa 53:7.

This is the one who delivered us
from slavery into freedom,
from darkness into light,
from death into life,
from tyranny into an eternal kingdom,
and who made us a new priesthood,
and a special people forever.

69 This one is the passover of our salvation.
This is the one who patiently endured many
    things in many people:
This is the one who was murdered in Abel,
and bound as a sacrifice in Isaac,
and exiled in Jacob,
and sold in Joseph,
and exposed in Moses,
and sacrificed in the lamb,
and hunted down in David,
and dishonored in the prophets.

70 This is the one who became human in a
    virgin,
who was hanged on the tree,
who was buried in the earth,
who was resurrected from among the dead,
and who raised humankind up
out of the grave below
to the heights of heaven.

71 This is the lamb that was slain.
This is the lamb that was silent.
This is the one who was born of Mary, that
    beautiful ewe-lamb.
This is the one who was taken from the flock,
and was dragged to sacrifice,
and was killed in the evening,
and was buried at night,
the one who was not broken while on the
    tree,
who did not see dissolution while in the earth,
who rose up from the dead,
and who raised up humankind
from the grave below.

72 This one was murdered.
And where was he murdered?
In the very center of Jerusalem!
Why?
Because he had healed their lame,
and had cleansed their lepers,
and had guided their blind with light,

and had raised up their dead.
For this reason he suffered.
Somewhere it has been written in the law and
    prophets,
"They paid me back evil for good,
and my soul with barrenness,
plotting evil against me,
saying, Let us bind this just man
because he is troublesome to us."[7]

73 Why, O Israel, did you do this strange in-
    justice?
You dishonored the one who had honored
    you.
You held in contempt the one who held you
    in esteem.
You denied the one who publicly acknowl-
    edged you.
You renounced the one who proclaimed you
    his own,
You killed the one who made you to live,
Why did you do this, O Israel?

74 Has it not been written for your benefit:
"Do not shed innocent blood
lest you die a terrible death"?
Nevertheless, Israel admits, I killed the Lord!
Why?
Because it was necessary for him to die.
You have deceived yourself, O Israel,
rationalizing thus about the death of the Lord.

75 It was necessary for him to suffer, yes,
but not by you;
it was necessary for him to be dishonored,
but not by you;
it was necessary for him to be judged,
but not by you;
it was necessary for him to be crucified,
but not by you,
nor by your right hand.

76 O Israel!
You ought to have cried aloud to God with
    this voice:
"O Lord,
if it was necessary for your Son to suffer,
and if this was your will,

---

[7]Ps 34:4, 12.

let him suffer indeed,
but not at my hands.
Let him suffer at the hands of strangers.
Let him be judged by the uncircumcised.
Let him be crucified by the tyrannical right
    hand,
but not by mine."

77 But you, O Israel,
    did not cry out to God with this voice,
    nor did you absolve yourself of guilt before
        the Lord,
    nor were you persuaded by his works.

78 The withered hand which was restored whole
        to its body
    did not persuade you;
    nor did the eyes of the blind which were
        opened by his hand;
    nor did the paralyzed bodies
    restored to health again through his voice;
    nor did that most extraordinary miracle per-
        suade you,
    namely, the dead man raised to life from the
        tomb
    where already he had been lying for four
        days.
    Indeed, dismissing these things,
    you, to your detriment, prepared the
        following
    for the sacrifice of the Lord at eventide;
    sharp nails,
    and false witnesses,
    and fetters,
    and scourges,

79 and vinegar,
    and gall,
    and a sword,
    and affliction,
    and all as though it were for a blood-stained
        robber.
    For you brought to him
    scourges for his body,
    and the thorns for his head.
    And you bound those beautiful hands of his,
    which had formed you from the earth.
    And that beautiful mouth of his,
    which had nourished you with life,
    you filled with gall.

And you killed your Lord
at the time of the great feast.

80 Surely you were filled with gaiety,
    but he was filled with hunger;
    you drank wine and ate bread,
    but he vinegar and gall;
    you wore a happy smile,
    but he had a sad countenance;
    you were full of joy,
    but he was full of trouble;
    you sang songs,
    but he was judged;
    you issued the command,
    he was crucified;
    you danced,
    he was buried;
    you lay down on a soft bed,
    but he in a tomb and coffin.

81 O lawless Israel,
    why did you commit this extraordinary crime
    of casting your Lord into new sufferings—
    your master,
    the one who formed you,
    the one who made you,
    the one who honored you,
    the one who called you Israel?

82 But you were found not really to be Israel,
    for you did not see God,
    you did not recognize the Lord,
    you did not know, O Israel.
    that this one was the firstborn of God.
    the one who was begotten before the morn-
        ing star,
    the one who caused the light to shine forth,
    the one who made bright the day,
    the one who parted the darkness,
    the one who established the primordial start-
        ing point,
    the one who suspended the earth,
    the one who quenched the abyss,
    the one who stretched out the firmament,
    the one who formed the universe,

83 the one who set in motion the stars of heaven,
    the one who caused those luminaries to shine,
    the one who made the angels in heaven,
    the one who established their thrones in that
        place,

the one who by himself fashioned humans
  upon the earth.
This was the one who chose you,
the one who guided you,
from Adam to Noah,
from Noah to Abraham,
from Abraham to Isaac and Jacob and the
  Twelve Patriarchs.

84 This was the one who guided you into Egypt,
and guarded you,
and himself kept you well supplied there.
This was the one who lighted your route with
  a column of fire,
and provided shade for you by means of a
  cloud,
the one who divided the Red Sea,
and led you across it,
and scattered your enemy abroad.

85 This is the one who provided you with manna
  from heaven,
the one who gave you water to drink from a
  rock,
the one who established your laws in Horeb,
the one who gave you an inheritance in the
  land,
the one who sent out his prophets to you,
the one who raised up your kings.

86 This is the one who came to you,
the one who healed your suffering ones
and who resurrected your dead.
This is the one whom you sinned against.
This is the one whom you wronged.
This is the one whom you killed
This is the one whom you sold for silver,
although you asked him for the didrachma.

87 O ungrateful Israel, come here
and be judged before me for your ingratitude.
How high a price did you place on being created by him?
How high a price did you place on the discovery of your fathers?
How high a price did you place on the descent into Egypt,
and the provision made for you there
through the noble Joseph?

88 How high a price did you place on the ten
  plagues?
How high a price did you place on the nightly
  column of fire,
and the daily cloud,
and the crossing of the Red Sea?
How high a price did you place on the gift of
  manna from heaven,
and the gift of water from the rock,
and the gift of law in Horeb,
and the land as an inheritance,
and the benefits accorded you there?

89 How high a price did you place on your suffering people
whom he healed when he was present?
Set me a price on the withered hand,
which he restored whole to its body.

90 Put me a price on the people born blind,
whom he led into light by his voice.
Put me a price on those who lay dead,
whom he raised up alive from the tomb.
Inestimable are the benefits that come to you
  from him.
But you, shamefully,
have paid him back with ingratitude,
returning to him
evil for good,
and affliction for favor
and death for life—

91 a person for whom you should have died.
Furthermore, if the king of some nation is
  captured by an enemy,
a war is started because of him,
fortifications are shattered because of him,
cities are plundered because of him,
ransom is sent because of him,
ambassadors are commissioned because of
  him
in order that he might be surrendered,
so that either he might be returned if living,
or that he might be buried if dead.

92 But you, quite to the contrary,
voted against your Lord,
whom indeed the nations worshipped,
and the uncircumcised admired,
and the foreigners glorified,

over whom Pilate washed his hands.
But as for you—
you killed this one at the time of the great
feast.

93 Therefore, the feast of unleavened bread
has become bitter to you
just as it was written:
"You will eat unleavened bread with bitter
herbs."
Bitter to you are the nails which you made
pointed.
Bitter to you is the tongue which you sharp-
ened.
Bitter to you are the false witnesses whom
you brought forward.
Bitter to you are the fetters which you prepared.
Bitter to you are the scourges which you wove.
Bitter to you is Judas whom you furnished
with pay.
Bitter to you is Herod whom who followed.
Bitter to you is Caiaphas whom you obeyed.
Bitter to you is the gall which you made
ready.
Bitter to you is the vinegar which you pro-
duced.
Bitter to you are the thorns which you
plucked.
Bitter to you are your hands which you
bloodied,
when you killed your Lord
in the midst of Jerusalem.

94 Pay attention, all families of the nations, and
observe!
An extraordinary murder has taken place
in the center of Jerusalem,
in the city devoted to God's law,
in the city of the Hebrews,
in the city of the prophets,
in the city thought of as just.
And who has been murdered?
And who is the murderer?
I am ashamed to give the answer,
but give it I must.
For if this murder had taken place at night,
or if he had been slain in a desert place,

it would be well to keep silent;
but it was in the middle of the main street,
even in the center of the city,
while all were looking on,
that the unjust murder of this just person took
place.

95 And thus he was lifted upon the tree,
and an inscription was affixed
identifying the one who had been murdered.
Who was he?
It is painful to tell,
but it is more dreadful not to tell.
Therefore, hear and tremble
because of him for whom the earth trembled.

96 The one who hung the earth in space, is himself hanged;
the one who fixed the heavens in place, is
himself impaled;
the one who firmly fixed all things, is himself firmly fixed to the tree.
The Lord is insulted,
God has been murdered,
the King of Israel has been destroyed
by the right hand of Israel.

97 O frightful murder!
O unheard of injustice!
The Lord is disfigured
and he is not deemed worthy of a cloak for
his naked body,
so that he might not be seen exposed.
For this reason the stars turned and fled,
and the day grew quite dark,
in order to hide that naked person hanging on
the tree,
darkening not the body of the Lord,
but the eyes of humans.

98 Yes, even though the people did not tremble,
the earth trembled instead;
although the people were not afraid,
the heavens grew frightened;
although the people did not tear their garments,
the angels tore theirs;
although the people did not lament,
the Lord thundered from heaven,
and the most high uttered his voice.

99 Why was it like this, O Israel?
    You did not tremble for the Lord.
    You did not fear for the Lord.
    You did not lament for the Lord,
    yet you lamented for your firstborn.
    You did not tear your garments at the cruci-
        fixion of the Lord,
    yet you tore your garments for your own who
        were murdered.
    You forsook the Lord;
    you were not found by him.
    You dashed the Lord to the ground;
    you, too, were dashed to the ground,
    and lie quite dead.

100 But he arose from the dead
    and mounted up to the heights of heaven.
    When the Lord had clothed himself with hu-
        manity,
    and had suffered for the sake of the sufferer,
    and had been bound for the sake of the im-
        prisoned,
    and had been judged for the sake of the con-
        demned,
    and buried for the sake of the one who was
        buried,

101 he rose up from the dead,
    and cried aloud with this voice:
    Who is he who contends with me?
    Let him stand in opposition to me.
    I set the condemned one free;
    I gave the dead one life;
    I raised up the one who had been entombed.

102 Who is my opponent?
    I, he says, am the Christ.
    I am the one who destroyed death,
    and triumphed over the enemy,
    and trampled Hades under foot,
    and bound the strong one,
    and carried off humanity
    to the heights of heaven,
    I, he says, am the Christ.

103 Therefore, come, all human families,
    you who have been befouled with sins,

and receive forgiveness for your sins.
I am your forgiveness,
I am the passover of your salvation,
I am the lamb which was sacrificed for you,
I am your ransom,
I am your light,
I am your savior,
I am your resurrection,
I am your king,
I am leading you up to the heights of heaven,
I will show you the eternal Father,
I will raise you up by my right hand.

104 This is the one who made the heaven and the
        earth,
    and who in the beginning created humans,
    who was proclaimed through the law and
        prophets,
    who became human via the virgin,
    who was hanged upon a tree,
    who was buried in the earth,
    who was resurrected from the dead,
    and who ascended to the heights of heaven,
    who sits at the right hand of the Father,
    who has authority to judge and to save every-
        thing,
    through whom the Father created everything
    from the beginning of the world to the end of
        the age.

105 This is the alpha and the omega.
    This is the beginning and the end—
    an indescribable beginning
    and an incomprehensible end.
    This is the Christ.
    This is the king.
    This is Jesus.
    This is the general.
    This is the Lord.
    This is the one who rose up from the dead.
    This is the one who sits at the right hand of
        the Father.
    He bears the Father
    and is borne by the Father,
    to whom be the glory
    and the power forever. Amen.

18. Tertullian: Answer to the Jews

Among Tertullian's writings (see Chapter 4) is a lengthy treatise against the Jews. Reproduced here is the first chapter, in which Tertullian states that following a public debate between a Jew and a Christian (Tertullian himself?), he decided to clarify matters at greater length in writing (possibly his public performance was not overly persuasive). His short discussion of Genesis 25 and Exodus 32 provides a nice, brief example of how Christians worked to turn the Scriptures of the Jews against them, claiming that God planned from the beginning to reject the Jews in favor of his new people, the Christians.

It happened very recently that a dispute was held between a Christian and a Jewish proselyte. Alternately with contentious cable they each spun out the day until evening. By the opposing din, moreover, of some partisans of the individuals, truth began to be overcast by a sort of cloud. It was therefore our pleasure that that which, owing to the confused noise of disputation, could be less fully elucidated point by point, should be more carefully looked into, and that the pen should determine, for reading purposes, the questions handled.

For the occasion, indeed, of claiming Divine grace even for the Gentiles derived a preeminent fitness from this fact, that the man who set up to vindicate God's Law as his own was of the Gentiles, and not a Jew of the stock of the Israelites. For this fact—that Gentiles are admissible to God's Law—is enough to prevent Israel from priding himself on the notion that the Gentiles are accounted as a little drop of a bucket, or else as dust out of a threshing-floor: although we have God himself as an adequate engager and faithful promiser, in that he promised to Abraham that "in his seed should be blest all nations of the earth";[1] and that out of the womb of Rebecca "two peoples and two nations were about to proceed,"[2]—

of course those of the Jews, that is, of Israel; and of the Gentiles, that is ours. Each, then, was called a *people* and a *nation*; lest, from the nuncupative appellation, any should dare to claim for himself the privilege of grace. For God ordained "two peoples and two nations" as about to proceed out of the womb of one woman: nor did grace make distinction in the nuncupative appellation, but in the order of birth; to the effect that, which ever was to be prior in proceeding from the womb, should be subjected to "the less," that is, the posterior. For thus unto Rebecca did God speak: "Two nations are in thy womb, and two peoples shall be divided from thy bowels; and people shall overcome people, and the greater shall serve the less."[3] Accordingly, since the *people* or *nation* of the Jews is anterior in time, and "greater" through the grace of primary favor in the Law, whereas ours is understood to be "less" in the age of times, as having in the last era of the world attained the knowledge of divine mercy: beyond doubt, through the edict of the divine utterance, the *prior* and "greater" people—that is, the Jewish—must

---

[1] Gen 22:18.
[2] Gen 25:23.
[3] Gen 25:23.

Tertullian: "Answers to the Jews," from *The Ante-Nicene Fathers*; vol. 3, *Latin Christianity: Its Founder, Tertullian*, ed. A. Cleveland. Reprinted; 2d ed. Grand Rapids, Mich.: Eerdmans, 1989.

necessarily serve the "less"; and the "less" people—that is, the Christian—overcome the "greater." For, withal, according to the memorial records of the divine Scriptures, the *people* of the Jews—that is, the more ancient—quite forsook God, and did degrading service to idols, and, abandoning the Divinity, was surrendered to images; while "the people" said to Aaron, "Make us gods to go before us."[4] And when the gold out of the necklaces of the women and the rings of the men had been wholly smelted by fire, and there had come forth a calf-like head, to this figment Israel with one consent (abandoning God) gave honor, saying, "These are the gods who brought us from the land of Egypt."[5] For thus, in the later times in which kings were governing them, did they again, in conjunction with Jeroboam, worship golden kine, and groves, and enslave themselves to Baal. Whence is proved that they have ever been depicted, out of the volume of the divine Scriptures, as guilty of the crime of idolatry; whereas our "less"—that is, posterior—*people*, quitting the idols which formerly it used slavishly to serve, has been converted to the same God from whom Israel, as we have above related, had departed. For thus has the "less"—that is, posterior—*people* overcome the "greater people," while it attains the grace of divine favor, from which Israel has been divorced.

---

[4]Exod 32:1, 23.
[5]Exod 32:4.

Chapter 6

The Diversity of Early Christianity

Writings Later Deemed Heretical

Arguably the most significant breakthrough in the modern understanding of early Christianity is the realization that, contrary to what had earlier been thought, this religion was exceptionally diverse. The older, traditional view (which prevailed till the mid-twentieth century) was that Christianity was basically monolithic, that there was one dominant form of Christianity reflected in the beliefs, practices, and ethics of most Christians everywhere throughout the first three centuries, a form of Christianity that was then ratified by the great church councils of the fourth century, which were organized principally to work out some of the more complicated details. To be sure, it was recognized that there were other "nonorthodox" views represented by scattered groups of "heretics," but these were seen as fringe groups with little historical significance.

In this traditional understanding of early Christianity, the term "orthodoxy" (from two Greek words meaning "correct belief" or "right doctrine") referred to the views promoted by Jesus and his apostles and subscribed to by a solid and pervasive core of the Christian church from the earliest of times; "heresies" (from a Greek word meaning "choice") comprised marginal groups that had willfully chosen to corrupt and depart from the true faith.

As already pointed out in Chapter 1, many scholars now recognize that this traditional understanding does not conform to historical realities. There were, in fact, numerous Christian groups in the second and third centuries, with a wide range of beliefs and practices. Each of these groups claimed to represent the original teachings of Jesus and his apostles; most of them had writings allegedly written by the apostles to sustain their claims. But, in the struggle to acquire the greatest number of adherents, only one of these groups "won out." It was this group that then deemed itself orthodox and marginalized every other group as heretical, insisting that it had held the majority position all along, maintaining that its views, and only its views, went back to the teachings of Jesus' apostles, and writing the history of its own movement as if it had been the only significant form of Christianity from the beginning (thus the *Ecclesiastical History* of Eusebius, who stood within this "orthodox" line).

Why did the "nonorthodox" Christians not simply read their New Testaments and realize that the "orthodox" views were right? In addressing this question, we need always to remember that the final collection of books that we call the "New Testament"—books also attributed to Jesus' apostles—was not yet in existence during this period. In fact, the decision concerning which books to include in the collection was largely made as a *result* of the struggles to determine which form of Christianity was "true" (= orthodox) and which ones were "false" (= heretical) (see Chapter 9). Before these books were collected into a canon that was to be authoritative for all Christians everywhere, there was a diversity of belief and practice that makes the varieties of Christianity today look altogether tame by comparison.

Throughout the second and third centuries, for example, there were Christians who believed that there was not just one God, but two; others believed in as many as twelve, or thirty-six, or 365. Whereas many Christians believed that the true God had created the world, others claimed that God was not the Creator and that he had never had any dealings with the world; for them, it had been created by an evil deity or group of deities. While many Christians accepted the Jewish Scriptures as the true word of God to be interpreted and followed literally, others insisted they were to be read allegorically, and yet others argued that they were not to be read at all, since they had been inspired by the Jewish God, who was not the one true God. Throughout this period we know of Christians who believed that Jesus was divine but not human, others who believed he was human but not divine, others who believed that he was two different creatures, one divine and one human, and yet others who believed he was one being, simultaneously both divine *and* human. There were some Christians who believed that Jesus had died for the sins of the world, other Christians who said that Jesus' death had nothing to do with the sins of the world, and yet others who said that he had never died. Second- and third-century Christianity was diverse in the extreme.

As already pointed out, all of the early Christian groups that maintained these various points of view had writings that authorized, explicated, or simply assumed them; many of these writings claimed to be written by apostles. Unfortunately, almost all of the "nonorthodox" writings have disappeared from memory; many of them were destroyed after one form of Christianity assumed such overwhelming dominance in the fourth century; many others simply passed out of use and were lost. During modern times, however, a number of these writings have been accidentally discovered. Far and away the most dramatic discovery occurred in 1945, when a bedouin digging for fertilizer near the village of Nag Hammadi, Egypt, uncovered a large earthenware jar containing thirteen leather-bound volumes. As scholars soon discovered, the papyrus leaves of these books contained some fifty-two documents, almost all of them produced by "nonorthodox" Gnostic Christians (on what such Christians believed, see pp. 144–145). The texts were written in Coptic, an ancient form of Egyptian, but they were clearly translations of works that had originally been composed in Greek. And even though the volumes themselves were manufactured in the fourth century, the treatises they contained were written much earlier. Some of them were already known, but by name only, from the writings of the antiheretical church writers of the second and third centuries. In other words, this cache included texts used by early Gnostic Christian groups that were later deemed heretical.

There continue to be debates over how these texts, now commonly called the Nag Hammadi Library, came to be hidden in an earthenware jar in the wilderness. Since an ancient Christian monastery was located nearby, many scholars have assumed that when such writings were proscribed in the late fourth century (i.e., when the contours of the New Testament canon were becoming fixed; see Chapter 9), resident monks who revered these books, or at least wanted to keep them intact, decided to hide rather than destroy them, possibly for later use (though the matter is hotly debated).

A selection of these texts is provided in this chapter, along with several other writings used widely among other, nongnostic forms of Christianity. It should be emphasized, however, that even with the new additions to our collections of "nonorthodox" texts, our knowledge of various early forms of Christianity is lamentably incomplete; this is particularly to be regretted since many scholars now recognize that in the second and third centuries, some regions of the Mediterranean were more or less dominated by these forms of Christianity, rather than the form that came to hold almost universal sway by the fourth century. A case in point involves the churches that followed the teachings of a second-century thinker and evangelist named Marcion. According to his opponents, Marcion's churches were nearly ubiquitous throughout large portions of Asia Minor. Unfortunately, all of the writings of Marcion and his followers are completely lost, except as they are quoted by his opponents among the "orthodox" (for some of Marcion's views, see Chapter 7).

The nonorthodox texts that have survived, however, do make for very interesting reading and provide a glimpse, at least, into the wide-ranging and rich diversity of the early Christian movement. The following selection organizes and introduces the surviving works into two major groups, Jewish-Christian and Gnostic-Christian.

For Further Reading

Bauer, Walter. *Orthodoxy and Heresy in Earliest Christianity*, ed. Robert Kraft and Gerhard Krodel, tr. Robert Kraft et al. Philadelphia: Fortress, 1971.

Elliott, J. K., ed. *The Apocryphal New Testament.* Oxford: Clarendon, 1993.

Hennecke, Edgar. *The New Testament Apocrypha*, 2 vols., ed. W. Schneemelcher, tr. R. McL. Wilson. 3rd ed. Louisville: Westminster/John Knox, 1991.

Klijn, A. F. J. *Jewish-Christian Gospel Tradition.* Leiden: E. J. Brill, 1992.

Layton, Bentley. *The Gnostic Scriptures.* Garden City, N.Y.: Doubleday, 1987.

Pagels, Elaine. *The Gnostic Gospels.* New York: Random House, 1976.

Robinson, James M., ed. *The Nag Hammadi Library in English.* 3rd ed. San Francisco: HarperSanFrancisco, 1988.

Rudolph, Kurt. *Gnosis: The Nature and History of Gnosticism*, tr. and ed. by R. McL. Wilson. San Francisco: HarperSanFrancisco, 1983.

JEWISH-CHRISTIAN TEXTS: INTRODUCTION

Since Jesus and his followers were all Jews, it is no surprise that some form of Jewish-Christianity was dominant throughout much of the first century. The earliest Christians kept the Jewish law as interpreted by Jesus and insisted that their converts do so as well (cf. Matt 5:17–20). Soon, though, the religion became predominantly Gentile, largely the result of the work of such missionaries as Paul, who was himself a Jew but who was dedicated to evangelizing pagans. Paul insisted that pagan converts did not need to become Jewish in order to be full-fledged members of the Christian church. The nature of the religion shifted as a result of such views, most Christians understanding themselves to be distinct from Judaism, which was itself seen, then, as misguided at best and demonic at worst (see Chapter 5).

But there were Jews who continued to convert to Christianity, even after the end of the first century. Many of these retained their Jewishness and believed that in doing so they were following the teachings of Jesus and the examples set by his apostles, especially the disciple Peter and Jesus' own brother James, the leader of the Christian church in Jerusalem. Jewish-Christian groups were found in various parts of the Mediterranean, though we know of them best in the area in and around Palestine. Many of them did not look favorably upon Paul and his teachings; most of them revered Moses and kept the laws of circumcision, kosher foods, and sabbath observance that he gave; some were known to pray towards the holy city Jerusalem three times a day and to follow other Jewish customs.

At least one of these groups was said to appeal to a Hebrew Gospel, allegedly written by Matthew, as the chief authority for their views. This Gospel was different from the Matthew that was eventually included in the New Testament in that it lacked what are now the first two chapters. For these Jewish-Christians did not think that Jesus was miraculously born of a virgin; he was a flesh-and-blood human being, with a nature and birth like all other humans. Even so, Jesus was special before God: as the most righteous person on earth, he had been adopted by God, at his baptism, to be his son, the messiah who would save his people by dying for their sins.

Other Jewish-Christian groups revered yet other Gospels, as seen in the readings that follow; some of these groups came to be influenced by still other forms of Christianity over a period of time. Some Jewish-Christians, for example, evidently adopted perspectives found more widely among Gnostics. Our sources for all these groups are quite sparse. The following are among the most important ones that survive.

19. The Gospel According to the Ebionites

The *Gospel According to the Ebionites* does not survive intact but exists only in quotations by an opponent of the Jewish Christians, the fourth-century heresy hunter Epiphanius of Salamis. These quotations, however, give us a good idea of what the entire Gospel must have looked like. It was written in Greek and represented a kind of harmony of the Gospels of Matthew, Mark, and Luke. This can be seen most clearly in the account of the voice at Jesus' baptism. In the three canonical versions, the voice says slightly different things. These differences are harmonized, however, in the *Gospel According to the Ebionites*, where the voice comes from heaven three times, saying something slightly different on each occasion (corresponding to the words found in each of the Synoptics).

Some of the Ebionites' distinctive concerns were embodied in their Gospel. For example, since they believed that Jesus' sacrifice on the cross had put an end to all animal sacrifices in fulfillment of the Mosaic law, they appear to have abstained from meat. Their convictions on this score are evident in their Gospel's account of the diet of John the Baptist, where the canonical statement that John ate locusts and wild honey is modified by the change of one letter, so that now the Baptist, in anticipation of the Ebionites themselves, maintains a strictly vegetarian cuisine, eating *pancakes* and wild honey.

It is difficult to assign a date to this Gospel, but since it betrays a knowledge of Matthew, Mark, and Luke and presupposes a thriving community of Jewish Christians, it is perhaps best to locate it sometime in the early or mid-second century. The following extracts are all that remain of the Gospel and are drawn from Epiphanius's work, *The Medicine Chest*, Book 30.

1. And there was a man named Jesus, and he was about thirty years old; he has chosen us and he came into Capernaum and entered into the house of Simon, surnamed Peter, and he opened his mouth and said, "As I walked by the sea of Tiberias, I chose John and James, the sons of Zebedee, and Simon and Andrew and Thaddaeus and Simon Zelotes, and Judas Iscariot; you also, Matthew, when you were sitting at the receipt of custom, did I call and you followed me. According to my intention you shall be twelve apostles for a testimony to Israel."

2. And it came to pass when John baptized, that the Pharisees came to him and were baptized, and all Jerusalem also. He had a garment of camels' hair, and a leathern girdle about his loins. And his meat was wild honey, which tasted like manna, formed like cakes of oil.[1]

3. The beginning of their Gospel reads thus: "It came to pass in the days of Herod, King of Judaea, that John came and baptized with the baptism of repentance in the river Jordan; he is said to be from the tribe of Aaron and a son of Zacharias the priest and of Elizabeth, and all went out to him."

4. And after many other words it goes on: "After the people had been baptized, Jesus came also, and was baptized by John. And as he came out of the water, the heavens opened, and he saw the Holy Spirit descending in the form of a dove and entering into him. And a voice was heard from heaven, 'You are my beloved Son, and in you am I well pleased.' And again, 'This day have I begotten you.' And suddenly a great light shone in that place. And John, seeing him, said, 'Who

[1]Matt 3:4–5; Mark 1:5–6.

are you, Lord?' Then a voice was heard from heaven, 'This is my beloved Son, in whom I am well pleased.' Threat John fell at his feet and said, 'I pray you, Lord, baptize me.' But he would not, saying, 'Suffer it, for thus it is fitting that all should be accomplished.'[2]

5. They also deny that he is a man, basing their assertion on the word which he said when he was told: "Behold your mother and your brethren stand outside." "Who is my mother and who are my brethren?" And he stretched forth his hand toward his disciples and said, "My brethren and my mother and sisters are those who do the will of my Father."[3]

6. They say that he is not begotten by God the Father but created like one of the archangels, being greater than they. He rules over the angels and the beings created by God and he

came and declared, as the gospel used by them records: "I have come to abolish the sacrifices: if you do not cease from sacrificing, the wrath [of God] will not cease from weighing upon you."

7. Those who reject meat have inconsiderately fallen into error and said, "I have no desire to eat the flesh of this Paschal Lamb with you." They leave the true order of words and distort the word which is clear to all from the connection of words and make the disciples say: "Where do you want us to prepare for you to eat the Passover."[4] To which he replied, "I have no desire to eat the flesh of this Paschal Lamb with you."

---

[2]Matt 3:13–17; Mark 1:9–11; Luke 3:21–22
[3]Matt 12:46–50; Mark 3:31–35; Luke 8:19–21
[4]Matt 26:17; Mark 14:12.

---

20. The Letter of Peter to James and Its Reception

The "Letter of Peter to James" is one of a number of early Christians writings pseudonymously written in the name of Jesus' disciple, Simon Peter (cf. the Gospel of Peter and the Apocalypses of Peter, Chapters 7 and 8). It does not survive as an independently transmitted letter but exists only as the preface to the "Homilies of Clement," a collection of legendary stories and sermons of Clement of Rome (see reading 21). The account of its "Reception" by James, the brother of Jesus and the leader of the church in Jerusalem, is also part of this preface. The date of the composition of these works is difficult to determine, but they are probably to be situated in the early third century.

In the letter, Peter urges James to pass along the accompanying sermons carefully, and only to those who are worthy to receive them. The clear concern is that Peter's teachings not be corrupted by those who have a different understanding of the truth. Both the Letter and the Reception are Jewish-Christian in their orientation, as seen in their em-

---

The Letter of Peter to James, from *New Testament Apocrypha*, vol. 2; ed. Wilhelm Schneemelcher, 2d ed. Cambridge/Louisville: Lutterworth Press/Westminster John Knox Press, 1991. Used with permission of Lutterworth Press and Westminster John Knox Press.

phasis on emulating the actions of Moses, on keeping the Law, and on opposing the person Peter calls "the man who is my enemy," commonly understood to be none other than the apostle Paul (cf. Gal 2:11–14), who taught that salvation comes to all people, Jew and Gentile, *apart* from following the Law of Moses, and who urged Gentiles *not* to be circumcised (see Galatians). This Pauline notion stood in sharp contrast to the views of Jewish Christians like the Ebionites, as seen here, for example, in the insistence by James (the brother of Jesus himself!) that only "one who has been circumcised is a believing Christian."

1 Peter to James, the lord and bishop of the holy church: Peace be with you always from the Father of all through Jesus Christ.

2 Knowing well that you, my brother, eagerly take pains about what is for the mutual benefit of us all, I earnestly beseech you not to pass on to any one of the Gentiles the books of my preachings which I (here) forward to you, nor to any one of our own tribe before probation. But if some one of them has been examined and found to be worthy, then you may hand them over to him in the same way as Moses handed over his office of a teacher to the seventy.

3 Wherefore also the fruit of his caution is to be seen up to this day. For those who belong to his people preserve everywhere the same rule in their belief in the one God and in their line of conduct, the Scriptures with their many senses being unable to incline them to assume another attitude.

4 Rather they attempt, on the basis of the rule that has been handed down to them, to harmonise the contradictions of the Scriptures, if haply some one who does not know the traditions is perplexed by the ambiguous utterances of the prophets.

5 On this account they permit no one to teach unless he first learn how the Scriptures should be used. Wherefore there obtain amongst them one God, one law, and one hope.

2 In order now that the same may also take place among us, hand over the books of my preachings in the same mysterious way to our seventy brethren that they may prepare those who are candidates for positions as teachers.

2 For if we do not proceed in this way, our word of truth will be split into many options. This I do not know as a prophet, but I have already the beginning of the evil before me.

3 For some from among the Gentiles have rejected my lawful preaching and have preferred a lawless and absurd doctrine of the man who is my enemy.

4 And indeed some have attempted, whilst I am still alive, to distort my words by interpretations of many sorts, as if I taught the dissolution of the law and, although I was of this opinion, did not express it openly. But that may God forbid!

5 For to do such a thing means to act contrary to the law of God which was made known by Moses and was confirmed by our Lord in its everlasting continuance. For he said: "The heaven and the earth will pass away, but one jot or one title shall not pass away from the law."[1]

6 This he said that everything might come to pass. But those persons who, I know not how, allege that they are at home in my thoughts wish to expound the words which they have heard of me better than I myself who spoke them. To those whom they instruct they say that this is my opinion, to which indeed I never gave a thought.

7 But if they falsely assert such a thing while I am still alive, how much more after my death will those who come later venture to do so?

3 In order now that such a thing may not happen I earnestly beseech you not to pass on the books of my preachings which I send you to any one of our own tribe or to any foreigner before probation, but if some one is examined and found

---

[1]Matt 24:35; 5:18.

to be worthy, let them then be handed over in the way

2 in which Moses handed over his office of a teacher to the seventy, in order that they may preserve the dogmas and extend farther the rule of the truth, interpreting everything in accordance with our tradition and not being dragged into error through ignorance and uncertainty in their minds to bring others into the like pit of destruction.

3 What seems to me to be necessary I have now indicated to you. And what you, my lord, deem to be right, do you carry fittingly into effect. Farewell.

The Reception of the Letter

1 Now when James had read the epistle he called the elders together, read it to them and said: "As is necessary and proper, our Peter has called our attention to the fact that we must be cautious in the matter of the truth, that we should pass on the books of his preachings that have been forwarded to us not indiscriminately, but only to a good and religious candidate for the position of a teacher, a man who as one who has been circumcised is a believing Christian, and indeed that we should not pass on all the books to him at once, so that, if he shows indiscretion in handling the first, he may not be entrusted with the others.

2 He ought therefore to be proved for not less than six years. Thereafter, according to the way of Moses, let him be brought to a river or a fountain where there is living water and the regeneration of the righteous takes place; not that he may swear, for that is not permitted, but he should be enjoined to stand by the water and to vow, as we also ourselves were made to do at the time of our regeneration, to the end that we might sin no more.

2 And let him say: 'As witness I invoke heaven, earth, and water, in which everything is comprehended, and also in addition the all-pervading air, without which I am unable to breathe, that I shall always be obedient to him who hands over to me the books of the preachings and shall not

pass on to any one in any way the books which he may give to me, that I shall neither copy them nor give a copy of them nor allow them to come into the hands of a copyist, neither shall I myself do this nor shall I do it through another, and not in any other way, through cunning or tricks, through keeping them carelessly, through depositing them with another or through underhand agreement, nor in any other manner or by means of any other artifice will I pass them on to a third party.

2 Only if I have proved someone to be worthy—proving him as I myself have been proved, or even more, in no case for less than six years—if he is a religious and good candidate for the position of a teacher, I will hand them over to him as I have received them and certainly in agreement with my bishop.

3 Otherwise, though he be either my son or a brother or a friend or any other relation, if he is unworthy, I shall keep information away from him since it does not befit him.

2 I shall allow myself neither to be frightened by persecutions nor to be deceived by gifts. And even if I should ever come to the conviction that the books of the preachings which have been handed to me do not contain the truth, then also I shall not pass them on but shall hand them back.

3 When I am on a journey, I shall carry with me all the books that are in my possession. And if I purpose not to take them with me, I shall not leave them behind in my house, but shall consign them to the care of my bishop, who is of the same faith and of like extraction.

4 If I am sick and see death before me, I shall, if I am childless, proceed in the same way. I shall do the like if at the time of my death my son is not worthy or is not yet of age. I shall deposit the books with my bishop that if, when my son has come of age, he should prove to be worthy of the trust that he may hand them over to him as a father's legacy according to the terms of the vow.

4 And that I shall proceed in this way, I again invoke as witnesses heaven, earth, and water, in which everything is comprehended, and also in addition the all-pervading air without which I am unable to breathe: I shall be obedient to him who hands over to me the books of the preachings, I shall keep them in every respect as I have vowed and even beyond that.

2 If now I observe the agreements, then will my portion be with the saints; but if I act against my vow, then may the universe and the all-pervading ether and God, who is over all and is mightier and more exalted than any other, be hostile to me.

3 And if even I should come to believe in another god, then I swear also by him, whether he now is or is not, that I shall not proceed otherwise. In addition to all that, if I am false to my word, I shall be accursed living and dead and suffer eternal punishment.' And thereupon let him partake of bread and salt with him who hands over the books to him."

5 When James had said this, the elders were pale with fright. Accordingly, observing that they feared greatly, James said, "Hear me, brethren and fellow-servants.

2 If we pass on the books to all without discrimination and if they are falsified by audacious people and are spoiled by interpretations— as indeed you have heard that some have already done—then it will come to pass that even those who earnestly seek the truth will always be led into error.

3 On this account it is better that we keep the books and, as we have said, hand them with all caution only to those who wish to live and to save others. But if any one, after that he has made such a vow, does not adhere to it, then will he rightly suffer eternal punishment.

4 For why should he not go to ruin who has been guilty of the corruption of others?" Then were the elders pleased with James's conclusion and said, "Praised be he who has foreseen all things and destined you to be our bishop." And when they had said this, we rose up and prayed to God the Father of all, to whom be glory for ever. Amen.

21. The Homilies of Clement

The "Homilies of Clement" is an example of a pseudonymous Christian writing produced in the name of a famous person living *after* the apostles: Clement, thought to be the third bishop of Rome at the end of the first century (for other examples, cf. 1 Clement in Chapter 10 and 2 Clement in Chapter 12). The Homilies comprise twenty legendary discourses allegedly delivered by Clement in Rome and sent to James of Jerusalem; in them Clement narrates his family background, his search for truth, and, principally, his travels to the East, where he meets Simon Peter, whom he then accompanies, observing his words, deeds, and controversies (especially with the magician Simon Magus).

As the following excerpts show, the Homilies embrace a Jewish-Christian perspective. Peter is shown to be the chief apostle, bearer of Christ's power and leader of Christ's

The Homilies of Clement, from *New Testament Apocrypha*, vol. 2; ed. Wilhelm Schneemelcher, 2d ed. Cambridge/ Louisville: Lutterworth Press/Westminster John Knox Press, 1991. Used with permission of Lutterworth Press and Westminster John Knox Press.

church; he claims ascendancy over his archrival, the magician Simon Magus, who is portrayed as the principal missionary to the Gentiles (and is sometimes, therefore, thought to be a cipher for the apostle Paul). Particularly striking are Peter's views of the relation of Jesus and Moses, the acceptance of either one of whom, he claims, can bring salvation.

The Homilies are closely related to another surviving work of the third century attributed to Clement, the *Recognitions*; both were evidently based on an earlier legendary account of Clement's travels that is now lost. The following excerpts follow the sequence of the chapters determined to be more likely original by master scholars.

Book 1

18 (Peter says to Clement:) The will of God has fallen into oblivion for many sorts of reasons,

2 above all in consequence of inadequate instruction, careless upbringing, bad company, unseemly conversation and erroneous statements.

3 Thence there comes ignorance, and there come also dissoluteness, unbelief, unchastity, avarice, vanity, and innumerable vices of this kind, which have occupied the world as it were a house which, like a cloud of smoke, they have filled; they have thus made muddy the eyes of those who dwell in the house and have prevented them from looking up and recognising the Creator God from his works and inferring his will.

4 Therefore the friends of truth who are in the house must cry from the depth of their heart for help for their truth-seeking souls, that if someone is outside the smoke-filled house, he may come and open the door, so that the sunlight from outside may invade the house and that the smoke within may be dissipated.

19 Now the man who can help here, I call the true prophet; he alone can enlighten the souls of people that with their own eyes they may be able to see the way to eternal salvation.

2 That is not possible in any other way, as indeed you yourself know; only just now you said

3 that every view has its friends and opponents and counts as true or false according to the qualification of its advocate, and in consequence different opinions do not come to light as what they are, but receive the semblance of worth or worthlessness from their advocates.

4 Wherefore the world needs the godly efforts of the true prophet that he may describe things to us as they actually are and tell us what we have to believe regarding everything.

5 First of all then we must examine the prophet with all seriousness and arrive at the certainty that he is a true prophet,

6 and then we should believe him in all matters and ought not to quibble at the least small particular in his teaching, but should accept all his words as valid, as it may appear in faith, yet actually on the ground of the sound examination that we have made. . . .

15 (Peter:) Now that he might bring people to the true knowledge of all things, God, who himself is a single person, made a clear separation by way of pairs of opposites, in that he, who from the beginning was the one and only God, made heaven and earth, day and night, life and death.

2 Among these he has gifted free-will to humans alone so that they may be just or unjust. For them he has also permuted the appearing of the pairs of opposites, in that he has set before their eyes first the small and then the great, first the world and then eternity, this world being transitory, but the one to come eternal; so also ignorance precedes knowledge.

3 In the same way he has ordered the bearers of the prophetic spirit. For since the present is womanly and like a mother gives birth to children, but the future, manly time on the other hand takes up its children in the manner of a father,

4 therefore there come first the prophets of this world (who prophesy falsely, and) those who have the knowledge of eternal things follow them because they are sons of the coming age.

5 Had the God-fearing known this secret, then they would never have been able to go wrong, and also they would even now have known that Simon, who now confounds all, is merely a helpmate of the feeble left hand (of God, i.e., the evil one).

16 As regards the disposition of the prophetic mission the case is as follows. As God, who is one person, in the beginning made first the heaven and then the earth, as it were on the right hand and on the left, he has also in the course of time established all the pairs of opposites. But with humans it is no longer so—rather does he invert the pairs.

2 For as with him the first is the stronger and the second the weaker, so with humans we find the opposite, first the weaker and then the stronger.

3 Thus directly from Adam, who was made in the image of God, there issued as the first son the unrighteous Cain and as the second the righteous Abel.

4 And in the same way from the man who amongst you is called Deucalion two symbols of the Spirit, the unclean and the clean, were sent out, the black raven and after it the white dove.

5 And also from Abraham, the progenitor of our people, there issued two sons, the older Ishmael and then Isaac, who was blessed by God.

6 Again from this same Isaac there sprang two sons, the godless Esau and the godly Jacob.

7 Likewise there came first, as first-born into the world, the high priest (Aaron) and then the law-giver (Moses).

17 The syzygy associated with Elijah, which ought to have come, willingly held off to another time, being resolved to take its place when the occasion arises.

2 Then in the same way there came first he who was among them that are born of women and only after that did he who belongs to the sons of men appear as the second.

3 Following up this disposition it would be possible to recognise where Simon belongs, who as first and before me went to the Gentiles, and where I belong, I who came after him and followed him as the light follows darkness, knowledge ignorance, and healing sickness.

4 Thus then, as the true prophet has said, a false gospel must first come from an impostor and only then, after the destruction of the holy place, can a true gospel be sent forth for the correction of the sects that are to come.

5 And thereafter in the end Antichrist must first come again and only afterwards must Jesus, our actual Christ, appear and then, with the rising of eternal light, everything that belongs to darkness must disappear.

18 Since now, as has been said, many do not know this conformity of the syzygies with law, they do not know who this Simon, my forerunner, is. For were it known, no one would believe him. But now, as he remains unknown, confidence is wrongly placed in him.

2 Thus he who does what haters do finds love; the enemy is received as a friend; people long for him who is death as a bringer of salvation; although he is fire, he is regarded as light; although he is a cheat, he obtains a hearing as a proclaimer of truth. . . .

Book 7

1 In Tyre not a few people from the neighbourhood and numerous inhabitants of the city came to Peter and cried to him: "May God have mercy upon us through you, and may he through you bring us healing!" And Peter, having mounted a high rock that he might be seen of all, greeted them in a godly way and began as follows:

2 "God, who has made heaven and the universe, is not wanting in power to save those who desire to be saved. . . .

4 "And what is pleasing to God is this, that we pray to him and ask from him as the one who dispenses everything according to a righteous law, that we keep away from the table of devils, that we do not eat dead flesh, that we do not touch blood, that we wash ourselves clean from all defilement.

3 "Let the rest be said to you also in one word, as the God-fearing Jews heard it, while you show yourselves, many as you are, of one mind: 'What good a person wishes for himself, let him confer the same also on his neighbor!'. . ."

5 After they had thus been instructed for some days by Peter and had been healed, they were baptized. At the time of his other miraculous deeds the rest sat beside one another in the middle of the market-place in sackcloth and ashes and did penance for their former sins.

2 When the Sidonians heard this, they did likewise; and because they themselves were not able on account of their diseases to come to Peter, they sent a petition to him.

3 After he had stayed for some days in Tyre and had instructed all the inhabitants and freed them from numerous sufferings, Peter founded a church and appointed a bishop for them from the number of the elders who were accompanying him; then he set out for Sidon.

6 When Peter entered Sidon, the people brought many sick folk in beds and set them down before him.

2 And he said to them: "Do not on any account believe that I, a mortal man, myself subject to many sufferings, can do anything to heal you! But I greatly desire to tell you in what way you can be delivered. . . .

7 "For I mention to you two ways, showing you in the first place in what way people fall into misfortune and in the second place in what way under God's guidance they are delivered.

2 "The way of those who perish is broad and very easy, but it leads straight away to misfortune; the way of those who are delivered is narrow and rough, but in the end it leads to salvation those who have taken its burdens upon themselves. Before these two ways there stand belief and unbelief. . . ."

8 Such were the addresses that Peter gave in Sidon. There also within a few days many were converted and believed and were healed. So Peter founded a church there and enthroned as bishop one of the elders who were accompanying him. He then left Sidon.

9 Immediately after the arrival of Peter in Berytus an earthquake took place; and people came to Peter saying: "Help, for we greatly fear that we shall all together perish!"

2 Then Simon dared, along with Appion, Annubion, Athenodorous and his other comrades, to turn against Peter in the presence of all the people: "Flee, people from this man;

3 "for he is a magician—you may believe me—and has himself occasioned this earthquake and has caused these diseases to frighten you, as if he himself was a god!"

4 And many other false charges of this sort did Simon and his followers bring against Peter, suggesting that he possessed superhuman power.

5 As soon as the multitude gave him a hearing, Peter with a smile and an impressive directness spoke the words: "Oh people, I admit that, God willing, I am capable of doing what these men here say and in addition am ready, if you will not hear my words, to turn your whole city upside down."

10 Now when the multitude took alarm and readily promised to carry out his commands, Peter said: "Let no one of you associate with these magicians or in any way have intercourse with them."

2 Scarcely had the people heard this summons when without delay they laid hold of cudgels and pursued these fellows till they had driven them completely out of the city. . . .

12 After he had stayed for several days with the inhabitants of Berytus, had made many conversant with the worship of the one God, and had baptized them, Peter enthroned as bishop one of the elders who were accompanying him and then journeyed to Byblus.

3 On coming there he learned that Simon had not waited for him even for a single day, but had started at once for Tripolis. Accordingly Peter remained a few days with the people of Byblus, effected not a few healings, and gave instruction in the Holy Scriptures. He then journeyed in the track of Simon to Tripolis, being resolved to pursue him rather than to make room for him.

Book 8

1 Along with Peter there entered into Tripolis people from Tyre, Sidon, Berytus, Byblus and neighboring places, who were eager to learn, and in numbers that were not smaller, people from the city itself crowded about him desiring to get to know him. . . .

4 Astonished at this eagerness of the multitudes, Peter answered: "You see, beloved brethren, how the words of our Lord are manifestly fulfilled. For I remember how he said: 'Many will come from east and west, from north and south, and repose in the bosom of Abraham, Isaac and Jacob.'[1] Nevertheless 'many are called, but few are chosen.'[2]

2 "In their coming in response to the call so much is fulfilled.

3 "But since it rests not with them but with God who has called them and permitted them to come, on this account alone they have no reward. . . .

4 "But if after being called they do what is good, and that rests with them themselves, for that they will receive their reward.

5 "For even the Hebrews who believe in Moses . . . are not saved unless they abide by what has been said to them.

2 "For their believing in Moses lies not with a decision of their own will but with God, who said to Moses. 'Behold, I come to you in a pillar of cloud that the people may hear me speaking to you and believe for ever!'[3] Since then it is granted to the Hebrews and to them that are called from the Gentiles to believe the teachers of truth, while it is left to the personal decision of each individual whether he will perform good deeds, the reward rightly falls to those who do well.

4 "For neither Moses nor Jesus would have needed to come if of themselves people had been willing to perceive the way of discretion. And there is no salvation in believing in teachers and calling them lords.

6 "Therefore is Jesus concealed from the Hebrews who have received Moses as their teacher, and Moses hidden from those who believe Jesus.

2 "For since through both one and the same teaching becomes known, God accepts those who believe in one of them.

3 "But belief in a teacher has as its aim the doing of what God has ordered.

4 "That this is the case our Lord himself declares, saying: 'I confess to you, Father of heaven and earth, that you have hidden this from the wise and elder, but have revealed it to simpletons and infants.'[4] Thus has God himself hidden the teacher from some since they know beforehand what they ought to do, and has revealed him to others since they know not what they have to do.

7 "Thus the Hebrews are not condemned because they did not know Jesus . . . provided only they act according to the instructions of Moses and do not injure him whom they did not know.

2 "And again the offspring of the Gentiles are not judged, who . . . have not known Moses, provided only they act according to the words of Jesus and thus do not injure him whom they did not know.

3 "Also it profits nothing if many describe their teachers as their lords, but do not do what it befits servants to do.

4 "Therefore our Lord Jesus said to one who again and again called him Lord, but at the same time did not abide by any of his commands. 'Why call me Lord and not do what I say?'[5] For it is not speaking that can profit any one, but doing.

5 "In all circumstances goods works are needed; but if a person has been considered worthy to know both teachers as heralds of a single doctrine, then that one is counted rich in God. . . ."

---

[1]Matt 8:11.
[2]Matt 22:14.
[3]Exod 19:9.
[4]Matt 11:25; Luke 10:21.
[5]Matt 7:21; Luke 6:46.

GNOSTIC-CHRISTIAN TEXTS: INTRODUCTION

(See also the Apocalypse of Peter and the Second Treatise of the Great Seth in Chapter 7 and the Gospel of Thomas in Chapter 8)

Prior to the discovery of the Nag Hammadi Library, we were ill informed concerning the beliefs and practices of early Christian Gnostics, since virtually all of our information came from attacks leveled against them by their proto-orthodox opponents. An enemy can scarcely be trusted to provide a fair or accurate portrayal of one's views.

The discovery of the Nag Hammadi texts did not completely remedy the problem, however. For one thing, these texts do not themselves present a unified view of what Gnosticism was but represent a remarkable range of opinion and belief. Even more problematic, these documents do not purport to lay out what the Gnostics believed and practiced but *presuppose* such matters as the backdrop for what they do want to discuss. That is to say, these books were written by Gnostics for Gnostics and so do not go to any great lengths to explain what the authors and readers together assumed to be true (any more than an article on the sports page about the first game of the World Series explains the rules and history of baseball). Modern readers who want to know what Gnosticism was *about*, then, are compelled to read between the lines to try to reconstruct the underlying assumptions about the divine realm, the world, and the place of humanity in it, as well as to see what ritual practices and ethical systems were found among such groups.

As a result, scholars devoted to uncovering such matters continue to dispute rather basic issues, such as where Gnosticism came from, whether it was originally connected with Christianity, and what its various permutations were. It is generally agreed, however, that (a) the term Gnosticism can be applied to a wide range of religious groups, many of them Christian, that thrived in the second century of the common era and (b) that most of these groups stressed "knowledge" (= gnosis, hence the term "gnostic") as a way of salvation from this evil world, which was not created by the one true God.

More specifically, based on a careful reading of the Gnostics' texts themselves and the reports of their enemies (the church fathers who opposed them), it appears that the overarching views of most Gnostics may be summarized under the following, rather simplified, rubrics (these will be of assistance to you as you try to read through the various gnostic texts):

1. *The World.* Most Gnostics differentiated between "matter," which was evil, and "spirit," which was good. This world, as a material realm, was evil.
2. *The Divine Realm.* The true God did not, therefore, create this world. He was completely spirit. According to the myths that Gnostics told, in eternity past the true

God generated other divine offspring (often called "aeons") who themselves, often in pairs, reproduced offspring. A catastrophe occurred in the divine realm (called the "pleroma," meaning the "fullness"), as one of these divine beings (sometimes named "Sophia," Greek for "Wisdom") became separated off from the rest and spontaneously generated another divine being. The latter, born outside the pleroma, was evil. With his minions that also then came into being, he created the material world as a place of imprisonment for the one who had fallen from the pleroma. He is therefore known as the "Demiurge."

3. *Humans.* The aeon that had fallen was captured and imprisoned in this material world in the bodies of humans. Many humans have this spark of the divine within them. People with the spark have a longing to escape this world; those that do not are simply animals like other animals, destined to die and cease, then, to exist.

4. *Salvation.* The divine spark within humans can escape only by learning where it came from, how it got here, and how it can return. Deliverance from this material world, in other words, can come only by liberating knowledge (gnosis).

5. *The Divine Redeemer.* This knowledge, though, cannot be gained from within this world, since the world is evil; it must, therefore, be brought from the outside. In Christian forms of Gnosticism, the one who brings this knowledge is Christ, who comes from above to convey the gnosis necessary for salvation. Since he cannot really belong to this world, he was not actually born here. Some Gnostics maintained that Jesus only seemed to be a human, that is, that his body was a phantasm, physical in appearance only; others claimed that Christ was a divine aeon who temporarily inhabited the real body of the man Jesus, starting with his baptism, and who then left him at the end of his life, prior to his crucifixion, only to raise him from the dead and repossess him so as to convey his secret teachings after his resurrection.

6. *The Church.* Many Gnostics maintained that Christians who have faith in Christ and do good works can have some modicum of salvation after they die, but the real and glorious afterlife will come only to the Gnostics themselves, those who have the divine spark within and who have come to acquire the full knowledge of the secrets of salvation. These are the "elect."

7. *Ethics.* As a rule, Gnostics appear to have believed that since the human body was evil, it was to be treated harshly to facilitate the spirit's escape from it. These Gnostics, then, urged a rigorously ascetic style of life.

Several of the texts from Nag Hammadi represent explications of the myths that convey these views; these are probably to be allowed poetic license rather than taken as propositional truths or historical sketches of what "really" happened in the mythic past. Many of these are interpretations of the Jewish Scriptures, especially the opening chapters of Genesis, which provided fuel for the mythological imagination. Other texts are poetical reflections on the divine realm, the need for liberating knowledge, and the nature of the world or of the human place in it; yet others contain attacks on literal-minded Christians who failed to recognize the truth (see Chapter 7). The few gnostic texts that have survived in other places (i.e., outside of Nag Hammadi), also seem to share many of these basic perspectives.

22. The Secret Book of John

The Secret Book (sometimes called "Apocryphon") of John was one of the most remarkable discoveries of the Nag Hammadi Library. Cast as a postresurrection discussion of Jesus with his disciple, John the son of Zebedee, the book contains one of the clearest expositions of the gnostic myth of creation and redemption, an exposition designed, ultimately, to explain the existence of evil in the world and the path of escape for those who recognize their plight.

In intricate detail the account discusses the propagation of the divine realm from the one invisible, imperishable, incomprehensible God prior to creation and the tragic mistake of the aeon Sophia, who produced an offspring apart from her divine consort. The result was the monster Creator God Yaltabaoth (the God of the Bible), ultimately responsible for the creation of the world and humans in the image of God. Much of this part of the myth represents an exposition of Genesis 1–4. The tale continues with the appearance of Christ from above to provide the knowledge necessary for escape to the divine souls entrapped within mortal bodies.

Since this particular version of the gnostic myth was known, in a slightly different form, to the late-second-century church father Irenaeus, most scholars date the Secret Book of John sometime prior to 180 C.E. (N.B.: the brackets [] used in this text and in the ones that follow indicate places where the original words have been lost because of holes in the manuscript but have been reconstructed by modern editors. The bold-face numerals represent the page numbers of the Nag Hammadi tractate in which it is found.)

The teaching [of the savior], and [the revelation] of the mysteries, [and the] things hidden in silence, [even these things which] he taught John, [his] disciple.

[And] it happened one [day], when John, [the brother] of James—who are the sons of Zebedee—had come up to the temple, that a Pharisee named Arimanius approached him and said to him, "Where is your master [whom] you followed?" And he [said] to him, "He has gone to the [place] from which he came." The Pharisee [said to him, "With deception did this Nazarene] deceive you (pl.), and he filled [your ears with lies], and closed [your hearts (and) turned you] from the traditions [of your fathers."]

[When] I, [John], heard these things [I turned] away from the temple [to a desert place]. And I grieved [greatly in my heart saying], "How [then was] the savior [appointed], and why was he sent [in to the world] by [his Father, and who is his] Father who [sent him, and of what sort] is [that] aeon [to which we shall go?] For what did he [mean when he said to us], 'This aeon to [which you will go is of the] type of the [imperishable] aeon,' [but he did not teach] us concerning [the latter of what sort it is."]

Straightway, [while I was contemplating these things,] behold, the [heavens opened and] the whole creation [which is] below heaven shone, and [the world] was shaken. **2** [I was afraid, and behold I] saw in the light [a youth who stood] by me. While I looked [at him he became] like an old man. And he [changed his] likeness (again) becoming like a servant. There was [not a plurality] before me, but there was a [likeness] with multiple forms in the light, and the [likenesses] appeared through each other, [and] the [likeness] had three forms.

He said to me, "John, John, why do you doubt, or why [are you] afraid? You are not unfamiliar with this image, are you?—that is, do not [be] timid!—I am one who is [with you (pl.)] always. I [am that Father], I am the Mother, I am the Son. I am the undefiled and incorruptible one. Now [I have come to teach you] what is [and what was] and what will come to [pass], that [you may know the] things which are not revealed [and those which are revealed, and to teach you] concerning the [unwavering race of] the perfect [Man]. Now, [therefore, lift up] your [face, that] you may [receive] the things that I [shall teach you] today, [and] may [tell them to your] fellow spirits who [are from] the [unwavering] race of the perfect Man."

[And I asked] to [know it, and he said] to me, "The Monad [is a] monarchy with nothing above it. [It is he who exists] as [God] and Father of everything, [the invisible] One who is above [everything, who exists as] incorruption, which is [in the] pure light into which no [eye] can look.

"He [is the] invisible [Spirit] of whom it is not right [to think] of him as a god, or something similar. For he is more than a god, since there is nothing above him, for no one **3** lords it over him. [For he does] not [exist] in something inferior [to him, since everything] exists in him. [For it is he who establishes] himself. [He is eternal] since he does [not] need [anything]. For [he] is total perfection. [He] did not [lack anything] that he might be completed by [it; rather] he is always completely perfect in [light]. He is [illimitable]

since there is no one [prior to him] to set limits to him. He is unsearchable [since there] exists no one prior to him to [examine him. He is] immeasurable since there [was] no one [prior to him to measure] him. [He is invisible since no] one saw [him. He is eternal] since he [exists] eternally. He is [ineffable since] no one was able to comprehend him to speak [about him]. He is unnameable since [there is no one prior to him] to give [him] a name.

"He is [immeasurable light] which is pure, holy, [(and) immaculate]. He is ineffable [being perfect in] incorruptibility. (He is) [not] in perfection, nor in blessedness, nor in divinity, but he is far superior. He is not corporeal [nor] is he incorporeal. He is neither large [nor] is he small. [There is no] way to say, 'What is his quantity?' or, 'What [is his quality?'], for no one can [know him]. He is not someone among (other) [beings, rather he is] far superior. [Not] that [he is (simply) superior], but his essence does not [partake] in the aeons nor in time. For he who partakes in [an aeon] was prepared beforehand. Time [was not] apportioned to him, [since] he does not receive anything from another, [for it would be received] on loan. For he who precedes someone does not [lack] that he may receive from [him]. For [rather] it is the latter that looks expectantly at him in **4** his light.

"For the [perfection] is majestic. He is pure, immeasurable [mind]. He is an aeon-giving aeon. He is [life]-giving life. He is a blessedness-giving blessed one. He is knowledge-giving knowledge. [He is] goodness-giving goodness. [He is] mercy and redemption-[giving mercy]. He is grace-giving grace, [not] because he possesses it, but because he gives [the] immeasurable, incomprehensible [light].

"[How am I to speak] with you about him? His [aeon] is indestructible, at rest and existing in [silence, reposing] (and) being prior [to everything. For he] is the head of [all] the aeons, [and] it is he who gives them strength in his goodness. For [we know] not [the ineffable things, and we] do not understand what [is immeasurable], except for him who came forth [from] him, namely (from) [the] Father. For it is he who [told] it to us [alone]. For it is he who looks at him[self] in his light which surrounds [him], namely the spring [of the] water of life. And it is he who gives to [all] the [aeons] and in every way, (and) who [gazes upon] his image which he sees in the spring of the [Spirit]. It is he who puts his desire in his [water]-light [which is in the] spring of the [pure light]-water [which] surrounds him.

"And [his thought performed] a deed and she came forth, [namely] she who had [appeared] before him in [the shine of] his light. This is the first [power which was] before all of them (and) [which came] forth from his mind. She [is the forethought of the All]—her light [shines like his] light—the [perfect] power which is [the] image of the invisible, virginal Spirit who is perfect. [The first power], the glory of Barbelo, the perfect **5** glory in the aeons, the glory of the revelation, she glorified the virginal Spirit and it was she who praised him, because thanks to him she had come forth. This is the first thought, his image; she became the womb of everything, for it is she who is prior to them all, the Mother-Father, the first man, the holy Spirit, the thrice-male, the thrice-powerful, the thrice-named androgynous one, and the eternal aeon among the invisible ones, and the first to come forth.

"<She> requested from the invisible, virginal Spirit—that is Barbelo—to give her foreknowledge. And the Spirit consented. And when he had [consented], the foreknowledge came forth, and it stood by the forethought; it originates from the thought of the invisible, virginal Spirit. It glorified him [and] his perfect power, Barbelo, for it was for her sake that it had come into being.

"And she requested again to grant her [indestructibility], and he consented. When he had [consented], indestructibility [came] forth, and it stood by the thought and the foreknowledge. It glorified the invisible One and Barbelo, the one for whose sake they had come into being.

"And Barbelo requested to grant her eternal life. And the invisible Spirit consented. And when he had consented, eternal life came forth, and [they attended] and glorified the invisible [Spirit]

and Barbelo, the one for whose sake they had come into being.

"And she requested again to grant her truth. And the invisible Spirit consented. And [when he had] consented truth came forth, and they attended and glorified the invisible, **6** excellent Spirit and his Barbelo, the one for whose sake they had come into being.

"This is the pentad of the aeons of the Father, which is the first man, the image of the invisible Spirit; it is the forethought, which is Barbelo, and the thought, and the foreknowledge, and the indestructibility, and the eternal life, and the truth. This is the androgynous pentad of the aeons, which is the decad of the aeons, which is the Father.

"And he looked at Barbelo with the pure light which surrounds the invisible Spirit and (with) his spark, and she conceived from him. He begot a spark of light with a light resembling blessedness. But it does not equal his greatness. This was an only-begotten child of the Mother-Father which had come forth; it is the only offspring, the only-begotten one of the Father, the pure Light.

"And the invisible, virginal Spirit rejoiced over the light which came forth, that which was brought forth first by the first power of his forethought which is Barbelo. And he anointed it with his goodness until it became perfect, not lacking in any goodness, because he had anointed it with the goodness of the invisible Spirit. And it attended him as he poured upon it. And immediately when it had received from the Spirit, it glorified the holy Spirit and the perfect forethought for whose sake it had come forth.

"And it requested to give it a fellow worker, which is the mind, and he consented [gladly]. And when the invisible Spirit had consented, **7** the mind came forth, and it attended Christ glorifying him and Barbelo. And all these came into being in silence.

"And the mind wanted to perform a deed through the word of the invisible Spirit. And his will became a deed and it appeared with the mind; and the light glorified it. And the word followed the will. For because of the word, Christ the divine Autogenes created everything. And the eternal life <and> his will and the mind and the foreknowledge attended and glorified the invisible Spirit and Barbelo, for whose sake they had come into being.

"And the holy Spirit completed the divine Autogenes, his son, together with Barbelo, that he may attend the mighty and invisible, virginal Spirit as the divine Autogenes, the Christ whom he had honored with a mighty voice. He came forth through the forethought. And the invisible, virginal Spirit placed the divine Autogenes of truth over everything. And he subjected to him every authority, and the truth which is in him, that he may know the All which had been called with a name exalted above every name. For that name will be mentioned to those who are worthy of it.

"For from the light, which is the Christ, and the indestructibility, through the gift of the Spirit the four lights (appeared) from the divine Autogenes. He expected that they might attend **8** him. And the three (are) will, thought, and life. And the four powers (are) understanding, grace, perception, and prudence. And grace belongs to the light-aeon Armozel, which is the first angel. And there are three other aeons with this aeon: grace, truth, and form. And the second light (is) Oriel, who has been placed over the second aeon. And there are three other aeons with him: conception, perception, and memory. And the third light is Daveithai, who has been placed over the third aeon. And there are three other aeons with him: understanding, love, and idea. And the fourth aeon was placed over the fourth light Eleleth. And there are three other aeons with him: perfection, peace, and wisdom. These are the four lights which attend the divine Autogenes, (and) these are the twelve aeons which attend the son of the mighty one, the Autogenes, the Christ, through the will and the gift of the invisible Spirit. And the twelve aeons belong to the son of the Autogenes. And all things were established by the will of the holy Spirit through the Autogenes.

"And from the foreknowledge of the perfect mind, through the revelation of the will of the invisible Spirit and the will of the Autogenes, <the> perfect Man (appeared), the first revelation, and the truth. It is he whom the virginal Spirit called Pigera-Adamas, and he placed him over **9** the first

aeon with the mighty one, the Autogenes, the Christ, by the first light Armozel; and with him are his powers. And the invisible one gave him a spiritual, invincible power. And he spoke and glorified and praised the invisible Spirit, saying, 'It is for your sake that everything has come into being and everything will return to you. I shall praise and glorify you and the Autogenes and the aeons, the three: the Father, the Mother, and the Son, the perfect power.'

"And he placed his son Seth over the second aeon in the presence of the second light Oriel. And in the third aeon the seed of Seth was placed over the third light Daveithai. And the souls of the saints were placed (there). And in the fourth aeon the souls were placed of those who do not know the Pleroma and who did not repent at once, but who persisted for a while and repented afterwards; they are by the fourth light Eleleth. These are creatures which glorify the invisible Spirit.

"And the Sophia of the Epinoia, being an aeon, conceived a thought from herself and the conception of the invisible Spirit and foreknowledge. She wanted to bring forth a likeness out of herself without the consent of the Spirit—he had not approved—and without her consort, and without his consideration. And though the person of her maleness had not approved, and she had not found her agreement, and she had thought without the consent of the Spirit and the knowledge of her agreement, (yet) she brought forth. **10** "And because of the invincible power which is in her, her thought did not remain idle and something came out of her which was imperfect and different from her appearance, because she had created it without her consort. And it was dissimilar to the likeness of its mother for it has another form.

"And when she saw (the consequences of) her desire, it changed into a form of a lion-faced serpent. And its eyes were like lightening fires which flash. She cast it away from her, outside that place, that no one of the immortal ones might see it, for she had created it in ignorance. And she surrounded it with a luminous cloud, and she placed a throne in the middle of the cloud that no one might see it except the holy Spirit who is called the mother of the living. And she called his name Yaltabaoth.

"This is the first archon who took a great power from his mother. And he removed himself from her and moved away from the places in which he was born. He became strong and created for himself other aeons with a flame of luminous fire which (still) exists now. And he joined with his arrogance which is in him and begot authorities for himself. The name of the first one is Athoth, whom the generations call [the reaper]. The second one is Harmas, who [is the eye] of envy. The third one is Kalila-Oumbri. The fourth one is Yabel. The fifth one is Adonaiou, who is called Sabaoth. The sixth one is Cain, whom the generations of men call the sun. The seventh is Abel. The eighth is Abrisene. The ninth is Yobel. **11** "The tenth is Armoupieel. The eleventh is Melceir-Ardonein. The twelth is Belias, it is he who is over the depth of Hades. And he placed seven kings—each corresponding to the firmaments of heaven—over the seven heavens, and five over the depth of the abyss, that they may reign. And he shared his fire with them, but he did not send forth from the power of the light which he had taken from his mother, for he is ignorant darkness.

"And when the light had mixed with the darkness, it caused the darkness to shine. And when the darkness had mixed with the light, it darkened the light and it became neither light nor dark, but it became dim.

"Now the archon who is weak has three names. The first name is Yaltabaoth, the second is Saklas, and the third is Samael. And he is impious in his arrogance which is in him. For he said, 'I am God and there is no other God beside me,'[1] for he is ignorant of his strength, the place from which he had come.

"And the archons created seven powers for themselves, and the powers created for themselves six angels for each one until they became 365 angels. And there are the bodies belonging with the names: the first is Athoth, he has a sheep's face; the second is Eloaiou, he has a donkey's face; the third is Astaphaios, he has a [hyena's] face; the fourth is Yao, he has a [serpent's] face with seven heads; the fifth is Sabaoth, he has a dragon's face;

the sixth is Adonin, he had a monkey's face; the seventh is Sabbede, he has a shining fire-face. This is the sevenness of the week.

"But Yaltabaoth had a multitude **12** of faces more than all of them so that he could put a face before all of them, according to his desire, when he is in the midst of seraphs. He shared his fire with them; therefore he became lord over them. Because of the power of the glory he possessed of his mother's light, he called himself God. And he did not obey the place from which he came. And he united the seven powers in his thought with the authorities which were with him. And when he spoke it happened. And he named each power beginning with the highest: the first is goodness with the first (authority), Athoth; the second is foreknowledge with the second one, Eloaio; and the third is Astraphaio; the fourth is lordship with the fourth one, Yao; the fifth is kingdom with the fifth one, Sabaoth; the sixth is envy with the sixth one, Adonein; the seventh is understanding with the seventh one, Sabbateon. And these have a firmament corresponding to each aeon-heaven. They were given names according to the glory which belongs to heaven for the [destruction of the] powers. And in the names which were given to [them by] their Originator there was power. But the names which were given them according to the glory which belongs to heaven mean for them destruction and powerlessness. Thus they have two names.

"And having created [   ] everything he organized according to the model of the first aeons which had come into being, so that he might **13** create them like the indestructible ones. Not because he had seen the indestructible ones, but the power in him, which he had taken from his mother, produced in him the likeness of the cosmos. And when he saw the creation which surrounds him and the multitude of the angels around him which had come forth from him, he said to them, 'I am a jealous God and there is no other God beside

---

[1]Isa 45:5–6, 12; cf. Exod 20:2–3.

me.'[2] But by announcing this he indicated to the angels who attended him that there exists another God. For if there were no other one, of whom would he be jealous?

"Then the mother began to move to and fro. She became aware of the deficiency when the brightness of her light diminished. And she became dark because her consort had not agreed with her."

And I said, "Lord, what does it mean that she moved to and fro?" But he smiled and said, "Do not think it is, as Moses said, 'above the waters.'[3] No, but when she had seen the wickedness which had happened, and the theft which her son had committed, she repented. And she was overcome by forgetfulness in the darkness of ignorance and she began to be ashamed. And she did not dare to return, but she was moving about. And the moving is the going to and fro.

"And the arrogant one took a power from his mother. For he was ignorant, thinking that there existed no other except his mother alone. And when he saw the multitude of the angels which he had created, then he exalted himself above them.

"And when the mother recognized that the garment of darkness was imperfect, then she knew that her consort had not agreed with her. She repented **14** with much weeping. And the whole pleroma heard the prayer of her repentance and they praised on her behalf the invisible, virginal Spirit. And he consented; and when the invisible Spirit had consented, the holy Spirit poured over her from their whole pleroma. For it was not her consort who came to her, but he came to her through the pleroma in order that he might correct her deficiency. And she was taken up not to her own aeon but above her son, that she might be in the ninth until she has corrected her deficiency.

"And a voice came forth from the exalted aeon-heaven: 'The Man exists and the son of Man.' And the chief archon, Yaltabaoth, heard (it) and thought that the voice had come from his mother. And he did not know from where it came. And he taught them, the holy and perfect Mother-Father, the complete foreknowledge, the image of the invisible one who is the Father of the all (and)

through whom everything came into being, the first Man. For he revealed his likeness in a human form.

"And the whole aeon of the chief archon trembled, and the foundations of the abyss shook. And of the waters which are above matter, the underside was illuminated by the appearance of his image which had been revealed. And when all the authorities and the chief archon looked, they saw the whole region of the underside which was illuminated. And through the light they saw the form of the image in the water. **15** "And he said to the authorities which attend him, 'Come, let us create a man according to the image of God and according to our likeness that his image may become a light for us.'[4] And they created by means of their respective powers in correspondence with the characteristics which were given. And each authority supplied a characteristic in the form of the image which he had seen in its natural (form). He created a being according to the likeness of the first, perfect Man. And they said, 'Let us call him Adam, that his name may become a power of light for us.'. . . **19** And all the angels and demons worked until they had constructed the natural body. And their product was completely inactive and motionless for a long time.

"And when the mother wanted to retrieve the power which she had given to the chief archon, she petitioned the Mother-Father of the All who is most merciful. He sent, by means of the holy decree, the five lights down upon the place of the angels of the chief archon. They advised him that they should bring forth the power of the mother. And they said to Yaltabaoth, 'Blow into his face something of your spirit and his body will arise.' And he blew into his face the spirit which is the power of his mother; he did not know (this), for he exists in ignorance. And the power of the mother went out of Yaltabaoth into the natural body which they had fashioned after

---

[2]Exod 20:5; Isa 45:5–6, 12.
[3]Gen 1:2.
[4]Gen 1:26.

the image of the one who exists from the beginning. The body moved and gained strength, and it was luminous.

"And in that moment the rest of the powers **20** became jealous, because he had come into being through all of them and they had given their power to the man, and his intelligence was greater than that of those who had made him, and greater than that of the chief archon. And when they recognized that he was luminous, and that he could think better than they, and that he was free from wickedness, they took him and threw him into the lowest region of all matter.

"But the blessed One, the Mother-Father, the beneficent and merciful One, had mercy on the power of the mother which had been brought forth out of the chief archon, for they (the archons) might gain power over the natural and perceptible body. And he sent, through his beneficent Spirit and his great mercy, a helper to Adam, luminous Epinoia which comes out of him, who is called Life. And she assists the whole creature, by toiling with him and by restoring him to his fullness and by teaching him about the descent of his seed (and) by teaching him about the way of ascent, (which is) the way he came down. And the luminous Epinoia was hidden in Adam, in order that the archons might not know her, but that the Epinoia might be a correction of the deficiency of the mother. . . .
21 "And the archons took him and placed him in paradise. And they said to him, 'Eat, that is at leisure,' for their luxury is bitter and their beauty is depraved. And their luxury is deception and their trees are godlessness and their fruit is deadly poison and their promise is death. And the tree of their life they had placed in the midst of paradise.

"And I shall teach you (pl.) what is the mystery of their life, which is the plan which they made together, which is the likeness of their spirit. The root of this (tree) is bitter and its branches are death, its shadow is hate and deception is in its leaves, and its blossom is the ointment of evil, and its fruit is death and desire is its seed, and it sprouts in darkness. The **22** dwelling place of those who taste from it is Hades and the darkness is their place of rest.

"But what they call the tree of knowledge of good and evil, which is the Epinoia of the light, they stayed in front of it in order that he (Adam) might not look up to his fullness and recognize the nakedness of his shamefulness. But it was I who brought about that they ate."

And I said to the savior, "Lord, was it not the serpent that taught Adam to eat?" The savior smiled and said, "The serpent taught them to eat from wickedness of begetting, lust, (and) destruction, that he (Adam) might be useful to him. And he (Adam) knew that he was disobedient to him (the chief archon) due to light of the Epinoia which is in him, which made him more correct in his thinking than the chief archon. And (the latter) wanted to bring about the power which he himself had given him. And he brought a forgetfulness over Adam. . . .

"Then the Epinoia of the light hid herself in him (Adam). And the chief archon wanted to bring her out of his rib. But the Epinoia of the light cannot be grasped. Although darkness pursued her, it did not catch her. And he brought a part of his power out of him. And he made another creature in the form of a woman according to the likeness of the Epinoia which had appeared to him. And he brought **23** the part which he had taken from the power of the man into the female creature, and not as Moses said, 'his rib-bone.'[5]

"And he (Adam) saw the woman beside him. And in that moment the luminous Epinoia appeared, and she lifted the veil which lay over his mind. And he became sober from the drunkenness of darkness. And he recognized his counter-image, and he said, 'This is indeed bone of my bones and flesh of my flesh.'[6] Therefore the man will leave his father and his mother and he will cleave to his wife and they will both be one flesh. For they will send him his consort, and he will leave his father and his mother.

"And our sister Sophia (is) she who came down in innocence in order to rectify her deficiency. Therefore she was called Life, which is

---

[5]Gen 2:21–22.
[6]Gen 2:23.

the mother of the living, by the foreknowledge of the sovereignty of heaven and [ ] to him [ ]. And through her they have tasted the perfect Knowledge. I appeared in the form of an eagle on the tree of knowledge, which is the Epinoia from the foreknowledge of the pure light, that I might teach them and awaken them out of the depth of sleep. For they were both in a fallen state and they recognized their nakedness. The Epinoia appeared to them as a light (and) she awakened their thinking.

"And when Yaldabaoth noticed that they withdrew from him, he cursed his earth. He found the woman as she was **24** preparing herself for her husband. He was lord over her though he did not know the mystery which had come to pass through the holy decree. And they were afraid to blame him. And he showed his angels his ignorance which is in him. And he cast them out of paradise and he clothed them in gloomy darkness. And the chief archon saw the virgin who stood by Adam, and that the luminous Epinoia of life had appeared in her. And Yaldabaoth was full of ignorance. And when the foreknowledge of the All noticed (it), she sent some and they snatched life out of Eve. . . .

"And the two archons he set over principalities so that they might rule over the tomb. And when Adam recognized the likeness of his own foreknowledge, he begot the likeness **25** of the son of man. He called him Seth according to the way of the race in the aeons. Likewise the mother also sent down her spirit which is in her likeness and a copy of those who are in the pleroma, for she will prepare a dwelling place for the aeons which will come down. And he made them drink water of forgetfulness, from the chief archon, in order that they might not know from where they came. Thus the seed remained for a while assisting (him) in order that, when the Spirit comes forth from the holy aeons, he may raise up and heal him from the deficiency, that the whole pleroma may (again) become holy and faultless."

And I said to the savior, "Lord, will all the souls then be brought safely into the pure light?" He answered and said to me, "Great things have arisen in your mind, for it is difficult to explain them to others except to those who are from the immovable race. Those on whom the Spirit of life will descend and (with whom) he will be with the power, they will be saved and become perfect and be worthy of the greatness and be purified in that place from all wickedness and the involvements in evil. Then they have no other care than the incorruption alone, to which they direct their attention from here on, without anger or envy or jealousy or desire and greed of anything. They are not affected by anything except the state of being in the flesh alone, which they bear while looking expectantly for the time when they will be met **26** by the receivers (of the body). Such then are worthy of the imperishable, eternal life and the calling. For they endure everything and bear up under everything, that they may finish the good fight and inherit eternal life."

I said to him, "Lord, the souls of those who did not do these works, (but) on whom the power and Spirit descended, will they be rejected?" He answered and said to me, "If the Spirit descended upon them, they will in any case be saved and they will change (for the better). For the power will descend on every one, for without it no one can stand. And after they are born, then, when the Spirit of life increases and the power comes and strengthens that soul, no one can lead it astray with works of evil. But those on whom the counterfeit spirit descends are drawn by him and they go astray."

And I said, "Lord, where will the souls of these go when they have come out of their flesh?" And he smiled and said to me, "The soul, in which the power will become stronger than the counterfeit spirit, is strong and it flees from evil and, through the intervention of the incorruptible one, it is saved and it is taken up to the rest of the aeons."

And I said, "Lord, those, however, who have not known to whom they belong, where will their souls be?" And he said to me, "In those the despicable spirit has **27** gained strength when they went astray. And he burdens the soul and draws it to the works of evil, and he casts it down into forgetfulness. And after it comes out of (the body), it is handed over to the authorities, who came into being through the archon, and they bind it with chains and cast it into prison and consort with it until it is liberated from the forgetfulness and acquires knowledge. And if thus it becomes perfect, it is saved." . . .

And I said, "Lord, these also who did not know but have turned away, where will their souls go?" Then he said to me, "To that place where the angels of poverty go they will be taken, the place where there is no repentance. And they will be kept for the day on which those who have blasphemed the spirit will be tortured, and they will be punished with eternal punishment. . . . **31** "And behold, now

I shall go up to the perfect aeon. I have completed everything for you in your hearing. And I have said everything to you that you might write them down and give them secretly to your fellow spirits, for this is the mystery of the immovable race."

And the savior presented these things to him that he might write them down and keep them secure. And he said to him, "Cursed be everyone who will exchange these things for a gift or for food or for drink or for clothing or for any other such thing." **32** And these things were presented to him in a mystery, and immediately he disappeared from him. And he went to his fellow disciples and related to them what the savior had told him.

>-+-◆>--O--<◆-+-<

23. The First Thought in Three Forms

Discovered at Nag Hammadi, the "First Thought in Three Forms" (sometimes called the "Trimorphic Protennoia") contains a series of three mystical discourses on the world, humans, and salvation through knowledge, placed on the lips of a female aeon. Comparable in many ways to the Secret Book of John, the discourses contain several of the key elements of the gnostic myth. Particularly emphasized in this account are the revelations of divine knowledge from on high, culminating in the incarnation of the Word (cf. John 1:1–18).

The "First Thought" (= Protennoia) is the first emanation from the one true inscrutable God. She begins her discourse by revealing her own mysterious and ineffable greatness and then describes the three descents that she made from the heavenly realm in order to bring to humans the heavenly knowledge that can illuminate their souls, delivering them from darkness into light. Each of these descents is associated with one of Barbelo's three forms, since she is the Thought of the Father (or Voice), the Mother (or Sound), and the Son (or Word, i.e., the Logos). It is her final descent in the appearance

The "First Thought in Three Forms," from "The Trimorphic Protennoia," translated by John D. Turner, *The Nag Hammadi Library in English*, 3d, completely revised ed., by James M. Robinson, General Editor. Copyright © 1978, 1988 by E. J. Brill, Leiden, The Netherlands. Reprinted by permission of HarperCollins Publishers, Inc.

of human flesh that brings the ultimate illumination to those who dwell in ignorance and darkness, leading to their ascent into the world of Light.

It is difficult to date this work, but many scholars think it was written around 200 C.E.

35 [I] am [Protennoia, the] Thought that [dwells] in [the Light. I] am the movement that dwells in the [All, she in whom the] All takes its stand, [the first]-born among those who [came to be, she who exists] before the All. [She (Protennoia) is called] by three names, although she dwells alone, [since she is perfect]. I am invisible within the Thought of the Invisible One. I am revealed in the immeasurable, ineffable (things). I am incomprehensible, dwelling in the incomprehensible. I move in every creature.

I am the life of my Epinoia that dwells within every Power and every eternal movement and (in) invisible Lights and within the Archons and Angels and Demons and every soul dwelling in [Tartaros] and (in) every material soul. I dwell in those who came to be. I move in everyone and I delve into them all. I walk uprightly, and those who sleep I [awaken]. And I am the sight of those who dwell in sleep.

I am the Invisible One within the All. It is I who counsel those who are hidden, since I know the All that exists in it. I am numberless beyond everyone. I am immeasurable, ineffable, yet whenever I [wish, I shall] reveal myself of my own accord. I [am the head of] the All. I exist before the [All, and] I am the All, since I [exist in] everyone.

I am a Voice [speaking softly]. I exist [from the first. I dwell] within the Silence [that surrounds every one] of them. 36 And [it is] the [hidden Voice] that [dwells within] me, [within the] incomprehensible, immeasurable [Thought, within the] immeasurable Silence.

I [descended to the] midst of the underworld and I shone [down upon the] darkness. It is I who poured forth the [water]. It is I who am hidden within [radiant] waters. I am the one who gradually put forth the All by my Thought. It is I who am laden with the Voice. It is through me that Gnosis comes forth. [I] dwell in the ineffable and

unknowable ones. I am perception and knowledge, uttering a Voice by means of thought. [I] am the real Voice. I cry out in everyone, and they recognize it (the voice), since a seed indwells [them]. I am the Thought of the Father and through me proceeded [the] Voice, that is, the knowledge of the everlasting things. I exist as Thought for the [All]—being joined to the unknowable and incomprehensible Thought—I revealed myself— yes, I—among all those who recognize me. For it is I who am joined with everyone by virtue of the hidden Thought and an exalted <Voice>, even a Voice from the invisible Thought. And it is immeasurable, since it dwells in the Immeasurable One. It is a mystery; it is [unrestrainable] by [the Incomprehensible One]. It is invisible [to all those who are] visible in the All. [It is a Light] dwelling in Light.

It is we [also who] alone [have separated] [from the] visible [world] since we [are saved by the] hidden [wisdom by means of the] 37 ineffable, immeasurable [Voice]. And he who is hidden within us pays the tributes of his fruit to the Water of Life.

Then the Son who is perfect in every respect— that is, the Word who originated through that Voice; who proceeded from the height; who has within him the Name; who is a Light—he (the Son) revealed the everlasting things and all the unknowns were known. And those things difficult to interpret and secret, he revealed, and as for those who dwell in Silence with the First Thought, he preached to them. And he revealed himself to those who dwell in darkness, and he showed himself to those who dwell in the abyss, and to those who dwell in the hidden treasuries he told ineffable mysteries, and he taught unrepeatable doctrines to all those who became Sons of the Light.

Now the Voice that originated from my Thought exists as three permanences: the Father, the Mother, the Son. Existing perceptibly as Speech, it (Voice) has within it a Word endowed with every <glory>, and it has three masculinities, three powers, and three names. They exist in the manner of Three □ □ □—which are quadrangles—secretly within a silence of the Ineffable One.

[It is he] alone who came to be, that [is, the Christ. And] as for me I anointed him as the glory [of the] Invisible [Spirit] with [goodness]. Now [the Three] I established [alone in] eternal [glory] over [the Aeons in the] Living [Water], that [is, the glory that surrounds him] **38** who first came forth to the Light of those exalted Aeons, and it is in glorious Light that he firmly perseveres. And [he] stood in his own Light that surrounds him, that is, the Eye of the Light that gloriously shines on me. He perpetuated the Father of all <the> Aeons, who am I, the Thought of the Father, Protennoia, that is, Barbelo, the [perfect] Glory and the [immeasurable] Invisible One who is hidden. I am the Image of the Invisible Spirit and it is through me that the All took shape, and (I am) the Mother (as well as) the Light which she appointed as Virgin, she who is called Meirothea, the incomprehensible Womb, the unrestrainable and immeasurable Voice.

Then the Perfect Son revealed himself to his Aeons who originated through him, and he revealed them and glorified them and gave them thrones and stood in the glory with which he glorified himself. They blessed the Perfect Son, the Christ, the only-begotten God. And they gave glory, saying, "He is! He is! The Son of God! The Son of God! It is he who is! The Aeon of Aeons beholding the Aeons which he begot! For you have begotten by your own desire! Therefore [we] glorify you: ma mō ō ō ō eia ei on ei! The [Aeon] of [Aeons! The] Aeon which he gave!"

Then, moreover, the [God who was begotten] gave them (the Aeons) a power of [life on which they might rely] and [he] established [them. The] first Aeon, he established [over the first]: Armedon, Nousa[nios, Armozel; the] second he established [over the second Aeon]: **39** Phaionios, Ainios, Oroiael; the third over the third Aeon:

Mellephaneus, Loios, Daveithai; the fourth over the fourth: Mousanios, Amethes, Eleleth. Now those Aeons were begotten by the God who was begotten—the Christ—and these Aeons received as well as gave glory. They were the first to appear, exalted in their thought, and each Aeon gave myriads of glories within great untraceable lights and they all together blessed the Perfect Son, the God who was begotten.

Then there came forth a word from the great Light Eleleth and said, "I am King! Who belongs to Chaos and who belongs to the underworld?" And at that instant his Light appeared radiant, endowed with the Epinoia. The Powers of the Powers did not entreat him and likewise immediately there appeared the great Demon who rules over the lowest part of the underworld and Chaos. He has neither form nor perfection, but on the contrary possesses the form of the glory of those begotten in the darkness. Now he is called "Saklas," that is, "Samael," "Yaltabaoth," he who had taken power; who had snatched it away from the innocent one (Sophia); who had earlier overpowered her who is the Light's Epinoia (Sophia) who had descended, her from whom he (Yaltabaoth) had come forth originally.

Now when the Epinoia of the [Light] realized that [he (Yaltabaoth)] had begged him (the Light), for another [order, even though he was lower] than she, she said, "Grant [me another order so that] you may become for me [a dwelling place lest I dwell] in disorder [forever." And the order of the] entire house of **40** glory [was agreed] upon her word. A blessing was brought for her and the higher order released it to her.

And the great Demon began to produce aeons in the likeness of the real Aeons, except that he produced them out of his own power.

Then I too revealed by Voice secretly, saying, "Cease! Desist, (you) who tread on matter; for behold I am coming down to the world of mortals for the sake of my portion that was in that place from the time when the innocent Sophia was conquered, she who descended, so that I might thwart their aim which the one revealed by her appoints." And all were disturbed, each one who dwells in the house of the ignorant light, and the abyss trembled. And the Archigenetor of ignorance reigned over Chaos and the underworld and produced a man in my likeness. But he neither knew that that one would become for him a sentence of dissolution nor does he recognize the power in him.

But now I have come down and reached down to Chaos. And I was [with] my own who were in that place. [I am hidden] within them, empowering [them and] giving them shape. And [from the first day] until the day [when I will grant mighty power] to those who [are mine, I will reveal myself to] those who have [heard my mysteries], **41** that is, the [Sons] of [the] Light.

I am their Father and I shall tell you a mystery, ineffable and indivulgeable by [any] mouth: Every bond I loosed from you, and the chains of the Demons of the underworld, I broke, these things which are bound on my members, restraining them. And the high walls of darkness I overthrew, and the secure gates of those pitiless ones I broke, and I smashed their bars. And the evil Force and the one who beats you, and the one who hinders you, and the Tyrant, and the Adversary, and the one who is King, and the present Enemy, indeed all these I explained to those who are mine, who are the Sons of the light, in order that they might nullify them all and be saved from all those bonds and enter into the place where they were at first.

I am the first one who descended on account of my portion which remains, that is, the Spirit that (now) dwells in the soul, (but) which originated from the Water of Life and out of the immersion of the mysteries, and I spoke, I together with the Archons and Authorities. For I had gone down below their language and I spoke my mysteries to my own—a hidden mystery—and the bonds and eternal oblivion were nullified. And I bore fruit in them, that is, the Thought of the unchanging Aeon, and my house, and their [Father]. And I went down [to those who were mine] from the first and I [reached them and broke] the first strands that [enslaved them. Then] everyone [of those] within me shone, and **42** I prepared [a pat-

tern] for those ineffable Lights that are within me. Amen.

The Discourse of Protennoia: [One]

I am the Voice that appeared through my Thought, for I am "He who is syzygetic," since I am called "the Thought of the Invisible One." Since I am called "the unchanging Speech," I am called "She who is syzygetic."

I am a single one (fem.) since I am undefiled. I am the Mother [of] the Voice, speaking in many ways, completing the All. It is in me that knowledge dwells, the knowledge of <things> everlasting. It is I [who] speak within every creature and I was known by the All. It is I who lift up the Speech of the Voice to the ears of those who have known me, that is, the Sons of the Light.

Now I have come the second time in the likeness of a female and have spoken with them. And I shall tell them of the coming end of the Aeon and teach them of the beginning of the Aeon to come, the one without change, the one in which our appearance will be changed. We shall be purified within those Aeons from which I revealed myself in the Thought of the likeness of my masculinity. I settled among those who are worthy in the Thought of my changeless Aeon.

For I shall tell you a mystery [of] this particular Aeon and tell you about the forces that are in it. The birth beckons: [hour] begets hour, [day begets day]. The months made known the [month. Time] has [gone round] succeeding [time]. This particular Aeon **43** was completed in [this] fashion, and it was estimated, and it (was) short, for it was a finger that released a finger and a joint that was separated from a joint. Then when the great Authorities knew that the time of fulfillment had appeared—just as in the pangs of the parturient it (the time) had drawn near, so also had the destruction approached—all together the elements trembled, and the foundations of the underworld and the ceilings of Chaos shook and a great fire shone within their midst, and the rocks and the earth were shaken like a reed shaken by the wind. And the lots of Fate and those who apportion the domiciles were greatly disturbed over a great thunder. And the thrones of the Powers were disturbed since they were overturned, and their King was afraid. And those who pursue Fate paid their allotment of visits to the path, and they said to the Powers, "What is this disturbance and this shaking that has come upon us through a Voice <belonging> to the exalted Speech? And our entire habitation has been shaken, and the entire circuit of our path of ascent has met with destruction, and the path upon which we go, which takes us up to the Archigenetor of our birth, has ceased to be established for us." Then the Powers answered, saying, "We too are at a loss about it since we did not know what was responsible for it. But arise, let us go up to the Archigenetor and ask him." And the Powers all gathered and went up to the Archigenetor. [They said to] him, "Where is your boasting in which [you boast]? Did we not [hear you say], 'I am God [and I am] your Father **44** and it is I who [begot] you and there is no [other] beside me'? Now behold, there has appeared [a] Voice belonging to that invisible Speech of [the Aeon] (and) which we know not. And we ourselves did not recognize to whom we belong, for that Voice which we listened to is foreign to us, and we do not recognize it; we did not know whence it was. It came and put fear in our midst and weakening in the members of our arms. So now let us weep and mourn most bitterly! As for the future, let us make our entire flight before we are imprisoned perforce and taken down to the bosom of the underworld. For already the slackening of our bondage has approached, and the times are cut short and the days have shortened and our time has been fulfilled, and the weeping of our destruction has approached us so that we may be taken to the place we recognize. For as for our tree from which we grew, a fruit of ignorance is what it has; and also its leaves, it is death that dwells in them, and darkness dwells under the shadow of its boughs. And it was in deceit and lust that we harvested it, this (tree) through which ignorant Chaos became for us a dwelling place. For behold, even

he, the Archigenetor of our birth, about whom we boast, even he did not know this Speech."

So now, O Sons of the Thought, listen to me, to the Speech of the Mother of your mercy, for you have become worthy of the mystery hidden from (the beginning of) the Aeons, so that [you might receive] it. And the consummation of this [particular] Aeon [and] of the evil life [has approached and there dawns **45** the] beginning of the [Aeon to come] which [has no change forever].

I am androgynous. [I am Mother (and) I am] Father since [I copulate] with myself. I [copulated] with myself [and with those who love] me, [and] it is through me alone that the All [stands firm]. I am the Womb [that gives shape] to the All by giving birth to the Light that [shines in] splendor. I am the Aeon to [come. I am] the fulfillment of the All, that is, Me[iroth]ea, the glory of the Mother. I cast [voiced] Speech into the ears of those who know me.

And I am inviting you into the exalted, perfect Light. Moreover (as for) this (Light), when you enter it you will be glorified by those [who] give glory, and those who enthrone will enthrone you. You will accept robes from those who give robes and the Baptists will baptize you and you will become gloriously glorious, the way you first were when you were <Light>.

And I hid myself in everyone and revealed [myself] within them, and every mind seeking me longed for me, for it is I who gave shape to the All when it had no form. And I transformed their forms into (other) forms until the time when a form will be given to the All. It is through me that the Voice originated and it is I who put the breath within my own. And I cast into them the eternally holy Spirit and I ascended and entered my Light. [I went up] upon my branch and sat [there among the] Sons of the [holy] Light. And [I withdrew] to their dwelling place **46** which [. . .] become [glorious. . . . Amen].

[On Fate: Two]

I am [the Word] who dwells [in the] ineffable [Voice]. I dwell in undefiled [Light] and a Thought [revealed itself] perceptibly through [the great] Speech of the Mother, although it is a male offspring [that supports me] as my foundation. And it (the Speech) exists from the beginning in the foundations of the All.

But there is a Light [that] dwells hidden in Silence and it was first to [come] forth. Whereas she (the Mother) alone exists as Silence, I alone am the Word, ineffable, unpolluted, immeasurable, inconceivable. It (the Word) is a hidden Light, bearing a Fruit of Life, pouring forth a Living Water from the invisible, unpolluted, immeasurable Spring, that is, the unreproducible Voice of the glory of the Mother, the glory of the offspring of God; a male Virgin by virtue of a hidden Intellect, that is, the Silence hidden from the All, being unreproducible, an immeasurable Light, the source of the All, the Root of the entire Aeon. It is the Foundation that supports every movement of the Aeons that belong to the mighty Glory. It is the Foundation of every foundation. It is the Breath of the Powers. It is the Eye of the Three Permanences, which exist as Voice by virtue of Thought. And it is a Word by virtue of Speech; it was sent to illumine those who dwell in the [darkness].

Now behold [I will reveal] to you [my mysteries] since you are my fellow [brethren, and you shall] know them all [. . .]. **47** I [told all of them about my mysteries] that exist in [the incomprehensible], inexpressible [Aeons]. I taught [them the mysteries] through the [Voice that exists] within a perfect Intellect [and I] became a foundation for the All, and [I empowered] them.

The second time I came in the [Speech] of my Voice. I gave shape to those who [took] shape until their consummation.

The third time I revealed myself to them [in] their tents as Word and I revealed myself in the likeness of their shape. And I wore everyone's garment and I hid myself within them, and [they] did not know the one who empowers me. For I dwell within all the Sovereignties and Powers and within the Angels and in every moment [that] exists in all matter. And I hid myself within them until I revealed myself to my [brethren]. And none of them (the Powers) knew me, [although] it is I

who work in them. Rather [they thought] that the All was created [by them] since they are ignorant, not knowing [their] root, the place in which they grew.

[I] am the Light that illumines the All. I am the Light that rejoices [in my] brethren, for I came down to the world [of] mortals on account of the Spirit that remains [in] that which [descended] (and) came forth [from] the innocent Sophia. [I came] and I delivered [. . .] and I [went] to **48** [. . .] which he had [formerly and I gave to him] from the Water [of Life, which strips] him of the Chaos [that is in the] uttermost [darkness] that exists [inside] the entire [abyss], that is, the thought of [the corporeal] and the psychic. All these I put on. And I stripped him of it and I put upon him a shining Light, that is, the knowledge of the Thought of the Fatherhood.

And I delivered him to those who gives robes— Yammon, Elasso, Amenai—and they [covered] him with a robe from the robes of the Light; and I delivered him to the Baptists and they baptized him—Micheus, Michar, and Mn[e]sinous—and they immersed him in the spring of the [Water] of Life. And I delivered him to those who enthrone— Bariel, Nouthan, Sabenai—and they enthroned him from the throne of glory. And I delivered him to those who glorify—Ariom, Elien, Phariel—and they glorified him with the glory of the Fatherhood. And those who snatch away snatched away— Kamaliel. [. . .]anen, Samblo, the servants of <the> great holy Luminaries—and they took him into the light-[place] of his Fatherhood. And [he received] the Five Seals from [the Light] of the Mother, Protennoia, and it was [granted] him [to] partake of [the mystery] of knowledge, and [he became a Light] in Light.

So, now [. . . **49** I was] dwelling in them [in the form of each] one. [The Archons] thought [that I] was their Christ. Indeed I [dwell in] everyone. Indeed within those in whom [I revealed myself] as Light [I eluded] the Archons. I am their beloved, [for] in that place I clothed myself [as] the Son of the Archigenetor, and I was like him until the end of his decree, which is the ignorance of Chaos. And among the Angels I revealed myself in their likeness, and among the Powers as if I were one of them, but among the Sons of Man as if I were a Son of Man, even though I am Father of everyone.

I hid myself within them all until I revealed myself among my members, which are mine, and I taught them about the ineffable ordinances, and (about) the brethren. But they are inexpressible to every Sovereignty and every ruling Power except to the Sons of the Light alone, that is, the ordinances of the Father. These are the glories that are higher than every glory, that is, [the Five] Seals complete by virtue of Intellect. He who possesses the Five Seals of these particular names has stripped off <the> garments of ignorance and put on a shining Light. And nothing will appear to him that belongs to the Powers of the Archons. Within those of this sort darkness will dissolve and [ignorance] will die. And the thought of the

creature which [is scattered will] present a single appearance and [dark Chaos] will dissolve and **50** [. . .] and the [. . .] incomprehensible [. . .] within the [. . .] until I reveal myself [to all my fellow brethren] and until I gather [together] all [my fellow] brethren within my [eternal kingdom]. And I proclaimed to them the ineffable [Five Seals in order that I might] abide in them and they also might abide in me.

As for me, I put on Jesus. I bore him from the cursed wood, and established him in the dwelling places of his Father. And those who watch over their dwelling places did not recognize me. For I, I am unrestrainable together with my Seed, and my Seed, which is mine, I shall [place] into the Holy Light within an incomprehensible Silence. Amen.

>→→→O→←→←

24. The Gospel of Truth

A moving expression of gnostic joy in experiencing enlightenment, the "Gospel of Truth" is one of the real treasures of the Nag Hammadi Library. The book is not a Gospel in the traditional sense—there is no account of the life or teachings of Jesus here; it is called a gospel because it presents the "good news" of God's gracious revelation of saving knowledge, gnosis, which comes through Jesus Christ. Some scholars believe that it was originally a sermon preached to a gnostic, or possibly a more broadly Christian, congregation; many are convinced that it was authored by the most famous Gnostic Christian of the second century, Valentinus himself.

The Gospel of Truth presupposes important aspects of gnostic myth, but it does not explicate them; there are only scattered hints about how the divine realm, the material world, and human beings came into existence. Instead, the book focuses on the truth that brings redemption to an anguished humanity languishing in darkness and ignorance, and especially on the one who brought this revealed truth, Jesus Christ, the Word who comes forth from the Father as his Son. Through Christ's revelation, the fog of error has been dissipated and the illusions of falsehood have been exposed, opening those who receive

The "Gospel of Truth," translated by Harold W. Attridge and George W. MacRae, from *Nag Hammadi Codex I (The Jung Codex); (NHX XXII)*, ed. Harold W. Attridge. Leiden: E. J. Brill, 1985. Used with permission.

the truth to understand who they are, allowing them to be reunited with the incomprehensible and inconceivable Father of all.

Whether or not the work actually came from the pen of Valentinus, it was known to the church father Irenaeus and so must date to before 180 C.E.

The gospel of truth is joy for those who have received from the Father of truth the grace of knowing him, through the power of the Word that came forth from the pleroma, the one who is in the thought and the mind of the Father, that is, the one who is addressed as the Savior, (that) being the name of the work he is to perform for the redemption of those who were **17** ignorant of the Father, while in the name [of] the gospel is the proclamation of hope, being discovery for those who search for him.

When the totality went about searching for the one from whom they had come forth—and the totality was inside of him, the incomprehensible, inconceivable one who is superior to every thought—ignorance of the Father brought about anguish and terror; and the anguish grew solid like a fog, so that no one was able to see. For this reason error became powerful; it worked on its own matter foolishly, not having known the truth. It set about with a creation, preparing with power and beauty the substitute for the truth.

This was not, then, a humiliation for him, the incomprehensible, inconceivable one, for they were nothing, the anguish and the oblivion and the creature of deceit, while the established truth is immutable, imperturbable, perfect in beauty. For this reason, despise error.

Thus it had no root; it fell into a fog regarding the Father, while it was involved in preparing works and oblivions and terrors, in order that by means of these it might entice those of the middle and capture them.

The oblivion of error was not revealed. It is not a **18** [. . .] from the Father. Oblivion did not come into existence from the Father, although it did indeed come into existence because of him. But what comes into existence in him is knowledge, which appeared in order that oblivion might vanish and the Father might be known. Since oblivion came into existence because the Father was not known, then if the Father comes to be known, oblivion will not exist from that moment on.

Through this, the gospel of the one who is searched for, which <was> revealed to those who are perfect through the mercies of the Father, the hidden mystery, Jesus, the Christ, enlightened those who were in darkness through oblivion. He enlightened them; he showed (them) a way; and the way is the truth which he taught them.

For this reason error grew angry at him, persecuted him, was distressed at him (and) was brought to naught. He was nailed to a tree (and) he became a fruit of the knowledge of the Father. It did not, however, cause destruction because it was eaten, but to those who ate it it gave (cause) to become glad in the discovery, and he discovered them in himself, and they discovered him in themselves.

As for the incomprehensible, inconceivable one, the Father, the perfect one, the one who made the totality, within him is the totality and of him the totality has need. Although he retained their perfection within himself which he did not give to the totality, the Father was not jealous. What jealously indeed (could there be) between himself and his members? **19** For, if this aeon had thus [received] their [perfection], they could not have come [. . .] the Father. He retains within himself their perfection, granting it to them as a return to him and a perfectly unitary knowledge. It is he who fashioned the totality, and within him is the totality and the totality was in need of him.

As in the case of a person of whom some are ignorant, he wishes to have them know him and love him, so—for what did the totality have need of if not knowledge regarding the Father?—he became a guide, restful and leisurely. In schools he appeared (and) he spoke the word as a teacher. There came the men wise in their own estimation, putting him to the test. But he confounded them because they were foolish. They hated him because they were not really wise.

After all these, there came the little children also, those to whom the knowledge of the Father belongs. Having been strengthened, they learned about the impressions of the Father. They knew, they were known; they were glorified, they glorified. There was manifested in their heart the living book of the living—the one written in the thought and the mind **20** [of the] Father, which from before the foundation of the totality was within his incomprehensibility—that (book) which no one was able to take, since it remains for the one who will take it to be slain. No one could have become manifest from among those who have believed in salvation unless that book had appeared. For this reason the merciful one, the faithful one, Jesus, was patient in accepting sufferings until he took that book, since he knows that his death is life for many.

Just as there lies hidden in a will, before it is opened, the fortune of the deceased master of the house, so (it is) with the totality, which lay hidden while the Father of the totality was invisible, being something which is from him, from whom every space comes forth. For this reason Jesus appeared; he put on that book; he was nailed to a tree; he published the edict of the Father on the cross. O such great teaching! He draws himself down to death though life eternal clothes him. Having stripped himself of the perishable rags, he put on imperishability, which no one can possibly take away from him. Having entered the empty spaces of terrors, he passed through those who were stripped naked by oblivion, being knowledge and perfection, proclaiming the things that are in the heart, **21** [. . .] teach those who will receive teaching.

But those who are to receive teaching [are] the living who are inscribed in the book of the living. It is about themselves that they receive instruction, receiving it from the Father, turning again to him. Since the perfection of the totality is in the Father, it is necessary for the totality to ascend to him. Then, if one has knowledge, he receives what are his own and draws them to himself. For he who is ignorant is in need, and what he lacks is great, since he lacks that which will make him perfect. Since the perfection of the totality is in the Father and it is necessary for the totality to ascend to him and for each one to receive what are his own, he enrolled them in advance, having prepared them to give to those who came forth from him.

Those whose name he knew in advance were called at the end, so that one who has knowledge is the one whose name the Father has uttered. For he whose name has not been spoken is ignorant. Indeed, how is one to hear if his name has not been called? For he who is ignorant until the end is a creature of oblivion, and he will vanish along with it. If not, how is it that these miserable ones have **22** no name, (how is it that) they do not have the call? Therefore, if one has knowledge, he is from above. If he is called, he hears, he answers, and he turns to him who is calling him, and ascends to him. And he knows in what manner he is called. Having knowledge, he does the will of the one who called him, he wishes to be pleasing to him, he receives rest. Each one's name comes to him. He who is to have knowledge in this manner knows where he comes from and where he is going. He knows as one who having become drunk has turned away from his drunkenness, (and) having returned to himself, has set right what are his own.

He has brought many back from error. He has gone before them to their places, from which they had moved away, since it was on account of the depth that they received error, the depth of the one who encircles all spaces while there is none that encircles him. It was great wonder that they were in the Father, not knowing him, and (that) they were able to come forth by themselves, since they were unable to comprehend or to know the one in whom they were. For if his will had not thus emerged from him—for he revealed it in view of a knowledge in which all its emanations concur.

This is the knowledge of the living book which he revealed to the **23** aeons, at the end, as [his letters], revealing how they are not vowels nor are they consonants, so that one might read them and think of something foolish, but they are letters of the truth which they alone speak who know them. Each letter is a complete <thought> like a complete book, since they are letters written by the Unity, the Father having written them for the aeons in order that by means of his letters they should know the Father.

While his wisdom contemplates the Word, and his teaching utters it, his knowledge has revealed <it>. While forebearance is a crown upon it, and his gladness is in harmony with it, his glory has exalted it, his image has revealed it, his repose has received it into itself, his love has made a body over it, his fidelity has embraced it. In this way the Word of the Father goes forth in the totality, as the fruit **24** [of] his heart and an impression of his will. But it supports the totality; it chooses them and also receives the impression of the totality, purifying them, bringing them back into the Father, into the Mother, Jesus of the infinite sweetness.

The Father reveals his bosom.—Now his bosom is the Holy Spirit.—He reveals what is hidden of him—what is hidden of him is his Son—so that through the mercies of the Father the aeons may know him and cease laboring in search of the Father, resting there in him, knowing that this is the rest. Having filled the deficiency, he abolished the form—the form of it is the world, that in which he served.—For the place where there is envy and strife is deficient, but the place where (there is) Unity is perfect. Since the deficiency came into being because the Father was not known, therefore, when the Father is known, from that moment on the deficiency will no longer exist. As in the case of the ignorance of a person, when he comes to have knowledge, his ignorance vanishes of itself, as the darkness vanishes when light appears, **25** so also the deficiency vanishes in the perfection. So from that moment on the form is not apparent, but it will vanish in the fusion of Unity, for now their works lie scattered. In time Unity will perfect the spaces. It is within Unity that each one will attain himself; within knowledge he will purify himself from multiplicity into Unity, consuming matter within himself like fire, and darkness by light, death by life.

If indeed these things have happened to each one of us, then we must see to it above all that the house will be holy and silent for the Unity. (It is) as in the case of some people who moved out of dwellings having jars that in spots were not good. They would break them and the master of the house would not suffer loss. Rather <he> is glad because in place of the bad jars (there are) full ones which are made perfect. For such is the judgment which has come from **26** above. It has passed judgment on everyone; it is a drawn sword, with two edges, cutting on either side. When the Word appeared, the one that is within the heart of those who utter it—it is not a sound alone but it became a body—a great disturbance took place among the jars because some had been emptied, others filled; that is, some had been supplied, others poured out, some had been purified, still others broken up. All the spaces were shaken and disturbed because they had no order nor stability. Error was upset, not knowing what to do; it was grieved, in mourning, afflicting itself because it knew nothing. When knowledge drew near it—this is the downfall of (error) and all its emanations—error is empty, having nothing inside.

Truth appeared; all its emanations knew it. They greeted the Father in truth with a perfect power that joins them with the Father. For, as for everyone who loves the truth—because the truth is the mouth of the Father; his tongue is the Holy Spirit—he who is joined **27** to the truth is joined to the Father's mouth by his tongue, whenever he is to receive the Holy Spirit, since this is the manifestation of the Father and his revelation to his aeons.

He manifested what was hidden of him; he explained it. For who contains, if not the Father alone? All the spaces are his emanations. They have known that they came forth from him like children who are from a grown man. They knew that they had not yet received form nor yet received a name, each one of which the Father begets. Then, when they receive form by his knowledge, though truly within him, they do not know him. But the Father is perfect, knowing every space within him. If he wishes, he manifests whomever he wishes by giving him form and giving him a name, and he gives a name to him and brings it about that those come into existence who, before they come into existence, are ignorant of him who fashioned them.

I do not say, then, that they are nothing (at all) who have not yet come into existence, but they are **28** in him who will wish that they come into existence when he wishes, like the time that is to come. Before all things appear, he knows what he will produce. But the fruit which is not yet manifest does not know anything, nor does it do anything. Thus, also, every space which is itself in the Father is from the one who exists, who established it from what does not exist. For he who has no root has no fruit either, but though he thinks to himself, "I have come into being," yet he will perish by himself. For this reason, he who did not exist at all will never come into existence. What, then, did he wish him to think of himself? This: "I have come into being like the shadows and phantoms of the night." When the light shines on the terror which that person had experienced, he knows that it is nothing.

Thus they were ignorant of the Father, he being the one **29** whom they did not see. Since it was terror and disturbance and instability and doubt and division, there were many illusions at work by means of these, and (there were) empty fictions, as if they were sunk in sleep and found themselves in disturbing dreams. Either (there is) a place to which they are fleeing, or without strength they come (from) having chased after others, or they are involved in striking blows, or they are receiving blows themselves, or they have fallen from high places, or they take off into the air though they do not even have wings. Again, sometimes (it is as) if people were murdering them, though there is no one even pursuing them, or they themselves are killing their neighbors, for they have been stained with their blood. When those who are going through all these things wake up, they see nothing, they who were in the midst of all these disturbances, for they are nothing. Such is the way of those who have cast ignorance aside from them like sleep, not esteeming it as anything, nor do they esteem its **30** works as solid things either, but they leave them behind like a dream in the night. The knowledge of the Father they value as the dawn. This is the way each one has acted, as though asleep at the time when he was ignorant. And this

is the way he has <come to knowledge>, as if he had awakened. {and} Good for the one who will return and awaken. And blessed is he who has opened the eyes of the blind.

And the Spirit ran after him, hastening from waking him up. Having extended his hand to him who lay upon the ground, he set him up on his feet, for he had not yet risen. He gave them the means of knowing the knowledge of the Father and the revelation of his Son. For, when they had seen him and had heard him, he granted them to taste him and to smell him and to touch the beloved Son.

When he had appeared instructing them about the Father, the incomprehensible one, when he had breathed into them what is in the thought, doing his will, when many had received the light, they turned **31** to him. For the material ones were strangers and did not see his likeness and had not known him. For he came by means of fleshly form, while nothing blocked his course because incorruptibility is irresistible, since he, again, spoke new things, still speaking about what is in the heart of the Father, having brought forth the flawless word.

When light had spoken through his mouth, as well as his voice which gave birth to life, he gave them thought and understanding and mercy and salvation and the powerful spirit from the infiniteness and the sweetness of the Father. Having made punishments and tortures cease—for it was they which were leading astray from his face some who were in need of mercy, in error and in bonds—he both destroyed them with power and confounded them with knowledge. He became a way for those who were gone astray and knowledge for those who were ignorant, a discovery for those who were searching, and a support for those who were wavering, immaculateness for those who were defiled.

He is the shepherd who left behind the ninety-**32** nine sheep which were not lost. He went searching for the one which had gone astray. He rejoiced when he found it, for ninety-nine is a number that is in the left hand which holds it. But when the one is found, the entire number passes to the right (hand). As that which lacks the one—that is, the entire right (hand)—draws what was deficient and takes it from the left-hand side and brings (it) to the right, so too the number becomes one hundred. It is the sign of the one who is in their sound; it is the Father. Even on the Sabbath, he labored for the sheep which he found fallen into the pit. He gave life to the sheep, having brought it up from the pit in order that you might know interiorly—you, the sons of interior knowledge—what is the Sabbath, on which it is not fitting for salvation to be idle, in order that you may speak from the day from above, which has no night, and from the light which does not sink because it is perfect.

Say, then, from the heart that you are the perfect day and in you dwells the light that does not fail. Speak of the truth with those who search for it and (of) knowledge to those who have committed sin in their error. **33** Make firm the foot of those who have stumbled and stretch out your hands to those who are ill. Feed those who are hungry and give repose to those who are weary, and raise up those who wish to rise, and awaken those who sleep. For you are the understanding that is drawn forth. If strength acts thus, it becomes even stronger. Be concerned with yourselves; do not be concerned with other things which you have rejected from yourselves. Do not return to what you have vomited to eat it. Do not be moths. Do not be worms, for you have already cast it off. Do not become a (dwelling) place for the devil, for you have already destroyed him. Do not strengthen (those who are) obstacles to you who are collapsing, as though (you were) a support (for them). For the lawless one is someone to treat ill rather than the just one. For the former does his work as a lawless person; the latter as a righteous person does his work among others. So you, do the will of the Father, for you are from him.

For the Father is sweet and in his will is what is good. He has taken cognizance of the things that are yours that you might find rest in them. For by the fruits does one take cognizance of the things that are yours because the children of the Father **34** are his fragrance, for they are from the grace of his countenance. For this reason the Father loves his fragrance and manifests it in every place, and if it mixes with matter he gives his fragrance to the light and in his repose he causes it to surpass every form (and) every sound. For it is not the ears that smell the fragrance, but (it is) the breath that has the sense of smell and attracts the fragrance to itself and is submerged in the fragrance of the Father, so that he thus shelters it and takes it to the place where it came from, from the first fragrance which is grown cold. It is something in a psychic form, being like cold water which has frozen (?), which is on earth that is not solid, of which those who see it think it is earth; afterwards it dissolves again. If a breath draws it, it gets hot. The fragrances, therefore, that are cold are from the division. For this reason faith came; it dissolved the division, and it brought the warm pleroma of love in order that the cold should not come again but there should be the unity of perfect thought.

———————

25. Ptolemy's Letter to Flora

One of the most famous disciples of Valentinus (see the Gospel of Truth) was Ptolemy, a renowned gnostic teacher who lived in Rome in the mid-second century. From Ptolemy's own hand comes one of the clearest expositions of gnostic ideas, in a letter addressed to a woman named Flora, a non-Gnostic Christian whom Ptolemy is concerned to educate into the higher realms of knowledge of the faith. The letter is just the beginning of Ptolemy's instruction (regrettably, his subsequent lessons have been lost), but it concerns a central component of his gnostic views, his understanding of the Bible.

The proper interpretation of the Bible, Ptolemy avers, depends on understanding the nature of its divine inspiration. Those who maintain that it was authored by the Perfect God and Father (e.g., the "proto-othodox" Christians) err, because a perfect being could not inspire laws that are imperfect; those who claim that it was written by his adversary, the Devil (e.g., other groups of Gnostics?) also err, because an evil deity could not inspire laws that are just. Instead, there is a god intermediate between these two, the just but imperfect (and harsh) god who created the world; it was he who inspired parts of the Bible. Other parts, though, derive from Moses himself, and yet others from the elders around him. Those that are from god can themselves be divided into three parts, those that Jesus fulfilled (e.g., the Ten Commandments), those that he abolished (e.g., "an eye for an eye"), and those that he symbolically transformed (e.g., ceremonial laws). Ptolemy explicitly bases his views on the teachings of Paul and, especially, of Jesus himself.

This letter has not been transmitted independently and was not present among the Nag Hammadi writings but can be found only in quotations in the writings of the fourth-century heresy hunter Epiphanius (Book 33 of *The Medicine Chest*).

3 The law established by Moses, my dear sister Flora, has in the past been misunderstood by many people, for they were not closely acquainted with the one who established it or with its commandments. I think you will see this at once if you study their discordant opinions on this topic.

2 For some say that this law has been ordained by god the father; while others, following the opposite course, stoutly contend that it has been established by the adversary, the pernicious devil; and so the latter school attributes the craftsmanship of the world to the devil, saying that he is "the father and maker of the universe."[1]

3 <But> they are <utterly> in error, they disagree with one another, and each of the schools utterly misses the truth of the matter.

4 Now, it does not seem that the law was established by the perfect god and father: for, it must be of the same character as its giver; and yet it is imperfect and needful of being fulfilled by another and contains commandments incongruous with the nature and intentions of such a god.

5 On the other hand to attribute a law that abolishes injustice to the injustice of the adversary is the false logic of those who do not comprehend the principle of which the savior spoke. For our savior declared that a house or city divided against itself will not be able to stand.

6 And, further, the apostle states that the craftsmanship of the world is his, and that "all things were made through him, and without him was not anything made,"[2] thus anticipating these liars' flimsy wisdom. And the craftsmanship is that of a god who is just and hates evil, not a pernicious one as believed by these thoughtless people, who take no account of the craftsman's forethought and so are blind not only in the eye of the soul but even in the eyes of the body.

7 Now, from what has been said it should be clear to you (sing.) that these (schools of thought) utterly miss the truth, though each does so in its

---

[1]Plato *Tim* 28e.
[2]John 1:3.

own particular way: one (school) by not being acquainted with the god of righteousness, the other by not being acquainted with the father of the entirety, who was manifested by him alone who came and who alone knew him.

8 It remains for us, who have been deemed worthy of <acquaintance> with both, to show you (sing.) exactly what sort of law the law is, and which legislator established it. We shall offer proofs of what we say by drawing from our savior's words, by which alone it is possible to reach a certain apprehension of the reality of the matter without stumbling.

4 Now, first you must learn that, as a whole, the law contained in the Pentateuch of Moses was not established by a single author, I mean not by god alone: rather, there are certain of its commandments that were established by human beings as well. Indeed, our savior's words teach us that the Pentateuch divides into three parts.

2 For one division belongs to god himself and his legislations; while <another division> belongs to Moses—indeed, Moses ordained certain of the commandments not as god himself ordained through him, rather based upon his own thoughts about the matter; and yet a third division belongs to the elders of the people, <who> likewise in the beginning must have inserted certain of their own commandments.

3 You will now learn how all this can be demonstrated from the savior's words.

4 When the savior was talking with those who were arguing with him about divorce—and it has been ordained (in the law) that divorce is permitted—he said to them: "For your (pl.) hardness of heart Moses allowed divorce of one's wife. Now, from the beginning it was not so."[3] For god, he says, has joined together this union, and "what the lord has joined together, let no man put asunder."[4]

5 Here he shows that <the> law of god is one thing, forbidding a woman to be put asunder from her husband; while the law of Moses is another, permitting the couple to be put asunder because of hard-heartedness.

6 And so, accordingly, Moses ordains contrary to what god ordains; for <separating> is contrary to not separating.

Yet if we also scrutinize Moses' intentions with which he ordained this commandment, we find that he created the commandment not of his own inclination but of necessity because of the weakness of those to whom it was ordained.

7 For the latter were not able to put into practice god's intentions, in the matter of their not being permitted to divorce their wives. Some of them were on very bad terms with their wives, and ran the risk of being further diverted into injustice and from there into their destruction.

8 Moses, wishing to excise this unpleasant element through which they also ran the risk of being destroyed, ordained for them of his own accord a second law, the law of divorce, choosing under the circumstances the lesser of two evils, as it were,

9 so that if they were unable to keep the former (that is, god's law) they could keep at least the latter and so not be diverted into injustice and evil, through which utter destruction would follow in consequence.

10 These are Moses' intentions, with which we find him ordaining laws contrary to those of god. At any rate, even if we have for the moment used only one example in our proof, it is beyond doubt that, as we have shown, this law is of Moses himself and is distinct from god's.

11 And the savior shows also that there are some traditions of the elders interwoven in the law. He says, "For god spoke: 'Honor your father and your mother, that it may be well with you.'

12 But you have declared," the savior says, addressing the elders, "'What you would have gained from me is given to god.' And for the sake of your tradition, O ancients, you have made void the law of god."[5]

13 And Isaiah declared this by saying, "This people honors me with their lips, but their heart is far from me; in vain do they worship me, teaching as doctrines the precepts of men."[6]

---

[3]Matt 19:8.
[4]Matt 19:6.
[5]Matt 15:4–5.
[6]Isa 29:3; Matt 15:8.

14 Thus it has been clearly shown from these passages that, as a whole, the law is divided into three parts. For we have found in it legislations belonging to Moses himself, to the elders, and to god himself. Moreover, the analysis of the law as a whole, as we have divided it here, has made clear which part of it is genuine.

5 Now, what is more, the one part that is the law of god himself divides into three subdivisions.

The first subdivision is the pure legislation not interwoven with evil, which alone is properly called law, and which the savior did not come to abolish but to fulfill. For what he fulfilled was not alien to him, <but stood in need of fulfillment>: for it did not have perfection.

And the second subdivision is the part interwoven with the inferior and with injustice, which the savior abolished as being incongruous with his own nature.

2 Finally, the third subdivision is the symbolic and allegorical part, which is after the image of the superior, spiritual realm: the savior changed (the referent of) this part from the perceptible, visible level to the spiritual, invisible one.

3 The first, the law of god that is pure and not interwoven with the inferior, is the decalogue of Ten Commandments inscribed on two stone tablets; they divide into the prohibition of things that must be avoided and the commanding of things that must be done. Although they contain pure legislation they do not have perfection, and so they were in need of fulfillment by the savior.

4 The second, which is interwoven with injustice, is that which applies to retaliation and repayment of those who have already committed a wrong, commanding us to pluck out an eye for an eye and a tooth for a tooth and to retaliate for murder with murder.[7] This part is interwoven with injustice, for the one who is second to act unjustly still acts unjustly, differing only in the relative order in which he acts, and committing the very same act.

5 But otherwise, this commandment both was and is just, having been established as a deviation from the pure law because of the weakness of those to whom it was ordained; yet it is incongruous with the nature and goodness of the father of the entirety.

6 Now perhaps this was apt; but even more, it was a result of necessity. For when one who does not wish even a single murder to occur—by saying, "You shall not kill"—when, I say, he ordains a second law and commands the murderer to be murdered,[8] acting as judge between two murders, he who forbade even a single murder[9] has without realizing it been cheated by necessity.

7 For this reason, then, the son who was sent from him abolished this part of the law, though he admits that it too belonged to god: this part is reckoned as belonging to the old school of thought, both where he says, "For god spoke: 'He who speaks evil of father or mother, let him surely die' "[10] and elsewhere.

8 And the third subdivision of god's law is the symbolic part, which is after the image of the superior, spiritual realm: I mean, what is ordained about offerings, circumcision, the Sabbath, fasting, Passover, the Feast of Unleavened Bread, and the like.

9 Now, once the truth had been manifested, the referent of all these ordinances was changed, inasmuch as they are images and allegories. As to their meaning in the visible realm and their physical accomplishment they were abolished; but as to their spiritual meaning they were elevated, with the words remaining the same but the subject matter being altered.

10 For the savior commanded us to offer offerings, but not dumb beasts or incense: rather, spiritual praises and glorifications and prayers of thanksgiving, and offerings in the form of sharing and good deeds.

11 And he wishes us to perform circumcision, but not circumcision of the bodily foreskin, rather of the spiritual heart;

12 and to keep the Sabbath, for he wants us to be inactive in wicked acts;

---

[7]Lev 24:17, 20.
[8]Exod 20:13.
[9]Exod 21:12.
[10]Matt 15:4.

13 and to fast, though he does not wish us to perform physical fasts, rather spiritual ones, which consist of abstinence from all bad deeds.

Nevertheless, fasting as to the visible realm is observed by our adherents, since fasting, if practiced with reason, can contribute something to the soul, so long as it does not take place in imitation of other people or by habit or because fasting has been prescribed <for> a particular day.

14 Likewise, it is observed in memory of true fasting, so that those who are not yet able to observe true fasting might have a remembrance of it from fasting according to the visible realm.

15 Likewise, the apostle Paul makes it clear that Passover and the Feast of Unleavened Bread were images, for he says that "Christ, our paschal lamb, has been sacrificed"[11] and, he says, be without leaven, having no share in leaven—now, by "leaven" he means evil—but rather "be fresh dough."

6 And so it can be granted that the actual law of god is subdivided into three parts. The first subdivision is the part that was fulfilled by the savior: for "you shall not kill," "you shall not commit adultery," "you shall not swear falsely" are subsumed under not being angry, not looking lustfully at another, and not swearing at all.[12]

2 The second subdivision is the part that was completely abolished. For the commandment of "an eye for an eye and a tooth for a tooth,"[13] which is interwoven with injustice and itself involves an act of injustice, was abolished by the savior with injunctions to the contrary,

3 and of two contraries one must "abolish" the other: "For I say to you (pl.), Do not in any way resist one who is evil. But if any one strikes you (sing.), turn to him the other cheek also."[14]

4 And the third subdivision is the part whose referent was changed and which was altered from the physical to the spiritual—the allegorical part, which is ordained after the image of the superior realm.

5 Now, the images and allegories are indicative of other matters, and they were well and good while truth was not present. But now that truth is present, one must do the works of truth and not those of its imagery.

6 His disciples made these teachings known, and so did the apostle Paul: he makes known to us the part consisting of images, through the passage on the paschal lamb and the unleavened bread, which we have already spoken of. The part consisting of a law interwoven with injustice, he made known by speaking of "abolishing the law of commandments and ordinances";[15] and the part not interwoven with the inferior, when he says, "The law is holy, and the commandment is holy and just and good."[16]

7 Thus I think I have shown you, as well as possible in a brief treatment, both that there is human legislation which has been slipped into the law and that the law of god himself divides into three subdivisions.

2 Now it remains for us to say what sort of being this god is, who established the law. But this too I believe I have demonstrated to you (sing.) in what I have already said, providing you have followed carefully.

3 For since this division of the law (that is, god's own law) was established neither by the perfect god, as we have taught, nor surely by the devil—which it would be wrong to say—then the establisher of this division of the law is distinct from them.

4 And he is the craftsman and maker of the universe or world and of the things within it. Since he is different from the essences of the other two <and> (rather) is in a state intermediate between them, he would rightfully be described by the term intermediateness.

5 And if the perfect god is good according to his nature—as indeed he is, for our savior showed that "one only is there who is good,"[17] namely his father whom he manifested—and if furthermore the law belonging to the nature of the adversary is both evil and wicked and is stamped in the mold of injustice, then a being that is in a state intermediate between these and is neither good, nor

---

[11]1 Cor 5:7.
[12]Matt 5:21, 27, 33.
[13]Lev 24:20.
[14]Matt 5:39.
[15]Eph 2:15.
[16]Rom 7:12.
[17]Matt 19:17.

evil or unjust, might well be properly called just, being a judge of the justice that is his.

6 And on the one hand this god must be inferior to the perfect god and less than his righteousness precisely because he is engendered and not unengendered—for "there is one unengendered father, from whom are all things,"[18] or more exactly, from whom all things depend; and on the other hand, he must have come into being as better and more authoritative than the adversary; and must be born of an essence and nature distinct from the essences of the other two.

7 For the essence of the adversary is both corruption and darkness, for the adversary is material and divided into many parts; while the essence of the unengendered father of the entirety is both incorruptibility and self-existent light, being simple and unique. And the essence of this intermediate produced a twofold capacity, for he is an image of the better god.

8 And now, given that the good by nature engenders and produces the things that are similar to itself and of the same essence, do not be bewil-

dered as to how these natures—that of corruption and <that> of intermediateness—which have come to be different in essence, arose from a single first principle of the entirety, a principle that exists and is confessed and believed in by us, and which is unengendered and incorruptible and good.

9 For, god permitting, you will next learn about both the first principle and the generation of these two other gods, if you are deemed worthy of the apostolic tradition, which even we have received by succession; and along with this you will learn how to test all the propositions by means of our savior's teaching.

10 I have not failed, my sister Flora, to state these matters to you briefly. And what I have just written is a concise account, though I have treated the subject adequately. In the future these teachings will be of the greatest help to you—at least if, like good rich soil that has received fertile seeds, you bear fruit.

---

[18]1 Cor 8:6.

><+>-O-<+><

26. On the Origin of the World

This Nag Hammadi tractate is not provided with a title in its manuscript; modern scholars have called it "On the Origin of the World" simply as a precise summation of its contents. Evidently speaking to outsiders, its unknown author explains in involved and intricate detail a gnostic view of how the world came into being. The account is largely based on an imaginative exposition of the opening chapters of Genesis, in which a number of the gaps of the narrative (including the events that transpired *before* Gen 1:1) are filled in. Many important aspects of gnostic mythology are covered here: the existence of the

---

"On the Origin of the World," translated by Hans-Gebhard Bethge and Bentley Layton, from *The Nag Hammadi Library in English*, 3d, completely revised ed., by James M. Robinson, General Editor. Copyright © 1978, 1988 by E. J. Brill, Leiden, The Netherlands. Reprinted by permission of HarperCollins Publishers, Inc.

divine pleroma before all things, the emergence of Yaldabaoth the creator God, his generation of other divine beings, the creation of the material world, and the formation of the human race. The following excerpt gives approximately two-thirds of the treatise, from its beginning through the creation of Adam.

Scholars debate the dating of the work; possibly it was written near the end of the third century.

Seeing that everybody, gods of the world and humankind, says that nothing existed prior to chaos, I in distinction to them shall demonstrate that they are all mistaken, because they are not acquainted with the origin of chaos, nor with its root. Here is the demonstration. How well it suits **98** all people, on the subject of chaos, to say that it is a kind of darkness! But in fact it comes from a shadow, which has been called by the name darkness. And the shadow comes from a product that has existed since the beginning. It is, moreover, clear that it (viz., the product) existed before chaos came into being, and that the latter is posterior to the first product.

Let us therefore concern ourselves with the facts of the matter; and furthermore, with the first product, from which chaos was projected. And in this way the truth will be clearly demonstrated.

After the natural structure of the immortal beings had completely developed out of the infinite, a likeness then emanated from Pistis (Faith); it is called Sophia (Wisdom). It exercised volition and became a product resembling the primeval light. And immediately her will manifested itself as a likeness of heaven, having an unimaginable magnitude; it was between the immortal beings and those things that came into being after them, like . . . : she (Sophia) functioned as a veil dividing mankind from the things above.

Now the eternal realm (aeon) of truth has no shadow outside it, for the limitless light is everywhere within it. But its exterior is shadow, which has been called by the name darkness. From it there appeared a force, presiding over the darkness. And the forces that came into being subsequent to them called the shadow "the limitless chaos." From it, every [kind] of divinity sprouted

up . . . together with the entire place, [so that] also, [shadow] is posterior to the first **99** product. It was <in> the abyss that [it] (shadow) appeared, deriving from the aforementioned Pistis.

Then shadow perceived that there was something mightier than it, and felt envy; and when it had become pregnant of its own accord, suddenly it engendered jealousy. Since that day, the principle of jealousy amongst all the eternal realms and their worlds has been apparent. Now as for that jealousy, it was found to be an abortion without any spirit in it. Like a shadow it came into existence in a vast watery substance. Then the bile that had come into being out of the shadow was thrown into a part of chaos. Since that day, a watery substance has been apparent. And what sank within it flowed away, being visible in chaos: as with a woman giving birth to a child—all her superfluities flow out; just so, matter came into being out of shadow and was projected apart. And it (viz., matter) did not depart from chaos; rather, matter was in chaos, being in a part of it.

And when these things had come to pass, then Pistis came and appeared over the matter of chaos, which had been expelled like an aborted fetus— since there was no spirit in it. For all of it (viz., chaos) was limitless darkness and bottomless water. Now when Pistis saw what had resulted from her defect, she became disturbed. And the disturbance appeared, as a fearful product; it rushed [to] her in the chaos. She turned to it and [blew] into its face in the abyss, which is below **100** all the heavens.

And when Pistis Sophia desired to cause the thing that had no spirit to be formed into a likeness and to rule over matter and over all her forces, there appeared for the first time a ruler, out of the waters, lionlike in appearance, androgynous, having great authority within him and ignorant of whence he had come into being. Now when Pistis Sophia saw him moving about in the depth of the waters she said to him, "Child, pass through to here," whose equivalent is "*yalda baōth.*"

Since that day there appeared the principle of verbal expression, which reached the gods and the angels and mankind. And what came into being as a result of verbal expression, the gods and the angels and mankind finished. Now as for the ruler Yaltabaoth, he is ignorant of the force of Pistis: he did not see her face, rather he saw in the water the likeness that spoke with him. And because of that voice, he called himself Yaldabaoth. But Ariael is what the perfect call him, for he was like a lion. Now when he had come to have authority over matter, Pistis Sophia withdrew up to her light.

When the ruler saw his magnitude—and it was only himself that he saw: he saw nothing else, except for water and darkness—then he supposed that it was he alone who existed. His [. . .] was completed by verbal expression: it **101** appeared as a spirit moving to and fro upon the waters. And when that spirit appeared, the ruler set apart the watery substance. And what was dry was divided into another place. And from matter he made for himself an abode, and he called it heaven. And from matter, the ruler made a footstool, and he called it earth.

Next, the ruler had a thought—consistent with his nature—and by means of verbal expression he created an androgyne. He opened his mouth and cooed to him. When his eyes had been opened, he looked at his father, and he said to him, "Eee!" Then his father called him Eee-a-o (Yao). Next he created the second son. He cooed to him. And he opened his eyes and said to his father, "Eh!" His father called him Eloai. Next he created the third son. He cooed to him. And he opened his eyes and said to his father, "Asss!" His father called him Astaphaios. These are the three sons of their father.

Seven appeared in chaos, androgynous. They have their masculine names and their feminine names. The feminine name is Pronoia (Fore-

thought) Sambathas, which is "week." And his son is called Yao: his feminine name is Lordship.

> Sabaoth: his feminine name is Deity.
> Adonaios: his feminine name is Kingship.
> Eloaios: his feminine name is Jealousy.
> Oraios: his feminine name is Wealth.
> And Astaphaios: his feminine name **102** is Sophia (Wisdom).

These are the [seven] forces of the seven heavens of [chaos]. And they were born androgynous, consistent with the immortal pattern that existed before them, according to the wish of Pistis: so that the likeness of what had existed since the beginning might reign to the end.

You (sg.) will find the effect of these names and the force of the male entities in the *Archangelic (Book) of the Prophet Moses*, and the names of the female entities in the first *Book (biblos) of Noraia*.

Now the prime parent Yaldabaoth, since he possessed great authorities, created heavens for each of his offspring through verbal expression—created them beautiful, as dwelling places—and in each heaven he created great glories, seven times excellent. Thrones and mansions and temples, and also chariots and virgin spirits up to an invisible one and their glories, each one has these in his heaven; mighty armies of gods and lords and angels and archangels—countless myriads—so that they might serve.

The account of these matters you (sg.) will find in a precise manner in the first *Account of Oraia*.

And they were completed from this heaven to as far up as the sixth heaven, namely that of Sophia. The heaven and his earth were destroyed by the troublemaker that was below them all. And the six heavens shook violently; for the forces of chaos knew who it was that had destroyed the heaven that was below them. And when Pistis knew about the breakage resulting from the disturbance, she sent forth her breath and bound him and cast him down into Tartaros. Since that day, the heaven, along with **103** its earth, has consolidated itself through Sophia the daughter of Yaldabaoth, she who is below them all.

Now when the heavens had consolidated themselves along with their forces and all their administration, the prime parent became insolent. And he was honored by all the army of angels. And all the gods and their angels gave blessing and honor to him. And for his part he was delighted and continually boasted, saying to them, "I have no need of anyone." He said, "It is I who am God, and there is no other one that exists apart from me."[1] And when he said this, he sinned against all the immortal beings who give answer. And they laid it to his charge.

Then when Pistis saw the impiety of the chief ruler she was filled with anger. She was invisible. She said, "You are mistaken, Samael," that is, "blind god." "There is an immortal man of light who has been in existence before you and who will appear among your modelled forms; he will trample you to scorn just as potter's clay is pounded. And you will descend to your mother, the abyss, along with those that belong to you. For at the consummation of your (pl.) works the entire defect that has become visible out of the truth will be abolished, and it will cease to be and will be like what has never been." Saying this, Pistis revealed her likeness of her greatness in the waters. And so doing she withdrew up to her light.

Now when Sabaoth the son of Yaldabaoth heard the voice of Pistis, he sang praises to her, and [he] condemned the father . . . 104 at the word of Pistis; and he praised her because she had instructed them about the immortal man and his light. Then Pistis Sophia stretched out her finger and poured upon him some light from her light, to be a condemnation of his father. Then when Sabaoth was illumined, he received great authority against all the forces of chaos. Since that day he has been called "Lord of the Forces."

He hated his father, the darkness, and his mother, the abyss, and loathed his sister, the thought of the prime parent, which moved to and fro upon the waters. And because of his light all the authorities of chaos were jealous of him. And when they had become disturbed, they made a great war in the seven heavens. Then when Pistis Sophia had seen the war, she dispatched seven archangels to Sabaoth from her light. They snatched him up to the seventh heaven. They stood before him as attendants. Furthermore she sent him three more archangels and established the kingdom for him over everyone so that he might dwell above the twelve gods of chaos.

Now when Sabaoth had taken up the place of repose in return for his repentance, Pistis also gave him her daughter Zoe (Life) together with great authority so that she might instruct him about all things that exist in the eighth heaven. And as he had authority, he made himself first of all a mansion. It is huge, magnificent, seven times as great as all those that exist in the seven heavens.

And before 105 his mansion he created a throne, which was huge and was upon a four-faced chariot called "Cherubin." Now the Cherubin has eight shapes per each of the four corners, lion forms and calf forms and human forms and eagle forms, so that all the forms amount to sixty-four forms— and (he created) seven archangels that stand before it; he is the eighth, and has authority. All the forms amount to seventy-two. Furthermore, from this chariot the seventy-two gods took shape; they took shape so that they might rule over the seventy-two languages of the peoples. And by that throne he created other, serpent-like angels, called "Saraphin," which praise him at all times.

Thereafter he created a congregation (*ekklesia*) of angels, thousands and myriads, numberless, which resembled the congregation in the eighth heaven; and a firstborn called Israel—which is, "the man that sees God"; and another being, called Jesus Christ, who resembles the savior above in the eighth heaven and who sits at his right upon a revered throne, and at his left, there sits the virgin of the holy spirit, upon a throne and glorifying him. And the seven virgins stand before her, . . . possessing thirty harps, and psalteries and 106 trumpets, glorifying him. And all the armies of the angels glorify him, and they bless him. Now where he sits is upon a throne of light <within a> great cloud that covers him. And there was no one with him in the cloud except Sophia <the daughter of> Pistis, instructing him about all the things that ex-

---

[1]Isa 45:5–6, 12.

ist in the eighth heaven, so that the likenesses of those things might be created, in order that his reign might endure until the consummation of the heavens of chaos and their forces.

Now Pistis Sophia set him apart from the darkness and summoned him to her right, and the prime parent she put at her left. Since that day, right has been called justice, and left called wickedness. Now because of this they all received a realm (*kosmos*) in the congregation of justice and wickedness, . . . stand . . . upon a creature . . . all.

Thus when the prime parent of chaos saw his son Sabaoth and the glory that he was in, and perceived that he was greatest of all the authorities of chaos, he envied him. And having become wrathful he engendered Death out of his death: and he (viz., Death) was established over the sixth heaven, <for> Sabaoth had been snatched up from there. And thus the number of the six authorities of chaos was achieved. Then Death, being androgynous, mingled with his (own) nature and begot seven androgynous offspring. These are the names of the male ones: Jealousy, Wrath, Tears, Sighing, Suffering, Lamentation, Bitter Weeping. And these are the names of the female ones: Wrath, Pain, Lust, Sighing, Curse, Bitterness, Quarrelsomeness. They had intercourse with one another, and each one begot seven, so that they amount to **107** forty-nine androgynous demons.

Their names and their effects you will find in the *Book of Solomon*.

And in the presence of these, Zoe, who was with Sabaoth, created seven good androgynous forces. These are the names of the male ones: the Unenvious, the Blessed, the Joyful, the True, the Unbegrudging, the Beloved, the Trustworthy. Also, as regards the female ones, these are their names: Peace, Gladness, Rejoicing, Blessedness, Truth, Love, Faith (Pistis). And from these there are many good and innocent spirits.

Their influences and their effects you will find in the *Configurations of the Fate of Heaven That Is Beneath the Twelve*.

And having seen the likeness of Pistis in the waters, the prime parent grieved very much, especially when he heard her voice, like the first voice that had called to him out of the waters. And when he knew that it was she who had given a name to him, he sighed. He was ashamed on account of his transgression. And when he had come to know in truth that an immortal man of light had been existing before him, he was greatly disturbed; for he had previously said to all the gods and their angels, "It is I who am god. No other one exists apart from me."[2] For he had been afraid they might know that another had been in existence before him, and might condemn him. But he, being devoid of understanding, scoffed at the condemnation and acted recklessly. He said, "If **108** anything has existed before me, let it appear, so that we may see its light."

And immediately, behold! Light came out of the eighth heaven above and passed through all of the heavens of the earth. When the prime parent saw that the light was beautiful as it radiated, he was amazed. And he was greatly ashamed. As that light appeared, a human likeness appeared within it, very wonderful. And no one saw it except for the prime parent and Pronoia, who was with him. Yet its light appeared to all the forces of the heavens. Because of this they were all troubled by it.

Then when Pronoia saw that emissary, she became enamored of him. But he hated her because she was on the darkness. But she desired to embrace him, and she was not able to. When she was unable to assuage her love, she poured out her light upon the earth. Since that day, that emissary has been called "Adam of Light," whose rendering is "the luminous man of blood," and the earth spread over him, holy Adaman, whose rendering is "the Holy Land of Adamantine." Since that day, all the authorities have honored the blood of the virgin. And the earth was purified on account of the blood of the virgin. But most of all, the water was purified through the likeness of Pistis Sophia, who had appeared to the prime parent in the waters. Justly, then, it has been said: "through the waters." The holy water, since it vivifies the all, **109** purifies it.

Out of that first blood Eros appeared, being androgynous. His masculinity is Himireris (i.e.,

---

[2]Isa 45:5–6, 12.

Himeros), being fire from the light. His femininity that is with him—a soul of blood—is from the stuff of Pronoia. He is very lovely in his beauty, having a charm beyond all the creatures of chaos. Then all the gods and their angels, when they beheld Eros, became enamored of him. And appearing in all of them he set them afire: just as from a single lamp many lamps are lit, and one and the same light is there, but the lamp is not diminished. And in this way Eros became dispersed in all the created beings of chaos, and was not diminished. Just as from the midpoint of light and darkness Eros appeared and at the midpoint of the angels and mankind the sexual union of Eros was consummated so out of the earth the primal pleasure blossomed. The woman followed earth. And marriage followed woman. Birth followed marriage. Dissolution followed birth.

After that Eros, the grapevine sprouted up out of that blood, which had been shed over the earth. Because of this, those who drink of it conceive the desire of sexual union. After the grapevine, a fig tree and a pomegranate tree sprouted up from the earth, together with the rest of the trees, all species, having within them their seed from the **110** seed of the authorities and their angels.

Then Justice created Paradise, being beautiful and being outside the orbit of the moon and the orbit of the sun in the Land of Wantonness, in the East in the midst of the stones. And desire is in the midst of the beautiful, appetizing trees. And the tree of eternal life is as it appeared by God's will, to the north of Paradise, so that it might make eternal the souls of the pure, who shall come forth from the modelled forms of poverty at the consummation of the age. Now the color of the tree of life is like the sun. And its branches are beautiful. Its leaves are like those of the cypress. Its fruit is like a bunch of grapes when it is white. Its height goes as far as heaven. And next to it (is) the tree of acquaintance (*gnosis*), having the strength of God. Its glory is like the moon when fully radiant. And its branches are beautiful. Its leaves are like fig leaves. Its fruit is like a good appetizing date. And this tree is to the north of Paradise, so that it might arouse the souls from the torpor of the demons, in order that they might ap-

proach the tree of life and eat of its fruit and so condemn the authorities and their angels.

The effect of this tree is described in the *Sacred Book*, to wit: "It is you who are the tree of acquaintance, which is in Paradise, from which the first man ate and which opened his mind; and he loved his female counterpart and condemned **111** the other, alien likenesses and loathed them."

Now after it, the olive tree sprouted up, which was to purify the kings and the high priests of righteousness, who were to appear in the last days, since the olive tree appeared out of the light of the first Adam for the sake of the unguent that they were to receive.

And the first soul (*psyche*) loved Eros, who was with her, and poured her blood upon him and upon the earth. And out of that blood the rose first sprouted up, out of the earth, out of the thorn bush, to be a source of joy for the light that was to appear in the bush. Moreover after this the beautiful, good-smelling flowers sprouted up from the earth, different kinds, from every single virgin of the daughters of Pronoia. And they, when they had become enamored of Eros, poured out their blood upon him and upon the earth. After these, every plant sprouted up from the earth, different kinds, containing the seed of the authorities and their angels. After these, the authorities created out of the waters all species of beast, and the reptiles and birds—different kinds—containing the seed of the authorities and their angels.

But before all these, when he had appeared on the first day, he remained upon the earth, something like two days, and left the lower Pronoia in heaven, and ascended towards his light. And immediately darkness covered all the universe. **112** Now when she wished, the Sophia who was in the lower heaven received authority from Pistis, and fashioned great luminous bodies and all the stars. And she put them in the sky to shine upon the earth and to render temporal signs and seasons and years and months and days and nights and moments and so forth. And in this way the entire region upon the sky was adorned.

Now when Adam of Light conceived the wish to enter his light—i.e., the eighth heaven—he was unable to do so because of the poverty that had mingled with his light. Then he created for himself a vast eternal realm. And within that eternal realm he created six eternal realms and their adornments, six in number, that were seven times better than the heavens of chaos and their adornments. Now all these eternal realms and their adornments exist within the infinity that is between the eighth heaven and the chaos below it, being counted with the universe that belongs to poverty.

If you (sg.) want to know the arrangement of these, you will find it written in the *Seventh Universe of the Prophet Hieralias.*

And before Adam of Light had withdrawn in the chaos, the authorities saw him and laughed at the prime parent because he had lied when he said, "It is I who am God. No one exists before me."[3] When they came to him, they said, "Is this not the god who ruined our work?" He answered and said, "Yes. If you do not want him to be able to ruin our work, come let us create a human being out of earth, according to the image of our body and according to the likeness **113** of this being (viz., Adam of Light), to serve us; so that when he (viz., Adam of Light) sees his likeness he might become enamored of it. No longer will he ruin our work; rather, we shall make those who are born out of the light our servants for all the duration of this eternal realm. Now all of this came to pass according to the forethought of Pistis, in order that a human being should appear after his likeness, and should condemn them because of their modelled form. And their modelled form became an enclosure of the light.

Then the authorities received the acquaintance (*gnosis*) necessary to create man. Sophia Zoe—she who is with Sabaoth—had anticipated them. And she laughed at their decision. For they are blind: against their own interests they ignorantly created him. And they do not realize what they are about to do. The reason she anticipated them and made her own human being first, was in order that he might instruct their modelled form how to despise them and thus to escape from them.

Now the production of the instructor came about as follows. When Sophia let fall a droplet of light, it flowed onto the water, and immediately a human being appeared, being androgynous. That droplet she molded first as a female body. Afterwards, using the body she molded it in the likeness of the mother which had appeared. And he finished it in twelve months. An androgynous human being was produced, whom the Greeks call Hermaphrodites; and whose mother the Hebrews call Eve of Life (Eve of Zoe), namely, the female instructor of life. Her offspring is the creature that is lord. Afterwards, the authorities **114** called it "Beast," so that it might lead astray their modelled creatures. The interpretation of "the beast" is "the instructor." For it was found to be the wisest of all beings.

Now, Eve is the first virgin, the one who without a husband bore her first offspring. It is she who served as her own midwife.

For this reason she is held to have said:

"It is I who am the part of my mother;
And it is I who am the mother;
It is I who am the wife;
It is I who am the virgin;
It is I who am pregnant;
It is I who am the midwife;
It is I who am the one that comforts pains
    of travail;
It is my husband who bore me;
And it is I who am his mother,
And it is he who is my father and my lord.
It is he who is my force;
What he desires, he says with reason.
I am in the process of becoming.
Yet I have borne a man as lord."

Now these through the will <. . .>. The souls that were going to enter the modelled forms of the authorities were manifested to Sabaoth and his Christ. And regarding these the holy voice said, "Multiply and improve! Be lord over all creatures." And it is they who were taken captive, according to their destinies, by the prime parent. And thus they were shut into the prisons of the modelled forms. . . . And at that time, the prime parent then rendered an opinion concerning man to those who were with him. Then each of them cast his sperm

---

[3]Isa 45:5–6, 12.

into the midst of the navel of the earth. Since that day, the seven rulers have fashioned man with his body resembling their body, but his likeness resembling the man that had appeared to them. His modelling took place by parts, one at a time. And their leader fashioned the brain and the nervous system. Afterwards he appeared as prior to him. He became **115** a soul-endowed man. And he was called Adam, that is, "father," according to the name of the one that existed before him.

▷·◆▷··○··◁·◆◁

27. The Wisdom of Jesus Christ

The "Wisdom (or Sophia) of Jesus Christ" recounts a discussion between Jesus and his disciples after his resurrection. In it, Jesus responds to the eager questions of his followers about the ultimate nature of reality. This kind of postresurrection dialogue was a popular form of gnostic writing; by placing the ultimate revelation of truth in the period after Jesus' life, the author was able to show its hidden, esoteric quality (see the Secret Book of John).

Here Jesus is shown to be a divine aeon, come to reveal the true nature of the Perfect God and Father; of the divine, celestial realm above; of the constitution of humans; and of the way of ultimate salvation through perfect knowledge, a salvation that involves a return to the one God in whom the enlightened will repose forever.

This tractate is closely related to another one discovered at Nag Hammadi, usually called "Eugnostos the Blessed." Since Eugnostos does not contain explicitly Christian elements but is cast as a philosophical letter sent by a teacher to his followers, many scholars think that the "Wisdom of Jesus Christ" represents a later, christianized version of the account, which evidently originated some time in the second century. (NB: the sequence of the chapter numbers becomes confused near the end of this text because it is drawn from two different manuscripts, neither one of which is complete.)

After he rose from the dead, his twelve disciples and seven women continued to be his followers and went to Galilee onto the mountain **91** called "Divination and Joy." When they gathered together and were perplexed about the underlying reality of the universe and the plan and the holy providence and the power of the authorities and about everything that the Savior is doing with them in the secret of the holy plan, the Savior appeared, not in his previous form, but in the invisible spirit. And his likeness resembles a great angel of light. But his resemblance I must not describe. No mortal flesh could endure it, but only pure (and) perfect flesh, like that which he taught

---

us about on the mountain called "Of Olives" in Galilee. And he said: "Peace be to you (pl.)! My peace I give to you!" And they all marveled and were afraid.

The Savior **92** laughed and said to them: "What are you thinking about? (Why) are you perplexed? What are you searching for?" Philip said: "For the underlying reality of the universe and the plan."

The Savior said to them: "I want you to know that all people born on earth from the foundation of the world until now, being dust, while they have inquired about God, who he is and what he is like, have not found him. Now the wisest among them have speculated from the ordering of the world and (its) movement. But their speculation has not reached the truth. For it is said that the ordering is directed in three ways by all the philosophers, (and) hence they do not agree. For some of them say about the world that it is directed by itself. **93** Others, that it is providence (that directs it). Others, that it is fate. But it is none of these. Again, of the three voices I have just mentioned, none is close to the truth, and (they are) from humans. But I, who came from Infinite Light, I am here—for I know him (Light)—that I might speak to you about the precise nature of the truth. For whatever is from itself is a polluted life; it is self-made. Providence has no wisdom in it. And fate does not discern.

But to you it is given to know; and whoever is worthy of knowledge will receive (it), whoever has not been begotten by the sowing of unclean rubbing but by First Who Was Sent, for he is an immortal in the midst of mortals."

Matthew said **94** to him: "Lord, no one can find the truth except through you. Therefore teach us the truth." The Savior said: "He Who Is is ineffable. No principle knew him, no authority, no subjection, nor any creature from the foundation of the world until now, except he alone and anyone to whom he wants to make revelation through him who is from First Light. From now on I am the Great Savior. For he is immortal and eternal. Now he is eternal, having no birth; for everyone who has birth will perish. He is unbegotten, having no beginning; for everyone who has a begin-

ning has an end. Since no one rules over him, he has no name; for whoever has a name is the creation of another. He is unnameable. He has no human form; for whoever has human form is the creation of another. And he has a semblance **95** of his own—not like what you have seen and received, but a strange semblance that surpasses all things and is better than the universe. It looks to every side and sees itself from itself. Since it is infinite, he is ever incomprehensible. He is imperishable and has no likeness (to anything). He is unchanging good. He is faultless. He is eternal. He is blessed. While he is not known, he ever knows himself. He is immeasurable. He is untraceable. He is perfect, having no defect. He is imperishably blessed. He is called 'Father of the Universe.'"

Philip said: "Lord, how, then, did he appear to the perfect ones?" The perfect Savior said to him: "Before anything is visible of those that are visible, the majesty and the authority are **96** in him, since he embraces the whole of the totalities, while nothing embraces him. For he is all mind. And he is thought and considering and reflecting and rationality and power. They all are equal powers. They are the sources of the totalities. And their whole race from first to last was in his foreknowledge, (that of) the infinite Unbegotten Father."

Thomas said to him: "Lord, Savior, why did these come to be, and why were these revealed?" The perfect Savior said: "I came from the Infinite that I might tell you all things. Spirit Who Is was the begetter, who had the power <of> a begetter **97** and form-[giver's] nature, that the great wealth that was hidden in him might be revealed. Because of his mercy and his love he wished to bring forth fruit by himself, that he might not <enjoy> his goodness alone but (that) other spirits of the Unwavering Generation might bring forth body and fruit, glory and honor in imperishableness and his infinite grace, that his treasure might be revealed by Self-begotten God, the father of every imperishableness and those that came to be afterward. But they had not yet come to visibility.

Now a great difference exists among the imperishables." He called out saying: "Whoever has ears to hear about the infinities, let him hear"; and "I have addressed those who are awake." Still he continued **98** and said: "Everything that came from the perishable will perish, since it came from the perishable. But whatever came from imperishableness does not perish but becomes imperishable since it is from imperishableness. So, many people went astray because they had not known this difference and they died."

Mary said to him: "Lord, then how will we know that?" The perfect Savior said: "Come (pl.) from invisible things to the end of those that are visible, and the very emanation of Thought will reveal to you how faith in those things that are not visible was found in those that are visible, those that belong to Unbegotten Father. Whoever has ears to hear, let him hear.

The Lord of the Universe is not called 'Father' but 'Forefather.' <For the Father is> the beginning (or principle) of those that will appear, but he (the Lord) **99** is [the] beginningless Forefather. Seeing himself within himself in a mirror, he appeared resembling himself, but his likeness appeared as Divine Self-Father and <as> Confronter 'over the confronted ones,' First Existent Unbegotten Father. He is indeed of equal age <with> the Light that is before him, but he is not equal to him in power.

"And afterward was revealed a whole multitude of confronting, self-begotten ones, equal in age and power, being in glory (and) without number, whose race is called 'The Generation over Whom There Is No Kingdom' 'from the one in whom you yourselves have appeared from these people.' And that whole multitude over which there is no kingdom is called **100** 'Sons of Unbegotten Father, God, [Savior], Son of God,' whose likeness is with you. Now he is the Unknowable, who is full of ever imperishable glory and ineffable joy. They all are at rest in him, ever rejoicing in ineffable joy in his unchanging glory and measureless jubilation; this was never heard or known among all the aeons and their worlds until now."

Matthew said to him: "Lord, Savior, how was Man revealed?" The perfect Savior said: "I want you to know that he who appeared before the universe in infinity, Self-grown **101** Self-constructed Father, being full of shining light and ineffable, in the beginning, when he decided to have his likeness become a great power, immediately the principle (or beginning) of that Light appeared as Immortal Androgynous Man, that through that Immortal Man they might attain their salvation and awake from forgetfulness through the interpreter who was sent, who is with you until the end of the poverty of the robbers. "And his consort is the Great Sophia who from the first was destined in him for union by Self-begotten Father, from Immortal Man 'who appeared as First and divinity and kingdom,' for the Father, who is **102** called 'Man, Self-Father,' revealed this. And he created a great aeon, whose name is Ogdoad, for his own majesty.

"He was given great authority, and he ruled over the creation of poverty. He created gods and angels <and> archangels, myriads without number for retinue from that Light and the tri-male Spirit, which is that of Sophia, his consort. For from this God originated divinity and kingdom. Therefore he was called 'God of gods,' 'King of kings.'

"First Man has his unique mind, within, and thought—just as he is it (thought)—(and) considering, reflecting, rationality, **103** power. All the attributes that exist are perfect and immortal. In respect to imperishableness, they are indeed equal. (But) in respect to power, they are different, like the difference between father and son, <and son> and thought, and the thought and the remainder.

"As I said earlier, among the things that were created, the monad is first. And after everything, all that was revealed appeared from his power. And from what was created, all that was fashioned appeared; from what was fashioned appeared what was formed; from what was formed, what was named. Thus came the difference among the unbegotten ones from beginning to end." Then Bartholomew said to him: "How (is it that) <he> was designated in **104** the Gospel 'Man' and 'Son of Man'? To which of them, then, is this Son related?" The Holy One said to him:

"I want you to know that First Man is called 'Begetter, Self-perfected Mind.' He reflected with Great Sophia, his consort, and revealed his first-

begotten, androgynous son. His male name is designated 'First Begetter Son of God'; his female
name, 'First Begettress Sophia, Mother of the Universe.' Some call her 'Love.' Now First-begotten
is called 'Christ.' Since he has authority from his
father, he created a multitude of angels **105** without number for retinue from Spirit and Light."

His disciples said to him: "Lord, reveal to us
about the one called 'Man' that we also may know
his glory exactly." The perfect Savior said: "Whoever has ears to hear, let him hear. First Begetter
Father is called 'Adam, Eye of Light,' because he
came from shining Light, [and] his holy angels,
who are ineffable (and) shadowless, ever rejoice
with joy in their reflecting, which they received
from their Father. The whole kingdom of Son of
Man, who is called 'Son of God,' is full of ineffable and shadowless joy, and unchanging jubilation, (they) rejoicing over his imperishable **106**
glory, which has never been heard until now, nor
has it been revealed in the aeons that came afterward and their worlds. I came from Self-begotten
and First Infinite Light that I might reveal everything to you."

Again, his disciples said: "Tell us clearly how
(it is that) they came down from the invisibilities,
from the immortal (realm) to the world that dies?"
The perfect Savior said: "Son of Man consented
with Sophia, his consort, and revealed a great androgynous light. His male name is designated
'Savior, Begetter of All Things.' His female name
is designated 'All-Begettress Sophia.' Some call
her 'Pistis.' All who come into the world, like **107**
a drop from the Light, are sent by him to the world
of Almighty, that they might be guarded by him.
And the bond of his forgetfulness bound him by the
will of Sophia, that the matter might be <revealed>
through it to the whole world in poverty concerning his (Almighty's) arrogance and blindness and
the ignorance that he was named. But I came from
the places above by the will of the great Light, (I)
who escaped from that bond; I have cut off the
work of the robbers; I have wakened that drop that
was sent from Sophia, that it might bear much fruit
through me and be perfected and not again be defective but be <joined> through me, the Great Savior, that his glory might be revealed, so that Sophia

might also be justified in regard to that defect, that
her **108** sons might not again become defective
but might attain honor and glory and go up to
their Father and know the words of the masculine
Light. And you were sent by the Son, who was
sent that you might receive Light and remove
yourselves from the forgetfulness of the authorities, and that it might not again come to appearance because of you, namely, the unclean rubbing
that is from the fearful fire that came from their
fleshly part. Tread upon their malicious intent."

Then Thomas said to [him]: "Lord, Savior
how many are the aeons of those who surpass the
heavens?" The perfect Savior said: "I praise you
(pl.) because you ask about the great aeons, for
your roots are in the infinities.

"Now when those whom I have discussed earlier were revealed, Self-Begetter Father very soon
created twelve aeons for retinue for the twelve angels. All these are perfect and good. Thus the defect in the female appeared."

And <he> said to him: "How many are the
aeons of the immortals, starting from the infinities?" The perfect Savior said: "Whoever has ears
to hear, let him hear. The first aeon is that of Son
of Man, who is called 'First Begetter,' who is
called 'Savior,' who has appeared. The second
aeon (is) that of Man, who is called 'Adam, Eye
of Light.'

"That which embraces these is the aeon over
which there is no kingdom, (the aeon) of the Eternal Infinite God, the Self-begotten aeon of the
aeons that are in it, (the aeon) of the immortals,
whom I described earlier, **109** (the aeon) above
the Seventh that appeared from Sophia, which is
the first aeon.

"Now Immortal Man revealed aeons and powers and kingdoms and gave authority to all who
appear in him that they might exercise their desires until the last things that are above chaos. For
these consented with each other and revealed every
magnificence, even from spirit, multitudinous
lights that are glorious and without number. These
110 were called in the beginning, that is, the first
aeon and <the second> and <the third>. The first
<is> called 'Unity and Rest.' Each one has its
(own) name; for the <third> aeon was designated

'Assembly' from the great multitude that appeared: in one, a multitude revealed themselves. Now because the multitudes **111** gather and come to a unity, we call them 'Assembly of the Eighth.' It appeared as androgynous and was named partly as male and partly as female. The male is called 'Assembly,' while the female is called 'Life,' that it might be shown that from a female came the life for all the aeons. And every name was received, starting from the beginning.

"For from his concurrence with his thought, the powers very soon appeared who were called 'gods'; and [the] gods of the gods from their wisdom revealed gods; <and the gods> from their wisdom revealed lords; and the lords of the lords from their thinkings revealed lords; and the lords from their power revealed archangels; the archangels from their words revealed angels; **112** from them semblances appeared with structure and form and name for all the aeons and their worlds.

"And the immortals, whom I have just described, all have authority from Immortal Man, who is called 'Silence' because by reflecting without speech all her own majesty was perfected.' For since the imperishabilities had the authority, each created a great kingdom in the Eighth and (also) thrones and temples (and) firmaments for their own majesties. For these all came by the will of the Mother of the Universe."

Then the Holy Apostles said to him: "Lord, Savior, tell us about those who are in the aeons, since it is necessary for us to ask about them." The perfect **113** Savior said: "If you ask about anything, I will tell you. They created hosts of angels, myriads without number for retinue and their glory. They created virgin spirits, the ineffable and unchangeable lights. For they have no sickness nor weakness, but it is will. And they came to be in an instant.

"Thus the aeons were completed quickly with the heavens and the firmaments in the glory of Immortal Man and Sophia, his consort: the area from which every aeon and the world and those that came afterward took (their) pattern for their creation of likenesses in the heavens of chaos and their worlds. And all natures, starting from the revelation of chaos, are in the Light that shines without shadow and joy that cannot be described and unutterable jubilation. They ever delight themselves on account of their unchanging glory **114** and the immeasurable rest, which cannot be described among all the aeons that came to be afterward and all their powers. Now all that I have just said to you, I said that you might shine in Light more than these." Mary said to him: "Holy Lord, where did your disciples come from and where are they going and (what) should they do here?" The perfect Savior said to them: "I want you to know that Sophia, the Mother of the Universe and the consort, desired by herself to bring these to existence without her male (consort). But by the will of the Father of the Universe, that his unimaginable goodness might be revealed, he created that curtain between the immortals and those that came afterward, that the consequence might follow every aeon and chaos, that the defect of the female might <appear>, and it might come about that Error would contend with her. And these became **119** the curtain of spirit. From <the> aeons above the emanations of Light, as I have said already, a drop from Light and Spirit came down to the lower regions of Almighty in chaos, that their molded forms might appear from that drop, for it is a judgment on him, Arch-Begetter who is called 'Yaldabaoth.' That drop revealed their molded forms through the breath, as a **120** living soul. It was withered and it slumbered in the ignorance of the soul. When it became hot from the breath of the Great Light of the Male, and it took thought, (then) names were received by all who are in the world of chaos and all things that are in it through that Immortal One, when the breath blew into him. But when this came about by the will of Mother Sophia—so that Immortal Man might piece together **121** the garments there for a judgment on the robbers—<he> then welcomed the blowing of that breath; but since he was soul-like, he was not able to take that power of himself until the number of chaos should be complete, (that is,) when the time determined by the great angel is complete.

"Now I have taught you about Immortal Man and have loosed the bonds of the robbers from him.

I have broken the gates of **122** the pitiless ones in their presence. I have humiliated their malicious intent, and they all have been shamed and have risen from their ignorance. Because of this, then, I came here, that they might be joined with that Spirit and Breath, **117** that [. . .] and Breath, and might from two become one, just as from the first, that you might yield much fruit and go up to Him Who Is from the Beginning, in ineffable joy and glory and [honor and] grace of [the Father of the Universe].

"Whoever, [then] knows [the Father in pure] knowledge [will depart] to the Father [and repose in] Unbegotten [Father]. But [whoever knows] [him defectively] will depart [to the defect] and the rest [of the Eighth. Now] whoever knows Immortal [Spirit] of Light in silence, through reflecting and consent in the truth, let him bring me signs of the Invisible One, and he will become a light in the Spirit of Silence. Whoever knows Son of Man in knowledge and love, let him bring me a sign **118** of Son of Man, that he might depart to the dwelling-places with those in the Eighth.

"Behold, I have revealed to you the name of the Perfect One, the whole will of the Mother of the Holy Angels, that the masculine [multitude] may be completed here, that there [might appear, in the aeons,] [the infinities and] those that [came to be in the] untraceable [wealth of the Great] Invisible [Spirit, that they] all [might take] [from his goodness,] even the wealth [of their rest] that has no [kingdom over it]. I came [from First] Who Was Sent, that I might reveal to you Him Who Is from the Beginning, because of the arrogance of Arch-Begetter and his angels, since they say about themselves that they are gods. And I came to remove them from their blindness that I might tell everyone about the God who is above the universe. **119** Therefore, tread upon their graves, humiliate their malicious intent and break their yoke and arouse my own. I have given you authority over all things as Sons of Light, that you might tread upon their power with [your] feet."

These are the things [the] blessed Savior [said,] [and he disappeared] from them. Then [all the disciples] were in [great, ineffable joy] in [the spirit from] that day on. [And his disciples] began to preach [the] Gospel of God, [the] eternal, imperishable [Spirit]. Amen.

><del>·<del>+·-O-<+·<del>·<

28. The Treatise on the Resurrection

Discovered at Nag Hammadi, the provocative philosophical discourse known as the "Treatise on the Resurrection" is a letter addressed by an unknown gnostic teacher to an inquirer, possibly a non-Gnostic Christian, named Rheginos. In response to Rheginos's questions, the treatise provides basic instruction about the nature of death and resurrection—both of Jesus and, more important, of humans.

The author assures Rheginos that the resurrection is by no means an illusion; it will certainly take place. But it will not involve some kind of crass revivification of the material body (which, he claims, is itself more illusory than real). After death, even though

The "Treatise on the Resurrection," translated by Malcolm L. Peel, from *Nag Hammadi Codex I (The Jung Codex); (NHS XXII)*, ed. Harold W. Attridge. Leiden: E. J. Brill, 1985. Used with permission.

the body passes away, a person's spirit will ascend to the heavenly realm, drawn up by Jesus himself. The flesh, in other words, is completely transitory, but the spirit is eternal. Those who live in such a way as to deny their flesh have begun to escape this bodily existence and started along the path to their heavenly home; for people like this, the resurrection has already occurred.

This teaching stands in sharp contrast with proto-orthodox notions of the future bodily resurrection (cf. 2 Tim 2:18). Although it is impossible to say when this intriguing treatise was written, many scholars date it to the late second century.

Some there are, my son Rheginos, who want to learn many things. They have this goal when they are occupied with questions whose answer is lacking. If they succeed with these, they usually think very highly of themselves. But I do not think that they have stood within the Word of Truth. They seek rather their own rest, which we have received through our Savior, our Lord Christ. **44** We received it (i.e., Rest) when we came to know the truth and rested ourselves upon it. But since you ask us pleasantly what is proper concerning the resurrection, I am writing you (to say) that it is necessary. To be sure, many are lacking faith in it, but there a few who find it. So then, let us discuss the matter.

How did the Lord proclaim things while he existed in flesh and after he had revealed himself as Son of God? He lived in this place where you remain, speaking about the Law of Nature—but I call it "Death!" Now the Son of God, Rheginos, was Son of Man. He embraced them both, possessing the humanity and the divinity, so that on the one hand he might vanquish death through his being Son of God, and that on the other through the Son of Man the restoration to the Pleroma might occur; because he was originally from above, a seed of the Truth, before this structure (of the cosmos) had come into being. In this (structure) many dominions and divinities came into existence.

I know that I am presenting **45** the solution in difficult terms, but there is nothing difficult in the Word of Truth. But since the Solution appeared so as not to leave anything hidden, but to reveal all things openly concerning existence—the destruction of evil on the one hand, the revelation of the elect on the other. This (Solution) is the emanation of Truth and Spirit, Grace is of the Truth.

The Savior swallowed up death—(of this) you are not reckoned as being ignorant—for he put aside the world which is perishing. He transformed [himself] into an imperishable Aeon and raised himself up, having swallowed the visible by the invisible, and he gave us the way of our immortality. Then, indeed, as the Apostle said, "We suffered with him, and we arose with him, and we went to heaven with him."[1] Now if we are manifest in this world wearing him, we are that one's beams, and we are embraced by him until our setting, that is to say, our death in this life. We are drawn to heaven by him, like beams by the sun, not being restrained by anything. This is the spiritual resurrection **46** which swallows up the psychic in the same way as the fleshly.

But if there is one who does not believe, he does not have the (capacity to be) persuaded. For it is the domain of faith, my son, and not that which belongs to persuasion: the dead shall arise! There is one who believes among the philosophers who are in this world. At least he will arise. And let not the philosopher who is in this world have cause to believe that he is one who returns himself by himself—and (that) because of our faith! For we have known the Son of Man, and we have believed that he rose from among the dead. This is he of whom we say, "He became the destruction of death, as he is a great one in whom they believe." <Great> are those who believe it.

The thought of those who are saved shall not perish. The mind of those who have known him shall not perish. Therefore, we are elected to salva-

---

[1]cf. 1 Tim 2:10–11.

tion and redemption since we are predestined from the beginning not to fall into the foolishness of those who are without knowledge, but we shall enter into the wisdom of those who have known the Truth. Indeed, the Truth which is kept cannot be abandoned, nor has it been. "Strong is the system of the Pleroma; small is that which broke loose (and) became (the) world. But the All is what is encompassed. It has not **47** come into being; it was existing." So, never doubt concerning the resurrection, my son Rheginos! For if you were not existing in flesh, you received flesh when you entered this world. Why will you not receive flesh when you ascend into the Aeon? That which is better than the flesh is that which is for it (the) cause of life. That which came into being on your account, is it not yours? Does not that which is yours exist with you? Yet, while you are in this world, what is it that you lack? This is what you have been making every effort to learn.

The afterbirth of the body is old age, and you exist in corruption. You have absence as a gain. For you will not give up what is better if you depart. That which is worse has diminution, but there is grace for it.

Nothing, then, redeems us from this world. But the All which we are, we are saved. We have received salvation from end to end. Let us think in this way! Let us comprehend in this way!

But there are some (who) wish to understand, in the enquiry about those things they are looking into, whether he who is saved, if he leaves his body behind, will be saved immediately. Let no one doubt concerning this. . . . indeed, the visible members which are dead **48** shall not be saved, for (only) the living [members] which exist within them would arise.

What, then, is the resurrection? It is always the disclosure of those who have risen. For if you remember reading in the Gospel that Elijah appeared and Moses with him,[2] do not think the resurrection is an illusion. It is no illusion, but it is truth! Indeed, it is more fitting to say that the world is an illusion, rather than the resurrection which has come into being through our Lord the Savior, Jesus Christ.

But what am I telling you now? Those who are living shall die. How do they live in an illusion? The rich have become poor, and the kings have been overthrown. Everything is prone to change. The world is an illusion!—lest, indeed, I rail at things to excess!

But the resurrection does not have this aforesaid character, for it is the truth which stands firm. It is the revelation of what is, and the transformation of things, and a transition into newness. For imperishability **49** [descends] upon the perishable; the light flows down upon the darkness, swallowing it up; and the Pleroma fills up the deficiency. These are the symbols and the images of the resurrection. He (Christ) it is who makes the good.

Therefore, do not think in part, O Rheginos, nor live in conformity with this flesh for the sake of unanimity, but flee from the divisions and the fetters, and already you have the resurrection. For if he who will die knows about himself that he will die—even if he spends many years in this life, he is brought to this—why not consider yourself as risen and (already) brought to this? If you have the resurrection but continue as if you are to die—and yet that one knows that he has died—why, then, do I ignore your lack of exercise? It is fitting for each one to practice in a number of ways, and he shall be released from this Element that he may not fall into error but shall himself receive again what at first was.

These things I have received from the generosity of my **50** Lord, Jesus Christ. [I have] taught you and your [brethren], my sons, concerning them, while I have not omitted any of the things suitable for strengthening you (pl.). But if there is one thing written which is obscure in my exposition of the Word, I shall interpret it for you (pl.) when you (pl.) ask. But now, do not be jealous of anyone who is in your number when he is able to help.

Many are looking into this which I have written to you. To these I say: peace (be) among them and grace. I greet you and those who love you (pl.) in brotherly love.

---

[2]Mark 9:4.

29. The Hymn of the Pearl

One of the most elegant compositions of early Christianity, the "Hymn of the Pearl" is embedded in the third-century Acts of Thomas (see Chapter 2). Most scholars agree, however, that the hymn was composed by a different hand and at an earlier date. On the surface, it appears to be a simple folktale of a prince sent by his royal parents on a mission to snatch a pearl from the lair of a ravenous dragon in Egypt, only to arrive at his destination and forget his task and his identity, needing a message from the royal court to be saved from his torpor; when he then remembers who he is, he seizes the pearl and returns to the glories of his father's realm.

The hymn may be something far more than a simple folktale, however. Hints within the text itself—such as the "knowledge" (literally "gnosis") intrinsic to the prince's heavenly garment (1. 88)—along with parallels to other literature, suggest in fact that the story represents a gnostic allegory of the incarnation of the soul, which enjoys a glorious heavenly existence ("my father's palace") from which it descends (to "Egypt") to become entrapped in matter ("clothed myself in garments like theirs"); forgetting whence it came, the soul eventually relearns its true nature from a divine emissary; when it awakens to its true identity ("son of kings"), it returns to its heavenly home, where it receives the full knowledge of itself.

108 (1) When I was a little child, in my father's palace,

2 And enjoyed the wealth and luxury of those who nurtured me,

3 My parents equipped me with provisions and sent me out from the East, our homeland.

4 From the wealth of our treasury they gave me a great burden,

5 Which was light so that I could carry it by myself:

6 Gold from the land above, silver from great treasuries,

7 And stones, chalcedonies of India and agates from Kushan.

8 And they girded me with steel,

9 And they took away from me the garment set with gems and spangled with gold Which they had made out of love for me

10 And the yellow robe which was made for my size,

11 And they made a covenant with me And wrote it in my mind that I might not forget:

12 "If you go down to Egypt and bring the one pearl

13 Which is in the land of the devouring serpent,

14 You shall put on again that garment set with stones and the robe which lies over it,

15 And with your brother, our next in command, you shall be a herald for our kingdom."

16 So I departed from the East on a difficult and frightening road led by two guides,

17 And I was very young to travel on it.

18 I passed over the borders of the Mosani, where there is the meeting-place of the merchants of the East,

---

The "Hymn of the Pearl," from *The Apocryphal New Testament*, ed. J.K. Elliott. © Oxford University Press, 1993. Reprinted by permission of Oxford University Press.

19 And reached the land of the Babylonians.

20 I went down to Egypt, and my companions
   parted from me.

21 I went straight to the serpent and stayed
   near his den

22 Until he should slumber and sleep, so that I
   might take the pearl from him.

23 Being alone I altered my appearance and
   seemed an alien even to my own people,

24 But I saw one of my kinsmen there, a free-
   born man from the East,

25 A youth fair and beautiful, the son of
   courtiers.

26 He came and kept me company.

27 And I made him my intimate friend, a com-
   rade with whom I communicated my
   business.

28 Being exhorted to guard against the Egyptians and against partaking of unclean things,

29 I clothed myself in garments like theirs, so
   that I would not be seen as a stranger

30 And as one who had come from abroad to
   take the pearl,
   Lest the Egyptians might arouse the serpent
   against me.

31 But somehow they learned that I was not
   their countryman.

32 They dealt with me treacherously, and I
   tasted their food.

33 I no longer recognized that I was a king's
   son, and I served their king.

34 I forgot the pearl for which my parents had
   sent me.

35 And I fell into a deep sleep because of the
   heaviness of their food.

110 36 While I was suffering these
   things my parents were aware of it
   and grieved over me.

37 And a proclamation was heralded in our
   kingdom that all should present themselves at our doors.

38 The kings of Parthia and those in office,
   and the great men of the East

39 Resolved that I should not be left in Egypt.

40 So the courtiers wrote me a letter:

41 "From your father the king of kings and
   your mother, the mistress of the East

42 And their brothers, who are second to us,
   To our son in Egypt, greetings!

43 Awake, and rise from your sleep.

44 Listen to the words in this letter,
   Remember you are the son of kings,
   You have fallen beneath the yoke of slavery.

45 Remember your gold-spangled garment,

46 Recall the pearl for which you were sent to
   Egypt,

47 Your name has been called to the book of
   life,

48 Together with that of your brother whom
   you have received in our kingdom."

111 49 And the king sealed it to make it
   an ambassador,

50 Because of the wicked Babylonian children and the tyrannical demons of the
   Labyrinth.

53 I rose from sleep when I recognized its voice,

54 I took it up and kissed it and I read.

55 And what was written concerned that which
   was engraved on my heart.

56 And I immediately remembered that I was
   a son of kings and that my freedom demanded my people.

57 I remembered the pearl for which I had
   been sent to Egypt,

58 And the fact that I had come to snatch it
   from the terrifying serpent.

59 I subdued it by calling out my father's name,

61 And I snatched the pearl and turned about
   to go to my parents.

62 And I took off the dirty clothing and left it
   behind in their land.

63 And directed my way forthwith to the light
   of our Eastern home.

64 And on the road I found a female who
   lifted me up.

65 She awakened me, giving me an oracle
   with her voice, and guided me to the light.

66 The Royal silken garment shone before my
   eyes.

68 And with familial love leading me and
   drawing me on

69 I passed by the Labyrinth,
   And leaving Babylon behind on the left,

70 I reached Meson which is a great coast.

112

75 But I could not recall my splendor,

For it had been when I was still a child and quite young that I had left it behind in my father's palace.

76 But, when suddenly I saw my garment reflected as in a mirror,

77 I perceived in it my whole self as well

And through it I knew and saw myself.

78 For though we originated from the one and the same we were partially divided,

Then again we were one, with a single form.

79 The treasurers too who had brought the garment

80 I saw as two beings, but there existed a single form in both,

One royal symbol consisting of two halves.

81 And they had my money and wealth in their hands and gave me my reward:

82 The fine garment of glorious colors,

83 Which was embroidered with gold, precious stones, and pearls to give a good appearance.

84 It was fastened at the collar.

86 And the image of the King of Kings was all over it.

87 Stones of lapis lazuli had been skillfully fixed to the collar,

88 And I saw in turn that motions of knowledge were stirring throughout it,

89 And that it was prepared to speak.

90 Then I heard it speak:

91 "It is I who belong to the one who is stronger than all people and for whose sake I was written about by the father himself."

92 And I took note of my stature,

93 And all the royal feelings rested on me as its energy increased.

94 Thrust out by his hand the garment hastened to me as I went to receive it,

95 And a longing aroused me to rush and meet it and to receive it.

96 And I stretched out and took it and adorned myself with the beauty of its colors.

97 And I covered myself completely with my royal robe over it.

98 When I had put it on I ascended to the land of peace and homage.

99 And I lowered my head and prostrated myself before the splendor of the father who had sent it to me.

100 For it was I who had obeyed his commands

And it was I who had also kept the promise,

101 And I mingled at the doors of his ancient royal building.

102 He took delight in me and received me in his palace.

103 All his subjects were singing hymns with harmonious voices.

104 He allowed me also to be admitted to the doors of the king himself,

105 So that with my gifts and the pearl I might appear before the king himself.

>─◆─○─◆─<

30. The Gospel of Philip

The Gospel of Philip was among the documents discovered at Nag Hammadi. Although it is easily recognized as gnostic, the book is notoriously difficult to understand in its details. In part this is due to the form of its composition; it is neither a narrative Gospel of the type found in the New Testament nor a group of self-contained sayings like the Gospel of Thomas (see Chapter 8). It is, instead, a collection of mystical reflections that have evidently been excerpted from previously existing sermons, treatises, and theological meditations, brought together here under the name of Philip (presumably Jesus' own disciple). Since they are given in relative isolation, without any real narrative context, the reflections are difficult to interpret. There are, at any rate, extensive uses of catchwords to organize some of the material, and several of the principal themes emerge upon a careful reading.

Among the clearest emphases is precisely the contrast between those who can understand and those who cannot, between knowledge that is exoteric (available to all) and that which is esoteric (available only to insiders), between the immature outsiders (regular Christians, called "Hebrews") and the mature insiders (Gnostics, called "Gentiles"). Those who do not understand, the outsiders with only exoteric knowledge, err in many of their judgments—for example, in taking such notions as the virgin birth (v. 17) or the resurrection of Jesus (v. 21) as literal statements of historical fact, rather than symbolic expressions of deeper truths.

Throughout much of the work, the Christian sacraments figure prominently. Five are explicitly named: baptism, anointing, eucharist, salvation, and bridal chamber (v. 68). It is hard to know what deeper meaning these rituals had for the author (especially the "bridal chamber," which has stirred considerable debate among scholars), or even what he imagined them to entail when practiced literally.

It is difficult to assign a date to this work, but it was probably compiled during the third century, although it draws on earlier sources.

1 A Hebrew person makes a Hebrew, and he is called a proselyte. But a proselyte does not make a proselyte . . . there are those who are as they are . . . and they make others . . . it is enough for them that they exist.

2 The slave seeks only to be free. However, he does not seek after his lord's properties. The son, however, is not only a son but writes himself into the inheritance of the father.

3 Those who inherit the dead are dead and inherit the dead. Those who inherit living things are alive, and they inherit the living and the dead. Those who are dead inherit nothing. For how will the one who is dead inherit? If the dead one inherits the living he will not die, but the dead one will live more.

4 A Gentile does not die. He has not lived, so he cannot die. He lives who has believed the truth; and he is in danger that he will die, for he is alive. Now that Christ has come

5 the world is created, the cities are bedecked, the dead are carried out.

6 When we were Hebrews, we were orphans. We had only our mother. But when we became Christians, we gained a father and mother.

7 Those who sow in winter reap in summer. The winter is the world; the summer is the other aeon. Let us sow in the world so that we may reap in the summer. On account of this it is seemly for us not to pray in the winter. That which comes out of the winter is the summer. But if someone reaps in the winter, he really will not be reaping, but he will be tearing things out,

8 since this will not produce . . . not only will it [not] produce . . . but on the Sabbath [his field] is unfruitful.

9 Christ came to ransom some, but others he saved, others he redeemed. Those who were strangers he ransomed and made them his, and he

set them apart. These he made as securities in his will. Not only when he appeared did he lay aside his life as he wished, but at the establishment of the world he laid aside his life. He came to take it when he wished to, because it had been set aside as a pledge. It came under the control of robbers, and it was held prisoner. But he saved it, and he ransomed the good ones and the evil ones who were in the world.

10 Light and darkness, life and death, the right and the left are each other's brothers. They cannot separate from one another. Therefore, the good are not good nor are the evil evil, nor is life life, nor death death. On account of this, each one will dissolve into its beginning origin. But those who are exalted above the world cannot dissolve; they are eternal.

11 The names which are given to the worldly things contain a great occasion for error. For they twist our consideration from the right meaning to the wrong meaning. For whoever hears (the word) "God," does not know the right meaning but the wrong meaning. It is the same way with (such words as) "the Father" and "the Son" and "the Holy Spirit" and "the life" and "the light" and "the resurrection" and "the Church" and all the other names. Folk do not know the right meaning; rather they know the wrong meaning [unless] they have come to know the right meaning . . . they are in the world . . . in the aeon they would never be used as names in the world, nor would they list them under worldly things. They have an end in the aeon.

12 There is only one name which one does not speak out in the world, the name which the Father gave to the Son. It is above everything. It is the name of the Father. For the Son will not become the Father, if he does not put on the name of the Father. Those who have this name truly know it, but they do not speak it. Those who do not have it do not know it.

But the truth engendered names in the world for us, because it is impossible to know it (the truth) without names. The truth is a single thing and is many things. It is this way for our sake, in order to teach us this one thing in love through its many-ness.

13 The archons wanted to deceive the human because they saw that he was kindred to the truly good ones. They took the name of the good ones and gave it to those that are not good, so that by names they could deceive him and bind them to the ones that are not good. If they do them a favor, they are taken away from those who are not good and given their place among those that are good. They knew these things. For they (the archons) wished to take the free person and enslave him forever. . . .

15 Before the Christ came there was no bread in the world. So also in paradise, the place where Adam was, there were many trees as food for the animals, but there was no wheat for human food. The human ate as the animals. But when the Christ, the perfect man came, he brought bread from heaven so that people could eat in a human way.

16 The archons believed that what they did was by their own power and will. However, the Holy Spirit secretly worked all through them as he willed. The truth is sown in every place; she (the truth) was from the beginning, and many see her as she is sown. But only a few see her being gathered in.

17 Some say Mary was impregnated by the Holy Spirit. They err. They do not know what they say. When did a woman become pregnant by a woman? Mary is the virgin whom no power corrupted. She is a great anathema to the Hebrews, who are the apostles and apostolic men. This virgin whom no power defiled . . . the powers defiled them (or, themselves). The Lord (would) not have said, "My [Father who is in] Heaven," if he had not had another Father. But he would have simply said: ["My Father."]

18 The Lord said to the disciples . . . "Enter the Father's house, but do not take anything in the Father's house, nor remove anything."

19 "Jesus" is a secret name; "Christ" is a revealed name. For this reason, "Jesus" does not exist in any (other) language, but his name is always "Jesus," as they say. "Christ" is also his name; in Syriac, it is "Messiah," but, in Greek, it is "Christ." Actually, everyone has it according to his own language. "The Nazarene" is the one who reveals secret things.

20 The Christ has everything in himself: man, angel, mystery, and the Father.

21 They err who say, "The Lord first died and then he arose." First he arose, and then he died. If someone does not first achieve the resurrection, will he not die? So truly as God lives, that one would . . . [text uncertain].

22 No one will hide an extremely valuable thing in something of equal value. However, people often put things worth countless thousands into a thing worth a penny. It is this way with the soul. It is a precious thing which came into a worthless body.

23 Some fear that they will arise naked. Therefore, they wish to arise in the flesh, and they do not know that those who carry the flesh are naked. They who . . . who disrobe themselves are not naked. Flesh [and blood can] not inherit the Kingdom [of God]. What is this which will not inherit? That which is on us. But what is this which will inherit? That which is of Jesus and of his blood. Therefore he said: "The one who does not eat my flesh and drink my blood does not have life in him."[1] What is it? His flesh is the Logos, and his blood is the Holy Spirit. Whoever has received these has food and drink and clothing. I blame those who say it will not rise. Then they are both to blame. You say, "The flesh will not rise." But tell me what will rise, so that we may praise you. You say, "The spirit in the flesh and this light in the flesh." This is also a Logos (or, saying) which is fleshly. Whatever you say, you do not say anything outside the flesh. It is necessary to rise in this flesh; everything is in it.

24 In this world those who put on clothes are worth more than the clothes. In the Kingdom of Heaven the clothes are worth more than those who have put them on. Through water and fire, which purify the whole place,

25 those things which are revealed are revealed by those which are manifest, those which are secret by those which are secret. Some are hidden through those which are manifest. There is water in water; there is fire in anointing.

26 Jesus secretly stole them all. For he showed himself not to be as he really was, but he appeared in a way that they could see him. To those . . . he appeared. [He appeared] to the great as great. [He appeared] to the small as small. [He appeared] to the angels as an angel and to humans as a human. Because of this, his Logos hid from everyone. Some, to be sure, saw him, and they thought that they saw themselves. But, when he appeared in glory to the disciples on the mountain he was not small. He became great; however, he made the disciples great, so that they were able to see him as he was, great.

He said on that day in the thanksgiving, "You who have united with the perfect, the light, the Holy Spirit, have united the angels also with us, with the images."

27 Do not scorn the Lamb. For without it one cannot see the King. No one who is naked will be able to find his way to the King.

28 The heavenly Man has many more children than the earthly man. If the children of Adam are more numerous, and still die, how much more the children of the Perfect One who do not die but are always begotten. . . .

32 There were three who always walked with the Lord: Mary, his mother and her sister and Magdalene, whom they call his lover. A Mary is his sister and his mother and his lover.

33 "The Father" and "the Son" are single names. The "Holy Spirit" is a double name. They are everywhere. They are above; they are below; they are in the secret; they are in the revealed. The Holy Spirit is in the revealed; it is below; it is in the secret; it is above.

34 The saints are ministered to by the evil powers, for the powers are blind because of the Holy Spirit. Therefore, they will believe that they serve a man when they work for the saints. Because of this, one day a disciple sought from the Lord something from the world. He said to him, "Ask your mother, and she will give you from a stranger's (things).". . .

50 God is a man eater. On account of this the Man [was killed] for him. Before they killed the Man, they killed animals, for those were not Gods for whom they killed.

---

[1]John 6:54.

51 Glass and pottery vessels are both made with fire. But if glass vessels are broken they are made again, for they are created with a breath. But if pottery vessels are broken, they are destroyed, for they are created without a breath.

52 An ass which turns a millstone in a circle went one hundred miles. When he was turned loose he found he was still at the same place. There are people who make many trips and get nowhere. When evening came upon them, they saw no city or town, no creation or nature, no power or angel. The poor fellows labored in vain.

53 The Eucharist is Jesus. For they call him in Syriac *pharisatha*, which is, "the one who is spread out." For Jesus came and he crucified the world.

54 The Lord went into the dye shop of Levi. He took seventy-two colors and threw them into the kettle. He took them all out white, and he said, "Thus the Son of man came, a dyer."

55 Wisdom (*sophia*), whom they call barren, is the mother of the angels, and the consort of Christ is Mary Magdalene. The [Lord loved Mary] more than all the disciples, and he kissed her on the [mouth many times]. The other [women/disciples saw] . . . him. They said to him, "Why do you [love her] more than all of us?" The Savior answered and said to them, "Why do not I love you as I do her?"

56 If a blind person and one who can see are in the dark, there is no difference between them. When the light comes, then the one who sees will see the light, and the one who is blind will stay in the darkness.

57 The Lord said, "Blessed is the one who exists before he came into being. For he who exists was and will be."

58 The greatness of the human being is not revealed, but it is hidden. Because of this he is lord of the animals that are stronger than he and are great according to that which is clear as well as hidden. And this mastery gives to them their stability. But if a person leaves them alone, they kill one another (and) bite one another. And they ate one another because they could find no food. But they have now found food because the person has worked the ground.

59 If anyone goes down into the water and comes up having received nothing and says, "I am a Christian," he has borrowed the name at interest. But if he receives the Holy Spirit, he has taken the name as a gift. If someone has received a gift, it is not taken back. But he who has borrowed something at interest has to meet the payment.

60 It is this way . . . if anyone should be in a mystery. . . .

62 Do not be afraid of the flesh nor love it. If you fear it, then it will be your master. If you love it, it will swallow and strangle you.

63 Either one is in this world, or in the resurrection, or in the places in the middle. God forbid that I be found in them. In this world there is good and evil. Its good is not good, and its evil is not evil. But there is evil after this world, true evil, which they call "the middle." It is death. As long as we are in this world, it is fitting to us to acquire the resurrection, so that when we peel off the flesh we will be found in repose, not making our way in "the middle." For many wander astray off the path. For it is good to come out of the world before one sins. . . .

67 The truth did not come naked into the world, but came in types and images. One will not receive the truth in any other way. There is a being-born-again, and an image of being-born-again. It is truly necessary that they become born again through the image. What else is the resurrection? It is necessary that the image arise through the image. The Bridal Chamber and the image necessarily enters into the truth through the image; this is the recapitulation. It is necessary not only that those who have it received the name of the Father and the Son and the Holy Spirit, but that they took it themselves. If someone does not take it himself, the name also will be taken away from him. But one receives them in the anointing of the power of [the cross] . . . the apostles call it "the right" and "the left." For this reason one is no longer a Christian, but a Christ.

68 The Lord [did?] all in a Mystery, a Baptism, an Anointing, a Eucharist, a Salvation, and a Bridal Chamber. . . .

82 Is it all right to speak a mystery? The Father of all joined himself with the virgin who came down, and a fire[?] was burned for him that day. He appeared in the great Bridal Chamber. Therefore, his body came into being that day. He came out of the Bridal Chamber as one who came into being from the bridegroom and the bride. Thus, Jesus established all through these. And it is fitting for each of the disciples to enter his repose.

83 Adam came into being from two virgins: from the Spirit and from the virgin earth. Therefore, the Christ was born from a virgin so that he could bring order to the stumbling which occurred in the beginning.

84 There are two trees in paradise. The one engenders a[nimals]; the other engenders people. Adam [ate] from the tree which brought forth animals; [he be]came a beast and he begot beasts. Because of this they worship . . . of Adam. The tree . . . fruit is . . . engenders people . . . the (person) . . . God created the p[erson . . . the perso]n created God.

85 It is like this in the world: people create Gods and they worship those whom they have created. It would be proper if the Gods worshipped people. . . .

99 The world came into being through an error. For he who created it intended to create it imperishable and immortal. He failed to attain his hope. For the world is not imperishable and neither is he who created the world. For there is no imperishability of things, but there is of sons. And no thing can attain imperishability if it does not become a son. But if someone cannot receive, how much more will he not be able to give?

100 The Cup of Prayer holds wine and it holds water. It serves as a type of the blood for which they give thanks. And it is full of the Holy Spirit and belongs to the completely perfect Man. When we drink this, we will take to ourselves the perfect Man.

101 The living water is a body. It is right that we clothe ourselves with the living Man. Therefore, when he comes to go down to the water, he disrobes in order that he may put this one on. . . .

125 As long as it is hidden, wickedness is really brought to nothing, but it is still not removed from the midst of the seed of the Holy Spirit. They are slaves of evil. When it is revealed, then the perfect light will pour over everyone, all those in it will receive the [anointing]. Then the slaves will become free, and the prisoners will be redeemed.

126 [Every] plant my Father in Heaven does not plant [will be] rooted out. Those who are alienated will be united. They will be filled. Everyone who [will go in] to the Bridal Chamber will [light the light]. For [it shines] as in the marriages which [are seen, although they] are in the night. The fire [burns] in the night, then it is extinguished. But the mysteries of this marriage are fulfilled in the day and the light. That day and its light do not set.

127 If anyone becomes a child of the Bridal Chamber, he will receive the light. If anyone does not receive it while he is in these places (i.e., this world), he will not be able to receive it in the other place. The one who has received light cannot be seen nor can he be held. And no one can torment him, even while he lives in the world. And further, when he goes out of the world, already he has received the truth in images. The world has become the aeon, for the aeon has become for him the fullness. It is thus; it is revealed only to him. It is not hidden in the darkness and the night, but it is hidden in a perfect day and a holy light.

Chapter 7

The Internal Conflicts of Christianity

Writings Against the "Heretics"

As odd as it might seem to modern persons, religions in the ancient world were not, as a rule, concerned with what people believed. Greco-Roman religions were principally concerned with appropriate *behavior* toward the gods, especially in the regular and proper observance of the sacrificial practices that had been handed down from antiquity. What one happened to *believe* about the gods was of very little importance. As a consequence, there was no such thing as orthodoxy or heresy in these religions, no written Scriptures to follow (except, of course, in Judaism), and no creeds to be confessed. Perhaps this is why none of these religions was exclusivistic, that is, why none of them insisted on a person's exclusive devotion (except, again, Judaism). People were free to participate in as many religions as they liked.

Christianity emerged as a major exception. From the earliest times, Christians insisted that what a person believed was absolutely essential to true religion, that a person's beliefs were either true or false, that true beliefs helped put a person in a proper standing before God and false beliefs permanently endangered a person's standing. As a result, Christianity from the outset had a strongly exclusivistic strain.

The emphasis on right and wrong belief is already evident in the writings of the earliest Christian author whose works have survived, the apostle Paul, who insisted that his opponents, for example, in Galatia or Corinth, advocated false notions about such matters as the importance of the Jewish law for salvation and the future reality of the resurrection. For Paul, failing to understand the gospel of Christ properly could lead to serious consequences, in both this life and the life to come.

As time progressed, Christians developed certain doctrinal perspectives that they imposed on all persons coming into the religion. The irony, of course, is that different Christians had different understandings about what these correct beliefs were (see Chapter 6); strikingly, most advocates of one or another view insisted that their perspectives had been taught by Jesus and his apostles. And to prove it, they usually could appeal to books that claimed to be written by the apostles.

Thus, along with the development of various kinds of doctrine—about God, Christ, salvation, the Spirit, creation—came heated disputes over which forms of these doctrines were correct (see further Chapter 14). A good deal of the Christian writings from the second and third century is "in-house" literature directed against proponents of views deemed, by the authors, to be "heretical" rather than "orthodox" (on these terms, see Chapter 6). Among the best-known authors of this period are such heresiologists (literally: describers of heresy) as Irenaeus of Lyons, Hippolytus of Rome, Tertullian of Carthage, and Origen of Alexandria. All of these writers, of course, stood within the doctrinal tradition that eventually became dominant and so declared *itself* "orthodox" by the end of the period. We can be sure, though, that Christians who took opposing views had a good deal to say for themselves, starting all the way back with Paul's opponents in Galatia and Corinth. But since the supporters of these alternative views lost the struggles, their writings were not preserved for us. As a result, we usually hear only one side of the argument.

It would be wrong to think, though, that this was the only side that was endorsed or that it necessarily proved to be the most persuasive for everyone everywhere. One of the most intriguing features of the Nag Hammadi Library, as we will see, is that some of these gnostic tractates attack *proto-orthodox* views for being completely misguided (i.e., "heretical")! Still, the vast preponderance of the surviving antiheretical literature comes, naturally enough, from the pens of those who won the conflicts.

For Further Reading

Bauer, Walter. *Orthodoxy and Heresy in Earliest Christianity*, ed. Robert Kraft and Gerhard Krodel, tr. Robert Kraft et. al. Philadelphia: Fortress, 1971.

Ehrman, Bart D. *The Orthodox Corruption of Scripture.* New York: Oxford University Press, 1993; esp. chap. 1.

Grant, Robert M. *Jesus After the Gospels: The Christ of the Second Century.* Louisville: Westminster/John Knox, 1990.

Pearson, Birger. "Anti-Heretical Warnings in Codex IX from Nag Hammadi," in *Essays on the Nag Hammadi Texts in Honour of Pahor Labib*, ed. M. Krause. NHS 6: Leiden: E. J. Brill, 1975, 145–54.

Valleé, Gérard. *A Study in Anti-Gnostic Polemics: Irenaeus, Hippolytus, and Epiphanius.* Studies in Christianity and Judaism 1. Waterloo, Ontario: Wilfred Laurier University, 1981.

Wisse, Frederik. "The Nag Hammadi Library and the Heresiologists," *Vigiliae Christianae* 25 (1971) 205–23.

PROTO-ORTHODOX HERESIOLOGISTS: INTRODUCTION

The constant barage of attacks on "heretical" views by the proto-orthodox of the first three Christian centuries should itself give us pause. If orthodox believers were always and everywhere in the solid majority, why were their opponents ubiquitous? And why were they so to be feared? Some scholars have suggested that the proto-orthodox claims—for example, that heretical groups were pestiferous but small minorities—may themselves indicate otherwise.

A particularly striking feature of the early debates over orthodoxy is that various Christian groups were forced to fight simultaneously on a number of different fronts. For the proto-orthodox, at least, this situation resulted in a highly paradoxical set of beliefs. Against groups like the Ebionites, for example, who maintained that Christ was fully human but not at all divine, the proto-orthodox had to insist that he was God; at the same time, against some groups of Gnostics, who maintained that Christ was fully divine but not human, they had to assert that he was a man. But how could he be both? And on yet a third front, other groups of Gnostics maintained that Christ was both human and divine because he was in fact two different entities: the man Jesus and the aeon Christ who temporarily indwelt him; in response, the proto-orthodox claimed that Jesus Christ was one being, not two. Out of these various conflicts, then, emerged the enigmatic doctrine of Christ that came to be embedded in the orthodox creed: Christ was fully human *and* fully divine, yet he was one person, not two.

The antiheretical writings of the second and third centuries are among the most interesting and vitriolic literature of early Christianity. Much of the vitriol is reserved for the followers of Marcion and the Gnostics; we might assume that these groups were widely seen as the most threatening to the proto-orthodox. Although wide-ranging differences appear among the specific attacks of one heresiologist or the other, their overall charges are fairly consistent:

1. The "heretics" subscribe to views that are absurdly complicated, self-contradictory, and contrary to "common sense." Often the heresiologists simply detail the myths told by such people and ridicule them as nonsense (as if the myths were meant to be taken as propositional truths).
2. The mind-boggling variety of heretical beliefs shows that none of them can possibly be true.
3. These absurd and contradictory views derive from faulty interpretations of the sacred Scriptures. Heretics are commonly attacked for not accepting a literal, straightforward understanding of the biblical text and for importing, instead, their own views by means of an allegorical reading.

4. The heretics cannot appeal to any apostolic authorization for their views; those who do so are either lying or deceived. According to the standard proto-orthodox position, Jesus delivered his true teachings to his apostles, who then entrusted them to the bishops of the churches they established. As a result the leaders of the apostolic churches of the heresiologists' own day were said to stand in a direct line of succession back to Jesus himself (this is the famous doctrine of "apostolic succession"). Anyone who disputed the teachings of these bishops, therefore, was charged with impugning Christ himself.

5. The alternative views fabricated by heretics become increasingly fantastic with the passing of time, as each new generation of heretics adds new perversions to the corrupt view of their forebears.

6. The perversion of the truth is closely tied to a perversion of morals. This is a constant weapon in the proto-orthodox arsenal: those who subscribe to heretical views engage in wild and profligate activities, immoral behavior that reflects the heretics' false beliefs.

As already pointed out, the opponents of these proto-orthodox writers certainly had plenty to say about each of these points. Unfortunately, nearly all of their own attacks and counterattacks have been lost.

31. Irenaeus: Against the Heresies

Ireneaus was the bishop of Lyons (in Gaul) during the final quarter of the second century. Although he had predecessors among proto-orthodox heresiologists—he himself quotes Justin's tractate against Marcion—none of these earlier works survives intact. Irenaeus wrote his own lengthy treatise, "Against the Heresies" (original title: "Refutation and Overthrow of Falsely Called Gnosis"), in Greek, around 180 C.E. It is preserved in its entirety only in Latin translation.

The attack is principally against Valentinian Gnostics, whose myths Irenaeus mocks as completely implausible. His detailed descriptions of these myths were evidently drawn from a gnostic treatise similar to the Secret Book of John (see Chapter 6). Some scholars think that Irenaeus somewhat misunderstood his opponents, however, taking their myths as propositional and historical statements rather than mystical reflections on the meaning of the universe. In any event, a longish excerpt of his exposition is included here to provide a taste. Irenaeus attacks other, non-Valentinian, heretics, in somewhat less de-

Irenaeus: "Against the Heresies," Book 1, from *St. Irenaeus of Lyons Against the Heresies*, ed. Dominic Unger. Mahway, N.J.: Paulist Press, 1992. Used by permission of Paulist Press; Book 3, from *The Ante-Nicene Fathers*, vol. 1, *The Apostolic Fathers with Justin Martyr and Irenaeus,* ed. A. Cleveland Coxe. Reprint; 2nd ed. Grand Rapids, Mich.: Eerdmans, 1987.

tail, as seen in the excerpts on Marcus, Saturninus, Basilides, Carpocrates, Marcion, and others that follow.

Throughout his refutation, Irenaeus maligns the heretics' emphasis on fragmentation and difference—within the divine realm, the world, and the church. In contrast, Irenaeus himself stresses unity: unity within the godhead (there is only one true God, unified in being and purpose), between God and creation, God and Christ, Jesus and Christ (he is one being, not two), Christ and the apostles, the apostles and the apostolic churches, and the apostolic churches with one another. Especially important for Irenaeus, in this connection, is his notion of the apostolic succession.

Irenaeus set the tone and provided the arguments for many of his heresiological successors, some of whom simply borrowed his descriptions and attacks for their own books. For another selection from "Against the Heresies," see Chapter 9.

Book 1

Preface

Certain people are discarding the truth and introducing deceitful myths and endless genealogies, which, as the Apostle says, "promote speculations rather than the divine training that is in faith."[1] By specious argumentation, craftily patched together, they mislead the minds of the more ignorant and ensnare them by falsifying the Lord's words. Thus they become wicked interpreters of genuine words. They bring many to ruin by leading them, under the pretense of knowledge, away from him who established and adorned this universe, as if they had something more sublime and excellent to manifest than the God who made heaven and . . . all things in heaven. By cleverness with words they persuasively allure the simple folk to this style of searching, but then, absurdly, bring them to perdition by trumping up their blasphemous and impious opinion against the Creator. In this matter they just cannot distinguish what is false from what is true.

2 Error, in fact, does not show its true self, lest on being stripped naked it should be detected. Instead, it craftily decks itself out in an attractive dress, and thus, by an outward false appearance, presents itself to the more ignorant, truer than truth itself, ridiculous as it is even to say this. With regard to such people, one greater than we has said: "An artful imitation in glass is a mockery to a pre-cious stone, though it is an emerald and highly prized by some people, so long as no one is at hand to evaluate it and skillfully expose the crafty counterfeit. And when copper is alloyed to silver, what person, if he is unskilled, will readily be able to evaluate it." Therefore, we will see to it that it will not be our fault if some are snatched away, like sheep by wolves, whom they would fail to recognize because of the treachery of the sheepskin, since they speak the same language we do, but intend different meanings. Of such the Lord admonished us to beware. And so, after chancing upon the commentaries of the disciples of Valentinus—as they style themselves—and after conversing with some of them and becoming acquainted with their doctrine, we thought it necessary to inform you, our dear friend, about these portentous and profound "mysteries" which not all grasp, because not all have purged their brains. Thus, having learned of these mysteries yourself, you can make them clear to all your people and warn them to be on guard against this profundity of nonsense and of blasphemy against God. To the best of our ability we will give you a concise and clear report on the doctrine of these people who are at present spreading false teaching. We are speaking of the disciples of Ptolemaeus, an offshoot of the Valen-

---

[1] 1 Tim 1:4.
[2] Matt 10:26.

tinian school. We will also offer suggestions, to the best of our limited capacity, for refuting this doctrine, by showing how utterly absurd, inconsistent, and incongruous with the truth their statements are. Not that we are accustomed to writing books, or practiced in the art of rhetoric; but it is love that prompts us to acquaint you and all your people with the teachings which up till now have been kept secret, which, however, by the grace of God have at last come to light. "For nothing is covered that will not be revealed, and nothing hidden that will not be known."[2]

Chapter 1

1 They claim that in the invisible and unnameable heights there is a certain perfect Aeon that was before all, the First-Being, whom they also call First-Beginning, First-Father, and Profundity. He is invisible and incomprehensible. And, since he is incomprehensible and invisible, eternal and ingenerate, he existed in deep quiet and stillness through countless ages. Along with him there existed Thought, whom they also name Grace and Silence. At one time this Profundity decided to emit from himself the Beginning of all things. This emission would be as a "seed" which he decided to emit and deposit as it were in the womb of Silence, who coexisted with him. After she had received this "seed" and had become pregnant, she gave birth to Mind, who was both similar and equal to his Father who emitted him; and he alone comprehended his (Father's) greatness. This Mind they also call Only-begotten, Father, and Beginning of all things. Truth was emitted at the same time he [Mind] was. Thus these four constitute the first and principal Pythagorean Tetrad, for there are Profundity and Silence, then Mind and Truth. This [Tetrad] they also style the root of all things. But when this Only-begotten perceived for what things he was emitted, he in turn emitted Word and Life, since he was Father of all who were to come after him and the beginning and formation of the entire Fullness. Thereupon by the conjugal union of Word and Life, Man and Church were emitted. That is the principal Ogdoad, the root and the substance of all

things, known among them by four names, Profundity, Mind, Word, and Man, because each of these is male and female; thus, in the first case, First-Father was united in marriage to Thought whom they call Grace and Silence; then Only-begotten, that is, Mind, to Truth; next Word, to Life; finally Man, to Church.

2 Since these Aeons themselves were emitted for their Father's glory, they in turn wished to glorify the Father by something of their own. So they sent forth emissions through conjugal unions. After Man and Church had been emitted, Word and Life emitted ten other Aeons, whose names are these: Profound and Mingling, Ageless and Union, Self-producing and Pleasure, Immobile and Blending, Only-begotten and Happiness. These are the ten Aeons which they assert were emitted by Word and Life. Moreover, Man himself, together with Church, emitted twelve Aeons, to whom they give these names: Advocate and Faith, Paternal and Hope, Maternal and Love, Praise and Understanding, Ecclesiastic and Blessedness, Desired and Wisdom.

3 Such are the thirty Aeons of their erroneous system. They are enveloped in silence and are known to no one. This indivisible and spiritual Fullness of theirs is tripartite, being divided into an Ogdoad, a Decad, and a Dodecad. And for this reason Savior—for they do not wish to call him Lord—did no work in public for thirty years,[3] thus manifesting the mystery of these Aeons. They also assert that these thirty Aeons are most plainly indicated in the parable of the laborers sent into the vineyard; for some are sent about the first hour, others about the third hour, others about the sixth hour, others about the ninth hour, others about the eleventh hour.[4] Now if the hours mentioned are added up, the sum total will be thirty; for one, three, six, nine, and eleven make thirty. Thus they hold that the Aeons have been indicated by these hours. Besides, they claim that these are great and wonderful and unutterable mysteries, which they themselves bear as fruit. And if anywhere anything of the many things mentioned in the Scriptures can

---

[3]Luke 3:23.
[4]Matt 20:1–16.

[be drawn to these things, they wish to] accommodate and adapt them to their fabrication.

Chapter 2

1 So they tell us that First-Father of theirs is known only to Only-begotten, that is, to Mind, who was born of him. To all the rest he is invisible and incomprehensible. According to them, Mind alone enjoyed himself in contemplating Father and exulted in considering his immeasurable greatness. He was thinking of communicating Father's greatness also to the rest of the Aeons, how vast and great he is, and that he is without beginning, immeasurable, and incapable of being seen. But at the will of Father, Silence restrained him, because she wished to get them all to have the mind and the desire to seek after their First-Father mentioned above. The rest of the Aeons, too, were in some manner quietly desiring to see the one who emitted their "Seed" and to be informed about their Root who was without beginning.

2 But the last and youngest Aeon of the Dodecad emitted by Man and Church, namely, Wisdom, advanced far ahead of all of them and suffered passion, though without the embrace of Desired, her consort. The passion began in Mind and Truth but spread as by infection to this estranged Aeon [Wisdom] under the pretense of love, but in reality out of temerity, because she had no fellowship with perfect Father, as even Mind did. The passion consisted in seeking after Father; for she wished, so they say, to comprehend his greatness. But then she was not able, inasmuch as she undertook an impossible affair, and she fell into extreme agony because of the immense height and unsearchable nature of Father and because of the affection for him. Since she was ever stretching forward to what was ahead, she would at last have been swallowed up by his charm and resolved into the entire substance unless she had met the power that strengthens all things and safeguards them outside the unspeakable greatness. This power they also call Limit. By it they say she was restrained and strengthened, and when with difficulty she had been brought to her senses and was convinced that Father is unfathomable, she laid aside the first Intention together with the subsequent

passion which had arisen from that amazing admiration [for Father].

3 Some of them, however, describe the passion and return of Wisdom in this mystical fashion. After she had undertaken the impossible and unattainable affair, she brought forth a formless substance, namely, such a nature as a woman could bring forth. When she looked at it, she was filled first with grief on account of the unfinished nature of her offspring, then with fear lest her very existence should come to an end. After that she was beside herself and perplexed as she sought the cause [of her offspring] and how she might conceal her. While involved in these passions, she changed her mind and tried to return to Father. When she had made the bold attempt for some time and her strength failed, she entreated Father. The other Aeons, too, especially Mind, made supplication together with her. Hence, they claim, material substance took its beginning from ignorance and grief, fear and bewilderment.

4 Afterwards Father, by means of Only-begotten, emitted the above-mentioned Limit as part of no conjugal couple, [but] bisexual. For they hold that sometimes Father emits with Silence as consort, then again he is above both male and female. This Limit they call Stake, Redeemer, Reaper, Limiter, and Restorer. They claim that Wisdom was purified by this Limit and strengthened and restored to her own consort [Desired]. For, after Intention, together with her subsequent passion, had been separated from her, she herself remained within the Fullness, but her Intention with her passion was separated by Limit and fenced out and kept outside of it. Intention is a spiritual substance, possessing some of the natural tendency of an Aeon, but she is formless and shapeless, because she had received nothing. For this reason they say she is a weak and feminine fruit.

5 After Intention had been separated outside the Fullness of the Aeons, and its Mother had been restored to her own conjugal partner, Only-begotten in accord with Father's forethought again emitted another conjugal couple, namely, Christ and Holy Spirit, for the stabilization and support of the Fullness, lest any of the Aeons have a sim-

ilar misfortune [as Wisdom]. Through them they say the Aeons were perfected. For, they claim, Christ taught them the nature of their conjugal union, that they would be able to know the comprehension of Ingenerate. He also announced among them the knowledge of Father [Profundity], namely, that he is immeasurable and incomprehensible, and that he can be neither seen nor heard. He is known only by Only-begotten. Father's incomprehensible nature is primarily the cause for the permanent existence of the rest of the Aeons; but what can be comprehended of him, namely, his Son, is the cause of their origin and formation. These things, then, Christ performed among them as soon as he had been emitted.

6 The [one] Holy Spirit taught them to give thanks that they had all been made equal, and he introduced [them to] the true rest. They say that in this manner the Aeons were made equal in form and mind, since all became Minds and all Words and all Men and all Christs. In like manner, the female Aeons all became Truths and Lives and Spirits and Churches. Thereupon, they tell us, when all the Aeons had been strengthened and brought to perfect rest, they sang hymns amid much rejoicing to First-Father, who himself took part in the great exultation. Then, in gratitude for this benefit, the entire Fullness of the Aeons, with one will and mind, and with the consent of Christ and Spirit and the approval of their Father, collected and combined whatever most beautiful and brilliant each one had in himself. These things they fittingly blended together and carefully united into one. To the honor and glory of Profundity they made this emission the most perfect beauty and constellation of the Fullness, the most perfect fruit, Jesus. They also gave him the name Savior and Christ, and patronymically, Word, and All, because he is emitted from all. And as an honor to themselves, they emitted together with him Angels of the same nature to be his bodyguard.

Chapter 3

1 Such, then, are the dealings in the inner circle of the Fullness, as they tell them. Such, too, was the misfortune of the Aeon who suffered pas-

sion and nearly perished when, because of her search after Father, she was involved in much material substance. Such was the stabilization, after her agony, by Limit, Stake, Redeemer, Reaper, Limiter, and Restorer. Such was likewise the later origin of the Aeons, namely, of the first Christ and Holy Spirit, both of whom were emitted by Father after the repentance of Wisdom. Such was the formation of the second Christ—whom they also style Savior—a creation out of the combined contributions [of the Aeons]. These things, however, were not declared openly, because not all are capable of grasping this knowledge. They were pointed out mystically by Savior through parables to those who were able to understand them. Thus, the thirty Aeons are pointed out, as we said above, by the thirty years during which they say Savior did not work in public and by the parable of the workers in the vineyard. Paul, on his part, very clearly and frequently names these Aeons, and even preserves their rank, when he speaks thus: "To all generations of the age [aeon] of ages [aeons]."[5] Even we ourselves at the giving of thanks, when we say: "To the ages [aeons] of the ages" [aeons], are said to point out those Aeons. Finally, whenever the word Aeon or Aeons occurs [in Scripture], they maintain there is reference to their Aeons.

2 The emission of the Dodecad of the Aeons is indicated [they claim] by the fact that the Lord was twelve years old when he disputed with the teachers of the Law;[6] likewise, by the choice of the apostles. Besides, the other eighteen Aeons were revealed by the fact that after his resurrection from the dead, he is said to have spent eighteen months with his disciples. Likewise, the ten Aeons are pointed out by iota, the first letter of his name. For this reason Savior said: "Not one iota or one tittle shall be lost . . . till all is accomplished."[7]

3 Now the passion experienced by the twelfth Aeon is pointed out, they say, by the apostasy of Judas, the twelfth of the apostles, when the be-

---

[5]Eph 3:21.
[6]Luke 2:41–51.
[7]Matt 5:18.

trayal took place. Also by the fact that [Jesus] suffered in the twelfth month; for they profess that he preached one year after his baptism. Furthermore, this is most clearly manifested by the case of the woman with the hemorrhage, since, after she had suffered for twelve years, she was healed by Savior's coming, when she touched the hem of his cloak. And because of that, Savior said: "Who touched me?"[8] By this he taught the disciples the mystery that had taken place among the Aeons and the healing of the Aeon that had suffered passion. For that power was pointed out through her who had suffered for twelve years, inasmuch as she was straining forward and her material substance was flowing out into immensity, as they say. And unless she had touched that Son's cloak, that is, the Truth of the First Tetrad, which is indicated by the hem, she would have been resolved into the universal substance. But she stopped and rested from her passion; for, when the power of the Son went out—this they hold is the power of Limit—he healed her and removed the passion from her.

4 Moreover, they assert that Savior, who was made from all things, is the All. This is proved by the following passage: "Every male who opens the womb;"[9] for he, being the All, opened the womb of Intention of the Aeon who suffered passion when she was cast out of the Fullness. He also calls this second Ogdoad, of which we shall speak a little later. They say that for this reason Paul said explicitly: "But he is all;"[10] and again: "To him and from him are all things;"[11] and further: "In him the whole fullness of deity dwells;"[12] and: "All things are recapitulated in Christ through God."[13] Thus they interpret these and similar passages. . . .

Chapter 8

1 Such is their system which neither the prophets preached, nor the Lord taught, nor the apostles handed down. They boast rather loudly of knowing more about it than others do, citing it from non-scriptural works; and, as people would say, they attempt to braid ropes of sand. They try to adapt to their own sayings in a manner worthy

of credence, either the Lord's parables, or the prophet's sayings, or the apostles' words, so that their fabrication might not appear to be without witness. They disregard the order and the connection of the Scriptures and, as much as in them lies, they disjoint the members of the Truth. They transfer passages and rearrange them; and, making one thing out of another, they deceive many by the badly composed phantasy of the Lord's words that they adapt. By way of illustration, suppose someone would take the beautiful image of a king, carefully made out of precious stones by a skillful artist, and would destroy the features of the man on it and change around and rearrange the jewels, and make the form of a dog, or of a fox, out of them, and that a rather bad piece of work. Suppose he would then say with determination that this is the beautiful image of the king that the skillful artist had made, at the same time pointing to the jewels which had been beautifully fitted together by the first artist into the image of the king, but which had been badly changed by the second into the form of a dog. And suppose he would through this fanciful arrangement of the jewels deceive the inexperienced who had no idea of what the king's picture looked like, and would persuade them that this base picture of a fox is that beautiful image of the king. In the same way these people patch together old women's fables, and then pluck words and sayings and parables from here and there and wish to adapt these words of God to their fables. We have already said how much of these words they adapt to the things within the Fullness. . . .

Chapter 10

1 The Church, indeed, though disseminated throughout the world, even to the ends of the earth, received from the apostles and their disciples the

---

[8]Mark 5:30.
[9]Exod 13:2; cf. Luke 2:23.
[10]Col 3:11.
[11]Rom 11:36.
[12]Col 2:9.
[13]Eph 1:10.

faith in one God the Father Almighty, the Creator of heaven and earth and the seas and all things that are in them; and in the one Jesus Christ, the Son of God, who was enfleshed for our salvation; and in the Holy Spirit, who through the prophets preached the Economies, the coming, the birth from a Virgin, the passion, the resurrection from the dead, and the bodily ascension into heaven of the beloved Son, Christ Jesus our Lord, and his coming from heaven in the glory of the Father to recapitulate all things, and to raise up all flesh of the whole human race, in order that to Christ Jesus, our Lord and God, Savior and King, according to the invisible Father's good pleasure, "Every knee should bow [of those] in heaven and on earth and under the earth, and every tongue confess him,"[14] and that he would exercise just judgment toward all; and that, on the other hand, he would send into eternal fire the spiritual forces of wickedness, and the angels who transgressed and became rebels, and the godless, wicked, lawless, and blasphemous people; but, on the other hand, by bestowing life on the righteous and holy and those who kept his commandments and who have persevered in his love—both those who did so from the beginning and those who did so after repentance—he would bestow on them as a grace the gift of incorruption and clothe them with everlasting glory.

2 The church, as we have said before, though disseminated throughout the whole world, carefully guards this preaching and this faith which she has received, as if she dwelt in one house. She likewise believes these things as if she had but one soul and the one and the same heart; she preaches, teaches, and hands them down harmoniously, as if she possessed but one mouth.

For, though the languages throughout the world are dissimilar, nevertheless the meaning of the tradition is one and the same. To explain, the churches which have been founded in Germany do not believe or hand down anything else; neither do those founded in Spain or Gaul or Libya or in the central regions of the world. But just as the sun, God's creation, is one and the same throughout the world, so too the light, the preaching of the truth, shines everywhere and enlightens all people who wish to come to the knowledge of the truth. Neither will any of those who preside in the churches, though exceedingly eloquent, say anything else (for no one is above the Master); nor will a poor speaker subtract from the tradition. For, since the faith is one and the same, neither he who can discourse at length about it adds to it, nor he who can say only a little subtracts from it. . . .

Chapter 13

1 A certain member of their company, Marcus by name, who boasts of correcting his teacher, is also very skilled in magical imposture. By this means he deceived many men and not a few women, and converted them to himself as to one most learned and most perfect, possessed of the greatest power from invisible and unnameable regions. In truth, he was the forerunner of the Antichrist. For example, he combines the buffooneries of Anaxilaus with the craftiness of so-called magicians. As a result those who have no sense and have lost their mind think he is working wonders.

2 As he feigns to give thanks over the cup mixed with wine, and draws out at great length the prayer of invocation, he makes the cup appear to be purple or red so that it seems that Grace, who is from the regions which are above all things, dropped her own blood into that cup because of his invocation, and that those who are present greatly desire to taste of that drink, so that Grace, who was invoked by this magician, might rain upon them too. Moreover, having handed mixed cups to the women, he commands them to give thanks over them in his presence. And when this has been done, he himself brings forward another cup much larger than that over which the duped woman gave thanks, and pours from the smaller cup, over which thanks had been given by the woman, into the one which he himself brought forward. At the same time he says over it these words: "May Grace who is before all things, unthinkable and unspeakable, fill your inner self and increase in you her own knowledge, by planting the mustard seed in good ground." By saying some such words and driving

---

[14]Phil 2:10–11.

the wretched woman to madness, he appears to have worked wonders, namely, that the large cup was filled from the small one, even to overflowing. Still other acts similar to these he performed and deceived many and drew them after himself.

3 It is probable that he possesses even some demon as a familiar, through whom he himself seems to prophesy, and through whom whatever woman he considers worthy to partake of his Grace he makes prophesy. Especially about women he is concerned, and that, about those who are well-dressed and clothed in purple and who are very rich, whom he often attempts to seduce. Flatteringly he says to them: "I want you to partake of my Grace, because the Father of all always sees your Angel in his presence. But the dwelling place of your Greatness [angel] is within us. It behooves us to be united. First receive Grace from me and through me. Adorn yourself as a bride awaiting her bridegroom that you may be what I am, and I may be what you are. Put the 'seed' of light in your bridal chamber. Take from me the bridegroom. Receive him [in yourself] and be received in him. Look, Grace is descending upon you. Open your mouth and prophesy." Now, if the woman should answer: "I have never prophesied and do not know how to prophesy," he will again utter some invocations to the amazement of the duped woman. He says to her: "Open your mouth and say anything whatsoever and prophesy." Thereupon she becomes puffed up and elated by those words, her soul becomes aroused at the prospect of prophesying, her heart beats faster than usual. She dares idly and boldly to say nonsensical things and whatever happens to come to mind, since she has been heated by an empty wind. (This is what one superior to us said about such people, "A soul that is heated by empty air is bold and impudent.") From now on she considers herself a prophetess and thanks Marcus for having given her of his Grace. She tries to reward him not only by the gift of her possessions—in that manner he has amassed a fortune—but by sharing her body, desiring to unite herself with him in every way so that she may become one with him.

4 But some of the most faithful women, who have the fear of God and could not be deceived—

whom he tried to beguile like the rest by commanding them to prophesy—rejected and condemned him, and withdrew from such company. They knew very well that the gift of prophecy does not enter a person through Marcus, the magician. On the contrary, upon whomever God sends his grace from above, they are the ones who possess the God-given prophetic power and then speak where and when God wills, but not when Marcus commands. For whoever commands is greater and of higher authority than the one who is commanded, since the one rules, but the other has been made subject. If, then, Marcus commands, or someone else—since they all have the custom of drawing lots at the banquets and of commanding one another to prophesy, and, in keeping with their own desires, of prophesying for their own benefit—the one who commands, though he is a human, will be greater and of higher authority than the prophetic spirit. This, of course, is impossible. On the contrary, such spirits that are commanded by these people and speak whatever the people wish are perishable and weak, bold and impudent, sent by Satan to deceive and destroy those who have not kept that vigorous faith, which they had received through the Church in the beginning.

5 Furthermore, often these women returned to the Church of God and confessed that this Marcus concocts love potions and charms for some of them, though not for all, in order to insult even their bodies; and that they were violated in body by him, and on their part loved him very erotically. So it happened that a certain deacon from among our own people in Asia, who while giving Marcus hospitality in his own house fell victim to such a misfortune. His wife, who was very beautiful, was defiled in mind and body by this magician. For a long time she traveled about with him. When, however, with much effort the brothers converted her, she spent the whole time doing penance amid weeping and lamentation over the defilement she had suffered through this magician. . . .

Chapter 22

1 The Rule of the Truth that we hold is this: There is one God Almighty, who created all

things through his Word; he both prepared and made all things out of nothing, just as Scripture says: "For by the word of the Lord the heavens were made, and all their host by the breath of His mouth."[15] And again: "All things were made through Him and without Him was made not a thing."[16] From this "all" nothing is exempt. Now, it is the Father who made all things through him, whether visible or invisible, whether sensible or intelligible, whether temporal for the sake of some dispensation or eternal. These he did not make through angels or some powers that were separated from his thought. For the God of all things needs nothing. No, he made all things by his Word and Spirit, disposing and governing them and giving all of them existence. This is the one who made the world, which indeed is made up of all things. This is the one who fashioned humans. This is the God of Abraham and Isaac and Jacob, above whom there is no other God, nor a Beginning, nor a Power, nor a Fullness. This is the Father of our Lord Jesus Christ, as we shall demonstrate. If, therefore, we hold fast this Rule, we shall easily prove that they have strayed from the truth, even though their statements are quite varied and numerous. It is true, nearly all the heretical sects, many as they are, speak of one God; but they alter him by their evilmindedness. They are thereby ungrateful to him who made them, just as the pagans by idolatry. Moreover, they hold in contempt God's handiwork by speaking against their own salvation; and they are thus their own most bitter accusers and false witnesses. Even though they do not wish to, they will surely rise again in the flesh in order to acknowledge the power of Him who raises them from the dead; they will, however, not be numbered with the righteous, because of their unbelief.

2 Since, therefore, the exposé and refutation of all the heretical sects is different and multiform, and since we have resolved to give an answer to everyone according to its own standard, we have deemed it necessary first of all to give an account of their source and root, in order that you may know their most sublime profundity, and understand the tree from which such fruits came forth.

Chapter 23

1 Simon, the Samaritan, was the famous magician of whom Luke, the disciple and follower of the apostles, said: "But there was a man named Simon, who had previously practiced magic in the city and seduced the people of Samaria, saying that he himself was somebody great. They all gave heed to him, from the least to the greatest, saying, 'This man is that Power of God which is called Great.' And they gave heed to him, because for a long time he had bewitched them with his magic."[17] This Simon, then, feigned faith; he thought that even the apostles themselves affected cures by magic and not by God's power. He suspected that, when by the imposition of hands the apostles filled with the Holy Spirit those who believed in God through Jesus Christ who was announced by them, they were doing this through some greater knowledge of magic. But when he offered the apostles some money so that he too might receive this power of bestowing the Holy Spirit on whomever he willed, he heard this from Peter: "Keep your money to yourself, to perish with you, because you thought you could obtain the gift of God with money. You have neither part nor lot in this matter, for your heart is not right before God. For I see that you are in the gall of bitterness and in the bond of iniquity."[18] But he believed still less in God and greedily intended to rival the apostles so that he too might appear famous. So he made yet a deeper investigation into the entire art of magic to the amazement of the crowds of people. This happened during the reign of Emperor Claudius, who, so they say, also honored him with a stature because of his magic. So this man was glorified by many as a god. He taught that he himself was the one who appeared among the Jews as the Son of God, while in Samaria he descended as the Father, and among the other nations he came as the Holy Spirit. He also taught that he was the most sublime Power, that is, the

---

[15]Ps 33:6.
[16]John 1:3.
[17]Acts 8:9–11.
[18]Acts 8:20–21, 23.

Father who is above all things. He permitted himself to be called whatever people might call him.

2 Now Simon, the Samaritan, from whom all heresies got their start, proposed the following sort of heretical doctrine. Having himself redeemed a certain Helen from being a prostitute in Tyre, a city of Phoenicia, he took her with him on his rounds, saying that she was the first Thought of his mind, the Mother of all things, through whom in the beginning he conceived in his mind to make the Angels and Archangels. For he asserted that this Thought leaped forth from him, since she knew what her Father wanted, and descended to the lower regions and gave birth to Angels and Powers, by whom also this world was made. But after she had given birth to them, she was detained by them out of envy, since they did not wish to be considered the offspring of anyone else. For he was entirely unknown to them. His Thought, however, who was detained by the Powers and Angels that had been emitted by her, also suffered all kinds of contumely at their hands, so that she could not return to her Father on high. [She suffered] even to the extent of being imprisoned in a human body and of transmigrating for ages into other female bodies, as from one vessel into another. For example, she was in the famous Helen on account of whom the Trojan war was fought; for that reason Stesichorus who reviled her in his verses was struck blind, but after he repented and had written what are called palinodes, in which he sang her praises, his sight was restored. Thus, passing from one body into another, and always suffering insults from the body, she was at last a prostitute in a public house. She was the lost sheep.

3 He himself came for this reason that he might first take her to himself, free her from the bonds, and then bring salvation to humankind by his own knowledge. The angels governed the world badly, because each one desired to be sovereign. So he came, he said, to set matters right; having been transformed and made like the principalities and powers and angels, he appeared in turn as a man, though he was not a man. He appeared to suffer in Judea, though he really did not suffer. Moreover, the prophets uttered their prophecies by virtue of inspirations received from

the angels who made the world. Wherefore, those who put their trust in Simon and his Helen do not give heed to them, but do whatever they will, since they are free. For they say that people are saved through his grace, and not through holy deeds, because deeds are holy not by nature but by accident. For example, the angels who made the world laid down precepts and through these made slaves of people. He, therefore, promised that the world would be destroyed so that those who belong to him would be freed from the domain of those who made the world.

4 The mystic priests of these people live licentious lives and practice magic, each one in whatever way he can. They make use of exorcisms and incantations, love-potions too and philters, and the so-called familiars, and dream-senders. They diligently practice whatever other magic arts there may be. They also have a statue of Simon patterned after Jupiter, and one of Helen patterned after Minerva. They worship these statues. They also have a name for themselves, the "Simonians" derived from Simon the author of this most impious doctrine, from whom the falsely called knowledge took its origin, as one can learn from their assertions. . . .

Chapter 24

1 Saturninus, who was of Antioch near Daphne, and Basilides got their start from these heretics. Still they taught different doctrines, the one in Syria, the other in Alexandria. Saturninus, following Menander, assumed there is one Father who is unknown to all and who made the angels and archangels, virtues and powers. But the world and all that is in it was made by certain seven Angels. Humanity too is the work of angels. When a shining image appeared from above from the sovereign power and they were not able to hold fast to it because it immediately ascended again, he said that they exhorted each other, saying, "Let us make man after an image and likeness."[19] When this first-formed-man was made and was not able

---

[19]Gen 1:26.

to stand erect because of the weakness of the angels, but wriggled on the ground as a worm, then the Power on high had pity on him, because he was made after its likeness, and he sent a spark of life which raised him up and set him upright and made him live. This spark of life, then, he claims, returns to its own kind after a human's death, and the rest of the things out of which he was made are again resolved into these same things.

2 He assumed, furthermore, that Savior was unbegotten, incorporeal, and formless; still he was believed to have appeared as man. He says the God of the Jews is one of the angels. On this account, because his Father wished to destroy all the principalities, Christ came to destroy the God of the Jews and to bring salvation to those who believe in him. These are the ones who have in themselves the spark of life. In truth, he says that two kinds of humans were formed by the angels, the one wicked, the other good. And since the demons aided the wicked, Savior came for the destruction of the evil people and the demons, but for the salvation of the good. Besides, he said that to marry and to beget children comes from Satan. Most of his followers even abstain from animal food, misleading many by this false type of temperance. As for the prophecies, some were uttered by the angels who made the world, others by Satan, whom he assumed to be the very angel who opposes those who made the world, especially the God of the Jews. . . .

Chapter 25

1 Carpocrates and his disciples assert that the world and the things in it were made by angels who are far inferior to the ingenerate Father, and that Jesus was begotten by Joseph and, though he was made like humans, he was superior to the rest. Moreover, since his soul was vigorous and innocent, he remembered what he had seen within the sphere which belongs to the ingenerate God. For this reason, a power was sent down upon him by God, that by means of it he could escape from the makers of the world and that this [soul], having passed through all their domains and so remained free in all, might ascend to him [Father].

The souls that embrace things similar to it [Jesus' soul] will in like manner [ascend to him]. Furthermore, they say, the soul of Jesus, though trained according to the law in the practices of the Jews, despised them, and for this reason received power by which he destroyed the passions which were in people as a punishment.

2 The soul, therefore, which is like that of Jesus, is able to hold in contempt those rulers and makers of the world, receiving like Jesus a power to perform the same things that he performed. Wherefore, some of them advanced to such a pitch of pride that they claim to be like Jesus; others even claim that they are more powerful than Jesus; some again assert that they are superior to his disciples, as, for instance, Peter and Paul and the rest of the apostles. They claim that they are in no way inferior to Jesus. Really, their souls, they claim, descend from the same sphere, and because in like manner they hold in contempt the makers of the world, they have been deemed worthy of the same power and return again to the same place. If, however, anyone has despised the things here below more than he did, such a one can be better than he.

3 These people, too, practice magic and make use of incantations, philtres, spells, familiars, dream-senders, and the rest of the evil magic. They assert that they have power even now to exercise dominion over the rulers and makers of this world; not only over them, but also over all the creatures in it. So some of them have been sent forth by Satan to the pagans to malign the holy name of the church, so that when people, in one way or another, hear their tenets and imagine that we all are like them, they would turn their ears from the preaching of the truth; or even as they see their conduct they would speak slander of us all. However, we have nothing in common with them in doctrine, morals, or daily conduct. On the contrary, they live licentious lives and hold godless doctrine. But they use the Name [of Jesus] only to veil their own wickedness. Their condemnation is just. They will be punished by God in keeping with the deserts of their deeds.

4 They have fallen into such unbridled madness that they boast of having in their power and

of practicing every kind of impious and godless deed. For they claim that deeds are good or bad only because of human opinion. Therefore, they say that the souls must have experience in every kind of life and in every act by means of transmigration from one body to another, unless some soul would preoccupy itself once and for all, and in an equivalent manner do in one coming [into this world] all the deeds—deeds which it is not only wrong for to us to speak of and to listen to, but which we may not even think or believe that such things are done among people who live in our cities. The purpose of this, according to their writings, is that the souls, having had every experience in life, may at their departure not be wanting in anything; moreover, they must take care lest they be again sent forth into a body because something was wanting to their liberation. For this reason they assert that Jesus uttered the following parable: "And as you with an accuser, make an effort to settle with him lest he drag you to the judge, and the judge hand you to the officer, and he put you in prison. Amen, I tell you, you will never get out till you have paid the very last copper."[20] They say that the adversary is one of the angels who are in the world. They call him Devil. They claim that he was made in order to lead from the world to the ruler those souls that perished. They also say he is the first of the authors of this world and he hands such souls over to another angel, who is his minister, that he might imprison them in other bodies; for the body is a prison, they assert. And this clause: "You will never get out till you have paid the very last copper," they interpret to mean that no one will escape from the power of the angels who made the world, but will always transmigrate from one body to another until he has had experience in absolutely every kind of action that exists in the world. And when nothing is wanting to him, his soul, having been liberated, escapes to the God who is above the angels, the makers of the world. In this manner all souls are saved—whether in one coming [into this world] they preoccupy themselves in being mixed up in every kind of action, whether they transmigrate from one body to another, or, what is the same, whether they have been sent into every kind of life. And having fulfilled the requirements and paid the debts, they are liberated, so that they no longer have to operate in a body.

5 Now, whether these impious, unlawful, and forbidden acts are really practiced by them, I would hardly believe. But in their writings it is so written, and they also explain it so. Jesus, they assert, spoke privately in mystery to his disciples and apostles and commissioned them to hand down privately these things to those who are worthy and believe; for they are saved by faith and love. But the other things are indifferent, some good, some bad, according to the view of people, inasmuch as nothing is bad by nature.

6 Some of them put a mark on their disciples, branding them on the underside of the lobe of the right ear. Marcellina belonged to their number. She came to Rome under Pope Anicetus and, since she belonged to this school, she led multitudes astray. They call themselves Gnostics and possess images, some of which are paintings, some made of other materials. They said Christ's image was copied by Pilate at the time that Jesus lived among humans. On these images they put a crown and exhibit them along with the images of the philosophers of the world, namely, with the image of Pythagoras, Plato, Aristotle, and the rest. Toward these [images] they observe other rites that are just like those of the pagans.

Chapter 26

1 A certain Cerinthus taught in Asia that the world was not made by the first God, but by some power which was separated and distant from the authority that is above all things, and which was ignorant of the God who is above all things. He proposes Jesus, not as having been born of a virgin—for this seemed impossible to him—but as having been born the son of Joseph and Mary like all other people, and that he excelled over every person in justice, prudence, and wisdom. After his baptism Christ descended on him in the shape of a dove from the authority that is above all things.

---

[20]Matt 5:25–26.

Then he preached the unknown Father and worked wonders. But at the end Christ again flew off from Jesus. Jesus indeed suffered and rose again from the dead, but Christ remained impassible, since he was spiritual.

2 The so-called Ebionites admit that the world was made by the true God, but in regard to the Lord they hold the same opinion as Cerinthus and Carpocrates. They use only the Gospel according to Matthew and reject the Apostle Paul, saying that he is an apostate from the law. The prophetical writings, however, they strive to interpret in a rather curious manner. They circumcise themselves and continue in the practices which are prescribed by the law and by the Judaic standard of living, so that they worship Jerusalem as the house of God. . . .

Chapter 27

1 A certain Cerdo also got his start from the disciples of Simon. He settled in Rome under Hyginus, who held the ninth place of the episcopacy by succession from the apostles. He taught that the God who had been proclaimed under the law and the prophets was not the Father of Our Lord Jesus Christ, for the former was known, but the latter was unknown; again, the former was just, whereas the latter was benevolent.

2 Marcion of Pontus succeeded Cerdo and amplified his doctrine. He uttered the impudent blasphemy that the God who was proclaimed by the law and the prophets was the author of evil, and desirous of war. He was inconsistent in his teaching and contradicted himself. Jesus, however, who has his origin in the Father who is above the God who made the world, came to Judea at the time when Pontius Pilate presided as procurator of Tiberius Caesar. He was manifested in the form of a man to those who were in Judea. He abolished the prophets and the law and all the works of the God who made the world, whom he also styled the World-Ruler. Besides all this, he mutilated the Gospel according to Luke, discarding all that is written about the birth of the Lord, and discarding also many of the Lord's discourses containing teaching in which it is most clearly written that

the Lord confessed his Father as the Maker of the universe. Marcion persuaded his disciples that he was more truthful than the apostles who handed down the Gospel, though he gave them not the Gospel, but only a portion of the Gospel. In like manner, he mutilated the letters of Paul, removing whatever was clearly said by the apostle about the God who made the world inasmuch as he is the Father of our Lord Jesus Christ; for the apostle taught by quoting from the prophetical writings that foretold the Lord's coming.

3 Only those souls that had learned his doctrine would attain salvation. The body, on the contrary, since it was taken from the earth, is incapable of sharing in salvation. Besides the blasphemy against God, he added this one (thus truly speaking with the devil's mouth and uttering all things contrary to the truth): Cain and those like him, the Sodomites and the Egyptians and those like them, and all the pagans who walked in every mess of wickedness were all saved by the Lord when he descended into the netherworld and they met him, and he took them into his kingdom. But Abel, Enoch, Noah, and the rest of the righteous and the patriarchs who came from Abraham, together with all the prophets and those who pleased God, did not share in salvation, as the Serpent that was in Marcion proclaimed. For, he says, since these people know that their God always tempted them, they had a suspicion that he was tempting them at that time, and they did not go to meet Jesus, nor did they believe in his preaching. As a result their souls remained in the netherworld.

4 Now, since this man alone was openly so bold as to mutilate the Scriptures and to calumniate God more impudently than all others, we will answer him separately and expose him by his own writings, and also from the discourses of the Lord and the apostles which he himself kept and used; and thus with God's grace we shall overthrow him. We have necessarily made mention of him at present that you might know that all those who in any way adulterate the truth and do injury to the preaching of the church are the disciples and successors of Simon, the magician of Samaria. For even though they do not acknowledge the name of

their teacher in order to mislead others, yet it is his doctrine they teach. By proposing the name of Christ Jesus as a kind of incentive, they put many to death by wickedly disseminating their own teaching by means of the good name [Jesus], and by handing them the bitter and wicked poison of the Serpent, the author of the apostasy, under the guise of the delight and beauty of this name.

Book 3

Chapter 3

1 It is within the power of all, therefore, in every church, who may wish to see the truth, to contemplate clearly the tradition of the apostles manifested throughout the whole world; and we are in a position to reckon up those who were by the apostles instituted bishops in the churches, and [to demonstrate] the succession of these men to our own times; those who neither taught nor knew of anything like what these [heretics] rave about. For if the apostles had known hidden mysteries, which they were in the habit of imparting to "the perfect" apart and secretly from the rest, they would have delivered them especially to those to whom they were also committing the churches themselves. For they were desirous that these men should be very perfect and blameless in all things, whom also they were leaving behind as their successors, delivering up their own place of government to these men; which men, if they discharged their functions honestly, would be a great boon [to the church], but if they should fall away, the direst calamity.

2 Since, however, it would be very tedious, in such a volume, as this, to reckon up the successions of all the churches, we do put to confusion all those who, in whatever manner, whether by an evil self-pleasing, by vainglory, or by blindness and perverse opinion, assemble in unauthorized meetings; [we do this, I say,] by indicating that tradition derived from the apostles, of the very great, the very ancient, and universally known church founded and organized at Rome by the two most glorious apostles, Peter and Paul; as also [by pointing out] the faith preached to people, which

comes down to our time by means of the successions of the bishops. For it is a matter of necessity that every church should agree with this church, on account of its preeminent authority, that is, the faithful everywhere, inasmuch as the apostolical tradition has been preserved continuously by those [faithful men] who exist everywhere.

3 The blessed apostles, then, having founded and built up the Church, committed into the hands of Linus the office of the episcopate. Of this Linus, Paul makes mention in the Epistles to Timothy. To him succeeded Anacletus; and after him, in the third place from the apostles, Clement was allotted the bishopric. This man, as he had seen the blessed apostles, and had been conversant with them, might be said to have the preaching of the apostles still echoing [in his ears], and their traditions before his eyes. Nor was he alone [in this], for there were many still remaining who had received instructions from the apostles. In the time of this Clement, no small dissension having occurred among the brethren at Corinth, the Church in Rome despatched a most powerful letter to the Corinthians, exhorting them to peace, renewing their faith, and declaring the tradition which it had lately received from the apostles, proclaiming the one God, omnipotent, the Maker of heaven and earth, the Creator of humans, who brought on the deluge, and called Abraham, who led the people from the land of Egypt, spoke with Moses, set forth the law, sent the prophets, and who has prepared fire for the devil and his angels. From this document, whosoever chooses to do so, may learn that he, the Father of our Lord Jesus Christ, was preached by the churches, and may also understand the apostolical tradition of the church, since this Epistle is of older date than these people who are now propagating falsehood, and who conjure into existence another god beyond the Creator and the Maker of all existing things. To this Clement there succeeded Evaristus. Alexander followed Evaristus; then, sixth from the apostles, Sixtus was appointed; after him, Telephorus, who was gloriously martyred; then Hyginus; after him, Pius; then after him, Anicetus. Soter having succeeded Anicetus, Eleutherius does now, in the twelfth place from the apostles, hold the inheritance of

the episcopate. In this order, and by this succession, the ecclesiastical tradition from the apostles, and the preaching of the truth, have come down to us. And this is most abundant proof that there is one and the same vivifying faith, which has been preserved in the church from the apostles until now, and handed down in truth.

4 But Polycarp also was not only instructed by apostles, and conversed with many who had seen Christ, but was also, by apostles in Asia, appointed bishop of the church in Smyrna, whom I also saw in my early youth, for he tarried [on earth] a very long time, and, when a very old man, gloriously and most nobly suffering martyrdom, departed this life, having always taught the things which he had learned from the apostles, and which the Church has handed down, and which alone are true. To these things all the Asiatic Churches testify, as do also those men who have succeeded Polycarp down to the present time—a man who was of much greater weight, and a more stedfast witness of truth, than Valentinus, and Marcion, and the rest of the heretics. He it was who, coming to Rome in the time of Anicetus, caused many to turn away from the aforesaid heretics to the Church of God, proclaiming that he had received this one and sole truth from the apostles—that, namely, which is handed down by the church. There are also those who heard from him that John, the disciple of the Lord, going to bathe at Ephesus, and perceiving Cerinthus within, rushed out of the bath-house without bathing, exclaiming, "Let us fly, lest even the bath-house fall down, because Cerinthus, the enemy of the truth, is within." And Polycarp himself replied to Marcion, who met him on one occasion, and said, "Do you know me?" "I do know you, the first-born of Satan." Such was the horror which the apostles and their disciples had against holding even verbal communication with any corrupters of the truth; as Paul also says, "A person that is an heretic, after the first and second admonition, reject; knowing that he that is such is subverted, and sins, being condemned of himself."[21] There is also a very powerful Epistle of Polycarp written to the Philippians, from which those who choose to do so, and are anxious about their salvation, can learn

the character of his faith, and the preaching of the truth. Then, again, the Church in Ephesus, founded by Paul, and having John remaining among them permanently until the times of Trajan, is a true witness of the tradition of the apostles.

Chapter 4

1 Since therefore we have such proofs, it is not necessary to seek the truth among others which it is easy to obtain from the church; since the apostles, like a rich person [depositing his money] in a bank, lodged in her hands most copiously all things pertaining to the truth: so that every one, whosoever will, can draw from her the water of life. For she is the entrance to life; all others are thieves and robbers. On this account are we bound to avoid them, but to make choice of the things pertaining to the church with the utmost diligence, and to lay hold of the tradition of the truth. For how stands the case? Suppose there arise a dispute relative to some important question among us, should we not have recourse to the most ancient churches with which the apostles held constant intercourse, and learn from them what is certain and clear in regard to the present question? For how should it be if the apostles themselves had not left us writings? Would it not be necessary, [in that case,] to follow the course of the tradition which they handed down to those to whom they did commit the churches?

2 To which course many nations of those barbarians who believe in Christ do assent, having salvation written in their hearts by the Spirit, without paper or ink, and, carefully preserving the ancient tradition, believing in one God, the Creator of heaven and earth, and all things therein, by means of Christ Jesus, the Son of God; who, because of his surpassing love towards his creation, condescended to be born of the virgin, he himself uniting people through himself to God, and having suffered under Pontius Pilate, and rising again, and having been received up in splendor, shall come in glory, the Savior of those who are saved, and the Judge of those who are judged, and sending into eternal fire those who transform the truth, and de-

---

[21]Tit 3:10.

spise his Father and his advent. Those who, in the absence of written documents, have believed this faith, are barbarians, so far as regards our language; but as regards doctrine, manner, and tenor of life, they are, because of faith, very wise indeed; and they do please God, ordering their conversation in all righteousness, chastity, and wisdom. If any one were to preach to these people the inventions of the heretics, speaking to them in their own language, they would at once stop their ears, and flee as far off as possible, not enduring even to listen to the blasphemous address. Thus, by means of that ancient tradition of the apostles, they do not suffer their mind to conceive anything of the [doctrines suggested by the] portentous language of these teachers, among whom neither church nor doctrine has ever been established.

3 For, prior to Valentinus, those who follow Valentinus had no existence; nor did those from Marcion exist before Marcion; nor, in short, had any of those malignant-minded people, whom I have above enumerated, any being previous to the initiators and inventors of their perversity. For Valentinus came to Rome in the time of Hyginus, flourished under Pius, and remained until Anicetus. Cerdo, too, Marcion's predecessor, himself arrived in the time of Hyginus, who was the ninth bishop. Coming frequently into the church, and making public confession, he thus remained, one time teaching in secret, and then again making public confession; but at last, having been denounced for corrupt teaching, he was excommunicated from the assembly of the brethren. Marcion, then, succeeding him, flourished under Anicetus, who held the tenth place of the episcopate. But the rest, who are called Gnostics, take rise from Menander, Simon's disciple, as I have shown; and each one of them appeared to be both the father and the high priest of that doctrine into which he has been initiated. But all these (the Marcosians) broke out into their apostasy much later, even during the intermediate period of the church.

⊳·◄►·○·◄►·◄

32. Tertullian: Prescription of the Heretics

Tertullian was one of the most brilliant and wide-ranging Christian authors of the first three centuries, as we have already seen in Chapter 4 (see that introduction). One of his most famous works is the heresiological treatise "Prescription of the Heretics." The title refers to an established Roman legal practice, the "prescription," in which a lawyer could prevent a case from coming to trial on the basis of a legal technicality. Tertullian makes a metaphorical use of this strategy: heretics do not need to be given a fair hearing—their case does not even need to be put on the docket—because they have forfeited their right to defend their views. In Tertullian's opinion, the Christian Scriptures are the only grounds for theological reflection. But since heretics have forsaken the church, they are not Christians; and since they are not Christians, they have no right to appeal to the Chris-

Tertullian: "Prescription of the Heretics," from *Early Latin Theology: Selections from Tertullian, Cyprian, Ambrose and Jerome*, ed. S. L. Greenslade [The Library of Christian Classics, V]. London: SCM Press, 1956. Used with permission of SCM Press and Westminster John Knox Press.

tian Scriptures. That is to say, since the Scriptures belong only to those who accept the faith proclaimed by the apostles—those within the apostolic churches (here Tertullian depends on the doctrine of apostolic succession)—the heretics' views can be "prescribed" without a trial.

Other significant ideas are developed in this treatise as well, including the notions that heretics have acquired their ideas from the pagan philosophers, that there is one rule of faith subscribed to by all true Christians, that heretics have modified the texts of Scripture to their own ends, and that their improper use of Scripture is paralleled by the undisciplined management of their churches. All in all, this is a brilliant tour de force, composed early in Tertullian's career, possibly around 200 C.E.

1 The times we live in provoke me to remark that we ought not to be surprised either at the occurrence of the heresies, since they were foretold, or at their occasional subversion of faith, since they occur precisely in order to prove faith by testing it. To be scandalized, as many are, by the great power of heresy is groundless and unthinking. What power could it have if it never occurred? When something is unquestionably destined to come into existence, it receives, together with the purpose of its existence, the force by which it comes to exist and which precludes its non-existence.

2 Fever, for example, we are not surprised to find in its appointed place among the fatal and excruciating issues which destroy human life, since it does in fact exist; and we are not surprised to find it destroying life, since that is why it exists. Similarly, if we are alarmed that heresies which have been produced in order to weaken and kill faith can actually do so, we ought first to be alarmed at their very existence. Existence and power are inseparable.

Faced with fever, which we know to be evil in its purpose and power, it is not surprise we feel, but loathing; and as it is not in our power to abolish it, we take what precautions we can against it. But when it comes to heresies, which bring eternal death and the heat of a keener fire with them, there are people who prefer to be surprised at their power rather than avoid it, although they have the power to avoid it. But heresy will lose its strength if we are not surprised that it is strong. . . .

6 I need say no more on that point, for it is the same Paul who elsewhere, when writing to the Galatians,[1] classes heresy among the sins of the flesh, and who counsels Titus to shun a heretic after the first reproof[2] because such a person is perverted and sinful, standing self-condemned. Besides, he censures heresy in almost every letter when he presses the duty of avoiding false doctrine, which is in fact the product of heresy. This is a Greek word meaning choice, the choice which anyone exercises when he teaches heresy or adopts it. That is why he calls a heretic self-condemned; he chooses for himself the cause of his condemnation. We Christians are forbidden to introduce anything on our own authority or to choose what someone else introduces on his own authority. Our authorities are the Lord's apostles, and they in turn chose to introduce nothing on their own authority. They faithfully passed on to the nations the teaching which they had received from Christ. So we should anathematize even an angel from heaven if he were to preach a different gospel.[3] The Holy Ghost had already at that time foreseen that an angel of deceit would come in a virgin called Philumene, transforming himself into an angel of light, by whose miracles and tricks Apelles was deceived into introducing a new heresy.

---

[1]Gal 5:20.
[2]Tit 3:10.
[3]Gal 1:8.

7 These are human and demonic doctrines, engendered for itching ears by the ingenuity of that worldly wisdom which the Lord called foolishness, choosing the foolish things of the world to put philosophy to shame. For worldly wisdom culminates in philosophy with its rash interpretation of God's nature and purpose. It is philosophy that supplies the heresies with their equipment. From philosophy come the aeons and those infinite forms—whatever they are—and Valentinus's human trinity. He had been a Platonist. From philosophy came Marcion's God, the better for his inactivity. He had come from the Stoics. The idea of a mortal soul was picked up from the Epicureans, and the denial of the restitution of the flesh was taken over from the common tradition of the philosophical schools. Zeno taught them to equate God and matter, and Heracleitus comes on the scene when anything is being laid down about a god of fire. Heretics and philosophers perpend the same themes and are caught up in the same discussions. What is the origin of evil, and why? The origin of humans, and how? And—Valentinus's latest subject—what is the origin of God? No doubt in Desire and Abortion! A plague on Aristotle, who taught them dialectic, the art which destroys as much as it builds, which changes its opinions like a coat, forces its conjectures, is stubborn in argument, works hard at being contentious and is a burden even to itself. For it reconsiders every point to make sure it never finishes a discussion.

From philosophy come those fables and endless genealogies and fruitless questionings, those words that creep like a canker. To hold us back from such things, the Apostle testifies expressly in his letter to the Colossians that we should beware of philosophy. "Take heed lest anyone circumvent you through philosophy or vain deceit, after the tradition of humans,"[4] against the providence of the Holy Spirit. He had been at Athens where he had come to grips with the human wisdom which attacks and perverts truth, being itself divided up into its own swarm of heresies by the variety of its mutually antagonistic sects. What has Jerusalem to do with Athens, the Church with the Academy, the Christian with the heretic? Our

principles come from the Porch of Solomon, who had himself taught that the Lord is to be sought in simplicity of heart. I have no use for a Stoic or a Platonic or a dialectic Christianity. After Jesus Christ we have no need of speculation, after the Gospel no need of research. When we come to believe, we have no desire to believe anything else; for we begin by believing that there is nothing else which we have to believe. . . .

13 The Rule of Faith—to state here and now what we maintain—is of course that by which we believe that there is but one God, who is none other than the Creator of the world, who produced everything from nothing through his Word, sent forth before all things; that this Word is called his Son, and in the Name of God was seen in divers ways by the patriarchs, was ever heard in the prophets and finally was brought down by the Spirit and power of God the Father into the Virgin Mary, was made flesh in her womb, was born of her and lived as Jesus Christ; who thereafter proclaimed a new law and a new promise of the kingdom of heaven, worked miracles, was crucified, on the third day rose again, was caught up into heaven and sat down at the right hand of the Father; that he sent in his place the power of the Holy Spirit to guide believers; that he will come with glory to take the saints up into the fruition of the life eternal and the heavenly promises and to judge the wicked to everlasting fire, after the resurrection of both good and evil with the restoration of their flesh.

This Rule, taught (as will be proved) by Christ, allows of no questions among us, except those which heresies introduce and which make heretics. To know nothing against the Rule is to know everything. . . .

14 . . . Grant that heretics are not enemies of the truth, grant that we were not warned to avoid them, what is the good of conferring with people who themselves profess that they are still seeking? If they are indeed still seeking, they have still found nothing certain. Whatever they hold is

---

[4]Col 2:8.

only provisional. Their continual searching shows up their hesitation. And so when you, a seeker like them, look to people who are seekers themselves, the doubter to the doubters, the uncertain to the uncertain, then, blind yourself, you must needs be led by the blind into the ditch. But, in fact, it is only for the sake of deceiving us that they pretend to be still seeking. By first filling us with anxiety, they hope to commend their own views to us. The moment they get near us they begin to defend the very propositions which, they had been saying, need investigation. We must be as quick to refute them, making them understand that it is not Christ we deny, but themselves. In that they are still seeking, they do not yet hold any convictions. In that they possess no convictions, they have yet come to believe. In that they have not yet come to believe, they are not Christians.

An objection is raised. "They do hold convictions and believe, but assert the necessity of 'seeking' in order to defend their faith." Yes, but before they defend it they deny it, confessing by their seeking that they have not yet believed. Not Christians even to themselves, how can they be to us? What sort of faith are they arguing when they come with deceit? What truth are they vindicating when they introduce it with a lie? Another objection. "They discuss and persuade on the basis of Scripture." Naturally. From what other source than the literature of the faith could they talk about the things of the faith?

15 So I reach the position I had planned. I was steering in this direction, laying the foundations by my introductory remarks. From this point onwards I shall contest the ground of my opponents' appeal. They plead Scripture, and some people are influenced from the outset by this audacious plea. Then, as the contest goes on, they weary even the strong, they capture the weak and send the waverers off torn with anxiety. Therefore I take my stand above all on this point: they are not to be admitted to any discussion of Scripture at all. If the Scriptures are to be their strong point (supposing they can get hold of them), we must first discover who are the rightful owners of the Scriptures, in case anyone is given access to them without any kind of right to them.

16 Do not suspect me of raising this objection from want of confidence or from a desire to enter upon the issues in some other way. My reason is primarily the obedience which our faith owes to the Apostle when he forbids us to enter upon questionings, to lend our ears to novel sayings, to associate with a heretic after one correction[5]—not, observe, after one *discussion*. In designating correction as the reason for meeting a heretic, he forbade discussion, and he says *one* correction because the heretic is not a Christian. He is to have no right to a second censure, like a Christian, before two or three witnesses, since he is to be censured for the very reason that forbids discussion with him. Besides, arguments about Scripture achieve nothing but a stomach-ache or a headache.

17 Any given heresy rejects one or another book of the Bible. What it accepts, it perverts with both additions and subtractions to suit its own teaching, and if, in some cases, it keeps books unmaimed, it none the less alters them by inventing different interpretations from ours. False exegesis injures truth just as much as a corrupt text. Baseless assumptions naturally refuse to acknowledge the instrument of their own refutation. They rely on passages which they have put together in a false context or fastened on because of their ambiguity. What will you accomplish, most learned of biblical scholars, if the other side denies what you affirmed and affirms what you denied? True, you will lose nothing in the dispute but your voice; and you will get nothing from their blasphemy but bile.

18 You submit yourself to a biblical disputation in order to strengthen some waverer. Will he in fact incline to the truth any more than to heresy? He sees that you have accomplished nothing, the rival party being allowed equal rights of denial and affirmation and an equal status. As a result he will go away from the argument even more uncertain than before, not knowing which he is to count as heresy. The heretics too can retort these charges upon us. Maintaining equally that the truth is with them, they are compelled to

---

[5]Tit 3:10.

say that it is we who introduce the falsifications of Scripture and the lying interpretations.

19 It follows that we must not appeal to Scripture and we must not contend on ground where victory is impossible or uncertain or not certain enough. Even if a biblical dispute did not leave the parties on a par, the natural order of things would demand that one point should be decided first, the point which alone calls for discussion now, namely, who holds the faith to which the Bible belongs, and from whom, through whom, when, and to whom was the teaching delivered by which people become Christians? For only where the true Christian teaching and faith are evident will the true Scriptures, the true interpretations, and all the true Christian traditions be found.

20 Our Lord Jesus Christ, whoever he is—if he will permit me to speak in this way for the moment—of whatever God he is Son, of whatever matter Man and God, whatever faith he taught, whatever reward he promised, himself declared, while he lived on earth, what he was, what he had been, how he was fulfilling his Father's will, what he was laying down as a person's duty. He declared all this either openly to the people or privately to the disciples, twelve of whom he had specially attached to his person and destined to be the teachers of the nations. One of them was struck off. The remaining eleven, on his return to his Father after the resurrection, he ordered to go and teach the nations, baptizing them into the Father and into the Son and into the Holy Spirit.

At once, therefore, the apostles (whose name means "sent") cast lots and added a twelfth, Matthias, in the place of Judas, on the authority of the prophecy in a psalm of David; and having obtained the promised power of the Holy Spirit to work miracles and to speak boldly, they set out through Judaea first, bearing witness to their faith in Jesus Christ and founding churches, and then out into the world, proclaiming the same doctrine of the same faith to the nations. Again they set up churches in every city, from which the other churches afterwards borrowed the transmission of the faith and the seeds of doctrine and continue to borrow them every day, in order to become churches. By this

they are themselves reckoned apostolic as being the offspring of apostolic churches. Things of every kind must be classed according to their origin. These churches, then, numerous as they are, are identical with that one primitive apostolic church from which they all come. All are primitive and all apostolic. Their common unity is proved by fellowship in communion, by the name of brother and the mutual pledge of hospitality—rights which are governed by no other principle than the single tradition of a common creed.

21 On this ground, therefore, we rule our prescription. If the Lord Christ Jesus sent the apostles to preach, none should be received as preachers except in accordance with Christ's institution. For no one knows the Father save the Son and the one to whom the Son has revealed him, nor is the Son known to have revealed him to any but the apostles whom he sent to preach—and of course to preach what he revealed to them. And I shall prescribe now that what they preached (that is, what Christ revealed to them) should be proved only through the identical churches which the apostles themselves established by preaching to them both *viva voce*, as one says, and afterwards by letters. If this is so, it follows that all doctrine which is in agreement with those apostolic churches, the wombs and sources of the faith, is to be deemed true on the ground that it indubitably preserves what the churches received from the apostles, the apostles from Christ, and Christ from God. It follows, on the other hand, that all doctrine which smacks of anything contrary to the truth of the churches and apostles of Christ and God must be condemned out of hand as originating in falsehood.

It remains for me to show whether this doctrine of ours, the Rule of which I have set out above, does originate in the tradition of the apostles and whether, in consequence, the other doctrines come from falsehood. We are in communion with the apostolic churches. That is not true of any other doctrine. This is evidence of truth. . . .

32 But if any heresies venture to plant themselves in the apostolic age, so that they may be thought to have been handed down by the apostles because they existed in their time, we can say,

Let them exhibit the origins of their churches, let them unroll the list of their bishops, coming down from the beginning by succession in such a way that their first bishop had for his originator and predecessor one of the apostles or apostolic men; one, I mean, who continued with the apostles. For this is how the apostolic churches record their origins. The church of Smyrna, for example, reports that Polycarp was placed there by John, the church of Rome that Clement was ordained by Peter. In just the same way the other churches produced men who were appointed to the office of bishop by the apostles and so transmitted the apostolic seed to them.

Let the heretics invent something of the sort for themselves. Blasphemers already, they will have no scruples. But even if they do invent something, it will be useless to them. If their teaching is compared with the teaching of the apostles, the differences and contradictions between them will cry out that theirs is not the work of any apostle or apostolic person. For the apostles would not have differed from each other in their teaching and the apostolic persons would not have contradicted the apostles. Or are we to believe that the people who learned from the apostles preached something different? Consequently they will be challenged according to this standard by those churches which, though they can produce no apostle or apostolic person as their direct founder, since they are much later foundations (churches are being founded every day), yet, because they agree in the same faith, are reckoned to be no less apostolic through their kinship in doctrine. So, when the heresies are challenged by our churches according to these two standards, let them one and all show how they regard themselves as apostolic. But they are not, and they cannot prove themselves to be what they are not. Nor can they be received into peace and communion by churches which are in any way apostolic when they are in no way apostolic on account of their disagreement in creed. . . .

37 If therefore truth must be adjudged to us "as many as walk according to this rule"[6] which the church has handed down from the apostles, the apostles from Christ, and Christ from God, the principle which we propounded is estab-

lished, the principle which ruled that heretics are not to be allowed to enter an appeal to Scripture, since, without using Scripture, we prove that they have nothing to do with Scripture. If they are heretics, they cannot be Christians, since the names which they accept come not from Christ but from the heretics whom they follow of their own choice. So, not being Christians, they acquire no right to Christian literature, and we have every right to say to them: "Who are you? When did you arrive, and where from? You are not my people; what are you doing on my land? By what right are you cutting down my timber, Marcion? By whose leave are you diverting my waters, Valentinus? By what authority are you moving my boundaries, Apelles? This property belongs to me. And all the rest of you, why are you sowing and grazing here at your will? It is my property. I have been in possession for a long time, I came into possession before you appeared. I have good title-deeds from the original owners of the estate. I am heir to the apostles. As they provided in their will, as they bequeathed it in trust and confirmed it under oath, so, on their terms, I hold it. You they permanently disinherited and disowned as strangers and enemies." And how can heretics be strangers and enemies to the apostles except through their difference in doctrine, which each of them, on his own judgment, has either produced or received against the apostles?

38 Corruption of the Scriptures and of their interpretation is to be expected wherever difference in doctrine is discovered. Those who proposed to teach differently were of necessity driven to tamper with the literature of doctrine, for they could not have taught differently had they not possessed different sources of teaching. Just as their corruption of doctrine would not have been successful without their corruption of its literature, so our doctrinal integrity would have failed us without the integrity of the sources by which doctrine is dealt with.

Now, in our sources, what is there to contradict our teaching? What have we imported of our own making, that we should find it contradicted in Scripture, and remedy the defect by subtraction

---

[6]Gal 6:16.

or addition or alteration? What we are, that the Scriptures have been from their beginning. We are of them, before there was any change, before you mutilated them. Mutilation must always be later than the original. It springs from hostility, which is neither earlier than, nor at home with, what it opposes. Consequently no person of sense can believe that it is we who introduced the textual corruptions into Scripture, we who have existed from the beginning and are the first, any more than he can help believing that it is they, who are later and hostile, who were the culprits. One man perverts Scripture with his hand, another with his exegesis. If Valentinus seems to have used the whole Bible, he laid violent hands on the truth with just as much cunning as Marcion. Marcion openly and nakedly used the knife, not the pen, massacring Scripture to suit his own material. Valentinus spared the text, since he did not invent scriptures to suit his matter, but matter to suit the Scriptures. Yet he took away, and added more, by taking away the proper meanings of particular words and by adding fantastic arrangements. . . .

41 I must not leave out a description of the heretics' way of life—futility, earthly, all too human, lacking in gravity, in authority, in discipline, as suits their faith. To begin with, one cannot tell who is a catechumen and who is baptized. They come in together, listen together, pray together. Even if any of the heathen arrive, they are quite willing to cast that which is holy to the dogs and their pearls (false ones!) before swine. The destruction of discipline is to them simplicity, and our attention to it they call affectation. They are in communion with everyone everywhere. Differences of theology are of no concern to them as long as they are all agreed in attacking the truth. They are all puffed up, they all promise knowledge. Their catechumens are perfect before they are fully instructed. As for the women of the heretics, how forward they are! They have the impudence to teach, to argue, to perform exorcisms, to promise cures, perhaps even to baptize. Their ordinations are hasty,

irresponsible, and unstable. Sometimes they appoint novices, sometimes people tied to secular office, sometimes renegades from us, hoping to bind them by ambition as they cannot bind them by the truth. Nowhere can you get quicker promotion than in the camp of the rebels, where your mere presence is a merit. So one man is bishop today, another tomorrow. The deacon of today is tomorrow's reader, the priest of today is tomorrow a layman. For they impose priestly functions even upon laymen.

42 What am I to say about the ministry of the word? Their concern is not to convert the heathen, but to subvert our folk. The glory they seek comes from bringing the upright down, not raising the fallen up. Since their work results from no constructive operations of their own, but from the destruction of the truth, they undermine our constructions to build their own. Take their complaints against the Law of Moses and the prophets and God the Creator away from them, and they have nothing to say. So it comes about that they find it easier to pull down standing buildings than to build up fallen ruins. In such labor only do they show themselves humble and suave and respectful. But they have no reverence for their own leaders. The reason why there are practically no schisms among the heretics is that when they occur they are not noticed, for their very unity is schism. I am much mistaken if among themselves they do not make alterations in their own rules of faith, each of them adapting what he has received to suit himself, just as the person who handed it down had put it together to suit himself. Its development does not belie its nature and the character of its origin. The Valentinians and Marcionites have taken the same liberty as Valentinus and Marcion themselves to make innovations in faith at their pleasure. In short, when heresies are closely examined, they are all found to be in disagreement on many points with their own founders. A great number of them even have no churches. Motherless and homeless, they wander about bereft of faith and banished from the truth.

33. Tertullian: On the Flesh of Christ

Although his "Prescription" maintains that heretical views do not need even to be considered, Tertullian himself attacked his Christian opponents at considerable length, summarizing, ridiculing, and refuting their views on the basis of the Christian Scriptures. In the present treatise he addresses those who maintained that Christ did not have real flesh, who taught that, although Christ *appeared* to be human, it was indeed all an appearance. This view is normally called "docetism," from the Greek word *dokeo*, "to seem" or "to appear."

A principal proponent of a docetic Christology was the mid-second-century thinker and evangelist Marcion, against whom Tertullian devoted an entire five-volume work ("Against Marcion"). Taking his cue from Paul's letters, Marcion maintained that there was a sharp disjuncture between the Law of Moses and the Gospel of Christ; for him, in fact, the God who gave the Law to his people, the Jews, was not the God of Jesus. The Jewish God was harsh and vindictive ("an eye for an eye"); the God of Jesus was gracious and merciful ("turn the other cheek"). The Jewish God had created the world; the God of Jesus had never had anything to do with it—until he sent Jesus to save people from its harsh Judge. Since this world belonged to the creator God, Jesus had no ties to it; he was not really born and did not have real flesh. Marcion supported his views by appealing to his own version of the Christian Scriptures, comprising a Gospel comparable to our Luke and ten of the Pauline epistles (excluding the Pastorals)—all edited by the removal of positive references to the Old Testament and its creator God.

In refuting Marcion's views, and those that he deemed similar, Tertullian makes extensive appeal to the words of his own Testament (not just Luke and Paul) and offers some very interesting interpretations, including one of the earliest Christian expositions of the parallels between Eve and Mary.

1 They who are so anxious to shake that belief in the resurrection which was firmly settled before the appearance of our modern Sadducees, as even to deny that the expectation thereof has any relation whatever to the flesh, have great cause for besetting the flesh of Christ also with doubtful questions, as if it either had no existence at all, or possessed a nature altogether different from human flesh. For they cannot but be apprehensive that, if it be once determined that Christ's flesh was human, a presumption would immediately arise in opposition to them, that that flesh must by all means rise again, which has already risen in Christ. Therefore we shall have to guard our belief in the resurrection from the same armory, whence they get their weapons of destruction. Let us examine our Lord's bodily substance, for about his spiritual nature all are agreed. It is his flesh that is in question. Its verity and quality are the points in dispute. Did it ever exist? Whence was

Tertullian: "On the Flesh of Christ," from *The Ante-Nicene Fathers*; vol. 3, *Latin Christianity: Its Founder, Tertullian*, ed. A. Cleveland Coxe. Reprint; 2d ed. Grand Rapids, Mich.: Eerdmans, 1989.

it derived? And of what kind was it? If we succeed in demonstrating it, we shall lay down a law for our own resurrection. Marcion, in order that he might deny the flesh of Christ, denied also his nativity, or else he denied his flesh in order that he might deny his nativity; because, of course, he was afraid that his nativity and his flesh bore mutual testimony to each other's reality, since there is no nativity without flesh, and no flesh without nativity. As if indeed, under the prompting of that license which is ever the same in all heresy, he too might not very well have either denied the nativity, although admitting the flesh—like Apelles, who was first a disciple of his, and afterwards an apostate—or, while admitting both the flesh and the nativity, have interpreted them in a different sense, as did Valentinus, who resembled Apelles both in his discipleship and desertion of Marcion. At all events, he who represented the flesh of Christ to be imaginary was equally able to pass off his nativity as a phantom; so that the virgin's conception, and pregnancy, and child-bearing, and then the whole course of her infant too, would have to be regarded as putative. These facts pertaining to the nativity of Christ would escape the notice of the same eyes and the same senses as failed to grasp the full idea of his flesh.

2 Clearly enough is the nativity announced by Gabriel.[1] But what has he to do with the Creator's angel? The conception in the virgin's womb is also set plainly before us. But what concern has he with the Creator's prophet, Isaiah?[2] He will not brook delay, since suddenly (without any prophetic announcement) did he bring down Christ from heaven. "Away," says he, "with that eternal plaguey taxing of Caesar, and the scanty inn, and the squalid swaddling-clothes, and the hard stable. We do not care a jot for that multitude of the heavenly host which praised their Lord at night. Let the shepherds take better care of their flock, and let the wise men spare their legs so long a journey; let them keep their gold to themselves. Let Herod, too, mend his manners, so that Jeremiah may not glory over him. Spare also the babe from circumcision, that he may escape the pain thereof; nor let him be brought into the temple, lest he burden his parents with the expense of the offering; nor let him be handed to Simeon, lest the old man be saddened at the point of death. Let that old woman also hold her tongue, lest she should bewitch the child."[3] After such a fashion as this, I suppose you have had, O Marcion, the hardihood of blotting out the original records (of the history) of Christ, that his flesh may lose the proofs of its reality. But on what grounds (do you do this)? Show me your authority. If you are a prophet, foretell us a thing; if you are an apostle, open your message in public; if a follower of apostles, side with apostles in thought; if you are only a (private) Christian, believe what has been handed down to us: if, however, you are nothing of all this, then (as I have the best reason to say) cease to live. For indeed you are already dead, since you are no Christian, because you do not believe that which by being believed makes people Christian—nay, you are the more dead, the more you are not a Christian; having fallen away, after you had been one, by rejecting what you formerly believed, even as you yourself acknowledge in a certain letter of yours, and as your followers do not deny, while our (brethren) can prove it. Rejecting, therefore, what you once believed, you have completed the act of rejection, by now no longer believing: the fact, however, of your having ceased to believe has not made your rejection of the faith right and proper; nay, rather, by your act of rejection you prove that what you believed previous to the said act was of a different character. What you believed to be of a different character, had been handed down just as you believed it. Now that which had been handed down was true, inasmuch as it had been transmitted by those whose duty it was to hand it down. Therefore, when rejecting that which had been handed down, you rejected that which was true. You had no authority for what you did. However, we have already in another treatise availed ourselves more fully of these prescriptive rules against all heresies. Our repetition of them here after that large

---

[1]Luke 1:26–38.
[2]Isa 7:14.
[3]Matt 1–2; Luke 1–2.

(treatise) is superfluous, when we ask the reason why you have formed the opinion that Christ was not born.

3 Since you think that this lay within the competency of your own arbitrary choice, you must needs have supposed that being born was either impossible for God, or unbecoming to him. With God, however, nothing is impossible but what he does not will. Let us consider, then, whether he willed to be born (for if he had the will, he also had the power, and was born). I put the argument very briefly. If God had willed not to be born, it matters not why, he would not have presented himself in the likeness of a human. Now who, when he sees a human, would deny that he had been born? What God therefore willed not to be, he would in no wise have willed the seeming to be. When a thing is distasteful, the very notion of it is scouted; because it makes no difference whether a thing exist or do not exist, if, when it does not exist, it is yet assumed to exist. It is of course of the greatest importance that there should be nothing false (or pretended) attributed to that which really does not exist. But, say you, his own consciousness (of the truth of his nature) was enough for him. If any supposed that he had been born, because they saw him as a man, that was their concern. Yet with how much more dignity and consistency would he have sustained the human character on the supposition that he was truly born; for if he were not born, he could not have undertaken the said character without injury to that consciousness of his which you on your side attribute to his confidence of being able to sustain, although not born, the character of having been born even against his own consciousness! Why, I want to know, was it of so much importance, that Christ should, when perfectly aware what he really was, exhibit himself as being that which he was not? You cannot express any apprehension that, if he had been born and truly clothed himself with human nature, he would have ceased to be God, losing what he was, while becoming what he was not. For God is in no danger of losing his own state and condition. But, say you, I deny that God was truly changed to a human in such wise

as to be born and endued with a body of flesh, on this ground, that a being who is without end is also of necessity incapable of change. For being changed into something else puts an end to the former state. Change, therefore, is not possible to a Being who cannot come to an end. Without doubt, the nature of things which are subject to change is regulated by this law, that they have no permanence in the state which is undergoing change in them, and that they come to an end from thus wanting permanence, whilst they lose that in the process of change which they previously were. But nothing is equal with God; his nature is different from the condition of all things. If, then, the things which differ from God, and from which God differs, lose what existence they had while they are undergoing change, wherein will consist the difference of the Divine Being from all other things except in his possessing the contrary faculty of theirs—in other words, that God can be changed into all conditions, and yet continue just as he is? On any other supposition, he would be on the same level with those things which, when changed, lose the existence they had before; whose equal, of course, he is not in any other respect, as he certainly is not in the changeful issues of their nature. You have sometimes read and believed that the Creator's angels have been changed into human form, and have even borne about so veritable a body, that Abraham even washed their feet,[5] and Lot was rescued from the Sodomites by their hands;[6] an angel, moreover, wrestled with a man so strenuously with his body, that the latter desired to be let loose, so tightly was he held.[7] Has it, then, been permitted to angels, which are inferior to God, after they have been changed into human bodily form, nevertheless to remain angels? and will you deprive God, their superior, of this faculty, as if Christ could not continue to be God, after his real assumption of the nature of a human? Or else, did those angels appear as phantoms of flesh? You will not, however, have the courage to say this; for if it be so held in your be-

---

[5]Gen 18:4.
[6]Gen 19:12–23.
[7]Gen 32:22–32.

lief, that the Creator's angels are in the same condition as Christ, then Christ will belong to the same God as those angels do, who are like Christ in their condition. If you had not purposely rejected in some instances, and corrupted in others, the Scriptures which are opposed to your opinion, you would have been confuted in this matter by the Gospel of John, when it declares that the Spirit descended in the body of a dove, and sat upon the Lord.[8] When the said Spirit was in this condition, he was as truly a dove as he was also a spirit; nor did he destroy his own proper substance by the assumption of an extraneous substance. But you ask what becomes of the dove's body, after the return of the Spirit back to heaven, and similarly in the case of the angels. Their withdrawal was effected in the same manner as their appearance had been. If you had seen how their production out of nothing had been effected, you would have known also the process of their return to nothing. If the initial step was out of sight, so was also the final one. Still there was solidity in their bodily substance, whatever may have been the force by which the body became visible. What is written cannot but have been.

4 Since, therefore, you do not reject the assumption of a body as impossible or as hazardous to the character of God, it remains for you to repudiate and censure it as unworthy of him. Come now, beginning from the nativity itself, declaim against the uncleanness of the generative elements within the womb, the filthy concretion of fluid and blood, of the growth of the flesh for nine months long out of that very mire. Describe the womb as it enlarges from day to day—heavy, troublesome, restless even in sleep, changeful in its feelings of dislike and desire. Inveigh now likewise against the shame itself of a woman in labor, which, however, ought rather to be honored in consideration of that peril or to be held sacred in respect of (the mystery of) nature. Of course you are horrified also at the infant, which is shed into life with the embarrassments which accompany it from the womb; you likewise, of course, loathe it even after it is washed, when it is dressed out in its swaddling-clothes, graced with repeated anointing,

smiled on with nurse's fawns. This reverend course of nature, you, O Marcion (are pleased to) spit upon; and yet, in what way were you born? You detest a human being at his birth; then after what fashion do you love anybody? Yourself, of course, you had no love of, when you departed from the church and the faith of Christ. But never mind, if you are not on good terms with yourself, or even if you were born in a way different from other people. Christ, at any rate, has loved even that person who was condensed in his mother's womb amidst all its uncleannesses, even that person who was brought into life out of the said womb, even that person who was nursed amidst the nurse's simpers. For his sake he came down (from heaven), for his sake he preached, for his sake "He humbled himself even unto death—the death of the cross."[9] He loved, of course, the being whom he redeemed at so great a cost. If Christ is the Creator's Son, it was with justice that he loved his own (creature); if he comes from another god, his love was excessive, since he redeemed a being who belonged to another. Well, then, loving the human he loved his nativity also, and his flesh as well. Nothing can be loved apart from that through which whatever exists has its existence. Either take away nativity, and then show us your human; or else withdraw the flesh, and then present to our view the being whom God has redeemed—since it is these very conditions which constitute the person whom God has redeemed. And are you for turning these conditions into occasions of blushing to the very creature whom he has redeemed, (censuring them), too, us unworthy of him who certainly would not have redeemed them had he not loved them? Our birth he reforms from death by a second birth from heaven; our flesh he restores from every harassing malady; when leprous, he cleanses it of the stain; when blind, he rekindles its light; when palsied, he renews its strength; when possessed with devils, he exorcises it; when dead, he reanimates it—then shall we blush to own it? If, to be sure, he had chosen to be born of a mere animal, and were to preach the kingdom of heaven invested with the body of

---

[8]John 1:33.
[9]Phil 2:8.

a beast either wild or tame, your censure (I imagine) would have instantly met him with this demurrer: "This is disgraceful for God, and this is unworthy of the Son of God, and simply foolish." For no other reason than because one thus judges. It is of course foolish, if we are to judge God by our own conceptions. But, Marcion consider well this Scripture, if indeed you have not erased it: "God has chosen the foolish things of the world, to confound the wise."[10] Now what are those foolish things? Are they the conversion of people to the worship of the true God, the rejection of error, the whole training in righteousness, chastity, mercy, patience, and innocence? These things certainly are not "foolish." Inquire again, then, of what things he spoke, and when you imagine that you have discovered what they are will you find anything to be so "foolish" as believing in a God that has been born, and that of a virgin, and of a fleshly nature too, who wallowed in all the before-mentioned humiliations of nature? But some one may say, "These are not the foolish things; they must be other things which God has chosen to confound the wisdom of the world." And yet, according to the world's wisdom, it is more easy to believe that Jupiter became a bull or a swan, if we listen to Marcion, than that Christ really became a human.

5 There are, to be sure, other things also quite as foolish (as the birth of Christ), which have reference to the humiliations and sufferings of God. Or else, let them call a crucified God "wisdom." But Marcion will apply the knife to this doctrine also and even with greater reason. For which is more unworthy of God, which is more likely to raise a blush of shame, that God should be born, or that he should die? that he should bear the flesh, or the cross? be circumcised, or be crucified? be cradled, or be coffined? be laid in a manger, or in a tomb? Talk of "wisdom!" You will show more of *that* if you refuse to believe this also. But, after all, you will not be "wise" unless you become a "fool" to the world, by believing "the foolish things of God." Have you, then, cut away all sufferings from Christ, on the ground that, as a mere phantom, he was incapable of ex-

periencing them? We have said that he might possibly have undergone the unreal mockeries of an imaginary birth and infancy. But answer me at once, you that murder truth: Was not God really crucified? And, having been really crucified, did he not really die? And, having indeed really died, did he not really rise again? Falsely did Paul "determine to know anything amongst us but Jesus and him crucified;"[11] falsely has he impressed upon us that he was buried; falsely inculcated that he rose again. False, therefore, is our faith also. And all that we hope for from Christ will be a phantom. O you most infamous of men, who acquits of all guilt the murderers of God! For nothing did Christ suffer from them, if he really suffered nothing at all. Spare the whole world's one only hope, you who are destroying the indispensable dishonor of our faith. Whatsoever is unworthy of God, is of gain to me. I am safe, if I am not ashamed of my Lord. "Whosoever," says He, "shall be ashamed of me, of him will I also be ashamed."[12] Other matters for shame find I none which can prove me to be shameless in a good sense, and foolish in a happy one, by my own contempt of shame. The Son of God was crucified; I am not ashamed because people must be ashamed of it. And the Son of God died; it is by all means to be believed, because it is absurd. And he was buried and rose again; the fact is certain, because it is impossible. But how will all this be true in him, if he was not himself true—if he really had not in himself that which might be crucified, might die, might be buried, and might rise again? I mean this flesh suffused with blood, built up with bones, interwoven with nerves, entwined with veins, a flesh which knew how to be born, and how to die, human without doubt, as born of a human being. It will therefore be mortal in Christ, because Christ is man and the Son of man. Else why is Christ man and the Son of man, if he has nothing of man, and nothing from man? Unless it be either that man is anything else than flesh, or man's flesh comes from any other source

---

[10]1 Cor 1:27.
[11]1 Cor 2:2.
[12]Mark 8:38.

than man, or Mary is anything else than a human being, or Marcion's man is as Marcion's god. Otherwise Christ could not be described as being man without flesh, nor the Son of man without any human parent; just as he is not God without the Spirit of God, nor the Son of God without having God for his father. Thus the nature of the two substances displayed him as man and God—in one respect born, in the other unborn; in one respect fleshly, in the other spiritual; in one sense weak in the other exceeding strong; in one sense dying, in the other living. This property of the two states—the divine and the human—is distinctly asserted with equal truth of both natures alike, with the same belief both in respect of the Spirit and of the flesh. The powers of the Spirit, proved him to be God, his sufferings attested the flesh of man. If his powers were not without the Spirit in like manner, were not his sufferings without the flesh. If his flesh with its sufferings was fictitious, for the same reason was the Spirit false with all its powers. Why halve Christ with a lie? He was wholly the truth. Believe me, he chose rather to be born, than in any part to pretend—and that indeed to his own detriment—that he was bearing about a flesh hardened without bones, solid without muscles, bloody without blood, clothed without the tunic of skin, hungry without appetite, eating without teeth, speaking without a tongue, so that his word was a phantom to the ears through an imaginary voice. A phantom, too, it was of course after the resurrection, when, showing his hands and his feet for the disciples to examine, he said, "Behold and see that it is I myself, for a spirit does not have flesh and bones, as you see that I have;"[13] without doubt, hands, and feet, and bones are not what a spirit possesses, but only the flesh. How do you interpret this statement, Marcion, you who tell us that Jesus comes only from the most excellent God, who is both simple and good? See how He rather cheats, and deceives, and juggles the eyes of all, and the senses of all, as well as their access to and contact with him! You ought rather to have brought Christ down, not from heaven, but from some troop of mountebanks, not as God besides humans, but simply as a human, a magician; not as the High Priest of our salvation, but as the con-

jurer in a show; not as the raiser of the dead, but as the misleader of the living,—except that, if he were a magician, he must have had a nativity!. . .

17 . . . Leaving Alexander with his syllogisms, which he so persuasively applies in his discussions, as well as with the hymns of Valentinus, which, with consummate assurance, he interpolates as the production of some respectable author, let us confine our inquiry to a single point—Whether Christ received flesh from the virgin?—that we may thus arrive at a certain proof that his flesh was human, if he derived its substance from his mother's womb, although we are at once furnished with clear evidences of the human character of his flesh, from its name and description as that of a human, and from the nature of its constitution, and from the system of its sensations, and from its suffering of death. Now, it will first be necessary to show what previous reason there was for the Son of God's being born of a virgin. He who was going to consecrate a new order of birth, must himself be born after a novel fashion, concerning which Isaiah foretold how that the Lord himself would give the sign. What, then, is the sign? "Behold a virgin shall conceive and bear a son."[14] Accordingly, a virgin did conceive and bear "Emmanuel, God with us."[15] This is the new nativity; a human is born in God. And in this human God was born, taking the flesh of an ancient race, without the help, however, of the ancient seed, in order that he might reform it with a new seed, that is, in a spiritual manner, and cleanse it by the removal of all its ancient stains. But the whole of this new birth was prefigured, as was the case in all other instances, in ancient type, the Lord being born as a human by a dispensation in which a virgin was the medium. The earth was still in a virgin state, reduced as yet by no human labor, with no seed as yet cast into its furrows, when, as we are told, God made man out of it into a living soul.[16] As, then, the first Adam is thus introduced

---

[13]Luke 24:39.
[14]Isa 7:14
[15]Matt 1:23.
[16]Gen 2:7.

to us, it is a just inference that the second Adam likewise, as the apostle has told us, was formed by God into a quickening spirit out of the ground—in other words, out of a flesh which was unstained as yet by any human generation. But that I may lose no opportunity of supporting my argument from the name of Adam, why is Christ called Adam by the apostle, unless it be that, as a human, he was of that earthly origin? And even reason here maintains the same conclusion, because it was by just the contrary operation that God recovered his own image and likeness, of which he had been robbed by the devil. For it was while Eve was yet a virgin, that the ensnaring word had crept into her ear which was to build the edifice of death. Into a virgin's soul, in like manner, must be introduced that Word of God which was to raise the fabric of life; so that what had been reduced to ruin by this sex, might by the selfsame sex be recovered to salvation. As Eve had believed the serpent,[17] so Mary believed the angel. The delinquency which the one occasioned by believing, the other by believing effaced. But (it will be said) Eve did not at the devil's word conceive in her womb. Well, she at all events conceived; for the devil's word afterwards became as seed to her that she should conceive as an outcast, and bring forth in sorrow. Indeed she gave birth to a fratricidal devil; while Mary, on the contrary, bore one who was one day to secure salvation to Israel, his own brother after the flesh, and the murderer of himself. God therefore sent down into the virgin's womb his Word, as the good brother, who should blot out the memory of the evil brother. Hence it was necessary that Christ should come forth for the salvation of humans, in that condition of flesh into which humanity had entered ever since his condemnation.

---

[17]Gen 3:1–7.

34. Tertullian: Against Praxeas

Among second- and third-century Christians who accepted the basic proto-orthodox understanding of Christ as both human and divine, yet one being instead of two, there was a range of opinion about how to work out all the details. One popular view near the end of the second century was that Jesus was God the Father himself, become human. Only later did this view come to be widely acknowledged as a heresy; its opponents derisively labeled it "patripassianism" ("father suffering"), for in it God the Father himself was said to have been crucified (see Chapter 14; the view is sometimes also called "Sabellianism" after one of its later proponents). Tertullian was among the first to attack this view; he did so by spurning one of its leading proponents, a prominent Roman Christian named Praxeas.

The refutation is significant for several reasons, seen even in the short excerpt that follows: it shows how the debates over the person of Christ were becoming increasingly

---

Tertullian: "Against Praxeas," from *The Ante-Nicene Fathers*; vol. 3, *Latin Christianity: Its Founder, Tertullian*, ed. A. Cleveland Coxe. Reprint; 2d ed. Grand Rapids, Mich.: Eerdmans, 1989.

nuanced in the late second and early third centuries; it suggests how and why Christians began to think of the godhead in terms of a trinity of beings, different in person but equal in substance (see Chapter 14); and it reveals Tertullian's own commitment to the Christian group known as the Montanists (after their leader, Montanus), who emphasized the ongoing revelatory work of the Holy Spirit and who were themselves later viewed as sectarian by the bulk of proto-orthodox Christians.

For a further selection from this work, see Chapter 14.

1 In various ways has the devil rivalled and resisted the truth. Sometimes his aim has been to destroy the truth by defending it. He maintains that there is one only Lord, the Almighty Creator of the world, in order that out of this doctrine of the unity he may fabricate a heresy. He says that the Father himself came down into the virgin, was himself born of her, himself suffered, indeed was himself Jesus Christ. Here the old serpent has fallen out with himself, since, when he tempted Christ after John's baptism, he approached him as "the Son of God;" surely intimating that God had a Son, even on the testimony of the very Scriptures, out of which he was at the moment forging his temptation: "If you are the Son of God, command that these stones be made bread."[1] Again: "If you are the Son of God, cast yourself down from here; for it is written, He shall give his angels charge concerning you"—referring no doubt, to the Father—"and in their hands they shall bear up, that you do not strike your foot against a stone."[2] Or perhaps, after all, he was only reproaching the Gospels with a lie, saying in fact: "Away with Matthew; away with Luke! Why heed their words? In spite of them, I declare that it was God himself that I approached; it was the Almighty himself that I tempted face to face; and it was for no other purpose than to attempt him that I approached him. If, on the contrary, it had been only the Son of God, most likely I should never have condescended to deal with him." However, he is himself a liar from the beginning, and whatever person he instigates in his own way; as, for instance, Praxeas. For he was the first to import into Rome from Asia this kind of heretical pravity, a man in other respects of restless dispo-

sition, and above all inflated with the pride of confessorship simply and solely because he had to bear for a short time the annoyance of a prison; on which occasion, even "if he had given his body to be burned, it would have profited him nothing,"[3] not having the love of God, whose very gifts he has resisted and destroyed. For after the Bishop of Rome had acknowledged the prophetic gifts of Montanus, Prisca, and Maximilla, and, in consequence of the acknowledgment, had bestowed his peace on the churches of Asia and Phrygia, he, by importunately urging false accusations against the prophets themselves and their churches, and insisting on the authority of the bishop's predecessors in the see, compelled him to recall the pacific letter which he had issued, as well as to desist from his purpose of acknowledging the said gifts. By this Praxeas did a twofold service for the devil at Rome: he drove away prophecy, and he brought in heresy; he put to flight the Paraclete, and he crucified the Father. Praxeas' tares had been moreover sown, and had produced their fruit here also, while many were asleep in their simplicity of doctrine; but these tares actually seemed to have been plucked up, having been discovered and exposed by him whose agency God was pleased to employ. Indeed, Praxeas had deliberately resumed his old (true) faith, teaching it after his renunciation of error; and there is his own handwriting in evidence remaining among the carnally-minded, in whose society the transaction then took place; afterwards nothing was heard of him. We indeed,

---

[1]Matt 4:3; Luke 4:3.
[2]Matt 4:6; Luke 4:9–11.
[3]1 Cor 13:3.

on our part, subsequently withdrew from the carnally-minded on our acknowledgment and maintenance of the Paraclete. But the tares of Praxeas had then everywhere shaken out their seed, which having lain hid for some while, with its vitality concealed under a mask, has now broken out with fresh life. But again shall it be rooted up, if the Lord will, even now; but if not now, in the day when all bundles of tares shall be gathered together, and along with every other stumbling-block shall be burnt up with unquenchable fire.[4]

2 In the course of time, then, the Father forsooth was born, and the Father suffered—God himself, the Lord Almighty, whom in their preaching they declare to be Jesus Christ. We, however, as we indeed always have done (and more especially since we have been better instructed by the Paraclete, who leads people indeed into all truth), believe that there is one only God, but under the following dispensation, or economy, as it is called, that this one only God has also a Son, his word, who proceeded from himself, by whom all things were made, and without whom nothing was made. Him we believe to have been sent by the Father into the virgin, and to have been born of her—being both man and God, the Son of Man and the Son of God, and to have been called by the name of Jesus Christ; we believe him to have suffered, died, and been buried, according to the Scriptures, and, after he had been raised again by the Father and taken back to heaven, to be sitting at the right hand of the Father, and that he will come to judge the living and the dead; who sent also from heaven from the Father, according to his own promise, the Holy Spirit, the Paraclete, the sanctifier of the faith of those who believe in the Father, and in the Son, and in the Holy Spirit. That this rule of faith has come

down to us from the beginning of the gospel, even before any of the older heretics, much more before Praxeas, a pretender of yesterday, will be apparent both from the lateness of date which marks all heresies, and also from the absolutely novel character of our new-fangled Praxeas. In this principle also we must henceforth find a presumption of equal force against all heresies whatsoever—that whatever is first is true, whereas that is spurious which is later in date. But keeping this prescriptive rule inviolate, still some opportunity must be given for reviewing (the statements of heretics), with a view to the instruction and protection of divers persons; were it only that it may not seem that each perversion of the truth is condemned without examination, and simply prejudged; especially in the case of this heresy, which supposes itself to possess the pure truth, in thinking that one cannot believe in One Only God in any other way than by saying that the Father, the Son, and the Holy Spirit are the very selfsame person. As if in this way also one were not all, in that all are of one, by unit (that is) of substance; while the mystery of the dispensation is still guarded, which distributes the Unity into a Trinity, placing in their order the three Persons—the Father, the Son, and the Holy Spirit; three, however, not in condition, but in degree; not in substance, but in form; not in power, but in aspect; yet of one substance, and of one condition, and of one power, inasmuch as he is one God, from whom these degrees and forms and aspects are reckoned, under the name of the Father, and of the Son, and of the Holy Spirit. How they are susceptible of number without division, will be shown as our treatise proceeds.

---

[4]Matt 13:30.

GNOSTIC HERESIOLOGISTS: THE TEXTS

(See also Ptolemy's Letter to Flora and the Treatise on the Resurrection in Chapter 6)

It is a real loss not to have other sides of the debates over Christian heresy and orthodoxy more fully preserved. We are fortunate, though, to have a couple of Nag Hammadi tractates that indicate how gnostic heresiologists attacked their proto-orthodox opponents. The basic line of attack, not surprisingly, is that their opponents propounded absurd and ridiculous views about Christ based on a wooden reading of sacred texts that, as divinely inspired, cannot simply be understood as bare-bones descriptions of divine realities. The inspired writings of the Old Testament and the events of Jesus' life are full of nuance and deeper meanings, far below the surface, and to understand them completely (rather than superficially, like the proto-orthodox opponents), one needs to be guided by divine revelation and to recognize in them the truths about the nature of God and his relation to this world through Christ. Christians without gnosis have been misled by simple-minded bishops who wrangle over words whose depths they cannot perceive and who discuss events (such as Jesus' crucifixion) whose meaning they cannot fathom.

35. The Coptic Apocalypse of Peter

There are three surviving apocalypses allegedly written by Simon Peter, the disciple of Jesus (for another one, see Chapter 8); the one given here was discovered at Nag Hammadi (see Chapter 6). The book contains a series of visions given by Jesus to Peter (hence the title "apocalypse" or "revelation"), which Peter then records in the first person. In these visions, Christ issues dire warnings against the teaching of heretics who propagate falsehoods. Strikingly, the heretics here are the bishops and deacons of the proto-orthodox churches, and their false teaching is that Jesus was himself the Christ who suffered a literal death on the cross. The author deems this staunchly orthodox view laughable; he labels its orthodox proponents blind.

For this author, the true significance of Jesus' death goes much deeper. Even though Jesus' flesh was killed, Christ himself was far removed from suffering; those who beheld the cross with full knowledge (gnosis) saw not the suffering Jesus but the living Christ, who was himself laughing at the entire proceeding. Jesus was merely his outward appearance, just as simple-minded Christians are nothing but the outward appearance of the living ones who have been fully enlightened by the spiritual truth of the immortal Christ.

Most scholars have dated this gnostic treatise to the third century.

The "Coptic Apocalypse of Peter," translated by James Brashler, from *Nag Hammadi Codex VII* (*NHS* XXX), ed. Birger Pearson. Leiden: E. J. Brill, 1996. Used with permission.

And when I said these things, the Savior said, "I have told you that these (people) are blind and deaf. Now then, listen to the things that are being told to you in a mystery, and guard them. Do not tell them to the children of this age. For you will be despised in these ages, since they are ignorant of you. But you will be praised in (the age of) knowledge. For many will accept our teaching in the beginning. But they will turn away again in accordance with the will of the father of their error, because they have done what he wanted. And he will make manifest in his judgment who the servants of the word are. But those who became **74** mingled with these will become their prisoners, since they are without perception. And the guileless, good, pure one is pushed to the executioner, even into the kingdom of those who praise a restored Christ. And they praise the men of the propagation of falsehood, who will succeed you. And they will hold fast to the name of a dead man, while thinking that they will become pure. But they will become greatly defiled. And they will fall into an explicit error and into the hand of an evil, cunning man with a multifarious doctrine. And they will be ruled heretically. For some of them will blaspheme the truth and proclaim evil teaching. And they will say evil things to each other.

"And some, because they stand by virtue of the archons, will be given a name of a man and a naked woman who is multifarious and very sensual. And **75** those who say these things will ask about dreams. And if they say that a dream came from a demon worthy of their error, then they will be given destruction instead of immortality. 'For evil cannot produce good fruit.' For each source produces what is like itself. For not every soul comes from the truth, nor from immortality. For every soul of these ages has death assigned to it, in our view. Consequently it is always a slave. It is created for its desires and their eternal destruction, for which they exist and in which they exist. They (the souls) love the material creatures which came forth with them. But the immortal souls are not like these, O Peter. But indeed, as long as the hour has not yet come, she (the immortal soul) will indeed resemble a mortal one. But she will

not reveal her nature, although she alone is the **76** immortal one and thinks about immortality. She has faith, and desires to renounce these (material) things. 'For people neither gather figs from thorns'—or from thorn trees if they are wise— 'nor grapes from brambles.' For on the one hand, a particular thing (masc.) always remains in that (condition) in which it exists. If it exists in a particular condition that is not good, that (condition) becomes its (fem.) destruction and death. On the other hand, this one (fem. = the immortal soul) abides in the Eternal One, in the one of life and immortality of life which are alike to Him.

"Therefore everything that does not abide will dissolve into that which does not exist. For deaf and blind ones join only with their own kind. But some will depart from evil words and deceptive mysteries. Others do not understand mysteries, although they speak of these things which they do not understand. Nevertheless they will boast that the mystery of the truth is theirs alone. And in haughtiness **77** they will begin {in haughtiness} to envy the immortal soul that has become dedicated (to God). For every authority, principality, and power of the ages always wanted to remain with these (immortal souls) from the foundation of the world, in order that those who do not abide, since they have been ignorant and have not been saved, may be glorified by those who do abide. And they have not been brought to the way by them, although they have always desired that they would become the imperishable ones. For if the immortal soul receives power through an intellectual spirit, then immediately she is joined by one of those who have been misled. And others, who are numerous and who oppose the truth, who are the messengers of error, will concoct their error and their law against these pure thoughts of mine. Since they see from one (perspective), they think that good and evil are from one (source).

78 "They do business in my word. And they will set forth a harsh fate in which the race of the immortal souls will run in vain until my return. For they will remain among them. And I have forgiveness of their transgressions into which they fell because of the adversaries. I accepted their ransom from the slavery in which they existed (and) I gave them freedom. For they will create an imitation remnant in the name of a dead man, who is Hermas, the first-born of unrighteousness, in order that the real light might not be believed by the little ones. But those of this sort (the adversaries) are the workers who will be cast into the outer darkness, away from the children of light. For they will not enter, but neither do they permit those (to enter) who are going up to their approval and for their release. And still others of them who have sensual (natures) think that they will perfect **79** the wisdom of the brotherhood that really exists, the spiritual friendship with those companions rooted in fellowship, those through whom the wedding of incorruptibility will be revealed.

"The kindred race of the sisterhood will appear as an imitation. These are the ones who oppress their brothers, saying to them, 'Through this our God has pity, since salvation (allegedly) comes to us through this.' They do not know the punishment of those who are delighted by what has been done to the little ones whom they sought out and imprisoned. And there will be others of those who are outside our number who name themselves 'bishop' and also 'deacons,' as if they have received their authority from God. They submit to the judgment of the leaders. Those people are dry canals."

But I said, "I am afraid because of what you have told me—that **80** indeed little ones are, in our view, counterfeit. Indeed, there are multitudes that will mislead other multitudes of living ones, and they will be destroyed among them. And when they speak your name, they will be believed."

The Savior said, "For a period of time determined for them in proportion to their error, they will rule over the little ones. But after the completion of the error, the ageless one of immortal understanding will be renewed, and they (the little ones) will rule over those who are their rulers. The root of their error he will pull out, and he will put it to shame, and it will be exposed in all the impudence that it has assumed to itself. And such persons shall remain unchanged, O Peter. Come, therefore! Let us proceed to the completion of the will of the undefiled Father. For behold, those who will bring judgment upon themselves are

coming. And they will put themselves to shame. But me they cannot touch. And you, O Peter, will stand in their midst. Do not be afraid because of your cowardice. **81** Their minds will be closed. For the invisible one has opposed them."

When he had said those things, I saw him apparently being seized by them. And I said, "What am I seeing, O Lord? Is it you yourself whom they take? And are you holding on to me? Who is this one above the cross, who is glad and laughing? And is it another person whose feet and hands they are hammering?"

The Savior said to me, "He whom you see above the cross, glad and laughing, is the living Jesus. But he into whose hands and feet they are driving the nails is his physical part, which is the substitute. They are putting to shame that which is in his likeness. But look at him and me."

But I, when I had looked, said, "Lord, no one is looking at you. Let us flee this place." But he said to me, "I have told you, 'Leave the blind alone!' And notice how they do not know what they are saying. **82** For the son of their glory, instead of my servant, they have put to shame."

And I saw someone about to approach us who looked like him, even him who was laughing above the cross. and he was <filled> with a pure spirit, and he (was) the Savior. And there was a great ineffable light around them and the multitude of ineffable and invisible angels blessing them. And it was I who saw him when this one who glorifies was revealed. And he said to me, "Be strong! For you are the one to whom these mysteries have been given, to know through revelation that he whom they crucified is the first-born, and the home of demons, and the clay vessel in which they dwell, belonging to Elohim, and belonging to the cross that is under the law. But he who stands near him is the living Savior, the primal part in him whom they seized. And he has been released. He stands joyfully looking at those who persecuted him. **83** They are divided among themselves. Therefore he laughs at their lack of perception, and he knows that they are born blind. Indeed, therefore, the suffering one must remain, since the body is the substitute. But that which was released was my incorporeal body. But I am the intellectual spirit filled with radiant light. He whom you saw coming to me was our intellectual pleroma, which unites the perfect light with my pure spirit. These things, therefore, which you saw, you shall present to those of another race, who are not of this age. For there will be no grace in any one who is not immortal, but (grace will) only (be in) those who were chosen from an immortal essence that has shown that it is able to accept him who gives his abundance.

"Therefore I said, 'To every one who has, it will be given, and that one will have plenty.[1] But the one who does not have'—that is, the one of this place, being completely dead and changed by the planting of creation and begetting, **84** who, if one of the immortal essence appears, think<s> that he (i.e. the one of immortal essence) is being seized—'it will be taken from him.' And it will be added to the one who is. You, therefore, be courageous and do not fear anything. For I will be with you so that none of your enemies will prevail over you. Peace be to you! Be strong!"

When he (the Savior) had said these things, he (Peter) came to his senses.
Apocalypse of Peter

---

[1]Matt 25:29.

---

36. The Second Treatise of the Great Seth

In the "Second Treatise of the Great Seth," Christ himself provides a firsthand description of how he descended into the man Jesus' body, occupied it for the length of his ministry, and then died only in appearance. Like other gnostic teachers, such as Basilides, the unknown author of this book thinks that Simon of Cyrene, who bore Jesus' cross, was mistakenly crucified in his place, while Jesus looked on and laughed. Those who ascribe to a literal understanding of Christ's death are said to proclaim "a doctrine of a dead man"; in so doing they subject themselves to "fear and slavery"; they are "small and ignorant."

As in the Coptic Apocalypse of Peter, these false believers are the proto-orthodox Christians, who foolishly believe that the Jewish Scriptures are true (from Adam to the Patriarchs, Moses, and the prophets) and that the Creator of the world is almighty. In fact, the ancient Jews and their God himself are all a "laughingstock." Those who do not see the deeper truths about God and Christ from the Scriptures—that is, those without gnosis—are "like dumb animals." They *think* that "they are advancing the name of Christ," especially in persecuting those who have been liberated (i.e., the Gnostics), but in fact they are completely ignorant.

The name Seth does not occur anywhere in the tractate except in the title; in the Old

---

The "Second Treatise of the Great Seth," translated by Greg Riley, from *Nag Hammadi Codex VII* (NHS XXX), ed. Birger Pearson. Leiden: E. J. Brill, 1996. Used with permission.

Testament, he is said to be the third son of Adam and Eve. Some gnostic groups maintained that he was the first to whom gnosis came, the progenitor of the Gnostics themselves. This book probably dates from the third century.

I visited a bodily dwelling. I cast out the one who was in it previously, and I went in. And the whole multitude of the archons was disturbed. And all the physical matter of the archons along with the powers born of the earth began to tremble when it saw the likeness of the image, since it was mixed. And I was the one who was in it, not resembling him who was in it previously. For he was a **52** worldly man, but I, I am from above the heavens. I did not refuse them, on the one hand, and I became Christ. But on the other, I did not reveal myself to them in the love which was coming forth from me. I was revealing that I am a stranger to the regions below.

There was a great disturbance in the whole earthly region, with confusion and flight, and (in) the plan of the archons. And some were persuaded, when they saw the acts of power which were being accomplished by me. And they flee, namely all these who are descended by race from the one who fled from the throne to the Sophia of Hope—since she had previously given indication concerning us and all those who were with me—these of the race of Adonaios. Yet others fled as though (sent) from the World Ruler and those with him, and brought every punishment upon me. And there was a flight of their mind about what counsel they would take concerning me, thinking that the(ir) Greatness is (the) All, and speaking lying witness against the Man also and the whole greatness **53** of the assembly. It was not possible for them to know who the Father of truth is, the Man of the greatness. And these took the name because of <pollution> and ignorance—which (is) a burning and a vessel which they created for destruction of Adam, which they had made in order to cover up those who are equally theirs.

But they, the archons belonging to the place of Yaldabaoth, lay bare the circuit of the angels.

This is what humanity was going around seeking because they did not know the Man of truth. For Adam appeared to them, the one whom they had fashioned. And a disturbance of fear occurred throughout their entire dwelling, lest perhaps the surrounding angels stand against them. For on account of those who were offering (him) praise I died, though not in reality, because their archangel was vain. And then a voice of the World Ruler came to the angels "I am God and there is no other beside me."[1] But I laughed with joy when I considered his conceit. And he kept saying all the more, "Who **54** is Man?"[2] And the entire army of his angels who had seen Adam and his dwelling were laughing at his smallness.

And in this way their thought came to be removed away from the Greatness of the heavens, who is the Man of truth, whose name they saw because he is in the smallness of a dwelling place. Since they are foolish in the senselessness of their vain thought, namely their laughter, it became defilement for them. The whole greatness of the Fatherhood of the Spirit was resting in its places, and I was with him, since I have a thought of a single emanation from the eternal ones and the unknowable ones, undefiled and immeasurable. I placed the small Ennoia in the world, having disturbed them and frightened the whole multitude of the angels and their ruler. And I examined them all with burning and fire on account of my thought. And each of their activities they did on account of me. And trouble and fighting arose around the Seraphim and Cherubim, since their glory will perish, **55** and the disturbance which is around Adonaios this side and that, and (around) their dwelling—(reaching) to the World Ruler and the

---

[1]Isa 45:5–6.
[2]Ps 8:4.

one who said "Let us seize him." Others again (said), "The counsel shall not come to be." For Adonaios knows me because of Hope.

And I was in the mouths of lions. And (as for) the counsel which they planned about me against destruction of their deception and their foolishness, I did not give in to them as they had devised. And I was not afflicted at all. Those there punished me, yet I did not die in solid reality but in what appears, in order that I not be put to shame by them, because these are part of me. I cut off the shame from me and I did not become faint-hearted at what happened to me at their hands. I was about to become a slave to fear, but I was struck (merely) according to their sight and thought, in order that no word might ever be found to speak about them. For my death which they think happened, (happened) to them in their error and blindness. They nailed their man up to their death. For their minds did not see **56** me, for they were deaf and blind. But in doing these things, they render judgment against themselves.

As for me, on the one hand they saw me; they punished me. Another, their father, was the one who drank the gall and the vinegar; it was not I. They were hitting me with the reed; another was the one who lifted up the cross on his shoulder, who was Simon. Another was the one on whom they put the crown of thorns. But I was rejoicing in the height over all the riches of the archons and the offspring of their error and their conceit, and I was laughing at their ignorance. And all their powers I brought into subjection. For when I came down no one saw me. For I kept changing my forms above, transforming from appearance to appearance. And on account of this, when I was at their gates I kept taking their likeness. For I passed them by quietly, and I was viewing the places, and I did not fear nor was I ashamed, for I was undefiled. And I was speaking with them, mixing among them through those who are mine, and I tread on those who **57** are harsh to them jealously, and the fire I extinguished.

And all these things I kept doing on account of my will in order that this which I willed in the will of the Father above I might complete. And the Son of the Greatness, who was hidden in the region below, we brought to the height, where I am with all these aeons, which no one has seen nor understood, where the wedding of the wedding robe is, the new (wedding) and not the old, nor does it perish. For the new bridal chamber is of the heavens and perfect.

I have revealed (that) there are three paths, (which are) an undefiled mystery in a spirit of this aeon, which does not perish, nor is it partial, nor is to be spoken of; rather, it is undivided, universal, and permanent. For the soul, which is from the height, will not speak about the error which is here, nor transport itself from these aeons, since it will be transported when it becomes a free person and experience nobility in the world, standing **58** before the Father without trouble and fear, always mixed with the mind of ideal power. They will see me from every side without hatred. For while they see me, they are being seen, being mixed with them. As for me, since they did not put me to shame, they were not shamed. As for me, since they were not afraid before me, they will pass by every gate without fear, and they will be perfected in the third glory. I was the one whose cross the world did not accept, (my) apparent exaltation, my third baptism in an apparent image, when they had fled from the fire of the seven authorities. And the sun of the powers of the archons set, darkness overtook them, and the world became poor.

After they bound him with many restraints, they nailed him to the cross, and they fastened him with four nails of bronze. The veil of his temple he tore with his hands. There was a trembling that overcame the chaos of the earth, for the souls which were in the sleep below were released, and they were resurrected. They walked about boldly, having laid **59** aside jealousy of ignorance and un-learnedness beside the dead tombs, having put on the new man, having come to know that blessed and perfect one of the eternal and incomprehensible Father and of the boundless light, which I am. When I came to my own and joined them with myself, there was no need for many words, for our thought was with their thought; on this account they understood what I was saying, for we took counsel concerning the destruction of the archons. And on this account I did the will of the Father, which I am.

When we went forth from our home, when we came down to this world and came into being in the world in bodies, we were hated and persecuted, not only (by) those who are ignorant, but by those also who think that they are advancing the name of Christ, since they are vain in ignorance. They do not know who they are, like unreasoning beasts. Those who were set free by me they persecute, since they hate them— those who, if they shut their mouth, would weep with groaning without profit because **60** they did not know me completely. Instead, they served two masters, even a multitude. But you (pl.) will be victorious in everything, in war and battles and schism of jealousy and anger. But in the uprightness of our love we are without deceit, pure, good, having the mind of the Father in an ineffable mystery. For it (the world) was a laughingstock. It is I who bear witness that it was a laughingstock— since the archons do not know that it is an ineffable union of undefiled truth, like that which exists among the children of the light, of which they made an imitation, proclaiming the doctrine of a dead man and falsehoods to resemble the freedom and purity of the perfect assembly, uniting themselves in their doctrine to fear and slavery and worldly concerns and discarded worship, being few (and) uninstructed.

They do not accept for themselves the nobility of the truth, hating the one for whom they exist and loving the one for whom they do not exist. For they did not know the **61** Gnosis of the Greatness, that it is from above and (from) the fountain of truth. And it is not from slavery and jealousy and fear and love of worldly matter. For that which is not theirs and that which is theirs they use without fear and with freedom. They do not covet because they have authority and a law from themselves over the things which they would desire. But those who do not have are poor, namely, those who do not possess something and yet they desire it. And they lead astray those who through them are like those who have the truth of their freedom, so as to constrain us under a yoke and compulsion of concern and fear. This one is

in slavery. And this one who is brought by compulsion of violence and threat has been guarded by God. But the noble-born one of the Fatherhood is not guarded, since he guards that which is his own by himself, without word or compulsion. He is united with his will, this one who is of the thought alone of the Fatherhood, that (the Fatherhood) may become perfect and unutterable through **62** the living water, if it exists in wisdom among yourselves not only in word of hearing but in deed and fulfilled word.

For the perfect are worthy to be established in this way. And they are joined with me in order that they may not share in any enmity. In a wholesome friendship I accomplish everything in the Good One, for this is the joining of truth, that they should have no adversary. But everyone who causes division—and he will learn none of their wisdom because he causes division and is not a friend—he is an enemy to them all. But the one who lives in agreement and friendship of brotherly love by nature and not by decree, wholly and not in part, this one is truly the will of the Father. This one is the universal and the perfect love.

For Adam was a laughingstock, and he was created from the image of a pattern of a man by the Hebdomad, as though he had become stronger than I and my brethren. We are innocent with respect to him, since we did not sin. And Abraham was a laughing stock, and Isaac and Jacob, since they were given a name by the Hebdomad, namely "the fathers from the image," as **63** though he had become stronger than I and my brethren. We are innocent with respect to him, since we did not sin. David was a laughingstock since his son was named the Son of Man, having been activated by the Hebdomad, as though he had become stronger than I and the friends of my race. But we are innocent with respect to him; we did not sin. Solomon was a laughingstock, since he thought that he was Christ, having become arrogant through the Hebdomad, as though he had become stronger than I and my brethren. But we are innocent with respect to him; I did not sin. The 12 prophets were laughingstocks, since they have come forth as imitations of the true prophets. They came into being from the image through the Hebdomad, as though it had become stronger than I and my brethren. But we are innocent with respect to it, since we did not sin. Moses was a laughingstock, a "faithful servant," being named "the friend"; they bore witness concerning him in iniquity, since he never knew me. Neither he nor those before him, from Adam to Moses and John the Baptist, none of them knew me nor **64** my brethren. For a doctrine of angels is what arose through them, to keep dietary rules and bitter slavery. They never knew truth nor will they know it, for there is a great deception upon their soul, and they have no ability to find a mind of freedom ever, in order to know him, until they come to know the Son of Man.

But concerning my Father, I am the one whom the world did not know, and on this account, it rose up against me and my brethren. But we are innocent with respect to it; we did not sin. For the Archon was a laughingstock because he said, "I am God, and there is none greater than I. I alone am the Father, the Lord, and there is no other beside me. I am a jealous God, bringing the sins of the fathers upon the children for three and four generations,"³ as though he had become stronger than I and my brethren. But we are innocent with

respect to him; for we did not sin. Though we mastered his doctrine in this way, he lives in conceit, and he does not agree with our Father. And thus through our friendship we prevailed over his doctrine, since he is arrogant in conceit and does not agree with our Father. For he was a laughingstock with (his) **65** judgment and false prophecy.

O those who do not see! You do not see your blindness that this is who was not known. Neither did they ever know him, nor did they understand him. Concerning him they would not listen to a valid report. On this account they trained in a judgment of error, and they raised their defiled, murderous hands against him as if they were striking the air. And the senseless and the blind are senseless always, being slaves always of law and worldly fear. I am Christ, the Son of Man, the one from you (pl.) who is in you. I am despised on your account, in order that you ourselves may forget what is changeable. And do not become female, lest you give birth to their evils and kindred things: to jealousy and schism, anger and wrath, fear and a divided heart and vain coveting which is not fulfilled. But I am an ineffable mystery to you.

---

³Isa 45:5–6; Exod 20:5.

Chapter 8

"Apostolic" Writings Outside the Canon

New Testament Apocrypha/ Pseudepigrapha

Early Christians chose to base their religious beliefs and practices on the writings of Jesus' apostles. It comes as no surprise, then, to find a large number of Christian writings forged in their names. We know of Christian forgeries even from within the New Testament itself: 2 Thess 2:2 mentions a letter forged in Paul's name. Ironically enough, many scholars have suspected that 2 Thessalonians *itself* is falsely attributed to Paul—along with as many as five of the other New Testament letters that bear his name and both of the letters attributed to Peter. Whether or not this view is right, there can be no doubt that the production of literary texts in the names of the apostles became something of a cottage industry in the second and third centuries. Numerous examples of such pseudonymous works still survive; traditionally they have been called the "New Testament Apocrypha."

The term "apocrypha" literally means "secret" and may be taken to refer to the secretive nature of the information conveyed in some of these works. But most of them are not at all esoteric; it may be better, then, simply to speak of them as New Testament Pseudepigrapha (i.e., writings falsely ascribed to a famous author). It has been customary to organize these books according to the genres preserved in the New Testament itself, that is, as Gospels (roughly understood to be accounts of the words, deeds, and/or experiences of Jesus), Acts (the activities of his apostles), Epistles (letters written in their names), and Apocalypses (revelations of the heavenly truths that can explain mundane realities, including the truths about the future of the world, the end of time, or the nature of the afterlife).

The Christian authors who forged these writings were by no means anomalous in their wider Greco-Roman culture. Forgery was a widely practiced, though not widely appreciated, practice. We know of numerous other forgeries of all kinds that survive from this period, both pagan and Jewish; ancient authors sometimes comment on the practice, usually disparagingly. Notwithstanding these strictures, there were always ample motivations for authors to forge documents. In some instances, there was a pure profit motive, as when major libraries were willing to pay hard cash for original works by a classical author (leading some enterprising authors to create a few); at other times, quite the opposite motivation was at work, as in some of the philosophical schools where students signed their master's name to their own treatises as an expression of humility, on the grounds that all their knowledge derived from the teachings of their revered leader. Probably the most common reason for forging a document, however, was to receive a hearing for one's views. Anyone writing a philosophical treatise in his or her own name might not find much of a readership; that could quickly change if the work were signed by "Plato."

Since none of the Christian authors who engaged in the practice left us any discussion of the matter, it is exceedingly difficult to know precisely *what* motivated them individually. Many of the surviving works appear to have been forged to allow the cherished views of the author to be more widely heard. In other instances, though, it is difficult to believe that this was the motivating factor: many of these works appear to be told simply for the pleasure of the reading, that is, as entertainment for their hearers.

The following collection of some of the most interesting of these texts has been arranged according to genre; each group is provided with a separate introduction.

For Further Reading

Bovon, Francois. *New Testament Traditions and Apocryphal Narratives.* Allison Park, Pa.: Pickwick, 1995.

Burris, Virginia. *Chastity as Autonomy: Women in the Stories of the Apocryphal Acts.* Lewiston, NY: Mellen, 1987.

Davies, Stevan. *The Revolt of the Windows: The Social World of the Apocryphal Acts.* Carbondale: Southern Illinois University, 1980.

Elliott, J. K., ed. *The Apocryphal New Testament.* Oxford: Clarendon, 1993.

Hennecke, Edgar. *The New Testament Apocrypha,* 2 vols., ed. W. Schneemelcher, tr. R. McL. Wilson, 3rd ed. Louisville: Westminster/John Knox, 1991.

Koester, Helmut. *Ancient Christian Gospels: Their History and Development.* London/Philadelphia: SCM Press Ltd/Trinity Press International, 1990.

MacDonald, Dennis R. *The Legend and the Apostle: The Battle for Paul in Story and Canon.* Philadelphia: Westminster, 1983.

APOCRYPHAL GOSPELS: THE TEXTS

(See also, e.g., the Gospel of the Ebionites, Secret Book of John and the Gospel of Philip in Chapter 6)

Of the thirty or so early Christian writings that can be classified as "Gospels," very few are structured like those of the New Testament, with portrayals of Jesus' public ministry of teaching and healing leading up to his passion and resurrection. Those that may have originally shared this form of narrative—for example, possibly, the Gospel of Peter (see reading 38) and the Gospel according to the Ebionites (see Chapter 6)—have survived not in their entirety but only in fragments. As a rule, most of the noncanonical Gospels instead cover materials not found in the canonical four: the "lost" years of Jesus life (especially his infancy and childhood, and sometimes the events leading up to his miraculous conception), the mysterious revelations that he conveyed to his disciples after his resurrection, and other collections of previously unknown and secret teachings.

Most of these other Gospels appear to embody particular doctrinal emphases or religious perspectives that the author wanted to convey to his readers under divine authorization; others of them (especially the stories of Jesus' childhood) may simply reflect pious and creative imaginations at work to entertain their readers and hearers.

37. The Gospel of Thomas

None of the fifty-two tractates discovered in the Nag Hammadi Library has attracted more attention than the Gospel of Thomas. For this book of Jesus' sayings claims to have been written by Didymus Judas Thomas, who, according to Christian legend, was Jesus' own twin brother (see the Acts of Thomas in Chapter 2).

The book records 114 "secret teachings" of Jesus. Unlike the Gospels of the New Testament, it includes no other material: no miracles, no passion narrative, no stories of any kind. Jesus' death and resurrection thus appear to be of no concern to this author (since he never discusses them); what matters instead are the mysterious teachings that

Jesus delivered. Indeed, the Gospel begins by stating that anyone who learns the interpretation of these words will have eternal life.

Many of the sayings closely approximate Jesus' words from the New Testament—for example, the warning against the "blind leading the blind" and the parables of the sower and of the mustard seed. Others, however, are quite different and appear to presuppose a gnostic point of view (see Chapter 6), in which people are understood to be spirits who have fallen from the divine realm and become entrapped in matter (i.e., in the prisons of their material bodies). Salvation, according to this perspective, comes to those who learn the truth of their plight and so are enabled to escape this impoverished material existence by acquiring the knowledge necessary for salvation. Jesus is the one who conveys this knowledge.

Some scholars maintain that the Gospel of Thomas is at least as old as The New Testament Gospels; but others point out that the theology of the more gnostic sayings cannot be confidently dated prior to the beginning of the second century. Thus, while some of these sayings may be quite old—may, in fact, go back to Jesus himself—the document as a whole was probably written somewhat after the New Testament Gospels (though perhaps independently of them), early in the second century.

These are the secret words which the living Jesus spoke, and Didymus Judas Thomas wrote them down.

1 And he said, "The one who finds the meaning of these words will not taste death."

2 Jesus said, "Let him who seeks not cease seeking until he finds, and when he finds, he shall be troubled, and when he is troubled, he will marvel, and he will rule over the All."

3 Jesus said, "If the ones who lead you say, 'There is the kingdom, in heaven,' then the birds of heaven shall go before you. If they say to you, 'It is in the sea,' then the fish shall go before you. Rather, the kingdom is within you and outside you. If you know yourselves, then you will be known, and you will know that you are sons of the living Father. But if you do not know yourselves, then you are in poverty and you are poverty."

4 Jesus said, "A man who is old in his days will not hesitate to ask a baby of seven days about the place of life and he will live. For many who are first shall (be) last, and they shall become a single one."

5 Jesus said, "Know what is in front of your face, and what is concealed from you will be revealed to you. For there is nothing concealed which will not be manifest."

6 His disciples asked him, "Do you want us to fast, and how shall we pray, and shall we give alms, and what food regulations shall we keep?" Jesus said, "Do not lie, and do not do what you hate, because all is revealed before Heaven. For nothing is hidden that will not be revealed, and nothing is covered that shall remain without being revealed."

7 Jesus said, "Blessed is the lion which the man eats, and the lion thus becomes man; and cursed is the man whom the lion shall eat, when the lion thus becomes man."

8 And he said, "The man is like a wise fisherman who threw his net into the sea. He drew it up from the sea; it was full of small fish. The fisherman found among them a large, good fish. He threw all the small fish back into the sea; with no trouble he chose the large fish. He who has ears to hear, let him hear."

9 Jesus said, "Behold, the sower went out; he filled his hand; he threw. Some fell on the road. The birds came; they gathered them up. Others fell on the rock and did not send roots into the earth and did not send ears up to heaven. Others fell among thorns. They choked the seed, and the worm ate (the seed). And others fell on good earth,

and it raised up good fruit to heaven. It bore sixty per measure and one hundred-twenty per measure."

10 Jesus said, "I have hurled fire on the world, and behold, I guard it until it burns."

11 Jesus said, "This heaven will pass away and your heaven above it will pass away, and the dead are not living and the living shall not die. In the days when you ate what is dead, you made it alive; when you come into the light, what will you do? On the day when you were one, you became two. But when you have become two, what will you do?"

12 The disciples said to Jesus, "We know that you will go away from us; who will become ruler over us?" Jesus said, "Wherever you may be, you will go to James the righteous; heaven and earth came into being for him."

13 Jesus said to his disciples, "Make a comparison and tell me whom I am like." Simon Peter said to him, "You are like a righteous angel." Matthew said to him, "You are like a wise man." Thomas said to him, "Master, my mouth will not be able to say what you are like." Jesus said, "I am not your master. Because you drank, you are drunk from the bubbling spring which I measured out." And he took him; he went aside. He spoke to him three words. When Thomas returned to his companions, they asked him, "What did Jesus say to you?" Thomas said to them, "If I tell you one of the words which he said to me, you will pick up stones; you will throw them at me. And fire will come from the stones and consume you."

14 Jesus said to them, "If you fast, you will bring sin upon yourselves and, if you pray, you will be condemned and, if you give alms, you will do evil to your spirits. And if you enter any land and wander through the regions, if they receive you, whatever they set before you, eat it. Heal the sick among them. For that which goes into your mouth will not defile you, but that which comes out of your mouth is what will defile you."

15 Jesus said, "When you see him who was not born of woman, throw yourself down on your faces (and) adore him; that one is your Father."

16 Jesus said, "People might think I have come to throw peace on the world, and they do not know that I have come to throw dissolution on the earth; fire, sword, war. For there shall be five in a house: three shall be against two and two against three, the father against the son and the son against the father, and they shall stand as solitary ones."

17 Jesus said, "I will give you what no eye has seen and what no ear has heard and no hand has touched and what has not come into the heart of a human."

18 The disciples said to Jesus, "Tell us how our end will occur." Jesus said, "Have you found the beginning that you search for the end? In the place of the beginning, there the end will be. Blessed is he who will stand at the beginning, and he will know the end, and he will not taste death."

19 Jesus said, "Blessed is he who was before he came into being. If you become my disciples (and) you hear my words, these stones shall serve you. For you have five trees in paradise which are immobile in summer or winter, and they do not shed their leaves. Whoever knows them shall not taste death."

20 The disciples said to Jesus, "Tell us, what is the Kingdom of Heaven like?" He said to them, "It is like a mustard seed, smaller than all seeds. But when it falls on plowed ground, it puts forth a large shrub and becomes a shelter for the birds of heaven."

21 Mary said to Jesus, "Whom are your disciples like?" He said, "They are like little children; they settle themselves in a field that is not theirs. When the owners of the field come, they (the owners) say, 'Give us our field.' They undress before them and release it (the field) to them and give back their field to them. Because of this I say, if the owner of the house knows that the thief is coming, he will watch before he comes and will not let him break into his house of his kingdom and carry away his goods. But you watch especially for the world; gird your loins with great power lest the robbers find a way to come upon you, because the trouble you expect will happen. Let there be a person of understanding among you. When the fruit ripened, he came quickly, his sickle in his hand (and) he reaped it. He who has ears to hear, let him hear."

22 Jesus saw babies being suckled. He said to his disciples, "These babies who are being suckled are like those who enter the Kingdom." They said to him, "We are children, shall we enter the Kingdom?" Jesus said to them, "When you make the two one, and when you make the inner as the outer and the outer as the inner and the upper as the lower, so that you will make the male and the female into a single one, so that the male will not be male and the female [not] be female, when you make eyes in the place of an eye, and hand in place of a hand, and foot in the place of a foot, (and) an image in the place of an image, then you shall enter [the Kingdom]."

23 Jesus said, "I shall choose you, one from a thousand, and two from ten thousand, and they shall stand; they are a single one."

24 His disciples said, "Show us the place where you are, for it is necessary for us to seek it." He said to them, "He who has ears to hear, let him hear. There is light within a person of light and he (or it) lights the whole world. When he (or, it) does not shine, there is darkness."

25 Jesus said, "Love your brother as your soul; keep him as the apple of your eye."

26 Jesus said, "The chip that is in your brother's eye you see, but the log in your own eye you do not see. When you take the log out of your eye, then you will see to remove the chip from your brother's eye."

27 "If you do not fast (in respect to) the world, you will not find the Kingdom; if you do not keep the Sabbath a Sabbath, you shall not see the Father."

28 Jesus said, "I stood in the midst of the world, and I appeared to them in the flesh. I found all of them drunk; I did not find any of them thirsting. And my soul was pained for the sons of men because they are blind in their hearts, and they do not see that they came empty into the world; they seek to go out of the world empty. However, they are drunk. When they have shaken off their wine, then they shall repent."

29 Jesus said, "If the flesh exists because of spirit, it is a miracle, but if spirit (exists) because of the body, it is a miracle of miracles. But I marvel at how this great wealth established itself in this poverty."

30 Jesus said, "Where there are three Gods, they are Gods; where there are two or one, I am with him."

31 Jesus said, "A prophet is not acceptable in his own village; a physician does not heal those who know him."

32 Jesus said, "A city being built and fortified upon a high mountain cannot fall, nor can it be hidden."

33 Jesus said, "What you will hear in your ear and in your [other] ear, preach from your housetops. For no one lights a lamp and puts it under a basket, nor does he put it in a hidden place, but he sets it on a lampstand so everyone who comes in and goes out will see its light."

34 Jesus said, "If a blind person leads a blind person, the two of them fall into a pit."

35 Jesus said, "It is impossible for one to enter the house of the strong man and rob it violently unless he bind his hands; then he can pillage his house."

36 Jesus said, "Do not be anxious from morning to evening and from evening to morning about what you will wear."

37 His disciples said, "On what day will you be revealed to us and on what day shall we see you?" Jesus said, "When you undress without being ashamed, and you take your clothes and put them under your feet as little children and tramp on them, then you shall see the Son of the Living [One], and you shall not fear."

38 Jesus said, "Many times you desired to hear these words which I say to you, and you have no one else from whom to hear them. There will be days when you will seek me, and you will not find me."

39 Jesus said, "The Pharisees and the scribes took the keys of knowledge; they hid them. They did not enter, and they did not allow those to enter who wanted to enter. But you be wise as serpents and as innocent as doves."

40 Jesus said, "A vine was planted without the Father and it has not strengthened; it will be pulled up by its roots (and) it will be destroyed."

41 Jesus said, "He who has something in his hand shall be given more; and he who does not have anything, even the little he has will be taken away from him."

42 Jesus said, "Be wanderers."

43 His disciples said to him, "Who are you that you say these things to us?" "By what I say to you, you do not know who I am, but you have become as the Jews. They love the tree, they hate its fruit; they love the fruit, they hate the tree."

44 Jesus said, "Whoever blasphemes the Father, it will be forgiven him, and whoever blasphemes the Son, it will be forgiven him, but he who blasphemes the Holy Spirit will not be forgiven either on earth or in Heaven."

45 Jesus said, "One does not pick grapes from thorns, nor does one gather figs from thistles; they do not give fruit. F[or a go]od man brings forth good from] his treasure; a b[ad] man brings forth evil from the evil treasure in his heart, and he speaks evil. For out of the abundance of his heart he brings forth evil."

46 Jesus said, "From Adam to John the Baptist, among those born of women no one is greater than John the Baptist, so that his eyes . . . [here the text is uncertain]. Yet I said that whoever among you shall become as a child shall know the Kingdom, and he shall become higher than John."

47 Jesus said, "A man cannot mount two horses; he cannot stretch two bows. A servant cannot serve two masters; either he will honor the one and the other he will scorn . . . No one drinks old wine and right away wants to drink new wine; and one does not put new wine into the old wineskins lest they tear; and one does not put old wine into new wineskins lest it spoil. One does not sew an old patch on a new garment, because there will be a tear."

48 Jesus said, "If two make peace between themselves in the same house, they shall say to the mountain, 'Move away,' and it will move."

49 Jesus said, "Blessed are the solitary and the chosen, because you will find the Kingdom; because you come from it, you will again go there."

50 Jesus said, "If they say to you, 'Where did you come from?' say to them, 'We come from the light, where the light came into being through itself. It stood . . . and reveals itself in their image.' If they say to you, '[Who] are you?' say to them, 'We are his sons and we are the chosen of the living Father.' If they ask you, 'What is the sign of your Father who is in you?' say to them, 'It is movement and repose.'"

51 His disciples said to him, "When will be the repose of the dead, and when will the new world come?" He said to them, "What you look for has come, but you do not know it."

52 His disciples said to him, "Twenty-four prophets spoke in Israel and all of them spoke in you." He said to them, "You have left out the Living One who is with you, and you have spoken about the dead."

53 His disciples said to him, "Is circumcision profitable or not?" He said to them, "If it were profitable, their father would beget them circumcized from their mother. But the true circumcision in the Spirit has found complete usefulness."

54 Jesus said, "Blessed are the poor, for yours is the Kingdom of Heaven."

55 Jesus said, "He who does not hate his father and his mother cannot be my disciple, and (he who) does not hate his brothers and sisters and (does not) carry his cross in my way will not be worthy of me."

56 Jesus said, "He who has known the world has found a corpse, and he who has found a corpse, the world is not worthy of him."

57 Jesus said, "The Kingdom of the Father is like a man who had [good] seed. His enemy came by night, (and) he sowed a weed among the good seed. The man did not let them pull up the weed. He said to them, 'I fear lest you go to pull up the weed, and you pull up the wheat with it.' For on the day of the harvest the weeds will be apparent; they will pull them up and burn them."

58 Jesus said, "Blessed is the one who has suffered; he has found the Life."

59 Jesus said, "Look upon the Living One as long as you live, lest you die and seek to see him and you cannot see."

60 (They saw) a Samaritan carrying a lamb; he was going to Judea. He said to his disciples, "Why does he carry the lamb?" They said to him, "That he may kill it and eat it." He said to them, "As long as it is alive he will not eat it, but only when he has killed it and it has become a corpse."

They said, "Otherwise he cannot do it." He said to them, "You yourselves seek a place for yourselves in repose, lest you become a corpse and be eaten."

61 Jesus said, "Two will be resting on a couch; the one will die, the one will live." Salome said, "Who are you, man? As if from the One you sat on my couch and you ate from my table." Jesus said to her, "I am he who is from him who is the same. The things from my Father have been given to me." (Salome said,) "I am your disciple." (Jesus said to her,) "Therefore, I say, if he is the same, he will be filled with light, but if he is divided, he will be filled with darkness."

62 Jesus said, "I tell my mysteries [to those who are worthy of my] mysteries. What your right (hand) will do, do not let your left (hand) know."

63 Jesus said, "There was a rich man who had many possessions. He said, 'I will use my goods so that I can sow and reap and plant and fill my warehouses with fruit so that I will not be in need of anything.' He truly believed this. And in that night he died. He who has ears, let him hear."

64 Jesus said, "A man had guests and, when he had prepared the banquet, he sent his servant to invite the guests. He went to the first; he said to him, 'My master invites you.' He said, 'Money is owed me by some merchants. They will come to me in the evening; I will go and I will give them orders. Please excuse me from the dinner.' He went to another; he said to him, 'My master invites you.' He said to him, 'I have bought a house and they have asked me (to come out) for a day (to close the deal). I will not have time.' He went to another; he said to him, 'My master invites you.' He said to him, 'My friend is going to marry, and I will prepare a dinner; I will not be able to come. Please excuse me from the dinner.' He went to another; he said to him, 'My master invites you.' He said to him, 'I have bought a farm, I go to collect the rent. I will not be able to come. Please excuse me from the dinner.' The servant returned; he said to his master, 'Those whom you invited asked to be excused from the dinner.' The master said to his servant, 'Go outside to the streets, bring those whom you find so that they may feast.' Buyers and merchants will not enter the places of my Father."

65 He said, "A good man had a vineyard. He rented it to some farmers so that they would work it, and he would give him the profits of the vineyard. They seized his servant, beat him, and almost killed him. The servant went back; he told his master. His master said, 'Perhaps he did not know them.' He sent another servant. The farmers beat him also. Then the master sent his son. He said, 'Perhaps they will respect my son.' Those farmers seized him, and they killed him, because they knew he was the heir of the vineyard. He who has ears, let him hear."

66 Jesus said, "Show me the stone rejected by those who built. It is the cornerstone."

67 Jesus said, "He who believes (that) the All is wanting in anything lacks all himself."

68 Jesus said, "Blessed are you when they hate and persecute you, and they will find no place wherever you have been persecuted."

69a Jesus said, "Blessed are those whom they have persecuted in their hearts; these are they who know the Father in truth."

69b "Blessed are those who are hungry, so that the belly of him who hungers will be filled."

70 Jesus said, "If you beget what is in you, what you have will save you. If you do not have it in you, what you do not have in you will kill you."

71 Jesus said, "I shall destroy [this] house and no one will be able to build it [again]."

72 [A man] s[aid] to him, "Speak to my brothers, so that they will divide my father's possessions with me." He said to him, "O man, who made me a divider?" He turned to his disciples; he said to them, "I am not a divider, am I?"

73 Jesus said, "The harvest is great, but the workers are few; but beseech the Lord to send workers to the harvest."

74 He said, "Lord, there are many standing around the cistern, but no one (or, nothing) in the cistern."

75 Jesus said, "Many are standing at the door, but the solitary will enter the Bridal Chamber."

76 Jesus said, "The Kingdom of the Father is like a merchant who had goods. Then he found a pearl. This was a prudent merchant. He gave up (i.e., sold) the goods, and he bought the single pearl for himself. You also must seek for the trea-

sure which does not perish, which abides where no moth comes near to eat, nor worm destroys."

77 Jesus said, "I am the light which is above all of them; I am the All. The All came forth from me and the All reached me. Split wood, I am there; lift up the stone, and you will find me there."

78 Jesus said, "Why did you come to the desert? To see a reed shaken by the wind? To see a [man clo]thed in soft clothes? [Behold, your] kings and your great ones are dressed in soft [clothes] and they are not able to know the truth."

79 A woman in the crowd said to him, "Blessed are the womb which bore you and the breasts which fed you." He said to [her], "Blessed are those who have heard the Word of the Father (and) have kept it in truth. For there will be days when you will say: 'Blessed are the womb which has not conceived and the breasts that have not suckled.'"

80 Jesus said, "He who has known the world has found the body, but he who has found the body, the world is not worthy of him."

81 Jesus said, "He who has become rich, let him become king; and he who has power, let him renounce it."

82 Jesus said, "He who is near me is near the fire, and he who is far from me is far from the Kingdom."

83 Jesus said, "The images are manifest to a person, and the light in them is hidden in the image of the light of the Father. He will reveal himself, and his image will be hidden by his light."

84 Jesus said, "When you see your likeness, you rejoice. But when you see your images which came into being before you, (which) do not die nor are manifest, how much you will bear!"

85 Jesus said, "Adam came into existence from a great power and a great wealth, and he was not worthy of you. For, if he had been worthy, he [would] not [have tasted] death."

86 Jesus said, "[The foxes have] h[oles] and the birds have [their] nests, but the Son of Man does not have any place to lay his head and to rest."

87 Jesus said, "The body is wretched which depends on a body, and the soul is wretched which depends on these two."

88 Jesus said, "The angels and the prophets shall come to you, and they shall give you that which is yours. You give them what is in your hands, (and) say to yourselves, 'On which day will they come and receive what is theirs?'"

89 Jesus said, "Why do you wash the outside of the cup? Do you not know that he who made the inside is also he who made the outside?"

90 Jesus said, "Come to me because my yoke is easy and my mastery is gentle, and you will find your repose."

91 They said to him, "Tell us who you are so that we can believe in you." He said to them, "You examine the face of the heavens and the earth, and (yet) you have not known him who is in front of your face, nor do you know how to examine this time."

92 Jesus said, "Search and you will find, but those things which you asked me in those days, I did not tell you then; now I want to speak them, and you do not ask about them."

93 "Do not give what is holy to the dogs, because they will throw it on the dung heap. Do not throw the pearls to the pigs, lest they make . . ." [text uncertain].

94 Jesus (said), "He who searches, will find . . . it will open to him."

95 Jesus (said), "If you have money, do not lend it at interest, but give (to those) from whom you will not receive it (back again)."

96 Jesus (said), "The Kingdom of the Father is like a woman, she took a bit of leaven, hid it in dough, and made big loaves. He who has ears, let him hear."

97 Jesus said, "The Kingdom of the [Father] is like a woman who was carrying a jar which was full of meal. While she was walking on a distant road, the handle of the jar broke; the meal spilled out behind her onto the road. She did not know; she was not aware of the accident. After she came to her house, she put the jar down, and found it empty."

98 Jesus said, "The Kingdom of the Father is like a man who wanted to kill a powerful man. He drew the sword in his own house; he thrust it into the wall so that he would know if his hand would stick it through. Then he killed the powerful one."

99 The disciples said to him, "Your brothers and your mother are standing outside." He said to them, "Those here who do the will of my Father are my brothers and mother; they will enter the Kingdom of my Father."

100 They showed Jesus a gold coin, and they said to him, "Caesar's men demand taxes from us." He said to them, "Give Caesar's things to Caesar; give God's things to God; and what is mine give to me."

101 "He who does not hate his [father] and his mother in my way will not be able to be my [disciple], and he who does [not] love his father and his mother in my way, will not be able to be my [disciple], for my mother. . . , but [my] true [mother] gave me life."

102 Jesus said, "Woe to the Pharisees; they are like a dog lying in the oxen's food trough, for she does not eat nor let the oxen eat."

103 Jesus said, "Blessed is the man who knows in which part . . . the robbers will come, so that he will rise and gather his . . . and gird up his loins before they come in. . ."

104 They said (to him), "Come, let us pray today, and let us fast." Jesus said, "Why? What sin have I committed, or by what have I been conquered? But after the bridegroom has left the Bridal Chamber, then let them fast and pray."

105 Jesus said, "He who acknowledges the father and the mother will be called the son of a harlot."

106 Jesus said, "When you make the two one, you shall be Sons of Man, and when you say, 'Mountain, move away,' it will move."

107 Jesus said, "The Kingdom is like a shepherd who had a hundred sheep. One of them, which was the largest, wandered off. He left the ninety-nine; he searched for the one until he found it. After he tired himself, he said

to the sheep, 'I love you more than the ninety-nine.'"

108 Jesus said, "He who drinks from my mouth will be as I am, and I will be he and the things that are hidden will be revealed to him."

109 Jesus said, "The Kingdom is like a man who had a treasure [hidden] in his field, and he did not know it. And [after] he died, he left it to his son. His son did not know; he received the field, and he sold [it]. The one who bought it went plowing; and [he found] the treasure. He began to lend money at interest to whomever he wished."

110 Jesus said, "He who finds the world and becomes rich, let him reject the world."

111 Jesus said, "The heavens and the earth will roll up in your presence, and he who lives by the Living One will not see death . . ." Because did not Jesus say, "He who finds himself, the world is not worthy of him"?

112 Jesus said, "Woe to the flesh which depends on the soul; woe to the soul which depends on the flesh."

113 His disciples said to him, "On what day will the Kingdom come?" (He said,) "It will not come by expectation. They will not say, 'Look here,' or, 'Look there,' but the Kingdom of the Father is spread out on the earth and people do not see it."

114 Simon Peter said to them, "Let Mary leave us, because women are not worthy of the Life." Jesus said, "Look, I shall guide her so that I will make her male, in order that she also may become a living spirit, being like you males. For every woman who makes herself male will enter the Kingdom of Heaven."

>—+—◇—◇—+—<

38. The Gospel of Peter

Although the *Gospel of Peter* was known and used as Scripture in some parts of the Christian church in the second century, its use was eventually disallowed by church leaders who considered some of its teachings heretical. Having fallen out of circulation, it was practically forgotten in all but name until a fragment of its text was discovered near the end of the nineteenth century in the tomb of an Egyptian monk.

The fragment narrates Jesus' passion and resurrection, beginning (in mid-sentence) with Pilate's washing of his hands. Although many of the stories are familiar from the New Testament, especially Matthew, some of the details are strikingly different, such as the statement that on the cross, Jesus was "silent as if he felt no pain" (v. 10). Yet more striking are several episodes found nowhere else among our Gospels, especially the impressive account of Jesus' emergence from his tomb as a giant, supported by two enormous angels and followed by a talking cross.

Scholars debate whether the Gospel of Peter consisted exclusively of a passion narrative or whether, like the New Testament Gospels, it simply ended with one. Nor is it clear whether the pseudonymous author derived his stories from the canonical accounts or, instead, from other sources, independent of them. What is clear is that his account, even more than the New Testament Gospels, goes out of its way to incriminate Jews for the death of Jesus (e.g., v. 25). This strong anti-Judaic slant may suggest a date from the early part of the second century.

1 . . . none of the Jews washed their hands, nor did Herod or any of his judges. As they did not wish to wash, Pilate stood up [to leave].

2 Then Herod the king ordered that the Lord be taken away, and he said to them, "What I ordered you to do to him, do it."

3 Joseph, a friend of Pilate and of the Lord, stood there, and, knowing that they were about to crucify him, he came to Pilate and asked for the body of the Lord for burial.

4 Pilate sent to Herod and asked for his [Jesus'] body.

5 Herod said, "Brother Pilate, even if no one asked for the body, we would bury him, since the Sabbath is about to begin. For it is written in the law: "The sun shall not set on one who has been executed."[1] And he delivered him to the people on the day before their feast of unleavened bread.

6 They took the Lord and hastily shoved him along and said, "Let us drag away the son of God now that we have power over him."

7 And they dressed him in a purple robe and set him on the judgment seat and said, "Judge rightly, King of Israel!"

8 And one of them fetched a crown of thorns and put it on the Lord's head.

9 Others who were standing there spat in his face; and others hit him on the cheeks; another struck him with a reed, and whipped him. And they said, "By this honor, we honor the son of God."

10 Then they brought two criminals and crucified the Lord between them. But he remained silent as if he felt no pain.

11 And when they erected the cross, they wrote on it "This is the King of Israel."

12 They laid down his garments, divided them in front of him, and cast lots for them.

13 One of the criminals reproached them, saying, "We suffer for the wrongs things we have actually done, but this one, who is the savior of humanity—how has he done you wrong?"

---

[1]Deut 21:22–23.

14 And they were furious with the thief and ordered that his legs should not be broken; thus he died in agony.

15 It was midday, and darkness covered all Judea. And they became very troubled and anxious lest the sun had already set, because he [Jesus] still lived. For it is written for them, "The sun shall not set upon one who has been executed."[2]

16 One of them said, "Give him gall with vinegar to drink." And they mixed it, and gave it to him to drink.

17 And thus they fulfilled everything and brought their sins to full fruition on their own heads.

18 Many of them walked around with lamps, thinking that it was night, and they fell down.

19 Then the Lord cried out, "My power! Power! You have left me." When he said this, he was taken up.

20 At the same hour the veil of the temple in Jerusalem was torn in two.

21 They pulled the nails from the Lord's hands and laid him on the ground. And the whole earth quaked, and they were terribly afraid.

22 Then the sun shone again; they realized it was the ninth hour.

23 The Jews rejoiced, and they gave his body to Joseph in order that he should bury it, since he had seen what good things he [Jesus] had done.

24 He took the Lord, washed him, wrapped him in linen, and took him to his own tomb, called "Joseph's Garden."

25 Then the Jews, the elders, and the priests, knowing what evil they had done to themselves, began to beat their breasts and say, "Woe, because of our sins; the judgment and the end of Jerusalem are at hand."

26 But I mourned with my companions; we were trembling, wounded in our hearts. And we hid, for we were sought by them as evil-doers and as those who threatened to burn the temple.

27 Because of all this we fasted and sat mourning night and day until the Sabbath.

28 The scribes and Pharisees and elders all gathered together, after hearing that all the people murmured and beat their breasts, and said, "If such great miracles have happened at his death, see just how righteous [or, innocent] he is!"

29 The elders were frightened, and they came begging to Pilate, and said,

30 "Give us soldiers, so that we may guard his tomb for three days, lest his disciples come and steal him, and the people believe that he is risen from the dead, and they harm us."

31 Pilate gave to them Petronius, the centurion, with soldiers to guard the tomb. The elders and scribes went with them to the grave.

32 Everyone who was there with the centurion and the troops together rolled a huge boulder, and placed it over the door of the tomb.

33 They put seven seals on it, pitched a tent there and set watch.

34 At early morning on the Sabbath, a crowd came from Jerusalem and the surrounding countryside to see the sealed tomb.

35 But in the night before the dawn of the Lord's day, while the others stood watch two at a time, there came a great sound [or, voice] from heaven.

36 And they saw the heavens open and two men who had great splendor come down from there and draw near to the tomb.

37 The stone which was set over the door rolled away by itself and moved to the side. The tomb was opened, and both the young men went in.

38 When the soldiers who were there saw this, they awakened the centurion and the elders—they were there also keeping watch.

39 While they narrated what they had seen, they then saw three men exit the tomb; two supported the one, and a cross followed them.

40 The heads of the two reached up to heaven, but the one whom they supported with their hands stretched beyond the heavens.

41 And they heard a voice from the heavens which said, "Have you preached to those who are asleep?"

42 And they heard an answer from the cross, "Yes."

43 Those who were there decided among themselves to go and to report these things to Pilate.

44 While they discussed the matter, the heavens again appeared—open—and a man descended and entered the tomb.

---

[2]Deut 21:22–23.

45 When those in the centurion's company saw this, they hurried by night to Pilate—quitting the tomb they guarded—and they narrated with great agitation to him everything they had seen, and said, "Truly he was a son of God."

46 Pilate answered, "I am pure in respect to the blood of the son of God; it was you who made the decision about this matter."

47 Then they all approached him and begged him to order the centurion and his troops to say nothing.

48 "It will be better for us," they said, "to bear the guilt of the greatest sin before God than to fall into the hands of the Jewish people and to be stoned."

49 Pilate therefore ordered the centurion and the troops to say nothing.

50 At the dawn of the Lord's day, Mary Magdalene, a disciple of the Lord—afraid of the Jews because they were inflamed with rage, she had not done at the burial what women are supposed to do by custom for their loved ones who have died—

51 took with her women friends and came to the tomb where he was buried.

52 They were afraid lest the Jews should see them and said, "Because we could not weep and mourn on the day he was crucified, let us at least now do so at the tomb.

53 "But who will roll away for us the boulder set at the door of the tomb, so that we may enter and sit beside him and do what we should do?

54 "For the boulder is huge, and we are afraid lest someone should see us. If we cannot [do as we should], at least we can set down at the door of the tomb what we have brought; and we may weep and mourn until we return to our house."

55 When they arrived, they found the tomb opened. They approached near, bent down, and saw there a young man seated inside the tomb; he was handsome and wore a brightly shining robe. He said to them.

56 "Why did you come? Whom do you seek? Not the one who was crucified? He is risen and gone. If you do not believe, bend down and see the place where he was laid, because he is not here. For, he is risen and has gone to the place from where he was sent."

57 Then the woman were stricken with fear, and they fled.

58 It was the last day of the feast of unleavened bread, and many had returned to their homes; the feast was over.

59 We, the twelve disciples of the Lord, cried and mourned. Each of us, mourning for what had happened, went to his own house.

60 But I, Simon Peter, and Andrew, my brother, took our nets and went to the sea. With us was Levi, the son of Alphaius, whom the Lord. . . [The text breaks off at this point.]

>─+◆>─O─◆+─◄

39. The Proto-Gospel of James

This book is sometimes called a "Proto-Gospel" because it narrates events that took place *prior* to Jesus' birth (although it includes an account of the birth as well). The ancient manuscripts that preserve the book call it "The Birth of Mary" or "The Story of the Birth of Saint Mary, Mother of God." Its author claims to be James, usually understood to be Jesus' (half-) brother known from the New Testament, here assumed to be Joseph's son by a previous marriage.

Focusing its attention on Jesus' mother, Mary, the book provides legendary accounts of (a) her miraculous birth to the wealthy Jew Joachim and his wife, Anna; (b) her sanctified upbringing in the Jerusalem Temple; (c) her marriage to Joseph, an old widower miraculously chosen to be her husband; and (d) her supernatural conception of Jesus through the Spirit. Parts of the book rely heavily on the infancy narratives of Matthew and Luke, but with numerous intriguing expansions, including information about Joseph's previous marriage and grown sons, Mary's work as a seamstress for the curtain in the temple, and the birth of Jesus in a cave with the assistance of Salome, a midwife who performs a postpartum inspection of Mary to be assured of her virginity.

Since the book was already known to Origen in the early third century, and probably to Clement of Alexandria at the end of the second, it must have been in circulation already soon after 150 C.E. The book was enormously popular in later centuries.

1 In the "Histories of the Twelve Tribes of Israel" Joachim was a very rich man, and he brought all his gifts to the Lord twofold, saying. "What I bring in excess shall be for the whole people, and what I bring as a sin-offering shall be for the Lord, as a propitiation for me."

2 Now the great day of the Lord drew near, and the children of Israel were bringing their gifts. And Reuben stood up and said, "It is not lawful for you to offer your gifts first, because you have begotten no offspring in Israel."

3 Then Joachim became very sad, and went to the record-book of the twelve tribes of the people and said, "I will look in the register to see whether I am the only one who has not begotten offspring in Israel," and he found that all the righteous had raised up offspring in Israel. And he remembered the patriarch Abraham to whom in his last days God gave a son, Isaac.

4 And Joachim was very sad, and did not show himself to his wife, but went into the wilderness; there he pitched his tent and fasted forty days and forty nights, saying to himself, "I shall not go down either for food or for drink until the Lord my God visits me; my prayer shall be food and drink."

2 Anna his wife sang two dirges and gave voice to a twofold lament:

"I will mourn my widowhood, and grieve for my childlessness."

2 Now the great day of the Lord drew near, and Judith her maid said, "How long do you intend to humble your soul, because the great day of the Lord is near and it is not lawful for you to mourn. But take this headband, which the mistress of work gave me; it is not right for me to wear it because I am a servant and it bears a royal cipher."

3 But Anna said, "Get away from me! I shall never do it. The Lord has greatly humbled me. Who knows whether a deceiver did not give it to you, and you came to make me share in your sin!" Judith answered, "Why should I curse you? The Lord God has shut up your womb to give you no fruit in Israel."

4 And Anna was very sad, but she took off her mourning garments, washed her head, put on her bridal garments, and about the ninth hour went into her garden to walk there. And she saw a laurel tree and sat down beneath it and implored the Lord saying, "O God of our fathers, bless me and heed my prayer, just as you blessed the womb of Sarah and gave her a son, Isaac."

3 And Anna sighed towards heaven and saw a nest of sparrows in the laurel tree and she sang a dirge to herself:

"Woe is me, who gave me life
What womb brought me forth?
For I was born a curse before them all and
    before the children of Israel,
And I was reproached, and they mocked me
    and thrust me out of the temple of the
    Lord.
2 Woe is me, to what am I likened?
I am not likened to the birds of the heaven;
for even the birds of the heaven are fruitful
    before you, O Lord.
Woe is me, to what am I likened?
I am not likened to the beasts of the earth;
for even the beasts of the earth are fruitful
    before you, O Lord.
3 Woe is me, to what am I likened?
I am not likened to these waters;
for even these waters are fruitful before you,
    O Lord.
Woe is me, to what am I likened?
I am not likened to this earth;
for even this earth brings forth its fruit in its
    season and praises you, O Lord."

4 And behold an angel of the Lord appeared to her and said, "Anna, Anna, the Lord has heard your prayer. You shall conceive and bear, and your offspring shall be spoken of in the whole world." And Anna said, "As the Lord my God lives, if I bear a child, whether male or female, I will bring it as a gift to the Lord my God, and it shall serve him all the days of its life."

2 And behold there came two angels, who said to her, "Behold, Joachim your husband is coming with his flocks for an angel of the Lord had come down to him and said to him, 'Joachim, Joachim, the Lord God has heard your prayer. Go down from here; behold, your wife Anna shall conceive.'"

3 And Joachim went down and called his herdsmen and said, "Bring me here ten female lambs without blemish and without spot; they shall be for the Lord my God. And bring me twelve tender calves and they shall be for the priests and council of elders, and a hundred young he-goats for the whole people."

4 And, behold, Joachim came with his flocks, and Anna stood at the gate and saw Joachim coming and ran immediately and threw her arms around his neck saying, "Now I know that the Lord God has greatly blessed me; for behold the widow is no longer a widow, and I, who was childless, shall conceive."

And Joachim rested the first day in his house.

5 The next day he offered his gifts, saying to himself, "If the Lord God is gracious to me the frontlet of the priest will make it clear to me."

And Joachim offered his gifts and observed the priest's frontlet when he went up to the altar of the Lord; and he saw no sin in himself. And Joachim said, "Now I know that the Lord God is gracious to me and has forgiven all my sins." And he came down from the temple of the Lord justified, and went to his house.

2 And her months were fulfilled; in the ninth month Anna gave birth. And she said to the midwife, "What have I brought forth?" And she said, "A female." And Anna said, "My soul is magnified this day." And she lay down. And when the days were completed, Anna purified herself and gave suck to the child, and called her Mary.

6 Day by day the child grew strong; when she was six months old her mother stood her on the ground to see if she could stand. And she walked seven steps and came to her bosom. And she took her up saying, "As the Lord my God lives, you shall walk no more upon this earth until I bring you into the temple of the Lord." And she made a sanctuary in her bedroom and did not permit anything common or unclean to pass through it. And she summoned the undefiled daughters of the Hebrews, and they served her.

2 On the child's first birthday Joachim made a great feast, and invited the chief priests and the priests and the scribes and the elders and all the people of Israel. And Joachim brought the child to the priests, and they blessed her saying, "O God

of our fathers, bless this child and give her a name eternally renowned among all generations." And all the people said, "So be it, so be it, Amen." And they brought her to the chief priests, and they blessed her saying, "O God of the heavenly heights, look upon this child and bless her with a supreme blessing which cannot be superseded." And her mother carried her into the sanctuary of her bedroom and gave her suck. And Anna sang this song to the Lord God:

> "I will sing a praise to the Lord my God,
> for he has visited me and removed from me
>   the reproach of my enemies.
> And the Lord gave me the fruit of his right-
>   eousness, unique yet manifold before
>   him.
> Who will proclaim to the sons of Reuben
>   that Anna gives suck?"

And she laid her down to rest in the bedroom of her sanctuary, and went out and served them. When the feast was ended they went down rejoicing and glorifying the God of Israel.

7 The months passed, and the child grew. When she was two years old Joachim said, "Let us take her up to the temple of the Lord, so that we may fulfil the promise which we made, lest the Lord send some evil to us and our gift be unacceptable." And Anna replied, "Let us wait until the third year, that the child may then no more long for her father and mother." And Joachim said, "Let us wait."

2 And when the child was three years old Joachim said, "Call the undefiled daughters of the Hebrews, and let each one take a torch, and let these be burning, in order that the child may not turn back and her heart be tempted away from the temple of the Lord." And they did so until they had gone up to the temple of the Lord. And the priest took her and kissed her and blessed her, saying, "The Lord has magnified your name among all generations; because of you the Lord at the end of the days will reveal his redemption to the sons of Israel."

3 And he placed her on the third step of the altar, and the Lord God put grace upon her and

she danced with her feet, and the whole house of Israel loved her.

8 And her parents returned marvelling, praising the Lord God because the child did not turn back. And Mary was in the temple of the Lord nurtured like a dove and received food from the hand of an angel.

2 When she was twelve years old, there took place a council of the priests saying, "Behold, Mary has become twelve years old in the temple of the Lord. What then shall we do with her lest she defile the temple of the Lord?" And they said to the high priest, "You stand at the altar of the Lord; enter the sanctuary and pray concerning her, and that which the Lord shall reveal to you we will indeed do."

3 And the high priest took the vestment with the twelve bells and went into the Holy of Holies and prayed concerning her. And behold, an angel of the Lord appeared and said to him, "Zacharias, Zacharias, go out and assemble the widowers of the people, and to whomsoever the Lord shall give a sign she shall be a wife." And the heralds went forth through all the country round about Judaea; the trumpet of the Lord sounded, and all came running.

9 And Joseph threw down his adze and went out to their meeting. And when they were gathered together, they took the rods and went to the high priest. He took the rods from them all, entered the temple, and prayed. When he had finished the prayer he took the rods, and went out and gave them to them; but there was no sign on them. Joseph received the last rod, and behold, a dove came out of the rod and flew on to Joseph's head. And the priest said to Joseph, "You have been chosen by lot to receive the virgin of the Lord as your ward."

2 But Joseph answered him, "I have sons and am old; she is but a girl. I object lest I should become a laughing-stock to the sons of Israel." And the priest said to Joseph, "Fear the Lord your God, and remember what God did to Dathan, Abiram, and Korah, how the earth was split in two and they were all swallowed up because of their rebellion. And now beware, Joseph, lest these things

happen in your house too." And Joseph was afraid and received her as his ward. And Joseph said to Mary, "I have received you from the temple of the Lord, and now I leave you in my house and go away to build my buildings. I will return to you; the Lord will guard you."

10 Now there was a council of the priests saying, "Let us make a veil for the temple of the Lord." And the priest said, "Call to me pure virgins of the tribe of David." And the officers departed and searched and they found seven virgins. And the priest remembered the child Mary, that she was of the tribe of David and was pure before God. And the officers went and fetched her.

2 Then they brought them into the temple of the Lord and the priest said, "Cast lots to see who shall weave the gold, the amiantus, the linen, the silk, the hyacinth-blue, the scarlet, and the pure purple." The pure purple and scarlet fell by lot to Mary. And she took them and went home. At that time Zacharias became dumb, and Samuel took his place until Zacharias was able to speak again. Mary took the scarlet and spun it.

11 And she took the pitcher and went out to draw water, and behold, a voice said, "Hail, highly favored one, the Lord is with you, you are blessed among women."[1] And she looked around to the right and to the left to see where this voice came from. And, trembling, she went to her house and put down the pitcher and took the purple and sat down on her seat and drew out the thread.

2 And behold, an angel of the Lord stood before her and said, "Do not fear, Mary; for you have found grace before the Lord of all things and shall conceive by his Word." When she heard this she considered it and said, "Shall I conceive by the Lord, the living God, and bear as every woman bears?"

3 And the angel of the Lord said, "Not so, Mary; for the power of the Lord shall overshadow you; wherefore that holy one who is born of you shall be called the Son of the Most High. And you shall call his name Jesus; for he shall save his people from their sins."[2] And Mary said, "Behold, (I am) the handmaid of the Lord before him: be it to me according to your word."[3]

12 And she made ready the purple and the scarlet and brought them to the priest. And the priest blessed her and said, "Mary, the Lord God has magnified your name, and you shall be blessed among all generations of the earth."[4] And Mary rejoiced and went to Elizabeth her kinswoman and knocked on the door. When Elizabeth heard it, she put down the scarlet and ran to the door and opened it, and when she saw Mary she blessed her and said, "How is it that the mother of my Lord should come to me? For behold, that which is in me leaped and blessed you."[5] But Mary forgot the mysteries which the archangel Gabriel had told her, and raised a sigh towards heaven and said, "Who am I, Lord, that all generations of the earth count me blessed?"

3 And she remained three months with Elizabeth. Day by day her womb grew, and Mary was afraid and went into her house and hid herself from the children of Israel. And Mary was sixteen years old when all these mysterious things happened.

13 Now when she was in her sixth month, behold, Joseph came from his buildings and entered his house and found her with child. And he struck his face, threw himself down on the ground on sackcloth and wept bitterly saying, "With what countenance shall I look towards the Lord my God? What prayer shall I offer for this maiden? For I received her as a virgin out of the temple of the Lord my God and have not protected her. Who has deceived me? Who has done this evil in my house and defiled the virgin? Has the story of Adam been repeated in me? For as Adam was absent in the hour of his prayer and the serpent came and found Eve alone and deceived her, so also has it happened to me."

2 And Joseph arose from the sackcloth and called Mary and said to her, "You who are cared for by God, why have you done this and forgotten the Lord your God? Why have you humiliated

---

[1] Luke 1:28.
[2] Luke 1:35, 31; Matt 1:21.
[3] Luke 1:38.
[4] Luke 1:42, 48.
[5] Luke 1:41–44.

your soul, you who were brought up in the Holy of Holies and received food from the hand of an angel?"

3 But she wept bitterly, saying, "I am pure, and know not a man." And Joseph said to her, "As the Lord my God lives, I do not know whence it has come to me."

14 And Joseph feared greatly and parted from her, pondering what he should do with her. And Joseph said, "If I conceal her sin, I shall be found to be in opposition to the law of the Lord. If I expose her to the children of Israel, I fear lest that which is in her may be from the angels and I should be found delivering innocent blood to the judgment of death. What then shall I do with her? I will put her away secretly." And the night came upon him.

2 And behold, an angel of the Lord appeared to him in a dream, saying, "Do not fear this child. For that which is in her is of the Holy Spirit. She shall bear a son, and you shall call his name Jesus; for he shall save his people from their sins."[6] And Joseph arose from sleep and glorified the God of Israel who had bestowed his grace upon him, and he guarded her.

15 And Annas the scribe came to him and said to him, "Joseph, why have you not appeared in our assembly?" And Joseph said to him, "Because I was weary from the journey and I rested the first day." And Annas turned and saw that Mary was pregnant.

2 And he went running to the priest and said to him, "Joseph, for whom you are a witness, has grievously transgressed." And the high priest said, "In what way?" And he said, "The virgin, whom he received from the temple of the Lord, he has defiled, and has secretly consummated his marriage with her, and has not disclosed it to the children of Israel." And the priest said to him, "Has Joseph done this?" And Annas said to him, "Send officers, and you will find the virgin pregnant." And the officers went and found as he had said, and brought her and Joseph to the court. And the priest said, "Mary, why have you done this? Why have you humiliated your soul and forgotten the Lord your God, you who were brought up in the

Holy of Holies and received food from the hand of an angel, and heard hymns, and danced before him? Why have you done this?" But she wept bitterly saying, "As the Lord my God lives, I am pure before him and I know not a man." And the priest said to Joseph, "Why have you done this?" And Joseph said, "As the Lord my God lives, I am pure concerning her." And the priest said, "Do not give false witness, but speak the truth. You have consummated your marriage in secret, and have not disclosed it to the children of Israel, and have not bowed your head under the mighty hand in order that your seed might be blessed." And Joseph was silent.

16 And the priest said, "Give back the virgin whom you have received from the temple of the Lord." And Joseph began to weep. And the priest said, "I will give you both to drink the water of the conviction of the Lord, and it will make your sins manifest in your eyes."

2 And the priest took it and gave it to Joseph to drink and sent him into the hill-country, and he returned whole. And he made Mary drink also, and sent her into the hill-country, and she returned whole. And all the people marvelled, because sin did not appear in them. And the priest said, "If the Lord God has not revealed your sins, neither do I judge you." And he released them. And Joseph took Mary and departed to his house, rejoicing and glorifying the God of Israel.

17 Now there went out a decree from the king Augustus that all those in Bethlehem in Judaea should be enrolled.[7] And Joseph said, "I shall enrol my sons, but what shall I do with this child? How shall I enrol her? As my wife? I am ashamed to do that. Or as my daughter? But all the children of Israel know that she is not my daughter. On this day of the Lord the Lord will do as he wills."

2 And he saddled his she-ass and sat her on it; his son led, and Joseph followed. And they drew near to the third milestone. And Joseph

---

[6]Matt 1:20–21.
[7]Luke 2:1.

turned round and saw her sad and said within himself, "Perhaps the child within her is paining her." Another time Joseph turned round and saw her laughing and said to her, "Mary, why is it that I see your face at one moment laughing and at another sad?" And Mary said to Joseph, "I see with my eyes two peoples, one weeping and lamenting and one rejoicing and exulting."

3 And having come half-way, Mary said to him, "Joseph, take me down from the she-ass, for the child within me presses me to come forth." And he took her down from the she-ass and said to her, "Where shall I take you and hide your shame? For the place is desert."

18 And he found a cave there and brought her into it, and left her in the care of his sons and went out to seek for a Hebrew midwife in the region of Bethlehem.

2 Now, I, Joseph, was walking, and yet I did not walk, and I looked up to the air and saw the air in amazement. And I looked up at the vault of heaven, and saw it standing still and the birds of the heaven motionless. And I looked down at the earth, and saw a dish placed there and workmen reclining, and their hands were in the dish. But those who chewed did not chew, and those who lifted up did not lift, and those who put something to their mouth put nothing to their mouth, but everybody looked upwards. And behold, sheep were being driven and they did not come forward but stood still; and the shepherd raised his hand to strike them with his staff but his hand remained upright. And I looked at the flow of the river, and saw the mouths of the kids over it and they did not drink. And then suddenly everything went on its course.

19 And behold, a woman came down from the hill-country and said to me, "Man, where are you going?" And I said, "I seek a Hebrew midwife." And she answered me, "Are you from Israel?" And I said to her, "Yes." And she said, "And who is she who brings forth in the cave?" And I said, "My betrothed." And she said to me, "Is she not your wife?" And I said to her, "She is Mary, who was brought up in the temple of the Lord, and I received her by lot as my wife,

and she is not my wife, but she has conceived by the Holy Spirit." And the midwife said to him, "Is this true?" And Joseph said to her, "Come and see." And she went with him.

2 And they stopped at the entrance to the cave, and behold, a bright cloud overshadowed the cave. And the midwife said, "My soul is magnified today, for my eyes have seen wonderful things; for salvation is born to Israel." And immediately the cloud disappeared from the cave and a great light appeared, so that our eyes could not bear it. A short time afterwards that light withdrew until the baby appeared, and it came and took the breast of its mother Mary. And the midwife cried, "This day is great for me, because I have seen this new sight."

3 And the midwife came out of the cave, and Salome met her. And she said to her, "Salome, Salome, I have a new sight to tell you about; a virgin has brought forth, a thing which her condition does not allow." And Salome said, "As the Lord my God lives, unless I insert my finger and test her condition, I will not believe that a virgin has given birth."

20 And the midwife went in and said to Mary, "Make yourself ready, for there is no small contention concerning you". And Salome inserted her finger to test her condition. And she cried out, saying, "Woe for my wickedness and my unbelief; for I have tempted the living God; and behold, my hand falls away from me, consumed by fire!"

2 And she bowed her knees before the Lord saying, "O God of my fathers, remember me; for I am the seed of Abraham, Isaac, and Jacob; do not make me pilloried for the children of Israel, but restore me to the poor. For you know, Lord, that in your name I perform my duties and from you I have received my hire."

3 And behold, an angel of the Lord appeared and said to her, "Salome, Salome, the Lord God has heard your prayer. Bring your hand to the child and touch him and salvation and joy will be yours."

4 And Salome came near and touched him, saying, "I will worship him, for a great king has

been born to Israel." And Salome was healed as she had requested, and she went out of the cave. And, behold, an angel of the Lord cried, "Salome, Salome, do not report what marvels you have seen, until the child has come to Jerusalem."

21 And behold, Joseph was ready to go to Judaea. And there took place a great tumult in Bethlehem of Judaea. For there came wise men saying, "Where is the new-born king of the Jews? For we have seen his star in the east and have come to worship him."[8]

2 When Herod heard this he was troubled and sent officers to the wise men, and sent for the high priests and questioned them, "How is it written concerning the Messiah? Where is he born?" They said to him, "In Bethlehem of Judaea; for thus it is written." And he let them go. And he questioned the wise men and said to them, "What sign did you see concerning the new-born king?" And the wise men said, "We saw how an indescribably greater star among these stars and dimmed them, so that the stars no longer shone; and so we knew that a king was born for Israel. And we have come to worship him." And Herod said, "Go and seek, and when you have found him, tell me, that I also may come to worship him."

3 And the wise men went out. And behold, the star which they had seen in the east went before them until they came to the cave. And it stood over the head of the cave. And the wise men saw the young child with Mary his mother, and they took out of their pouch gifts: gold, and frankincense, and myrrh.

4 And having been warned by the angel that they should not go into Judaea, they went to their own country by another route.

22 But when Herod realized that he had been deceived by the wise men he was angry and sent his murderers and commanded them to kill all the babies who were two years old and under.[9]

2 When Mary heard that the babies were to be killed, she was afraid and took the child and wrapped him in swaddling clothes and laid him in an ox-manger.

3 But Elizabeth, when she heard that John was sought for, took him and went up into the hill-country. And she looked around to see where she could hide him, and there was no hiding-place. And Elizabeth groaned aloud and said, "O mountain of God, receive a mother with a child." For Elizabeth could not ascend. And immediately the mountain was rent asunder and received her. And a light was shining for them; for an angel of the Lord was with them and protected them.

23 Herod was searching for John, and sent officers to Zacharias saying, "Where have you hidden your son?" And he answered and said to them, "I am a minister of God and serve in the temple of the Lord. I do not know where my son is."

2 And the officers departed and told all this to Herod. Then Herod was angry and said, "His son is to be king over Israel!" And he sent to him again saying, "Tell the truth. Where is your son? You know that you are at my mercy." And the officers departed and told him these things.

3 And Zacharias said, "I am a witness of God. Pour out blood! But the Lord will receive my spirit, for you shed innocent blood at the threshold of the temple of the Lord." And about daybreak Zacharias was slain. And the children of Israel did not know that he had been slain.

24 But at the hour of the salutation the priests were departing, and the customary blessing of Zacharias did not take place. And the priests stood waiting for Zacharias, to greet him with prayer and to glorify the Most High.

2 But when he failed to come they were all afraid. But one of them took courage and went in and he saw beside the altar congealed blood; and a voice said, "Zacharias has been slain, and his blood shall not be wiped away until his avenger comes." And when he heard these words, he was afraid and went out and told the priests what he had seen.

---

[8]Matt 2:1–12.
[9]Matt 2:16.

3 And they took courage and entered and saw what had happened. And the ceiling panels of the temple wailed, and they split their clothes from the top to the bottom. And they did not find his body, but they found his blood turned into stone. And they were afraid, and went out and told all the people that Zacharias had been slain. And all the tribes of the people heard and they mourned him and lamented three days and three nights.

4 And after the three days the priests took counsel whom they should appoint in his stead and the lot fell upon Symeon. Now it was he to whom it had been revealed by the Holy Spirit that he should not see death until he had seen the Christ in the flesh.

25 Now I, James, wrote this history in Jerusalem when tumult arose on the death of Herod, and withdrew into the desert until the tumult in Jerusalem ceased. And I praise the Lord God who gave me the wisdom to write this history. Grace shall be with all those who fear our Lord Jesus Christ, to whom be glory for ever and ever, Amen.

40. The Infancy Gospel of Thomas

The "Infancy Gospel of Thomas," not to be confused with the Coptic Gospel of Thomas from Nag Hammadi, is one of the earliest legendary accounts of Jesus' life as a young boy. The author calls himself "Thomas, the Israelite"; it is not clear whether he wanted himself to be recognized as Judas Thomas, allegedly Jesus' twin brother (see the Coptic Gospel of Thomas).

The narrative begins with Jesus as a supernaturally endowed and somewhat mischievous five-year-old. Included are anecdotes of Jesus at play with his childhood companions (sometimes harming them with his divine power, sometimes healing them), in confrontation with his elders (usually bettering them), at school with his teachers (revealing their ignorance), and in the workshop with his father (miraculously correcting his mistakes). For modern readers it is difficult to know whether such stories were meant as serious accounts of Jesus' early years or simply as speculative and entertaining episodes in the life of the youthful Son of God. The book concludes with the story, familiar from the Gospel of Luke, of Jesus as a twelve-year-old in the Temple.

Many scholars believe that such "infancy Gospels" began to circulate during the beginning or middle of the second century; the Infancy Gospel of Thomas may have been one of the earliest among them.

1 I, Thomas the Israelite, announce and make known to all you brethren from the Gentiles the childhood and great deeds of our Lord Jesus Christ, which he did when he was born in our country. This is the beginning.

2 When this child Jesus was five years old, he was playing at the ford of a stream. He made pools of the rushing water and made it immediately pure; he ordered this by word alone.

2 He made soft clay and modeled twelve sparrows from it. It was the Sabbath when he did this. There were many other children playing with him.

3 A certain Jew saw what Jesus did while playing on the Sabbath; he immediately went and announced to his father Joseph, "See, your child is at the stream, and has taken clay and modeled twelve birds; he has profaned the Sabbath."

4 Joseph came to the place, and seeing what Jesus did he cried out, "Why do you do on the Sabbath what it is not lawful to do?" Jesus clapped his hands and cried to the sparrows, "Be gone." And the sparrows flew off chirping.

5 The Jews saw this and were amazed. They went away and described to their leaders what they had seen Jesus do.

3 The son of Annas the scribe was standing there with Joseph. He took a branch of a willow and scattered the water which Jesus had arranged.

2 Jesus saw what he did and became angry and said to him, "You unrighteous, impious ignoramus, what did the pools and the water do to harm you? Behold, you shall also wither as a tree, and you shall not bear leaves nor roots nor fruit."

3 And immediately that child was all withered. Jesus left and went to the house of Joseph. The parents of the withered one bore him away, bemoaning his lost youth. They led him to Joseph and reproached him, "What kind of child do you have who does such things?"

4 Once again he was going through the village, and a child who was running banged into his shoulder. Jesus was angered and said to him, "You shall go no further on your way." And immedi-

ately the child fell down dead. Some people saw this happen and said, "From whence was this child begotten, for his every word is an act accomplished?"

2 The parents of the dead boy went to Joseph and blamed him: "Because you have such a boy, you cannot live with us in the village; your alternative is to teach him to bless and not to curse, for he is killing our children."

5 Joseph took the child aside privately and warned him, saying, "Why do you do such things? These people are suffering and they hate us and are persecuting us!" Jesus said, "I know that these are not your words, but on account of you I will be silent. However, they shall bear their punishment. Immediately, those who accused him were blinded.

2 Those who saw were very frightened and puzzled, and they said about him, "Every word he speaks, whether good or evil, happens and is a miracle." When he saw what Jesus had done, Joseph arose and took hold of Jesus' ear and pulled it hard.

3 The child was angry and said to him, "It is fitting for you to seek and not find. You have acted very stupidly. Do you not know I am yours? Do not vex me."

6 A man named Zaccheus, a teacher, was standing there and he heard, in part, Jesus saying these things to his father. He was greatly astonished that he said such things, since he was just a child.

2 And after a few days he approached Joseph and said to him. "You have a smart child, and he has a mind. Come, hand him over to me so that he may learn writing. I will give him all understanding with the letters, and teach him to greet all the elders and to honor them as grandfathers and fathers and to love his peers."

3 He told him all the letters from the Alpha to the Omega plainly, with much discussion. But Jesus looked at Zaccheus the teacher, and said to him, "You do not know the Alpha according to nature, how do you teach others the Beta? You hypocrite! First, if you know it, teach the Alpha, then we shall believe you about the Beta." Then

he began to question the teacher about the first letter and he could not answer him.

4 Many heard as the child said to Zaccheus, "Listen, teacher, to the order of the first element, and pay attention to this, how it has lines, and a central mark which goes through the two lines you see, (they) converge, go up, again come to head, become the same three times, subordinate, and hypostatic, isometric . . . [The text is unreliable.] You now have the lines of Alpha."

7 When the teacher, Zaccheus, heard so many such allegories of the first letter spoken by the child, he was puzzled about such expoundings and his teaching. He said to those present, "Woe is me, I am wretched and puzzled; I have shamed myself trying to handle this child.

2 "I beg you, brother Joseph, take him away. I cannot bear the severity of his glance. I cannot understand his speech at all. This child is not earthborn; he is able to tame even fire. Perhaps he was begotten before the world's creation. What belly bore him, what womb nurtured him, I do not know. Woe is me, friend, he completely confuses me. I cannot follow his understanding. I have fooled myself; I am thrice wretched. I worked anxiously to have a disciple, and I found myself with a teacher.

3 "I consider my shame, friends; I am an old man and have been conquered by a child; for at this hour I cannot look into his gaze. When they all say that I have been conquered by a little child, what can I say? What can I discuss about the lines of the first element he spoke to me? I do not know, O friends, for I do not know its beginning and end. Therefore, I beg you, brother Joseph, take him into your house. He is something great: a God, an angel, or what I should say I do not know."

8 While the Jews were comforting Zaccheus, the child gave a great laugh, saying, "Now let what is yours bear fruit, and the blind in heart see. I am from above in order that I may curse them and call them into the things which are above, because he who sent me on your account ordered it."

2 And as the child ceased talking, immediately all those who had fallen under his curse were saved (or, healed). And after that no one dared to anger him, lest he should curse him, and he should be crippled.

9 After some days Jesus was playing upstairs in a certain house, and one of the children playing with him fell from the house and died. And when the other children saw this they ran away, and Jesus remained alone.

2 The parents of the dead child came and accused Jesus of throwing him down. Jesus replied, "I did not throw him down." But still they accused him.

3 Then Jesus leaped down from the roof and stood by the body of the child and cried out in a great voice, saying "Zenon!"—that was his name—"rise up and tell me, did I throw you down?" He immediately rose up and said: "No, Lord, you did not throw me down, but you raised me." Those who saw this were astonished. The parents of the child glorified God because of this sign that happened, and they worshipped Jesus.

10 After a few days a young man was splitting wood in the vicinity; the axe fell and split the bottom of his foot, and he was bleeding to death.

2 There was an outcry and people gathered. The child Jesus ran there. He pushed through the crowd, and seized the injured foot of the youth; immediately he was healed. He said to the youth, "Now get up, split your wood, and remember me." The crowd, seeing what had happened, worshiped the child, saying, "Truly, the Spirit of God lives in this child!"

11 When he was six, his mother sent him to draw water and to bring it into the house, giving him a pitcher. But in the crowd, he had a collision; the water jug was broken.

2 Jesus spread out the garment he had on, filled it with water, and bore it to his mother. When his mother saw the miracle she kissed him, and she kept to herself the mysteries which she saw him do.

12 Again, during planting time the child went with his father to sow seed in their field. While they planted, his father sowed, and the child Jesus planted one grain of wheat.

2 When he had reaped and threshed it, it yielded one hundred measures, and he called all the poor of the village to the threshing floor and gave them the grain. Joseph took the remainder of the grain. He was eight when he did this sign.

13 His father was a carpenter and at that time made ploughs and yokes. He received an order from a certain rich man to make a bed for him. One beam came out shorter than the other, and he did not know what to do. The child Jesus said to Joseph his father, "Lay the two pieces of wood alongside each other, and make them even at one end."

2 Joseph did as the child told him. Jesus stood at the other end and grasped the shorter beam; he stretched it and made it equal with the other. His father Joseph saw and was astonished, and embracing the child he kissed him and said, "I am blessed because God has given this child to me."

14 When Joseph saw the mind and age of the child, that he was growing up, he again wished him not to be ignorant of letters. And he took him and gave him to another teacher. But the teacher said to Joseph, "First I will teach him Greek, and then Hebrew." For the teacher knew the child's learning and feared him. Nevertheless he wrote the alphabet and taught him for many hours, but Jesus did not answer him.

2 Then Jesus said to him, "If you really are a teacher, and you know the letters well, tell me the power of Alpha and I will tell you that of Beta." The teacher was angered and hit Jesus on the head. The child was hurt and cursed him. Immediately the teacher fainted, falling to the ground upon his face.

3 The child returned to the house of Joseph. But Joseph was grief-stricken and gave this order to his mother: "Do not let him go outside the door, because anyone who angers him dies."

15 After some time there was another teacher, a good friend of Joseph. He said to him, "Bring the child to me at school, maybe by flattery I can teach him letters." Joseph said, "If you dare, brother, take him with you." He took him with fear and much anxiety, but the child went with pleasure.

2 Jesus went boldly into the school and found a book lying on the lectern, and taking it, did not read the letters in it, but opened his mouth and spoke by the Holy Spirit and taught the Law to those standing nearby. A great crowd gathered and stood listening to him. They were astonished at the beauty of his teaching and the eloquence of his words, that being a babe he could say such things.

3 Joseph heard and was frightened. He ran into the school, wondering whether this teacher was also without skill, but the teacher said to Joseph, "Know, brother, that I took the child as a disciple, but he is full of much grace and wisdom, and I beg you brother, take him into your house."

4 When the child heard this, immediately he smiled at him and said, "Since you spoke correctly and witnessed correctly, on account of you the one who was stricken shall be healed." And immediately the other teacher was healed. Joseph took the child and returned home.

16 Joseph sent his son James to gather wood and to bring it into the house. The child Jesus followed him. While James was gathering the sticks, a snake bit James's hand.

2 As he lay dying, Jesus came near and breathed on the bite. Immediately James ceased suffering, the snake burst, and James was healed.

17 After this, in the neighborhood of Joseph a certain child took sick and died. His mother wept bitterly. Jesus, hearing the great mourning and clamor, ran quickly and found the child dead. He touched his breast and said, "I say to you, child, do not die, but live and be with your mother!" And immediately the child looked up and laughed. Jesus said to the woman, "Pick him up and give him milk, and remember me."

2 The crowd standing around saw and was amazed, and they said, "Truly this child is a God or an angel of God, because his every word becomes a finished deed." And Jesus left there and played with the other children.

18 After some time a house was being built and there was a great clamor. Jesus arose and went there. Seeing a man lying dead he took his hand and said, "I say to you, man, arise, to your work!" And immediately he arose and worshiped him.

2 Seeing this, the crowd was astonished and said, "This is a heavenly child, for he saved many souls from death, and can save them all his life."

19 When he was twelve his parents, according to custom, went to Jerusalem to the Passover with their traveling companions. After the Passover they returned to their home. While they were going home, the child Jesus went back to Jerusalem. His parents thought that he was in the caravan.

2 After a day's travel, they sought him among their kinfolk and when they did not find him they were troubled. They returned again to the city to seek him. After three days they found him in the Temple, seated in the midst of the teachers, listening and questioning them. They all were attentive and amazed at how he, being a child, could argue with the elders and teachers of the people, solving the chief problems of the Law and the parables of the prophets.

3 His mother, Mary, came up and said to him, "How can you have done this to us, child? Behold, we have looked everywhere for you, grieving." And Jesus said to them, "Why did you look for me? Do you not know that I must be in my Father's house?"

4 The scribes and Pharisees said, "Are you the mother of this child?" She said, "I am." They said to her, "You are blessed among women, because God has blessed the fruit of your womb. We have never before seen or heard such glory or such excellence and wisdom."

5 Jesus arose and followed his mother and was obedient to his parents. But his mother kept (in her heart) all that had happened. Jesus grew in wisdom and stature and grace. Glory be to him forever and ever. Amen.

>—+—◇—<◇>—+—<

41. The Epistle of the Apostles

Completely unknown until the end of the nineteenth century, when a Coptic version of it was uncovered in Cairo, the "Epistle of the Apostles" gives a dialogue that Jesus allegedly had with his eleven remaining disciples after his resurrection (Judas having already hanged himself), which is then passed along by them in a letter, written in the first person, to Christians around the world. The so-called "postresurrection dialogue" was a genre highly favored among Gnostics (see the "Wisdom of Jesus Christ" in Chapter 6). But the orientation of this particular book is completely anti-gnostic. In particular, it seeks to counter the views of Simon Magus and Cerinthus, two Gnostics most despised among the heresiologists of the second century, by insisting on the fleshly nature of Christ's body, the reality of his incarnation, death, resurrection, and future return in glory, and the importance of his followers' fleshly existence in this world and in the world to come (see Chapter 6).

The "Epistle of the Apostles," from *New Testament Apocrypha*, vol. 1, ed. Wilhelm Schneemelcher, 2d ed. Cambridge/Louisville: Lutterworth Press/Westminster John Knox Press, 1991. Used with permission of Lutterworth Press and Westminster John Knox Press.

The nature of its argument and the opponents that it names suggests that the book was written some time in the mid-second century. Originally penned in Greek, the text is now preserved only in other languages; the following excerpt is drawn from the Ethiopic translation.

1 What Jesus Christ revealed to his disciples as a letter, and how Jesus Christ revealed the letter of the council of the apostles, the disciples of Jesus Christ, to the Catholics; which was written because of the false apostles Simon and Cerinthus, that no one should follow them—for in them is deceit with which they kill people—that you may be established and not waver, not be shaken, and not turn away from the word of the Gospel that you have heard. As we have heard (it), kept (it), and have written (it) for the whole world, so we entrust (it) to you, our sons and daughters, in joy and in the name of God the Father, the ruler of the world, and in Jesus Christ. May grace increase upon you.

2 (We,) John and Thomas and Peter and Andrew and James and Philip and Bartholomew and Matthew and Nathanael and Judas Zelotes and Cephas, we have written to the churches of the East and West, towards North and South, recounting and proclaiming to you concerning our Lord Jesus Christ, as we have written; and we have heard and felt him after he had risen from the dead; and how he has revealed to us things great, astonishing, real. . . .

6 And these things our Lord and Savior revealed and showed to us, and likewise we to you, that you, reflecting upon eternal life, may be associates in the grace of the Lord and in our service and in our glory. Be firm, without wavering, in the knowledge and investigation of our Lord Jesus Christ, and he will prove gracious and will save always in all never-ending eternity.

7 Cerinthus and Simon have come to go through the world. But they are enemies of our Lord Jesus Christ, who in reality alienate those who believe in the true word and deed, namely Jesus Christ. Therefore take care and beware of them,

for in them is affliction and contamination and death, the end of which will be destruction and judgment.

8 Because of that we have not hesitated with the true testimony of our Lord and Savior Jesus Christ, how he acted while we saw him, and how he constantly both explained and caused our thoughts within us.

9 He of whom we are witnesses we know as the one crucified in the days of Pontius Pilate and of the prince Archelaus, who was crucified between two thieves;[1] and was taken down from the wood of the cross together with them; and he was buried in a place which is called the place of the skull, to which three women came, Sarah, Martha, and Mary Magdalene. They carried ointment to pour out upon his body, weeping and mourning over what had happened. And they approached the tomb and found the stone where it had been rolled away from the tomb, and they opened the door and did not find his body.

10 And as they were mourning and weeping, the Lord appeared to them and said to them, "Do not weep; I am he whom you seek. But let one of you go to your brothers and say to them, 'Come, our Master has risen from the dead.' "

And Mary came to us and told us. And we said to her, "What have we to do with you, O woman? He that is dead and buried, can he then live?" And we did not believe her, that our Savior had risen from the dead.

Then she went back to our Lord and said to him, "None of them believed me concerning your resurrection." And he said to her, "Let another one of you go saying this again to them." And Sarah came and gave us the same news, and we

---

[1]Matt 27–28; Mark 15–16; Luke 23–24; John 19–21.

accused her of lying. And she returned to our Lord and spoke to him as Mary had.

11 And then the Lord said to Mary and to her sisters, "Let us go to them." And he came and found us inside, veiled. And we doubted and did not believe. He came before us like a ghost and we did not believe that it was he. But it was he. And thus he said to us. "Come, and do not be afraid. I am your teacher whom you, Peter, denied three times before the cock crowed, and now do you deny again?" And we went to him, thinking and doubting whether it was he. And he said to us, "Why do you doubt and why are you not believing that I am he who spoke to you concerning my flesh, my death, and my resurrection? And that you may know that it is I, lay your hand, Peter (and your finger) in the nailprint of my hands; and you, Thomas, in my side; and also you, Andrew, see whether my foot steps on the ground and leaves a footprint. For it is written: 'But a ghost, a demon, leaves no print on the ground.' "

12 But now we felt him, that he had truly risen in the flesh. And then we fell on our faces before him, asked him for pardon, and entreated him because we had not believed him. Then our Lord and Savior said to us, "Stand up and I will reveal to you what is on earth, and what is above heaven, and your resurrection that is in the kingdom of heaven, concerning which my Father has sent me, that I may take up you and those who believe in me."

13 And what he revealed is this, as he said to us, "While I was coming from the Father of all, passing by the heavens, wherein I put on the wisdom of the Father and by his power clothed myself in his power, I was like the heavens. And passing by the angels and archangels in their form and as one of them, I passed by the orders, dominions, and princes, possessing the measure of the wisdom of the Father who sent me. And the archangels Michael and Gabriel, Raphael and Uriel followed me until the fifth firmament of heaven, while I appeared as one of them. This kind of power was given me by the Father. Then I made the archangels to become distracted with

the voice and go up to the altar of the Father and serve the Father in their work until I should return to him. I did this thus in the likeness of his wisdom. For I became all in all with them, that I, fulfilling the will of the mercy of the Father and the glory of him who sent me, might return to him.

14 "Do you know that the angel Gabriel came and brought the message to Mary?" And we said to him, "Yes, O Lord." And he answered and said to us, "Do you not remember that I previously said to you that I became like an angel to the angels?" And we said to him, "Yes, O Lord." And he said to us, "At that time I appeared in the form of the archangel Gabriel to the virgin Mary and spoke with her, and her heart received (me); she believed and laughed; and I, the Word, went into her and became flesh; and I myself was servant for myself; and in the likeness of an angel, like him will I do, and after it I will go to my Father."

15 "And you therefore celebrate the remembrance of my death, which is the Passover; the one who stands beside me will be thrown into prison for my name's sake, and he will be very grieved and sorrowful, for while you celebrate the passover he who is in custody did not celebrate it with you. And I will send my power in the form of (my) angel, and the door of the prison will open, and he will come out and come to you to watch with you and to rest. And when you complete my Agape and my remembrance at the crowing of the cock, he will again be taken and thrown in prison for a testimony, until he comes out to preach, as I have commanded you." And we said to him, "O Lord, have you then not completed the drinking of the passover? Must we, then, do it again?" And he said to us, "Yes, until I come from the Father with my wounds."

16 And we said to him, "O Lord, great is this that you say and reveal to us. In what kind of power and form are you about to come?" And he said to us, "Truly I say to you, I will come as the sun which bursts forth; thus will I, shining seven times brighter than it in glory, while I am carried on the wings of the clouds in splendor with my cross going on before me, come to the earth to judge the living and the dead."

17 And we said to him, "O Lord, how many years yet?" And he said to us, "When the hundred and fiftieth year is completed, between pentecost and passover will the coming of my Father take place." And we said to him, "O Lord, now you said to us, 'I will come,' and then you said, 'he who sent me will come.' " And he said to us, "I am wholly in the Father and the Father in me."[2] Then we said to him, "Will you really leave us until your coming? Where will we find a teacher?" And he answered and said to us, "Do you not know that until now I am both here and there with him who sent me?" And we said to him, "O Lord, is it possible that you should be both here and there?" And he said to us, "I am wholly in the Father and the Father in me after his image and after his likeness and after his power and after his perfection and after his light, and I am his perfect word."

18 This is, when he was crucified, had died and risen again, as he said this, and the work that was thus accomplished in the flesh, that he was crucified, and his ascension—this is the fulfilling of the number. "And the wonders and his image and everything perfect you will see in me with respect to redemption which takes place through me, and while I go to the Father and into heaven. . . ."

23 And we said again to him, "O Lord, but it is necessary, since you have commanded us to preach, prophesy, and teach, that we, having heard accurately from you, may be good preachers and may teach them, that they may believe in you. Therefore we question you."

24 He answered and said to us, "Truly I say to you, the flesh of every one will rise with his soul alive and his spirit." And we said to him, "O Lord, then can what is departed and scattered become alive? Not as if we deny it do we ask; rather we believe that what you say has happened and will happen." And he said to us, being angry, "You of little faith, how long yet do you ask me? And inquire (only) without anguish after what you wish to hear.

"Keep my commandments, and do what I tell you, without delay and without reserve and without respect of persons; serve in the strait, direct, and narrow way. And thereby will the Father in every respect rejoice concerning you."

25 And we said again to him, "O Lord, look; we have you to derision with the many questions." And he said to us, "I know that in faith and with your whole heart you question me. And I am glad because of you. Truly I say to you I am pleased, and my Father in me rejoices, that you thus inquire and ask. Your boldness makes me rejoice, and it affords yourselves life." And when he had said this to us, we were glad, for he had spoken to us in gentleness. And we said again to him, "Our Lord, in all things you have shown yourself gracious toward us and grant us life; for all we have asked you you have told us." Then he said to us, "Does the flesh or the spirit fall away?" And we said to him, "The flesh." And he said to us, "Now what has fallen will arise, and what is ill will be sound, that my Father may be praised therein; as he has done to me, so I (will do) to you and to all who believe in me.

26 "Truly I say to you, the flesh will rise with the soul, that they may confess and be judged with the work which they have done, whether it is there may be a selection and exhibition for those who have believed and have done the commandment of my Father who sent me. Then will the righteous judgment take place; for thus my Father wills, and he said to me, 'My son, on the day of judgment you will not fear the rich and not spare the poor; rather deliver each one to eternal punishment according to his sins.' But to those who have loved me and do love me and who have done my commandment I will grant rest in life in the kingdom of my heavenly Father."

---

[2]John 10:38; 14:10–21.

APOCRYPHAL ACTS: THE TEXTS

(See also the Acts of John and the Acts of Thomas in Chapter 1)

In addition to extracanonical accounts of Jesus' words and deeds, we have numerous accounts of the activities and experiences of his apostles after his death. Some of these may have been modeled on the canonical Acts of the Apostles, but in most instances the noncanonical accounts concern the missionary exploits of only one or the other of the apostolic band, such Thomas, Peter, or John. It is difficult, in most instances, to determine the theological proclivities of these accounts: their allusions to doctrine often defy any clear classification into "gnostic" or "docetic" or "proto-orthodox." To be sure, many of them do appear to be written for didactic or hortatory purposes—for example, to urge a life of strict asceticism or the need of martyrdom—and not infrequently they push for one doctrinal idea or another. But by and large these works appear to be chiefly intent on providing entertaining accounts of the miraculous lives of Jesus' apostles, their passion for spreading the gospel, and the supernatural support they receive from God himself in exchange for their devotion to his work.

42. The Acts of Peter

Closely related to the tales about Peter found in the "Homilies of Clement" (see Chapter 6), the Acts of Peter provides a number of entertaining accounts of the escapades of the leader of the apostles, including several of his sermons and a number of his miracles. Much of the narrative concerns a series of contests between Peter and his nemesis, the Satanically inspired sorcerer Simon Magus, who presents himself as the true representative of God on earth. The same Simon is elsewhere portrayed as the first Gnostic and arch-heretic (see, e.g., the Epistle of the Apostles, reading 41), although here there is less attention paid to his theology than to his claims of divine superiority. These claims are completely refuted by Peter, who through the true power of God is able to make dogs and newborns speak and to restore smoked tunas and dead people to life. The contests reach a climax in a passage not excerpted here, when Simon uses his powers to fly like a bird over the temples and hills of Rome; Peter responds by

The "Acts of Peter," from *The Apocryphal New Testament*, ed. J. K. Elliott. © Oxford University Press, 1993. Reprinted by permission of Oxford University Press.

calling upon God to smite him in midair. When Simon crashes to the ground, the crowds, convinced of Peter's superior power, rush to the scene to stone Simon and leave him for dead.

This account appears to have been in circulation some time before the end of the second century.

4 After a few days there was a great commotion in the congregation, for some said that they had seen things done by a man named Simon, who was at Aricia. They also added, "He claims to be the great power of God, doing nothing without God. Is he then Christ? We, however, believe in him whom Paul has preached to us. For through him we saw the dead raised and some healed from various diseases. This power seeks conflicts, we know. For it is no small disturbance that has come upon us. Perhaps he has already come to Rome. For yesterday he was invited with great acclamation to do so, being told, 'You are God in Italy, you are the savior of the Romans; hasten to Rome as quickly as possible.' And Simon addressed the people and said with a shrill voice, 'On the following day about the seventh hour you shall see me fly over the gate of the city in the same form in which I now speak to you.' Wherefore, brethren, if you agree, let us go and diligently await the end of the matter." And they all went out and came to the gate. About the seventh hour there suddenly appeared afar off a dust-cloud in the sky, looking like smoke shining with a glare of fire. And when it reached the gate it suddenly disappeared. Then he appeared standing in the midst of the people. They all worshipped him and knew that it was he whom they had seen the day before. And the brethren were exceedingly disturbed, especially as Paul was not at Rome, nor Timothy and Barnabas, whom Paul had sent to Macedonia, nor anyone who could strengthen us (sic) in the faith, especially the neophytes. As Simon's authority grew more and more, some of those among whom he worked in their daily conversations called Paul a sorcerer and a deceiver and all of the great multitude which had been confirmed in the faith were led astray, excepting the presbyter Narcissus, and two women in the hospice of the Bithynians, and four others who could not leave their house;

and day and night they entreated the Lord either that Paul might return as soon as possible or that some one else might come to care for his servants, whom the devil by his wickedness had perverted.

5 While they were grieving and fasting God was already preparing Peter at Jerusalem for the future. After the twelve years had passed, according to the direction of the Lord to Peter, Christ showed to him the following vision, saying, "Peter, Simon, whom you expelled from Judaea after having exposed him as a magician, has forestalled you at Rome. And in short, all who believed in me he has perverted by the cunning and power of Satan, whose agent he proves to be. But do not delay. Go tomorrow to Caesarea, and there you will find a ship ready to sail to Italy. And within a few days I will show you my grace which is boundless." Instructed by this vision, Peter did not delay to mention it to the brethren and said, "I must go up to Rome to subdue the enemy and opponent of the Lord and of our brethren." And he went down to Caesarea and at once boarded the ship, which was ready to sail, without having obtained for himself any provisions. But the steersman, named Theon, looked at Peter and said, "What we have belongs to you. For what grace is it for us in receiving a man like ourselves in difficult circumstances, without sharing with him what we have? Let us have a safe journey." Peter thanked him for his offer. And he fasted in the ship, being dejected, and yet again comforted because God regarded him as a servant worthy of his service. A few days later the captain got up at meal time and asked Peter to eat with him, saying to him, "Whoever you are, I hardly know you. You are either a God or a man. But as far as I can see, I think that you are a servant of God. As I was steering my ship in the middle of the night I fell asleep. It seemed to me as if a human voice from heaven

said to me, "Theon, Theon!" Twice it called me by name and said to me, 'Amongst all the passengers treat Peter in the most honorable way. For, with his help, you and the rest will escape safe from an unexpected incident.'" Peter, however, thinking that God wished to show his providence to all those who were in the ship, began at once to speak to Theon of the great deeds of God, and how the Lord had chosen him among the apostles and for what cause he was sailing to Italy. Daily he spoke to him the word of God. After they had become better acquainted Peter found out that Theon was one with him in the faith and a worthy servant. When the ship was detained by the calm of the Adriatic Sea, Theon remarked on the calm to Peter and said, "If you think me worthy to be baptized with the sign of the Lord, you have the chance now." All the others in the ship were in a drunken stupor. Peter let himself down by a rope and baptized Theon in the name of the Father and of the Son and of the Holy Spirit. He came up out of the water rejoicing with great joy. Peter also had become more cheerful because God had deemed Theon worthy of his name. And it happened that in the same place where Theon was baptized, a young man, radiant in splendor, appeared and said to them, "Peace be with you." And both Peter and Theon immediately went up and entered the cabin; and Peter took bread and gave thanks to the Lord, who had deemed him worthy of his holy service, and because a young man had appeared to them saying, "Peace be with you." Peter said, "Most excellent and the only Holy One, for you appeared to us, O God Jesus Christ. In your name I have spoken, and he was signed with your holy sign. Therefore also I give to him, in your name, your eucharist, that he may for ever be your servant, perfect and without blemish." When they were eating and rejoicing in the Lord, suddenly a moderate wind, not a violent one, arose at the prow of the ship and lasted six days and six nights till they came to Puteoli.

6 Having landed at Puteoli, Theon left the ship and went to the inn where he usually stayed, to make preparations for the reception of Peter. The inn-keeper's name was Ariston, a God-fearing man, and to him he went for the sake of the Name. And when he had come to the inn and found Ariston, Theon said to him, "God, who counted you worthy to serve him, has also made known to me his grace through his holy servant Peter, who has just arrived with me from Judaea, being bidden by our Lord to go to Italy." When Ariston heard this, he fell upon Theon's neck, embraced him and asked him to bring him to the ship and show Peter to him. For Ariston said, "Since Paul has gone to Spain there was not one of the brethren who could strengthen me. Besides, a certain Jew named Simon has invaded the city. By means of his magical sayings and his wickedness he has completely perverted the entire fraternity, so that I have fled from Rome hoping for the arrival of Peter. For Paul had spoken of him, and I saw many things in a vision. Now I believe in my Lord, that he will again establish his ministry, that all deception be extinguished from his servants. For our Lord Jesus Christ is faithful, and he can renew our thoughts." When Theon heard this from the weeping Ariston, his confidence was restored, and he was even more strengthened in his faith, knowing that he believed in the living God. When they came to the ship, Peter saw them and, filled with the Spirit, he smiled, so that Ariston fell upon his face to the feet of Peter and said, "Brother and Lord, who makes known the sacred mysteries and teaches the right way, which is in the Lord Jesus Christ, our God, through you he has shown us his coming. All whom Paul entrusted to us we have lost through the power of Satan. But now I trust in the Lord, who sent his messenger and told you to hasten to us, that he has deemed us worthy to see his great and wonderful deeds done by your hands. I therefore beg you, come quickly to the city. For I left the brethren who had stumbled, whom I saw fall into the snares of the devil, and fled here saying to them, 'Brethren, stand firm in the faith; for it is to be that within the next two months the mercy of our Lord will bring you his servant.' I saw a vision of Paul speaking to me and saying, 'Ariston, flee from the city.' Having heard this, I believed without wavering, departed from the city in the Lord, and though the flesh which I bear is weak, yet I came here, stood daily by the shore, and asked the sailors, 'Has Peter come with you?' And now that the grace of the Lord abounds, I beseech you to go up to Rome without delay, lest the teaching of the wicked man increases still more." When Ariston had spoken amidst tears Peter gave him his hand and lifted him up from the ground, and said with tears and sighs, "He who tempts the world by his angels forestalled us; but he who has the power to deliver his servants from all temptation will destroy his deceits and put them under the feet of those who believe in Christ, whom we preach." And when they entered by the gate Theon entreated Peter and said, "During the long sea voyage you never refreshed yourself on the ship, and now will you go from the ship on such a rough road? No, stay, refresh yourself and then go. From here to Rome the road is rocky, and I fear you might hurt yourself with the shaking." But Peter answered and said to them, "But what would have happened if about my neck and that of the enemy of the Lord a millstone were hanged (as my Lord said to us, if any one should offend one of the brethren[1]), and we be drowned in the depths of the sea? Not only would it be a millstone, but what is worse, I the opponent of this persecutor of his servants would die far away from those who have believed in the Lord Jesus Christ." In no way could Theon persuade him to remain a day longer. Whereupon Theon gave everything that was in the ship to be sold at a fair price, and followed Peter to Rome, and accompanied Ariston to the house of the presbyter Narcissus.

7 Soon it became known among the scattered brethren of the city that Peter had come to Rome on account of Simon, to prove that he was a seducer and persecutor of the good. And the whole multitude came together to see the apostle of the Lord, confirming the congregation in Christ. When they gathered on the first day of the week to meet Peter he began to speak with a loud voice, "You people who are here, hoping in Christ, you who suffered a brief temptation, learn why God sent his Son into the world, or why he begot him by the virgin Mary, if it were not to dispense some mercy or means of salvation. For he meant to an-

nul every offence and every ignorance and every activity of the devil, his instigations and powers, by means of which he once had the upper hand, before our God shone forth in the world. Since with their many and manifold weaknesses they fell to death by their ignorance, Almighty God had compassion and sent his Son into the world, and I was with him. And I walked on the water and survive as a witness; I confess I was there when he was at work in the world performing signs and wonders. Dearest brethren, I denied our Lord Jesus Christ, not once, but thrice; for those who ensnared me were wicked gods, just as the prophet of the Lord said. But the Lord did not lay it to my charge; he turned to me and had mercy on the weakness of my flesh, so that I wept bitterly; and I mourned for my little faith, having been deceived by the devil and disobeyed the word of my Lord. And now I tell you, men and brethren, who are convened in the name of Jesus Christ, Satan the deceiver sends his arrows upon you too, to make you leave the way. But do not be disloyal, brethren, nor fail in your mind, but strengthen yourselves, stand fast, and doubt not. For if Satan has subverted me, whom the Lord esteemed so highly, so that I denied the light of my hope, causing me to fall and persuading me to flee as if I believed in a man, what do you think will happen to you, who have just become converted? Do you imagine that he will not subvert you to make you enemies of the Kingdom of God and to bring you by the worst error into perdition? For every one whom he deprives of the hope in our Lord Jesus Christ is a child of perdition for all eternity. Repent, therefore, brethren whom the Lord has chosen, and be firmly established in the Almighty Lord, the Father of our Lord Jesus Christ, whom no one has ever seen nor can see except he who believes in him. Understand whence the temptation has come for you. For I came not only for the sake of convincing you with words that he whom I preach is the Christ, but by reason of miraculous deeds and powers I exhort you by faith in Jesus Christ. Let no one wait for another savior besides

---

[1]Matt 18:6.

him who was despised and whom the Jews reviled, this crucified Nazarene, who died and rose again on the third day."

8 The brethren repented and asked Peter to overcome Simon's claim that he was the power of God. Simon was staying at the house of the senator Marcellus whom he had won over by his magic. "Believe us, brother Peter", they said, "none among humans was so wise as this Marcellus. All the widows who hoped in Christ took their refuge in him; all the orphans were fed by him. Will you know more, brother? All the poor called Marcellus their patron; his house was called the house of the pilgrims and poor. To him the emperor said, 'I will give you no office, lest you rob the provinces to benefit the Christians.' To this Marcellus replied, 'Yet everything that is mine is yours.' Caesar said to him, 'It would be mine if you kept it for me, but now it is not mine, since you give it to whom you please, and who knows to what low people?' This, brother Peter, we know and report to you, now that the great benevolence of the man has been turned into blasphemy. For had he not been changed we certainly should not have left the holy faith in God our Lord. Now this Marcellus is enraged and repents of his good deeds and says, 'So much wealth have I spent for such a long time in the foolish belief that I spent it for the knowledge of God.' In his rage he even goes so far that when a pilgrim comes to the door of his house he beats him with a stick or has him driven off and says, 'If only I had not spent so much money on those imposters!' And he utters many more blasphemies. But if you have something of the compassion of our Lord in you and the goodness of his commandments, help this man in his error for he has shown goodness to a great many of God's servants." When Peter learned this he was very greatly moved and said, "Oh, the manifold arts and temptations of the devil! Oh, the cunnings and devices of the evil one, treasuring up to himself the great fire in the day of wrath, destruction of simple people, a ravening wolf devouring and destroying eternal life! You enticed the first man to evil lust and by your former wickedness and bodily bond bound him to you.

You are the fruit of bitterness, which is entirely bitter, inducing various desires. You have forced my fellow disciple and co-apostle Judas to act wickedly and betray our Lord Jesus Christ; you must be punished. You hardened the heart of Herod and kindled Pharaoh and made him fight against Moses, the holy servant of God; you emboldened Caiaphas to deliver our Lord Jesus Christ to the cruel multitude; and now you are still firing your poisonous arrows at innocent souls. You wicked foe of all, you shall be cursed from the church of the Son of the holy, almighty God and extinguished like a firebrand thrown from the fireplace by the servants of our Lord Jesus Christ. Let your blackness turn against you and against your sons, the wicked seed; let your wickedness turn against you, also your threats, and let your temptations turn against you and your angels, you beginning of iniquity, abyss of darkness! Let the darkness which you have be with you and your vessels which you own. Depart, therefore, from those who shall believe in God; depart from the servants of Christ and from those who will serve in his army. Keep for yourself your garments of darkness; without cause you knock at strange doors which belong not to you but to Christ Jesus who keeps them. For you, ravening wolf, will carry off the sheep which do not belong to you but to Christ Jesus, who keeps them with the greatest diligence."

9 When Peter had spoken with great sorrow of soul many more believers were added to the congregation. And the brethren entreated Peter to fight with Simon and not allow him to disturb the people any longer. And without delay Peter left the meeting and went to the house of Marcellus where Simon was staying. And a great multitude followed him. When he came to the door he summoned the keeper and said to him, "Go and tell Simon, 'Peter, on whose account you left Judaea, awaits you at the door!'" The door-keeper answered and said to Peter, "I do not know, sir, if you are Peter. But I have instructions. Knowing that you arrived yesterday in the city, he said to me, 'Whether he comes in the day or at night or at whatever hour, say that I am not at home.'" But

Peter said to the young man, "You were right to tell me this, although you have been forced by him not to tell me." And Peter, turning around to the people, who followed him, said, "You are about to see a great and wonderful sign." And Peter saw a big dog, tied by a big chain, and he went and loosened him. The dog, being loosed, became endowed with a human voice and said to Peter, "What will you have me do, servant of the ineffable living God?" to which Peter said, "Go inside and tell Simon in the presence of the people, 'Peter sends word to you to come outside. For on your account I have come to Rome, you wicked man and destroyer of simple souls.'" And the dog ran away at once and went into the midst of the people who were with Simon, and lifting his front legs he said with a very loud voice, "Simon, Peter, who stands at the door, bids you to come outside in public; for he says 'On your account have I come to Rome, you wicked man and destroyer of simple souls.'" When Simon heard this and saw the incredible occurrence he lost the words with which he was deceiving the onlookers, and all were amazed.

10 When Marcellus saw this he ran outside and fell down before Peter and said, "Peter, holy servant of the holy God, I embrace your feet. I have committed many sins; do not punish my sins if you have some true faith in Christ, whom you preach. If you remember the commandments, to hate none, to do no evil to anyone, as I have learned from your fellow-apostle Paul, do not consider my sins but pray for me to the Lord, the holy Son of God, whom I angered by persecuting his servants. Pray, therefore, for me, like a good advocate of God, that I may not be given over with the sins of Simon to the everlasting fire. For by his persuasion it came about that I erected a statue to him with the following inscription: 'To Simon, the young god.' If I knew, Peter, that you could be won over with money I would give you all my property. I would give it to you, to save my soul. If I had sons I would esteem them for nothing if only I could believe in the living God. I confess, however, that he seduced me only because he said that he was the power of

God. Nevertheless I will tell you, dearest Peter: I was not worthy to hear you, servant of God, and I was not firmly established in the belief in God which is in Christ: for this reason I was made to stumble. I pray you, therefore, be not angry at what I am about to say. Christ our Lord, whom you preach in truth, said to your fellow-apostles in your presence, 'If you have faith like a grain of mustard-seed, you will say to this mountain: Remove yourself, and at once it shall move.'[2] But this Simon called you, Peter, an unbeliever, because you lost faith on the water. And I heard that he also said, 'Those who are with me understood me not.' If, therefore, you, upon whom he laid his hands, whom he has also chosen, with whom he even performed miraculous deeds—if you doubted, therefore I also repent, and relying upon his testimony I resort to your intercession. Receive me, who have fallen away from our Lord and his promise. But I believe that by repenting he will have mercy on me. For the Almighty is faithful to forgive my sins." And Peter said with a loud voice, "Glory and praise be unto our Lord, Almighty God, Father of our Lord Jesus Christ. To you be praise and honor for ever and ever. Amen. Since you have now fully strengthened us and fully established us in you in the sight of all who see it, holy Lord, confirm Marcellus and give him and his house your peace today. But all who are lost or erring, you alone can restore. We worship you, O Lord, the Shepherd of the sheep which once were scattered, but now will be brought together through you. So receive Marcellus also as one of your sheep, and do not permit him to walk about any longer in error or in ignorance but receive him among the number of your sheep. Yes, Lord, receive him, since he beseeches you with sorrow and with tears."

11 Having thus spoken, and having embraced Marcellus, Peter turned to the multitude who stood beside him, when he saw one man laughing, in whom was a very bad devil. Peter said to him, "Whoever you are who have been laughing, show yourself in public." When the

---

[2]Matt 17:20.

young man heard this he ran into the courtyard of the house, cried with a loud voice, threw himself against the wall, and said, "Peter, there is a mighty contest between Simon and the dog, which you sent inside. For Simon says to the dog, 'Say I am not here.' But the dog tells him more things than you commanded. And when he has fulfilled your wish he will die at your feet." And Peter said, "Demon, whoever you are, in the name of our Lord Jesus Christ depart from this young man without hurting him. Show yourself to all present." When the young man heard this he rushed forward, took hold of a large marble statue, which stood in the courtyard of the house, and kicked it to pieces. It was a statue of Caesar. When Marcellus saw this he beat his forehead and said to Peter, "A great crime has been committed, for should Caesar hear of it through one of his spies he will greatly punish us." Peter answered, "I see that you are not the man you were a short time ago when you said you were ready to spend everything for the salvation of your soul. But if you are truly repentant and believe in Christ with all your heart, take running water into your hands and, beseeching the Lord, sprinkle it in his name on the pieces of the statue and it shall be a whole as before." Marcellus did not doubt, but believed with his whole heart, and before taking the water he lifted up his hands and said, "I believe in you, Lord Jesus Christ. For your apostle Peter has examined me whether I truly believe in your holy name. Therefore I take water in my hands and sprinkle these stones in your name that the statue become whole again as before. If it is your will, O Lord, that I live and receive no punishment from Caesar, let this statute be whole as before." And he sprinkled water on the stones, and the statue became whole, Peter, therefore, exulted that he had not hesitated to petition the Lord, and Marcellus also rejoiced in the Spirit, that the first miracle took place by his hands. He believed therefore, with all his heart in the name of Jesus Christ, the Son of my God, by whom all things impossible become possible.

12 And Simon, being inside, spoke thus to the dog, "Tell Peter that I am not in." But the dog said to him in the presence of Marcellus, "You most wicked and shameless man, worst enemy of all who live and believe in Christ Jesus. A dumb animal, which received a human voice, has been sent to you to convict you and to prove that you are a cheat and deceiver. Did it require so many hours for you to say, 'Say I am not here!' You have not been ashamed to lift up your weak and useless voice against Peter, the servant and apostle of Christ, as if you could be hidden from him who told me to speak to your face. And this is not for your sake, but on account of those whom you deceived and brought to perdition. You shall therefore be accursed, enemy and destroyer of the way of Christ's truth. He shall punish your iniquities, which you have done, with imperishable fire and you shall be in outer darkness." Having spoken these words the dog ran away. And the multitude followed so that Simon remained alone. And the dog came to Peter who was with the crowd who had come to see the face of Peter; and the dog reported what had happened with Simon. To the messenger and apostle of the true God the dog said as follows, "Peter, you shall have a hard fight with Simon, the enemy of Christ, and with his adherents, but many whom he deceived you shall convert to the faith. For this you shall receive a reward for your work from God." Having thus spoken the dog fell at the feet of Peter and expired. When the multitude with great astonishment saw the talking dog, many fell down at the feet of Peter, but others said, "Show us another miracle that we may believe in you as a servant of the living God, for Simon too did many wonders in our presence, and on that account we followed him."

13 And Peter turning around saw a smoked tuna fish hanging in a window. He took it, saying to the people, "When you see this swimming in water like a fish, will you be able to believe in him whom I preach?" And all said with one voice, "Indeed we shall believe you." So he went to the pond near by, saying, "In your name, O Jesus Christ, in whom they do not yet believe, I say, 'Tuna, in the presence of all these, live and swim like a fish.' " And he cast the tuna into the pond, and it became alive and began to swim. The multitude saw the swimming fish and he made it swim not only for that hour but, lest they said that it was a deception, he made it swim longer, thereby attracting crowds from all parts and showing that the smoked tuna had again become a living fish. The success was such that many threw pieces of bread into the water, seeing that the fish was whole. Very many who had witnessed this followed Peter and believed in the Lord, and met day and night in the house of Narcissus the presbyter. And Peter spoke to them of the prophetical writings and of the things done by our Lord Jesus Christ in word and deed.

14 Marcellus was more firmly established in the faith, seeing the signs which Peter did by the grace of Jesus Christ, which was given to him. And Marcellus attacked Simon, who sat in the dining-room of his house. Cursing him, he said to him, "O you most malevolent and most pestilential of men, destroyer of my soul and of my house, who intended to lead me away from Christ, my Lord and Savior." And he laid his hand on him and ordered that he be thrown out of his house. And the servants, having obtained permission, treated him in the most shameful way; some struck him in the face, some beat him with a rod, some flung stones at him, some emptied vessels containing filth over his head. Those who, for his sake, had left their master and were imprisoned, and other servants whom he had maligned to their master, reviled him and said to him, "Now we repay to you the worthy reward, according to the will of God, who had mercy upon us and upon our master." And Simon, thus treated, left the house and went to the house in which Peter was staying. Standing at the door of the house of the presbyter Narcissus, he cried, "Behold, here am I, Simon. Come down, Peter, and I will prove that you believed in a Jewish man and the son of a carpenter."

15 When Peter heard these things he sent to him a woman with her suckling child and said to her, "Go down quickly and you shall see someone seeking me. As for you, do not speak, but keep silent and listen to what the child which

you hold will say to him." And the woman went down. And her baby was seven months old. Assuming a manly voice it said to Simon, "You abomination before God and people, O destroyer of truth and most wicked seed of corruption, O unfaithful fruit of nature! After only a little while an everlasting punishment awaits you. Son of a shameless father, never taking root in good soil but in poison; unfaithful creature, destitute of all hope: when the dog accused you, you were not ashamed. I, a child, am forced by God to speak and still you do not blush. But against your will, on the coming Sabbath day, another shall lead you to the forum of Julius that you may be shown what you are. Leave by the doorway at which the saints enter. For no more shall you corrupt innocent souls whom you perverted and led away from Christ. Your whole evil nature will therefore be manifested, and your machinations will be spoiled. Now I say to you a last word: Jesus Christ says to you, 'Be speechless by the power of my name and leave Rome till the coming Sabbath.' "

At once he became speechless, and being constrained he left Rome till the next Sabbath and lodged in a stable. The woman returned to Peter with the baby and told Peter and the other brethren what the child had said to Simon. And they praised the Lord who had shown these things to humans.

16 When night came Peter, still awake, saw Jesus clothed with a shining garment, smiling and saying to him, "The greatest part of the brethren has already come back through me and through the signs which you have made in my name. But on the coming Sabbath you shall have a contest of faith, and many more Gentiles and Jews shall be converted in my name to me who was reviled, despised, and spat upon. For I shall show myself to you when you shall ask for signs and wonders and you shall convert many, but you will have Simon opposing you through the works of his father. But all his doings shall be manifested as sorcery and magical deception. And do not delay and you shall confirm in my name all those whom I shall send to you." When it was day he told the brethren how the Lord had appeared to him and what he had commanded him. . . .

20 When Peter had entered he saw one of the old women who was blind, and her daughter led her by the hand and conducted her into the house of Marcellus. And Peter said to her, "Come here, mother; from this day Jesus gives you his right hand; through him we have light unapproachable which darkness cannot hide. Through me he says to you, 'Open your eyes, see and walk on your own.'" And the widow at once saw Peter put his hand upon her. When Peter came into the dining-room he saw that the gospel was being read. And rolling it up he said, "People, who believe in Christ and hope in him, you shall know how the holy scriptures of our Lord must be explained. What we have written down according to his grace, though it may seem to you as yet so little, contains what is endurable to be understood by humanity. It is necessary that we first know God's will or his goodness; for when deceit was spread and many thousands of people were plunging into perdition the Lord was moved by compassion to show himself in another form and to appear in the image of man, by whom neither the Jews nor we are worthy to be enlightened. For each of us saw him as his capacity permitted. Now, however, I will explain to you that which has been read to you. Our Lord wished to let me see his majesty on the holy mountain;[3] but when I with the sons of Zebedee saw his brightness I fell at his feet as dead, closed my eyes, and heard his voice in a manner which I cannot describe. I imagined I had been deprived of my eyesight by his splendor. I recovered a little and said to myself, 'Perhaps the Lord has brought me here to deprive me of my eyesight.' And I said, 'If such is your will, O Lord, I shall not resist.' And he took me by the hand and lifted me up. And when I arose I saw him again in a form which I could not comprehend. So the merciful God, most beloved brethren, has borne our infirmities and carried our transgressions, as the prophet says, 'He bears our griefs; and is afflicted for us; yet we did esteem him stricken and afflicted.'[4] For he is in the Father and the Father in him; in him also is the fullness of all majesty, who has shown us all his benefits. He ate and drank on our account though he was neither hungry nor thirsty; he suffered and bore reproaches for us, he died and rose for us. He also defended and strengthened me through his greatness when I sinned; he will also comfort you, so that you may love him, this Great and Small One, this Beautiful and Ugly One, this Young Man and Old Man, appearing in time, yet utterly invisible in eternity; whom a human hand has not grasped, yet is held by his servants; whom flesh has not seen and now sees; who has not been heard, but is known now as the word which is heard; never chastised, but now chastised; who was before the world and is now perceived in time, beginning greater than all dominion, yet delivered to the princes; glorious, but lowly among us; ugly, yet foreseeing. This Jesus you have, brethren, the door, the light, the way, the bread, the water, the life, the resurrection, the refreshment, the pearl, the treasure, the seed, the abundance, the grain of mustard seed, the vine, the plough, the grace, the faith, the word: he is everything, and there is none greater than he; to him be praise in all eternity. Amen."...

23 The brethren and all who were in Rome came together, and on payment of a piece of gold each occupied a seat. Senators and prefects and officers also assembled. But when Peter came in he stood in the center. All cried aloud, "Show us, Peter, who your God is or which majesty it is which gave you such confidence. Be not disaffected to the Romans; they are lovers of the gods. We have had evidence from Simon, let us have yours also; show us, both of you, whom we must believe." And when they had spoken Simon also came. Dismayed, he stood by the side of Peter gazing closely at him. After a long silence Peter said, "Roman men, you shall be our true judges. I say that I believe in the living and true God, of whom I will give you proof already known to me, and to which many among you testify. You see that this man is silent because he has been refuted and because I have driven him from Judaea on account of the frauds perpetrated upon Eubola, a highly respected but simple woman, by means

---

[3]Mark 9:2–8.
[4]Isa 53:4.

of his magic. Having been expelled by me from there, he has come here believing that he could remain hidden among you; and now here he stands face to face with me. Tell me, Simon, did you not fall at my feet and those of Paul, when in Jerusalem you saw the miraculous cures which took place by our hands, and say, 'I pray you, take as much money from me as you wish, that I too by laying on of hands may perform such deeds'? And when we heard this from you, we cursed you: do you think that we try to possess money? And now are you afraid? My name is Peter, because the Lord Christ had the grace to call me to be ready for every cause. For I believe in the living God, through whom I shall destroy your magic arts. Let Simon perform in your presence the wonderful things which he used to do. And will you not believe me what I just told you about him?" And Simon said, "You have the impudence to speak of Jesus the Nazarene, the son of a carpenter, himself a carpenter, whose family is from Judaea. Listen Peter. The Romans have understanding, they are no fools." And turning to the people he said, "Men of Rome, is a God born? Is he crucified? Whoever has a master is no God." And when he spoke, many said, "You are right, Simon."

24 And Peter said, "Cursed be your words against Christ. You spoke in these terms whereas the prophet says of him, 'Who shall declare his generation?'[5] And another prophet says, 'And we have seen him, and he had no form nor beauty.'[6] And 'In the last days a child shall be born of the Holy Spirit; his mother knows not a man and no one claims that he is his father.' And again he says, 'She has given birth and has not given birth.' And again, 'Is it a very little thing for you to go to battle? Behold, in the womb a virgin shall conceive.'[7] And another prophet says in honor of the Father, 'We neither heard her voice, nor did a midwife come.'[8] Another prophet says, 'He came not out of the womb of a woman but descended from a heavenly place,' and 'A stone cut out without hands and has broken all kingdoms,'[9] and 'The stone which the builders rejected has become the headstone of the corner,'[10] and he calls him 'the tried, precious' stone.[11] And again, the

prophet says of him, 'I saw him come on a cloud like the Son of man.'[12] And what more shall I say? Men of Rome, if you knew the prophetical writings I would explain everything to you. It was necessary that through them it should be a mystery and the Kingdom of God be completed. But these things shall be revealed to you afterwards. Now I turn to you, Simon; do one of the signs whereby you deceived them before and I shall frustrate it through my Lord Jesus Christ." Simon took courage and said, "If the prefect permits."

25 The prefect wished to show his impartiality to both, so that he might not appear to be acting unjustly. And the perfect summoned one of his slaves and spoke to Simon, "Take him and kill him." To Peter he said, "And you revive him." And to the people the prefect said, "It is for you to decide which of these is accepted before God, he who kills, or he who revives." And Simon whispered something into the ear of the slave and made him speechless, and he died. But when the people began to murmur, one of the widows who had been cared for by Marcellus cried out, "Peter, servant of God, my son also is dead, the only one I had." The people made room for her, and they brought her to Peter. And she fell down at his feet and said, "I had only one son; by the labor of his hands he provided for me; he lifted me up, he carried me. Now he is dead, who will give me a hand?" Peter said to her, "In the presence of these witnesses go and bring your son, that they may be able to see and believe that he was raised up by the power of God; the other shall see it and perish." And Peter said to the young men, "We need young men such as shall believe." And at once thirty young men offered themselves to carry the widow and to fetch her dead son. When the widow had recovered, the young men lifted her up. But she cried and said, "Behold my

---

[5]Isa 53:8.
[6]Isa 53:2.
[7]Isa 7:14.
[8]Asc. of Isa 11:13.
[9]Dan 2:34.
[10]Ps 118:22; Mark 12:10.
[11]Isa 28:16.
[12]Dan 7:13.

son, the servant of Christ has sent for you," and she tore her hair and scratched her face. And the young men who had come examined the nose of the boy to see if he were really dead. When they perceived that he was dead they comforted his mother and said, "If you really believe in the God of Peter, we will lift him up and bring him to Peter, that he may revive him and restore him to you."

26 While the young men were saying this the prefect in the forum looked at Peter and said, "What do you say, Peter? Behold, the lad is dead; the emperor liked him, and I spared him not. I had indeed many other young men; but I trusted in you and in your Lord whom you proclaim, if indeed you are sure and truthful: therefore I allowed him to die." And Peter said, "God is neither tempted nor weighed in the balance. But he is to be worshipped with the whole heart by those whom he loves and he will hear those who are worthy. Since, however, my God and Lord Jesus Christ is now tempted among you, he is doing many signs and miracles through me to turn you from your sins. In your power, revive now through my voice, O Lord, in the presence of all, him whom Simon killed by his touch." And Peter said to the master of the lad, "Come, take hold of him by the right hand and you shall have him alive and walking with you." And the prefect Agrippa ran and came to the lad, took his hand, and restored him to life. And when the multitude saw this they cried, "There is only one God, the God of Peter."

27 Meanwhile the widow's son was brought in on a bier by the young men. The people made room, and they brought him to Peter. Peter, however, lifted up his eyes towards heaven, stretched forth his hands, and said, "Holy Father of your Son Jesus Christ who has given us power to ask and to obtain through you and to despise everything that is in this world and follow you only, who are seen by few and wish to be known by many; shine round, O Lord, enlighten, appear, revive the son of the aged widow, who is helpless without him. And I take the word of my Lord Christ and say to you, 'Young man, arise and walk with your mother as long as you can be of use to her. Afterward you shall be called to a higher min-

istry and serve as deacon and bishop.'" And the dead man rose immediately, and the multitude saw and were amazed, and the people cried, "You, God the Savior, you, God of Peter, invisible God and Savior." And they spoke with one another and wondered at the power of a man who with his word called upon his Lord, and they accepted what had taken place for their sanctification.

28 When the news had spread through the entire city, the mother of a senator came, and making her way through the multitude she threw herself at Peter's feet and said, "I heard many people say that you are a minister of the merciful God and that you impart his mercy to all who desire this light. Bestow, therefore, also to my son this light, since I have learned that you are not ungenerous towards any one; do not turn way from a lady, who entreats you." Peter said to her, "Do you believe in my God through whom your son shall rise?" And the mother, weeping, said with a loud voice, "I believe, Peter, I believe." The whole multitude cried out, "Give the mother her son." And Peter said, "Let him be brought here into the presence of all." And Peter, turning to the people, said, "Men of Rome, I, too, am one of you! I have human flesh and I am a sinner, but I have obtained mercy. Do not imagine that what I do, I do in my own power; I do it in the power of my Lord Jesus Christ who is the judge of the living and the dead. I believe in him, I have been sent by him, and I dare to call upon him to raise the dead. Go, therefore, woman, and have your son brought here and have him raised." And the woman made her way through the multitude, ran into the street with great joy, and believed with her heart; coming to the house she made her slaves carry him and came back to the forum. And she told the young men to cover their heads and go before the bier and carry everything that she intended to spend on the body of her son in front of the bier, so that Peter, seeing this, might have pity on the body and on her. With them all as mourners she came to the assembly, followed by a multitude of senators and ladies who came to see God's wonderful deeds. And Nicostratus (the man who had died) was very noble and respected in the senate. They brought him and placed him be-fore Peter. And Peter asked them to be silent and said with a very loud voice, "Romans, let a right-eous judgment now take place between me and Simon, and judge which of us believes in the liv-ing God, he or I. Let him revive the body which is before us, and believe in him as an angel of God. If he is not able I will call upon my God. I will restore the son alive to his mother and then you shall believe that he is a sorcerer and de-ceiver, this man who enjoys your hospitality." When they heard this, it seemed right to them what Peter had said. They encouraged Simon say-ing, "Show yourself publicly what you can do; ei-ther you convince us or you shall be convicted. Why do you stand still? Commence."

When Simon perceived that they all pushed him, he stood in silence. When the people had be-come quiet and were looking at him, Simon cried out and said, "Romans, when you see that the dead man is raised, will you cast Peter out of the city?" And the whole multitude said, "We shall not only cast him out but also burn him at once." Simon came to the head of the dead man, bowed three times, and he showed the people how the dead man had lifted up his head and moved it, and opened his eyes and lightly bowed to Simon. And immediately they began to gather wood to burn Peter. But Peter, having received the power of Christ, lifted up his voice and said to those who were shouting against him, "Now I see, Romans, that I must not call you foolish and silly so long as your eyes and your ears and your senses are blinded. So long as your mind is darkened you do not perceive that you are bewitched, since you seemingly believe that a dead man rose who has not risen. I would have been content, Romans, to keep silent and to die in silence and to leave you among the illusions of this world. But the punish-ment of the unquenchable fire is before my eyes. If you agree, let the dead man speak, let him rise; if he is alive, let him untie the band from his chin, let him call his mother and say to you, 'Bawlers, why are you crying?' Let him beckon to you with his hand. If, therefore, you wish to see that he is dead and you are spellbound, let this man step back from the bier, this one who persuaded you to

withdraw from Christ, and you shall see the dead man as you saw him when you brought him in." And the prefect Agrippa could no longer restrain himself but rose and with his own hand pushed Simon away. And the dead man looked as he had before. And the people were enraged and, con-verted from the magical spell of Simon, began to cry, "Hear, O Caesar, should the dead not rise let Simon be burned instead of Peter, because he has really deceived us." But Peter stretched forth his hand and said, "Romans, be patient. I do not say that Simon should be burned if the boy is restored; it is only when I tell you to do it, that you will." And the people cried, "Even if you should not wish it, Peter, we shall do it." Peter said to them, "If you continue, the boy shall not rise. We have learned not to recompense evil for evil, but we have learned to love our enemies and to pray for those who persecute us. For should even he re-pent, it is better. For God will not remember the evil. Let him, therefore, come to the light of Christ. But if he cannot, let him inherit the portion of his father, the devil. But do not let your hands be con-taminated." Having thus spoken to the people he came to the boy, and before raising him he said to his mother, "These young men, whom you set free in honor of your son, can as free men obey their living master. For I know that the souls of some among them will be wounded when they see your risen son and serve again as slaves. But let them all be free and receive their subsistence as be-fore—for your son shall rise again—and let them be with him." And Peter looked at her for some time awaiting the answer. And the mother of the boy said, "How can I do otherwise? Therefore I declare before the prefect that they should possess all that which I had to spend on the corpse of my son." Peter said to her, "Let the rest be divided among the widows." And Peter rejoiced in his soul and said in the spirit, "O Lord, who are mer-ciful, Jesus Christ, manifest yourself to your ser-vant Peter who calls upon you, as you always show mercy and goodness. In the presence of all these who have been set free, that they may be able to serve, let Nicostratus now arise." And Pe-ter touched the side of the lad and said, "Arise." And the lad arose, took up his garment and sat and untied his chin, asked for other garments, came down from the bier, and said to Peter, "I beg you, man, let us go to our Lord Christ, whom I heard speak to you; he said to you, pointing at me, 'Bring him here, for he belongs to me.'" When Peter heard this he was still more strengthened in the spirit by the help of the Lord and said to the people, "Romans, thus the dead are awakened, thus they speak, thus they walk when they are raised; they live for so long as it pleases God. But now I turn to you who came to see the spectacle. If you repent now from your sins and from all your human-made gods and from all uncleanness and lust, you shall receive the communion of Christ in faith so that you may obtain life for eternity."

29 From that hour on they worshipped him like a god, and the sick, whom they had at home, they brought to his feet to be cured by him. And when the prefect perceived that such a great multitude adhered to Peter he asked him to depart. And Peter bade the people come into the house of Marcellus. And the mother of the lad asked Peter to come to her house. But Peter had arranged to go to Marcellus on Sunday to see the widows, as Marcellus had promised, so that he might minister to them with his own hand. And the lad who had been raised said, "I shall not leave Peter." And his mother returned joyfully and cheerfully to her house. And on the day after the Sabbath she came into the house of Marcellus and brought two thousand pieces of gold and said to Peter, "Divide these among the virgins of Christ who minister to him." But the lad who had been raised, perceiving that he had not yet given anything to anyone, ran to his house, opened a chest, and brought four thousand pieces of gold, and said to Peter, "See, I also, who have been raised, offer the double gift and present myself from now on as a living sacrifice to God."

---

43. The Acts of Paul

The "Acts of Paul" is not preserved in its entirety but exists only in large fragments that are difficult to piece together. The complete book is usually thought to have included the Acts of Thecla and the pseudonymous letter of 3 Corinthians (see readings 44 and 46). Together, the various fragments narrate legendary episodes from Paul's life, including the account, not excerpted here, of a talking lion that Paul converts and baptizes and that, at a later time, spares Paul when loosed upon him in the arena.

The following extract was no doubt the conclusion of the book, for it describes Paul's martyrdom. Put on trial before the evil emperor Nero, Paul announces that, even if executed, he will reappear as proof that he can never really die but will live forever. When Paul is then beheaded, we are told that milk (a symbol of life?), rather than blood, squirts from his wound and that after his death, Paul fulfills his word by appearing to Nero and pronouncing the emperor's own imminent doom.

Most scholars identify the Acts of Paul with a book known to the church father Tertullian, who, around 200 C.E., claimed that it had been forged by a presbyter of Asia Minor who, after being caught, indicated that he had done it "out of love for Paul."

1 Luke, who had come from Gaul, and Titus, who had come from Dalmatia, expected Paul at Rome. When Paul saw them he rejoiced and rented a barn outside Rome where he and the brethren taught the word of truth. He became famous and many souls were added to the Lord, so that it was noised about in Rome and a great many from the house of the emperor came to him and there was much joy.

A certain Patroclus, a cupbearer of the emperor, who had come too late to the barn and could not get near to Paul on account of the throng of the people sat on a high window, and listened as he taught the word of God. But Satan, being wicked, became jealous of the love of the brethren and Patroclus fell down from the window and died; speedily it was reported to Nero. Paul, however, having learned it by Spirit said, "Brethren, the evil one has obtained a way to tempt you; go forth and you will find a boy who has fallen down and is dying. Lift him up and bring him here." This they did. When the people saw him they were frightened. Paul said to them, "Now, brethren, show your faith. Come, let us mourn to our Lord Jesus Christ, that the boy might live and we remain unharmed." When all began to lament, the boy took breath and, having put him on an animal, they sent him away alive with all those who were of the emperor's house.

2 And Nero, having heard of Patroclus' death, became very sad, and as he came out from his bath he ordered another to be appointed for the wine. But his servants said, "Emperor, Patroclus is alive and stands at the sideboard." When the emperor heard that Patroclus was alive he was frightened and would not come in. But when he came in and saw Patroclus he cried out, "Patroclus, are you alive?" He answered, "I am alive, Caesar." But he said, "Who is he who made you alive?" And the boy, uplifted by the confidence of faith, said, "Christ Jesus, the king of the ages." The emperor asked in dismay, "Is he to be king of the ages and destroy all kingdoms?" Patroclus said to him, "Yes, he destroys all kingdoms under heaven, and he alone shall remain in all eternity, and there will be no kingdom which escapes him." And he struck his face and cried out, "Patroclus, are you also fighting for that king?" He answered, "Yes, my lord and Caesar, for he has raised me from the dead."

And Barsabas Justus the flat-footed and Urion the Cappadocian and Festus of Galatia, the chief men of Nero, said, "And we, too, fight for him, the king of the ages." After having tortured those men whom he used to love he imprisoned them and ordered that the soldiers of the great king be sought, and he issued an edict that all Christians and soldiers of Christ that were found should be executed.

3 And among the many Paul also was brought in fetters. Those who were imprisoned with him looked at him, so that the emperor observed that he was the leader of the soldiers. And he said to him, "Man of the great king, now my prisoner, what induced you to come secretly into the Roman empire and to enlist soldiers in my territory?" But Paul, filled with the Holy Spirit, said in the presence of all, "Caesar, we enlist soldiers not only in your territory but in all lands of the earth. For thus we are commanded to exclude none who wishes to fight for my king. If it seems good to you, serve him, for neither riches nor the splendors of this life will save you; but if you become his subject and beseech him you shall be saved. For in one day he will destroy the world."

Having heard this Nero commanded all the prisoners to be burned with fire, but Paul to be beheaded according to the law of the Romans. But Paul was not silent and communicated the word to Longus the prefect and Cestus the centurion. And Nero, being instigated by the evil one, raged in Rome and had many Christians executed without trial, so that the Romans stood before the palace and cried, "It is enough, Caesar; these people are ours. You destroy the strength of the Romans."

Being thus convinced, he desisted and commanded that no Christian was to be touched till his case had been investigated.

4 After the issuing of the edict Paul was brought before him, and he insisted that he should be executed. And Paul said, "Caesar, I live not merely for a short time for my king; and if you have me executed I shall do the following: I will rise again and appear to you, for I shall not be dead but alive to my king, Christ Jesus, who shall come to judge the earth."

And Longus and Cestus said to Paul, "Whence have you this king that you believe in him without changing your mind even at point of death?" And Paul answered and said, "You men, who are now ignorant and in error, change your mind and be saved from the fire which comes over the whole earth. For we fight not, as you suppose, for a king who is from the earth but for one who is from heaven: he is the living God who comes as judge because of the lawless deeds which take place in this world. And blessed is he who will believe in him and live in eternity when he shall come with fire to purge the earth." And they besought him and said, "We entreat you, help us, and we will release you." But he answered, "I am not a deserter from Christ but a faithful soldier of the living God. If I knew that I should die I would still have done it, Longus and Cestus, but since I live to God and love myself I go to the Lord that I may come again with him in the glory of his Father." And they said to him, "How can we live after you have been beheaded?"

5 And while they were speaking Nero sent a certain Parthenius and Pheretas to see whether Paul had already been beheaded. And they found him still alive. He summoned them beside him and said, "Believe in the living God who will raise me, as well as all those who believe in him, from the dead." But they said, "We will now go to Nero but when you have died and have been raised up we will believe in your God."

But when Longus and Cestus continued to ask about salvation he said to them, "In the early

dawn come quickly to my grave and you will find two men at prayer, Titus and Luke; they will give you the seal in the Lord."

And turning toward the east, Paul lifted up his hands to heaven and prayed at length; and after having conversed in Hebrew with the fathers during prayer he bent his neck, without speaking any more. When the executioner cut off his head milk splashed on the tunic of the soldier. And the soldier and all who stood near by were astonished at this sight and glorified God who had thus honored Paul. And they went away and reported everything to Caesar.

6 When he heard of it he was amazed and did not know what to say. While many philosophers and the centurion were assembled with the emperor, Paul came about the ninth hour, and in the presence of all he said, "Caesar, behold, here is Paul, the soldier of God; I am not dead but live in my God. But upon you, unhappy one, many evils and great punishment will come because you have unjustly shed the blood of the righteous not many days ago." And having spoken this Paul departed from him. When Nero had heard, he commanded that the prisoners be released, Patroclus as well as Barsabas with his friends.

7 And, as Paul had told them, Longus and Cestus, the centurion, came in fear very early to the grave of Paul. And when they drew near they found two men in prayer and Paul with them, and they became frightened when they saw the unexpected miracle, but Titus and Luke, being afraid at the sight of Longus and Cestus, turned to run away.

But they followed and said to them, "We follow you not in order to kill you, blessed men of God, as you imagine, but in order to live, that you may do to us as Paul promised us. We have just seen him in prayer beside you." Upon hearing this Titus and Luke gave them joyfully the seal in the Lord, glorifying God and the Father of our Lord Jesus Christ to whom be glory for ever and ever. Amen.

>-+-0-+-<

44. The Acts of Thecla

The "Acts of Thecla" is a legendary account of the adventures of Thecla, a woman converted to the Christian faith through the preaching of the apostle Paul. Paul himself appears on the fringes of the story as a socially disruptive evangelist who converts women to a life of strict asceticism sexual renunciation, much to the chagrin of their husbands and fiancés.

Upon hearing Paul's message, Thecla abandons her fiancé to join the apostle on his journeys, liberated from the concerns of marriage and the potential domination by a future husband. Seeking revenge, however, Thecla's finacé brings her up before the authorities on charges of being a Christian. But, in a remarkable series of episodes (in which, among other things, Thecla baptizes herself in a pool of ravenous seals), God intervenes on Thecla's behalf, preserving her from death and reuniting her with her beloved apostle, who authorizes her to share fully in his ministry of teaching the word.

The Acts of Thecla was evidently in circulation near the end of the second century, along with the other narratives found in the "Acts of Paul" (see readings 43 and 46). Soon thereafter, and for centuries after, Thecla served as a model for Christian women.

1 As Paul was going to Iconium after his flight from Antioch, his fellow-travellers were Demas and Hermogenes, the copper-smith, who were full of hypocrisy and flattered Paul as if they loved him. Paul, looking only to the goodness of Christ, did them no harm but loved them exceedingly so that he made sweet to them all the words of the Lord and the interpretation of the gospel concerning the birth and resurrection of the Beloved; and he gave them an account, word for word, of the great deeds of Christ as they were revealed to him.

2 And a certain man, by name Onesiphorus, hearing that Paul was to come to Iconium, went out to meet him with his children Simmias and Zeno and his wife Lectra, in order that he might entertain him. Titus had informed him what Paul looked like, for he had not seen him in the flesh, but only in the spirit.

3 And he went along the royal road to Lystra and kept looking at the passers-by according to the description of Titus. And he saw Paul coming, a man small in size, bald-headed, bandy-legged, of noble mien, with eyebrows meeting, rather hook-nosed, full of grace. Sometimes he seemed like a man, and sometimes he had the face of an angel.

4 And Paul, seeing Onesiphorus, smiled; and Onesiphorus said, "Hail, O servant of the blessed God." And he said, "Grace be with you and your house." And Demas and Hermogenes were jealous and showed greater hypocrisy, so that Demas said, "Are we not of the blessed God that you have not thus saluted us?" And Onesiphorus said, "I do not see in you the fruit of righteousness, but if such you be, come also into my house and refresh yourselves."

5 And after Paul had gone into the house of Onesiphorus there was great joy and bowing of knees and breaking of bread and the word of God about abstinence and the resurrection. Paul said, "Blessed are the pure in heart, for they shall see God, blessed are those who have kept the flesh chaste, for they shall become a temple of God; blessed are the continent, for God shall speak with them; blessed are those who have kept aloof from this world, for they shall be pleasing to God; blessed are those who have wives as not having them, for they experience God; blessed are those who have fear of God, for they shall become angels of God.

6 "Blessed are those who respect the word of God, for they shall be comforted; blessed are those who have received the wisdom of Jesus Christ, for they shall be called the sons of the Most High; blessed are those who have kept the baptism, for they shall be refreshed by the Father and the Son; blessed are those who have come to a knowledge of Jesus Christ, for they shall be in the light; blessed are those who through love of God no longer conform to the world, for they shall judge angels, and shall be blessed at the right hand of the Father; blessed are the merciful, for they shall obtain mercy and shall not see the bitter day of judgment; blessed are the bodies of the virgins, for they shall be well pleasing to God and shall not lose the reward of their chastity. For the word of the Father shall become to them a work of salvation in the day of the Son, and they shall have rest for ever and ever."

7 And while Paul was speaking in the midst of the church in the house of Onesiphorus a certain virgin named Thecla, the daughter of Theoclia, betrothed to a man named Thamyris, was sitting at the window close by and listened day and night to the discourse of virginity, as proclaimed by Paul. And she did not look away from the window, but was led on by faith, rejoicing exceedingly. And when she saw many women and virgins going in to Paul she also had an eager desire to be deemed worthy to stand in Paul's presence and hear the word of Christ. For she had not yet seen Paul in person, but only heard his word.

8 As she did not move from the window her mother sent to Thamyris. And he came gladly as if already receiving her in marriage. And Thamyris said to Theoclia, "Where, then, is my Thecla [that I may see her]?" And Theoclia answered, "I have a strange story to tell you, Thamyris. For three days and three nights Thecla does not rise from the window either to eat or to drink; but looking earnestly as if upon some pleasant sight she is devoted to a foreigner teaching deceitful and artful discourses, so that I wonder how a virgin of her great modesty exposes herself to such extreme discomfort.

9 "Thamyris, this man will overturn the city of the Iconians and your Thecla too; for all the women and the young men go in to him to be taught by him. He says one must fear only one God and live in chastity. Moreover, my daughter, clinging to the window like a spider, lays hold of what is said by him with a strange eagerness and fearful emotion. For the virgin looks eagerly at what is said by him and has been captivated. But go near and speak to her, for she is betrothed to you."

10 And Thamyris greeted her with a kiss, but at the same time being afraid of her overpowering emotion said, "Thecla, my betrothed, why do you sit thus? And what sort of feeling holds you distracted? Come back to your Thamyris and be ashamed." Moreover, her mother said the same, "Why do you sit thus looking down, my child, and answering nothing, like a sick woman?" And those who were in the house wept bitterly, Thamyris for the loss of a wife, Theoclia for that of a child, and the maidservants for that of a mistress. And there was a great outpouring of lamentation in the house. And while these things were going on Thecla did not turn away but kept attending to the word of Paul.

11 And Thamyris, jumping up, went into the street, and watched all who went in to Paul and came out. And he saw two men bitterly quarrelling with each other and he said to them, "Men, who are you and tell me who is this man among you, leading astray the souls of young men and deceiving virgins so that they should not marry but remain as they are? I promise you money enough if you tell me about him, for I am the chief man of this city."

12 And Demas and Hermogenes said to him, "Who he is we do not know. But he deprives the husbands of wives and maidens of husbands, saying, 'There is for you no resurrection unless you remain chaste and do not pollute the flesh.'"

13 And Thamyris said to them, "Come into my house and refresh yourselves." And they went to a sumptuous supper and much wine and great wealth and a splendid table. And Thamyris made them drink, for he loved Thecla and wished to take her as wife. And during the supper Thamyris said, "Men, tell me what is his teaching that I also may know it, for I am greatly distressed about Thecla, because she so loves the stranger and I am prevented from marrying."

14 And Demas and Hermogenes said, "Bring him before the Governor Castellius because he persuades the multitude to embrace the new teaching of the Christians, and he will destroy him and you shall have Thecla as your wife. And we shall teach you about the resurrection which he says is to come, that it is has already taken place in the children[1] and that we rise again, after having come to the knowledge of the true God."

15 And when Thamyris heard these things he rose up early in the morning and, filled with jealousy and anger, went into the house of Onesiphorus with rulers and officers and a great crowd with batons and said to Paul, "You have deceived the city of the Iconians and especially my betrothed bride so that she will not have let me! Let us go to the governor Castellius!" And the whole crowd cried, "Away with the sorcerer for he has misled all our wives!" And the multitude was also incited.

16 And Thamyris standing before the tribunal said with a great shout, "O proconsul, this man—we do not know where he comes from—makes virgins averse to marriage. Let him

say before you why he teaches thus." But Demas and Hermogenes said to Thamyris, "Say that he is a Christian and he will die at once." But the governor kept his resolve and called Paul, saying, "Who are you and what do you teach? For they bring no small accusation against you."

17 And Paul, lifting up his voice, said, "If I today must tell any of my teachings then listen, O proconsul. The living God, the God of vengeance, the jealous God, the God who has need of nothing, who seeks the salvation of people, has sent me that I may rescue them from corruption and uncleanness and from all pleasure, and from death, that they may sin no more. On this account God sent his Son whose gospel I preach and teach, that in him people have hope, who alone has had compassion upon a world led astray, that people may be no longer under judgment but may have faith and fear of God and knowledge of honesty and love of truth. If then I teach the things revealed to me by God what harm do I do, O proconsul?" When the governor heard this he ordered Paul to be bound and sent to prison until he had time to hear him more attentively.

18 And Thecla, by night, took off her bracelets and gave them to the gatekeeper; and when the door was opened to her she went into the prison. To the jailer she gave a silver mirror and was thus enabled to go in to Paul and, sitting at his feet, she heard the great deeds of God. And Paul was afraid of nothing, but trusted in God. And her faith also increased and she kissed his bonds.

19 And when Thecla was sought for by her family and Thamyris they were hunting through the streets as if she had been lost. One of the gatekeeper's fellow slaves informed them that she had gone out by night. And they examined the gatekeeper who said to them, "She has gone to the foreigner in the prison." And they went and found her, so to say, chained to him by affection. And having gone out from there they incited the people and informed the governor what had happened.

---

[1] 2 Tim 2:18.

20 And he ordered Paul to be brought before the tribunal, but Thecla was riveted to the place where Paul had sat while in prison. And the governor ordered her also to be brought to the tribunal, and she came with an exceedingly great joy. And when Paul had been led forth the crowd vehemently cried out, "He is a sorcerer. Away with him!" But the governor gladly heard Paul speak about the holy works of Christ. And having taken counsel, he summoned Thecla and said, "Why do you not marry Thamyris, according to the law of the Iconians?" But she stood looking earnestly at Paul. And when she gave no answer Theoclia, her mother, cried out saying, "Burn the wicked one; burn her who will not marry in the midst of the theater, that all the women who have been taught by this man may be afraid."

21 And the governor was greatly moved, and after scourging Paul he cast him out of the city. But Thecla he condemned to be burned. And immediately the governor arose and went away to the theater. And the whole multitude went out to witness the spectacle. But as a lamb in the wilderness looks around for the shepherd, so Thecla kept searching for Paul. And having looked into the crowd she saw the Lord sitting in the likeness of Paul and said, "As if I were unable to endure, Paul has come to look after me." And she gazed upon him with great earnestness, but he went up into heaven.

22 And the boys and girls brought wood and straw in order that Thecla might be burned. And when she came in naked the governor wept and admired the power that was in her. And the executioners arranged the wood and told her to go up on the pile. And having made the sign of the cross she went up on the pile. And they lighted the fire. And though a great fire was blazing it did not touch her. For God, having compassion upon her, made an underground rumbling, and a cloud full of water and hail overshadowed the theater from above, and all its contents were poured out so that many were in danger of death. And the fire was put out and Thecla saved.

23 And Paul was fasting with Onesiphorus and his wife and his children in a new tomb on the way which led from Iconium to Daphne. And after many days had been spent in fasting the children said to Paul, "We are hungry." And they had nothing with which to buy bread, for Onesiphorus had left the things of this world and followed Paul with all his house. And Paul, having taken off his cloak, said, "Go, my child, sell this and buy some loaves and bring them." And when the child was buying them he saw Thecla their neighbor and was astonished and said, "Thecla, where are you going?" And she said, "I have been saved from the fire and am following Paul." And the child said, "Come, I shall take you to him; for he has been mourning for you and praying and fasting six days already."

24 And when she had come to the tomb Paul was kneeling and praying, "Father of Christ, let not the fire touch Thecla but stand by her, for she is yours'; she, standing behind him, cried out, "O Father who made the heaven and the earth, the Father of your beloved Son Jesus Christ, I praise you that you have saved me from the fire that I may see Paul again." And Paul, rising up, saw her and said, "O God, who knows the heart, Father of our Lord Jesus Christ, I praise you because you have speedily heard my prayer."

25 And there was great love in the tomb as Paul and Onesiphorus and the others all rejoiced. And they had five loaves and vegetables and water, and they rejoiced in the holy works of Christ. And Thecla said to Paul, "I will cut my hair off and I shall follow you wherever you go." But he said, "Times are evil and you are beautiful. I am afraid lest another temptation come upon you worse than the first and that you do not withstand it but become mad after men." And Thecla said, "Only give me the seal in Christ, and no temptation shall touch me." And Paul said, "Thecla, be patient; you shall receive the water."

26 And Paul sent away Onesiphorus and all his family to Iconium and went into Antioch, taking Thecla with him. And as soon as they had arrived a certain Syrian, Alexander by name, an influential citizen of Antioch, seeing Thecla, became enamored of her and tried to bribe Paul with gifts and presents. But Paul said, "I know not the woman of whom you speak, nor is she mine." But he, being of great power, embraced her in the street. But she would not endure it and looked about for Paul. And she cried out bitterly, saying, "Do not force the stranger; do not force the servant of God. I am one of the chief persons of the Iconians and because I would not marry Thamyris I have been cast out of the city." And taking hold of Alexander, she tore his cloak and pulled off his crown and made him a laughing-stock.

27 And he, although loving her, nevertheless felt ashamed of what had happened and led her before the governor; and as she confessed that she had done these things he condemned her to the wild beasts. The women of the city cried out before the tribunal, "Evil judgment! Impious judgment!" And Thecla asked the governor that she might remain pure until she was to fight with the wild beasts. And a rich woman named Queen Tryphaena, whose daughter was dead, took her under her protection and had her for a consolation.

28 And when the beasts were exhibited they bound her to a fierce lioness, and Queen Tryphaena followed her. And the lioness, with Thecla sitting upon her, licked her feet; and all the multitude was astonished. And the charge on her inscription was "Sacrilegious." And the women and children cried out again and again, "O God, outrageous things take place in this city." And after the exhibition Tryphaena received her again. For her dead daughter Falconilla had said to her in a dream, "Mother, receive this stranger, the forsaken Thecla, in my place, that she may pray for me and I may come to the place of the just."

29 And when, after the exhibition, Tryphaena had received her she was grieved because Thecla had to fight on the following day with the wild beasts, but on the other hand she loved her dearly like a daughter Falconilla and said, "Thecla, my second child, come, pray for my child that she may live in eternity, for this I saw in my sleep." And without hesitation she lifted up her voice and said, "My God, Son of the Most High, who are in heaven, grant her wish

that her daughter Falconilla may live in eternity." And when Thecla had spoken Tryphaena grieved very much, considering that such beauty was to be thrown to the wild beasts.

30 And when it was dawn Alexander came to her, for it was he who arranged the exhibition of wild beasts, and said, "The governor has taken his seat and the crowd is clamoring for us; get ready, I will take her to fight with the wild beasts." And Tryphaena put him to flight with a loud cry, saying, "A second mourning for my Falconilla has come upon my house, and there is no one to help, neither the child for she is dead, nor kinsman for I am a widow. God of Thecla, my child, help Thecla."

31 And the governor sent soldiers to bring Thecla. Tryphaena did not leave her but took her by the hand and led her away saying, "My daughter Falconilla I took away to the tomb, but you, Thecla, I take to fight the wild beasts." And Thecla wept bitterly and sighed to the Lord, "O Lord God, in whom I trust, to whom I have fled for refuge, who did deliver me from the fire, reward Tryphaena who has had compassion on your servant and because she kept me pure."

32 And there arose a tumult: the wild beasts roared, the people and the women sitting together were crying, some saying, "Away with the sacrilegious person!", others saying, "O that the city would be destroyed on account of this iniquity! Kill us all, proconsul; miserable spectacle, evil judgment!"

33 And Thecla, having been taken from the hands of Tryphaena, was stripped and received a girdle and was thrown into the arena. And lions and bears were let loose upon her. And a fierce lioness ran up and lay down at her feet. And the multitude of the women cried aloud. And a bear ran upon her, but the lioness went to meet it and tore the bear to pieces. And again a lion that had been trained to fight against men, which belonged to Alexander, ran upon her. And the lioness, encountering the lion, was killed along with it. And the women cried the more since the lioness, her protector, was dead.

34 Then they sent in many beasts as she was standing and stretching forth her hands and praying. And when she had finished her prayer she turned around and saw a large pit full of water and said, "Now it is time to wash myself." And she threw herself in saying, "In the name of Jesus Christ I baptize myself on my last day." When the woman and the multitude saw it they wept and said, "Do not throw yourself into the water!"; even the governor shed tears because the seals were to devour such beauty. She then threw herself into the water in the name of Jesus Christ, but the seals, having seen a flash of lightning, floated dead on the surface. And there was round her a cloud of fire so that the beasts could neither touch her nor could she be seen naked.

35 But the women lamented when other and fiercer animals were let loose; some threw petals, others nard, others cassia, others amomum, so that there was an abundance of perfumes. And all the wild beasts were hypnotized and did not touch her. And Alexander said to the governor, "I have some terrible bulls to which we will bind her." And the governor consented grudgingly, "Do what you will." And they bound her by the feet between the bulls and put red-hot irons under their genitals so that they, being rendered more furious, might kill her. They rushed forward but the burning flame around her consumed the ropes, and she was as if she had not been bound.

36 And Tryphaena fainted standing beside the arena, so that the servants said, "Queen Tryphaena is dead." And the governor put a stop to the games and the whole city was in dismay. And Alexander fell down at the feet of the governor and cried, "Have mercy upon me and upon the city and set the woman free, lest the city also be destroyed. For if Caesar hear of these things he will possibly destroy the city along with us because his kinswoman, Queen Tryphaena, has died at the theater gate."

37 And the governor summoned Thecla out of the midst of the beasts and said to her, "Who are you? And what is there about you that not one of the wild beasts touched you?" She answered, "I am a servant of the living God and, as

to what there is about me, I have believed in the Son of God in whom he is well pleased; that is why not one of the beasts touched me. For he alone is the goal of salvation and the basis of immortal life. For he is a refuge to the tempest-tossed, a solace to the afflicted, a shelter to the despairing; in brief, whoever does not believe in him shall not live but be dead forever."

38 When the governor heard these things he ordered garments to be brought and to be put on her. And she said, "He who clothed me when I was naked among the beasts will in the day of judgment clothe me with salvation." And taking the garments she put them on.

And the governor immediately issued an edict saying, "I release to you the pious Thecla, the servant of God." And the women shouted aloud and with one voice praised God, "One is the God, who saved Thecla," so that the whole city was shaken by their voices.

39 And Tryphaena, having received the good news, went with the multitude to meet Thecla. After embracing her she said, "Now I believe that the dead are raised! Now I believe that my child lives. Come inside and all that is mine I shall assign to you." And Thecla went in with her and rested eight days, instructing her in the word of God, so that many of the maidservants believed. And there was great joy in the house.

40 And Thecla longed for Paul and sought him, looking in every direction. And she was told that he was in Myra. And wearing a mantle that she had altered so as to make a man's cloak, she came with a band of young men and maidens to Myra, where she found Paul speaking the word of God and went to him. And he was astonished at seeing her and her companions, thinking that some new temptation was coming upon her. And perceiving this, she said to him, "I have received baptism, O Paul; for he who worked with you for the gospel has worked with me also for baptism."

41 And Paul, taking her, led her to the house of Hermias and heard everything from her, so that he greatly wondered and those who heard were strengthened and prayed for Tryphaena. And Thecla rose up and said to Paul, "I am going to Iconium." Paul answered, "Go, and teach the word of God." And Tryphaena sent her much clothing and gold so that she could leave many things to Paul for the service of the poor.

42 And coming to Iconium she went into the house of Onesiphorus and fell upon the place where Paul had sat and taught the word of God, and she cried and said, "My God and God of this house where the light shone upon me, Jesus Christ, Son of God, my help in prison, my help before the governors, my help in the fire, my help among the wild beasts, you alone are God and to you be glory for ever. Amen."

43 And she found Thamyris dead but her mother alive. And calling her mother she said, "Theoclia, my mother, can you believe that the Lord lives in heaven? For if you desire wealth the Lord will give it to you through me; or if you desire your child, behold, I am standing beside you."

And having thus testified, she went to Seleucia and enlightened many by the word of God; then she rested in a glorious sleep.

><del>+</del>+<del>O</del>+<del>+</del>≺

45. The Acts of John

Some of the most entertaining stories found among the apocryphal accounts of the apostles are in the "Acts of John," stories of the exploits of the son of Zebedee, the disciple commonly regarded as Jesus' closest companion. Two of the book's episodes have already been excerpted in Chapter 2. Like those earlier accounts, the stories in this reading demonstrate the uncanny power of God at work within his great apostle. The first is the amusing tale of the obedient bed bugs, which allow John to get some much-needed rest. The second is a gripping story of passion gone awry, in a love triangle involving the beautiful but ascetic Christian Drusiana, her loving husband, Andronicus, and the unbeliever Callimachus, whose unsatisfied lust becomes known to Drusiana, causing her to die of grief for being the object of temptation. In a fit of passion, however, Callimachus bribes his way into the burial vault, where he plans to fulfill his lust on Drusiana's corpse, only to be attacked by a preternatural serpent that stands as her guardian.

Razor-sharp in its contrast between ascetic virtue and lustful vice, this intriguing account stresses both the need for purity before God and the power of the apostle, who is able to raise the dead and to right all that has gone wrong in the world (the pure Drusiana, too, it should be noted, performs a resurrection in the account). The account was probably composed during the second half of the second century.

60 On the first day we came to a lonely inn, and when we were trying to find a bed for John we experienced a strange event. There was one bedstead with covers over which we spread our cloaks which we had brought and requested him to lie down and to rest, whilst we slept on the floor. He had hardly lain down, when he was molested by bugs. But as they became more and more troublesome, and as it was midnight already, we all heard him say to them, "I say to you, you bugs, be considerate; leave your home for this night and go to rest in a place which is far away from the servants of God!" And while we laughed and talked, John fell asleep. And we conversed quietly, and thanks to him we remained undisturbed.

61 When it was day, I rose first, and with me Verus and Andronicus. And in the door of the room which we had taken was a mass of bugs. And having called all the brethren, we went outside to have a full view of them. John was still asleep. When he woke up we showed him what we had seen. And sitting up in bed and seeing them, he said, "Since you have been wise to heed my warning, go back to your place!" When he had spoken and had risen from the bed, the bugs hastened from the door to the bed, ran up the legs into the joints and disappeared. And John said again, "This creature heard the voice of a man and kept quiet and was obedient. We, however, hear God's voice, and yet irresponsibly transgress his commandments. And how long will this go on?"

62 After this we came to Ephesus. And when the brethren who lived there had learned that John had returned after this long time, they met in the house of Andronicus, where he was also staying, grasped his feet, put his hands to their faces, and kissed them because they had touched his clothes.

63 And while great love and endless joy prevailed among the brethren, one, a servant of Satan, coveted Drusiana, although he saw and knew that she was the wife of Andronicus. Very many people remonstrated with him, "It is impossible for you to obtain this woman, especially since she has separated even from her husband out of piety. Or do you alone not know that Andron-

icus, who was not the godly man he now is, had locked her up in a tomb, saying, 'Either I'll have you as a wife, as I had you before, or you must die?' And she preferred to die rather than to commit the repugnant act. Now, if out of piety she withheld her consent to sexual intercourse with her husband and master, but persuaded him to become like-minded, should she consent to you, who wish to commit adultery with her? Desist from your passion, which gives you no rest! Desist from your scheme, which you cannot accomplish!"

64 Though his intimate friends remonstrated with him, they could not persuade him. He was even so impudent as to send word to her. When Drusiana heard of his disgraceful passion and shameless demands, she became very despondent, and after two days she was feverish. She said, "Oh, if I only had not come back to my native city where I have become a stumbling-block to a man who believes not in the worship of God! For if he were filled with God's word, he would not fall into such a passion. Therefore, O Lord, since I have become accessory to a blow which struck an ignorant soul, deliver me from this prison and take me soon to you!" And without being understood by anyone Drusiana departed this life in the presence of John, not rejoicing but sorrowing over the physical trouble of that man.

65 And Andronicus was sad and carried a hidden sorrow in his heart, and wept bitterly, so that John could only silence him by saying to him, "Drusiana has departed this unjust life for a better hope." To this answered Andronicus, "Of this I am certain, John, and I have no doubt in the belief in my God. My hopes are grounded on the fact, that she departed this life pure."

66 After she was interred, John took Andronicus aside, and having learned of the cause he sorrowed more than Andronicus. And he kept silence, considering the threats of the enemy, and sat still a little. When the brethren were assembled to hear which words he would say concerning the departed, he began to speak:

67 "When the helmsman who crosses the ocean has landed with the ship and passengers in a quiet haven free from storms, he feels secure. The husbandman who sowed the seed-grains in the ground and cared for them with great pains is only then to enjoy a rest from his labors when he has harvested abundant corn in his barns. Whoever promises to take part in a race should rejoice only when he has obtained the prize. He whose name is entered on the list of prize-fighting should triumph only after he receives the crowns. And thus it is with all races and skills, when they do not fail at the end, but are carried out, as they were intended.

68 "So I think it is with the faith which every one of us practises, and which can only be decided as having been the true one when it remains the same to the end of life. For there are many obstacles which cause unrest to human reasoning: cares, children, parents, glory, poverty, flattery, youth, beauty, boasting, desire for riches, anger, pride, frivolity, envy, passion, carelessness, violence, lust, slaves, money, pretence, and all the other similar obstacles which exist in life; it is the same for the helmsman who takes his course for a quiet journey and is opposed by the adverse winds and a great tempest and a mighty wave, when the heaven is serene; it is the same for the husbandman who is opposed by untimely weather and blight and creeping worms appearing from the ground; for the athletes, the near miss, and for the craftsman the obstacles to their skills.

69 "The believer must above all things consider the end and carefully examine how it will come, whether energetic and sober and without impediment, or in confusion and flattering worldly things and bound by passions. Thus one can praise the beauty of the body only when it is completely naked; and the greatness of the general when he has happily finished the whole campaign as he promised; and the excellence of the physician when he has succeeded in every cure; and so one praises a soul filled with faith and worthy of God if it has happily accomplished that which it promised, not one of which made a good beginning, and gradually descended into the errors of life and became weak, nor the numb soul which made an effort to attain higher things and

was afterwards reduced to perishable, nor that which loved the temporal more than the eternal, nor that which exchanged the perishable for the lasting, nor that which honored what was not to be honored and loved works of dishonor, nor that which accepted pledges from Satan and received the serpent into its house, nor one which was reviled for God's sake and afterwards was ashamed, nor one which consented with the mouth but did not show it by the deed; but we praise one which refused to be inflamed by filthy lust, to succumb to levity, to be ensnared by thirst after money, or to be betrayed by the strength of the body and anger."

70 While John continued to preach to the brethren that they despise earthly goods for the sake of the eternal ones, the lover of Drusiana, inflamed by the influence of the polymorphous Satan to the most ardent passions, bribed the greedy steward of Andronicus with money. And he opened the tomb of Drusiana and left him to accomplish on the body that which was once denied to him. Since he had not procured her during her lifetime, he continually thought of her body after she was dead, and exclaimed, "Although when living you refused to unite with me in love, after your death I will dishonor your corpse." Being in such a frame of mind he obtained the opportunity to execute his impious plan through the accursed steward, and both went to the tomb. Having opened the door, they began to take the graveclothes from the corpse, and said, "What have you gained, unhappy Drusiana? Could you not have done this while you were alive? It need not have grieved you if you had done it willingly."

71 While they spoke and only the shift remained, there appeared something wonderful, which people that do such things deserve to experience. A serpent appeared from somewhere, bit the steward, and killed him. And the serpent did not bite the young man, but encircled his feet, hissing fearfully, and when he fell down, the serpent sat on him.

72 On the following day John and Andronicus and the brethren went at the break of day to the tomb in which Drusiana had been for three days, so that we might break bread there. And when we were about to start, the keys were not to be found. And John said to Andronicus, "It is right that they are lost, for Drusiana is not in the tomb. Nevertheless, let us go, that you do not appear neglectful, and the doors will open of themselves, since the Lord has already given us many other things."

73 When we came to the place, the doors opened at the master's behest, and at the tomb of Drusiana we saw a beautiful youth smiling. When John saw him, he exclaimed and said, "Do you come before us here also, noble one? And why?" And he heard a voice saying to him, "For the sake of Drusiana, whom you are to raise up. I found her almost defiled on account of the dead man lying near the tomb." And when the noble one had thus spoken to John he ascended to heaven before the eyes of all. And John turned to the other side of the tomb and saw a young man, the very prominent Ephesian Callimachus—for this is what he was called—and on him a huge snake sleeping, also the steward of Andronicus, named Fortunatus, dead. On seeing both, he stood helpless and said to the brethren, "What does all this mean? Or why did the Lord not reveal to me what took place here, for he was always concerned for me?"

74 When Andronicus saw these bodies, he jumped up and went to the tomb of Drusiana. And when he saw her in her shift, he said to John, "I understand what took place, blessed servant of God. This Callimachus loved my sister. And as he could not get her, although he tried it often, he no doubt bribed this accursed steward of mine with a great sum of money with the intention—as one can now see—to accomplish his purpose through him. For this Callimachus said to many, 'If she will not yield to be me alive, rape shall be committed on her death.' This, O master, the noble one saw and did not allow her earthly remains to be violated. That is why those who engineered this are dead. And the voice which came to you 'Raise Drusiana!' foretold this. For she departed this life through sorrow. And I believe him who said that this is one of the men who was led astray. For you were asked to raise him. As for the other I know that he does not deserve salvation.

But one thing I ask of you. Raise Callimachus first, and he shall confess what took place."

75 And John looked at the corpse and said to the poisonous snake, "Depart from him who is to serve Jesus Christ!" Then he rose and prayed, "God, whose name is rightly praised by us; God, who overcomes each harmful work; God, whose will is done, who always hears us, make your grace now efficacious on this youth! And if through him some dispensation is to take place, make it known to us, when he is raised!" And the young man immediately arose and kept silence for a whole hour.

76 When the man had regained his senses, John asked what his intrusion into the tomb meant. And having learned from him what Andronicus had already told him, how he passionately loved Drusiana, John asked further whether he had accomplished his wicked design to commit rape on the holy earthly remains. And he replied, "How could I have accomplished this when this fearful beast killed Fortunatus with one bite before my eyes? And this deservedly so, for he encouraged me to such madness, after I had already desisted from the ill-timed and dreadful frenzy—but he frightened me and put me in the state in which you saw me, before I arose. But I will tell you another great miracle, which nearly slew me and almost killed me. When my soul was seized with mad passion and the incurable disease was troubling me, when I had already robbed her of the grave-clothes with which she was dressed, and went from the grave to put them down as you see, I turned back to perpetrate the abominable deed. And I saw a beautiful youth covering her with this cloak. Rays of light fell from his face upon hers, and he turned to me also and said, "Callimachus, die, that you may live." Who it was, I knew not, servant of God. Since you have come here, I know that it was an angel of God. And this I truly know, that the true God is preached by you; and I am sure of it. But I pray you, see to it that I may be delivered from this fate and dreadful crime, and bring me to your God as a man who had gone astray in scandalous, abominable, deceit. On my knees I ask for your help. I will become one of those who hope in Christ so that the voice may also prove true, which spoke here to me, 'Die to live!' And it is already fulfilled. For that unbeliever, godless, lawless man, is dead; I am raised by you as a believer, faithful and godly, that I may know the truth, which I ask of you to reveal to me."

77 And John, rejoicing, contemplated the whole spectacle of the salvation of people and said, "O Lord Jesus Christ, I do not know what your power is. I am amazed at your great mercy and endless forbearance. Oh, what greatness descended to servitude! O unspeakable freedom, which was enslaved by us! O inconceivable glory, which has come upon us! You have kept the grave from shame, and redeemed that man who contaminated himself with blood, and taught him to be chaste who meant to violate dead bodies. Father, full of mercy and compassion toward him who disregarded you, we praise, glorify, and honor you and thank you for your great goodness and long-suffering, holy Jesus, for you alone are God and none else; you against whose power all devices can do nothing now and in all eternity! Amen!"

78 After these words, John took Callimachus, kissed him, and said, "Glory be to our God, who had mercy upon you, child, and deemed me worthy to praise his power, and delivered you by a wise method from that madness and intoxication and called you to rest and renewal of life."

79 When Andronicus saw that Callimachus had been raised from the dead, he and the brethren besought John to raise Drusiana also, and said, "John, let her be raised and happily complete life's short space, which she gave up out of sorrow for Callimachus, because she thought she was a temptation to him! And when it pleases the Lord, he will take her to himself." And without delay John went to the grave, seized her hand and said, "You who alone are God, I call upon you, the immense, the unspeakable, the incomprehensible, to whom all worldly power is subject, before whom every authority bows, before whom every pride falls down and is silent, before whose voice the demons are confounded, at whose contemplation

the whole creation surrenders in quiet meditation. Your name will be hallowed by us. Raise Drusiana that Callimachus be still further strengthened in you who alone can do what is wholly impossible with man, and have given salvation and resurrection, and let Drusiana come out comforted because, in consequence of the conversion of the youth, she no more has the least impediment to long for you!"

80 Having spoken thus John said, "Drusiana, arise!" And she arose and came from the tomb. And when she saw that she wore nothing but her shirt, she was perplexed how to explain what had happened. Having learned everything from Andronicus, while John was upon his face and Callimachus with tears praised God, she also rejoiced and praised God.

81 Having dressed herself and looked around, she saw Fortunatus. And she said to John, "Father, he too shall rise, though he tried so much to become my betrayer." When Callimachus heard her speaking thus, he said, "No, I beg you, Drusiana. For the voice which I heard did not mention him, but only concerned you, and when I saw I believed. If he were good, God out of mercy would have certainly raised him through the blessed John. He knew that the man should have a bad death." And John answered him, "My son, we have not learnt to recompense evil with evil. For God has not recompensed the evil which we have done to him, but has given us repentance. And although we did not know his name, he did not forget us, but had mercy upon us. And when we reviled him, he forsook us not, but was merciful. And when we were disbelieving, he remembered not the evil. And when we persecuted his brethren, he did not requite us, but made us repent, turn away from sin, and called us to himself, as he called you also, child Callimachus, and, without remembering your former sins, made you his servant through his long-suffering mercy. If you do not wish me to raise Fortunatus, let Drusiana do it."

82 Without wavering, but in the joy of her spirit and soul, she went to the body of Fortunatus and said, "God of the ages, Jesus Christ, God of truth, you allowed me to see signs and wonders and granted me to partake of your name. You breathed into me your spirit with your polymorphous face, and showed much compassion. With your rich goodness, you protected me when my former husband, Andronicus, did violence to me, and gave me your servant Andronicus as a brother. Until now you have kept me, your maiden, pure. You raised me when I was dead through your servant John. To me, risen and freed from offence, you showed me him who was offended at me. You gave me perfect rest in you, and delivered me from the secret madness. I love you with all my heart. I beseech you, Christ, not to dismiss Drusiana's petition, who asks of you the resurrection of Fortunatus, though he tried so much to become my betrayer."

83 And she took the hand of the dead man and said, "Rise, Fortunatus, in the name of our Lord Jesus Christ!" And Fortunatus rose up. And seeing John in the tomb and Andronicus and Drusiana risen from the dead and Callimachus now a believer, he said, "O how far the power of these awful people has spread! I wish I were not raised, but remained dead, so as not to see them." And with these words he ran from the tomb.

84 And when John perceived the unchangeable soul of Fortunatus, he said, "O nature, unchanged for the better! O source of the soul, remaining in the filth! O essence of corruption, full of darkness! O death, dancing among those belonging to you! Of fruitless tree, full of fire! O wood, producing coal as fruit! O forest, with trees full of unhealthy shoots, neighbor of unbelief! You showed us who you are, and you will always be convicted with your children. And the power of praising higher things is unknown to you, for you do not have it. Therefore as your issue is, so is your root and nature. Vanish away from those who hope in the Lord—from their thoughts, from their mind, from their souls, from their bodies, from their action, from their life, from their conversation, from their activity, from their deeds, from their counsel, from their resurrection to God, from their fragrance which you will share, from their fastings, from their prayers, from their holy baptism, from their eucharist, from the nourishment of their flesh, from their drink, from their dress, from their agape, from their acts of mourning, from their continence, and from their righteousness. From all these, most unholy and abominable Satan, shall Jesus Christ, our God and judge of those who are like you and your nature, remove you."

85 After these words John prayed, fetched a loaf of bread to the tomb to break it, and said, "We praise your name, who have converted us from error and unmerciful lusts. We praise you who have brought before our eyes that which we saw. We bear witness to your goodness manifested to us in various ways. We hallow your gracious name, Lord, and thank you who have convicted those who are convicted by you. We thank you, Lord Jesus Christ, that we believe in your unchangeable mercy. We thank you that you are in need of a saved human nature. We thank you that you gave this sure faith, that you alone are God, now and for ever. We, your servants, thank you, O holy One, we who are assembled with good reason and risen from the dead."

86 Having thus prayed and praised God, he made all the brethren partake of the eucharist of the Lord and then left the tomb. And when he had come into the house of Andronicus, he said to the brethren, "Dear brethren, a spirit within me has prophesied that, in consequence of the bite of the serpent, Fortunatus would die of blood-poisoning. Let someone make haste and inquire whether it is so!" And one of the young men ran and found him dead already, the poison having spread and reached his heart. And he returned to John, reporting that he had been dead three hours already. And John said, "You have your child, devil!"

Thus John rejoiced with the brethren in the Lord.

APOCRYPHAL EPISTLES: THE TEXTS

(See also the Epistle of the Apostles, above, and the Epistle of Peter to James, Chapter 7)

Although the earliest Christian pseudepigrapha were epistles (e.g., the disputed Pauline epistles in the New Testament), apocryphal epistles are not particularly numerous. Of the ones that do survive, some are clearly meant to advance a particular doctrinal perspective or to oppose the doctrinal views of others (e.g., 3 Corinthians, directed explicitly against certain Gnostics), others serve to promote the status and importance of a particular apostolic hero (e.g., the forged correspondence between Paul and the Roman philosopher Seneca), and yet others claim to be otherwise lost letters referred to elsewhere in our literature (e.g., Paul's letter to the Laodiceans).

46. Paul's Third Letter to the Corinthians

The letter traditionally called 3 Corinthians is a pseudonymous reply of "Paul" to a letter from the Christians in Corinth, sent to him while he was in prison in Philippi. Both letters eventually came to be incorporated into the apocryphal Acts of Paul (see reading 43).

The letter from the Corinthians asks for Paul's advice about the teaching of two heretics, Simon (Magus?) and Cleobius, who maintain, among other things, that (a) God was not the creator, (b) the Jewish prophets were not from God, (c) Jesus did not come in the flesh, and (d) the flesh will not be raised. All of these clearly gnostic ideas (see Chapter 6); the pseudonymous author of 3 Corinthians replies by refuting each of them in turn. The letter concludes with dire warnings of eternal torment for those who embrace the heretical teachings of Paul's opponents.

If, as most scholars now think, these letters were originally composed and transmitted independently of the Acts of Paul, they must have been in circulation no later than the middle of the second century.

"Paul's Third Letter to the Corinthians," from "3 Corinthians," *The Apocryphal New Testament*, ed. J. K. Elliott. © Oxford University Press, 1993. Reprinted by permission of Oxford University Press.

Letter of the Corinthians to Paul

1 Stephanus and his fellow-presbyters Daphnus and Eubulus and Theophilus and Zeno to Paul, the brother in the Lord—greeting!

2 Two individuals have come to Corinth, named Simon and Cleobius, who overthrow the faith of some through pernicious words.

3 These you shall examine yourself.

4 For we never heard such things either from you or from the other apostles.

5 But we keep what we have received from you and from the others.

6 Since the Lord has shown us mercy, while you are still in the flesh we should hear this from you once more.

7 Come to us or write to us.

8 For we believe, as it has been revealed to Theonoe, that the Lord has delivered you from the hands of the godless.

9 What they say and teach is as follows:

10 They assert that one must not appeal to the prophets

11 and that God is not almighty,

12 there is no resurrection of the body,

13 man has not been made by God,

14 Christ has neither come in the flesh, nor was he born of Mary,

15 and the world is not the work of God but of angels.

16 Wherefore we beseech you, brother, be diligent to come to us that the Corinthian church may remain without stumbling and the foolishness of these men be confounded. Farewell in the Lord!. . .

Paul's Epistle to the Corinthians

1 Paul, the prisoner of Jesus Christ, to the brethren at Corinth—greeting!

2 Being in many afflictions, I marvel not that the teachings of the evil one had such rapid success.

3 For my Lord Jesus Christ will quickly come, since he is rejected by those who falsify his teaching.

4 For I delivered to you first of all what I received from the apostles before me who were always with Jesus Christ,

5 that our Lord Jesus Christ was born of Mary of the seed of David, the Father having sent the spirit from heaven into her

6 that he might come into this world and save all flesh by his own flesh and that he might raise us in the flesh from the dead as he has presented himself to us as our example.

7 And since humankind is created by his Father,

8 for this reason was he sought by him when he was lost, to become alive by adoption.

9 For the almighty God, maker of heaven and earth, sent the prophets first to the Jews to deliver them from their sins,

10 for he wished to save the house of Israel; therefore he took from the spirit of Christ and poured it out upon the prophets who proclaimed the true worship of God for a long period of time.

11 For the wicked prince who wished to be God himself laid his hands on them and killed them and bound all flesh of humans to his pleasure.

12 But the almighty God, being just, and not wishing to repudiate his creation had mercy

13 and sent his Spirit into Mary the Galilean,

15 that the evil one might be conquered by the same flesh by which he held sway, and be convinced that he is not God.

16 For by his own body Jesus Christ saved all flesh,

17 presenting in his own body a temple of righteousness

18 through which we are saved.

19 They who follow them are not children of righteousness but of wrath, who despise the wisdom of God and in their disbelief assert that heaven and earth and all that is in them are not a work of God.

20 They have the accursed belief of the serpent.

21 Turn away from them and keep aloof from their teaching.

24 And those who say that there is no resurrection of the flesh shall have no resurrection,

25 for they do not believe him who had thus risen.

26 For they do not know, O Corinthians, about the sowing of wheat or some other grain that it is cast naked into the ground and having perished rises up again by the will of God in a body and clothed.

27 And he not only raises the body which is sown, but blesses it manifold.

28 And if one will not take the parable of the seeds

29 let him look at Jonah, the son of Amathios who, being unwilling to preach to the Ninevites, was swallowed up by the whale.

30 And after three days and three nights God heard the prayer of Jonah out of deepest hell, and nothing was corrupted, not even a hair nor an eyelid.

31 How much more will he raise you up, who have believed in Christ Jesus, as he himself was raised up.

32 When a corpse was thrown on the bones of the prophet Elisha by one of the children of Israel the corpse rose from death; how much more shall you rise up on that day with a whole body, after you have been thrown upon the body and bones and Spirit of the Lord.

34 If, however, you receive anything else let no one trouble me,

35 for I have these bonds on me that I may win Christ, and I bear his marks that I may attain to the resurrection of the dead.

36 And whoever accepts this rule which we have received by the blessed prophets and the holy gospel, shall receive a reward,

37 but for whomsoever deviates from this rule fire shall be for him and for those who preceded him therein

38 since they are Godless people, a generation of vipers.

39 Resist them in the power of the Lord.

40 Peace be with you.

>─◆>─○─<◆─<

47. The Correspondence Between Paul and Seneca

In an effort to heighten the worldly significance of Paul, who in fact is never mentioned in any of the writings of his Jewish and Roman contemporaries, an unknown Christian author forged a series of fourteen letters between the apostle and the well-known philosopher and statesman, Seneca. Seneca, the most famous philosopher of his day, had been the tutor of the young Nero; when Nero later became emperor of Rome, he appointed Seneca to be his political adviser. The pseudonymous correspondence between Seneca and Paul presupposes that historical context, as Seneca indicates that he has shown Paul's letters to the emperor, who was extremely impressed. Apart from a show of mutual admiration, there is otherwise little of substance in the correspondence, with the exception

The Correspondence between Paul and Seneca, from *New Testament Apocrypha*, vol. 2, ed. Wilhelm Schneemelcher, 2d ed. Cambridge/Louisville: Lutterworth Press/Westminster John Knox Press, 1991. Used with permission of Lutterworth Press and Westminster John Knox Press.

of letter eleven, which mentions the fire in Rome allegedly started by Nero but blamed on the Christians (see Chapter 3).

This entire correspondence is often thought to have been composed some time in the late third century, although some scholars now suggest an even later date. The following are the final eight letters, given in their entirety.

Letter 7: From Seneca

I confess that I was much taken with the reading of your letters which you sent to the Galatians, the Corinthians, and the Achaeans, and let us both live in the spirit which with sacred awe you show in them. For the Holy Spirit is in you and above all exalted ones gives expression by your sublime speech to the most venerable thoughts. I could wish therefore that when you express such lofty thoughts a cultivated form of discourse should not be lacking to their majesty. And that I may conceal nothing from you, brother, or burden my conscience, I confess that the emperor was moved by your sentiments. When I had read to him about the origin of the power in you, he said that he could only wonder that a man who had not enjoyed the usual education should be capable of such thoughts. To which I answered that the gods are wont to speak through the mouths of the innocent, not of those who by their education are able to prevaricate. I gave him the example of Vatienus, an uneducated countryman, to whom two men appeared in a field at Reate who afterwards are named as Castor and Pollux; with that he seems sufficiently instructed. Farewell.

Letter 8: From Paul

I am not unaware that our emperor, if ever he is despondent, is a lover of marvellous things; however, he allows himself not to be injured, but only admonished. For I think you have gravely erred that you have wished to bring to his notice what is contrary to his belief and tenets. Since he worships the gods of the nations, I do not see what was your purpose in wishing him to know this, unless I am to think that you are doing this out of undue love for me. I beg you for the future not to do it. For you must beware lest in loving me you cause offence to the empress, whose displeasure will indeed only do harm if it persists, but also will be of no profit if that is not so. Even if as empress she is not affronted, as a woman she will be offended. Farewell.

Letter 9: From Seneca

I know that you are not so much disturbed for your own sake by the letter which I wrote to you about the giving of your letters to the emperor as by the nature of things which so hold back the minds of people from all arts and right customs. Today I do not wonder, especially since I now know it well from many documents. Therefore let us make a new beginning, and if in the past anything has been done too lightly, you will grant me forgiveness. I have sent you a book on "verbosity." Farewell, most beloved Paul.

Letter 10: From Paul

As often as I write to you and set my name behind yours, I commit a serious fault which is not congruent with my religion. For I ought, as I have often professed, to be all things to all people, and as concerns your person to observe what Roman law has conceded to the honor of the Senate, namely after perusal of a letter to choose the last place, that I may not with embarrassment and shame seek to do what was within my power. Farewell, my highly revered teacher.

Given on 27 June in the consulship of Nero (for the third time) and Messala (58 C.E.).

Letter 11: From Seneca

Greetings, my dearest Paul! Do you think that I am not saddened and distressed that capital punishment is still visited upon your innocence? And also that all the populace judges you people so hard-hearted and so ready for any crime, believing that whatever happens amiss in the city is done by you? But let us bear with equanimity and make use of the forum which fate provides, until invincible good fortune makes an end of evils. The time of the ancients suffered the Macedonian, the son of Philip, the Cyruses, Darius, and Dionysius, our own time also Gaius Caesar (= Caligula), men for whom all that they wished was legitimate. It is clear at whose hands the city of Rome so often suffers burning. But if human humility could declare what is the cause of it, and in this darkness was free to speak with impunity, then all would see everything. Christians and Jews are—forsooth!—executed as fire-raisers, as a matter of common custom. Whoever that delinquent is, who takes pleasure in murder and uses lies as a disguise, his days are numbered, and just as the best is sometimes offered up as one life for many, so also will this accursed one be burned in the fire for all. 132 palaces, 4000 apartment houses were burned in six days; the seventh brought a pause. I wish you good health, brother.

Given on 28 March in the consulship of Frugi and Bassus.

Letter 12: From Seneca

Greetings, my dearest Paul! If a man so distinguished as you and in every way beloved by God is, I do not say united but of necessity interwoven with me and my name, then it will be for the best with your Seneca. Since you are the crown and peak of all most lofty mountains, do you not wish me to rejoice that I am so close to you that I may be thought your second self? You should therefore not think that you are unworthy to be named in the first place in the letters, that you may not seem to tempt rather than to praise me, especially since you know yourself to be a Roman citizen. For I could wish that my place could be yours in your letters and yours mine. Fare well, dearest Paul.

Given on 23 March in the consulship of Apronianus and Capito (59 C.E.).

Letter 13: From Seneca

Many things are brought together by you, allegorically and enigmatically, from every quarter, and therefore the great power granted to you, in your material and in your office, ought to be adorned not with verbal trappings but with a certain refinement. Nor should you be afraid—as I recall, I have said this often already—that many who concern themselves with such things may corrupt the sense and weaken the power of the material. Certainly I could wish that you make me the concession to have regard for the Latinity and with noble words find the proper form, that you may worthily fulfil the honorable task entrusted to you. Fare well.

Given on 6 July in the consulship of Lurco and Sabinus (58 C.E.).

Letter 14: From Paul

In your reflection things have been revealed to you which the Deity has granted only to a few. With assurance therefore I sow in a field already fertile most powerful seed, not indeed matter that seems to be decaying but the firm word of God, the outflow of him who grows and abides for ever. What your discernment has grasped must remain unfailing: that the observances of the Gentiles and the Jews are to be avoided. Make yourself a new herald of Christ Jesus, showing by your rhetorical proclamations the irrefutable wisdom which you have almost attained. This you will teach to the temporal king and his servants and faithful friends. For them persuasion will be hard and above their capacity, for several of them are but little swayed by your expositions. But if the word of God is instilled in them as a vital blessing, it begets a new person without corruption, an animal ever in motion, which hastens hence towards God. Farewell, Seneca most dear to us!

Given on 1 August in the consulship of Lurco and Sabinus (58 C.E.).

48. Paul's Letter to the Laodiceans

The New Testament book of Colossians mentions a letter by Paul to the church of Laodicea in Asia Minor (Col 4:16). No letter addressed to the Laodiceans survives from Paul's own hand, but we know that one had been placed in circulation already in the second century, since the Muratorian canon (see Chapter 9) warns against it as a Marcionite forgery (on Marcion, see Chapter 7). It is difficult to know whether the letter given here is the one mentioned in the Muratorian canon, for, even though it shares its name, it shows no clear and compelling Marcionite tendencies.

In fact, the letters show few tendencies of *any* kind. It instead represents a kind of pastiche of statements drawn from Paul's canonical writings, especially Philippians: it evidences no specific occasion and addresses no clear theological or ethical issues. Nonetheless, the letter came to be widely copied by Latin scribes and is included in a number of Latin manuscripts of the New Testament itself.

It is difficult to determine the date of this letter, but it appears to have been written sometime during the second or third centuries.

1 Paul, an apostle not of humans and not through humans, but through Jesus Christ, to the brethren who are in Laodicea:

2 Grace to you and peace from God the Father and the Lord Jesus Christ.

3 I thank Christ in all my prayer that you continue in him and persevere in his works, in expectation of the promise at the day of judgment.

4 And may you not be deceived by the vain talk of some people who tell tales that they may lead you away from the truth of the gospel which is proclaimed by me.

5 And now may God grant that those who come from me for the furtherance of the truth of the gospel (. . .) may be able to serve and to do good works for the well-being of eternal life.

6 And now my bonds are manifest, which I suffer in Christ, on account of which I am glad and rejoice.

7 This to me leads to eternal salvation, which itself is brought about through your prayers and by the help of the Holy Spirit, whether it be through life or through death.

8 For my life is in Christ and to die is joy.

9 And his mercy will work in you, that you may have the same love and be of one mind.

10 Therefore, beloved, as you have heard in my presence, so hold fast and work in the fear of God, and eternal life will be yours.

11 For it is God who works in you.

12 And do without hesitation what you do.

13 And for the rest, beloved, rejoice in Christ and beware of those who are out for sordid gain.

14 May all your requests be manifest before God, and be steadfast in the mind of Christ.

15 And do what is pure, true, proper, just and lovely.

16 And what you have heard and received, hold in your heart, and peace will be with you.

17 Salute all the brethren with the holy kiss.

18 The saints salute you.

19 The grace of the Lord Jesus Christ be with your spirit.

20 And see that (this epistle) is read to the Colossians and that of the Colossians to you.

Paul's "Letter to the Laodiceans," from *The Apocryphal New Testament*, ed. J. K. Elliott. © Oxford University Press, 1993. Reprinted by permission of Oxford University Press.

APOCRYPHAL APOCALYPSES: THE TEXTS

Apocalypses were a popular kind of writing in ancient Judaism and Christianity. Most apocalypses present a first-person narrative of revelations given by God to a prophet through an angelic mediator (and interpreter); these revelations are either of the future course of world events or of the heavenly truths that explain the realities of life on earth. Normally they are given in wild dreams or visions loaded with bizarre (though sometimes transparent) symbolism; often they have a triumphalistic progression, providing hope that the horrible suffering of the present is simply a prelude to the glorious end that God has planned for his people from eternity past.

Like the Jewish apocalypses from the period, the noncanonical Christian apocalypses are, as a rule, written pseudonymously (unlike the Revelation to John in the New Testament, whose author does not claim to be any John in particular). Most of these books are concerned not so much with the course of future events on earth as with the fate of souls after death (cf. the Acts of John in Chapter 2). The typical narrative framework involves an apostle's journey through heaven and hell to witness the glorious afterlife of the saved and the cruel torments of the damned. The hortatory purpose of these accounts is clear: to ensure the blessings of heaven and avoid the tortures of hell, one must follow Christ and live an upright and moral life.

49. The Apocalypse of Peter

Three different Christian apocalypses claim to have been written by Jesus' disciple Peter (for one of the others, see Chapter 7). The one given here was discovered in 1887 in the tomb of an Egyptian monk, along with the *Gospel of Peter* (see reading 38); it was subsequently found in a fuller Ethiopic translation. Written in the early second century, the book was considered canonical in some proto-orthodox churches.

The bulk of the account gives Jesus' response to a query by Peter about the coming judgment, in which he describes the terrors of the last days, details the torments of the

---

The "Apocalypse of Peter," from *New Testament Apocrypha*, vol 2; ed. Wilhelm Schneemelcher, 2d ed. Cambridge/Louisville: Lutterworth Press/Westminster John Knox Press, 1991. Used with permission of Lutterworth Press and Westminster John Knox Press.

damned, and describes (more briefly) the blessings of the saved. It is not clear whether Jesus actually takes Peter on a journey of these two abodes of the dead or simply depicts them in such vivid detail that it *seems* as if Peter is seeing them. There is no ambiguity, however, concerning the ecstasies and torments awaiting those destined for one place or the other—particularly those in hell, whose horrific punishments are made to fit their crimes. The book ends with Peter's firsthand description of what he saw on the Mount of Transfiguration (not excerpted here), possibly given in order to validate the legitimacy of the rest of his vision (cf. 2 Pet 1:17–18).

The following excerpt gives the entire first fourteen chapters, from the Ethiopic version.

1 And when he was seated on the Mount of Olives, his own came to him, and we entreated and implored him severally and besought him, saying to him, "Make known to us what are the signs of your Parousia and of the end of the world, that we may perceive and mark the time of your Parousia and instruct those who come after us, to whom we preach the word of your gospel and whom we install in your Church, in order that they, when they hear it, may take heed to themselves that they mark the time of your coming."[1] And our Lord answered and said unto us, "Take heed that people deceive you not and that you do not become doubters and serve other gods. Many will come in my name saying 'I am Christ.' Believe them not and draw not near unto them. For the coming of the Son of God will not be manifest, but like the lightning that flashes from the east to the west, so shall I come on the clouds of heaven with a great host in my glory; with my cross going before my face will I come in my glory, shining seven times as bright as the sun will I come in my glory, with all my saints, my angels, when my Father will place a crown upon my head, that I may judge the living and the dead and recompense every one according to his work.

2 "And you, receive the parable of the fig-tree: as soon as its shoots have gone forth and its boughs have sprouted, the end of the world will come."[2] And I, Peter, answered and said to him, "Explain to me concerning the fig-tree, and how we shall perceive it, for throughout all its days does the fig-tree sprout and every year it brings forth its fruit for its master. What does the parable of the fig-tree mean? We know it not."—And the Master answered and said to me, "Do you not understand that the fig-tree is the house of Israel? Even as a person planted a fig-tree in his garden and it brought forth no fruit, and he sought its fruit for many years. When he found it not, he said to the keeper of his garden, 'Uproot the fig-tree that our land may not be unfruitful for us.' And the gardener said to God, 'We your servants wish to clear it (of weeds) and to dig the ground around it and to water it. If it does not then bear fruit, we will immediately remove its roots from the garden and plant another one in its place.' Have you not grasped that the fig-tree is the house of Israel? Truly, I say to you, when its boughs have sprouted at the end, then shall deceiving Christs come, and awaken hope (with the words): 'I am the Christ, who am (now) come into the world.' And when they shall see the wickedness of his (the false Messiah's) deeds, they shall turn away after them and deny him to whom our fathers gave praise, who crucified the first Christ and thereby sinned exceedingly. But this deceiver is not the Christ. And when they reject him, he will kill with the sword (dagger) and there shall be many martyrs. Then shall the boughs of the fig-tree, i.e., the house of Israel, sprout, and there shall be many

---

[1]See Matt 24; Mark 13; Luke 21.
[2]Mark 13:28–29.

martyrs by his hand: they shall be killed and become martyrs. Enoch and Elias will be sent to instruct them that this is the deceiver who must come into the world and do signs and wonders in order to deceive. And therefore shall they that are slain by his hand be martyrs and shall be reckoned among the good and righteous martyrs who have pleased God in their life."

3 And he showed me in his right hand the souls of all (people) and on the palm of his right hand the image of that which shall be fulfilled at the last day; and how the righteous and the sinners shall be separated and how those will do who are upright in heart, and how the evil-doers will be rooted out for all eternity. We saw how the sinners wept in great distress and sorrow, until all who saw it with their eyes wept, whether righteous, or angels, or himself also. And I asked him and said, "Lord, allow me to speak your word concerning these sinners: 'It were better for them that they had not been created.' "[3] And the Savior answered and said "O Peter, why speak thus, 'that not to have been created were better for them'? You resist God. You would not have more compassion than he for his image, for he has created them and has brought them forth when they were not. And since you have seen the lamentation which sinners shall encounter in the last days, therefore your heart is saddened; but I will show you their works in which they have sinned against the Most High.

4 "Behold now what they shall experience in the last days, when the day of God comes. On the day of the decision of the judgment of God, all the children of mortals from the east unto the west shall be gathered before my Father who ever lives, and he will command hell to open its bars of steel and to give up all that is in it. And the beasts and the fowls shall he command to give back all flesh that they have devoured, since he desires that people should appear (again); for nothing perishes for God, and nothing is impossible with him, since all things are his. For all things (come to pass) on the day of decision, on the day of judgment, at the word of God, and as all things came to pass when he created the world and com-

manded all that is therein, and it was all done— so shall it be in the last days; for everything is possible with God, and he says in the Scripture: 'Son of man, prophesy upon the several bones, and say to the bones—bone unto bone in joints, sinews, nerves, flesh and skin and hair thereon.'[4] And soul and spirit shall the great Uriel give at the command of God. For him God has appointed over the resurrection of the dead on the day of judgment. Behold and consider the corns of wheat which are sown in the earth. As something dry and without a soul does a person sow (them) in the earth; and they live again, bear fruit, and the earth gives (them) back again as a pledge entrusted to it. And this which dies, which is sown as seed in the earth and shall become alive and be restored to life, is humanity. How much more shall God raise up on the day of decision those who believe in him and are chosen by him and for whom he made (the earth); and all this shall the earth give back on the day of decision, since it shall be judged with them, and the heaven with it.

5 "And these things shall come to pass in the day of judgment of those who have fallen away from faith in God and have committed sin: cataracts of fire shall be let loose; and obscurity and darkness shall come up and cover and veil the entire world, and the waters shall be changed and transformed into coals of fire, and all that is in it (the earth?) shall burn and the sea shall become fire; under the heaven there shall be a fierce fire that shall not be put out and it flows for the judgment of wrath. And the stars shall be melted by flames of fire, as if they had not been created, and the fastnesses of heaven shall pass away for want of water and become as though they had not been created. And the lightnings of heaven shall be no more and, by their enchantment, they shall alarm the world. And the spirits of the dead bodies shall be like to them and at the command of God will become fire. And as soon as the whole creation is dissolved, the people who are in the east shall flee to the west [and those in the west] to the east;

---

[3]Mark 14:21.
[4]Ezek 37:4–8.

those that are in the south shall flee to the north and those in the [north to the] south, and everywhere will the wrath of the fearful fire overtake them; and an unquenchable flame shall drive them and bring them to the judgment of wrath in the stream of unquenchable fire which flows, flaming with fire, and when its waves separate one from another, seething, there shall be much gnashing of teeth among the children of mortals.

6 "And all will see how I come upon an eternal shining cloud, and the angels of God who will sit with me on the throne of my glory at the right hand of my heavenly Father. He will set a crown upon my head. As soon as the nations see it, they will weep, each nation for itself. And he shall command them to go into the river of fire, while the deeds of each individual one of them stand before them. [Recompense shall be given] to each according to his work. As for the elect who have done good, they will come to me and will not see death by devouring fire. But the evil creatures, the sinners and the hypocrites will stand in the depths of the darkness that passes not away, and their punishment is the fire, and angels bring forward their sins and prepare for them a place wherein they shall be punished for ever, each according to his offence. The angel of God, Uriel, brings the souls of those sinners who perished in the flood, and of all who dwell in all idols, in every molten image, in every love and in paintings, and of them that dwell on all hills and in stones and by the wayside, (whom) people call gods: they shall be burned with them (i.e., the objects in which they lodge) in eternal fire. After all of them, with their dwelling places, have been destroyed, they will be punished eternally.

7 "Then will men and women come to the place prepared for them. By their tongues with which they have blasphemed the way of righteousness will they be hung up. There is spread out for them unquenchable fire. . . .

"And behold again another place: this is a great pit filled, in which are those who have denied righteousness; and angels of punishment visit (them) and here do they kindle upon them the fire of their punishment. And again two women: they

are hung up by their neck and by their hair and are cast into the pit. These are they who plaited their hair, not to create beauty, but to turn to fornication, and that they might ensnare the souls of men to destruction. And the men who lay with them in fornication are hung by their thighs in that burning place, and they say to one another, 'We did not know that we would come into everlasting torture.'

"And the murderers and those who have made common cause with them are cast into the fire, in a place full of venomous beasts, and they are tormented without rest, as they feel their pains, and their worms are as numerous as a dark cloud. And the angel Ezrael will bring forth the souls of them that have been killed and they shall see the torment [of those who] killed [them] and shall say to one another, 'Righteousness and justice is the judgment of God. For we have indeed heard, but did not believe that we would come to this place of eternal judgment.'

8 "And near this flame there is a great and very deep pit and into it there flow all kinds of things from everywhere: judgment, horrifying things, and excretions. And the women (are) swallowed up (by this) up to their necks and are punished with great pain. These are they who have procured abortions and have ruined the work of God which he has created. Opposite them is another place where the children sit, but both alive, and they cry to God. And lightnings go forth from those children which pierce the eye of those who, by fornication, have brought about their destruction. Other men and women stand above them naked. And their children stand opposite to them in a place of delight. And they sigh and cry to God because of their parents, 'These are they who neglected and cursed and transgressed your commandment. They killed us and cursed the angel who created (us) and hung us up. And they withheld from us the light which you have appointed for all.' And the milk of the mothers flows from their breasts and congeals and smells foul, and from it come forth beasts that devour flesh, which turn and torture them for ever with their husbands, because they forsook the commandment of God and killed their children. And the children shall be given to the angel Temlakos. And those who slew them will be tortured for ever, for God wills it to be so.

9 "Ezrael, the angel of wrath, brings men and women with the half of their bodies burning and casts them into a place of darkness, the hell of humans; and a spirit of wrath chastises them with all manner of chastisement, and a worm that never sleeps consumes their entrails. These are the persecutors and betrayers of my righteous ones.

"And near to those who live thus were other men and women who chew their tongues, and they are tormented with red hot irons and have their eyes burned. These are the slanderers and those who doubt my righteousness.

"Other men and women—whose deeds (were done) in deception—have their lips cut off and fire enters into their mouths and into their entrails. [These are those] who slew the martyrs by their lying.

"In another place situated near them, on the stone pillar of fire, and the pillar is sharper than swords—men and women who are clad in rags and filthy garments, and they are cast upon it, to suffer the judgment of unceasing torture. These are they which trusted in their riches and despised widows and the woman (with) orphans . . . in the sight of God.

10 "And into another place near by, saturated with filth, they throw men and women up to their knees. These are they who lent money and took usury.

"And other men and women thrust themselves down from a high place and return again and run, and demons drive them. These are the worshippers of idols, and they drive them to the end of their wits (the slope?) and they plunge down from there. And this they do continually and are tormented for ever. These are they who have cut their flesh as apostles of a man, and the women who were with them . . . and thus are the men who defiled themselves with one another in the fashion of women.

"And beside them . . . [an untranslatable word], and beneath them the angel Ezrael prepares a place of much fire, and all the golden and silver idols, all idols, the works of human hands, and what resembles the images of cats and lions, of reptiles and wild beasts, and the men and women who manufactured the images, shall be in chains of fire; they shall be chastised because of their error before them (the images) and this is their judgment for ever. And near them other men and women who burn in the flames of the judgment, whose torture is for ever. These are they who have forsaken the commandment of God and followed . . . (unknown word) of the devils.

11 "And another very high place . . . (some unintelligible words), the men and women who make a false step go rolling down to where the fear is. And again, while the (fire) that is prepared flows, they mount up and fall down again and continue their rolling. They shall be punished thus for ever. These are they who have not honored their father and mother, and of their own accord withdrew themselves from them. Therefore shall they be punished eternally. Furthermore the angel Ezrael brings children and maidens to show to them those who are punished. They will be punished with pain, with hanging up and with many wounds which flesh-eating birds inflict. These are they that have confidence in their sins, are not obedient to their parents, and do not follow the instruction of their fathers and do not honor those who are older than they. Beside them, maidens clad in darkness for raiment, and they shall be seriously punished and their flesh will be torn in pieces. These are they who retained not their virginity till they were given in marriage; they shall be punished with these tortures, while they feel them.

"And again other men and women who ceaselessly chew their tongues and are tormented with eternal fire. These are the slaves who were not obedient to their masters. This then is their judgment for ever.

12 "And near to this torment are blind and dumb men and women whose raiment is white. They are packed closely together and fall on coals of unquenchable fire. These are they who give alms and say, 'We are righteous before God,' while they have not striven for righteousness.

"The angel of God, Ezrael, allows them to come forth out of this fire and sets forth a judgment of decision (?). This then is their judgment. (And) a stream of fire flows and all those judged are drawn into the midst of the stream. And Uriel sets them down (there). And there are wheels of fire, and men and women hung thereon by the power of their whirling. Those in the pit burn. Now these are the sorcerers and sorceresses. These wheels (are) in all decision by fire without number (?).

13 "Then the angels brought my elect and righteous, who are perfect in all righteousness, bearing them on their hands, clothed with the garments of eternal life. They shall see (their desire) on those who hated them, when he punishes them. Torment for every one (is) forever according to his deeds. And all those who are in torment will say with one voice, 'Have mercy upon us, for now we know the judgment of God, which he declared to us beforehand, and we did not believe.' And the angel Tatirokos (= Tartarouchos) will come and chasten them with even greater torment and will say unto them, 'Now do you repent when there is no more time for repen-

tance, and nothing of life remains.' And all shall say, 'Righteous is the judgment of God: for we have heard and perceived that his judgment is good, since we are punished according to our deeds.'

14 "Then will I give to my elect and righteous the baptism and the salvation for which they have besought me, in the field Akrosja (= Acherusia) which is called Aneslesleja (= Elysium). They shall adorn with flowers the portion of the righteous and I will go. . . . I will rejoice with them. I will cause the nations to enter into my eternal kingdom and show to them that eternal thing to which I have directed their hope, I and my heavenly Father. I have spoken it to you, Peter, and make it known to you. Go forth then and journey to the city in the west in the vineyard which I will tell you of . . . by the hand of my Son who is without sin, that his work . . . of destruction may be sanctified. But you are chosen in the hope which I have given to you. Spread my gospel throughout the whole world in peace! For there will be rejoicing (?) at the source of my word, the hope of life, and suddenly the world will be carried off."

><+>·O·<+><

50. The Apocalypse of Paul

In a well-known passage from 2 Corinthians 12, Paul claims that he had once been caught up into heaven to behold a vision of things that could not be uttered. A later Christian nonetheless decided to give utterance to these things, and the present apocalypse is the result. The book describes Paul's ascent into heaven to receive a revelation concerning the fate of individual souls after death. He observes souls who leave their bodies to appear before God, who knows every detail about their lives and metes out rewards or punishments accordingly. The vision continues with a narrative description of Paradise and

The "Apocalypse of Paul," from *The Apocryphal New Testament*, ed. J. K. Elliott. © Oxford University Press, 1993. Reprinted by permission of Oxford University Press.

a graphic portrayal of the torments of the damned, which parallel in many ways those found in the Apocalypse of Peter (see reading 49).

The Apocalypse of Paul in its present form dates from the end of the fourth century, but it contains materials that were composed earlier, as they are apparently alluded to by Origen in the early third century. The portions excerpted here may be among the older portions of the book.

In the consulship of Theodosius Augustus the Younger and Cynegius, a certain nobleman was then living in Tarsus, in the house which was that of Saint Paul; an angel appeared in the night and revealed it to him, saying that he should open the foundations of the house and should publish what he found, but he thought that these things were dreams.

2 But the angel coming for the third time beat him and forced him to open the foundation. And digging he found a marble box, inscribed on the sides; there was the revelation of Saint Paul, and his shoes in which he walked teaching the word of God. But he feared to open that box and brought it to the judge; when he had received it, the judge, because it was sealed with lead, sent it to the emperor Theodosius, fearing lest it might be something else; when the emperor had received it he opened it, and found the revelation of Saint Paul, a copy of which he sent to Jerusalem, and retained the original himself.

3 While I was in the body in which I was snatched up to the third heaven, . . .

14 And I said to the angel, "I wish to see the souls of the just and of sinners, and to see in what manner they go out of the body." And the angel answered and said to me, "Look again upon the earth." And I looked and saw all the world, and people were as naught and growing weak; and I looked carefully and saw a certain man about to die, and the angel said to me, "This one whom you see is a just man." And I looked again and saw all his works, whatever he had done for the sake of God's name, and all his desires, both what he remembered, and what he did not remember; they all stood in his sight in the hour of need; and

I saw the just man advance and find refreshment and confidence, and before he went out of the world the holy and the impious angels both attended; and I saw them all, but the impious found no place of habitation in him, but the holy angels took possession of his soul, guiding it till it went out of the body; and they roused the soul saying, "Soul, know the body you leave, for it is necessary that you should return to the same body on the day of the resurrection, that you may receive the things promised to all the just." Receiving therefore the soul from the body, they immediately kissed as if it were familiar to them, saying to it, "Be of good courage, for you have done the will of God while placed on earth." And there came to meet it the angel who watched it every day, and said to it, "Be of good courage, soul; I rejoice in you, because you have done the will of God on earth; for I related to God all your works just as they were." Similarly also the spirit proceeded to meet it and said, "Soul, fear not, nor be disturbed, until you come to a place which you have never known, but I will be a helper to you: for I found in you a place of refreshment in the time when I dwelt in you, while I was on earth." And his spirit strengthened it, and his angel received it, and led it into heaven; and an angel said, "Where are you running to, O soul, and do you dare to enter heaven? Wait and let us see if there is anything of ours in you; and behold we find nothing in you. I see also your divine helper and angel, and the spirit is rejoicing along with you, because you have done the will of God on earth." And they led it along till it should worship in the sight of God. And when it had ceased, immediately Michael and all the army of angels, with one voice, adored the footstool of his feet and his doors, saying at the same time to the soul, "This is your God of all things, who made you in his own image and likeness." Moreover, the angel ran on ahead and pointed him out, saying, "God, remember his labors; for this is the soul, whose works I related to you, acting according to your judgment." And the spirit said likewise, "I am the spirit of vivification inspiring it; for I had refreshment in it, in the time when I dwelt in it, acting according to your judgment." And there came the voice of God and said, "In as much as this man did not grieve me, neither will I grieve him; as he had pity, I also will have pity. Let it therefore be handed over to Michael, the angel of the Covenant, and let him lead it into the Paradise of joy, that it may become coheir with all the saints." And after these things I heard the voices of a thousand thousand angels and archangels and cherubim and twenty-four elders, saying hymns and glorifying the Lord and crying, "You are just, O Lord, and just are your judgments, and there is no respect of persons with you, but you reward every one according to your judgment." And the angel answered and said to me, "Have you believed and known that whatever each one of you has done he sees in the hour of need?" And I said, "Yes, sir."

15 And he said to me, "Look again down on the earth, and watch the soul of an impious man going out of the body, which grieved the Lord day and night, saying, "I know nothing else in this world, I eat and drink, and enjoy what is in the world; for who is there who has descended into hell and, ascending, has declared to us that there is judgment there!'" And again I looked carefully, and saw all the scorn of the sinner, and all that he did, and they stood together before him in the hour of need; and it was done to him in that hour, when he was led out of his body at the judgment, and he said, "It were better for me if I had not been born." And after these things, there came at the same time the holy angels and the evil angels, and the soul of the sinner saw both and the holy angels did not find a place in it. Moreover the evil angels cursed it; and when they had drawn it out of the body the angels admonished it a third time, saying, "O wretched soul, look upon your flesh from which you have come out; for is it nec-

essary that you should return to your flesh in the day of resurrection, that you may receive what is the due for your sins and your impieties."

16 And when they had led it forth the guardian angel preceded it, and said to it, "O wretched soul, I am the angel belonging to you, relating daily to the Lord your evil works, whatever you did by night or day; and if it were in my power, not for one day would I minister to you, but none of these things was I able to do: the judge is full of pity and just, and he himself commanded us that we should not cease to minister to the soul till you should repent, but you have lost the time of repentance. I have become a stranger to you and you to me. Let us go on then to the just judge; I will not dismiss you before I know from today I am to be a stranger to you." And the spirit afflicted it, and the angel troubled it. When they had arrived at the powers, when it started to enter heaven, a burden was imposed upon it, above all other burden: error and oblivion and murmuring met it, and the spirit of fornication, and the rest of the powers, and said to it, "Where are you going, wretched soul, and do you dare to rush into heaven? Hold, that we may see if we have our qualities in you, since we do not see that you have a holy helper." And after that I heard voices in the height of heaven saying, "Present that wretched soul to God, so it may know that it is God whom it despised." When, therefore, it had entered heaven all the angels saw it; a thousand thousand exclaimed with one voice, all saying, "Woe to you, wretched soul, for the sake of your works which you did on earth; what answer are you about to give to God when you have approached to adore him?" The angel who was with it answered and said, "Weep with me, my beloved, for I have not found rest in this soul." And the angels answered him and said, "Let such a soul be taken away from our midst, for from the time it entered the stink of it crosses to us angels." And after these things it was presented, that it might worship in the sight of God, and an angel of God showed it God who made it after his own image and likeness. Moreover its angel ran before it saying, "Lord God Almighty, I am the angel of this soul, whose works

I presented to you day and night, not acting in accordance with your judgment. And the spirit likewise said, "I am the spirit who dwelt in it from the time it was made; in itself I know it, and it has not followed my will; judge it, Lord, according to your judgment." And there came the voice of God to it and said, "Where is your fruit which you have made worthy of the goods which you have received? Have I put a distance of one day between you and the just person? Did I not make the sun to arise upon you as upon the just?" But the soul was silent, having nothing to answer, and again there came a voice saying, "Just is the judgment of God, and there is no respect of persons with God, for whoever shall have done mercy, on him shall he have mercy, and whoever shall not have been merciful, neither shall God pity him. Let it therefore be handed over to the angel Tartaruchus, who is set over the punishments, and let him cast it into outer darkness, where there is weeping and gnashing of teeth, and let it be there till the great day of judgment." And after these things I heard the voice of angels and archangels saying, "You are just, Lord, and your judgment is just."

17 And again I saw and, behold, a soul which was led forward by two angels, weeping and saying, "Have pity on me, just God, God the judge, for today it is seven days since I went out of my body, and I was handed over to these two angels, and they brought me to those places which I had never seen." And God, the just judge, said to it, "What have you done? For you never showed mercy, therefore you were handed over to such angels as have no mercy, and because you did no right, so neither did they act compassionately with you in your hour of need. Confess your sins which you committed when placed in the world." And it answered and said, "Lord, I did not sin." And the Lord, the just Lord, was angered in fury when it said, "I did not sin," because it lied; and God said, "Do you think you are still in the world where any one of you, sinning, may conceal and hide his sin from his neighbor? Here nothing whatever shall be hidden, for when the souls come to worship in sight of the throne both the good works and the

sins of each one are made manifest." And hearing these things the soul was silent, having no answer. And I heard the Lord God, the just judge, again saying, "Come, angel of this soul, and stand in the midst." And the angel of the sinful soul came, having in his hands a document, and said, "These, Lord, in my hands, are all the sins of this soul from its youth till today, from the tenth year of its birth; and if you command, Lord, will also relate its acts from the beginning of its fifteenth year." And the Lord God, the just judge, said, "I say to you, angel, I do not expect of you an account of it since it began to be fifteen years old, but state its sins for five years before it died and before it came hither." And again God, the just judge, said, "For by myself I swear, and by my holy angels, and by my virtue, that if it had repented five years before it died, on account of a conversion one year old, oblivion would now be thrown over all the evils which it sinned before, and it would have indulgence and remission of sins; now indeed it shall perish." And the angel of the sinful soul answered and said, "Lord, command that angel to exhibit those souls."

18 And in that same hour the souls were exhibited in the midst, and the soul of the sinner knew them; and the Lord said to the soul of the sinner, "I say to you, soul, confess your work which you wrought in these souls whom you see, when they were in the world." And it answered and said, "Lord, it is not yet a full year since I slew this one and poured his blood upon the ground, and with another I committed fornication; not only this, but I also greatly harmed her in taking away her goods." And the Lord God, the just judge, said, "Did you not know that if someone does violence to another and the person who sustains the violence dies first, he is kept in this place until the one who was committed the offence dies, and then both stand in the presence of the judge, and now each receives according to his deed." And I heard a voice of one saying, "Let that soul be delivered into the hands of Tartarus, and led down into hell; he shall lead it into the lower prison, and it shall be put in torments and left there till the great day of judgment." And again I heard a thousand thousand angels saying hymns to the Lord, and crying, "You are just, O Lord, and just are your judgments."

19 The angel answered and said to me, "Have you perceived all these things?" And I said, "Yes, sir." And he said to me, "Follow me again, and I will take you, and show you the places of the just." And I followed the angel, and he raised me to the third heaven and placed me at the entry of the door; and looking, I saw that the door was of gold, and two columns of gold above it full of golden letters, and the angel turned again to me and said, "Blessed are you if you enter through these doors, for it is not permitted for any to enter except those who have goodness and purity of body in all things. . . ."

22 And I looked around upon that land, and I saw a river flowing with milk and honey, and there were trees planted by the bank of that river, full of fruit; moreover, each single tree bore twelve fruits in the year, having various and diverse fruits; and I saw the created things which are in that place and all the work of God, and I saw there palms of twenty cubits, but others of ten cubits; and that land was seven times brighter than silver. And there were trees full of fruits from the roots to the highest branches, of ten thousand fruits of palms upon ten thousand fruits. The grapevines had ten thousand plants. Moreover in the single vines there were ten thousand thousand bunches and in each of these a thousand single grapes; moreover these single trees bore a thousand fruits. And I said to the angel, "Why does each tree bear a thousand fruits?" The angel answered and said to me, "Because the Lord God gives an abounding profusion of gifts to the worthy and because they of their own will afflicted themselves when they were placed in the world doing all things on account of his holy name." And again I said to the angel, "Sir, are these the only promises which the Most Holy God makes?" And he answered and said to me, "No! There are seven times greater than these. But I say to you that when the just go out of the body they shall see the promises and the good things which God has prepared for them. Till then, they shall sigh

and lament, saying, "Have we uttered any word from our mouth to grieve our neighbor even on one day?'" I asked and said again, "Are these alone the promises of God?" And the angel answered and said to me, "These whom you now see are the souls of the married and those who kept the chastity of their nuptials, controlling themselves. But to the virgins and those who hunger and thirst after righteousness and those who afflicted themselves for the sake of the name of God, God will give seven times greater than these, which I shall now show you.". . .

26 Again he led me where there is a river of milk, and I saw in that place all the infants whom Herod slew because of the name of Christ, and they greeted me, and the angel said to me, "All who keep their chastity and purity, when they have come out of the body, after they adore the Lord God are delivered to Michael and are led to the infants, and they greet them, saying that they are our brothers and friends and members; among them they shall inherit the promises of God."

27 Again he took me up and brought me to the north of the city and led me where there was a river of wine, and there I saw Abraham and Isaac and Jacob, Lot and Job and other saints, and they greeted me; and I asked and said, "What is this place, my lord?" The angel answered and said to me, "All who have given hospitality to strangers when they go out of the world first adore the Lord God, and are delivered to Michael and by this route are led into the city, and all the just greet them as son and brother, and say to them, 'Because you have observed humanity and helped pilgrims, come, have an inheritance in the city of the Lord our God: every righteous person shall receive good things of God in the city, according to his own action.'"

28 And again he carried me near the river of oil on the east of the city. And I saw there men rejoicing and singing psalms, and I said, "Who are those, my lord?" And the angel said to me, "These are they who devoted themselves to God with their whole heart and had no pride in themselves. For all those who rejoice in the Lord

God and sing psalms to the Lord with their whole heart are here led into this city. . . ."

31 When he had ceased speaking to me, he led me outside the city through the midst of the trees and far from the places of the land of the good, and put me across the river of milk and honey; and after that he led me over the ocean which supports the foundations of heaven.

The angel answered and said to me, "Do you understand why you go hence?" And I said, "Yes, sir." And he said to me, "Come and follow me, and I will show you the souls of the godless and sinners, that you may know what manner of place it is." And I went with the angel, and he carried me towards the setting of the sun, and I saw the beginning of heaven founded on a great river of water, and I asked, "What is this river of water?" And he said to me, "This is the ocean which surrounds all the earth." And when I was at the outer limit of the ocean I looked, and there was no light in that place, but darkness and sorrow and sadness; and I sighed.

And I saw there a river boiling with fire, and in it a multitude of men and women immersed up to the knees, and other men up to the navel, others even up to the lips, others up to the hair. And I asked the angel and said, "Sir, who are those in the fiery river?" And the angel answered and said to me, "They are neither hot nor cold, because they were found neither in the number of the just nor in the number of the godless. For those spent the time of their life on earth passing some days in prayer, but others in sins and fornications, until their death." And I asked him and said, "Who are these, sir, immersed up to their knees in fire?" He answered and said to me, "These are they who when they have gone out of church occupy themselves with idle disputes. Those who are immersed up to the navel are those who, when they have taken the body and blood of Christ, go and fornicate and do not cease from their sins till they die. Those who are immersed up to the lips are those who slander each other when they assemble in the church of God; those up to the eyebrows are those who nod to each other and plot spite against their neighbor."

32 And I saw to the north a place of various and diverse punishments full of men and women, and a river of fire ran down into it. I observed and I saw very deep pits and in them several souls together, and the depth of that place was about three thousand cubits, and I saw them groaning and weeping and saying, "Have pity on us, O Lord!", and no one had pity on them. And I asked the angel and said, "Who are these, sir?" And the angel answered and said to me, "These are they who did not hope in the Lord, that they would be able to have him as their helper." And I asked and said, "Sir, if these souls remain for thirty or forty generations thus one upon another, I believe the pits would not hold them unless they were dug deeper." And he said to me, "The Abyss has no measure, for beneath it there stretches down below that which is below it; and so it is that if perchance anyone should take a stone and throw it into a very deep well after many hours it would reach the bottom, such is the abyss. For when the souls are thrown in there, they hardly reach the bottom in fifty years."

33 When I heard this, I wept and groaned over the human race. The angel answered and said to me, "Why do you weep? Are you more merciful than God? For though God is good, he knows that there are punishments, and he patiently bears with the human race, allowing each one to do his own will in the time in which he dwells on the earth."

34 I observed the fiery river and saw there a man being tortured by Tartaruchian angels having in their hands an iron instrument with three hooks with which they pierced the bowels of that old man; and I asked the angel and said, "Sir, who is that old man on whom such torments are imposed?" And the angel answered and said to me, "He whom you see was a presbyter who did not perform his ministry well: when he had been eating and drinking and committing fornication he offered the host to the Lord at his holy altar."

35 And I saw not far away another old man led on by evil angels running with speed, and they pushed him into the fire up to his knees, and they struck him with stones and wounded his face like a storm and did not allow him to say, "Have pity on me!" And I asked the angel, and he said to me, "He whom you see was a bishop and did not perform his episcopate well, who indeed accepted the great name but did not enter into the witness of him who gave him the name all his life, seeing that he did not give judgment and did not pity widows and orphans, but now he receives retribution according to his iniquity and his works."

36 And I saw another man in the fiery river up to his knees. His hands were stretched out and bloody, and worms proceeded from his mouth and nostrils, and he was groaning and weeping, and crying he said, "Have pity on me! For I am hurt more than the rest who are in this punishment." And I asked, "Sir, who is this?" And he said to me, "This man whom you see was a deacon who devoured the oblations and committed fornication and did not do right in the sight of God; for this cause he unceasingly pays this penalty."

And I looked closely and saw alongside of him another man, whom they delivered up with haste and cast into the fiery river, and he was in it up to the knees; and the angel who was set over the punishments came with a great fiery razor, and with it he cut the lips of that man and the tongue likewise. And sighing, I lamented and asked, "Who is that, sir?" And he said to me, "He whom you see was a reader and read to the people, but he himself did not keep the precepts of God; now he also pays the proper penalty."

37 And I saw another multitude of pits in the same place, and in the midst of it a river full with a multitude of men and women, and worms consumed them. But I lamented, and sighing asked the angel and said, "Sir, who are these?" And he said to me, "These are those who exacted interest on interest and trusted in their riches and did not hope in God that he was their helper."

And after that I looked and saw another place, very narrow, and it was like a wall, and fire round about it. And I saw inside men and women gnawing their tongues, and I asked, "Sir, who are these?" And he said to me, "These are they who

in church disparage the Word of God, not attending to it, but as it were making naught of God and his angels; for that reason they now likewise pay the proper penalty."

38 And I observed and saw another pool in the pit and its appearance was like blood, and I asked and said, "Sir, what is this place?" And he said to me, "Into that pit stream all the punishments." And I saw men and women immersed up to the lips, and I asked, "Sir, who are these?" And he said to me, "These are the magicians who prepared for men and women evil magic arts and did not cease till they died."

And again I saw men and women with very black faces in a pit of fire, and I sighed and lamented and asked, "Sir, who are these?" And he said to me, "These are fornicators and adulterers who committed adultery, having wives of their own; likewise also the women committed adultery, having husbands of their own; therefore they unceasingly suffer penalties."

39 And I saw there girls in black raiment, and four terrifying angels having in their hands burning chains, and they put them on the necks of the girls and led them into darkness; and I, again weeping, asked the angel, "Who are these, sir?" And he said to me, "These are they who, when they were virgins, defiled their virginity unknown to their parents; for which cause they unceasingly pay the proper penalties."

And again I observed there men and women with hands cut and their feet placed naked in a place of ice and snow, and worms devoured them. Seeing them I lamented and asked, "Sir, who are these?" And he said to me, "These are they who harmed orphans and widows and the poor, and did not hope in the Lord, for which cause they unceasingly pay the proper penalties."

And I observed and saw others hanging over a channel of water, and their tongues were very dry, and many fruits were placed in their sight, and they were not permitted to take of them, and I asked, "Sir, who are these?" And he said to me, "These are they who broke their fast before the appointed hour; for this cause they unceasingly pay these penalties."

And I saw other men and women hanging by their eyebrows and their hair, and a fiery river drew them, and I said, "Who are these, sir?" And he said to me, "These are they who join themselves not to their own husbands and wives but to whores, and therefore they unceasingly pay the proper penalties."

And I saw other men and women covered with dust, and their countenance was like blood, and they were in a pit of pitch and sulphur running in a fiery river, and I asked, "Sir, who are these?" And he said to me, "These are they who committed the iniquity of Sodom and Gomorrah, the male with the male, for which reason they unceasingly pay the penalties.". . .

The New Scriptures

Canonical Lists in Early Christianity

Christianity started out as a religion that revered a sacred book. The Hebrew Bible was accepted, interpreted, and taught by Jesus and his followers. As the Christian movement developed away from its Jewish roots (see Chapter 5), it maintained its literary emphasis, both reinterpreting the Jewish Scriptures in light of its own emerging theology and producing and accepting other writings as standing on a par with them. The movement to adopt a new authority may have started as soon as Christians began to accept Jesus' own words as authoritative; clearly his teachings functioned this way for the earliest Christian communities (see 1 Cor 7:10; 9:14) and by the end of the first century they were sometimes quoted as "Scripture" (1 Tim 5:18). Moreover, the writings of Jesus' apostles were also seen as carrying particular weight; they were read in early Christian worship services and, by the close of the New Testament period, were occasionally referred to as Scripture (2 Pet 3:16).

The second and third centuries saw a movement within Christian circles to establish a fixed "canon" of Scripture ("canon": a Greek word literally meaning "straight edge" or "ruler," used to refer to a normative collection of writings, in this case, an authoritative collection of authoritative books). Several factors facilitated this movement, including the following: (a) the desire of Christians to have their own authorities in addition to those inherited from their mother religion (Judaism) and thereby to differentiate themselves from non-Christian Jews; (b) the widely perceived need to have an authoritative basis for the doctrines and practices central to the religion, and the concomitant sense that the "right" beliefs and practices required a foundation in the "right" books (i.e., those produced by Jesus' own apostles); and (c) the production of documents falsely claiming to be written by Jesus' apostles and embracing alterative views of belief and practice (see Chapter 8).

Many people do not realize that the formation of the New Testament was a long and drawn out process; the twenty-seven book canon familiar today did not come into being immediately at the end of the first century. For several hundred years Christians debated over which books to include. The first Christian known to make an authoritative pronouncement on the canon was Marcion (see Chapter 7), who maintained that the Christian Scriptures comprised the Gospel of Luke and ten of Paul's letters (all severely edited)—no other apostolic writings and none of the Old Testament. Other Christian groups had other favorite books, some preferring one or the other Gospel that eventually made it into the New Testament, possibly with the addition of other books like the Gospel of Peter or the Gospel of Thomas, others of them favoring a kind of mega-Gospel produced in the middle of the second century by a Christian named Tatian, whose work, the Diatesseron ("Through the Four"), compiled the stories of all four Gospels into one. Even among proto-orthodox groups there was no firm agreement, although by the end of the second century most such Christians accepted Matthew, Mark, Luke, and John, along with the book of Acts, the thirteen letters of Paul, 1 Peter, and 1 John. But even then there continued to be wide-ranging disputes concerning the status of such books as Hebrews, Revelation, the Shepherd of Hermas, and the Letter of Barnabas.

Christians engaged in these disputes generally appealed to several considerations. It was widely conceded that to be accepted as Scripture, a book needed to be (a) ancient (not representing any recent innovations), (b) apostolic (written by an apostle or one of their own followers), (c) catholic (used widely among Christian churches everywhere), and, perhaps most important, (d) orthodox (presenting the "right" beliefs as opposed to the wrong ones; what those beliefs *were*, of course, varied from one Christian group to another).

The canonical debates raged far beyond our period. In fact, the first known instance of any Christian author insisting on the twenty-seven books now in the canon, and only these twenty-seven, came in 367 C.E.—nearly three hundred years after much of the New Testament had been written—in a letter sent by Athanasius, the powerful and influential bishop of Alexandria, to his churches. Even then, however, the matter was far from resolved; orthodox Christians continued to dispute the fringes of the canon for well over a century.

The following texts are several of the canon lists of the second and third centuries, that is, lists of books considered canonical by various authors of the period.

For Further Reading

Bruce, F. F. *The Canon of Scripture*. Downers Grove, Ill.: Intervarsity Press, 1988.

Campenhausen, Hans von. *The Formation of the Christian Bible*, tr. J. A. Baker. Philadelphia: Fortress, 1972.

Gamble, Harry. *The New Testament Canon: Its Making and Meaning*. Philadelphia: Fortress, 1985.

———. "The Canon of the New Testament," in the *Anchor Bible Dictionary*, ed. David Noel Freedman. New York: Doubleday, 1992; I.852–861.

Metzger, Bruce M. *The Canon of the New Testament: Its Origin, Development, and Significance*. Oxford: Clarendon, 1987.

THE TEXTS

51. The Muratorian Canon

Named after L. A. Muratori, the Italian scholar who discovered it in the early eighteenth century, the Muratorian Canon is the earliest list of New Testament books known to exist. Written on a fragmentary manuscript in ungrammatical Latin, the list begins in mid-sentence by describing the production of an unnamed Gospel; since it continues by explicitly calling Luke the "third book of the Gospel" and John, then, the "fourth," the list evidently began with Matthew and Mark.

Twenty-two of the twenty-seven books of the New Testament canon are included here; Hebrews, James, 1 & 2 Peter, and 3 John are excluded. The author also accepted the Wisdom of Solomon and the Apocalypse of Peter (see Chapter 8). The Shepherd of Hermas is accepted for reading but not as part of sacred scripture for the church; the author explicitly rejects "Paul's" letters to Laodicea and Alexandria as Marcionite forgeries and condemns many others that he does not name.

The time and place of composition of this list is in great dispute, but, since the author shows a particular concern with the false teachings of Marcion, Valentinus, Basilides, and others who lived in the middle of the second century and knows something of the family of bishop Pius of Rome (d. 154), many scholars think he was living in the second half of the second century, possibly in Rome.

But he was present among them, and so he put [the facts down in his Gospel.] The third book of the Gospel [is that] according to Luke. Luke, the physician, after the ascension of Christ, when Paul had taken him with him as a companion of his traveling, [and after he had made] an investigation, wrote in his own name—but neither did he see the Lord in the flesh—and thus, as he was able to investigate, so he also begins to tell the story [starting] from the nativity of John. The fourth [book] of the Gospels is that of John, [one] of the disciples. When his fellow-disciples and bishops urged [him], he said: "Fast together with me today for three days and, what shall be revealed to each, let us tell [it] to each other." On the same night it was revealed to Andrew, [one] of the Apostles, that, with all of them reviewing [it], John should describe all things in his own name. And so, although different beginnings might be taught in the separate books of the Gospels, nevertheless it makes no difference to the faith of believers, since all things in all [of them] are declared by the one sovereign Spirit—concerning [his] nativity, concerning [his] passion, concerning [his] resurrection, concerning [his] walk with his dis-

The "Muratorian Canon," from *Evidence of Tradition*, ed. Daniel J. Theron. 2d ed. Grand Rapids, Mich.: Baker Book House, 1980.

ciples, and concerning his double advent: the first in humility when he was despised, which has been; the second in royal power, glorious, which is to be. What marvel, therefore, if John so constantly brings forward particular [matters] also in his Epistles, saying of himself: "What we have seen with our eyes and have heard with [our] ears and our hands have handled, these things we have written to you."[1] For thus he declares that he was not only an eyewitness and hearer, but also a writer of all the wonderful things of the Lord in order.

The Acts of all the Apostles, however, were written in one volume. Luke described briefly "for" most excellent Theophilus particular [things], which happened in his presence, as he also evidently relates indirectly the death of Peter (?) and also Paul's departure from the city as he was proceeding to Spain.

The Epistles of Paul themselves, however, show to those, who wish to know, which [they are], from what place, and for what cause they were sent. First of all he wrote to the Corinthians, admonishing against schism of heresy; thereupon to the Galatians [admonishing against] circumcision; to the Romans, however, [he wrote] rather lengthily pointing out with a series of Scripture quotations that Christ is their main theme also. [But] it is necessary that we have a discussion singly concerning these, since the blessed Apostle Paul himself, imitating the example of his predecessor, John, wrote to seven churches only by name [and] in this order: The first [Epistle] to the Corinthians, the second to the Ephesians, the third to the Philippians, the fourth to the Colossians, the fifth to the Galatians, the sixth to the Thessalonians, and the seventh to the Romans. But, although he wrote twice to the Corinthians and to the Thessalonians, for reproof, nevertheless [it is evident that] one

Church is made known to be diffused throughout the whole globe of the earth. For John also, though he wrote in the Apocalypse to seven churches, nevertheless he speaks to them all. But he [wrote] one [letter] to Philemon and one to Titus, but two to Timothy for the sake of affection and love. In honor of the General Church, however, they have been sanctified by an ordination of the ecclesiastical discipline. There is extant also [an epistle] to the Laodiceans, and another to the Alexandrians, forged in the name of Paul according to the heresy of Marcion. There are also many others which cannot be received in the General Church, for gall cannot be mixed with honey.

The Epistle of Jude indeed and the two with the superscription, "Of John," are accepted in the General [Church]—so also the Wisdom of Solomon written by friends in his honor. We accept only the Apocalypses of John and of Peter, although some of us do not want it to be read in the Church. But Hermas composed The Shepherd quite recently in our times in the city of Rome, while his brother, Pius, the bishop, occupied the [episcopal] seat of the city of Rome. And therefore, it should indeed be read, but it cannot be published for the people in the Church, neither among the Prophets, since their number is complete, nor among the Apostles for it is after their time.

But we accept nothing at all of Arsinoes, or Valentinus, or Metiades. Those also [are rejected] who composed a new book of Psalms for Marcion together with Basilides and the Cataphrygians of Asia. . . .

---

[1] 1 John 1:1.

52. Irenaeus: Against the Heresies

Writing in 180 C.E. in Gaul, the great proto-orthodox heresiologist Irenaeus (see Chapter 7) did not provide a complete list of books that he considered to be canonical. But he did attack various heretical groups for accepting only one or the other of the Gospels (while maintaining that the heretics would not have gone astray had they correctly interpreted even the one book they accepted). Irenaeus then mounted the following argument for his own view that there were four and only four Gospels, an argument that many interpreters suspect was convincing chiefly to those who already agreed with it.

So firm is the ground upon which these Gospels rest, that the very heretics themselves bear witness to them, and, starting from these [documents], each one of them endeavours to establish his own peculiar doctrine. For the Ebionites, who use Matthew's Gospel only, are confuted out of this very same, making false suppositions with regard to the Lord. But Marcion, mutilating that according to Luke, is proved to be a blasphemer of the only existing God, from those [passages] which he still retains. Those, again, who separate Jesus from Christ, alleging that Christ remained impassible, but that it was Jesus who suffered, preferring the Gospel by Mark, if they read it with a love of truth, may have their errors rectified. Those, moreover, who follow Valentinus, making copious use of that according to John, to illustrate their conjunctions, shall be proved to be totally in error by means of this very Gospel, as I have shown in the first book. Since, then, our opponents do bear testimony to us, and make use of these [documents], our proof derived from them is firm and true.

It is not possible that the Gospels can be either more or fewer in number than they are. For, since there are four zones of the world in which we live, and four principal winds, while the church is scattered throughout all the world, and the pillar and ground of the church is the Gospel and the spirit of life; it is fitting that she should have four pillars, breathing out immortality on every side, and vivifying afresh. From which fact, it is evident that the Word, the Artificer of all, he that sits upon the cherubim, and contains all things, he who was manifested to humans, has given us the Gospel under four aspects, but bound together by one Spirit.

Irenaeus's Gospel Canon, from *The Ante-Nicene Fathers*; vol. 1, *The Apostolic Fathers with Justin Martyr and Irenaeus*, ed. A. Cleveland Coxe. Reprint; 2ᵈ ed. Grand Rapids, Mich.: Eerdmans, 1987.

53. Origen of Alexandria

None of the surviving writings of Origen, the great Christian scholar of Alexandria (see Chapter 4), provides a full listing of the books that he considered to be part of the New Testament canon. Origen does make scattered references to the canon, however; the following partial lists are drawn from his Commentaries on Matthew and John and his Homilies on the Epistle to the Hebrews. As can be seen, Origen accepted the four Gospels that were eventually agreed upon: the Pauline epistles (which he does not enumerate in this fragment), one letter of Peter, allowing for the possibility of a second, one letter of John and possibly two more, and the Apocalypse to John. In the final fragment given here, he addresses the problem posed by the book of Hebrews, accepting it as canonical but expressing his doubts about whether Paul was actually its author.

These excerpts are drawn from Book VI of the *Ecclesiastical History* of the famous fourth-century church historian Eusebius (see reading 54), who devoted a significant portion of an entire volume of his history to the life and work of Origen.

1. From Origen's
Commentary on Matthew

I accept the traditional view of the four Gospels which alone are undeniably authentic in the church of God on earth. First to be written was that of the one-time exciseman who became an apostle of Jesus Christ—Matthew; it was published for believers of Jewish origin, and was composed in Aramaic. Next came that of Mark, who followed Peter's instructions in writing it, and who in Peter's general epistle was acknowledged as his son: "Greetings to you from the church in Babylon, chosen like yourselves, and from my son Mark."[1] Next came that of Luke, who wrote for Gentile converts the Gospel praised by Paul. Last of all came John's.

2. From Origen's
Commentary on John

The man who was enabled to become a minister of the New Covenant, not of the letter but of the spirit, Paul, proclaimed the Gospel from Jerusalem, in a wide sweep as far as Illyricum. But he did not write to all the churches he had taught; and to those to which he did write he sent only a few lines. Peter, on whom is built Christ's Church, over which the gates of Hades shall have no power, left us one acknowledged epistle, possibly two—though this is doubtful. Need I say anything about the man who leant back on Jesus' breast, John? He left a single

---

[1] 1 Pet 1:13.
[2] John 21:25.

Origen's New Testament Canon, from *Eusebius: The History of the Church from Christ to Constantine*, trans. G. A. Williamson, rev. Andrew Louth (Penguin Classics 1965, rev. ed. 1989). Copyright © G. A. Williamson, 1965. Revisions copyright © Andrew Louth, 1989. Used with permission.

Gospel, though he confessed that he could write so many that the whole world would not hold them.[2] He also wrote the Revelation, but was ordered to remain silent and not write the utterances of the seven thunders.[3] In addition, he left an epistle of a very few lines, and possibly two more, though their authenticity is denied by some. Anyway, they do not total a hundred lines between them.

3. From Origen's
Homilies on Hebrews

In the epistle entitled *To the Hebrews* the diction does not exhibit the characteristic roughness of speech or phraseology admitted by the Apostle himself, the construction of the sentences is closer to Greek usage, as anyone capable of recognizing differences of

style would agree. On the other hand the matter of the epistle is wonderful, and quite equal to the Apostle's acknowledged writings: the truth of this would be admitted by anyone who has read the Apostle carefully. . . . If I were asked my personal opinion, I would say that the matter is the Apostle's but the phraseology and construction are those of someone who remembered the Apostle's teaching and wrote his own interpretation of what his master had said. So if any church regards this epistle as Paul's, it should be commended for so doing, for the primitive Church had every justification for handing it down as his. Who wrote the epistle is known to God alone: the accounts that have reached us suggest that it was either Clement, who became Bishop of Rome, or Luke, who wrote the Gospel and the Acts.

----

[3] Rev 10:3–4.

---

54. Eusebius: Ecclesiastical History

As noted in Chapter 1, Eusebius of Caesarea, commonly known as the "Father of Church History," wrote in the early decades of the fourth century, immediately after the period otherwise represented here. But it may be useful to include at least one brief passage from Book III of his work, the *Ecclesiastical History*, to show that the debates over the canon had not been resolved, even within proto-orthodox circles, some two hundred years after the last of the books of the New Testament had been produced. Of particular interest in Eusebius's list is his categorization of apostolic books as (a) "recognized," that is, accepted as canonical by all churches, (b) "disputed," that is, recognized by some churches but not others (some of these books he labels "spurious," that is, orthodox but pseudonymous and so not to be accepted), and (c) rejected, that is, heretical forgeries.

Eusebius's New Testament Canon, from *Eusebius: The History of the Church from Christ to Constantine,* trans. by G. A. Williamson, rev. Andrew Louth (Pengiun Classics 965, rev. ed. 1989). Copyright © G. A. Williamson, 1965. Revisions copyright © Andrew Louth, 1989. Used with permission.

It will be well, at this point, to classify the New Testament writings already referred to. We must, of course, put first the holy quartet of the Gospels, followed by the Acts of the Apostles. The next place in the list goes to Paul's epistles, and after them we must recognize the epistle called 1 John; likewise 1 Peter. To these may be added, if it is thought proper, the Revelation of John, the arguments about which I shall set out when the time comes. These are classed as Recognized Books. Those that are disputed, yet familiar to most, include the epistles known as James, Jude, and 2 Peter, and those called 2 and 3 John, the work either of the evangelist or of someone else with the same name.

Among Spurious Books must be placed the "Acts" of Paul, the "Shepherd," and the "Revelation of Peter"; also the alleged "Epistle of Barnabas," and the "Teachings of the Apostles," together with the Revelation of John, if this seems the right place for it: as I said before, some reject it, others include it among the Recognized Books. Moreover, some have found a place in the list for the "Gospel of Hebrews," a book which has a special appeal for those Hebrews who have accepted Christ. These would all be classed with the Disputed Books, but I have been obliged to list the latter separately, distinguishing those writings which according to the tradition of the Church are true, genuine, and recognized, from those in a different category, not canonical but disputed, yet familiar to most church people; for we must not confuse these with the writings published by heretics under the name of the apostles, as containing either Gospels of Peter, Thomas, Matthias, and several others besides these, or Acts of Andrews, John, and other apostles. To none of these has any church person of any generation ever seen fit to refer in his writings. Again, nothing could be farther from apostolic usage than the type of phraseology employed, while the ideas and implications of their contents are so irreconcilable with true orthodoxy that they stand revealed as the forgeries of heretics. It follows that so far from being classed even among Spurious Books, they must be thrown out as impious and beyond the pale.

Chapter 10

The Structure of Early Christianity

The Development of Church Offices

Early Christian communities had none of the formal structures that characterized the church throughout the Middle Ages, with a pope in Rome, powerful regional bishops, ordained priests, and sundry other church officers with positions of influence. First-century sources do not attest even a basic division between priests and laity.

The earliest Christian churches we know about were those associated with the apostle Paul, the first Christian writer whose works have survived. Rather than being organized around highly qualified and well-trained professional ministers, these gatherings of Christians were charismatic communities, that is, groups of believers who were *all* understood to have been provided with a spiritual gift (Greek: *charisma*) to enable them to minister to the spiritual and physical needs of the entire congregation, gifts like wisdom, teaching, and healing (see 1 Corinthians 12–14). These gifts were endowments from the Spirit, given, evidently, at baptism. They were for the mutual upbuilding and edification of the church, in the interim period between the resurrection of Jesus (the "beginning of the end") and his return from heaven (its consummation). Paul and his congregations apparently believed that this interim would be very brief, that Christ would return within their own generation (see, e.g., 1 Thess 4:13–5:11). No surprise, then, that they made scant efforts to organize the church for the long haul.

As a result, these communities did not have "officially" appointed leaders. They did not even meet in public buildings constructed for the purpose. The first church building known to have existed (from literary sources) dates to 201 C.E; the first one actually discovered by archaeologists was built (out of a private home) nearly half a century after that. Christians of the first two centuries met in the homes of their wealthier members, who had places large enough to accommodate the congregation. There were several, possibly many, such house churches in the large urban areas around the Mediterranean. The earliest leaders of these communities were evidently the persons who owned the homes, that is, the wealthiest and, probably, the most highly educated members of the church, who provided not only a place to meet but possibly other resources for the church as well. They may also have taken the responsibility of running the meetings.

Women may have enjoyed a significant representation among these unofficial early church leaders. Although women in that world were for the most part denied access to public avenues of power, since men tended to assert their dominance in the public arena, they were by and large granted authority in the home. As a result, women in *house* churches appear to have played a much more prominent role than they did in the community at large.

In any event, in the small house churches of earliest Christianity, there were no ordained officers in charge of the spiritual lives of the congregation. Everyone had an endowment of the spirit and so was responsible for a set task. As a result, problems that arose were sometimes hard to deal with, as can be seen just from Paul's letters themselves. When severe ethical and doctrinal difficulties arose in Corinth, for example, Paul wrote a letter to the entire congregation urging them to act and believe in appropriate ways. Why did he not write the pastor of the church to urge him to set his congregation in order? There *was* no pastor.

It is not difficult to image the long-term problems that might set in with churches organized under a charismatic model. As more people flocked into the church, decisions had to be made concerning the direction the church was to take. If all church members had an equal endowment of the Spirit and felt that the Spirit was speaking directly to them, how was one to decide which course of action to take when different people felt led differently? How was one to deal with different theological opinions, some of them completely at odds with one another, and with different senses of how the congregation's worship services were to be run, its alms were to be distributed, and so on?

Largely as a result of the chaos that could (and did) develop without a more rigorous structure, these charismatic communities eventually transformed themselves into more structured social groups, with leaders of set qualification and specified function. Already by the end of the first century, the churches Paul had founded some decades earlier were organized around "bishops" (literally: overseers), who were ultimately in charge of the community, and "deacons" (literally: ministers or servers). The churches, rapidly becoming public institutions, were principally run by men; women were increasingly demoted from positions of active involvement.

These developments can be seen already in the Pastoral epistles of the New Testament (1 and 2 Timothy and Titus), which most scholars see as pseudonymous, written in Paul's name by a member of one of his churches near the end of the first century. By the mid-second century, much of the church structure that would later develop into the hierarchy of the Roman Catholic Church was already in place, in nucleus at least, in proto-orthodox communities (the ones about which we are best informed) throughout the Mediterranean. Procedures were developed for determining which persons were to serve as bishops; moreover, these bishops were understood as standing in a spiritual line of descent from the apostles of Jesus themselves (the "apostolic succession"; see Chapter 7). Under the bishop served a board of "elders" (literally: presbyters), who assisted him in his administration and instruction of the congregation. Below them was a group of "deacons," who assisted during the worship services and in the collection and distribution of alms. Other offices are in evidence as well, including "widows," single women appointed specifically to engage in prayer and acts of charity for the poor and sick.

There are various theories of how these offices developed; it is generally agreed that Christians followed models of organization already known to them from other kinds of social groups with which they are intimately familiar, such as the household (which tended to be organized hierarchically, with the *paterfamilias* as the undisputed head), the synagogue (which also had boards of "elders"), and the voluntary associations that were ubiquitous throughout the empire (for example, various trade organizations, in which members of the same profession gathered periodically for meals and other social events, including the worship of the patron deity). It is likely that churches in different localities were organized and structured differently, depending on local conditions (such as whether most members came from the synagogue or out of pagan cults), especially in the early part of our period, when the diversity of the Christian movement is particularly evident.

Already by the early second century, we find proto-orthodox Christians urging that the bishop have supreme control over the congregation and be respected like God himself and that the presbyters who serve with him be accorded all the respect of Jesus' own apostles. Authoritative tractates specify the qualifications for these offices, the specific duties they comprise, and instructions for carrying them out. Bishops of certain localities are widely recognized authorities in matters pertaining to the church throughout the entire world, not just in their own locality; the authority of the bishop of Rome is becoming widely recognized throughout the church. Moreover, women are by and large being excluded from leadership roles, at least within the proto-orthodox communities (not so elsewhere, especially among Gnostics).

And so, well before the end of our period, the hierarchical structures that were to become such a key feature of later medieval Christianity are already essentially in place, as can be seen in the following selection of texts.

For Further Reading

Burtchaell, James T. *From Synagogue to Church: Public Services and Offices in the Earliest Christian Communities.* Cambridge: Cambridge University Press, 1992.

Campenhausen, Hans von. *Ecclesiasical Authority and Spiritual Power in the Early Church.* Peabody, Mass: Hendrickson, 1997 (reprint of 1969 ed.).

Kaufman, Peter I. *Church, Book, and Bishop: Conflict and Authority in Early Latin Christianity.* Boulder: Westview Press, 1996.

Maier, Harry O. *The Social Setting of the Ministry as Reflected in the Writings of Hermas, Clement, and Ignatius.* Waterloo, Ont.: Wilfrid Laurier University, 1991.

Torjesen, Karen Jo. *When Women Were Priests: Women's Leadership in the Early Church and the Scandal of the Subordination in the Rise of Christianity.* San Francisco: HarperSanFrancisco, 1993.

White, L. Michael. "Christianity: Early Social Life and Organization," in the *Anchor Bible Dictionary,* ed. David Noel Freedman. New York: Doubleday, 1992; I.927–35.

THE TEXTS

55. First Clement

Sent from "the church of God in Rome" to "the church of God in Corinth" (1:1), this letter has been traditionally ascribed to Clement, the third bishop of Rome. The letter itself, however, never names its actual author or mentions Clement. The purpose of the writing, in any event, is perfectly clear. There has been a division in the church in Corinth in which the elders have been ousted from their positions (3:2–4). For the Roman Christians, this is an altogether unacceptable situation, "shameful in the extreme" (47:6), which should be rectified at once. The new leaders are to relinquish their authority to the old.

At the core of the letter's argument is one of the earliest expressions of the notion of "apostolic succession." The leaders of the Christian churches were appointed by the successors of the apostles who had been chosen by Christ who was sent by God: anyone who opposes those in authority, therefore, is in rebellion against God himself (chaps. 42–44). Much of the argument revolves around the history of the people of God as known from the Jewish Scriptures, where envy and strife were always promoted by sinners opposed to the righteous. The new leaders of the Corinthian congregation stand within this nefarious line.

Because of several hints within the letter itself (e.g., personal references to Peter and Paul in chap. 5 and the designation of the Corinthian church as "ancient" in chap. 47), most scholars date it near the end of the first century, possibly around 95 C.E. during the reign of Domitian.

The church of God, living in exile in Rome, to the church of God, exiled in Corinth—to you who are called and sanctified by God's will through our Lord Jesus Christ. Abundant grace and peace be yours from God Almighty through Jesus Christ.

1 Due, dear friends, to the sudden and successive misfortunes and accidents we have encountered, we have, we admit, been rather long in turning our attention to your quarrels. We refer to the abominable and unholy schism, so alien and foreign to those whom God has chosen, which a few impetuous and headstrong fellows have fanned to such a pitch of insanity that your good name, once so famous and dear to us all, has fallen into the gravest ill repute.

2 Has anyone, indeed, stayed with you without attesting the excellence and firmness of your faith? without admiring your sensible and considerate Christian piety? without broadcasting your spirit of unbounded hospitality? without praising your perfect and trustworthy knowledge?

3 For you always acted without partiality and walked in God's laws. You obeyed your rulers

and gave your elders the proper respect. You disciplined the minds of your young people in moderation and dignity. You instructed your women to do everything with a blameless and pure conscience, and to give their husbands the affection they should. You taught them, too, to abide by the rule of obedience and to run their homes with dignity and thorough discretion.

2 You were all humble and without any pretensions, obeying orders rather than issuing them, more gladly giving than receiving. Content with Christ's rations and mindful of them, you stored his words carefully up in your hearts and held his sufferings before your eyes.

2 In consequence, you were all granted a profound and rich peace and an insatiable longing to do good, while the Holy Spirit was abundantly poured out on you all.

3 You were full of holy counsels, and, with zeal for the good and devout confidence, you stretched out your hands to almighty God, beseeching him to have mercy should you involuntarily have fallen into any sin.

4 Day and night you labored for the whole brotherhood, that by your pity and sympathy the sum of his elect might be saved.

5 You were sincere and guileless and bore no grudges.

6 All sedition and schism were an abomination to you. You wept for the faults of your neighbors, while you reckoned their shortcomings as your own.

7 You never regretted all the good you did, being ready for any good deed.

8 Possessed of an excellent and devout character, you did everything in his fear. The commands and decrees of the Lord were engraven on the tablets of your heart.

3 You were granted great popularity and growing numbers, so that the word of Scripture was fulfilled: "My beloved ate and drank and filled out and grew fat and started to kick."[1]

2 From this there arose rivalry and envy, strife and sedition, persecution and anarchy, war and captivity.

3 And so the dishonored rose up against those who were held in honor, those of no reputation

against the notable, the stupid against the wise, the young against their elders.

4 For this reason righteousness and peace are far from you, since each has abandoned the fear of God and grown purblind in his faith, and ceased to walk by the rules of his precepts or to behave in a way worthy of Christ. Rather does each follow the lusts of his evil heart, by reviving that wicked and unholy rivalry, by which, indeed, death came into the world.

42 The apostles received the gospel for us from the Lord Jesus Christ; Jesus, the Christ, was sent from God.

2 Thus Christ is from God and the apostles from Christ. In both instances the orderly procedure depends on God's will.

3 And so the apostles, after receiving their orders and being fully convinced by the resurrection of our Lord Jesus Christ and assured by God's word, went out in the confidence of the Holy Spirit to preach the good news that God's Kingdom was about to come.

4 They preached in country and city, and appointed their first converts, after testing them by the Spirit, to be the bishops and deacons of future believers.

5 Nor was this any novelty, for Scripture had mentioned bishops and deacons long before. For this is what Scripture says somewhere: "I will appoint their bishops in righteousness and their deacons in faith."[2] . . .

44 Now our apostles, thanks to our Lord Jesus Christ, knew that there was going to be strife over the title of bishop.

2 It was for this reason and because they had been given an accurate knowledge of the future, that they appointed the officers we have mentioned. Furthermore, they later added a codicil to the effect that, should these die, other approved men should succeed to their ministry.

3 In the light of this, we view it as a breach of justice to remove from their ministry those who were appointed either by them [i.e., the apostles]

---

[1]Deut 32:15.
[2]Isa 60:17.

or later on and with the whole church's consent, by others of the proper standing, and who, long enjoying everybody's approval, have ministered to Christ's flock faultlessly, humbly, quietly, and unassumingly.

4 For we shall be guilty of no slight sin if we eject from the episcopate men who have offered the sacrifices with innocence and holiness.

5 Happy, indeed, are those presbyters who have already passed on, and who ended a life of fruitfulness with their task complete. For they need not fear that anyone will remove them from their secure positions.

6 But you, we observe, have removed a number of people, despite their good conduct, from a ministry they have fulfilled with honor and integrity.

45 Your contention and rivalry, brothers, thus touches matters that bear on our salvation.

2 You have studied Holy Scripture, which contains the truth and is inspired by the Holy Spirit.

3 You realize that there is nothing wrong or misleading written in it. You will not find that upright people have ever been disowned by holy people.

4 The righteous, to be sure, have been persecuted, but by wicked people. They have been imprisoned, but by the godless. They have been stoned by transgressors, slain by people prompted by abominable and wicked rivalry.

5 Yet in such sufferings they bore up nobly.

6 What shall we say, brothers? Was Daniel cast into a den of lions by those who revered God?

7 Or was Ananias, Azarias, or Mishael shut up in the fiery furnace by people devoted to the magnificent and glorious worship of the Most High? Not for a moment! Who, then, was it that did such things? Detestable people, thoroughly and completely wicked, whose factiousness drove them to such a pitch of fury that they tormented those who resolutely served God in holiness and innocence. They failed to realize that the Most High is the champion and defender of those who worship his excellent name with a pure con-

science. To him be the glory forever and ever. Amen.

8 But those who held out with confidence inherited glory and honor. They were exalted, and God inscribed them on his memory forever and ever. Amen.

46 Brothers, *we* must follow such examples.

2 For it is written: "Follow the saints, because those who follow them will become saints."

3 Again, it says in another place: "In the company of the innocent, you will be innocent; in the company of the elect, you will be elect; and in a crooked man's company you will go wrong."[3]

4 Let us, then, follow the innocent and the upright. They, it is, who are God's elect.

5 Why is it that you harbor strife, bad temper, dissension, schism, and quarreling?

6 Do we not have one God, one Christ, one Spirit of grace which was poured out on us? And is there not one calling in Christ?

7 Why do we rend and tear asunder Christ's members and raise a revolt against our own body? Why do we reach such a pitch of insanity that we are oblivious of the fact we are members of each other? Recall the words of our Lord Jesus.

8 For he said: "Woe to that man! It were better for him not to have been born than to be the occasion of one of my chosen ones stumbling. It were better for him to have a millstone around his neck and to be drowned in the sea, than to pervert one of my chosen"[4]

9 Your schism has led many astray; it has made many despair; it has made many doubt; and it has distressed us all. Yet it goes on!

47 Pick up the letter of the blessed apostle Paul.

2 What was the primary thing he wrote to you, when he started preaching the gospel?

3 To be sure, under the Spirit's guidance, he wrote to you about himself and Cephas and Apollos, because even then you had formed cliques.

---

[3]Ps 18:25–26.
[4]Matt 26:24; Mark 14:21; Matt 18:6; Mark 9:42; Luke 17:2.

4 Factiousness, however, at that time was a less serious sin, since you were partisans of notable apostles and of a man they endorsed.

5 But think now who they are who have led you astray and degraded your honorable and celebrated love of the brethren.

6 It is disgraceful, exceedingly disgraceful, and unworthy of your Christian upbringing, to have it reported that because of one or two individuals the solid and ancient Corinthian Church is in revolt against its presbyters.

7 This report, moreover, has reached not only us, but those who dissent from us as well. The result is that the Lord's name is being blasphemed because of your stupidity, and you are exposing yourselves to danger.

48 We must, then, put a speedy end to this. We must prostrate ourselves before the

Master, and beseech him with tears to have mercy on us and be reconciled to us and bring us back to our honorable and holy practice of brotherly love.

2 For it is this which is the gate of righteousness, which opens the way to life, as it is written: "Open the gates of righteousness for me, so that I may enter by them and praise the Lord.

3 "This is the Lord's gate: the righteous shall enter by it."[5]

4 While there are many gates open, the gate of righteousness is the Christian gate. Blessed are all those who enter by it and direct their way in holiness and righteousness, by doing everything without disorder.

_____

[5]Ps 118:19–20.

---

56. The Didache

Discovered in 1873 in a monastery library in Constantinople (Istanbul), the "Didache (literally, The Teaching) of the Twelve Apostles," has made a significant impact on our understanding of the social life and ritual practices of the early church. It is, in fact, the first "church manual" to have survived from early Christianity.

The bulk of the book gives instructions for the ritual observances and social interactions of the Christian community (for further excerpts, see Chapters 11 and 13). But, near the end, the author addresses the problem of wandering "apostles," "teachers," and "prophets" of dubious moral character; evidently, some Christians had become itinerant preachers simply for financial gain. The communities are to test the sincerity of these wandering ministers and to limit the length of their stay at the community's expense; moreover, the communities are to appoint leaders of their own to direct their affairs.

Because the book represents an early attempt to deal with such itinerant Christian leaders, a well-attested feature of earliest Christianity (cf. Mark 6:7–13 and the book of

The "Didache," reproduced from _Early Christian Fathers,_ ed. Cyril C. Richardson (Library of Christian Classics Series), 1970. Used by permission of Westminster John Knox Press.

Acts), and does not evidence the rigid form of church hierarchy that developed later in the second century (even though it speaks of bishops and deacons), most scholars think it was written around 100 C.E.

11 Now, you should welcome anyone who comes your way and teaches you all we have been saying.

2 But if the teacher proves himself a renegade and by teaching otherwise contradicts all this, pay no attention to him. But if his teaching furthers the Lord's righteousness and knowledge, welcome him as the Lord.

3 Now about the apostles and prophets: Act in line with the gospel precept.

4 Welcome every apostle on arriving, as if he were the Lord.

5 But he must not stay beyond one day. In case of necessity, however, the next day too. If he stays three days, he is a false prophet.

6 On departing, an apostle must not accept anything save sufficient food to carry him till his next lodging. If he asks for money, he is a false prophet.

7 While a prophet is making ecstatic utterances, you must not test or examine him. For "every sin will be forgiven," but this sin "will not be forgiven."[1]

8 However, not everybody making ecstatic utterances is a prophet, but only if he behaves like the Lord. It is by their conduct that the false prophet and the [true] prophet can be distinguished.

9 For instance, if a prophet marks out a table in the Spirit, he must not eat from it. If he does, he is a false prophet.

10 Again, every prophet who teaches the truth but fails to practice what he preaches is a false prophet.

11 But every attested and genuine prophet who acts with a view to symbolizing the mystery of the Church, and does not teach you to do all he does, must not be judged by you. His judgment rests with God. For the ancient prophets too acted in this way.

12 But if someone says in the Spirit, "Give me money, or something else," you must not heed him. However, if he tells you to give for others in need, no one must condemn him.

12 Everyone who comes to you in the name of the Lord must be welcomed. Afterward, when you have tested him, you will find out about him, for you have insight into right and wrong.

2 If it is a traveler who arrives, help him all you can. But he must not stay with you more than two days, or, if necessary, three.

3 If he wants to settle with you and is an artisan, he must work for his living.

4 If, however, he has no trade, use your judgment in taking steps for him to live with you as a Christian without being idle.

5 If he refuses to do this, he is trading on Christ. You must be on your guard against such people.

13 Every genuine prophet who wants to settle with you has a right to his support.

2 Similarly, a genuine teacher himself, just like a workman, has a right to his support.

3 Hence take all the first fruits of vintage and harvest, and of cattle and sheep, and give these first fruits to the prophets. For they are your high priests.

4 If, however, you have no prophet, give them to the poor.

5 If you make bread, take the first fruits and give in accordance with the precept.

6 Similarly, when you open a jar of wine or oil, take the first fruits and give them to the prophets.

7 Indeed, of money, clothes, and of all your possessions, take such first fruits as you think right, and give in accordance with the precept.

---

[1]Matt 12:31.

15 You must, then, elect for yourselves bishops and deacons who are a credit to the Lord, men who are gentle, generous, faithful, and well tried. For their ministry to you is identical with that of the prophets and teachers.

2 You must not, therefore, despise them, for along with the prophets and teachers they enjoy a place of honor among you.

3 Furthermore, do not reprove each other angrily, but quietly, as you find it in the gospel. Moreover, if anyone has wronged his neighbor, nobody must speak to him, and he must not hear a word from you, until he repents.

4 Say your prayers, give your charity, and do everything just as you find it in the gospel of our Lord.

><del>·<del>·O·<del>·<del>

57. The Letters of Ignatius to the Ephesians, Magnesians, and Smyrneans

We have already seen Ignatius of Antioch as an important figure in early proto-orthodox Christianity (see Chapter 3). The letters that Ignatius wrote on his path to martyrdom are principally concerned with two issues in the churches of Asia Minor: heresy and division. For both problems, Ignatius has a single, overarching solution: each church must adhere closely to the authority of its bishop, along with his ruling board of elders (the "presbytery") and the group of ministering deacons. The bishop has the authority of God himself; the elders are to be obeyed like the apostles. Nothing is to be done in the church without the bishop's sanction. Those who fail to follow the bishop's lead are outside the church, which is the only possible sphere of salvation.

Ignatius's notion of the "monarchial episcopate," that is, of the sole authority of the ruling bishop, became standard fare within proto-orthodox Christian circles of the later second and third centuries as they wrestled with the problems of heresy and schism. These particular letters were written around 110 C.E.

1. To the Ephesians

Heartiest greetings of pure joy in Jesus Christ from Ignatius, the "God-inspired," to the church at Ephesus in Asia. Out of the fullness of God the Father you have been blessed with large numbers and are predestined from eternity to enjoy forever continual and unfading glory. The source of your unity and election is genuine suffering which you undergo by the will of the Father and of Jesus Christ, our God. Hence you deserve to be considered happy. . . .

The Letters of Ignatius to the Ephesians, Magnesians, and Smyrneans, reproduced from *Early Christian Fathers*, ed. Cyril C. Richardson (Library of Christian Classics Series), 1970. Used by permission of Westminster John Knox Press.

3 I do not give you orders as if I were somebody important. For even if I am a prisoner for the Name, I have not yet reached Christian perfection. I am only beginning to be a disciple, so I address you as my fellow students. I needed your coaching in faith, encouragement, endurance, and patience.

2 But since love forbids me to keep silent about you, I hasten to urge you to harmonize your actions with God's mind. For Jesus Christ—that life from which we can't be torn—is the Father's mind, as the bishops too, appointed the world over, reflect the mind of Jesus Christ.

4 Hence you should act in accord with the bishop's mind, as you surely do. Your presbytery, indeed, which deserves its name and is a credit to God, is as closely tied to the bishop as the strings to a harp. Wherefore your accord and harmonious love is a hymn to Jesus Christ.

2 Yes, one and all, you should form yourselves into a choir, so that, in perfect harmony and taking your pitch from God, you may sing in unison and with one voice to the Father through Jesus Christ. Thus he will heed you, and by your good deeds he will recognize you are members of his Son. Therefore you need to abide in irreproachable unity if you really want to be God's members forever.

5 If in so short a time I could get so close to your bishop—I do not mean in a natural way, but in a spiritual—how much more do I congratulate you on having such intimacy with him as the Church enjoys with Jesus Christ, and Jesus Christ with the Father. That is how unity and harmony come to prevail everywhere.

2 Make no mistake about it. If anyone is not inside the sanctuary, he lacks God's bread. And if the prayer of one or two has great avail, how much more that of the bishop and the total Church.

3 He who fails to join in your worship shows his arrogance by the very fact of becoming a schismatic. It is written, moreover, "God resists the proud."[1] Let us, then, heartily avoid resisting the bishop so that we may be subject to God.

6 The more anyone sees the bishop modestly silent, the more he should revere him. For

everyone the Master of the house sends on his business, we ought to receive as the One who sent him. It is clear, then, that we should regard the bishop as the Lord himself.

2 Indeed, Onesimus spoke very highly of your godly conduct, that you were all living by the truth and harboring no sectarianism. Nay, you heed nobody beyond what he has to say truthfully about Jesus Christ. . . .

2. To The Magnesians

Every good wish in God the Father and in Jesus Christ from Ignatius, the "God-inspired," to the church at Magnesia on the Maeander. In Christ Jesus, our Savior, I greet your church which, by reason of its union with him, is blessed with the favor of God the Father.

1 I was delighted to hear of your well-disciplined and godly love; and hence, impelled by faith in Jesus Christ, I decided to write to you.

2 Privileged as I am to have this distinguished and godly name, I sing the praises of the churches, even while I am a prisoner. I want them to confess that Jesus Christ, our perpetual Life, united flesh with spirit. I want them, too, to unite their faith with love—there is nothing better than that. Above all, I want them to confess the union of Jesus with the Father. If, with him to support us, we put up with all the spite of the prince of this world and manage to escape, we shall get to God.

2 Yes, I had the good fortune to see you, in the persons of Damas your bishop (he's a credit to God!), and of your worthy presbyters, Bassus and Apollonius, and of my fellow slave, the deacon Zotion. I am delighted with him, because he submits to the bishop as to God's grace, and to the presbytery as to the law of Jesus Christ.

3 Now, it is not right to presume on the youthfulness of your bishop. You ought to respect him as fully as you respect the authority of God the Father. Your holy presbyters, I know, have not taken unfair advantage of his apparent youthful-

---

[1]Prov 3:34.

ness, but in their godly wisdom have deferred to him—nay, rather, not so much to him as to the Father of Jesus Christ, who is everybody's bishop.

2 For the honor, then, of him who loved us, we ought to obey without any dissembling, since the real issue is not that a person misleads a bishop whom he can see, but that he defrauds the One who is invisible. In such a case he must reckon, not with a human being, but with God who knows his secrets.

4 We have not only to be called Christians, but to *be* Christians. It is the same thing as calling a man a bishop and then doing everything in disregard of him. Such people seem to me to be acting against their conscience, since they do not come to the valid and authorized services.

5 Yes, everything is coming to an end, and we stand before this choice—death or life—and everyone will go to his own place. One might say similarly, there are two coinages, one God's, the other of the world's. Each bears its own stamp—unbelievers that of this world; believers, who are spurred by love, the stamp of God the Father through Jesus Christ. And if we do not willingly die in union with his passion, we do not have his life in us.

6 I believed, then, that I saw your whole congregation in these people I have mentioned, and I loved you all. Hence I urge you to aim to do everything in godly agreement. Let the bishop preside in God's place, and the presbyters take the place of the apostolic council, and let the deacons (my special favorites) be entrusted with the ministry of Jesus Christ who was with the Father from eternity and appeared at the end [of the world].

2 Taking, then, the same attitude as God, you should all respect one another. Let no one think of his neighbor in a carnal way; but always love one another in the spirit of Jesus Christ. Do not let there be anything to divide you, but be in accord with the bishop and your leaders. Thus you will be an example and a lesson of incorruptibility.

7 As, then, the Lord did nothing without the Father (either on his own or by the apostles) because he was at one with him, so you must not

do anything without the bishop and presbyters. Do not, moreover, try to convince yourselves that anything done on your own is commendable. Only what you do together is right. Hence you must have one prayer, one petition, one mind, one hope, dominated by love and unsullied joy—that means you must have Jesus Christ. You cannot have anything better than that.

2 Run off—all of you—to one temple of God, as it were, to one altar, to one Jesus Christ, who came forth from one Father, while still remaining one with him, and returned to him. . . .

3. To the Smyrneans

Heartiest greetings in all sincerity and in God's Word from Ignatius, the "God-inspired," to the church of God the Father and the beloved Jesus Christ, which is at Smyrna in Asia. By God's mercy you have received every gift; you abound in faith and love, and are lacking in no gift. You are a wonderful credit to God and real saints. . . .

6 Let no one be misled: heavenly beings, the splendor of angels, and principalities, visible and invisible, if they fail to believe in Christ's blood, they too are doomed. "Let the one accept it who can." Let no one's position swell his head, for faith and love are everything—there is nothing preferable to them.

2 Pay close attention to those who have wrong notions about the grace of Jesus Christ, which has come to us, and note how at variance they are with God's mind. They care nothing about love: they have no concern for widows or orphans, for the oppressed, for those in prison or released, for the hungry or the thirsty.

7 They hold aloof from the Eucharist and from services of prayer, because they refuse to admit that the Eucharist is the flesh of our Savior Jesus Christ, which suffered for our sins and which, in his goodness, the Father raised [from the dead]. Consequently those who wrangle and dispute God's gift face death. They would have done better to love and so share in the resurrection.

2 The right thing to do, then, is to avoid such people and to talk about them neither in private nor in public. Rather pay attention to the prophets and above all to the gospel. There we get a clear picture of the passion and see that the resurrection has really happened.

8 Flee from schism as the source of mischief. You should all follow the bishop as Jesus Christ did the Father. Follow, too, the presbytery as you would the apostles; and respect the deacons as you would God's law. Nobody must do anything that has to do with the Church without the bishop's approval. You should regard that Eucharist as valid which is celebrated either by the bishop or by someone he authorizes.

2 Where the bishop is present, there let the congregation gather, just as where Jesus Christ is,

there is the Catholic Church. Without the bishop's supervision, no baptisms or love feasts are permitted. On the other hand, whatever he approves pleases God as well. In that way everything you do will be on the safe side and valid.

9 It is well for us to come to our senses at last, while we still have a chance to repent and turn to God. It is a fine thing to acknowledge God and the bishop. He who pays the bishop honor has been honored by God. But he who acts without the bishop's knowledge is in the devil's service.

2 By God's grace may you have an abundance of everything! You deserve it. You have brought me no end of comfort; may Jesus Christ do the same for you! Whether I was absent or present, you gave me your love. May God requite you! If for his sake you endure everything, you will get to him. . . .

58. Hippolytus: The Apostolic Tradition

Hippolytus of Rome (160–235 C.E.) was one of the intriguing figures of early Christianity about whom we would like to know far more than we do. A prominent presbyter in the church of Rome near the end of the second century and the beginning of the third, his most important literary work was a ten-volume catalogue and refutation of heresies. His struggle against false teaching became particularly acute when he charged the bishop of Rome himself with embracing a heretical Christology. A schism erupted around 217 C.E., with the followers of Hippolytus appointing him as a kind of rival pope.

Hippolytus's concern to follow the early, unpolluted traditions of the church affected not only his theology but also his view of church administration. One of his treatises, the so-called "Apostolic Traditions," provides guidance for conducting the affairs of the church; most scholars think that it reflects the organization of the Roman church of Hippolytus's own day, and possibly earlier. In any event, the treatise clearly advances a particular form of church structure: firm instructions are given for ordaining bishops, presbyters, and deacons and for appointing other officials—church widows, readers, virgins, and subdeacons. Moreover, some of the official duties of these positions are discussed. For further excerpts dealing with the closely related issues of Christian liturgy, see Chapter 11.

Hippolytus: "The Apostolic Tradition," from *The Apostolic Tradition of Hippolytus,* ed. B. S. Easton. Cambridge: Cambridge University Press, 1934. Reprinted with the permission of Cambridge University Press.

2 Let the bishop be ordained after he has been chosen by all the people.

2 When he has been named and shall please all, let him, with the presbytery and such bishops as may be present, assemble with the people on a Sunday.

3 While all give their consent, the bishops shall lay their hands upon him, and the presbytery shall stand by in silence.

4 All indeed shall keep silent, praying in their heart for the descent of the Spirit.

5 Then one of the bishops who are present shall, at the request of all, lay his hand on him who is ordained bishop, and shall pray as follows, . . .

8 But when a presbyter is ordained, the bishop shall lay his hand upon his head, while the presbyters touch him, and he shall say according to those things that were said above, as we have prescribed above concerning the bishop, . . .

9 But the deacon, when he is ordained, is chosen according to those things that were said above, the bishop alone in like manner laying his hands upon him, as we have prescribed.

2 When the deacon is ordained, this is the reason why the bishop alone shall lay his hands upon him: he is not ordained to the priesthood but to serve the bishop and to carry out the bishop's commands.

3 He does not take part in the council of the clergy; he is to attend to his own duties and to make known to the bishop such things as are needful.

4 He does not receive that Spirit that is possessed by the presbytery, in which the presbyters share; he receives only what is confided in him under the bishop's authority.

5 For this cause the bishop alone shall make a deacon.

6 But on a presbyter, however, the presbyters shall lay their hands because of the common and like Spirit of the clergy.

7 Yet the presbyter has only the power to receive; but he has no power to give.

8 For this reason a presbyter does not ordain the clergy; but at the ordination of a presbyter he seals while the bishop ordains. . . .

10 On a confessor, if he has been in bonds for the name of the Lord, hands shall not be laid for the diaconate or the presbyterate, for he has the honor of the presbyterate by his confession. But if he is to be ordained bishop, hands shall be laid upon him.

2 But if he is a confessor who was not brought before the authorities nor was punished with bonds nor was shut up in prison, but was insulted casually or privately for the name of the Lord, even though he confessed, hands are to be laid upon him for every office of which he is worthy.

3 The bishop shall give thanks [in all ordinations] as we have prescribed.

4 It is not, to be sure, necessary for anyone to recite the exact words that we have prescribed, by learning to say them by heart in his thanksgiving to God; but let each one pray according to his ability.

5 If, indeed, he is able to pray competently with an elevated prayer, it is well.

6 But even if he is only moderately able to pray and give praise, no one may forbid him; only let him pray sound in the faith.

11 When a widow is appointed, she shall not be ordained but she shall be appointed by the name.

2 If her husband has been long dead, she may be appointed [without delay].

3 But if her husband has died recently, she shall not be trusted; even if she is aged she must be tested by time, for often the passions grow old in those who yield to them.

4 The widow shall be appointed by the word alone, and [so] she shall be associated with the other widows; hands shall not be laid upon her because she does not offer the oblation nor has she a sacred ministry.

5 Ordination is for the clergy on account of their ministry, but the widow is appointed for prayer, and prayer is the duty of all.

12 The reader is appointed by the bishop's giving him the book, for he is not ordained.

13 Hands shall not be laid upon a virgin, for it is her purpose alone that makes her a virgin.

14 Hands shall not be laid upon a subdeacon, but his name shall be mentioned that he may serve the deacon.

15 If anyone says, "I have received the gift of healing," hands shall not be laid upon him: the deed shall make manifest if he speaks the truth. . . .

25 Widows and virgins shall fast frequently and shall pray for the church; presbyters, if they wish, and lay people may fast likewise.

2 But the bishop may fast only when all the people fast.

26 For it constantly happens that some one wishes to make an offering—and such a one must not be denied—and then the bishop, after breaking the bread, must in every case taste and eat it with the other believers.

2 [At such an offering] each shall take from the bishop's hand a piece of [this] bread before breaking his own bread. [This service has a special ceremonial] for it is "a Blessing," not "a Thanksgiving," as is [the service of] the Body of the Lord.

3 But before drinking, each one, as many of you as are present, must take a cup and give thanks over it, and so go to your meal.

4 But to the catechumens is given exorcised bread, and each of them must offer the cup.

5 No catechumen shall sit at the Lord's Supper.

6 But at each act of offering, the offerer must remember his host, for he was invited to the latter's home for that very purpose.

7 But when you eat and drink, do so in an orderly manner and not so that anyone may mock, or your host be saddened by your unruliness, but behave so that he may pray to be made worthy that the saints may enter his dwelling: "for you," it is said, "are the salt of the earth."[1]

8 If the offering should be one made to all the guests jointly, take your portion from your host [and depart].

9 But if all are to eat then and there, do not eat to excess, so that your host may likewise send some of what the saints leave to whomsoever he will and [so] may rejoice in the faith.

10 But while the guests are eating, let them eat silently, not arguing, [attending to] such things as the bishop may teach, but if he should ask any question, let an answer be given him; and when he says anything, everyone in modest praise shall keep silence until he asks again.

11 And even if the bishop should be absent when the faithful meet at a supper, if a presbyter or a deacon is present they shall eat in a similar orderly fashion, and each shall be careful to take the blessed bread from the presbyter's or deacon's hand; and in the same way the catechumens shall take the same exorcised bread.

12 But if [only] lay people meet, let them not act presumptuously, for a layperson cannot bless the blessed bread.

13 Let each one eat in the name of the Lord; for this is pleasing to the Lord that we should be jealous [of our good name] even among the heathen, all sober alike.

27 If anyone wishes to give a meal to widows of mature years, let him dismiss them before evening.

2 But if, on account of existing conditions, he cannot [feed them in his house], let him send them away, and they may eat of his food at their homes in any way they please.

28 As soon as first-fruits appear, all shall hasten to offer them to the bishop.

2 And he shall offer them, shall give thanks and shall name him who offered them, saying:

3 We give you thanks, O God, and we offer you the first-fruits; which you have given us to enjoy, nourishing them through your word, commanding the earth to bring forth her fruits for the gladness and the food of humans and all beasts.

4 For all these things we praise you, O God, and for all things wherewith you have blessed us, who for us adorns every creature with divers fruits.

5 Through your Servant Jesus Christ, our Lord, through whom be to you glory, world without end. Amen.

6 Only certain fruits may be blessed, namely grapes, the fig, the pomegranate, the olive, the

---

[1]Matt 5:13.

pear, the apple, the mulberry, the peach, the cherry, the almond, the plum.

7 Not the pumpkin, nor the melon, nor the cucumber, nor the onion nor garlic nor anything else having an odor.

8 But sometimes flowers too are offered; here the rose and the lily may be offered, but no other.

9 But for everything that is eaten shall they [who eat it] give thanks to the Holy God, eating unto his glory.

29 Let no one at the paschal season eat before the offering is made, otherwise he shall not be credited with the fast.

2 But if any woman is with child, or if anyone is sick and cannot fast for two days, let such a one, on account of his need, [at least] fast on Saturday, contenting himself with bread and water.

3 But if anyone on a voyage or for any other necessary cause should not know the day, when he has learned the truth he shall postpone his fast until after Pentecost.

4 For the ancient type has passed away, and so the [postponed] fast in the second month has ceased.[2] and each one ought to fast in accord with his knowledge of the truth.

30 Each of the deacons, with the subdeacons, shall be alert on the bishop's behalf, for the bishop must be informed if any are sick so that, if he pleases, he may visit them; for a sick person is greatly comforted when the high priest is mindful of him.

33 Let the deacons and the presbyters assemble daily at the place which the bishop may appoint; let the deacons [in particular] never fail to assemble unless prevented by sickness.

2 When all have met they shall instruct those who are in the church, and then, after prayer, each shall go to his appointed duties.

34 No exorbitant charge shall be made for burial in the cemetery, for it belongs to all the poor; only the hire of the grave-digger and the cost of the tile [for closing the niche in the catacombs] shall be asked.

2 The wages of the caretakers are to be paid by the bishop, lest any of those who go to that place be burdened [with a charge].

35 Let all the faithful, whether men or women, when early in the morning they rise from their sleep and before they undertake any tasks, wash their hands and pray to God; and so they may go to their duties.

2 But if any instruction in God's word is held [that day], everyone ought to attend it willingly, recollecting that he will hear God speaking through the instructor and that prayer in the church enables him to avoid the day's evil; any godly person ought to count it a great loss if he does not attend the place of instruction, especially if he can read.

3 If a [specially gifted] teacher should come, let none of you delay to attend the place where the instruction is given, for grace will be given to the speaker to utter things profitable to all, and you will hear new things, and you will be profited by what the Holy Spirit will give you through the instructor; so your faith will be strengthened by what you hear, and in that place you will learn duties at home; therefore let everyone be zealous to go to the church, the place where the Holy Spirit abounds.

36 But if on any day there is no instruction, let everyone at home take the Bible and read sufficiently in passages that he finds profitable.

2 If at the third hour you are at home, pray then and give thanks to God; but if you chance to be abroad at that hour, make your prayer to God in your heart.

3 For at that hour Christ was nailed to the tree; therefore in the old [covenant] the law commanded the showbread to be offered continually for a type of the body and blood of Christ, and commanded the sacrifice of the dumb lamb, which was a type of the perfect Lamb; for Christ is the Shepherd, and he is also the Bread that came down from heaven.

4 At the sixth hour likewise pray also, for, after Christ was nailed to the wood of the cross, the day was divided and there was a great darkness; wherefore let [the faithful] pray at that hour

---

[2]See Num 9:11.

with an effectual prayer, likening themselves to the voice of him who prayed [and] caused all creation to become dark for the unbelieving Jews.

5 And at the ninth hour let a great prayer and a great thanksgiving be made, such as made the souls of the righteous ones, blessing the Lord, the God who does not lie, who was mindful of his saints and sent forth his Word to enlighten them.

6 At that hour, therefore, Christ poured forth from his pierced side water and blood, and brought the rest of the time of that day with light to evening; so, when he fell asleep, by making the beginning of another day he completed the pattern of his resurrection.

7 Pray again before your body rests on your bed.

8 At midnight arise, wash your hands with water and pray.

9 And if your wife is with you, both of you pray together; but if she is not yet a believer, go into another room and pray, and again return to your bed; be not slothful in prayer.

10 He who has used the marriage bed is not defiled; for they who are bathed have no need to wash again, for they are clean.

11 By signing yourself with your moist breath, and so spreading spittle on your body with your hand, you are sanctified to your feet; for the gift of the Spirit and the sprinkling with water, when it is brought with a believing heart as it were from a fountain, sanctifies him who believes.

12 It is needful to pray at this hour; for those very elders who gave us the tradition taught us that at this hour all creation rests for a certain moment, that all creatures may praise the Lord: stars and trees and waters stand still with one accord, and all the angelic host does service to God by praising him, together with the souls of the righteous.

13 For this cause believers should be zealous to pray at this hour; for the Lord, testifying to this, says: "Behold at midnight is a cry, Behold the Bridegroom comes! Rise up to meet him!"; and he

adds insistently: "Watch therefore, for you know not at what hour he comes".[3]

14 And at cockcrow rise up and pray likewise, for at that hour of cockcrow the children of Israel denied Christ, whom we have known by faith; by which faith, in the hope of eternal life at the resurrection of the dead, we look for his Day.

15 And so, all you faithful, if you thus act, and are mindful of these things, and teach them to one another, and cause the catechumens to be zealous, you can neither be tempted nor can you perish, since you have Christ always in your minds.

37 But imitate him always, by signing your forehead sincerely; for this is the sign of his Passion, manifest and approved against the devil if so you make it from faith; not that you may appear to people, but knowingly offering it as a shield.

2 For the adversary, seeing its power coming from the heart, that a person displays the publicly formed image of baptism, is put to flight; not because you spit, but because the Spirit in you breathes him away.

3 When Moses formed it by putting the blood of the Paschal lamb that was slain on the lintel and anointing the side-posts, he signified the faith which now we have in the perfect Lamb.

38 And so, if these things are accepted with thanksgiving and right faith, they give edification in the church and eternal life to believers.

2 I counsel that these things be kept by all who know aright; for over all who hear the apostolic tra[dition] and keep it, no heretics or any other person will prevail to lead them astray.

3 For the many heresies have increased because their leaders would not learn the purpose of the apostles but acted according to their own wills, following their lusts and not what was right.

4 Now, beloved, if we have omitted anything, God will reveal it to those who are worthy, guiding the holy church to its mooring in [God's] quiet haven.

---

[3]Matt 25:1–13.

59. The Didascalia

The "Didascalia (literally: Teaching) of the Apostles" is a church manual pseudony-mously written in the name of the twelve apostles along with the apostles Paul and James, the brother of Jesus. Originally produced in the early third century, only fragments of the book survive in the original Greek; it was translated early on, however, most notably into Syriac (modern editions are largely based on this version), and later authors sometimes incorporated portions of it wholesale into their own manuals.

As the following excerpts show, the book provides a full account of the qualifica-tions, duties, and conduct of persons holding various offices in the church, especially the bishop, but also presbyters, deacons, widows, and readers. In addition, the book instructs Christians regarding how they should relate to their leaders. Other portions of the Didas-calia deal more directly with aspects of Christian liturgy, as will be seen in Chapter 11.

3 But concerning the bishop, hear likewise. The shepherd who is appointed bishop and head among the presbyterate in the church in every con-gregation—"It is required of him that he shall be blameless, in nothing reproachable,"[1] one remote from all evil, a man not less than fifty years of age, who is now removed from the conduct of youth and from the lusts of the adversary, and from the slander and blasphemy of false brethren, which they bring against many because they understand not that word which is said in the Gospel: "Everyone that shall say an idle word shall give an answer regarding it to the Lord in the day of judgment; for from your words shall you be justified, and from your words shall you be convicted."[2] But if it is possible, let him be in-structed and able to teach; but if he does not know letters, he shall be capable and skilful in the word; and let him be advanced in years.

However, if the congregation is a small one, and there is not found a man advanced in years of whom they testify that he is wise and suitable to stand in the episcopacy, but there shall be found a brother who is young, of whom these who are with him testify that

he deserves to stand in the episcopacy, and who even if he is young through humility and quietness of con-duct demonstrates maturity—he shall be tried whether everyone testifies concerning him, and so let him sit in peace. Because Solomon also at the age of twelve years ruled over Israel. And Josiah at the age of eight years ruled in righteousness, and again, Joash also ruled when seven years old.

On this account, even if he is young, yet let him be humble and fearful and quiet; for the Lord God said in Isaiah: "On whom shall I look and be at rest, but on the quiet and humble, that tremble at my sayings?"[3] In the Gospel also he says thus: "Blessed are the humble, for they shall inherit the earth."[4] And let him be merciful—for he said again in the Gospel thus: "Blessed are the merci-ful, for mercy shall be upon them."[5] And again let

---

[1] 1 Tim 3:2; Tit 1:7.
[2] Matt 12:36–37.
[3] Isa 66:2.
[4] Matt 5:5.
[5] Matt 5:7.

The "Didascalia," from *The Didascalia Apostolorum Corpus Scriptorum Christianorum Orientalium*, ed. Arthur Vööbus. Louvain: Peeters, 1979. Used with permission.

him be a peacemaker—for he said: "Blessed are the peacemakers, for they shall be called the sons of God."[6] And let him be pure of all evil and injustice and inequity—for he said again: "Blessed are those who are pure in heart, for they shall see God."[7]

And let him be vigilant and chaste and stable and orderly; and let him not be violent, and let him not be one who exceeds in wine; and let him not be malicious; but let him be quiet and not be contentious; and let him not be money-loving. And let him not be youthful in mind, lest he be lifted up and fall into the judgment of Satan, for everyone that exalts himself is humbled.

But it is required that the bishop shall be "a man that has taken one wife, and who has managed his house well."[8] And thus let him be proved when he receives the imposition of hands to sit in the position of the episcopacy: whether he is chaste, and whether his wife also is a believer and chaste; and whether he has brought up his children in the fear of God, and admonished and taught them; and whether his household fear and reverence him and all of them obey him. For if his household in the flesh stands against him and does not obey him, how shall they who are without his house become his, and be subject to him? . . .

And let him be very diligent in his teaching, and constant in reading the divine Scripture diligently in order that he may interpret and expound the Scriptures thoroughly. And let him compare the Law and the prophets with the Gospel in order that the sayings of the Law and the prophets may agree with the Gospel. But before all let him be a good discerner between the Law and the second legislation in order that he may distinguish and demonstrate what is the Law of the faithful, and what are the bonds of them who do not believe, lest anyone of those under your dominion may hold the bonds for the Law, and may put upon himself heavy burdens, and become a child of perdition. Be diligent therefore and take care of the Word, bishop, in order that, if you can, you explain every saying so that with much instruction you may richly nourish and give drink to your people—for it is written in Wisdom: "Be careful of the herb of the field, that you may sheer your

flock: and gather the grass of summer, that you may have sheep for your garments; take care and take pains of your pasture, in order that you may have lambs."[9]

Thus let not the bishop be "a lover of defiled lucre,"[10] especially from the heathen. Let him be cheated and not (himself) cheat (others). And let him not love riches. And let him not think (ill) of any one nor bear false witness. And let him not be angry, nor loving strife. And let him not love the governorship. And let him not be double-minded or double-tongued, nor one who loves to incline his ear to words of slander and disparagement. And let him have no favoritism for persons. And let him not love the festivals of the heathen, nor occupy himself with vain error. And let him not be lustful nor money-loving because all these things are of the activity of demons.

All these things, however, let the bishop command and admonish all the people. And let him be wise and ascetic. And let him be admonishing and teaching in the instruction and discipline of God. And let his mind be fair, and remote from all the evil crafts of this world, and from all the evil lust of the heathen. And let his mind be sharp to estimate, in order that he may know beforehand those who are evil and to keep you from them. But let him be the friend of all, being an upright judge.

And whatever of good there is and is found in people, let those be in the bishop. For as the shepherd is remote from all evil, so shall he be able to constrain also his disciples and encourage them through his good manners to be imitators of his good works—as the Lord has said in the Twelve Prophets: "The people shall be as the priest."[11] For it is required of you to be an example to the people, because you also have Christ for an example. Be you then also a good example to your people, for the Lord said in Ezekiel: "And the utterance of the Lord was upon me, saying:

---

[6]Matt 5:9.

[7]Matt 5:8.

[8]1 Tim 3:2, 4.

[9]Prov 27:25–27.

[10]1 Tim 3:8.

[11]Hos 4:9.

Son of Man, speak to the sons of your people, and say unto them: When I bring the sword upon a land, the people of that land shall take one man from among them and make him their watchman: and he shall see the sword that comes upon the land, and shall blow the horn and warn the people: and everyone who hears the sound of the horn shall obey; and if he shall not take heed, and the sword shall come and taken him away, his blood shall be upon his head. Because he heard the sound of the horn, and took not heed, his blood shall be upon his head. But he that took heed has saved himself. But if the watchman shall see the sword coming, and shall not blow the horn, and the people shall not be warned, and the sword shall come and take away a soul from them: he has been taken away in his sins, and I shall demand his blood from the hands of the watchman."[12] Now the sword is the judgment, and the horn is the Gospel, but the watchman is the bishop who is set over the church. . . .

5 . . . But if also the bishop (himself) is not of a clean conscience, and shall accept persons for the sake of defiled gains, or for the sake of the presents he receives, and shall spare one who iniquitously sins, and shall allow him to stay in the church—a bishop who is such has defiled his congregation with God. Again also people, and with many of the partakers who are young in their minds, or with the hearers; and again he destroys youth and maidens beside with him. For because of the wantonness of a wicked person, when they have seen such a one among them, they too will doubt in themselves, and will imitate him, and they also will stumble and be seized by the same passion, and will perish with him.

But if he who sins shall see that the bishop and the deacons are free from rebuke and the entire flock pure, first of all he will not dare to enter the congregation, because he will be reproved by his conscience. But if, however, it should happen that he is bold, and shall come to the church in his obstinacy, and shall be reproved and convicted by the bishop, and shall look upon all and shall find no offense in any of them, neither in the bishop nor in those who are with him, he will then

be confused and in great shame will go out quietly, weeping and in remorse of soul. And so shall the flock remain pure. Moreover, when he is gone out, he will repent of his sin and weep and groan before God and there shall be hope for him. But again the entire flock itself also, when it sees the weeping and tears of that one, will fear, knowing and understanding that everyone who sins perishes.

On this account, bishop, take pains now to be pure in your works. And know your place, (namely) that you are set in the likeness of God Almighty, and do hold the place of God Almighty. And so sit in the church and teach as having authority to judge those who sin—instead of God Almighty. For to you bishops it is said in the Gospel: "Something that you shall bind on earth, it shall be bound in heaven. . . .[13]

6 . . . It is required of you therefore, O bishops, to judge according to the Scripture those who sin, with kindness and with mercy. For he who is walking on the brink of the river and is (ready) to slip—if you leave him, you have thrust (and) cast him into the river, and you have committed murder. But if a person were to slip on the brink of a river and be near to perish, stretch out quickly a hand to him and drag him out, so that he will not perish altogether. Thus, therefore do (all) that your people may learn and also act wisely, and (that) on the other hand he who sins may not utterly perish.

But when you have seen one who has sinned, be angry at him, and command that they cast him out. And when he is cast out, let them be angry at him, and contend with him and keep him outside of the church. And then let them come in and plead for him. For even our Savior was pleading with His father for those who sinned, as it is written in the Gospel: "My brethren, they know not what they do, nor what they speak; but if it be possible forgive them."[14] And then, O bishop, command him to come in, and ask him whether

---

[12]Ezek 33:1–6.
[13]Matt 18:18.
[14]Luke 23:34; Matt 26:39.

he repents. And if he is worthy to be received into the church, appoint him days of fasting according to his transgression, two weeks, or three, or five, or seven. And so dismiss him that he may go, saying to him all that is right for admonition and instruction. And rebuke him and say to him that he should be by himself in humiliation, and that he should pray and beseech in the days of his fast to be found worthy of the forgiveness of sins—as it is written in Genesis: "Have you sinned? Be silent: your repentance shall be with you, and you shall have power over it."[15] To Miriam the sister of Moses also, when she had spoken against Moses and afterwards repented and was esteemed worthy of forgiveness, it was said by the Lord: "If her father had but spit in her face, it were right for her to be ashamed, and to be separated seven days without the camp, and then to come in."[16] Likewise it also is required of you to do: to put out of the church those who promise to repent of their sins as is right for their transgressions—and afterwards receive them as merciful fathers. . . .

8 You shall not be lovers of wine, nor drunken, and you shall not be much puffed up nor luxurious, nor incurring expense that is not right, as not your own you should make use of the gifts of God, in as much as you are appointed good stewards of God who is ready to require at your hands an account of the management of the stewardship with which you are entrusted. Let then that suffice you which is enough for you, food and clothing and whatever else is necessary. And you shall not make use of these (things) that come in (as gifts) beyond what is right, as from alien (funds), but in moderation. And you shall not enjoy yourselves and be luxurious from these things that come into the church—for to a laborer his clothing and his food are sufficient.

As good stewards of God, therefore, do well in dispensing those things that are given and come into the church according to the commandment to orphans and widows and those who are afflicted and to strangers, like people who know that you have God who will require an account at your hands, who committed his stewardship to you. Thus distribute and give to all who are in want.

But be you also nourished and live from these things which come in to the church. And do not consume them by yourselves alone, but let those who are in want be sharers with you, and you shall be without offense with God. For God accuses those bishops who in greed and for themselves make use of these things which come in to the church, and do not make the poor to be sharers with them, saying thus: "You eat the milk, and with the wool you clothe yourselves." For it is required of you, the bishops, that you shall be nourished from these things which come into the church, but not to devour them; for it is written: "You shall not muzzle the ox that grinds."[17] As then the ox which works in the threshing floor without a muzzle, eats, indeed, but does not consume it all, so also you, who work in the threshing floor which is the church of God, be nourished from the church, in the manner of the Levites who served in the tabernacle of witness, which in everything was a type of the church. Indeed, even by its name, it tells (us this), for the tabernacle "of witness" manifested the church beforehand. Thus, the Levites who ministered therein were nourished unhindered from those things which were given to the offerings of God by all the people: gifts, and oblations, and first fruits, and tithes, and sacrifices, and offerings, and whole burnt offerings, they and their wives and their sons and their daughters, because their work was the ministry of the tabernacle alone. And therefore they received no inheritance of land among the children of Israel, because the inheritance of Levi and his tribe was the produce of the people.

9 Hear these things now, you lay people also, the elect church of God. For the former people also were called a church; you, however, are the catholic Church, the holy and perfect, a royal priesthood, a holy assembly, a people for inheritance, the great Church, the bride adorned for the Lord God. Those things then which were said before, hear also now. Set apart oblations and tithes

---

[15]Gen 4:7.
[16]Num 12:14.
[17]Deut 25:4; 1 Cor 9:9; 1 Tim 5:18.

and firstfruits to Christ, the true High Priest, and to his servants, tithes of salvation (to him) the beginning of whose name is the Decade. Hear, you catholic Church of God, that were rescued from the ten plagues and did receive the ten sayings, and did learn the Law, and hold the faith and believe in the Yod in the beginning of the Name, and are fixed in the perfection of his glory: instead of the sacrifices of that time, offer now prayers and supplications and thanksgivings. At that time there were firstfruits and tithes and oblations and gifts, but today the offerings which are presented through the bishops to the Lord God, for they are your high priests. But the priests and Levites now are the presbyters and deacons, and the orphans and widows—but the Levite and high priest is the bishop. He is a servant of the word and mediator, but to you a teacher, and your father after God, who has begotten you through the water. This is your chief and your leader and he is a mighty king to you. He guides in the place of the Almighty. But let him be honored by you as God (is), because the bishop sits for you in the place of God Almighty. But the deacon stands in the place of Christ, and you should love him. The deaconess, however, shall be honored by you in the place of the Holy Spirit. But the presbyters shall be to you in the likeness of the apostles, and the orphans and the widows shall be reckoned by you in the likeness of the altar. For as it was not lawful for a stranger, that is for one who was not a Levite, to approach the altar or to offer anything apart from the high priest, so you also shall do nothing apart from the bishop. But if any one should do something apart from the bishop, he does it in vain, for it shall not be accounted to him for a work, for it is not right that any one should do something apart from the high priest.

Present therefore your offerings to the bishop, either you yourselves, or through the deacons. And from that which what he has received he distributes justly. For the bishop is well acquainted with those who are afflicted and dispenses and gives to each one as it is right for him, so that one may not receive several times in the same day or in the same week, whereas another would not receive even a little. For whomever the priest and steward of God knows to be much afflicted, to him he does good as it is required of him.

And to those who invite widows to the agapes, let him frequently send her whom he knows to be afflicted in particular. And again, if anyone gives gifts to widows, let him send in particular her who is in want.

But let the portion of the shepherd be separated and be divided for him according to rule at the agapes or the gifts, even though he be not pres- ent, in honor of Almighty God. But however much is given to one of the widows, let the double be given to each of the deacons in honor of Christ, (but) twice double to the leader for the glory of the Almighty.

But if anyone wished to honor the presbyters also, let him give him a double, as to the deacons, for it is required for them that they should be honored as the apostles, and as the counsellors of the bishop, and as the crown of the church, for they are the fashioners and counsellors of the church.

But if there be also a lector, let him also receive with the presbyters. To every position, therefore, let each of the laity pay the honor which is right to him, by gifts and honors and with earthly reverence.

But let them have great boldness with the deacons, and let them not be troubling the leader at all hours; but rather (let them) make known whatever they require through the servants, that is through the deacons. For not even to the Lord God Almighty can one approach except through Christ. Everything therefore that they desire to do, let them make known to the bishop through the deacons, and (only) then do them. . . .

On this account, for the honor of the bishop, make known to him everything that you do. And let them be completed through him. And if you know that one is much afflicted, but the bishop does not know of him, inform him.

But apart from him do not do anything, to his dishonor, that you bring no shame upon him as a despiser of the poor.

For he who puts forth an evil report against the bishop, whether by word or by deed, offends God Almighty. And again, if any one shall speak evil against a deacon, whether by word or by deed, he stumbles against Christ. Wherefore also in the Law it is written: "You shall not revile your gods, and you shall not speak evil of the chiefs of your people."[18] Now let no one think that (here) the Lord speaks of idols of stone, but he calls "gods" those who stand as representing you. Moses also says again in the Book of Numbers, when the people had murmured against him and against Aaron: "You do not murmur against us, but against the Lord God".[19] Also our Savior said: "Everyone that wrongs you, wrongs me, and him that sent me."[20]

What hope, indeed, is there, even a little, for him who speaks evil against the bishop, or against a deacon? For if one called a layperson "fool or raca, he is liable to the assembly,"[21] as one of those who rise up against Christ—because that he calls "empty" his brother, him, in whom Christ dwells, who is not empty but fulfilled; or a "fool" him in whom the Holy Spirit of God dwells, fulfilled with all wisdom—as though he should become a fool from the Spirit that dwells in him! If then one who should say one of these things to a layperson is found to fall into all this condemnation, how much more if he should dare to say anything against the deacon, or against the bishop, through whom the Lord gave you the Holy Spirit, and through whom you have learned the word and have known God, and through whom you have been known of God, and through whom you were sealed, and through whom you became children of the light, and through whom the Lord in baptism, by the laying on of the hand of the bishop, bore witness to each one of you and caused his holy voice to be heard that said: "You are my son: this day have I begotten you."[22]

On this account, know your bishops, those through whom you were made a child of God, and the right hand, your mother. And love him who is become, after God, your father and your mother—for "whosoever shall revile his father or his mother, shall die the death."[23] But honor the bishops, those who have loosed you from sins, those who by the water have begotten you anew, those who filled you with the Holy Spirit, those who brought you up with the word as with milk, those who established you with doctrine, those who confirmed you with admonition, and made you to partake of the holy

eucharist of God, and made you partakers and joint heirs of the promise of God. Indeed, reverence these, and honor them with all honor for they have received from God the authority of life and death, not as judging those who sin and condemning them to death in fire everlasting, but excommunicating and expelling those who are judged—God forbid and may this never happen!—but that they may receive and revive those who return and repent.

14 Appoint as a widow one who is not less than fifty years of age, who in some way, by reason of her years, is remote from the reflection of having a second husband. But if you appoint one who is young to the office of a widow, and she does not endure widowhood because of her youth, and she become (a wife) to a man, she will bring a shame upon the glory of widowhood, (for which) she shall have to given an account to God. First, because she has become (a wife) for two husbands; and again, because she promised to be a widow unto God, and was receiving (alms) as a widow, but did not abide in widowhood.

But if there be one who is young, who has been a short time with her husband and her husband die, or for some other cause there be a separation, and she remains by herself alone, being in the honor of widowhood—she shall be blessed by God. For she resembles the widow of Sarepta of Sidon with whom the holy angel, the prophet of God, rested.[24] Or again, she shall be like Annah,[25] who praised the coming of Christ and there was a (good) testimony to her; and she shall be honored because of her gift, honor (being given) her by people, and praise from God in heaven.

But let not widows, those who are young, be appointed to the office of widows, yet let them be taken care of and helped in order that by cause of their being in need they may not desire to become

---

18Exod 22:28.
19Exod 16:8; cf. Num 14:2.
20Luke 10:16.
21Matt 5:22.
22Ps 2:7; Luke 3:22.
23Exod 21:16.
241 Kings 17:8–24.
25Luke 2:36–38.

(a wife) to a man for a second time, which would be an act of damage. This, indeed, you know—she who has had one husband may lawfully become (wife) for a second (but) beyond this she is (to be accounted) a harlot. On this account, support those who are young that they may continue in chastity unto God. And thus take care of them, O bishop.

And remember also the poor, hold them by the hand and nourish them even though there be among them those who are not widowers or widows, yet are in need of help because of poverty or because of sickness or because of the rearing of children, and are afflicted. . . .

15 . . . A widow should care for nothing else except this, to pray for those who give, and for the whole church. And when she is asked regarding an affair by anyone, let her not too quickly give an answer, except only about righteousness and about faith in God.

But let her send those who desire to be instructed to the leader. And to those who ask them let them (namely the widows) give answer only about the destruction of idols and about this, that there is only one God. It is not right for the widows to teach nor for a layperson. About punishment and about the rest, and about the kingdom of the name of Christ, and about his dispensation, neither a widow nor a layperson ought to speak. Indeed, when they speak without the knowledge of doctrine, they bring blasphemy against the word. For our Lord likened the word of his Gospel to mustard.[26] But mustard if it is not prepared with skill, is bitter and sharp to those who use it. On this account our Lord said in the Gospel, to widows and to all the laity: "Do not throw your pearls before swine, lest they trample upon them and turn against you and rend you.[27] Indeed, when the Gentiles, those who are being instructed, hear the word of God spoken not firmly, as it ought to be, unto edification of life everlasting—and especially because it is spoken to them by a woman— about how our Lord clothed himself in the body, and about the passion of Christ, they will deride and mock, instead of praising the word of doc-

trine. And she shall be guilty of a hard judgment for sin.

Therefore, it is not required nor necessary that women should be teachers, and especially about the name of Christ and about the redemption of his passion. Indeed, you have not been appointed to this, O women, and especially widows, that you should teach, but that you should pray and entreat the Lord God. For he, the Lord God, Jesus Christ our teacher, sent us the Twelve to instruct the people and the nations. And there were with us women disciples, Mary Magdalene and Mary the daughter of James, and the other Mary, and he did not send (them) to instruct the people with us. If it were required, indeed, that women should teach, our teacher himself would have commanded these to give instruction with us.

But let a widow know that she is the altar of God. And let her constantly sit at home, and let her not wander or run about among the houses of the faithful to receive. The altar of God, indeed, never wanders or runs about anywhere, but is fixed in one place.

A widow must not therefore wander or run about among the houses. For those who are roving and who have no shame cannot stay quiet even in their houses. For they are not widows, but blind, and they care for nothing else but making themselves ready to receive. And because they are talkative and chatterers and murmurers, they incite strifes, and they are bold and they have no shame. They that are such, indeed, are unworthy of him who called them. For neither in the fellowship of the assembly of rest on the Sunday, once they have come, are such women or men watchful, but they either fall asleep or whisper about something else, so that through them others also are taken captive by the enemy Satan, who does not allow them, those who are such, to be watchful unto the Lord. . . .

---

[26]Mark 4:31.
[27]Matt 7:6.

60. Cyprian: On the Unity of the Catholic Church

A wealthy and prominent rhetorician prior to his conversion in 246 C.E., Cyprian was to become one of the most significant church leaders of the mid-third century. Just two years after joining the church he was elected its bishop, a position he was to hold until his martyrdom in 258.

It was early in his bishopric that the empire-wide persecution under Decius broke out (see Chapter 3). Cyprian fled Carthage to rule his church in exile. Upon returning in 251, he found his Christian community split over what to do with those who had "lapsed" during the persecution—that is, those who, under pressure from the persecuting authorities, had sacrificed to the pagan deities or bribed their way into securing a certificate to indicate they had done so. In Cyprian's absence and against his own better judgment, some of his presbyters were urging that such people were to be allowed back into the good graces of the church without a long period of public penance. Moreover, it soon became known that a schism had occurred in Rome over just this issue, as a popular leader named Novatian insisted, in opposition to the Roman bishop, Cornelius, that the lapsed undergo a long and rigorous course of repentance. Novatian's followers soon elected him to be a rival pope.

Cyprian wrote his treatise, "On the Unity of the Church," to address such problems of schism, urging the bishops of the various churches to become unified among themselves for the sake of the body of Christ. Because some of his readers understood him to embrace the rightly elected bishop of Rome as the sole and ultimate authority over the church universal (i.e., as the "pope")—a meaning that Cyprian evidently did not intend—he later revised his treatise. Both versions are given in the excerpt that follows.

> The Lord says to Peter: "I say to you, that you are Peter and upon this rock I will build my Church, and the gates of hell shall not overcome it. I will give to you the keys of the kingdom of heaven. And what you shall bind upon earth shall be bound also in heaven, and whatsoever you shall loose on earth shall be loosed also in heaven.[1]

[1st edition]

And he says to him again after the resurrection: "Feed my sheep."[2] It is on him that he builds the Church, and to him that he entrusts the sheep to feed. And although he assigns a like power to all the apostles, yet he founded a single Chair, thus establishing by his own authority the source and hallmark of the [church's] oneness. No doubt the

[2nd edition]

It is on one person that he builds the Church, and although he assigns a like power to all the apostles after his resurrection, saying: "As the Father sent me, I also send you. . . . Receive the Holy

---

[1]Matt 16:18–19.
[2]John 21:17.

Cyprian: "The Unity of the Catholic Church," from *St. Cyprian: The Lapsed: The Unity of the Catholic Church,* ed. Maurice Bévenot. Mahway, N.J.: Paulist Press, 1956. Used by permission of Paulist Press.

others were all that Peter was, but a primacy is given to Peter, and it is [thus] made clear that there is but one church and one chair. So too, even if they are all shepherds, we are shown but one flock which is to be fed by all the apostles in common accord. If a person does not hold fast to this oneness of Peter, does he imagine that he still holds the faith? If he deserts the chair of Peter upon whom the church was built, has he still confidence that he is in the church?

Spirit: if you forgive any one his sins, they shall be forgiven him; if you retain any one's, they shall be retained,"[3] yet, in order that the oneness might be unmistakable, he established by his own authority a source for that oneness having its origin in one man alone. No doubt the other apostles were all that Peter was, endowed with equal dignity and power, but the start comes from him alone, in order to show that the church of Christ is unique. Indeed this oneness of the church is figured in the Canticle of Canticles when the Holy Spirit, speaking in our Lord's name, says: "One is my dove, my perfect one: to her mother she is the only one, the darling of her womb."[4] If a person does not hold fast to this oneness of the church, does he imagine that he still holds the faith? If he resists and withstands the church, has he still confidence that he is in the church, when the blessed apostle Paul gives us this very teaching and points to the mystery of oneness saying: "One body and one Spirit, one hope of your calling, one Lord, one Faith, one Baptism, one God"?[5]

Now this oneness we must hold to firmly and insist on—especially we who are bishops and exercise authority in the church—so as to demonstrate that the episcopal power is one and undivided too. Let none mislead the brethren with a lie, let none corrupt the true content of the faith by a faithless perversion of the truth.

---

[3]John 20:21–23.
[4]Song of Sol 6:8.
[5]Eph 4:4–6.

The authority of the bishops forms a unity, of which each holds his part in its totality. And the church forms a unity, however far she spreads and multiples by the progeny of her fecundity; just as the sun's rays are many, yet the light is one, and a tree's branches are many, yet the strength deriving from its sturdy root is one. So too, though many streams flow from a single spring, though its multiplicity seems scattered abroad by the copiousness of its welling waters, yet their oneness abides by reason of their starting point. Cut off one of the sun's rays—the unity of that body permits no [such] division of its light; break off a branch from the tree, it can bud no more; dam off a stream from its source, it dries up below the cut. So too our Lord's church is radiant with light and pours her rays over the whole world; but it is one and the same light which is spread everywhere, and the unity of her body suffers no division. She spreads her branches in generous growth over all the earth, she extends her abundant streams ever further; yet one is the head-spring, one the source, one the mother who is prolific in her offspring, generation after generation: of her womb are we born, of her milk are we fed, of her Spirit our souls draw their life breath.

The spouse of Christ cannot be defiled, she is inviolate and chaste; she knows one home alone, in all modesty she keeps faithfully to one only couch. It is she who rescues us for God, she who seals for the kingdom the children whom she has borne. Whoever breaks with the church and enters on an adulterous union, cuts himself off from the promises made to the church; and he who has turned his back on the church of Christ shall not come to the rewards of Christ: he is an alien, a worldling, an enemy. You cannot have God for your Father if you have not the church for your mother. If there was escape for anyone who was outside the ark of Noah, there is escape too for one who is found to be outside the church. Our Lord warns us when he says: "He that is not with me is against me, and he that gathers not with me, scatters."[6] Whoever breaks the peace and harmony of Christ acts against Christ; whoever gathers elsewhere than in the church, scatters the church of Christ. Our Lord says: "I and the Father are One"[7]; and again, of Father, Son, and Holy Spirit it is written: "And the three are One."[8] Does anyone think then that this oneness, which derives from the stability of God and is welded together after the celestial pattern, can be sundered in the church and divided by the clash of discordant wills? If a person does not keep this unity, he is not keeping the law of God; he has lost his faith about Father and Son, he has lost his life and his soul.

---

[6]Matt 12:30.
[7]John 10:30.
[8]1 John 5:8.

Chapter 11

The Development of the Liturgy
Ritual Practices in Early Christianity

Early Christians understood themselves to be the "body" of Christ, a distinct social group that stood over against the rest of the world, united together and different from everyone else. The distinctiveness of those within the group came especially in their unique relationship with the one true God. To that extent, Christians understood themselves to be a worshipping community.

Early Christian forms of worship were taken over principally from the Jewish synagogue, the place of worship for Jesus himself and his original followers, rather than from pagan cultic practices (although the celebration of the Lord's supper does share numerous similarities with cultic meals celebrated widely in pagan associations). Thus, unlike pagan cults, Christians had no sacred statues, no temples (other than the Jewish Temple in Jerusalem), and no rituals of sacrifice. Instead, Christian worship, much like Jewish, stressed the reading and exposition of Scripture (originally the Jewish Bible; see Chapter 9), prayer, confession, exhortation, the singing of psalms and hymns, and the collection of alms. Christians were distinguished from Jews, however, in having their own places of worship (see Chapter 10), in worshipping on a different day (the day of the resurrection, Sunday, rather than the Sabbath, Saturday), in accepting a different locus of authority (a new set of Scriptures and a new way of understanding the Old in light of Christ), and, perhaps most obvious, in having a different focus of worship (in seeing Christ as Lord of all, whose death was the ultimate sacrifice for sins). Eventually, ritualistic practices that were shared with Jews, such as fasting, came to be differentiated from them, as some Christians insisted, for example, on fasting on Wednesdays and Fridays instead of Mondays and Thursdays, as in the Jewish tradition.

In order to secure and maintain their unique status against the rest of the world, Christians had clear boundary markers to show who was "in" the group and who was not. In particular, from the earliest of times, these boundary markers included a one-time initiatory rite, baptism, and a periodic ritual meal, the eucharist (i.e., the Lord's supper), reserved for those who belonged to the group. Both ritual practices were believed to have been inaugurated by Jesus himself in his great commission after his resurrection (Matt 28:19–20) and in his own Last Supper (e.g., Matt 26:26–30). As might be expected, the practice and understanding of both rituals changed over time, probably in different ways in different Christian communities.

343

Our earliest sources indicate that baptism was initially practiced immediately upon conversion for those who came to believe in Christ, as well as for their entire households (which included their extended families, slaves, and, possibly, for wealthier people, their clients and other dependents; see, e.g., 1 Cor 1:16; Acts 16:15). The earliest known interpretation of the act comes in the writings of Paul, who saw baptism as a ritualistic (and actual) unification with Christ in his death, which enabled the baptized Christian to experience his or her death to the powers of sin that dominated the rest of humankind (Rom 6:1–6). Later the rite came to be understood as an official step to joining the church, to be preceded by a lengthy period of catechetical instruction, prayer, confession, fasting, and exorcism. Only later did Christian theologians begin to reflect on the efficacy of the act for the removal of original sin.

The eucharist evidently began as a weekly meal for the worshipping community, a celebration in which people shared food and drink with one another in commemoration of Jesus' last meal (and the sacrifice it presaged) and in anticipation of his imminent return (1 Cor 11:23–25). It soon took on other overtones, however, particularly as it symbolized both the unity of the Christian community implicit in the act of sharing (1 Cor 11:17–34) and the union of this community with God through the death of Christ. It was not long before the mystical significance of the meal itself, evident to some extent already in our earliest sources (e.g., 1 Cor 11:28–32), became increasingly pronounced. Thus, in the early second century, when the weekly celebration may have already become less an actual meal than a ritualistic service of remembrance of Christ's salvation, Ignatius speaks of the eucharist as the "bread that is the medicine of immortality, the antidote that wards off death" (Ign. *Eph* 20:2). The salvific effect of this spiritual food, of course, could come only to those who were within the church, that is, those who had been baptized and allowed to participate in the Christian services of worship.

The significance of these rituals for Christians appears to have been known outside the Christian communities, although the nature of the actual practices was not (since they were done in private). Their secretive character, however, led to widespread apprehensions among suspicious non-Christians, who had heard rumors about Christians coming together at night or early in the morning, calling one another brother and sister, greeting each other with a ritual kiss, and eating the body of the Son and drinking his blood. Rumors began to circulate that Christians engaged in incestuous nocturnal orgies (brothers and sisters kissing at will) that involved murder and cannibalism (see Chapter 4). In part to ward off such charges, starting in the middle of the second century, Christian apologists like Justin and Tertullian began to explain openly what Christians did in their private meetings and rituals. These public explanations, along with the in-house discussions that were passed along among the Christians themselves for purposes of instruction and correction, provide us with our best information concerning how the liturgical practices of the early Christians were conducted over the course of the first three centuries.

We are less informed about other Christian rituals known as far back as the New Testament period itself but referred to only briefly in our later sources, such as the "kiss" given during the services of worship (see Rom 16:16; 1 Cor 16:20), the "anointing with oil" practiced for healing (e.g., James 5:14; Mark 6:13), and the "laying on of hands" for healing or consecrating an individual (Acts 3:7; 1 Tim 4:14).

For Further Reading

Aune, David. "Worship: Early Christian," in the *Anchor Bible Dictionary*, ed. David Noel Freedman. New York: Doubleday, 1992; VI. 973–89.

Bradshaw, Paul F. *The Search for the Origins of Christian Worship*. Oxford: Oxford University Press, 1992.

Dix. Gregory. *The Shape of the Liturgy*. London: Dacre, 1945.

Ferguson, Everett, ed. *Worship in Early Christianity*. New York: Garland, 1993 (a collection of classic essays).

Jungmann, Josef A. *The Early Liturgy, To the Time of Gregory the Great*, tr. Francis A. Brunner. Notre Dame: University of Notre Dame, 1959.

THE TEXTS

61. The Didache

Outside of the New Testament, the first explicit discussion of early Christian ritual is found in the Didache (see Chapter 10). After an introductory section that provides ethical instruction for his readers (see Chapter 13), the unknown author gives directions for how Christians are to perform baptisms (preferably in cold, running water), when they are to fast (every Wednesday and Friday), what they are to pray (the Lord's Prayer, three times a day), and how they are to celebrate the Eucharist (first giving thanks for the cup, then for the bread—an order reversed from other early accounts; see 1 Cor 11:22–24; Mark 14:22–24). Some scholars believe that the words of thanksgiving that the author cites in the context of the eucharist may represent the prayers actually said in his own community. Unfortunately, the text gives no clear indications as to where that community was located.

7 Now about baptism: this is how to baptize. Give public instruction on all these points, and then "baptize" in running water, in the name of the Father and of the Son and of the Holy Spirit.

2 If you do not have running water, baptize in some other.

3 If you cannot in cold, then in warm. If you have neither, then pour water on the head three times in the name of the Father, Son, and Holy Spirit.

4 Before the baptism, moreover, the one who baptizes and the one being baptized must fast, and any others who can. And you must tell the one being baptized to fast for one or two days beforehand.

8 Your fasts must not be identical with those of the hypocrites. They fast on Mondays and Thursdays; but you should fast on Wednesdays and Fridays.

2 You must not pray like the hypocrites but pray as follows, as the Lord bid us in his gospel:

"Our Father in heaven, hallowed by your name; your Kingdom come; your will be done on earth as it is in heaven; give us today our bread for the morrow; and forgive us our debts as we forgive our debtors. And do not lead us into temptation, but save us from the evil one, for yours is the power and the glory forever."[1]

3 You should pray in this way three times a day.

9 Now about the eucharist: This is how to give thanks:

2 First in connection with the cup:

"We thank you, our Father, for the holy vine of David, your child, which you have revealed through Jesus, your child. To you be glory forever."

3 Then in connection with the piece [broken off the loaf]: "We thank you, our Father, for the life

---

[1]Matt 6:9–13.

The "Didache," reproduced from *Early Christian Fathers*, ed. Cyril C. Richardson (Library of Christian Classics Series), 1970. Used by permission of Westminster John Knox Press.

and knowledge which you have revealed through Jesus, your child. To you be glory forever."

4 "As this piece [of bread] was scattered over the hills and then was brought together and made one, so let your church be brought together from the ends of the earth into your Kingdom. For yours is the glory and the power through Jesus Christ forever."

5 You must not let anyone eat or drink of your eucharist except those baptized in the Lord's name. For in reference to this the Lord said, "Do not give what is sacred to dogs."[2]

10 After you have finished your meal, say grace in this way:

2 "We thank you, holy Father, for your sacred name which you have lodged in our hearts, and for the knowledge and faith and immortality which you have revealed through Jesus, your child. To you be glory forever.

3 "Almighty Master, you have created everything for the sake of your name, and have given

people food and drink to enjoy that they may thank you. But to us you have given spiritual food and drink and eternal life through Jesus, your child.

4 "Above all, we thank you that you are mighty. To you be glory forever.

5 "Remember Lord, your church, to save it from all evil and to make it perfect by your love. Make it holy, and gather it together from the four winds into your Kingdom which you have made ready for it. For yours is the power and the glory forever."

6 "Let grace come and let this world pass away."

"Hosanna to the God of David!" "If anyone is holy, let him come. If not, let him repent." "Our Lord, come!"

"Amen."

7 In the case of prophets, however, you should let them give thanks in their own way.

---

[2]Matt 7:6.

---

62. Justin: First Apology

One of the clearest accounts of early Christian ritual comes in the First Apology of Justin Martyr, written, possibly, in 155 C.E. (see Chapters 2 and 4). In order to defend Christians against charges of nefarious activities during their secret rites, Justin describes what actually took place during baptism, the eucharist, and the weekly services of worship. The account is interspersed with scriptural justifications for these practices and theological explanations of several important features. Moreover, it is interlaced with apologetic concerns (see esp. Chapter 4), as Justin stresses that Jesus is the fulfillment of prophecy, that Christians are upright, law-abiding citizens, that their secret rituals are completely innocuous, and that these rituals have been imitated by the evil demons in pagan cults.

The description of the Sunday worship service, with its readings, exhortations, prayers, eucharist, and collection, is the earliest to survive. The entire account is usually thought to reflect the actual practices of the Roman church in the mid-second century.

Justin: "First Apology," from *St. Justin Martyr: The First and Second Apologies*, ed. Leslie William Barnard. Mahway, N.J.: Paulist Press, 1997. Used by permission of Paulist Press.

61 I will also explain the manner in which we dedicated ourselves to God when we were made new through Christ, since if we left this out in our exposition we would seem to falsify something. As many as are persuaded and believe that the things we teach and say are true, and undertake to live accordingly, are instructed to pray and ask God with fasting for the remission of their past sins, while we pray and fast with them. Then they are brought by us where there is water, and are born again in the same manner of rebirth by which we ourselves were born again, for they then receive washing in water in the name of God the Father and Master of all, and of our Savior, Jesus Christ, and of the Holy Spirit. For Christ also said, "Except you are born again, you will not enter into the Kingdom of heaven."[1] Now it is clear to all that it is impossible for those who have once come into being to enter into their mothers' wombs. And it is said through Isaiah the prophet, as we wrote before, in what manner those who have sinned and repent shall escape from their sins. He thus spoke: "Wash, become clean, put away evil doings from our souls, learn to do good, judge the orphan and plead for the widow, and come and let us reason together, says the Lord. And though your sins be as scarlet, I will make them white as wool, and though they be as crimson, I will make them white as snow. But if you will not listen to me, a sword will devour you; for the mouth of the Lord has spoken these things."[2] And we have learned from the apostles this reason for this [rite]. Since at our first birth we were born of necessity without our knowledge, from moist seed by the intercourse of our parents with each other, and were brought up in bad habits and wicked behavior; in order that we should not remain children of necessity and ignorance, but of free choice and knowledge, and obtain remission of the sins formerly committed, there is named at the water over him who has chosen to be born again, and has repented of his sinful acts, the name of God the Father and Master of all; they who lead to the washing the one who is to be washed call on this [name] alone. For no one can give a name to the ineffable God; and if anyone should dare say there is one, he raves with a hopeless insanity. And this washing is called illu-

mination, as those who learn these things are illuminated in the mind. And he who is illuminated is washed in the name of Jesus Christ, who was crucified under Pontius Pilate, and in the name of the Holy Spirit, who through the prophets foretold all the things about Jesus. . . .

65 But we, after thus washing the one who has been convinced and has assented [to our instruction], lead him to those who are called brethren, where they are assembled; and we offer prayers in common for ourselves and for the one who has been illuminated and for all others everywhere, that we may be accounted worthy, having learned the truth, by our deeds also to be found good citizens and guardians of what is commanded, so that we may be saved with eternal salvation. Having ended the prayers we greet one another with a kiss. Then there is brought to the Ruler of the Brethren bread and a cup of water and [a cup] of wine mixed with water, and he taking them sends up praise and glory to the Father of the universe through the name of the Son and of the Holy Spirit, and offers thanksgiving at some length for our being accounted worthy to receive these things from him. When he has concluded the prayers and the thanksgiving, all the people present assent by saying, "Amen." Amen in the Hebrew language signifies "so be it." And when the Ruler has given thanks and all the people have assented, those who are called by us deacons give to each of those present a portion of the eucharistized bread and wine and water, and they carry it away to those who are absent.

66 And this food is called among us eucharist, of which no one is allowed to partake except one who believes that the things which we teach are true, and has received the washing that is for the remission of sins and for rebirth, and who so lives as Christ handed down. For we do not receive these things as common bread nor common drink; but in like manner as Jesus Christ our Savior having been incarnate by God's logos took both flesh and blood for our salvation, so also we

---

[1]John 3:3.
[2]Isa 1:16–20.

have been taught that the food eucharistized through the word of prayer that is from him, from which our blood and flesh are nourished by transformation, is the flesh and blood of that Jesus who became incarnate. For the apostles in the memoirs composed by them, which are called Gospels, thus handed down what was commanded them: that Jesus took bread and having given thanks said: "Do this for my memorial, this is my body"; and likewise he took the chalice and having given thanks said: "This is my blood"; and gave it to them alone.[3] Which also the wicked demons have imitated in the mysteries of Mithra and handed down to be done; for that bread and a cup of water are placed with certain words said over them in the secret rites of initiation, you either know or can learn.

67 And afterward we constantly remind each other of these things. And the wealthy come to the aid of the poor, and we are always together. Over all that we receive we bless the Maker of all through his Son Jesus Christ and through the Holy Spirit. And on the day called Sunday all who live in cities or in the country gather together in one place, and the memoirs of the apostles or the writings of the prophets are read, as long as time permits. Then when the reader has finished, the Ruler in a discourse instructs and exhorts to the imitation of these good things. Then we all stand up together and offer prayers; and, as we said before, when we have finished the prayer, bread is brought and wine and water, and the Ruler likewise offers up prayers and thanksgivings to the best of his ability, and the people assent, saying the Amen; and the distribution and the partaking of the eucharistized elements is to each, and to those who are absent a portion is sent by the deacons. And those who prosper, and so wish, contribute what each thinks fit; and what is collected is deposited with the Ruler, who takes care of the orphans and widows, and those who, on account of sickness or any other cause, are in want, and those who are in bonds, and the strangers who are sojourners among us, and in a word [he] is the guardian of all those in need. But we all hold this common gathering on Sunday, since it is the first day, on which God transforming darkness and matter made the universe, and Jesus Christ our Savior on the same day rose from the dead. For they crucified him on the day before Saturday, and on the day after Saturday, he appeared to his apostles and disciples and taught them these things which we have passed on to you also for your consideration.

---

[3]Matt 26:26–27; Mark 14:22–24.

⊱┈✦┈◯┈✦┈⊰

63. Tertullian: Apology

Some forty years after Justin, and in a different city (Carthage, in North Africa), Tertullian provided another discussion of the Christian services of worship (see Chapter 4). Like Justin, Tertullian sought to explain the Christians' practices to his pagan critics in order to defend the church against charges leveled against it. In particular, he described the so-called

---

Tertullian: "Apology," from *Tertullian: Apologetical Works and Minucius Felix: Octavius*, ed. Rudolph Arbesmann. Fathers of the Church, 10; 2 ed. Washington, D.C.: Catholic University Press of America, 1977. Used with permission.

"agapé meal" (i.e., the "love feast," a term that raised eyebrows outside the community), to show that it was in no way scandalous but involved a simple meal that benefited the poor, along with a hymn, reading of Scripture, and prayer. Throughout the description, Tertullian emphasizes the community benefits reaped by the love of Christians both for one another and for those in need, and lays particular stress on the high morality embodied by members of the Christian family, where "all things are held in common among us, except our wives."

Chapter 39

1 Now I myself will explain the practices of the Christian Church, that is, after having refuted the charges that they are evil, I myself will also point out that they are good. We form one body because of our religious convictions, and because of the divine origin of our way of life and the bond of common hope.

2 We come together for a meeting and a congregation, in order to besiege God with prayers, like an army in battle formation. Such violence is pleasing to God. We pray, also, for the emperors, for their ministers and those in power, that their reign may continue, that the state may be at peace, and that the end of the world may be postponed.

3 We assemble for the consideration of the holy Scriptures, [to see] if the circumstances of the present times demand that we look ahead or reflect. Certainly, we nourish our faith with holy conversation, we uplift our hope, we strengthen our trust, intensifying our discipline at the same time by the inculcation of moral precepts.

4 At the same occasion, there are words of encouragement, of correction, and holy censure. Then, too, judgment is passed which is very impressive, as it is before people who are certain of the presence of God, and it is a deeply affecting foretaste of the future judgment, if anyone has so sinned that he is dismissed from sharing in common prayer, assembly, and all holy intercourse.

5 Certain approved elders preside, men who have obtained this honor not by money, but by the evidence of good character. For, nothing that pertains to God is to be had for money.

Even if there is some kind of treasury, it is not accumulated from a high initiation fee as if the religion were something bought and paid for. Each person deposits a small amount on a certain day of the month or whenever he wishes, and only on condition that he is willing and able to do so. No one is forced; each makes his contribution voluntarily.

6 These are, so to speak, the deposits of piety. The money therefrom is spent not for banquets or drinking parties or good-for-nothing eating houses, but for the support and burial of the poor, for children who are without their parents and means of subsistence, for aged men who are confined to the house; likewise, for shipwrecked sailors, and for any in the mines, on islands or in prisons. Provided only it be for the sake of fellowship with God, they become entitled to loving and protective care for their confession.

7 The practice of such a special love brands us in the eyes of some. "See," they say, "how they love one another"; (for *they* hate one another), "and how ready they are to die for each other." (They themselves would be more ready to kill each other.)

8 Over the fact that we call ourselves brothers, they fall into a rage—for no other reason, I suppose, than because among them every term of kinship is only a hypocritical pretense of affection. But, we are your brothers, too, according to the law of nature, our common mother, although you are hardly men since you are evil brothers.

9 But, with how much more right are they called brothers and considered such who have acknowledged one father, God, who have drunk one spirit of holiness, who in fear and wonder have come forth from the one womb of their common ignorance to the one light of truth!

10 Perhaps this is why we are considered less legitimate brothers, because no tragic drama has our brotherhood as its theme, or because we are

brothers who use the same family substance which, among you, as a rule, destroys brotherhood.

11 So, we who are united in mind and soul have no hesitation about sharing what we have. Everything is in common among us—except our wives.

12 In this matter—which is the only matter in which the rest of humankind practise partnership—we dissolve partnership. They not only usurp the marriage rights of their friends, but they even hand over their own rights to their friends with the greatest equanimity. This results, I suppose, from the teaching they have learned from those who were older and wiser, the Greek Socrates and the Roman Cato, who shared with their friends the wives whom they had married, so that they could bear children in other families, too.

13 As a matter of fact, perhaps the wives were not exactly unwilling. For, why should they care about a chastity which their husbands had so readily given away? Oh, what an example of Attic wisdom and Roman dignity! The philosopher a pander, and the censor, too!

14 Why wonder, then, if such dear friends take their meals together? You attack our modest repasts—apart from saying that they are disgraced by crimes—as being extravagant. It was, of course, to us that Diogenes's remark referred: "The people of Megara purchase supplies as if they were to die tomorrow, but put up buildings as though they were never to die."

15 However, anyone sees the bit of straw in another's eye more easily than a mote in his own. With so many tribes, courts, and sub-courts belching, the air becomes foul: if the Salii are going to dine, someone will have to give a loan; the city clerks will have to count up the cost of the tithes and extravagant banquets in honor of Hercules; for the festival of the Apaturia, for the Dionysiac revels, for the mysteries of Attica, they proclaim a draft of cooks; at the smoke of a feast of Serapis the firemen will become alarmed. But, only about the repast of the Christians is any objection brought forth.

16 Our repast, by its very name, indicates its purpose. It is called by a name which to the Greeks means "love." Whatever it costs, it is gain to incur expense in the name of piety, since by this refreshment we comfort the needy, not as, among you, parasites contend for the glory of reducing their liberty to slavery for the price of filling their belly amidst insults, but as, before God, greater consideration is given to those of lower station.

17 If the motive of our repast is honorable, then on the basis of that motive appraise the entire procedure of our discipline. What concerns the duty of religion tolerates no vulgarity, no immorality. No one sits down to table without first partaking of a prayer to God. They eat as much as those who are hungry take; they drink as much as temperate people need.

18 They satisfy themselves as people who remember that they must worship God even throughout the night; they converse as people who know that the Lord is listening. After this, the hands are washed and lamps are lit, and each one, according to his ability to do so, reads the Holy Scriptures or is invited into the center to sing a hymn to God. This is the test of how much he has drunk. Similarly, prayer puts an end to the meal.

19 From here they depart, not to unite in bands for murder, or to run around in gangs, or for stealthy attacks of lewdness, but to observe the same regard for modesty and chastity as people do who have partaken not only of a repast but of a rule of life.

20 Such is the gathering of Christians. There is no question about it—it deserves to be called illegal, provided it is like those which are illegal; it deserves to be condemned, if any complaint is lodged against it on the same ground that complaints are made about other secret societies.

21 But, for whose destruction have we ever held a meeting? We are the same when assembled as when separate; we are collectively the same as we are individually, doing no one any injury, causing no one any harm. When people who are upright and good assemble, when the pious and virtuous gather together, the meeting should be called not a secret society but a senate.

64. Tertullian: On the Crown

In his treatise, "On the Crown," written around 205 C.E., Tertullian addresses the issue of whether it was right for a Christian to serve in the Roman army, since, among other things, doing so meant paying homage to the Roman emperor by wearing a ceremonial crown associated with pagan worship. In reply to those who pointed out that the practice is not forbidden in Scripture, Tertullian argues that some Christian practices are prescribed or forbidden not by Scripture but by venerable Christian tradition. As a case in point, he discusses traditions associated with the liturgy, thereby providing a rare glimpse into some of the specific customs involved in the practices of baptism (e.g., the renunciation of the devil beforehand, a threefold immersion, the drink of milk and honey afterward, and the refusal to bathe for the week that follows), eucharist (taken before daybreak), and worship (e.g., the refusal to kneel on Sundays and the use of the sign of the cross). These particular practices appear to reflect the traditions of Tertullian's own church in early third-century Carthage.

How can anything come into use, if it has not first been handed down? Even in pleading tradition, written authority, you say, must be demanded. Let us inquire, therefore, whether tradition, unless it be written, should not be admitted. Certainly we shall say that it ought not to be admitted, if no cases of other practices which, without any written instrument, we maintain on the ground of tradition alone, and the countenance thereafter of custom, affords us any precedent. To deal with this matter briefly, I shall begin with baptism. When we are going to enter the water, but a little before, in the presence of the congregation and under the hand of the president, we solemnly profess that we disown the devil, and his pomp, and his angels. Hereupon we are thrice immersed, making a somewhat ampler pledge than the Lord has appointed in the Gospel. Then, when we are taken up (as new-born children), we taste first of all a mixture of milk and honey, and from that day we refrain from the daily bath for a whole week. We take also, in congrega-tions before daybreak, and from the hand of none but the presidents, the sacrament of the Eucharist, which the Lord both commanded to be eaten at meal-times, and enjoined to be taken by all alike. As often as the anniversary comes round, we make offerings for the dead as birthday honors. We count fasting or kneeling in worship on the Lord's day to be unlawful. We rejoice in the same privilege also from Easter to Whitsunday. We feel pained should any wine or bread, even though our own, be cast upon the ground. At every forward step and movement, at every going in and out, when we put on our clothes and shoes, when we bathe, when we sit at table, when we light the lamps, on couch, on seat, in all the ordinary actions of daily life, we trace upon the forehead the sign.

If, for these and other such rules, you insist upon having positive Scripture injunction, you will find none. Tradition will be held forth to you as the originator of them, custom as their strengthener, and faith as their observer.

Tertullian: "On the Crown," from "Chaplet," *The Ante-Nicene Fathers*; vol. 3, *Latin Christianity: Its Founder, Tertullian*, ed. A. Cleveland Coxe. Reprint; 2 ed. Grand Rapids, Mich.: Eerdmans, 1989.

65. Hippolytus: The Apostolic Tradition

The "Apostolic Tradition" of Hippolytus (see Chapter 10) describes not only the ordination and duties of church leaders but also Christian liturgical practices. The following excerpt details the entire baptism ritual, including the examination of recent converts to Christianity (in which anyone found to be engaged in an "unchristian" occupation was required to find a different job), the instruction of catechumens anticipating baptism (for three years), the detailed preparations for the baptism itself, and a full description of the actual ritual, including the creed that was recited, the prayer that was said, and the eucharist that was then celebrated.

16 New converts to the faith, who are to be admitted as hearers of the word, shall first be brought to the teachers before the people assemble.

2 And they shall be examined as to their reason for embracing the faith, and they who bring them shall testify that they are competent to hear the word.

3 Inquiry shall then be made as to the nature of their life; whether a man has a wife or is a slave.

4 If he is the slave of a believer and he has his master's permission, then let him be received; but if his master does not give him a good character, let him be rejected.

5 If his master is a heathen, let the slave be taught to please his master, that the word be not blasphemed.

6 If a man has a wife or a woman a husband, let the man be instructed to content himself with his wife and the woman to content herself with her husband.

7 But if a man is unmarried, let him be instructed to abstain from impurity, either by lawfully marrying a wife or else remaining as he is.

8 But if any man is possessed with demons, he shall not be admitted as a hearer until he is cleansed.

9 Inquiry shall likewise be made about the professions and trades of those who are brought to be admitted to the faith.

10 If a man is a pander, he must desist or be rejected.

11 If a man is a sculptor or painter, he must be charged not to make idols; if he does not desist he must be rejected.

12 If a man is an actor or pantomimist, he must desist or be rejected.

13 A teacher of young children had best desist, but if he has no other occupation, he may be permitted to continue.

14 A charioteer, likewise, who races or frequents races, must desist or be rejected.

15 A gladiator or a trainer of gladiators, or a huntsman [in the wild-beast shows], or anyone connected with these shows, or a public official in charge of gladiatorial exhibitions must desist or be rejected.

16 A heathen priest or anyone who tends idols must desist or be rejected.

17 A soldier of the civil authority must be taught not to kill people and to refuse to do so if he is commanded, and to refuse to take an oath; if he is unwilling to comply, he must be rejected.

18 A military commander or civic magistrate that wears the purple must resign or be rejected.

Hippolytus: "The Apostolic Tradition," from *The Apostolic Tradition of Hippolytus*, ed. B. S. Easton. Cambridge: Cambridge University Press, 1934. Reprinted with the permission of Cambridge University Press.

19 If a catechumen or a believer seeks to become a soldier, he must be rejected, for he has despised God.

20 A harlot or licentious man or one who has castrated himself, or any other who does things not to be named, must be rejected, for they are defiled.

21 A magician must not [even] be brought for examination.

22 An enchanter, an astrologer, a diviner, a soothsayer, a user of magic verses, a juggler, a mountebank, an amulet-maker must desist or be rejected.

23 A concubine, who is a slave and has reared her children and has been faithful to her master alone, may become a hearer; but if she has failed in these matters she must be rejected.

24 If a man has a concubine, he must desist and marry legally; if he is unwilling, he must be rejected.

25 If, now, we have omitted anything (any trade?), the facts [as they occur] will instruct your mind; for we all have the spirit of God.

17 Let catechumens spend three years as hearers of the word.

2 But if a person is zealous and perseveres well in the work, it is not the time but his character that is decisive.

18 when the teacher finishes his instruction, the catechumens shall pray by themselves, apart from the believers.

2 And [all] women, whether believers or catechumens, shall stand for their prayers by themselves in a separate part of the church.

3 And when [the catechumens] finish their prayers, they must not give the kiss of peace, for their kiss is not yet pure.

4 Only believers shall salute one another, but men with men and women with women; a man shall not salute a woman.

5 And let all the women have their heads covered with an opaque cloth, not with a veil of thin linen, for this is not a true covering.

19 At the close of their prayer, when their instructor lays his hand upon the catechumens, he shall pray and dismiss them; whoever

gives the instruction is to do this, whether a cleric or a layperson.

2 If a catechumen should be arrested for the name of the Lord; let him not hesitate about bearing his testimony; for if it should happen that they treat him shamefully and kill him, he will be justified, for he has been baptized in his own blood.

20 They who are to be set apart for baptism shall be chosen after their lives have been examined: whether they have lived soberly, whether they have honored the widows, whether they have visited the sick, whether they have been active in well-doing.

2 When their sponsors have testified that they have done these things, then let them hear the Gospel.

3 Then from the time that they are separated from the other catechumens, hands shall be laid upon them daily in exorcism and, as the day of their baptism draws near, the bishop himself shall exorcise each one of them that he may be personally assured of their purity.

4 Then if there is any of them who is not good or pure, he shall be put aside as not having heard the word in faith; for it is never possible for the alien to be concealed.

5 Then those who are set apart for baptism shall be instructed to bathe and free themselves from impurity and wash themselves on Thursday.

6 If a woman is menstruous, she shall be set aside and baptized on some other day.

7 They who are to be baptized shall fast on Friday, and on Saturday the bishop shall assemble them and command them to kneel in prayer.

8 And, laying his hand upon them, he shall exorcise all evil spirits to flee away and never to return; when he has done this he shall breathe in their faces, seal their foreheads, ears and noses, and then raise them up.

9 They shall spend all that night in vigil, listening to reading and instruction.

10 They who are to be baptized shall bring with them no other vessels than the one each will bring for the eucharist; for it is fitting that he who is counted worthy of baptism should bring his offering at that time.

21 At cockcrow prayer shall be made over the water.

2 The stream shall flow through the baptismal tank or pour into it from above when there is no scarcity of water; but if there is a scarcity, whether constant or sudden, then use whatever water you find.

3 They shall remove their clothing.

4 And first baptize the little ones; if they can speak for themselves, they shall do so; if not, their parents or other relatives shall speak for them.

5 Then baptize the men, and last of all the women; they must first loosen their hair and put aside any gold or silver ornaments that they were wearing: let no one take any alien thing down to the water with them.

6 At the hour set for the baptism the bishop shall give thanks over oil and put it into a vessel: this is called the "oil of thanksgiving."

7 And he shall take other oil and exorcise it: this is called "the oil of exorcism." [The anointing is performed by a presbyter.]

8 A deacon shall bring the oil of exorcism, and shall stand at the presbyter's left hand; and another deacon shall take the oil of thanksgiving, and shall stand at the presbyter's right hand.

9 Then the presbyter, taking hold of each of those about to be baptized, shall command him to renounce, saying:

I renounce you, Satan, and all your servants and all your works.

10 And when he has renounced all these, the presbyter shall anoint him with the oil of exorcism, saying:

Let all spirits depart from you.

11 Then, after these things, let him give him over to the presbyter who baptizes, and let the candidates stand in the water, naked, a deacon going with them likewise.

12 And when he who is baptized goes down into the water, he who baptizes him, putting his hand on him, shall say thus:

Do you believe in God, the Father Almighty?

13 And he who is being baptized shall say:

I believe.

14 Then holding his hand placed on his head, he shall baptize him once.

15 And then he shall say:

Do you believe in Christ Jesus, the Son of God, who was born of the Holy Spirit of the Virgin Mary, and was crucified under Pontius Pilate, and was dead and buried, and rose again the third day, alive from the dead, and ascended into heaven, and sat at the right hand of the Father, and will come to judge the living and the dead?

16 And when he says: I believe, he is baptized again.

17 And again he shall say:

Do you believe in [the] Holy Spirit, and the holy church and the resurrection of the flesh?

18 He who is being baptized shall say accordingly:

I believe, and so he is baptized a third time.

19 And afterward, when he has come up [out of the water], he is anointed by the presbyter with the oil of thanksgiving, the presbyter saying:

I anoint you with holy oil in the name of Jesus Christ.

20 And so each one, after drying himself, is immediately clothed, and then is brought into the church.

22 Then the bishop, laying his hand upon them shall pray, saying:

O Lord God, who has made them worthy to obtain remission of sins through the laver of regeneration of [the] Holy Spirit, send into them your grace, that they may serve you according to your will; for yours is the glory, to the Father and the Son, with [the] Holy Spirit in the holy church, both now and world without end. Amen.

2 Then, pouring the oil of thanksgiving from his hand and putting it on his forehead, he shall say:

I anoint you with holy oil in the Lord, the Father Almighty and Christ Jesus and [the] Holy Spirit.

3 And signing them on the forehead he shall say:

The Lord be with you;

And he who is signed shall say:

And with your spirit.

4 And so he shall do to each one.

5 And immediately thereafter they shall join in prayer with all the people, but they shall not pray with the faithful until all these things are completed.

6 And at the close of their prayer they shall give the kiss of peace.

23 And then the offering is immediately brought by the deacons to the bishop, and by thanksgiving he shall make the bread into an image of the body of Christ, and the cup of wine mixed with water according to the likeness of the blood, which is shed for all who believe in him.

2 And milk and honey mixed together for the fulfillment of the promise to the fathers, which spoke of a land flowing with milk and honey; namely, Christ's flesh which he gave, by which they who believe are nourished like babes, he making sweet the bitter things of the heart by the gentleness of his word.

3 And the water into an offering in a token of that laver, in order that the inner part of the person, which is a living soul, may receive the same as the body.

4 The bishop shall explain the reason of all these things to those who partake.

5 And when he breaks the bread and distributes the fragments he shall say:

The heavenly bread in Christ Jesus.

6 And the recipient shall say, Amen.

7 And the presbyters—or if there are not enough presbyters, the deacons—shall hold the cups, and shall stand by with reverence and mod-

esty; first he who holds the water, then the milk, thirdly the wine.

8 And the recipients shall taste of each three times, he who gives the cup saying:

In God the Father Almighty:

9 and the recipient shall say, Amen. Then:

In the Lord Jesus Christ;

10 [and he shall say, Amen. Then:

In] [the] Holy Spirit and the holy church;

11 and he shall say, Amen. So it shall be done to each.

12 And when these things are completed, let each one hasten to do good works, and to please God and to live aright, devoting himself to the church, practising the things he has learned, advancing in the service of God.

13 Now we have briefly delivered to you these things concerning the holy baptism and the holy oblation, for you have already been instructed concerning the resurrection of the flesh and all other things as taught in Scripture.

14 Yet if there is any other thing that ought to be told [to converts], let the bishop impart it to them privately after their baptism; let not unbelievers know it, until they are baptized: this is the white stone of which John said: "There is upon it a new name written, which no one knows but he that receives the stone."[1]

---

[1]Rev. 2:17.

⊱⊱⊷•O•⊶⊰

66. The Didascalia

Among the interesting features of the church manual known as the "Didascalia" (see Chapter 10) are its detailed guidelines for certain church practices. As is seen in the following excerpts, this kind of church manual was becoming increasingly detailed in its

---

The "Didascalia," from *The Didascalia Apostolorum Corpus Scriptorum Christianorum Orientalium*, ed. Arthur Vööbus. Louvain: Peeters, 1979. Used with permission.

prescriptions of what was and what was not to be done in the context of the church's worship and ministry. Covered are such matters as the practice of excommunication, including instructions for how those who were excommunicated could return to the church's good graces and how they could be involved with the church in the meantime, the seating arrangements of the congregation during the worship services, and the subsidiary role of women in ministry, particularly in teaching and baptizing.

10

"... As a heathen," thus, "and as a publican let him be accounted by you"[1] who has been convicted of evil deeds and of falsehood. And afterwards, if he promise to repent as in the case when the heathen desire and promise to repent, and say "we believe," we receive them into the congregation that they may hear the word. But we do not communicate with them until they receive the seal and become perfected. Thus also do we not communicate with these until they show the fruits of repentance. But let them certainly come in, if they wish to hear the word, that they may not completely perish. But let them not communicate in prayer, but go outside. For they also, when they have seen that they do not communicate with the church, will subdue themselves, and repent of their former deeds, and strive to be received into the church for prayer. And again they likewise who see and hear them go forth like the heathen and publicans, will fear and take warning to take heed to themselves not to sin, lest it happens thus to them also, and being convicted of sin or falsehood they go out from the church.

But you shall by no means hinder them to enter the church and to hear the word, O bishop. For even our Lord and Savior did not completely put away and cast out publicans and sinners, but did even eat with them. On this account the Pharisees murmured against him and said: "He eats with publicans and sinners."[2] Then our Savior answered and said against their thoughts and their murmuring, and said: "The whole ones have no need of a physician, but they that are sick."[3] Therefore, deal with those who have been convicted of sins and are sick, and associate them with yourselves, and take care of their fate, and speak to them and console them, and keep hold of them, and make them to return. And afterwards, as each one of them re-

pents and shows the fruits of repentance, then receive him for prayer in the same way as a heathen. And so as you baptize a heathen and receive him, so also lay the hand upon this person while everyone is praying for him, and then bring him in and let him communicate with the church. Indeed, the laying on of the hand shall be to him instead of baptism—indeed, whether by the laying on of the hand, or by baptism, that they receive the fellowship of the Holy Spirit.

On this account, as a compassionate physician, heal all those who sin. And distribute with all skill, and offer healing for the remedy of their lives. And you shall not be ready to cut off the members of the church, but use the word of bandages and the admonitions of fomentations and the compresses of intercession. But if the ulcer goes deep and decreases his flesh, nourish it and counter-act it with healing medicine. And if there be filth in it, cleanse it with sharp medicine, that is with a word of reproof. But if the flesh be overswollen, reduce it and counter-act it with a strong medicine, that is with the threat of judgment. But if gangrene should be in it, cauterize it with branding irons, that is, with incisions of much fasting cut away and clear out the foulness of the ulcer. But again if the gangrene should gain strength and prevail even over the burnings, give judgment. And then, whichever member it be that is decayed, then with advice and much consultation with other physicians, cut off that decayed member, that it may not corrupt the whole body. Yet be not ready to amputate hastily, and do not hasten very quickly and run to the saw of many teeth, but use first the

---

[1]Matt 18:17.
[2]Matt 9:11.
[3]Matt 9:12.

scalpel and cut the ulcer, that it may be known what is the cause of the pain that is hidden inside, so that the whole body may be kept uninjured. But if you see that a person will not repent, but has completely cut off hope for himself, then with grief and mourning cut him off and cast him out of the church. . . .

12 But in your congregations in the holy churches hold your assemblies in (accordance with) all good manners, and fashion the places for the brethren carefully in sobriety. And for the presbyters let there be separated a place on the eastern side of the house, and let the bishop's chair be among them and let the presbyters sit with him.

And again, let the laymen sit in another eastern part of the house. For thus is it required that the presbyters shall sit in the eastern part of the house with the bishops, and afterwards the laymen, and then the women; so that when you stand up to pray, the leaders may stand first, and after them the laymen, and then also the women.

Indeed, it is required that you pray toward the east, as knowing that which is written: "Give glory to God, who rides upon the heaven of heavens toward the east."

As for the deacons, let one continue and stand by the oblations of the eucharist, but let another stand outside the door and observe those who come in. And afterwards, when you offer, let them serve together in the church. And if anyone be found sitting in a place which is not his, let the deacon who is within reprove him and make him rise up and sit in the place that is proper for him.

Indeed, our Lord likened the church to a lodge: for, as we see, the dumb animals, we mean oxen and sheep and goats, lie down and rise up according to their families, and feed and mate, none of them separating itself from its race. And again the wild beasts also go severally upon the mountains with those who are like them. So it is likewise required in the church that those who are young shall sit by themselves, if there be room, and if not, let them stand up; and those who are advanced in years shall sit by themselves. However, let the children stand on one side, or let their fathers and mothers take them to themselves; and let them stand up. And again let those who are girls also sit by themselves; but if there be no room, let them stand up behind the women. And let those who are married and young and have children stand by themselves, and let the aged women and widows sit by themselves. And let the deacons see that as each of them enters, he goes to his place, so that no one may sit in a place that is not his. And again let the deacon also observe that no one whispers or sleeps or laughs or makes signs. For thus it is required that with good manners and (great) care they watch in the church, and with their ears open to the word of the Lord.

But if there comes a person from another congregation, a brother or a sister, let the deacon ask and learn whether she is a wife of a man, or again whether she is a widow, a believer; and whether she is a daughter of the church, or whether she is of one of the heresies; and then let him conduct her and set her in a place that is right for her. But if a presbyter should come from another congregation, you the presbyters receive him with fellowship into your place.

And if it be a bishop, let him sit with the bishop, and let him be esteemed worthy of the honor of his rank, even as himself. And you, O bishop, tell him that he preach to your people. Indeed, the intercession and admonition of strangers is very helpful, especially because it is written: "There is no prophet that is acceptable in his country."[4] And when you offer the oblation, let him speak. But if he is wise and gives the honor to you, and does not wish to offer, yet let him speak over the cup.

But if, as you are sitting, another person should come, whether a man or a woman, who has honor in the world, either of the same locus or of another congregation—you, O bishop, if you are speaking the word of God, or hearing, or reading, shall not respect persons and leave off the service of your word and set them a place. But remain still as you are and do not interrupt your work, and let the brethren themselves receive them. And if there be no place, let one of the

---

[4]Luke 4:24.

brethren who is full of charity and loves his brethren, who is (prone) to honor, rise and give them place, but let himself stand up.

If, however, these who are younger men or women sit, (and) an older man or woman should rise and give up their place, you, O deacon, look at those who are sitting and see which man or woman of them is younger than his companions, and make them stand up, and cause him to sit who had risen and given up his place. And him whom you have caused to stand up, lead him away and make him stand behind his companions—that others also may be educated and learn to give place to others who are more honorable than themselves.

But if a poor man or woman should come, whether from the members of your congregation or from another congregation, and especially if they are advanced in years, and there be no place for those as such, do you, O bishop, with all your heart appoint a place for them—and even if you have to sit upon the ground, that you be not as one who respects the persons of others, but that your ministry be acceptable with God. . . .

15 Everyone who shall pray or communicate with one who is expelled from the church must rightly be reckoned with him. Indeed, these things lead to the dissolution and destruction of souls. For if one communicate and pray with him who is expelled from the church, and obey not the bishop, he does not obey God, and he is defiled with him (who is expelled). And moreover he does not allow him to repent. For if no one communicate with him, he will repent and weep, and will ask and beseech to be received, and he will repent of what he has done, and he will be saved.

About this, however, that a woman should baptize, or that one should be baptized by a woman, we do not counsel, for it is a transgression of the commandment and a great peril to her who baptizes and to him who is baptized. Indeed, if it were lawful to be baptized by a woman, our Lord and teacher himself would have been baptized by Mary his Mother. Now he was baptized by John, like other also of the people. Therefore do not bring danger upon yourselves, brethren and sisters, by acting beyond the law of the Gospel.

16 Therefore, O bishop, appoint yourself workers of righteousness, helpers who cooperate with you unto life. Those that please you out of all the people, you shall choose and appoint as deacons: on the one hand, a man for the administration of many things that are required, on the other hand a woman for the ministry of women.

For there are houses where you cannot send a deacon to the women, on account of the pagans, but (where) you may send a deaconess; also, because in many other matters the office of a deaconess is required. In the first place, when women go down into the water, it is required that those who go down into the water shall be anointed by deaconesses with the oil of anointing. And where there is no woman present, and especially no deaconess, it is necessary for him who baptizes to anoint her who is being baptized. But where there is a woman, and especially a deaconess, it is not right that women should be seen by men, but with the laying on of hand anoint the head only. As of old time the priests and kings in Israel were anointed, so in like manner, anoint the head of those who receive baptism, whether of men or of women. And afterwards, whether you yourself baptize or you command the deacons or presbyters to baptize—let a woman deacon, as we have said before, anoint the women. But let a man recite over them the invocation of the divine names in the water.

And when she who is being baptized has come up from the water, let the deaconess receive her, and teach and educate her in order that the unbreakable seal of baptism shall be (kept) in chastity and holiness. On this account, we say that the ministry of a woman deacon is especially required and urgent. For our Lord and Savior also was ministered unto by deaconesses who were Mary Magdalene, and Mary the daughter of James and mother of Jose, and the mother of the sons of Zebedee, with other women as well. Also for you the ministry of a deaconess is necessary for many things. Indeed, a deaconess is required for the houses of the pagans where there are believing women, that they enter and visit those who are sick, and to minister to them in something which is required for them, and to wash those who have begun to recover from sickness.

And let the deacons imitate the bishops in their conversation. However, let them labor even more than he. And let them not love polluted lucre, but let them be diligent in the ministry.

And in accordance with the number of the congregation of the people of the church, so let there be the deacons, that they may be able to distinguish (each) severally and give rest to every-one, so that for the aged women, those who have no strength, and for brethren and sisters, those who are in sickness—for everyone of them—they may provide the ministry which is proper for him. But let a woman especially be diligent in the service of women, and a man, a deacon to the service of men. And let him be ready to obey and submit himself to the command of the bishop.

12

The Proclamation of the Word

Homilies in Early Christianity

One of the central components of early Christian worship (see Chapter 11) was the oral exposition of Scripture. Early Christian homilies tended too be both hortatory (telling Christians how they ought to behave) and theological (indicating what they ought to believe). Usually they were based on specific texts of Scripture—originally the Jewish Bible but also, by the late first century, the writings ascribed to Jesus' apostles. It appears likely that the practice of having a leader within the community interpret Scripture for the gathered faithful was taken over from Judaism; in the New Testament, Jesus and Paul are themselves said to have delivered sermons in Jewish synagogues (see, e.g., Luke 4:16–30; Acts 13:15–43).

Examples of Christian sermons are scattered throughout the book of Acts (many of these are actually evangelistic sermons to outsiders); it is commonly thought among scholars that these addresses were composed by Luke himself, the author of the book. The earliest surviving homily that was actually delivered (possibly in writing) from a Christian leader to a Christian congregation is the anonymous book of Hebrews, also preserved in the New Testament. Despite the popularity of this mode of communication, we do not have an abundant number of surviving sermons prior to the fourth century, when their publication came to be widespread. The one exception involves the numerous homilies of Origen of Alexandria, the most prolific early Christian author.

Already in the second century, evidently, Christian homilies were based on rhetorical models of oral discourse taught and analyzed in Greek institutions of higher learning (i.e., rhetorical schools). With the passing of time, the use of Greek rhetoric in Christian sermons became increasingly pronounced. Among other things, this shows that Christian preachers were among the most highly educated and sophisticated members of the church. The views they express, therefore, and the ways they express them, may *not* be completely representative of Christendom at large.

We have already seen one example of a Christian sermon in the Passover Homily of Melito of Sardis (Chapter 5) and another, possibly, in the Gnostic-Christian Gospel of Truth (Chapter 6); the following texts of the second and third centuries may also be taken as broadly representative of the genre.

For Further Reading

Black, Clifton C. "The Rhetorical Form of the Hellenistic Jewish and Christian Sermon," *Harvard Theological Review* 81 (1988): 1–18.

Donfried, Karl. *The Setting of Second Clement in Early Christianity*. Leiden: E. J. Brill, 1974.

Kennedy, G. *Classical Rhetoric and Its Christian and Secular Tradition from Ancient to Modern Times*. Chapel Hill: University of North Carolina, 1980.

Wills, L. "The Form of the Sermon in Hellenistic Judaism and Early Christianity" *Harvard Theological Review* 77 (1984): 277–99.

THE TEXTS

67. Second Clement

The earliest surviving Christian homily outside of the New Testament appears to be the book commonly called "The Second Epistle of Clement." In parts of early Christianity, down to at least the fifth century, the book was regarded as Scripture. All the same, the traditional title is probably wrong: the book is not a letter but a sermon (see 19:1), and it was not produced by the author of 1 Clement (as is evident on stylistic grounds).

The audience, and probably the author, were former pagans who had converted to Christianity (see 1:6). The sermon is not based on a particular text of Scripture but consists of exhortations backed up by sayings of Jesus, along with the writings of the Old Testament and the apostles. Interestingly, one of the author's sources appears to have been a gnostic Gospel, possibly the Gospel of Thomas (12:2). He uses these sacred texts to urge his audience to repent and return to upright moral behavior in light of the coming day of judgment. In the course of his exhortation, he stresses the reality of the future resurrection of the flesh and attacks those (presumably Gnostics) who deny it (8:1).

It is difficult to say when, exactly, this sermon was written, but scholars usually date it to the mid-second century and locate its anonymous author possibly in Corinth or Alexandria.

1 Brothers, we ought to think of Jesus Christ as we do of God—as the judge of the living and the dead. And we ought not to belittle our salvation.

2 For when we belittle him, we hope to get but little; and they that listen as to a trifling matter, do wrong. And we too do wrong when we fail to realize whence and by whom and into what circumstances we were called, and how much suffering Jesus Christ endured for us.

3 How, then, shall we repay him, or what return is worthy of his gift to us? How many blessings we owe to him!

4 For he has given us light; as a Father he has called us sons; he has rescued us when we were perishing.

5 How, then, shall we praise him, or how repay him for what we have received?

6 Our minds were impaired; we worshiped stone and wood and gold and silver and brass, the works of humans; and our whole life was nothing else but death. So when we were wrapped in darkness and our eyes were full of such mist, by his will we recovered our sight and put off the cloud which infolded us.

7 For he took pity on us and in his tenderness saved us, since he saw our great error and ruin, and that we had no hope of salvation unless it came from him.

8 For he called us when we were nothing, and willed our existence from nothing.

2 "Rejoice, you who are barren and childless; cry out and shout, you who were never in labor; for the desolate woman has many more children than the one with the husband."[1] When he says, "Rejoice, you who are barren and childless," he refers to us; for our church was barren before it was given children.

2 And when he says, "Shout, you who were never in labor," this is what he means: we should offer our prayers to God with sincerity, and not lose heart like women in labor.

3 And he says, "The desolate woman has many more children than the one with the husband," because our people seemed to be abandoned by God. But now that we believe, we have become more numerous than those who seemed to have God.

4 And another Scripture says, "I did not come to call the righteous, but sinners."[2]

5 This means that those perishing must be saved.

6 Yes, a great and wonderful thing it is to support, not things which are standing, but those which are collapsing.

7 Thus it was that the Christ willed to save what was perishing; and he saved many when he came and called us who were actually perishing.

3 Seeing, then, that he has had such pity on us, firstly, in that we who are alive do not sacrifice to dead gods or worship them, but through him have come to know the Father of truth—what is knowledge in reference to him, save refusing to deny him through whom we came to know the Father?

2 He himself says, "He who acknowledges me before people, I will acknowledge before my Father."[3]

3 This, then, is our reward, if we acknowledge him through whom we are saved.

4 But how do we acknowledge him? By doing what he says and not disobeying his commands; by honoring him not only with our lips, but with all our heart and mind.

5 And he says in Isaiah as well, "This people honors me with their lips but their heart is far from me."[4]

4 Let us not merely call him Lord, for that will not save us.

2 For he says, "Not everyone who says to me, Lord, Lord, will be saved, but he who does what is right."[5]

3 Thus, brothers, let us acknowledge him by our actions, by loving one another, by refraining from adultery, backbiting, and jealousy, and by being self-controlled, compassionate, kind. We ought to have sympathy for one another and not to be avaricious. Let us acknowledge him by acting in this way and not by doing the opposite.

4 We ought not to have greater fear of people than of God.

5 That is why, if you act in this way, the Lord said, "If you are gathered with me in my bosom and do not keep my commands, I will cast you out and will say to you: 'Depart from me. I do not know whence you come, you workers of iniquity.' "[6]

5 Therefore, brothers, ceasing to tarry in this world, let us do the will of him who called us, and let us not be afraid to leave this world.

2 For the Lord said, "You will be like lambs among wolves."

3 But Peter replied by saying, "What if the wolves tear the lambs to pieces?"

4 Jesus said to Peter: "After their death the lambs should not fear the wolves, nor should you fear those who kill you and can do nothing more to you. But fear him who, when you are dead, has power over soul and body to cast them into the flames of hell."[7]

5 You must realize, brothers, that our stay in this world of the flesh is slight and short, but Christ's promise is great and wonderful, and means rest in the coming Kingdom and in eternal life.

---

[1] Isa 54:1; Gal 4:27.
[2] Matt 9:13; Mark 2:17; Luke 5:32.
[3] Matt 10:32; Luke 12:8.
[4] Isa 29:13.
[5] Matt 7:21.
[6] Gospel of the Egyptians?
[7] Gospel of the Egyptians?

6 What, then, must we do to get these things, except to lead a holy and upright life and to regard these things of the world as alien to us and not to desire them?

7 For in wanting to obtain these things we fall from the right way.

6 The Lord says, "No servant can serve two masters."[8] If we want to serve both God and money, it will do us no good.

2 "For what good does it do a person to gain the whole world and forfeit his life?"[9]

3 This world and the world to come are two enemies.

4 This one means adultery, corruption, avarice, and deceit, while the other gives them up.

5 We cannot, then, be friends of both. To get the one, we must give the other up.

6 We think that it is better to hate what is here, for it is trifling, transitory, and perishable, and to value what is there—things good and imperishable.

7 Yes, if we do the will of Christ, we shall find rest, but if not, nothing will save us from eternal punishment, if we fail to heed his commands.

8 Furthermore, the Scripture also says in Ezekiel, "Though Noah and Job and Daniel should rise, they shall not save their children in captivity."[10]

9 If even such upright people as these cannot save their children by their uprightness, what assurance have we that we shall enter God's Kingdom if we fail to keep our baptism pure and undefiled? Or who will plead for us if we are not found to have holy and upright deeds?

7 So, my brothers, let us enter the contest, recognizing that it is at hand and that, while many come by sea to corruptible contests, not all win laurels, but only those who have struggled hard and competed well.

2 Let us, then, compete so that we may all be crowned.

3 Let us run the straight race, the incorruptible contest; and let many of us sail to it and enter it, so that we too may be crowned. And if we cannot all be crowned, let us at least come close to it.

4 We must realize that if a contestant in a corruptible contest is caught cheating, he is flogged, removed, and driven from the course.

5 What do you think? What shall be done with the person who cheats in the contest for the incorruptible?

6 For in reference to those who have not guarded the seal, it says, "Their worm shall not die and their fire shall not be quenched, and they shall be a spectacle to all flesh."[11]

8 So while we are on earth, let us repent. For we are like clay in a worker's hands.

2 If a potter makes a vessel and it gets out of shape or breaks in his hands, he molds it over again; but if he has once thrown it into the flames of the furnace, he can do nothing more with it. Similarly, while we are in this world, let us too repent with our whole heart of the evil we have done in the flesh, so that we may be saved by the Lord while we have a chance to repent.

3 For once we have departed this world we can no longer confess there or repent any more.

4 Thus, brothers, by doing the Father's will and by keeping the flesh pure and by abiding by the Lord's commands, we shall obtain eternal life.

5 For the Lord says in the Gospel: "If you fail to guard what is small, who will give you what is great? For I tell you that he who is faithful in a very little, is faithful also in much."[12]

6 This, then, is what he means: keep the flesh pure and the seal undefiled, so that we may obtain eternal life.

9 Moreover, let none of you say that this flesh will not be judged or rise again.

2 Consider this: In what state were you saved? In what state did you regain your sight, if it was not while you were in this flesh?

3 Therefore we should guard the flesh as God's temple.

---

[8]Luke 16:13; Matt 6:24.
[9]Matt 16:26; Mark 8:36; Luke 9:25.
[10]Ezek 14:14–20.
[11]Isa 66:24; Mark 9:48.
[12]Luke 16:10–12.

4 For just as you were called in the flesh, you will come in the flesh.

5 If Christ the Lord who saved us was made flesh though he was at first spirit, and called us in this way, in the same way we too in this very flesh will receive our reward.

6 Let us, then, love one another, so that we may all come to God's Kingdom.

7 While we have an opportunity to be healed, let us give ourselves over to God, the physician, and pay him in return.

8 How? By repenting with a sincere heart.

9 For he foreknows everything, and realizes what is in our hearts.

10 Let us then praise him, not with the mouth only, but from the heart, so that he may accept us as children.

11 For the Lord said, "My brothers are those who do the will of my Father."[13]

10 So, my brothers, let us do the will of the Father who called us, so that we may have life; and let our preference be the pursuit of virtue. Let us give up vice as the forerunner of our sins, and let us flee impiety, lest evils overtake us.

2 For if we are eager to do good, peace will pursue us.

3 This is the reason people cannot find peace. They give way to human fears, and prefer the pleasures of the present to the promises of the future.

4 For they do not realize what great torment the pleasures of the present bring, and what delight attaches to the promises of the future.

5 If they did these things by themselves, it might be tolerable. But they persist in teaching evil to innocent souls, and do not realize that they and their followers will have their sentence doubled.

11 Let us therefore serve God with a pure heart and we shall be upright. But if, by not believing in God's promises, we do not serve him, we shall be wretched.

2 For the word of the prophet says, "Wretched are the double-minded, those who doubt in their soul and say, 'We have heard these things long ago, even in our fathers' times, and

day after day we have waited and have seen none of them.'

3 "You fools! Compare yourselves to a tree. Take a vine: first it sheds its leaves, then comes a bud, and after this a sour grape, then a ripe bunch.

4 "So my people too has had turmoils and troubles; but after that it will receive good things."[14]

5 So, my brothers, we must not be double-minded. Rather must we patiently hold out in hope so that we may also gain our reward.

6 For he can be trusted who promised to pay each one the wages due for his work.

7 If, then, we have done what is right in God's eyes, we shall enter his Kingdom and receive the promises which ear has not heard or eye seen, or which man's heart has not entertained.

12 Loving and doing what is right, we must be on the watch for God's Kingdom hour by hour, since we do not know the day when God will appear.

2 For when someone asked the Lord when his Kingdom was going to come, he said, "When the two shall be one, and the outside like the inside, and the male with the female, neither male or female."[15]

3 Now "the two" are "one" when we tell each other the truth and two bodies harbor a single mind with no deception.

4 "The outside like the inside" means this: "the inside" means the soul and "the outside" means the body. Just as your body is visible, so make your soul evident by your good deeds.

5 Furthermore "the male with the female, neither male nor female," means this: that when a brother sees a sister he should not think of her sex, any more than she should think of his.

6 When you do these things, he says, my Father's Kingdom will come.

13 Right now, my brothers, we must repent, and be alert for the good, for we are full of much stupidity and wickedness. We must wipe

---

[13]Matt 12:50; Mark 13:35; Luke 8:21.

[14]Source unknown.

[15]Gosp. Thom. 22.

off from us our former sins and by heartfelt repentance be saved. And we must not seek to please people or desire to please only ourselves, but by doing what is right to please even outsiders, so that the Name may not be scoffed at on our account.

2 For the Lord says, "My name is continually scoffed at by all peoples";[16] and again, "Alas for him through whom my name is scoffed at!"[17] How is it scoffed at? By your failing to do what I want.

3 For when the heathen hear God's oracles on our lips they marvel at their beauty and greatness. But afterwards, when they mark that our deeds are unworthy of the words we utter, they turn from this to scoffing, and say that it is a myth and a delusion.

4 When, for instance, they hear from us that God says, "It is no credit to you if you love those who love you, but it is to your credit if you love your enemies and those who hate you,"[18] when they hear these things, they are amazed at such surpassing goodness. But when they see that we fail to love not only those who hate us, but even those who love us, then they mock at us and scoff at the Name.

14 So, my brothers, by doing the will of God our Father we shall belong to the first church, the spiritual one, which was created before the sun and the moon. But if we fail to do the Lord's will, that passage of Scripture will apply to us which says, "My house has become a robber's den."[19] So, then, we must choose to belong to the church of life in order to be saved.

2 I do not suppose that you are ignorant that the living church is the body of Christ. For Scripture says, "God made man male and female."[20] The male is Christ; the female is the church. The Bible, moreover, and the apostles say that the church is not limited to the present, but existed from the beginning. For it was spiritual, as was our Jesus, and was made manifest in the last days to save us.

3 Indeed, the church which is spiritual was made manifest in the flesh of Christ, and so indicates to us that if any of us guard it in the flesh and do not corrupt it, he will get it in return by the Holy Spirit. For this flesh is the antitype of the spirit. Consequently, no one who had corrupted the antitype will share in the reality. This, then, is what it means, brothers: Guard the flesh so that you may share in the spirit.

4 Now, if we say that the church is the flesh and the Christ is the spirit, then he who does violence to the flesh, does violence to the church. Such a person, then, will not share in the spirit, which is Christ.

5 This flesh is able to share in so great a life and immortality, because the Holy Spirit cleaves to it. Nor can one express or tell what things the Lord has prepared for his chosen ones.

15 The advice I have given about continence is not, I think, unimportant; and if a person acts on it, he will not regret it, but will save himself as well as me who advised him. For no small regard attaches to converting an errant and perishing soul, so that it may be saved.

2 For this is how we can pay back God who created us, if the one who speaks and the one who hears do so with faith and love.

3 Consequently, we must remain true to our faith and be upright and holy, so that we may petition God in confidence, who says, "Even while you are speaking, I will say, 'See, here I am.' "[21]

4 Surely this saying betokens a great promise; for the Lord says of himself that he is more ready to give than we to ask.

5 Let us, then, take our share of such great kindness and not begrudge ourselves the obtaining of such great blessings. For these sayings hold as much pleasure in store for those who act on them, as they do condemnation for those who disregard them.

16 So, brothers, since we have been given no small opportunity to repent, let us take

---

[16]Isa 52:5.
[17]Source unknown.
[18]Luke 6:32, 35.
[19]Jer 7:11; Matt 21:13.
[20]Gen 1:27.
[21]Isa 58:9.

the occasion to turn to God who has called us, while we still have one to accept us.

2 For if we renounce these pleasures and master our souls by avoiding their evil lusts, we shall share in Jesus' mercy.

3 Understand that the day of judgment is already on its way like a furnace ablaze, and the powers of heaven will dissolve and the whole earth will be like lead melting in fire. Then people's secret and overt actions will be made clear.

4 Charity, then, like repentance from sin, is a good thing. But fasting is better than prayer, and charity than both. Love covers a multitude of sins, and prayer, arising from a good conscience, rescues from death. Blessed is everyone who abounds in these things, for charity lightens sin.

17 Let us, then, repent with our whole heart, so that none of us will be lost. For if we have been commanded to do this too—to draw people away from idols and instruct them—how much more is it wrong for the soul which already knows God to perish?

2 Consequently we must help one another and bring back those weak in goodness, so that we may all be saved; and convert and admonish one another.

3 Not only at this moment, while the presbyters are preaching to us, should we appear believing and attentive. But when we have gone home, we should bear in mind the Lord's commands and not be diverted by worldly passions. Rather should we strive to come here more often and advance in the Lord's commands, so that with a common mind we may all be gathered together to gain life.

4 For the Lord said, "I am coming to gather together all peoples, clans, and tongues."[22] This refers to the day of his appearing, when he will come to redeem us, each according to his deeds.

5 And unbelievers will see his glory and power, and they will be surprised to see the sovereignty of the world given to Jesus, and they will say, "Alas for us, for you really existed, and we neither recognized it nor believed, and we did not obey the presbyters who preached to us our salvation." And their worm will not die and their fire

will not be quenched, and they will be a spectacle to all flesh.

6 He refers to that day of judgment when people will see those who were ungodly among us and who perverted the commands of Jesus Christ.

7 But the upright who have done good and patiently endured tortures and hated the pleasures of the soul, when they see those who have done amiss and denied Jesus in word and act being punished with dreadful torments and undying fire, will give "glory to their God" and say, "There is hope for him who has served God with his whole heart."

18 Consequently we too must be of the number of those who give thanks and have served God, and not of the ungodly who are sentenced.

2 For myself, I too am a grave sinner, and have not yet escaped temptation. I am still surrounded by the devil's devices, though I am anxious to pursue righteousness. My aim is to manage at least to approach it, for I am afraid of the judgment to come.

19 So, my brothers and sisters, after God's truth I am reading you an exhortation to heed what was there written, so that you may save yourselves and your reader. For compensation I beg you to repent with all your heart, granting yourselves salvation and life. By doing this we will set a goal for all the young who want to be active in the cause of religion and of God's goodness.

2 We should not, moreover, be so stupid as to be displeased and vexed when anyone admonishes us and converts us from wickedness to righteousness. There are times when we do wrong unconsciously because of the double-mindedness and unbelief in our hearts, and out understanding is darkened by empty desires.

3 Let us, then, do what is right so that we may finally be saved. Blessed are they who observe these injunctions; though they suffer briefly in this world, they will gather the immortal fruit of the resurrection.

[22]Isa 66:18.

4 A religious person must not be downcast if he is miserable in the present. A time of blessedness awaits him. He will live again in heaven with his forefathers, and will rejoice in an eternity that knows no sorrow.

20 But you must not be troubled in mind by the fact that we see the wicked in affluence while God's slaves are in straitened circumstances.

2 Brothers and sisters, we must have faith. We are engaged in the contest of the living God and are being trained by the present life in order to win laurels in the life to come.

3 None of the upright has obtained his reward quickly, but he waits for it.

4 For were God to give the righteous their reward at once, our training would straightway be in commerce and not in piety, since we would give an appearance of uprightness, when pursuing, not religion, but gain. That is why the divine judgment punishes a spirit which is not upright, and loads it with chains.

5 To the only invisible God, the Father of truth, who dispatched to us the Savior and prince of immortality, through whom he also disclosed to us the truth and the heavenly life—to him be glory forever and ever. Amen.

68. Origen: Homilies on Luke

No Christian author of the second and third centuries published more homilies than Origen (see Chapter 4)—more than three hundred, according to ancient sources. Nearly two-thirds that number still survive, although principally only in Latin translation. These represent actual sermons that Origen delivered during worship services, either on weekday mornings (services were held daily), on Wednesday or Friday mid-afternoon services (when devoted Christians broke their fast with the eucharistic meal), or at the Sunday morning eucharist. Normally, the services included the reading of Scripture followed by an exposition of its meaning (see Chapter 11).

As public interpretations of Scripture for the common Christian (in contrast with Origen's biblical commentaries, written for serious students of the Bible), these homilies were meant to instruct the congregation in the meaning of the text for their beliefs and ethics. Throughout them one can see Origen's distinctive view of the Bible, a view that played a significant role in the development of later Christian theology (see Chapter 14).

In many instances, Origen can be seen to expound and embrace the literal meaning of the scriptural text. But he often found that the literal meaning leads to a contradiction or an absurdity. In such cases, he maintained, one must dig deeper into the text to find its less obvious, hidden, spiritual meaning. To do this, Origen used the Bible as its own interpreter, typically appealing to one passage of Scripture to assist in the interpretation

Origen: "Homilies on Luke," from *Origen: Homilies on Luke; Fragments on Luke*, ed. Joseph T. Lienhard. Fathers of the Church, 94; Washington, D.C.: Catholic University Press of America, 1996. Used with permission.

and exploration of another. This approach was rooted in Origen's understanding of the Bible as God's word in its fullness; any word, phrase, or verse could therefore lead him to consider related words, phrases, and verses in other passages. The Bible, then, provided a kind of closed system of meaning, any part of which could be used as an entree into issues of profound theological and practical importance.

Thirty-nine of Origen's homilies on Luke have survived. The following are four rather short expositions taken from the story of the birth of John the Baptist in Luke 1. The homilies are normally thought to have been written around 240 C.E. in Caesarea.

Homily 3

Luke 1:11

On the passage, "The angel of the Lord appeared to him, standing at the right side of the altar of incense."

OF THEMSELVES, beings that are corporeal and lack sensation do nothing to be seen by another. The observer's eye is simply directed toward them. Whenever the observer directs his gaze and his regard at them, he sees them, whether the objects will it or not. What can a person or any other object that is enclosed in a solid body do to avoid being seen, when they are in fact there? In contrast, things that are from above and divine are not seen, even when they are there, unless they themselves will it. It lies within their will to be seen or not. It was by an act of his grace that God appeared to Abraham and the other prophets. The eye of Abraham's heart was not the only cause that allowed him to see God; God offered his grace to the sight of a just man to let him see.

2 You should understand this not only of God the Father, but also of our Lord and Savior and of the Holy Spirit and —to come to lesser beings— of cherubim and seraphim. Perhaps an angel is helping us as we are speaking now, but we cannot see him because we do not deserve to. Even though the eye of our body or our soul makes an effort to see, the person who wants to see will not, unless the angel willingly appears and offers himself to sight. Thus, wherever Scripture says, "God appeared" to someone—just as here, for example, "The angel of

the Lord appeared to him, standing at the right side of the altar of incense"—understand it as I explained. Whether it is God or an angel, and whether he appears to Abraham or to Zechariah, he will be seen or not, depending on whether he wishes it or not.

3 And we say this not only of the present age but also of the age to come. When we depart from the world, God or the angels do not appear to everyone, as if anyone who departs from the body immediately deserves to see the angels, the Holy Spirit, the Lord and Savior, and God the Father himself. Only one who has a pure heart and shows himself worthy of the vision of God will see them. One will be pure of heart; another will still be stained with some filth. Although they will be in the same place, the place itself will not be able to help or hinder them. Whoever has a pure heart will see God. Whoever does not will not see what the other beholds. I think we should understand something similar of Christ, too, when he was seen in the body. Not everyone who laid eyes on him was able to see him.

4 They saw his body, but, insofar as he was Christ, they could not see him. But his disciples saw him and beheld the greatness of his divinity. I think this is why, when Philip entreated the Savior and said, "Show us the Father and it is enough for us," the Savior answered him, "Have I been with you for so long a time, and you do not know me? Philip, he who sees me sees the Father also."[1] Pilate, who saw Jesus, did not gaze upon the Father.

---

[1] John 14:8–9.

Neither did Judas the traitor. Neither Pilate nor Judas saw Christ as Christ. Nor did the crowd, which pressed around him. Only those whom Jesus judged worthy of beholding him really saw him. Let us, too, therefore, work so that God might appear to us at this moment. The holy word of Scripture has promised, "He is found by those who do not test him, and he appears to those who do not doubt him."[2] In the age to come may he not be hidden from us; may we see him face to face. May we have the assurance of a good life and enjoy the vision of Almighty God in Christ Jesus and in the Holy Spirit, to whom is glory and power for ages of ages. Amen.

Homily 4

Luke 1.13–17

On the passage from, "Do not be afraid, Zechariah," up to the point where it is said of John, "He will go before him in the spirit and power of Elijah."

WHEN ZECHARIAH SAW the angel, he was terrified. If the human gaze beholds a strange form, the mind is agitated and the soul is unsettled. The angel understands that human nature reacts in this way, so he first settles Zechariah's agitation and says, "Do not be afraid, Zechariah." He revives the trembling man and gladdens him by announcing his news. He says, "Your prayer has been heard. Your wife Elizabeth will bear a son. You shall name him John. He will bring you joy and elation."[3] When a just person is born into the world and enters the course of this life, those responsible for his birth rejoice, and their hearts soar upward. But, when someone who is destined for an evil life is born, one who is virtually banished to a prison as a punishment, the one responsible for his birth is thrown into confusion and loses heart.

2 Do you want an example of a holy man, all of whose deeds are praiseworthy? Consider Jacob. He fathered twelve male offspring. All of them became patriarchs, princes of God's people and of Jacob's heritage. Jacob, their father, rejoiced in all of them. The Gospel proclaims joy for all people because of John's birth. Once a man engages in the task of begetting children to benefit others and willingly devotes himself to this service, he should pray to God and ask that any son of his who comes into the world might be like John, one whose birth would bring him joy. Scripture says of John, "He will be great in the Lord's sight."[4] This phrase, "He will be great in the Lord's sight," shows the greatness of John's soul. God's eyes beheld this greatness. There is also a "smallness" of soul, which properly looks to the soul's virtue.

3 This is how I understand the passage in the Gospel that says, "Do not despise one of these least ones in the Church."[5] "Least one" is to be understood in contrast with someone greater. The Gospel does not command me not to despise a great one; a great one cannot be despised. But it tells me, "Do not despise one of these least ones." You should realize that the words "least" and "little" are not used haphazardly. Scripture says, for the reason we just mentioned, "whoever scandalizes one of these least ones."[6] A "least one" can be scandalized; a great one cannot.

4 Then the Gospel says of John, "He will be filled with the Holy Spirit even from his mother's womb."[7] John's birth is filled with miracles. An archangel announced the coming of our Lord and Savior; an archangel also announces John's birth: "He will be filled with the Holy Spirit even from his mother's womb." The Jewish people did not recognize our Lord when he performed signs and wonders and cured their illnesses. But, when John is still in his mother's womb, he rejoices and cannot be restrained. When Jesus' mother arrives, he tries to burst out of the womb. Elizabeth says, "For behold, when your greeting sounded in my ears, the infant leapt for joy in my womb"[8] John was still in his mother's womb when he received the Holy Spirit, but the Spirit was not the principle of his being or nature.

[2]Wis 1:2.
[3]Luke 1:13–14.
[4]Luke 1:15.
[5]Matt 18:10.
[6]Matt 18:6.
[7]Luke 1:15.
[8]Luke 1:44.

5 Then Scripture says, "He will convert many of the children of Israel to the Lord their God."[9] John converts many; the Lord converts not many but all. This is the Lord's work, to convert all to God the Father. "He will go before Christ in the spirit and power of Elijah."[10] Luke does not say, "in the soul of Elijah," but, "in the spirit and power of Elijah." Power and spirit dwelt in Elijah as in all the prophets and, with regard to his humanity, in the Lord and Savior as well. A little later in the Gospel the angel says to Mary, "The Holy Spirit will come upon you, and the power of the Most High will overshadow you."[11] So the spirit that had been in Elijah came upon John as well, and the power that Elijah had also appeared in John. Elijah was carried off to heaven. John was the Lord's precursor and died before so that he could go down to the underworld and proclaim his coming.

6 I believe that the mystery of John is still being achieved in the world today. If anyone is going to believe in Christ Jesus, John's spirit and power first come to his soul and "prepare a perfect people for the Lord."[12] It makes the roads in the heart's rough places level and straightens out its paths. Not only at that time were the roads made ready and the paths straight; even today John's spirit and power precede the coming of our Lord and Savior. How great are the Lord's mysteries and his plan! Angels go before Jesus, and today angels go up or down for the salvation of people in Christ Jesus, to whom is glory and power for ages of ages. Amen.

Homily 5

Luke 1.22

On the fact that Zechariah fell mute.

WHEN THE PRIEST Zechariah offers incense in the temple, he is condemned to silence and cannot speak. Or better, he speaks only with gestures. He remains mute until the birth of his son John. What does this mean? Zechariah's silence is the silence of prophets in the people of Israel. God no longer speaks to them. His "Word, which was

with the Father from the beginning, and was God,"[13] has passed over to us. For us Christ is not silent; for the Jews he is silent even to this day. Therefore, Zechariah the prophet was also silent. His words make it quite clear that he was both a prophet and a priest. But what does the phrase that follows mean, namely, "He kept nodding to them"[14]—that is, he compensated for the loss of his voice with signs? I think that there are deeds that are no different from empty signs because they lack words and reason. But, when words and reason come first and the deed follows, the deeds are not mere signs; they are endowed with rationality.

2 Consider the Jewish practices. They lack words and reason. The Jews cannot give a reason for their practices. Realize that what happened in the past in Zechariah is a type of what is fulfilled in the Jews even to this day. Their circumcision is like an empty sign. Unless the meaning of circumcision is provided, it remains an empty sign, a mute deed. Passover and other feasts are empty signs rather than the truth. To this very day the people of Israel are mute and dumb. The people who rejected the Word from their midst could not be anything but mute and dumb.

3 Moses himself once said, "I am *alogos*[15] (wordless)." After he said this, he received reason and speech, which he admitted that he did not have before. When the people of Israel were in Egypt, before they had received the Law, they too were without words and reason and thus, in a sense, mute. Then they received the Word; Moses was the image of it. So these people do not admit now what Moses had once admitted—that they are mute and wordless—but show by signs and silence that they have neither words nor reason. Do you not realize that the Jews are confessing their

---

[9]Luke 1:16.
[10]Luke 1:17.
[11]Luke 1:35.
[12]Luke 1:17.
[13]John 1:1–2.
[14]Luke 1:22.
[15]Exod 4:10.

folly when none of them can give a reasonable explanation of the precepts of their Law and of the predictions of their prophets?

4 Christ ceased to be in them. The Word deserted them. What Isaiah wrote was fulfilled, "The daughter of Zion will be deserted like a tent in the vineyard or like a hut in the cucumber patch; she is as desolate as a plundered city."[16] The Jews were left behind and salvation passed to the Gentiles. God meant to spur on the Jews with envy. We contemplate God's mysterious plan, how for our salvation he rejected Israel. We ought to be careful. The Jews were rejected for our sake; on our account they were abandoned. We would deserve even greater punishment if we did nothing worthy of our adoption by God and of his mercy. In his mercy God adopted us and made us his sons in Christ Jesus, to whom is glory and power for ages of ages. Amen.

Homily 6

Luke 1.24–32

On the passage from, "But, when Elizabeth conceived, she kept herself hidden" up to the point where it says, "He will be great."

WHEN ELIZABETH CONCEIVED, "she kept herself hidden for five months. She said, 'The Lord did this for me when he showed concern for me and took away the reason people reproach me.'"[17] I ask why she avoided public notice after she realized that she was pregnant. Unless I am mistaken, the reason is this. Even those who are joined in marriage do not consider every season free for intercourse. At times they abstain from the use of marriage. If the husband and wife are both aged, it is a disgraceful for them to yield to lust and turn to mating. The decline of the body, old age itself, and God's will all inhibit this act. But Elizabeth had relations with her husband once again, because of the angel's word and God's dispensation. She was embarrassed because she was an old and feeble woman, and had gone back to what young people do.

2 Hence "she kept herself hidden for five months"—not until the ninth month, when childbirth was impending, but until Mary also conceived. When Mary conceived and came to Elizabeth, and "her greeting resounded in [her] ears, the child in [Elizabeth's] womb leapt for joy."[18] Elizabeth prophesied. She was filled with the Holy Spirit. She spoke the words recorded in the Gospel account and "these words spread through the entire hill country."[19] A rumor spread among the people that Elizabeth bore a prophet in her womb, and that what she was carrying was greater than a human. Then she does not hide her condition. In full freedom she appears in public and rejoices, because she is bearing the precursor of the Savior in her womb.

3 Scripture then relates that, six months after Elizabeth conceived, "the angel Gabriel was sent by God to a town of Galilee named Nazareth, to a virgin betrothed to a man named Joseph of the house of David, and the virgin's name was Mary."[20] Again I turn the matter over in my mind and ask why, when God had decided that the Savior should be born of a virgin, he chose not a girl who was not betrothed, but precisely one that was already betrothed. Unless I am mistaken, this is the reason. The Savior ought to have been born of a virgin who was not only betrothed, but as Matthew writes, had already been given to her husband, although he had not yet had relations with her. Otherwise, if the virgin were seen growing big with child, the state of virginity itself would be a cause of disgrace.

4 I found an elegant statement in the letter of a martyr—I mean Ignatius, the second bishop of Antioch after Peter. During a persecution, he fought against wild animals at Rome. He stated, "Mary's virginity escaped the notice of the ruler of this age."[21] It escaped his notice because of

[16]Isa 1:8.
[17]Luke 1:24–25.
[18]Luke 1:44.
[19]Luke 1:65.
[20]Luke 1:26–27.
[21]Ign Eph 19:1.

Joseph, and because of their wedding, and because Mary was thought to have a husband. If she had not been betrothed or not had (as people thought) a husband, her virginity could never have been concealed from the ruler of this age. Immediately, a silent thought would have occurred to the devil: "How can this woman, who has not slept with a man, be pregnant? This conception must be divine. It must be something more sublime than human nature." But the Savior had so arranged his plan that the devil did not know that he had taken on a body. When he was conceived, he escaped the devil's notice. Later he commanded his disciples "not to make him known."[22]

5 When the Savior was tempted by the devil himself, he never admitted that he was the Son of God. He merely said, "It is not right for me to adore you or to turn these stones into loaves of bread or to throw myself down from a high place."[23] He said that, but never said he was the Son of God. Look in other books of Scripture, too. You will find that it was Christ's will that the devil should be ignorant of the coming of God's Son. For, the apostle maintains that the opposing powers were ignorant of his passion. He writes, "We speak wisdom among the perfect, but not the wisdom of this age or the wisdom of the rulers of this age. They are being destroyed. We speak God's wisdom, hidden in a mystery. None of the rulers of this age knows it. If they had known it, they would never have crucified the Lord of glory."[24] Thus the mystery of the Savior was hidden from the rulers of this age.

6 An objection to this explanation can be raised, and I think I should resolve it before someone else raises it. The problem is why something that was hidden from the rulers of this age was not hidden from the demon who said in the Gospel, "Have you come here to torture us before the assigned time? We know who you are—the Son of God."[25] Bear this in mind. The demon, who is less evil, knew the Savior, But the devil's wickedness is greater; he is fickle and depraved. The fact that his wickedness is greater prevents him from knowing the Son of God. We ourselves can ad-

vance to virtue more easily if we are less sinful. But, if we are more sinful, then we need sweat and hard labor to be freed from our greater evil. This is my explanation of why Mary was betrothed.

7 The angel greeted Mary with a new address, which I could not find anywhere else in Scripture. I ought to explain this expression briefly. The angel says, "Hail, full of grace."[26] The Greek word is *kecharitōmenē*. I do not remember having read this word elsewhere in Scripture. An expression of this kind, "Hail, full of grace," is not addressed to a male. This greeting was reserved for Mary alone. Mary knew the Law; she was holy, and had learned the writings of the prophets by meditating on them daily. If Mary had known that someone else had been greeted by words like these, she would never have been frightened by this strange greeting. Hence the angel says to her, "Do not be afraid, Mary! You have found grace in God's eyes. Behold, you will conceive in your womb. You will bear a son, and you will name him 'Jesus.' He will be great, and will be called 'Son of the Most High.'"[27]

8 Scripture also says of John, "He will be great,"[28] and the angel Gabriel attests to this. But, when Jesus (who is truly great and truly exalted) comes, then John (who earlier had been "great") becomes less. Jesus said, "He was a lamp, burning and shining, and at that hour you wished to rejoice in his light."[29] The greatness of our Savior was not manifested when he was born. It has shone forth only afterward, when his enemies seemed to have extinguished it.

9 Behold the Lord's greatness. "The sound of his teaching has gone out into every land, and

---

[22]Matt 12:16.
[23]cf. Matt 4:3–10; Luke 4:3–13.
[24]1 Cor 2:6–8.
[25]Matt 8:29.
[26]Luke 1:28.
[27]Luke 1:30–32.
[28]Luke 1:15.
[29]John 5:35.

his words to the ends of the earth."[30] Our Lord Jesus has been spread out to the whole world, because he is God's power. And now he is with us, according to the apostle's words: "You are gathered together in my spirit also, with the power of the Lord Jesus."[31] The power of the Lord and Savior is with those who are in Britain, separated from our world, and with those who are in Mauretania, and with everyone under the sun who has believed in his name. Behold the Savior's greatness. It extends to all the world. And still I have not expounded his true greatness.

10 Go up to the heavens. See how he fills the celestial regions: "He appeared to the angels."[32] Go down in your mind to the nether world. See that he went down there, too, "He went down, the one who also went up, to fulfill everything,"[33] "so that at Jesus' name every knee might bend—those of heavenly beings, and earthly beings, and beings in the nether world."[34] Ponder the Lord's

power, how it has filled the world—that is, the heavens, the earth, and the nether regions. He passed through heaven itself and rose to the regions above. We have read that the Son of God "passed through the heavens."[35]

If you understand this, you will also realize that Scripture does not say, "He will be great," carelessly, but the word has been fulfilled in deed. Jesus our Lord is great, both present and absent. He has endowed this assembly and gathering of ours with a share of his fortitude. That each of us may deserve to receive it, we pray the Lord Jesus, to whom it glory and power for all ages. Amen.

---

[30]Ps 19:4; Rom 10:18.
[31]1 Cor 5:14.
[32]1 Tim 3:16.
[33]Eph 4:10.
[34]Phil 2:10.
[35]Heb 4:14.

---

69. Origen: Homilies on Genesis

For Origen, the Old Testament was very much a Christian book, part of the entire revelation of God that conveys its full meaning only in relation to the salvation brought by Christ as set forth in the writings of the New Testament. Origen is able therefore to interpret the Old Testament, even the creation account of the book of Genesis, in light of his knowledge of Christ. This becomes particularly clear in his Homilies on Genesis, written about 240 C.E. and delivered, probably, to the Christian congregation in Caesarea in Palestine.

The following excerpt comprises the first part of Homily 1, based on the story of creation found in the first chapter of Genesis.

Origen: "Homilies on Genesis," from *Origen: Homilies on Genesis and Exodus*, ed. Ronald Heine. Fathers of the Church, 71; Washington, D.C.: Catholic University Press of America, 1996. Used with permission.

Homily 1

"In the beginning God made heaven and earth."[1]
What is the beginning of all things except our
Lord and Savior of all, Jesus Christ "the firstborn
of every creature"?[2] In this beginning, therefore,
that is, in his Word, "God made heaven and earth,"
as the evangelist John also says in the beginning
of his Gospel: "In the beginning was the Word,
and the Word was with God, and the Word was
God. The same was in the beginning with God.
All things were made by him and without him
nothing was made."[3] Scripture is not speaking
here of any temporal beginning, but it says that
the heaven and the earth and all things which were
made were made "in the beginning," that is, in the
Savior.

"And the earth was invisible and disordered
and darkness was upon the abyss, and the spirit of
God moved over the waters."[4] "The earth was invisible and disordered" before God said: "Let there
be light," and before he divided the light from the
darkness, as the order of the account shows.[5] But
since in the words which follow he orders the firmament to come into existence and calls this
heaven, when we come to that place the reason for
the difference between heaven and the firmament
will be explained there and also why the firmament was called heaven. But now the text says:
"Darkness was upon the abyss."[6] What is "the
abyss"? That place, of course, where the devil and
his angels will be. This indeed is most clearly designated also in the Gospel when it is said of the
Savior: "And the demons which he was casting
out were asking him that he not command them to
go into the abyss.[7]

For this reason, therefore, God dissolved the
darkness as the Scripture says: "And God said,
'Let there be light,' and there was light. And God
saw that the light was good; and God divided between the light and the darkness. And God called
the light day and he called the darkness night.
And there was evening and there was morning,
one day."[8]

According to the letter God calls both the
light day and the darkness night. But let us see according to the spiritual meaning why it is that

when God, in that beginning which we discussed
above, "made heaven and earth," and said, "let
there be light" and "divided between the light and
the darkness and called the light day and the darkness night," and the text said that "there was
evening and there was morning," it did not say:
"the first day," but said, "one day." It is because
there was not yet time before the world existed.
But time begins to exist with the following days.
For the second day and the third and the fourth
and all the rest begin to designate time.

2 "And God said: 'Let there be a firmament in
the midst of the water and let it divide water
from water.' And it was so done. And God made
the firmament."[9]

Although God had already previously made
heaven, now he makes the firmament. For he made
heaven first, about which he says, "heaven is my
throne."[10] But after that he makes the firmament,
that is, the corporeal heaven. For every corporeal
object is, without doubt, firm and solid; and it is
this which "divides the water which is above
heaven from the water which is below heaven."[11]

For since everything which God was to make
would consist of spirit and body, for that reason
heaven, that is, all spiritual substance upon which
God rests as on a kind of throne or seat, is said to
be made "in the beginning" and before everything.
But this heaven, that is, the firmament, is corporeal. And, therefore, that first heaven indeed,
which we said is spiritual, is our mind, which is
also itself spirit, that is, our spiritual person which
sees and perceives God. But that corporeal heaven,
which is called the firmament, is our outer person
which looks at things in a corporeal way.

---

[1]Gen 1:1.
[2]Col 1:15.
[3]John 1:1–3.
[4]Gen 1:2.
[5]Gen 1:3.
[6]Gen 1:2.
[7]Luke 8:31.
[8]Gen 1:3–5.
[9]Gen 1:6–7.
[10]Isa 66:1.
[11]Gen 1:7.

As therefore, heaven is called the firmament because it divides between those waters which are above it and those which are below it, so also a human, who has been placed in a body, will also himself be called heaven, that is, heavenly person, in the opinion of the apostle Paul who says: "But our citizenship is in heaven."[12] if he can divide and discern what the waters are which are higher, "above the firmament," and what those are which are below the firmament.

The very words of Scripture, therefore, contain it thus: "And God made the firmament, and divided the water which is under the firmament from the water which is above the firmament. And God called the firmament heaven. And God saw that it was good; and there was evening and there was morning, the second day."[13] Let each of you, therefore, be zealous to become a divider of that water which is above and that which is below. The purpose, of course, is that, attaining an understanding and participation in that spiritual water which is above the firmament one may draw forth "from within himself rivers of living water springing up into life eternal,"[14] removed without doubt and separated from that water which is below, that is, the water of the abyss in which darkness is said to be, in which the prince of this world and the adversary, the dragon and his angels dwell, as was indicated above.

Therefore, by participation in that celestial water which is said to be above the heavens, each of the faithful becomes heavenly, that is, when he applies his mind to lofty and exalted things, thinking nothing about the earth but totally about heavenly things. "seeking the things which are above, where Christ is at the right hand of the Father."[15] For then he also will be considered worthy of that praise from God which is written here when the text says: "And God saw that it was good."[16]

And then also those things which are described in the following statements about the third day signify this same meaning. For the text says: "And God said, 'Let the water which is under heaven be gathered into one gathering, and let the dry land appear.' And it was so done."[17]

Let us labor, therefore, to gather the water which is under heaven and cast it from us that the dry land, which it our deeds done in the flesh, might appear when this has been done so that, of course, "people seeing our good works may glorify our Father who is in heaven."[18] For if we have not separated from us those waters which are under heaven, that is, the sins and vices of our body, our dry land will not be able to appear nor have the courage to advance to the light. "For everyone who does evil hates the light and does not come to the light [lest his works be reproved. But he that does truth comes to the light that] his works may be made manifest" and appear, if "they are done in God."[19] This courage certainly will not be given unless like the waters, we cast off from us and remove the vices of the body which are the materials of sins. Once this has been done our dry land will not remain "dry land" as is shown from what follows.

For the text says: "And the water which is under heaven was gathered into its gatherings and the dry land appeared. And God called the dry land earth, and the gathering together of the waters he called seas."[20] As, therefore, this dry land, after the water was removed from it, as we said above, did not continue further as "dry land," but is now named "earth," in this manner also our bodies, if this separation from them takes place, will no longer remain "dry land." They will, on the contrary, be called "earth" because they can now bear fruit for God.

Whereas indeed "in the beginning God made heaven and earth," but later made "the firmament" and the "the dry land"; and "the firmament" indeed "he called heaven" giving it the name of that heaven which he had created earlier, but he called "the dry land" "earth" because he bestowed on it the capability of bearing fruits. If, therefore, anyone by his failure still remains dry and offers no

---

[12]Phil 3:20.
[13]Gen 1:7–8.
[14]John 7:38; 4:14.
[15]Col 3:1.
[16]Gen 1:8.
[17]Gen 1:9.
[18]Matt 5:16.
[19]John 3:20–21.
[20]Gen 1:9.

fruit but thorns and thistles, producing, as it were, fuel for the fire, in accordance with those things which he brought forth from himself, he also himself becomes fuel for the fire. But if, after the waters of the abyss, which are the thoughts of demons, have been separated from himself, he has shown himself fruitful earth by his zeal and diligence, he ought to expect similar things because he also is led by God into a land flowing with milk and honey.

3 But let us see from the following words what those fruits are which God orders the earth, on which he himself bestowed this name, to produce. "And God saw," the text says, "that it was good, and God said: 'Let the earth bring forth vegetation producing seed according to its kind and likeness, and the fruit tree bearing fruit whose seed is within it according to its likeness on the earth.' And it was so done."[21]

According to the letter, the fruits are clearly those which "the earth," not "the dry land" produces. But again let us also relate the meaning to ourselves. If we have already been made "earth," if we are no longer "dry land," let us offer copious and diverse fruits to God, that we also may be blessed by the Father who says: "Behold the smell of my son is as the smell of a plentiful field which the Lord has blessed,"[22] and that that which the apostle said might be fulfilled in us: "For the earth that receives the rain which comes frequently upon it and brings forth vegetation fit for those by whom it is cultivated will receive blessings from God. But that which brings forth thorns and briars is reprobate and very near a curse, whose end is to be burned.[23]

4 "And the earth brought forth green vegetation producing seed according to its kind and likeness and the fruit tree bearing fruit containing seed producing fruit according to its kind on the earth. And God saw that it was good. And there was evening and there was morning, the third day.[24]

Not only does God order the earth to bring forth "green vegetation," but also to bring forth "seed" that it can always bear fruit. And not only does God order that there be "the fruit tree," but

also that it "produce fruit containing seed according to its kind" that is, that it can always bear fruit from these seeds which it contains.

And we, therefore, ought thus both to bear fruit and to have seeds within ourselves, that is, to contain in our heart the seeds of all good works and virtues, that, having these fixed in our minds, from them now we might justly perform all the acts which occur to us. For those are the fruits of that seed, namely our acts, which are brought forth from the good treasure of our heart.

But if, on the one hand, we hear "the word" and from the hearing "immediately" our earth produces vegetation, and this vegetation "wither" before it should come to maturity or fruit, our earth will be called "rocky." But if those things which are said should press forward in our hearts with deeper roots so that they both "bear fruit" of works and contain the seeds of future works, then truly the earth of each of us will bear fruit in accordance with its potential, some "a hundred fold," some "sixty," other "thirty." But also we have considered it necessary to admonish that our fruit have no "darnel," that is, no tares, that it not be "beside the way," but be sown in the way itself, in that way which says, "I am the way,"[25] that the birds of heaven may not eat our fruits nor our vine. If, however, any of us should deserve to be a vine, let him beware lest he bear thorns for grapes, and for this reason "will no longer be pruned or digged" nor will "the clouds" be ordered "to rain upon it," but on the contrary it will be left "deserted" that "thorns" may overgrow it.[26]

5 But now, after this, the firmament deserves also to be adorned with lights. For God says: "Let there be lights in the firmament of heaven, that they may give light on the earth and divide between day and night."[27]

---

[21]Gen 1:10–11.
[22]Gen 27:27.
[23]Heb 6:7–8.
[24]Gen 1:12–13.
[25]John 14:6.
[26]Isa 5:2, 6.
[27]Gen 1:14.

As in that firmament which had already been called heaven God orders lights to come into existence that "they might divide between day and night," so it also can happen in us if only we also are zealous to be called and made heaven. We shall have lights in us which illuminate us, namely, Christ and his church. For he himself is "the light of the world"[28] who also illuminates the church by his light. For just as the moon is said to receive light from the sun so that the night likewise can be illuminated by it, so also the church, when the light of Christ has been received, illuminates all those who live in the night of ignorance.

But if someone progresses in this so that he is already made a "child of the day," so that "he walks honestly in the day," as "a child of the day and a child of light,"[29] this person is illuminated by Christ himself just as the day is illuminated by the sun.

6 " 'And let them be for signs and seasons, and for days and years; and let them be for illumination in the firmament of heaven, to give light on the earth.' And it was so done."[30]

As those lights of heaven which we see have been set "for signs and seasons and days and years," that they might give light from the firmament of heaven for those who are on the earth, so also Christ, illuminating his church, gives signs by his precepts, that one might know how, when the sign has been received, to escape the wrath to come, lest that day overtake him like a thief, but that rather he can reach the acceptable year of the Lord.

Christ, therefore, is "the true light which enlightens every man coming into this world."[31] From his light the church itself also having been enlightened is made "the light of the world" enlightening those "who are in darkness," as also Christ himself testifies to his disciples saying: "You are the light of the world."[32] From this it is shown that Christ indeed is the light of the apostles, but the apostles are "the light of the world." For they, "not having spot or wrinkle or anything of this kind," are the true Church, as also the Apostle says: "That he might present it to himself a glorious Church not having spot or wrinkle or any such thing."[33]

7 "And God made two great lights, a greater light to rule the day and a lesser light to rule the night, and the stars. And God set them in the firmament of heaven to shine upon the earth and to have authority over the day and the night and to divide between the light and the darkness. And God saw that it was good. And there was evening and there was morning, the fourth day."[34]

Just as the sun and the moon are said to be the great lights in the firmament of heaven, so also are Christ and the church in us. But since God also placed stars in the firmament, let us see what are also stars in us, that is, in the heaven of our heart.

Moses is a star in us, which shines and enlightens us by his acts. And Abraham, Isaac, Jacob, Isaiah, Jeremiah, Ezechiel, David, Daniel, and all to whom the Holy Scriptures testify that they pleased God. For just as "star differs from star in glory,"[35] so also each of the saints, according to his own greatness, sheds his light upon us.

Moreover, just as the sun and the moon enlighten our bodies so also our minds are enlightened by Christ and the church. We are enlightened in this way, however, if we are not blind in our minds. For although the sun and moon shine on those who are blind in their bodily eyes, they, nevertheless, cannot receive the light. In the same way also Christ offers his light to our minds, but it will so enlighten us only if blindness of mind impede in no way. But even if this happen, those who are blind must follow Christ saying and crying out: "Have mercy on us, son of David,"[36] that also receiving sight from him they can then also be radiant in the splendor of his light.

But all who see are not equally enlightened by Christ, but individuals are enlightened accord-

---

[28]John 8:12.
[29]1 Thes 5:5; Rom 13:13.
[30]Gen 1:14–15.
[31]John 1:9.
[32]Matt 5:14.
[33]Eph 5:27.
[34]Gen 1:16–19.
[35]1 Cor 15:41.
[36]Matt 9:27.

ing to the measure in which they are able to receive the power of the light. And just as the eyes
of our body are not equally enlightened by the
sun, but to the extent that one shall have ascended
to higher places and contemplated its risings with
a gaze form a higher vantage point, to such an extent will he perceive more of both its splendor and
its heat. So also to the extent that our mind shall
have approached Christ in a more exalted and
lofty manner and shall have presented itself nearer
the splendor of his light, to such an extent will it
be made to shine more magnificently and clearly
in his light as also he himself says through the
prophet: "Draw near to me and I shall draw near
to you, says the Lord,"[37] And again he says: "I
am a God who draws near, and not a God afar
off."[38]

We do not, however, all come to him in the
same way, but each one according to his own
proper ability. For either we come to him with
the crowds and he refreshes us by parables to
this end only, lest we faint in the way from many
fasts, or, of course, we sit always and inces-
santly at his feet, being free for this alone, that
we might hear his word, not at all disturbed
about "much serving," but choosing "the best
part which shall not be taken away" from us.[39]
And certainly those who thus approach him obtain much more of his light. But if, as the apostles, we should be moved from him in no way at
all, but should always remain with him in all his
tribulations, then he expounds and solves for us
in secret those things which he has spoken to the
crowds and enlightens us much more clearly.
But if in addition someone should be such as
can also ascend the mountain with him, as Peter, James, and John, he will be enlightened not
only by the light of Christ, but also by the voice
of the Father himself.

8 "And God said: 'Let the waters bring forth
creeping creatures having life and birds fly-
ing over the earth in the firmament of heaven.'
And it was so done."[40]

According to the letter,"creeping creatures"
and "birds" are brought forth by the waters at the
command of God and we recognize by whom

these things which we see have been made. But
let us see how also these same things come to be
in our firmament of heaven, that is, in the firmness of our mind or heart.

I think that if our mind has been enlightened
by Christ, our sun, it is ordered afterwards to bring
forth from these waters which are in it "creeping
creatures" and "birds which fly," that is, to bring
out into the open good or evil thoughts that there
might be a distinction of the good thoughts from
the evil, which certainly both proceed from the
heart. For both good and evil thoughts are brought
forth from our heart as from the waters. But by the
word and precept of God let us offer both to God's
view and judgment that, with his enlightenment
we may be able to distinguish what is evil from
the good, that is, that we may separate from ourselves those things which creep upon the earth
and bear earthly cares.

But let us permit those things which are better, that is, the "birds," to fly not only "above the
earth," but also "in the region of the firmament of
heaven," that is, let us explore in ourselves the
meaning and plan of heavenly things as well as
earthly, that we can also understand which of the
creeping creatures in us may be harmful. If we
should see "a woman to lust after her,"[41] that is
a poisonous reptile in us. But if we have the disposition of continence, even if an Egyptian mistress
love us deeply, we become birds and, leaving the
Egyptian garments in her hands, will fly away
from the indecent snare. If we should have in inclination inciting us to steal, that is a most evil
reptile. But if we have an inclination that even if
we should have "two mites" we would offer these
very mites out of mercy as a "gift of God,"[42] that
inclination is a bird thinking nothing about earthly
things, but striving for the firmament of heaven in
its flights. If an inclination should come to us persuading us that we ought not bear the tortures of

[37]Zech 1:3; James 4:8.
[38]Jer 23:23.
[39]Luke 10:39–42.
[40]Gen 1:20.
[41]Matt 5:28.
[42]Luke 21:2.

martyrdom, that will be a poisonous reptile. But if an inclination and thought such as this should spring up in us, that we struggle for the truth even to death, this will be a bird straining from earthly things to the things above. In the same manner also we should perceive and distinguish concerning other forms of either sins or virtues, which are "creeping creatures" and which are "birds" which our waters are commanded to bring forth for separation before God.

9 "And God made the great whales, and every creeping creature having life which the waters brought forth according to their kind, and every winged bird according to its kind."[43]

And we should observe concerning these words in the same way as those which we discussed above, that we too ought to bring forth "great whales" and "creeping creatures having life according to their kind." I think impious thoughts and abominable understandings which are against God are indicated in those great whales. All of these, nevertheless, are to be brought forth in the sight of God and placed before him that we may divide and separate the good from the evil, that the Lord might allot to each its place, as is shown from these words which follow. . . .

---

[43]Gen 1:21.

13

Leading the Upright Life

The Role of Ethics in
Early Christianity

High ethical standards appear to have played an important role in the Christian religion from the very beginning. This helped set Christianity off from other religions in the Greco-Roman world. It is not that non-Christians tended to be immoral; quite the contrary, ethical behavior was as important to people in antiquity as it is today. But, for the most part, ethics had little to do with established religion: pagan cults were concerned principally with performing sacrificial acts that were accepted as pleasing to the gods. How one *behaved* in one's daily life—how one acted towards one's friends, family, and neighbors—was generally left outside the cult as a matter of social norm and, for the more highly educated, of philosophy.

Judaism, of course, was an exception, in that Jews had an ancient law that specified not only how one was to worship God but also how one was to treat one's family and neighbors. Christians took over the ethical norms of Judaism, since, starting with Jesus and the apostles themselves, they subscribed to the law of Moses. In fact, many early Christians maintained that believers in Christ were to follow the ethical prescriptions of the Mosaic law even better than the religious leaders of the Jews (see Matt 5:17–20). Even when Gentiles were not required to follow the ceremonial aspects of the law, which provided social boundary markers for those who considered themselves Jews (e.g., circumcision and kosher food laws), they were expected to follow the laws that pertained to social relations, such as the law to "love your neighbor as yourself" (Lev 19:18; see Matt 22:39; Gal 5:14).

At the outset, Christians understood that proper moral behavior involved following not only the laws of the Old Testament but also the teachings of Jesus, which were understood to unpack the true meaning of the Jewish law. These teachings were seen to apply to believers' everyday lives in all their relations—with their families, fellow believers, governing officials, and so forth. In some situations, the upright lives of Christians proved important for their relationship with those outside the faith, for example, when attracting converts by their high ethical standards (see Chapter 2) or when defending themselves against charges of rampant and flagrant immorality (see Chapter 4). This emphasis on strong ethical behavior led Christian leaders to go far beyond the teachings of Jesus himself to become increasingly specific concerning what Christians were and were not allowed to do, what was required, what was permitted, and what was forbidden.

In particular, a number of early Christian groups developed a strong ascetic bent, as believers in Christ insisted that the body's desires were not to be indulged but that, in one way or another, the body was to be denied, trained, or punished. This ascetic impulse may have originally been rooted, at least in part, in Christianity's apocalyptic message. Christians like the apostle Paul, who believed that the end of the age was imminent, saw little sense in accomodating bodily passions and desires. This world, along with all its pleasures, great and small, was soon to be destroyed. Christians should prepare for the coming judgment and not be overly attached to that which was soon to pass away (see, e.g., 1 Cor 7:26–31).

Eventually, this ascetic strain experienced a range of permutations. We have already seen the writings of Christian Gnostics, for example, who believed that the material world was inherently evil and inimical to the true God; for such Christians, the body participated in evil materiality and was therefore itself an enemy to be overcome and punished (see Chapter 6). And there were early Christian women, both gnostic and proto-orthodox, who saw sexual renunciation as a way of liberation from the constraints and domination of the patriarchal institutions of marriage and family (see Chapter 8, esp. the *Acts of Thecla*).

The goal of Christian distinctiveness and the earnestness of some of the early Christian writers become especially evident in the moral treatises that have been preserved from the first three centuries of the church. Examples of moral guidelines can be found in numerous texts scattered throughout this volume. The following excerpts, however, are particularly germane, as they give some idea of the range of ethical issues that challenged Christians (at least in the eyes of their leaders) and the firm guidelines they were expected to follow when confronting them.

For Further Reading

Brown, Peter R. L. *The Body and Society: Men, Women and Sexual Renunciation in Early Christianity.* New York: Columbia University Press, 1988.

Meeks, Wayne. *The Origins of Christian Morality: The First Two Centuries.* New Haven: Yale University Press, 1993.

Murphy, Francis Xavier. *The Christian Way of Life.* Wilmington, Del.: M. Glazier, 1986.

Osborn, Eric, F. *Ethical Patterns in Early Christian Thought.* Cambridge: Cambridge University Press, 1976.

Wogaman, J. Philip. *Christian Ethics: A Historical Introduction.* Louisville: Westminster John Knox, 1993; chapters 1–2.

Womer, Jan. *Morality and Ethics in Early Christianity.* Philadelphia: Fortress, 1987.

THE TEXTS

70. The Didache

The opening section of the Didache (see Chapter 10) contains a number of ethical injunctions portrayed as the "Two Ways of Life and Death" (cf. Matt 7:13–14). The Way that leads to Life (chaps. 1–4) is paved with upright behavior: those who choose it are to love one another, avoid evil desires, jealousy, and anger, give alms to the poor, obey God's commandments, and generally lead morally respectable lives. Many of these instructions reflect the teachings of Jesus from the Sermon on the Mount in Matthew 5–7 (e.g., praying for one's enemies, turning the other cheek, and going the extra mile). As might be expected, the Way that leads to Death (chap. 5) involves the opposite sorts of behavior: "murders, adulteries, lusts, fornication, thefts," and sundry other transgressive activities.

A similar doctrine of the Two Ways is found near the end of the epistle of Barnabas (see Chapter 5), leading most scholars to think that it was drawn from an earlier source, possibly Jewish, that was more widely available.

1 There are two ways, one of life and one of death; and between the two ways there is a great difference.

2 Now, this is the way of life: First, you must love God who made you, and second, your neighbor as yourself. And whatever you want people to refrain from doing to you, and must not do to them.

3 What these maxims teach is this: Bless those who curse you, and pray for your enemies. Moreover, fast for those who persecute you. For what credit is it to you if you love those who love you? Is that not the way the heathen act? But you must love those who hate you, and then you will make no enemies. Abstain from carnal passions.

4 If someone strikes you on the right cheek, turn to him the other too, and you will be perfect. If someone forces you to go one mile with him, go along with him for two; if someone robs you of your overcoat, give him your suit as well. If someone deprives you of your property, do not ask for it back. (You could not get it back anyway!)

5 Give to everybody who begs from you, and ask for no return. For the Father wants his own gifts to be universally shared. Happy is the one who gives as the commandments bids him, for he is guiltless! But alas for the one who receives! If he receives because he is in need, he will be guiltless. But if he is not in need he will have to stand trial why he received and for what purpose. He will be thrown into prison and have his action investigated; and he will not get out until he has paid back the last cent.

6 Indeed, there is a further saying that relates to this: Let your donation sweat in your hands until you know to whom to give it.

The "Didache," reproduced from *Early Christian Fathers,* ed. Cyril C. Richardson (Library of Christian Classics Series), 1970. Used by permission of Westminster John Knox Press.

2 The second commandment of the Teaching:

2 Do not murder; do not commit adultery; do not corrupt boys; do not fornicate; do not steal; do not practice magic; do not go in for sorcery; do not murder a child by abortion or kill a newborn infant.

3 Do not covet your neighbor's property; do not commit perjury; do not bear false witness; do not slander; do not bear grudges.

4 Do not be double-minded or double-tongued, for a double tongue is a deadly snare.

5 Your words shall not be dishonest or hollow, but substantiated by action.

6 Do not be greedy or extortionate or hypocritical or malicious or arrogant. Do not plot against your neighbor.

7 Do not hate anybody; but reprove some, pray for others, and still others love more than your own life.

3 My child, flee from all wickedness and from everything of that sort.

2 Do not be irritable, for anger leads to murder. Do not be jealous or contentious or impetuous, for all this breeds murder.

3 My child, do not be lustful, for lust leads to fornication. Do not use foul language or leer, for all this breeds adultery.

4 My child, do not be a diviner, for that leads to idolatry. Do not be an enchanter or an astrologer or a magician. Moreover, have no wish to observe or heed such practices, for all this breeds idolatry.

5 My child, do not be a liar, for lying leads to theft. Do not be avaricious or vain, for all this breeds thievery.

6 My child, do not be a grumbler, for grumbling leads to blasphemy. Do not be stubborn or evil-minded, for all this breeds blasphemy.

7 But be humble since the humble will inherit the earth.

8 Be patient, merciful, harmless, quiet, and good; and always have respect for the teaching you have been given. Do not put on airs or give yourself up to presumptuousness. Do not associate with the high and mighty; but be with the upright and humble. Accept whatever happens to you as good, in the realization that nothing occurs apart from God.

4 My child, day and night you should remember him who preaches God's word to you, and honor him as you would the Lord. For where the Lord's nature is discussed, there the Lord is.

2 Every day you should seek the company of saints to enjoy their refreshing conversation.

3 You must not start a schism, but reconcile those at strife. Your judgments must be fair. You must not play favorites when reproving transgressions.

4 You must not be of two minds about your decision.

5 Do not be one who holds his hand out to take, but shuts it when it comes to giving.

6 If your labor has brought you earnings, pay a ransom for your sins.

7 Do not hesitate to give and do not give with a bad grace; for you will discover who he is that pays you back a reward with a good grace.

8 Do not turn your back on the needy, but share everything with your brother and call nothing your own. For if you have what is eternal in common, how much more should you have what is transient!

9 Do not neglect your responsibility to your son or your daughter, but from their youth you shall teach them to revere God.

10 Do not be harsh in giving orders to your slaves and slave girls. They hope in the same God as you, and the result may be that they cease to revere the God over you both. For when he comes to call us, he will not respect our station, but will call those whom the Spirit has made ready.

11 You slaves, for your part, must obey your masters with reverence and fear, as if they represented God.

12 You must hate all hypocrisy and everything which fails to please the Lord.

13 You must not forsake the Lord's commandments, but observe the ones you have been given, neither adding nor subtracting anything.

14 At the church meeting you must confess your sins, and not approach prayer with a bad conscience. That is the way of life.

5 But the way of death is this: First of all, it is wicked and thoroughly blasphemous: murders, adulteries, lusts, fornications, thefts, idola-

tries, magic arts, sorceries, robberies, false witness, hypocrisies, duplicity, deceit, arrogance,
malice, stubbornness, greediness, filthy talk, jealousy, audacity, haughtiness, boastfulness.

2 Those who persecute good people, who hate
truth, who love lies, who are ignorant of the reward
of uprightness, who do not abide by goodness or
justice, and are on the alert not for goodness but for
evil: gentleness and patience are remote from them.
They love vanity, look for profit, have no pity for
the poor, do not exert themselves for the oppressed,
ignore their Maker, murder children, corrupt God's
image, turn their backs on the needy, oppress the
afflicted, defend the rich, unjustly condemn the
poor, and are thoroughly wicked. My children,
may you be saved from all this!

>-+-◆>-O-<◆-+-<

71. Clement of Alexandria: The Educator

Although his writings have been among the most studied of early Christianity, little is
known about the life of Clement of Alexandria (150–215 C.E.). He is often thought to
have been born to pagan parents in Athens and then converted to Christianity, possibly
as a young adult. Ancient legend indicates that he was Origen's predecessor as the head
of the famous Alexandrian catechetical school, a kind of institution for higher Christian
learning. When a persecution arose in 202 C.E., Clement fled Alexandria, never to return.

Among Clement's best known writings are the *Stromateis* (literally, Miscellanies), a
collection of reflections on theological, philosophical, and ethical issues, and a sermon
called "What Rich Person Will Be Saved?" Of particular importance for understanding
the ethical impulse of early Christianity is his three-volume treatise called the *Paeda-
gogas*, literally, "The Educator." Here Clement portrays Christ as the teacher who molds
his followers' character by revealing how they ought to live. The following selection is
important for showing how, already by the beginning of the third century, church leaders
were concerned with every aspect of a Christian's public and private life, including such
matters as personal eating and drinking habits, sleep and exercise, use of humor, public
manners, sexual activities (even within marriage), and the use of public baths.

Book 2

1 In keeping with the purpose we have in mind,
we must now select passages from the Scriptures that bear on education in the practical needs
of life, and describe the sort of life he who is
called a Christian should live throughout his life.
We should begin with ourselves, and with the way
we should regulate [our actions]. . . .

Other people, indeed, live that they may eat,
just like unreasoning beasts; for them life is only

Clement of Alexandria: "The Educator," from *Clement of Alexandria: Christ the Educator,* ed. Simon P. Wood. Fathers of the
Church, 23; Washington, D.C.: Catholic University Press of America, 1954. Used with permission.

their belly. But as for us, our Educator has given the command that we eat only to live. Eating is not our main occupation, nor is pleasure our chief ambition. Food is permitted us simply because of our stay in this world, which the Word is shaping for immortality by his education. Our food should be plain and ungarnished, in keeping with the truth, suitable to children who are plain and unpretentious, adapted to maintaining life, not self-indulgence. . . .

We must shun gluttony and partake of only a few things that are necessary. And if some unbeliever invites us to a banquet and we decide to accept—although it is well not to associate with the disorderly—[the apostle] bids us eat what is set before us, "asking no question for conscience' sake."[1] We do not need to abstain from rich foods completely, but we should not be anxious for them. We must partake of what is set before us, as becomes a Christian, out of respect for him who has invited us and not to lessen or destroy the sociability of the gathering. We should consider the rich variety of dishes that are served as a matter of indifference, and despise delicacies as things that after a while will cease to be. "Let not him who eats despise him who does not eat, and let not him who does not eat judge him who eats."[2] A little later [the apostle] explains the reason for his command: "He who eats," he says, "eats for the Lord and he gives thanks to God. And he who does not eat, abstains for the Lord and gives thanks to God."[3] We conclude, then, that the true food is thanksgiving. At any rate, he who always offers up thanks will not indulge excessively in pleasure. . . .

Only a fool will hold his breath and gape at what is set before him at a public banquet, expressing his delight in words. But it is only a greater fool who will let his eyes become enslaved to these exotic delicacies, and allow self-control to be swept away, as it were, with the various dishes. Is it not utterly inane to keep leaning forward from one's couch, all but falling on one's nose into the dishes, as though, according to the common saying, one were leaning out from the nest of the couch to catch the escaping vapors with the nostrils? Is it not completely contrary to reason to keep dipping

one's hands into these pastries or to be forever stretching them out for some dish, gorging oneself intemperately and boorishly, not like a person tasting a food, but like one taking it by storm? It is easy to consider such people swine or dogs rather than humans, because of their voraciousness. They are in such a hurry to stuff themselves that both cheeks are puffed out at the same time, all the hollows of their face are filled out, and sweat even rolls down as they exert themselves to satisfy their insatiable appetite, wheezing from their intemperance, and cramming food into their stomachs with incredible energy, as though they were gathering a crop for storage rather than nourishment.

Lack of moderation, an evil wherever it is found, is particularly blameworthy in the matter of food. Gourmandising, at least, is nothing more than immoderate use of delicacies; gluttony is a mania for glutting the appetite, and belly-madness, as the name itself suggests, is lack of self-control with regard to food. The apostle, in speaking of those who offend at a banquet, exclaims: "For at the meal, each one takes first his own supper, and one is hungry, and another drinks overmuch. Have you not houses for your eating and drinking? Or do you despise the church of God and put to shame the needy?"[4] If a person is wealthy, yet eats without restraint and shows himself insatiable, he disgraces himself in a special way and does wrong on two scores: first, he adds to the burden of those who do not have, and lays bare, before those who do have, his own lack of temperance. Little wonder, then, that the apostle, after having taken to task those who were shamelessly lavish with their meals, and those who were voracious, never getting their fill, cried out a second time with an angry voice: "Wherefore, my brethren, when you come together to eat, wait for one another. If anyone is hungry, let him eat at home, lest you come together unto judgment."[5]

---

[1] 1 Cor 10:27.
[2] Rom 14:3.
[3] Rom 14:6.
[4] 1 Cor 11:21.
[5] 1 Cor 11:23.

Therefore, we must keep ourselves free of any suspicion of boorishness or of intemperance, by partaking of what is set before us politely, keeping our hands, as well as our chin and our couch, clean, and by preserving proper decorum of conduct, without twisting about or acting unmannerly while we are swallowing our food. Rather, we should put our hand out only in turn, from time to time; keep from speaking while eating, for speech is inarticulate and ill-mannered when the mouth is full, and the tongue, impeded by the food, cannot function properly but utters only indistinct sounds. It is not polite to eat and drink at the same time, either, because it indicates extreme intemperance to try to do two things together that need to be done separately. . . .

Lavishness is not capable of being enjoyed alone; it must be bestowed upon others. That is why we should shy away from foods that arouse the appetite and lead us to eat when we are not hungry. Even in moderate frugality, is there not a rich and wholesome variety? Roots, olives, all sorts of green vegetables, milk, cheese, fruits, and cooked vegetables of all sorts, but without the sauces. And should there be need for meat, boiled, or dressed, let it be given. "Have you anything here to eat?" the Lord asked his apostles after his resurrection. "And they offered him a piece of broiled fish," because he had taught them to practise frugality. "And when he had finished eating, he said to them," and Luke goes on to record all that he said.[6] We should not overlook the fact, either, that they who dine according to reason, or, rather, according to the Word, are not required to leave sweetmeats and honey out of their fare. Surely, of all the foods available, the most convenient are those which can be used immediately without being cooked. Inexpensive foods come next in order, since these are so accessible, as we have already said.

As long as those other fellows stay hunched over their groaning tables, catering to their lusts, the devil of gluttony leads them by the nose. I, for one, would not hesitate to call that devil the devil of the belly, the most wicked and deadly of them all. He is very much like the so-called *engastrimythos*, because he speaks, as it were,

through his belly. It is far better to possess happiness than to have any daemon as a companion; happiness is the practise of the virtues.

Matthew the apostle used to make his meal on seeds and nuts and herbs, without flesh meat; John, maintaining extreme self-restraint, ate locusts and wild-honey, and Peter abstained from pork. But, "he fell into an ecstasy," it is written in the Acts of the Apostles, "and saw heaven standing open and a certain vessel let down by the four corners to the earth; and in it were all the four-footed beasts and creeping things of the earth and birds of the air. And there came a voice to him: Arise and kill and eat. But Peter said: Far be it from me, Lord, for never did I eat anything common or unclean. And there came a voice a second time to him: What God has cleansed, do not thou call common."[7] The use of these foods is a matter of indifference for us, too, "for not that which goes into the mouth defiles a person."[8] but the barren pursuit of wantonness. When God formed man, He said: "All these things will be food for you."[9]

"Herbs with love rather than a fatted calf with deceit."[10] This is reminiscent of what we said before, that herbs are not the agapê, but that meals should be taken with charity. A middle course is good in all things, and no less so in serving a banquet. Extremes, in fact, are dangerous, but the mean is good, and all that avoids dire need is a mean. Natural desires have a limit set to them by self-sufficiency. . . .

2   "Use a little wine," the apostle cautions the water-drinking Timothy, "use a little wine for your stomach's sake."[11] Shrewdly, he recommends a stimulating remedy for a body become ill-disposed and requiring medical attention, but he adds "a little," lest the remedy, taken too freely, itself come to need a cure.

Now, the natural and pure drink demanded by ordinary thirst is water. This it was that the Lord

[6]Luke 24:41–44.
[7]Acts 10:10–15.
[8]Matt 15:11.
[9]Gen 1:29.
[10]Prov 15:17.
[11]1 Tim 5:23.

supplied for the Hebrews, causing it to gush from the split rock, as their only drink, a drink of sobriety; it was particularly necessary that they who were still wandering should keep far from wine. . . .

I have, then, only admiration for those who profess an austere life, limiting their desires to water, nourishment of sobriety, and avoiding wine as completely as they can, as they would the least threat of fire. It is conceded that boys and girls should, as a general rule, be kept from this sort of drink. It is not well for flaming youth to be filled with the most inflamable of all liquids, wine, for that would be like pouring fire upon fire. When they are under its influence, wild impulses, festering lusts, and hot-bloodedness are aroused; youths already on fire within are so much on the verge of satisfying their passions that the injury inflicted on them becomes evident by anticipation in their bodies, that is, the organs of lust mature before they should. I mean that, as the wine takes effect, the youths begin to grow heated from passion, without inhibition, and the breasts and sexual organs swell as a harbinger and an image of the act of fornication. The wound in their soul compels the body to manifest all the signs of passion, and the unrestrained throbbings aroused by temptation drive on into sin the curiosity of him who before had been sinless. At that point, the freshness of youth has exceeded the bounds of modesty. Therefore, it is imperative to attempt to extinguish the beginnings of passion in the young, as far as posible: first, by excluding them from all that will inflame them—Bacchus and his threat—and second, by pouring on the antidote that will restrain the smouldering soul, contain the aroused sexual movements, and calm the agitation of the storm-tossed desires.

As for adults, when they take their midday lunch, if that is their practise, let them take only a little bread and no liquids at all, so that the excessive moisture in their bodies may be assimilated and absorbed by the dry food. It is an indication, in fact, of disorder in the body caused by an excessive accumulation of liquids flowing through it, if we need to blow our noses constantly and experience a persistent urge to urinate. If they should become thirsty, let them relieve their thirst with water, but not too much of it. It is not good to drink water too freely, lest the food be simply washed away; the meal should be masticated to prepare it for digestion, only a little of it finally passing off as waste.

Minds that bear something of the divine should not be overcome with wine for another reason, too. "Strong wine," in the words of the comic poet, "keeps a man from thinking many thoughts"[12]—or, in fact, from being wise at all. But toward evening, near the time for supper, we may use wine, since we are no longer engaged in the public lectures which demand the absence of wine. At that time of day, the temperature has turned cooler than it was at midday, so that we need to stimulate the failing natural heat of the body with a little artificial warmth. But, even then, we must use only a little wine; certainly, we should not go so far as to demand whole bowls of it, because that would be sheer extravagance.

Again, those who have already passed the prime of life may be permitted more readily to enjoy their cup. They are but harmlessly making use of the medicine of wine to stimulate new warmth for the growing chill of old age as its heat dies down with the years. The passions of the aged are, for the most part, no longer storm-tossed with the threat of shipwreck from intemperance. Securely moored by the anchors of reason and of maturity, they easily bear the violent storm of passion aroused by drink, and they can even indulge in the merriment of feasts with composure. But, even for them, there is a limit: the point where they can still keep their minds clear, their memories active, and their bodies steady and under control, despite the wine. Those who know about these things call this the last drop before too much. It is well to stop short before this point, for fear of disaster.

A certain Artorius, I recall, in a book on longevity, is of the opinion that we should drink only so much as is needed to moisten our food, if we would live a long life. It is certainly a good idea to use wine, as some do, only for the sake of

---

[12]Menander *Frag* 779.

health, as a tonic, or for relaxation and enjoyment, as others do. Wine makes the person who drinks more mellow toward himself, better disposed toward his servants, and more genial with his friends. But, when he is overcome by wine, then he returns every offense of a drunken neighbor.

Wine is warm and gives out a sweet smell; therefore, in the proper mixture it thaws out the constipation of the intestines and with its sweetness dilutes every pungent or offensive odor. A quotation from Scripture will express it aptly: "Wine drunken with moderation was created from the beginning as the joy of the soul and of the heart."[13] But it is wise to dilute the wine with as much water as possible (and to avoid depending upon it as we do water), as well as to restrain our appetite for drinking bouts and to keep from drinking wine like water simply from intemperance. Both are creatures of God, and so the mixture of both, water and wine, contributes to our health. Life is made up of what is necessary, together with what is merely useful. The merely useful should be combined with a very large part of what is necessary, that is, with water.

When wine is indulged in too freely, the tongue becomes thick, the jaw sags, the eyes begin to roll, for all the world as if they were swimming in pools of moisture, and the vision, forced to deceive, conceives everything as going round in a circle, and is not sure whether things are single or double. "Indeed, I think I see two suns," the old Theban in his cups complained.[14] Truly, the sense of sight is deranged by the heat of wine and imagines it sees many times over what is only one. But there is no difference between deranging the sense of sight and distorting the object that is seen: in either case, the vision is affected the same way in its derangement and cannot accurately perceive the object. Similarly, the gait takes on the appearance of being swept along in a stream, and then there arises, as maids-in-waiting, hiccoughing, retching, and silliness. For, "every man overcome by wine," says the tragedian, "becomes subject to his passions and empty of mind, pours out idle chatter and is forced to hear against his will things he had said so willingly."[15] Even before these words were written, Wisdom had warned:

"Wine drunken with excess raises quarrels and many ruins."[16] . . .

5 . . . As for laughter itself, it, too, should be kept under restraint. Of course, when it rings out as it should, it proves the presence of discipline, but if it gets out of hand, it is a sure index of lack of self-control. We need not take away from a person any of the things that are natural to him, but only set a limit and due proportion to them. It is true that a human is an animal who can laugh; but it is not true that he therefore should laugh at everything. The horse is an animal that neighs, yet it does not neigh at everything. As rational animals, we must ever maintain proper balance, gently relaxing the rigor of seriousness and intensity without dissipating it out of all bounds.

Now, the proper relaxation of the features within due limits—as though the face were a musical instrument—is called a smile (that is the way joy is reflected on the face); it is the good humor of the self-contained. But the sudden loss of control over one's composure, in the case of women, is called a giggle, the laugh of harlots, and in the case of men, a guffaw, the laughter of idle suitors, offensive to the ear. "A fool lifts up his voice in laughter," Scripture says, "but a cunning person will scarce laugh low to himself."[17] The one called cunning here is really the prudent person, just the opposite of a fool. On the other hand, we should not become gloomy, either; only serious-minded. I certainly welcome the smiling fellow who showed up with a smile on his grim face, for then his laughter would be less disdainful.

It is well that even the smile be kept under the influence of the Educator. If it is a question of indecencies, we should make it plain that we are blushing in shame, rather than smiling, lest we be thought to give consent and agreement. If it is some misfortune, we should not manifest a light-hearted appearance, but look sorrowfully sober. That indicates human tact; the other would be cruelty. But,

[13]Sirach 31:27–28.
[14]Euripidus, *Bacch.* 918.
[15]Sophocles *Frag* 843.
[16]Sirach 31:29.
[17]Sirach 21:20.

we should not be always laughing—that would be lack of judgment—nor should we laugh in the presence of older persons or of those who deserve respect, unless, perhaps, they themselves make some witticism to put us at our ease. Nor should we give way to laughter with every chance companion, nor in every place, nor at everything, nor with everyone. Laughter can easily give rise to misunderstandings, particularly among boys and women. . . .

7 . . . If we meet at banquets for charity's sake, and if the purpose of such feasts is the good-fellowship created among the guests, with the food and drink merely accessories of charity, then should we not maintain a behavior that bespeaks the control of reason? (Incidentally, we need not impoverish ourselves to practise charity.) And if we gather with the intention of showing good-will toward one another, then why do we stir up ill-will by railing at others? It is better to keep silent than to engage in bickering, adding the fault of deed to that of boorishness. Surely, "blessed is the one that has not slipped by a word out of his mouth, and is not pricked with the remorse of sin."[18] or at least has repented of the sins committed in speech, or has conversed without inflicting pain on anyone. . . .

Let young men and women be kept from banquets of this sort, as a general rule, so that they may not fall into any improper misconduct. There can be no doubt that the indecent things heard, and the unbecoming things seen, unsettle their faith, set their imagination afire, and add fuel to the natural fickleness of their youth to make them ready victims of their passions. At times, too, they are to blame for the fall of others, proving how dangerous an occasion such a banquet can be. It is a good command that Wisdom gives: "Sit not at all with another man's wife, nor repose upon a couch with her," that is, do not dine or eat with her too often. Then it adds: "Do not have a meal with her in wine, lest perhaps your heart decline toward her, and by your blood, you fall into destruction."[19] Drinking unrestrainedly is dangerous because it can so easily degenerate into licentiousness. Scripture speaks of "another man's

wife," because there is a greater danger in such a case of destroying the wedding bond.

But, if there arise any need for women to be present, let them be amply clothed: exteriorly with a cloak, interiorly with modesty. The worst accusation that can be brought against any woman not subject to a husband is that she was present at a party for men, and, at that, for men in their cups. And as for young men, let them keep their eyes fixed on their own couch, lean on their elbow without too much fidgeting, and be present only with their ears. If they should be sitting down, let them not put their feet one on top of the other, nor cross their legs, nor rest their chin on their hands. It is lack of good breeding to fail to support oneself, yet a fault common in the young. To be forever restlessly shifting one's position argues for levity of character. . . .

Then, too, whistling and hissing and snapping the fingers—all sounds made to summon servants—should not be used by people who have the ability to speak, since these are wordless signals. At banquets, we should not be forever spitting or violently coughing or blowing our nose. We must consider the feelings of our companions at table, and avoid disgusting or nauseating them by our crude conduct, testifying to our own lack of self-control. Not even cattle or asses relieve nature at their feeding troughs, yet many people blow their nose and keep spitting while engaged at table. Again, if a sneeze take us by surprise, or, even more so, a belch, we need not deafen our neighbor with the noise and in so doing exhibit our lack of manners. A belch should be released silently, as we exhale, with our mouths shut, not wide open and gaping like the masks of the tragedy. The irritation that causes a sneeze may be relieved by quietly holding the breath; therefore, we should suppress the accumulated force of the breath politely by controlling our exhaling, so as to try to pass unnoticed if some of the excessive air, under pressure, escapes.

It is a sign of boorishness and of lack of discipline to want to add to the noises, rather than

---

[18]Sirach 14:1.
[19]Sirach 9:9.

lessen them. And those who scrape their teeth so much that they draw blood from their gums, besides injuring themselves, also annoy their companions. And beyond a doubt, scratching the ear and irritations to prompt sneezing are gestures proper to swine, suggestive of the search for immoral pleasures. Unbecoming glances and indecent conversations about such things must be renounced. Let the gaze be composed, and the movement of the head and the gestures be steady, as well as the motion of the hands in conversation. In general, the Christian is, by nature, a person of gentleness and quiet, of serenity and peace. . . .

9 Now we must discuss the way we are to sleep, still mindful of the precepts of temperance. After our dinner, once we have given thanks to God for having granted us such pleasures and for the completion of the day, then we should dispose our minds for sleep. We must forbid ourselves the use of expensive bedding, gold-sprinkled rugs and plain carpets embroidered in gold, rich purple bed robes or precious thick cloaks, purple blankets of elaborate art, with fleecy cloaks thrown over them, and beds too soft to be slept in. The habit of sleeping in soft down is injurious, apart from the danger of pampering the body, because those who sleep in it sink deep into the softness of the bed; it is not healthy for the sleeper who cannot move about in it because of the high elevation on either side of his body. Sleep is the time for digesting food, but such a bed causes the food simply to burn up and be destroyed, while those who can toss about on their beds, level as though a natural place of exercise during sleep, digest their food more easily and prepare themselves the better to face any contingencies. . . .

Following the dictates of reason, then, we should make use of a bed that is level and unadorned, yet affording some minimum of convenience: of protection, if it be summer; of warmth, if it be winter. Let the couch, too, be unadorned and its posts plain, for ornamented and molded wood readily and frequently becomes an easy path for creeping animals, providing them sure footing in the grooves carved by the craftsmen. But we must specially keep the softness of the bed within limits, for sleep is

meant to relax the body, not to debilitate it. For that reason, I say that sleep should be taken not as self-indulgence, but as rest from activity. . . .

10 It remains for us now to consider the restriction of sexual intercourse to those who are joined in wedlock. Begetting children is the goal of those who wed, and the fulfillment of that goal is a large family, just as hope of a crop drives the farmer to sow his seed, while the fulfillment of his hope is the actual harvesting of the crop. But he who sow in a living soil is far superior, for the one tills the land to provide food only for a season, the other to secure the preservation of the whole human race; the one tends his crop for himself, the other, for God. We have received the command: "Be fruitful,"[20] and we must obey. In this role man becomes like God, because he co-operates, in his human way, in the birth of another person.

Now, not every land is suited to the reception of seed, and, even if it were, not at the hands of the same farmer. Seed should not be sown on rocky ground nor scattered everywhere, for it is the primary substance of generation and contains imbedded in itself the principle of nature. It is undeniably godless, then, to dishonor principles of nature by wasting them on unnatural resting places. In fact, you recall how Moses, in his wisdom, once denounced seed that bears no fruit, saying symbolically: "Do not eat the hare nor the hyena."[21] He does not want a person to be contaminated by their traits nor even to taste of their wantonness, for these animals have an insatiable appetite for coition. As regards the hare, legend claims that it needs to void excrement only once a year, and possesses as many anuses as the years it has lived. Therefore, the prohibition against eating the hare is nothing else than a condemnation of pederasty. And with regard to the hyena, it is said that the male changes every year successively into a female, so that Moses means that he who abstains from the hyena is commanded not to lust after adultery.[22]

[20]Gen 1:28.
[21]Deut 14:7.
[22]*Barn.* 10:6–7.

While I agree that the all-wise Moses means, by this prohibition just mentioned, that we should not become like these beasts, I do not entirely agree with the explanation given these symbolic prohibitions. A nature can never be made to change; what has been once formed in it cannot be reformed by any sort of change. Change does not involve the nature itself; it necessarily modifies, but does not transform the structure. For instance, although many birds are said to change their color and their voice according to the season (like the blackbird which changes its black feathers to yellow, and its melodious voice to a harsh one, or the nightingale which changes its plumage and song at the same time), even so, their nature itself is not so affected that a male becomes female. Rather, a new growth of feathers, like a new garment, is bright with one color, but a little later, as winter threatens, it fades away, like a flower when its color goes. In the same way, the voice, affected unfavorably by the cold, loses its vibrancy: the surface of the whole body contracts with the climate, and the bronchial tubes, narrowly constricted in the throat, restrict the breath to the point that it is made quite muffled and capable of producing only harsh sounds. Later on, in the spring, responding to the weather and relaxing, the breath is once again freed of all constraint and is carried through passages that were tightly closed but are now wide open. No longer does the voice croak in dying tones, but bursts forth clear, pouring out in full-throated voice, and now in springtime there arises melodious song from the throats of the birds.

Therefore, we should not believe at all that the hyena changes its sex. Neither does it possess both the male and the female sexual organs at the same time, as some claim, conjuring up some freakish hermaphrodite and creating this female-male, a third new category halfway in between the male and the female. Erroneously they misconstrue the strategy of nature, mother of all and author of all existence. Because the hyena is of all animals the most sensual, there is a knob of flesh underneath its tail, in front of the anus, closely resembling the female sex organ in shape. It is not a passage, I mean it serves no useful purpose,

opening neither into the womb nor into the intestines. It has only a good-sized opening to permit an ineffective sexual act when the vagina is preparing for childbirth and is impenetrable. This is characteristic of both male and female hyena, because of hyperactive abnormal sexuality; the male lies with the male so that it rarely approaches the female. For that reason, births are infrequent among hyenas, because they so freely sow their seed contrary to nature.

This is the reason, I believe, that Plato, in excoriating pederasty in *Phaedrus,* terms it bestiality and says that these libertines who have so surrendered to pleasure, "taking the bit in their own mouths, like brutish beasts rush on to enjoy and beget."[23] Such godless people "God has given over," the apostle says, "to shameful lusts. For the women change their natural use to that which is against nature, and in like manner the men, also, having abandoned the natural use of the women, have burned in their lusts one towards another, men with men doing shameful things, and receiving in themselves the fitting recompense of their perversity."[24] Yet, nature has not allowed even the most sensual of beasts to sexually misuse the passage made for excrement. Urine she gathers into the bladder; undigested food in the intestines; tears in the eyes; blood in the veins; wax in the ear, and mucous in the nose; so, too, there is a passage connected to the end of the intestines by means of which excrement is passed off. In the case of hyenas, nature, in her diversity, has added this additional organ to accomodate their excessive sexual activity. Therefore, it is large enough for the service of the lusting organs, but its opening is obstructed within. In short, it is not made to serve any purpose in generation. The clear conclusion that we must draw, then, is that we must condemn sodomy, all fruitless sowing of seed, any unnatural methods of holding intercourse and the reversal of the sexual role in intercourse. We must rather follow the guidance of nature, which obviously disapproves of such practises from the very way she has fashioned the male organ, adapted not for re-

---

[23]*Phaedr* 254, 250E.
[24]Rom 1:26–27.

ceiving the seed, but for implanting it. When Jeremiah, or, rather, the Spirit through him, said: "The cave of the hyena is my home,"[25] he was resorting to an expressive figure to excoriate idolatry and to manifest his scorn for the nourishment provided for dead bodies. The house of the living God surely ought to be free of idols.

Again, Moses issued a prohibition against eating the hare. The hare is forever mounting the female, leaping upon her crouching form from behind. In fact, this manner of having intercourse is a characteristic of the hare. The female conceives every month, and, even before the first offspring is born, she become pregnant again. She conceives and begets, and as soon as she gives birth is fertilized again by the first hare she meets. Not satisfied with one mate, she conceives again, although she is still nursing. The explanation is that the female hare has a double womb, and therefore her desire for intercourse is stimulated not only by the emptiness of the womb, in that every empty space seeks to be filled, but also, when she is with young, her other womb begins to feel lustful desires. That is why hares have one birth after the other. So the mysterious prohibition [of Moses] in reality is but counsel to restrain violent sexual impulses, and intercourse is too frequent succession, relations with a pregnant woman, pederasty, adultery, and lewdness. . . .

We should consider boys as our sons, and the wives of other men as our daughters. We must keep a firm control over the pleasures of the stomach, and an absolutely uncompromising control over the organs beneath the stomach. If, as the Stoics teach, we should not move even a finger on mere impulse, how much more necessary is it that they who seek wisdom control the organ of intercourse? I feel that the reason this organ is also called the private part is that we are to treat it with privacy and modesty more than we do any other member. In lawful wedlock, as with eating, nature permits whatever is comfortable to nature and helpful and decent; it allows us to desire the act of procreation. However, whoever is guilty of excess sins against nature and, by violating the laws regulating intercourse, harms himself. First of all, it is decidedly wrong ever to touch youths in any

sexual way as though they were girls. The philosopher who learned from Moses taught; "Do not sow seeds on rocks and stones, on which they will never take root."[26] The Word, too, commands emphatically, through Moses: "You shall not lie with mankind as with womankind, for it is an abomination."[27] Again, further on, noble Plato advises: "Abstain from every female field of increase,"[28] because it does not belong to you. (He had read this in the holy Scripture and from it had taken the law: "You shall not give the coition of your seed to your neighbor's wife, to be defiled because of her."[29]) Then he goes on to say: "Do not sow the unconsecrated and bastard seed with concubines, where you would not want what is sown to grow."[30] In fact, he says: 'Do not touch anyone, except your wedded wife,'[31] because she is the only one with whom it is lawful to enjoy the pleasures of the flesh for the purpose of begetting lawful heirs. This is a share in God's own work of creation, and in such a work the seed ought not be wasted nor scattered thoughtlessly nor sown in a way it cannot grow. As an illustration of this last restriction, the same Moses forbade the Jews to approach even their own wives if they happened to be in the period of menstruation.[32] The reason is that it is wrong to contaminate fertile seed, destined to become a human being, with corrupt matter of the body, or to allow it be diverted from the furrow of the womb and swept away in a fetid flow of matter and excrement.

He discouraged the ancient Jews, also, from having relations with a wife already with child. Pleasure sought for its own sake, even within the marriage bonds, is a sin and contrary both to law and to reason. Moses cautioned them, then, to keep away from their pregnant wives until they be delivered. In fact, the womb, situated just below the bladder and above the part of the intestine

---

[25]Jer 12:9.
[26]Plato, *Laws* 328E.
[27]Lev 18:22.
[28]*Laws* 828E.
[29]Lev 18:20.
[30]*Laws* 839A.
[31]*Laws* 841D.
[32]Lev 15:19.

known as the rectum, extends its neck in between the edges of the bladder, and the outlet of this neck, by which the sperm enters, closes tight when the womb is full, opening again only when delivered of the fetus. It is only when it has become empty of its fruit that it can receive the sperm again. (It is not wrong for us to name the organs of generation, when God is not ashamed of their function.) The womb welcomes the seed when it yearns for procreation, but it refuses the seed when intercourse is contrary to nature; that is, once impregnated, it makes immoral relations impossible by drawing its neck tight together. All its instincts, up to now aroused by loving intercourse, begin to be directed differently, absorbed in the development of the child within, co-operating with the Creator. It is wrong, indeed, to interfere with the workings of nature by indulging in the extravagances of wantonness. . . .

In my treatise on continence, I have discussed in a general way the question whether we should marry or not (and this is the point of our investigation). Now, if we have to consider whether we may marry at all, then how can we possibly permit ourselves to indulge in intercourse each time without restraint, as we would food, as if it were a necessity? Certainly, we can see at a glance that the nerves are strained by it as on a loom and, in the intense feeling aroused by intercourse, are stretched to the breaking point. It spreads a mist over the senses and tires the muscles. This is obvious in irrational animals and in men in training. Of these last, those who practise abstinence while engaging in contests get the best of their opponents; while animals are easily captured if they are caught at and all but torn from coition, because then they are entirely emptied of strength and energy.

The sophist of Abdera called intercourse "a minor epilepsy," and considered it an incurable disease. Indeed, does not lassitude succeed intercourse because of the quantity of seed lost? "For a man is formed and torn out of a man."[33] See how much harm is done. A whole man is torn out when the seed is lost in intercourse. "This is bone of my bone, and flesh of my flesh,"[34] Scripture says. Man is emptied of as much seed as is needed

for a body that can be seen. After all, that which is separated from him is the beginning of a new birth. Besides that, the very agitation of matter upsets and disturbs the harmony of his whole body. Wise indeed was he who replied to someone asking him his attitude toward the pleasures of sex: "O man, quiet! I have been supremely happy in avoiding them as a fierce and wild tyrant."[35]

Yet marriage in itself merits esteem and the highest approval, for the Lord wished people to "be fruitful and multiply."[36] He did not tell them, however, to act like libertines, nor did he intend them to surrender themselves to pleasure as though born only to indulge in sexual relations. Let the Educator put us to shame with the word of Ezechiel: "Put away your fornications."[37] Why, even unreasoning beasts know enough not to mate at certain times. To indulge in intercourse without intending children is to outrage nature, whom we should take as our instructor. Her wise directions concerning the periods of life are meant to be obeyed; I mean that she allows us to marry at any time but after the advent of old age and during childhood (for she does not permit the one to marry yet, the other, any more). The attempt to procreate children is marriage, but the promiscuous scattering of seed contrary to law and to reason definitely is not. If we should but control our lusts at the start and if we would not kill off the human race born and developing according to the divine plan, then our whole lives would be lived according to nature. But women who resort to some sort of deadly abortion drug kill not only the embryo but, along with it, all human kindness.

Those whom nature has joined in wedlock need the Educator that they might learn not to celebrate the mystic rites of nature during the day, nor like the rooster copulate at dawn, or after they have come from church, or even from the market, when they should be praying or reading or performing the good works that are best done by day.

---

[33]Democritus *Frag* 86?
[34]Gen 2:23.
[35]Sophocles? cf. Plato *Republic* 329 B.C.
[36]Gen 1:28.
[37]Ezek 43:9.

In the evening, after dinner, it is proper to retire after giving thanks for the good things that have been received. Sometimes, nature denies them the opportunity to accomplish the marriage act so that it may be all the more desirable because it is delayed. Yet, they must not forget modesty at night time under the pretext of the cover of darkness; like the light of reason, modesty must ever dwell in their souls. If we weave the ideals of chastity by day and then unravel them in the marriage bed at night, we do not better than Penelope at her loom. Certainly, if we are required to practise self-control—as we are—we ought to manifest it even more with our wives, in the way we avoid every indecency in intimate embraces. Let the reliability and trustworthiness of the husband's purity in his dealings with his neighbor be present also in his home. He cannot possibly enjoy a reputation for self-control with his wife if she can see no signs of self-control in such intense acts of pleasure. Love, which tends toward sexual relations by its very nature, is in full bloom only for a time, then grows old with the body; but sometimes, if immoral pleasure mars the chastity of the marriage bed, desire becomes insipid and love ages before the body does. The hearts of lovers have wings; affection can be quenched by a change of heart, and love can turn into hate if there creep in too many grounds for loss of respect. . . .

Book 3

9 There are four reasons prompting us to frequent the baths (it was at this point that I digressed a while back in my discussion): either for cleanliness, for warmth, for health, or for the satisfaction of pleasure. We must not think of bathing for pleasure, because we must ruthlessly expel all unworthy pleasure. Women may make use of the bath for the sake of cleanliness and of health; men, only for the sake of their health. The motive of seeking warmth is scarcely urgent, since we can find relief from cold in other ways.

The continued use of baths undermines a man's strength, weakening the muscles of his body and often inducing lassitude and even fainting spells. Bodies drink up water in a definite way in the baths, like trees, not only by mouth, but also, as they say, through the pores of the whole body. A proof of this is that, often, when a man has been thirsty, his thirst is quenched on entering the water. Therefore, if the bath has no real benefit to offer, it should be completely avoided. The ancients called it a fulling shop for men, since it wrinkles the body before time, and forces the body to become old early; in much the way that iron is tempered by heat, the flesh is made soft by heat. We need to be hardened, as it were, by being doused in cold.

We ought not bathe on every occasion, either, but if at times we are too hungry, or too full, we should omit it. As a matter of fact, [it should be adjusted] to the age of the individual, and to the season of the year. It is not useful at all times, nor to everyone at all times, as those versed in these things agree. Due proportion is sufficient guide for us; we call upon it for help in every part of our life. Again, we should not linger in the bath so long that we will need someone to lead us out by the hand, nor should we loiter long or frequently in it, as we might in the public square. Finally, to have a score of servants pouring water over one is grievously to offend a neighbor; it is a sign of one far advanced in self-indulgence and unwilling to understand that the bath should be common, on an equal footing to all who bathe there.

It is our souls, above all, that we should wash in the purifying Word; only now and then, our bodies, to get rid of the dirt that adheres to them, and, sometimes, to refresh ourselves after hard labor. "Woe to you, Scribes and Pharisees," the Lord says, "hypocrites! For you are like whitened tombs; outwardly the tomb appears beautiful, but within it is full of dead men's bones and of all uncleanness."[38] And again he said to them: "Woe to you, because you clean the outside of the cup and of the plate, but within are full of uncleanness. Cleanse first the inside of the cup that the outside may also become clean."[39]

---

[38]Matt 23:27.
[39]Matt 23:25.

The most excellent cleansing is that which removes the filth of the soul, and is a spiritual bath; the inspired word says about such a cleansing: "The Lord shall wash away the filth of the sons and daughters of Israel and shall wash away the blood from their midst,"[40] that is, the blood of immorality, as well as the slaughtering of the prophets; that is the purification he meant, because he adds: "by the spirit of judgment and by the spirit of burning." But the washing of the body is something material and is accomplished only by water; in fact, it can be done even in fields away from the baths.

10 The gymnasium is sufficient for the needs of young boys, even if there is a bath at hand. This is all the more true when even men may legitimately make use of it in preference to the bath. It offers considerable benefit to the health of the young, and besides, instils in them a desire and ambition to develop not only a healthy constitution, but also a wholesome character. If physical exercise is engaged in without distracting them from more worthwhile deeds, it is entertaining and not without profit.

For that reason, even women should be allowed some sort of physical exercise, not on the wrestling-mat or the racecourse, but in spinning and weaving and supervising the cooking, if need arise. Again, the women should themselves bring whatever we need from the storeroom, and it is no disgrace for them to take their place at the mill. Then, too, for her to busy herself about the meals that they may be pleasing to her husband is a deed one who is housewife, spouse, and helpmate will not be reproached for performing. If she should also make the beds herself, and bring her husband drink when he is thirsty, and prepare the food, she would be exercising herself in a very becoming way, and maintaining her health by self-restraint. The Educator approves of such a woman who "stretches forth her hands to useful things, and who applies her fingers vigorously to the spindle, who opens her hands to the needy and stretches forth fruit to the poor,"[41] and who, in imitation of Sarah, is not ashamed to serve wayfarers generously. Abraham said to Sarah: "Quick, three measures of fine flour! Knead it, and make loaves."[42]

Again, Scripture says: "Rachel, daughter of Jacob, arrived with her father's sheep," and, as if this was not enough, it adds, to give a convincing lesson of lowliness: "for it was her custom to tend them."[43] There are innumerable examples given in the Scriptures both of frugality and of self-service, as well as of physical exercise.

As for the men, let some of them engage in wrestling stripped; let others play the game called *phaenind* with a small ball, particularly out in the sun. A walk will be sufficient for others, either strolling out into the country or into town. If, besides all this, they lay hold of the mattock, such a money-saving way of taking exercise will not be beneath their dignity. But I am almost forgetting to mention Pittacus, king of the Mitylenians, who wandered about taking energetic exercise.[44] It is well if a person draws his own water for his needs, and himself cuts the wood that he uses. Jacob pastured the sheep that Laban had given him with a rod of storax (which is a sign of royalty), and he took care to influence their nature for the better with such a rod.[45] Sometimes, reading out loud will be a good exercise for many.

But let them especially engage in wrestling, which we approve of, not for vain competition's sake, which serves no end, but to get rid of manly sweat. They should not cultivate the tricks meant only for display, but only the art of wrestling erect, keeping the neck and hands and sides free. Such movements are much more orderly and manly, are performed with controlled strength, and are clearly undertaken to benefit one's health—a very desirable thing. The other exercises of the gymnasium demand the practise of postures beneath our dignity. We must aim for moderation in all things. For, just as it is better for labor to precede meals, so, too, to labor beyond measure is both harmful and tiring, and leads to sickness. We should not be idle, yet we should not become completely exhausted by our labor, either. We were just dis-

---

[40]Isa 4:4.
[41]cf. Prov 31:19–20.
[42]Gen 18:6.
[43]Gen 29:9.
[44]Diog. Laertius 1:81.
[45]cf. Gen 30:37–43.

cussing the proper conduct to be observed in taking food; similarly, in every thing and every place
we should not live for pleasure nor for immorality; neither should we go to the other extreme. We
should, instead, choose a course of life in between,
well-balanced, temperate, and free from either
evil: extravagance or parsimony.

As we have already said, self-service is an
exercise without any trace of pride: for example,
to put on one's own sandals, wash one's own feet,
and also to rub off the oil that has been put on. To
rub down someone who has done the same for us
is both a physical exercise and an act of commu-

nal justice, as is also sleeping by a sick friend,
waiting on someone who cannot wait on himself,
and providing for someone in need. "And Abraham set before the three men a lunch under the
tree and he stood by while they ate."[46] So is fish-
ing, as it was for Peter, if we have leisure left over
from the instruction we need in the word. But the
best catch is the one the Lord entrusted to his disciples, when he taught them to catch people, as
though fish from a sea.

---

[46]Gen 18:8.

72. Tertullian: To His Wife

The proto-orthodox writer Tertullian has turned up a number of times already in this collection (Chapters 4, 5, 7, 11; see also Chapter 14). In an effort to promote more rigorous
standards among his fellow Christians, Tertullian devoted a good deal of his time to writing about ethical issues, urging stringent behavior and condemning those who refused to
adopt it. Among his surviving ethical treatises are discussions of monogamy, chastity,
women's head coverings and make-up, and other issues relevant for his views of gender
relations. The following example shows the fervor with which Tertullian could set forth
his views and is particularly interesting because it deals with a personal matter. As a kind
of "open letter" to his wife, the treatise instructs her about what do if he preceeds her in
death. In short, Tertullian marshals arguments from far and wide to convince her that she
should never remarry.

I thought it would be well, my dearest companion
in the service of the Lord, to give some consideration, even at this early date, to the manner of life
that ought to be yours after my departure from
this world, should I be called before you. I trust
your own loyalty to follow the suggestions I shall
offer. For if we pursue our purposes with such
diligence when worldly issues are at stake, even
drawing up legal instruments in our anxiety to secure each other's interests, ought we not to be all

---

Tertullian: "To His Wife," from *Tertullian: Treatises on Marriage and Remarriage,* ed. William P. Le Saint. Mahway, N.J.: Paulist Press, 1951. Used by permission of Paulist Press.

the more solicitous in providing for the welfare of those we leave behind us when there is question of securing their best advantage in matters concerning God and heaven? Ought we not, acting as it were before the event, bequeath them legacies of loving-counsel, and make clear our will respecting goods which constitute the eternal portion of their heavenly inheritance? God grant that you may be disposed to receive in its entirety the loving-counsel I now commit in trust to your fidelity. To him be honor, glory, splendor, grandeur, and power, now and forever.

This charge, then, I lay on you—that, exercising all the self-control of which you are capable, you renounce marriage after I have passed away. You will not, on that account, confer any benefit on me, apart from the good you do yourself. I would not want you to think that I now advise you to remain a widow because I fear to suffer hardship if you fail to preserve your person inviolate for myself alone. No, when the future time arrives, we shall not resume the gratification of unseemly passion. It is not such worthless, filthy things that God promises to those who are his own. Moreover, there is no promise given Christians who have departed this life that on the day of their resurrection they will be restored once more to the married state. They will, it is clear, be changed to the state of holy angels.[1] For this reason they will remain undisturbed by feelings of carnal jealousy. Even that woman who was said to have married seven brothers in succession, will give no offense to a single one of all her husbands when she rises from the dead; nor does a single one of them await her there to put her in the blush. The teaching of our Lord has settled this quibble of the Sadducees. Yet it is still permitted us to consider whether the course of action I recommend is of advantage to you personally or, for that matter, to the advantage of any other woman who belongs to God.

2 Of course, we do not reject the union of man and woman in marriage. It is an institution blessed by God for the reproduction of the human race. It was planned by him for the purpose of populating the earth and to make provision for the propagation of mankind. Hence, it was permitted;

but only once may it be contracted. For Adam was the only husband that Eve had and Eve was his only wife; one rib, one woman.

Now, everybody knows that it was allowed our forefathers, even the Patriarchs themselves, not only to marry but actually to multiply marriages. They even kept concubines. But, although figurative language is used in speaking of both church and synagogue, yet we may explain this difficult matter simply by saying that it was necessary in former times that there be practices which afterwards had to be abrogated or modified. For the Law had first to intervene; too, at a later date, the Word of God was to replace the law and introduce spiritual circumcision. Therefore, the licentiousness and promiscuity of earlier days—and there must needs have been abuses which called for the institution of a law—were responsible for that subsequent corrective legislation by which the Lord through his gospel, and the apostle in these latter days did away with excesses or controlled irregularities.

3 But I would not have you suppose that I have premised these remarks on the liberty which was allowed in former times and the severity of later legislation, because I wish to lay the foundation of an argument proving that Christ has come into the world for the purpose of separating those who are joined in wedlock and forbidding the conjugal relationship, as though from now on all marriages were to be outlawed. This is a charge they must be prepared to answer who, among other perversions of doctrine, teach their followers to divide those who are two in one flesh, opposing the will of him who first subtracted woman from man and then, in the mathematics of marriage, added two together again who had originally been substantially one. Finally, we do not read anywhere at all that marriage is forbidden; and this for the obvious reason that marriage is actually a good.

The apostle, however, teaches us what is better than this "good," when he says that he permits marriage, but prefers celibacy[2]—the former be-

---

[1]Matt 22:23–30.
[2]1 Cor 7:1–2.

cause of the snares of the flesh, the latter because the times are straitened. Hence, if we consider the reasons which he gives for each of these views, we shall have no difficulty in seeing that marriage is conceded to us on the principle that marry we may because marry we must. But what necessity proffers necessity cheapens. Scripture says that it is better to marry than to burn;[3] but what sort of good, I ask you, can that be which is such only when it is compared to what is bad? Marriage, forsooth, is better because burning is worse! How much better it is neither to marry nor to burn!

In time of persecution it is better to flee from place to place, as we are permitted, than to be arrested and to deny the faith under torture. Yet, far happier are they who find courage to bear witness and to undergo martyrdom for the faith. It can be said that what is merely tolerated is never really good. Suppose I am doomed to die. If I quail at this, then it is good to flee. If, however, I hesitate to use the permission given, this itself shows that there is something suspect about the very reasons for which the permission is granted. Nobody merely *permits* that which is better, since this is something of which there can be no doubt; it is a thing which recommends itself by its own transparent goodness.

Nothing is to be sought after for the sole reason that it is not forbidden. When we come to think of it, even such things are, in a sense, forbidden because other things are preferred to them. To prefer the lofty is to exclude the low. Nothing is good just because it is not bad, nor is it, therefore, not bad simply for the reason that it does you no hurt. A thing that is good in the full sense of the word is to be preferred because it helps us, not merely because it does not harm us. You ought to choose things that are good for you rather than things which are merely not bad for you.

Every contest is a straining for the first prize. When a person comes out second, he has consolation, but he does not have victory. If we listen to the apostle, then, "forgetting the things that are behind, let us stretch forth to those that are before,"[4] and be "zealous for the better gifts."[5] Thus, although the apostle does not cast a snare upon us, he does show us where our advantage lies when

he writes: "The unmarried woman . . . thinks on the things of the Lord, that she may be holy both in body and in spirit. But she that is married is solicitous . . . how she may please her husband."[6] In other places, also, the apostle is nowhere so tolerant of marriage that he fails to point out his own preference, and this is that we strive to follow his example. Blessed is he who is like Paul!

4 But we read that the flesh is weak; and this serves us as an excuse for pampering ourselves in a number of ways. We also read, however, that the spirit is strong. Both statements are made in the same sentence.[7] The flesh is of the earth, the spirit is of heaven. Now, why is it that, habitually seeking excuses for ourselves, we plead the weakness of our nature and disregard its strength? Should not the things of earth yield to the things of heaven? If the spirit, being nobler in origin, is stronger than the flesh, then we have no one to blame but ourselves when we yield to the weaker force.

There are two weaknesses in human nature which appear to make it necessary that those who have lost a spouse should marry again. First, there is the concupiscence of the flesh, and this has the strongest pull; second, there is the concupiscence of the world. We servants of God ought to scorn both weaknesses, since we renounce both lust and ambition.

Concupiscence of the flesh urges in its defense the right to exercise the functions of maturity; it seeks to pluck the fruits of beauty; it glories in its shame; it declares that woman's sex requires a husband to be her strength and comfort, or to protect her good name from ugly gossip.

But as for you, do you oppose against such specious arguments the example of those sisters of ours—their names are known to the Lord—who, having seen their husbands go to God, prefer chastity to the opportunities of marriage afforded them by their youth and beauty. They

---

[3]1 Cor 7:9.
[4]Phil 3:13.
[5]1 Cor 12:31.
[6]1 Cor 7:34–35.
[7]Matt 26:41.

choose to be wedded to God. They are God's fair ones, God's beloved. With him they live, with him they converse, with him they treat on intimate terms day and night. Prayers are the dowry they bring the Lord and for them they receive his favors as marriage gifts in return. Thus they have made their own a blessing for eternity, given them by the Lord; and, remaining unmarried, they are reckoned, even while still on earth, as belonging to the household of the angels. Train yourself to imitate the example of continence furnished by such women as these and, in your love for things of the spirit, you will bury concupiscence of the flesh. You will root out the fleeting, vagrant desires which come of beauty and youth, and make compensation for their loss with the blessings of heaven, which last forever.

The concupiscence of the world which I mentioned has its roots in pride, avarice, ambition, and the plea that one is unable to get along alone. Arguments drawn from sources such as these it uses to urge the necessity of marriage; and, of course, it promises heavenly rewards in return: to queen it over another man's household; to gloat over another man's wealth; to wheedle the price of a wardrobe out of another man's pocket; to be extravagant at no cost to yourself!

Far be it from Christians to desire such things as these! We are not solicitous about how we are to be supplied with the necessities of life—unless we have no confidence in the promises of God. He it is who clothes the lilies of the field in such great beauty; who feeds the birds of the air, though they labor not; who bids us not to be concerned about the morrow, what we shall eat or what we shall put on. He assures us that he knows what is necessary for each of his servants. And this, certainly, is not a mass of jeweled pendants, nor a surfeit of clothing, nor mules brought from Gaul, nor porters from Germany. Such things do lend lustre to a wedding, but what is necessary for us is, rather, a sufficiency which is consistent with sobriety and modesty. You may take it for granted that you will have need of nothing, if you but serve the Lord; indeed, all things are yours if you possess the Lord of all. Meditate on the things of heaven and you will despise the things of earth. The widow whose life is stamped with the seal of God's approval has need of nothing—except perseverance!

5 In addition to the reasons already advanced, some say that they wish to contract marriage because they desire to live on in their posterity and because they seek the bitter sweet which comes of having children. To us this is sheer nonsense. For, why should we be so anxious to propagate children since, when we do, it is our hope—in view, that is, of the straitened times which are at hand—that they will go to God before us. We ourselves desire, as did the Apostle, to be delivered from this wicked world and received into the arms of our Lord.

Of course, to the servant of God posterity is a great necessity! We are so sure of our own salvation that we have time for children! We must hunt up burdens for ourselves with which, for the most part, even pagans refuse to be encumbered—burdens which are forced upon people by law, but of which they rid themselves by resorting to murder of their own flesh and blood; burdens, in fine, which are especially troublesome to us because they constitute a danger to the faith. Why did our Lord prophesy, "Woe to them that are with child and that give suck,"[8] if he did not mean that on the day of our great exodus children will be a handicap to those who bear them? This is what comes of marriage. There will be no problem here for widows, however. At the first sound of the angel's trumpet they will leap forth lightly, easily able to endure any distress or persecution, with none of the heaving baggage of marriage in their wombs or at their breasts.

Accordingly, whether marriage be for the flesh or for the world or for the sake of posterity, the servant of God is above all such supposed necessities. I should think it quite enough to have succumbed once to any one of them and to have satisfied all such wants as these in a single marriage.

Are we to have weddings every day and, in the midst of nuptials, to be overtaken by the day of dread, even as were Sodom and Gomorrha? For in those places they were not just getting married

---

[8]Matt 24:19.

and transacting business! When our Lord says that they were marrying and they were buying, he wishes to stigmatize those gross vices of the flesh and the world which most withdraw people from the things of God—the one by the sweet seduction of lust, the other by greed for gain.[9] And yet, these people were afflicted by blindness of this kind at a time when the end of the world was still far off. How shall we fare, if the vices God then found detestable keep up back from divine things now? "The time is short," Scripture says; "it remains that they who have wives, act as if they had none."[10]

6 But now, if those who actually have wives are to put them out of their minds, how much more are those who have none prohibited from seeking a second time what they no longer have! Accordingly, she whose husband has departed this life ought to refrain from marrying and have done with sex forever. This is what many a pagan woman does in order to honor the memory of a beloved spouse.

When something seems difficult to us, let us think of those who put up with difficulties greater than our own. For example, how many are there who vow virginity from the very moment of their baptism! How many, too, who in wedlock abstain, by mutual consent, from the use of marriage! They have "made themselves eunuchs because of their desire for the kingdom of Heaven."[11] If they are able to practice continence while remaining married, how much easier is it to do so when marriage has been dissolved! For I rather imagine it is more difficult to sacrifice something we actually have than it is to be indifferent about something we no longer possess.

A hard thing it is, forsooth, and arduous, that a Christian woman, out of love for God, should practice continence after her husband's death, when pagans use the priestly offices of virgins and widows in the service of their own Satan! At Rome, for example, those women are called "virgins" who guard a flame which typifies the unquenchable fire, watching over that which is an omen of the punishment which awaits them together with the Dragon himself. At the town of Aegium a virgin is selected for the cult of the

Achaean Juno; and the women who rave at Delphi do not marry. Further, we know that "widows" minister to the African Ceres, women whom a most harsh insensibility has withdrawn from married life. For, while their husbands are still living, they not only separate from them but even introduce new wives to take their place—no doubt with the cheerful acquiescence of the husbands themselves! Such "widows" deprive themselves of all contact with men, even to the exclusion of kissing their own sons. Yet they become used to this discipline and persevere in a widowhood which rejects even those consolations which are found in the sacred bonds of natural affection. This is what the devil teaches his disciples. And they obey! As though on equal terms, the chastity of his followers challenges that of the servants of God. The very priests of hell are continent. For Satan has discovered how to turn the cultivation of virtue itself to a man's destruction, and it makes no difference to him whether he ruins souls by lust or chastity.

7 We have been taught by the Lord and God of salvation that continence is a means of attaining eternal life, a proof of the faith that is in us, a pledge of the glory of that body which will be ours when we put on the garb of immortality, and, finally, an obligation imposed upon us by the will of God. Regarding this last statement, I suggest that you reflect seriously on the following: if it is a fact that not a leaf falls to the ground unless God wills it, then it is equally true that no one departs this life unless God wills it. For it is necessary that he who brought us into the world should also usher us forth from it. Therefore, when God wills that a woman lose her husband in death, he also wills that she should be done with marriage itself. Why attempt to restore what God has put asunder? Why spurn the liberty which is offered you by enslaving yourself once more in the bonds of matrimony? "Are you bound in marriage?" Scripture says, "seek not to be loosed. Are you loosed from marriage? seek not to be

---

[9]Luke 17:28–30.
[10]1 Cor 7:29.
[11]Matt 19:12.

bound."[12] For, though you sin not in remarrying, yet, according to Scripture, "tribulation of the flesh will follow"[13] if you do.

Hence, as far as such a sentiment is possible, let us be grateful for the opportunity offered us of practicing continence and let us embrace it immediately, once it is offered. Thus, what we were unable to do in marriage we will be able to do in bereavement. We ought to make the most of a situation which removes what necessity imposed.

The law of the church and the precept of the apostle show clearly how prejudicial second marriages are to the faith and how great an obstacle to holiness. For men who have been married twice are not allowed to preside in the church[14] nor is it permissible that a widow be chosen unless she was the wife of but one man.[15] The altar of God must be an altar of manifest purity and all the glory which surrounds the Church is the glory of sanctity.

The pagans have a priesthood of widows and celibates—though, of course, this is part of Satan's malevolence; and the ruler of this world, their Pontifex Maximus, is not permitted to marry a second time. How greatly purity must please God, since even the Enemy affects it! He does this, not because he has any real affinity with virtue but because it is his purpose to make a mockery of what is pleasing to the Lord God.

8 There is a brief saying, revealed through the mouth of the prophet, which shows how greatly God honors widowhood: "Deal justly with the widow and the orphan and then come and let us reason together, saith the Lord."[16] The two groups mentioned here have no human means of support whatever; they are dependant on God's mercy, and the Father of all takes it upon himself to be their protector. See how familiarly the widow's benefactor is treated by God! In what esteem, then, is the widow herself held when he who is her advocate will reason with the Lord! Not even to virgins themselves, I fancy, is so much given.

Although virgins, because of their perfect integrity and inviolate purity, will look upon the face of God most closely, yet the life a widow leads is the more difficult, since it is easy not to desire that of which you are ignorant and easy to turn your back upon what you have never desired. Chastity is most praiseworthy when it is sensible of the right it has sacrificed and knows what it has experienced. The condition of the virgin may be regarded as one of greater felicity, but that of the widow is one of greater difficulty; the former has always possessed the good, the latter has had to find it on her own. In the former it is grace which is crowned, in the latter, virtue. For some things there are which come to us from the divine bounty, and others we have of our own efforts. Those which are bestowed upon us by the Lord are governed by his generosity; those which are achieved by humans are won at the cost of personal endeavor.

Therefore, cultivate the virtue of self-restraint, which ministers to chastity; cultivate industry, which prevents idleness; temperance, which spurns the world. Keep company and converse worthy of God, remembering the quotation sanctified by the apostle: "Evil associations corrupt good manners."[17] Chattering, idle, winebibbing, scandalmongering women do the greatest possible harm to a widow's high resolve. Their loquaciousness leads to the use of words offensive to modesty; their slothfulness engenders disloyalty to the austere life; their tippling issues in every sort of evil and their prurient gossip is responsible for inciting others to engage in the lustful conduct which such talk exemplifies. No woman of this kind can have anything good to say about monogamy. "Their god is their belly,"[18] as the apostle says; and so also is that which lies adjacent to it.

Here, then, my dearest fellow servant, is the counsel which even now I leave with you. And, really, although my words are superfluous after what the apostle has written on the subject, yet for you they will be words of consolation as often as, in thinking on them, you think of me.

---

[12]1 Cor 7:27.
[13]1 Cor 7:28.
[14]1 Tim 3:2; Tit 1:6.
[15]1 Tim 5:9.
[16]Isa 1:17–18.
[17]1 Cor 15:33.
[18]Phil 3:19.

14

The Emergence of Orthodoxy

Theological Writings of
Proto-orthodox Christians

Throughout this volume we have seen that two distinctive features of early Christianity were its exclusivity and its focus on doctrine. Christians maintained that they alone worshipped the true God and that this worship involved believing the right things about him. In tandem, these features made Christianity a confessional religion, unlike any other in the Greco-Roman world.

The Christian emphasis on theological affirmation brought with it a cluster of problems unparalleled in ancient religion. As people poured into the church from a wide range of backgrounds and with a host of perspectives, different, sometimes mutually exclusive, viewpoints were propounded as true and apostolic. Given the importance of right belief, these differences quickly led to harsh and vitriolic debates over "orthodoxy" and "heresy" (see Chapters 6 and 7). The views that eventually became dominant were developed over a long period of time and largely in opposition to views set forth by opposing parties. Just within the realm of Christology, for example, when "docetists" argued that Jesus was divine but not human, proto-orthodox Christians insisted that he was fully human; when "adoptionists" argued that he was fully human but not divine, proto-orthodox Christians maintained that he was fully divine as well; when Gnostics concluded that he was divine and human because he was two separate beings, the proto-orthodox claimed that he was one solitary and unitary being, both divine and human. This "orthodox" view eventually came to be embodied in the Christian confessions of faith, such as the Apostles' Creed and the Nicene Creed, formulations that were devised in the fourth century and have come down to us today.

Before the creeds were formalized, proto-orthodox Christians subscribed to a set of beliefs that they labeled the "Rule of Faith" (Latin: "regula fidei"). This "rule" strongly insisted on such antiheretical views as the belief in one God, the creator of the entire material world, and in Christ his son, who was both fully God and fully man. Such basic beliefs, though, still left a huge arena of interpretation, even within proto-orthodox circles. In part, the complexities were created by the paradoxes found within the proto-orthodox doctrines themselves, paradoxes that were created precisely because these doctrines were established in opposition to the unpalatable views of others. How was it possible, for example, to reconcile two of the most basic proto-orthodox beliefs, (a) that there was only one true God (against, for example, Marcion and the Gnostics) and (b) that Christ himself was fully divine? If God is God and Christ is God, are there not *two* Gods? And what about the Spirit, who was also thought to be God? Are there not *three* Gods?

No, proto-orthodox Christians insisted, there was only one God. But how can there be one if there are three? Is it possible, for example, that Christ was actually God himself on earth and that there was no other God than he, that in fact the Father became the Son to die for the sins of the world? That was the view of one group of Christians near the end of the second century, a group labeled by their opponents "patripassianists" (literally: "father sufferers") because they were forced by the logic of their position to maintain that the Father himself had suffered and died on the cross, a view unpalatable to other proto-orthodox Christians (see Chapter 7). But if the patripassianists were wrong, that is, if Jesus was not himself the Father, yet at the same time he really was fully God, how *could* one avoid being called a ditheist (i.e., one who believes in two gods) or, if the Spirit were included in the mix, a tritheist?

The debates over how to resolve these issues were long and hard and became increasingly complicated and nuanced with the passing of time. Near the end of the second and throughout the third centuries, Christians began to speak of the "trinity" as a way of resolving the problem, but proto-orthodox thinkers worked out the details in various ways until a view emerged that eventually became widely accepted as orthodox: to put the matter simply, the relationship of the three—Father, Son, and Spirit—was a mystery (i.e., above and beyond reason) that involved three distinct "persons" all sharing one "substance."

The philosophical sophistication required to work through these problems was far beyond the ability of average Christians, of course, most of whom were not even literate, let alone philosophically trained. Many of our surviving literary texts from the period, however, are heavily invested in precisely such questions, as they come from the pens of the Christian literary elite. As a rule, these authors attempt to solve the problems of right doctrine by applying philosophically sophisticated arguments to the text of Scripture, understood by them to be the ultimate revelation of divine truth. One of the reasons for their wide-ranging disagreements is that the authors of Scripture themselves did not deal with these kinds of theological problems or anything like them; proto-orthodox theologians were thus set on systematizing the doctrinal innuendos of authors who were addressing entirely different issues and concerns.

In this early period of Christian theology, some of the prominent spokespersons for proto-orthodox views developed their ideas in ways later deemed, by those with the benefit of hindsight, to be completely wrongheaded and dangerous. At the time, however, such views were seen as both acceptable and attractive. The clearest instance is the writings of Origen, the greatest intellect and the most prolific Christian author of the second and third centuries, known and respected as a leading voice among the proto-orthodox. Origen's views provided the foundation upon which much subsequent theology came to be built; yet he himself was condemned as a heretic some three centuries after his death.

The following selections, including an important portion of Origen's theological writing, "On First Principles," represent some of the more interesting attempts by second- and third-century Christians to make sense of the doctrines that they understood to be central to the faith.

For Further Reading

Grillmeier, Aloys. *Christ in the Christian Tradition*. Atlanta: John Knox, 1975.

Harnack, Adolf von. *History of Dogma*, tr. Neil Buchanan. New York: Dover, 1961.

Lyman, Rebecca. *Christology and Cosmology: Models of Divine Activity in Origen. Eusebius, and Athanasius*. Oxford: Clarendon, 1993.

Norris, Richard. *The Christological Controversy*. Philadelphia: Fortress, 1980.

Pelikan, *The Christian Tradition*, vol. 1. Chicago: University of Chicago Press, 1971.

Rusch, William G. *The Trinitarian Controversy*. Philadelphia: Fortress, 1980.

THE TEXTS

73. Tertullian: Against Praxeas

In the early part of the third century, Tertullian (see Chapter 4) wrote a vitriolic treatise against a man named Praxeas, who evidently maintained that Christ was God the Father himself become flesh, so there was no distinction between the Father and Son (for another selection, see Chapter 7). Some scholars have suspected that "Praxeas" is actually a cipher for someone else in the Roman church. He is not mentioned by other ancient sources, yet Tertullian assigns an inordinate significance to him; Praxeas is said not only to have infected the church with his patripassianist views but also to have driven out the Montanists, a rigorist Christian sect, eventually joined by Tertullian himself, that stressed the ongoing work of the Spirit.

Tertullian bars no holds in his attack, maintaining that Praxeas's notions have been inspired directly by the devil. In support of his counterposition, Tertullian provides a detailed exposition of the regula fidei allegedly confessed by all Christians, giving a creative and influential elaboration of the relation of the Father and the Son and developing in his own way, then, the doctrine of the trinity: there is *one* God who exists in *three* persons, "three not in condition but in degree; not in substance but in form . . . of one substance and of one condition, and of one power, inasmuch as he is one God . . . susceptible of number without division" (*Against Praxeas*, ch. 2; see Chapter 7).

Particularly notable are Tertullian's closely argued logic and, especially, his detailed appeals to the very words of inspired Scripture.

4 . . . We have been already able to show that the Father and the Son are two separate Persons, not only by the mention of their separate names as Father and the Son, but also by the fact that he who delivered up the kingdom, and he to whom it is delivered up—and in like manner, he who subjected (all things), and he to whom they were subjected—must necessarily be two different beings.

5 But since they [the followers of Praxeas] will have the two to be but one, so that the Father shall be deemed to be the same as the Son, it is only right that the whole question respecting the Son should be examined, as to whether he exists, and who he is and the mode of his existence. Thus shall the truth itself secure its own sanction from the Scriptures, and the interpretations which guard them. There are some who allege that even Genesis opens thus in Hebrew: "In the beginning God made for himself a Son." As there is no ground for this, I am led to other arguments derived from God's own dispensation, in which he existed before the creation of the world, up to the genera-

Tertullian: "Against Praxeas," from *The Ante-Nicene Fathers*; vol. 3, *Latin Christianity: Its Founder Tertullian*, ed. A. Cleveland Coxe. Reprint, 2d ed. Grand Rapids, Mich.: Eerdmans, 1989.

tion of the Son. For before all things God was alone—being in himself and for himself universe, and space, and all things. Moreover, he was alone, because there was nothing external to him but himself. Yet even not then was he alone; for he had with him that which he possessed in himself, that is to say, his own Reason. For God is rational, and Reason was first in him; and so all things were from himself. This reason is his own Thought (or Consciousness) which the Greeks call *logos* by which term we also designate Word or Discourse and therefore it is now usual with our people, owing to the mere simple interpretation of the term, to say that the Word was in the beginning with God; although it would be more suitable to regard Reason as the more ancient; because God had not Word from the beginning, but he had Reason even before the beginning; because also Word itself consists of Reason, which it thus proves to have been the prior existence as being its own substance. Not that this distinction is of any practical moment. For although God had not yet sent out his word, he still had him within himself, both in company with and included within his very Reason, as he silently planned and arranged within himself everything which he was afterwards about to utter through his Word. Now, while he was thus planning and arranging with his own Reason, he was actually causing that to become Word which he was dealing with in the way of Word or Discourse. And that you may the more readily understand this, consider first of all, from your own self, who are made in the image and likeness of God, for what purpose it is that you also possess reason in yourself, who are a rational creature, as being not only made by a rational artificer, but actually animated out of his substance. Observe, then, that when you are silently conversing with yourself, this very process is carried on within you by your reason, which meets you with a word at every movement of your thought, at every impulse of your conception. Whatever you think, there is a word; whatever you conceive, there is reason. You must speak it in your mind; and while you are speaking, you admit speech as an interlocutor with you, involved in which there is this very reason, whereby, while in thought you are holding converse with your word, you are (by reciprocal action) producing thought by means of that converse with your word. Thus, in a certain sense, the word is a second person within you, through which in thinking you utter speech, and through which also, (by reciprocity of process,) in uttering speech you generate thought. The word is itself a different thing from yourself. Now how much more fully is all this transacted in God, whose image and likeness even you are regarded as being, inasmuch as he has reason within himself even while he is silent, and involved in that Reason his word! I may therefore without rashness first lay this down (as a fixed principle) that even then before the creation of the universe God was not alone, since he had within himself both Reason, and, inherent in Reason, his Word, which he made second to himself by agitating it within himself. . . .

9 Bear always in mind that this is the rule of faith which I profess; by it I testify that the Father, and the Son, and the Spirit are inseparable from each other, and so will you know in what sense this is said. Now, observe, my assertion is that the Father is one, and the Son one, and the Spirit one, and that they are distinct from each other. This statement is taken in a wrong sense by every uneducated as well as every perversely disposed person, as if it predicated a diversity, in such a sense as to imply a separation among the Father, and the Son, and the Spirit. I am, moreover, obliged to say this, when (extolling the Monarchy at the expense of the Economy) they contend for the identity of the Father and Son and Spirit, that it is not by way of diversity that the Son differs from the Father, but by distribution: it is not by division that he is different, but by distinction; because the Father is not the same as the Son, since they differ one from the other in the mode of their being. For the Father is the entire substance, but the Son is a derivation and portion of the whole, as he himself acknowledges: "My Father is greater than I."[1] In the Psalm his inferiority is described as being "a little lower than the

---

[1]John 14:28.

angels."[2] Thus the Father is distinct from the Son, being greater than the Son, inasmuch as he who begets is one, and he who is begotten is another; he, too, who sends is one, and he who is sent is another; and he, again, who makes is one, and he through whom the thing is made is another. Happily the Lord himself employs this expression of the person of the Paraclete, so as to signify not a division or severance, but a disposition (of mutual relations in the Godhead); for he says, "I will pray the Father, and he shall send you another Comforter. . . . even the Spirit of truth,"[3] thus making the Paraclete distinct from himself, even as we say that the Son is also distinct from the Father; so that he showed a third degree in the Paraclete, as we believe the second degree is in the Son, by reason of the order observed in the Economy. Besides, does not the very fact that they have the distinct names of Father and Son amount to a declaration that they are distinct in personality? For, of course, all things will be what their names represent them to be; and what they are and ever will be, that will they be called; and the distinction indicated by the names does not at all admit of any confusion, because there is none in the things which they designate. "Yes is yes, and no is no; for what is more than these; come of evil."[4]

10 So it is either the Father or the Son, and the day is not the same as the night; nor is the Father the same as the Son, in such a way that both of them should be one, and one or the other should be both,—an opinion which the most conceited "Monarchians" maintain. He himself, they say, made himself a Son to himself. Now a Father makes a Son, and a Son makes a Father; and they who thus become reciprocally related out of each other to each other cannot in any way by themselves simply become so related to themselves, that the Father can make himself a Son to himself, and the Son render himself a Father to himself. And the relations which God establishes, them does he also guard. A father must have a son, in order to be a father; so likewise a son, to be a son, must have a father. It is, however, one thing to have, and another thing to be. For instance, in order to be a husband, I must have a

wife; I can never myself be my own wife. In like manner, in order to be a father, I have a son, for I never can be a son to myself; and in order to be a son, I have a father, it being impossible for me ever to be my own father. And it is these relations which make me (what I am), when I come to possess them: I shall then be a father, when I have a son; and a son, when I have a father. Now, if I am to be to myself any one of these relations, I no longer have what I am myself to be: neither a father, because I am to be my own father; nor a son, because I shall be my own son. Moreover, inasmuch as I ought to have one of these relations in order to be the other; so, if I am to be both together, I shall fail to be one while I possess not the other. For if I must be myself my son, who am also a father, I now cease to have a son, since I am my own son. But by reason of not having a son, since I am my own son, how can I be a father? For I ought to have a son, in order to be a father. Therefore I am not a son, because I have not a father, who makes a son. . . .

11 It will be your duty, however, to adduce your proofs out of the Scriptures as plainly as we do, when we prove that he made his Word a Son to himself. For if he calls him Son, and if the Son is none other than he who has proceeded from the Father himself, and if the Word has proceeded from the Father himself, he will then be the Son, and not himself from whom he proceeded. For the Father himself did not proceed from himself. Now, you who say that the Father is the same as the Son, do really make the same Person both to have sent forth from himself (and at the same time to have gone out from himself as) that Being which is God. If it was possible for him to have done this, he at all events did not do it. You must bring forth the proof which I require of you—one like my own; that is, (you must prove to me) that the Scriptures show the Son and the Father to be the same, just as on our side the Father and the Son are demonstrated to be distinct; I say distinct,

---

[2]Ps 8:5.
[3]John 14:16.
[4]Matt 5:37.

but not separate: for as on my part I produce the words of God Himself, "My heart has emitted my most excellent Word,"[5] so you in like manner ought to adduce in opposition to me some text where God has said, "My heart has emitted myself as my own most excellent Word," in such a sense that he is himself both the emitter and the emitted, both he who sent forth and he who was sent forth, since he is both the Word and God. I bid you also observe, that on my side I advance the passage where the Father said to the Son, "You are my Son, this day have I begotten."[6] If you want me to believe him to be both the Father and the Son, show me some other passage where it is declared, "The Lord said to himself, I am my own Son, today have I begotten myself"; or again, "Before the morning did I beget myself"[7]; and likewise, "I the Lord possessed myself the beginning of my ways for my own works; before all the hills, too, did I beget myself"[8]; and whatever other passages are to the same effect. . . .

12 If the number of the trinity also offends you, as if it were not connected in the simple unity, I ask you how it is possible for a being who is merely and absolutely one and singular, to speak in plural phrase, saying, "Let us make man in our own image, and after our own likeness";[9] whereas he ought to have said, "Let me make man in my own image, and after my own likeness," as being a unique and singular being? In the following passage, however, "Behold the man is become as one of us,"[10] he is either deceiving or amusing us in speaking plurally, if he is one only and singular. Or was it to the angels that he spoke, as the Jews interpret the passage, because these also acknowledge not the Son? Or was it because he was at once the Father, the Son, and the Spirit, that he spoke to himself in plural terms, making himself plural on that very account? Nay, it was because he had already his Son close at his side, as a second person, his own Word, and a third person also, the Spirit in the Word, that he purposely adopted the plural phrase, "Let *us* make"; and, "in *our* image"; and, "become as one *of us*." For with whom did he make man? and to whom did he make him like? (The answer must

be), the Son on the one hand, who was one day to put on human nature; and the Spirit on the other, who was to sanctify humans. With these did he then speak, in the unity of the trinity, as with his ministers and witnesses. In the following text also he distinguishes among the persons: "So God created man in his own image; in the image of God created he him."[11] Why say "image of God"? Why not "his own image" merely, if he was only one who was the Maker, and if there was not also one in whose image he made man? But there was one in whose image God was making man, that is to say, Christ's image, who, being one day about to become man (more surely and more truly so), had already caused the man to be called his image, who was then going to be formed of clay—the image and similitude of the true and perfect man. But in respect of the previous works of the world what says the Scripture? Its first statement indeed is made, when the Son has not yet appeared: "And God said, Let there be light, and there was light."[12] Immediately there appears the Word, "that true light, which light humans on his coming into the worlds,"[13] and through him also came light upon the world. From that moment God willed creation to be effected in the Word, Christ being present and ministering to him: and so God created. And God said, "Let there be a firmament, . . . and God made the firmament";[14] and God also said, "Let there be lights (in the firmament); and so God made a greater and a lesser light."[15] But all the rest of the created things did he in like manner make, who made the former ones—I mean the Word of God, "through whom all things were made, and without whom nothing was made."[16]

---

[5]Ps 45:1.
[6]Ps 2:7.
[7]cf. Ps 110:3.
[8]cf. Prov 8:22.
[9]Gen 1:26.
[10]Gen 3:22.
[11]Gen 1:27.
[12]Gen 1:3.
[13]John 1:9.
[14]Gen 1:6, 7.
[15]Gen 1:14, 16.
[16]John 1:3.

Now if he too is God, according to John, (who says,) "The Word was God,"[17] then you have two beings—one that commands that the things be made, and the other that executes the order and creates. In what sense, however, you ought to understand him to be another, I have already explained, on the ground of personality, not of substance—in the way of distinction, not of division. But although I must everywhere hold one only substance in three coherent and inseparable (persons), yet I am bound to acknowledge, from the necessity of the case, that he who issues a command is different from him who executes it. For, indeed, he would not be issuing a command if he were all the while doing the work himself, while ordering it to be done by the second. But still he did issue the command, although he would not have intended to command himself if he were only one; or else he must have worked without any command, because he would not have waited to command himself. . . .

27 . . . Now what Divine Person was born in [the flesh]? The Word, and the Spirit which became incarnate with the Word by the will of the Father. The Word, therefore, is incarnate; and this must be the point of our inquiry: How the Word became flesh—whether it was by having been transfigured, as it were, in the flesh, or by having really clothed himself in flesh. Certainly it was a real clothing of himself in flesh. For the rest, we must believe God to be unchangeable, and incapable of form, as being eternal. But transfiguration is the destruction of that which previously existed. For whatsoever is transfigured into some other thing ceases to be that which it had been, and begins to be that which it previously was not. God, however, neither ceases to be what he was, nor can he be any other thing than what he is. The Word is God, and the Word of the Lord remains for ever—even by holding on unchangeably in his own proper form. Now, if he admits not of being transfigured, it must follow that he be understood in this sense to have become flesh, when he comes to be in the flesh, and is manifested, and is seen, and is handled by means of the flesh; since all the other points likewise require to

be thus understood. For if the Word became flesh by a transfiguration and change of substance, it follows at once that Jesus must be a substance compounded of two substances—of flesh and spirit—a kind of mixture, like *electrum*, composed of gold and silver; and it begins to be neither gold (that is to say, spirit) nor silver (that is to say, flesh), the one being changed by the other, and a third substance produced. Jesus, therefore, cannot at this rate be God, for he has ceased to be the Word, which was made flesh; nor can he be man incarnate, for he is not properly flesh, and it was flesh which the Word became. Being compounded, therefore, of both, he actually is neither; he is rather some third substance, very different from either. But the truth is, we find that he is expressly set forth as both God and man; the very psalm which we have quoted intimating (of the flesh), that "God became man in the midst of it, he therefore established it by the will of the Father"[18]—certainly in all respects as the Son of God and the Son of Man, being God and man, differing no doubt according to each substance in its own especial property, inasmuch as the Word is nothing else but God, and the flesh nothing else but man. Thus does the apostle also teach respecting his two substances, saying, "who was made of the seed of David"[19]; in which words he will be man and Son of Man. "Who was declared to be the Son of God, according to the Spirit";[20] in which words he will be God, and the Word—the Son of God. We see plainly the twofold state, which is not confounded, but conjoined in one person—Jesus, God and man. Concerning Christ, indeed, I defer what I have to say. (I remark here), that the property of each nature is so wholly preserved, that the Spirit on the one hand did all things in Jesus suitable to itself, such as miracles and mighty deeds and wonders; and the flesh, on the other hand, exhibited the affections which belong to it. It was hungry under the devil's temptation, thirsty with the Samaritan woman, wept

---

[17]John 1:1.
[18]Ps 87:5.
[19]Rom 1:3.
[20]Rom 1:4.

over Lazarus, was troubled even unto death, and at last actually died. If, however, it was only a *tertium quid*, some composite essence formed out of the two substances, like the *electrum* (which we have mentioned), there would be no distinct proofs apparent of either nature. But by a transfer of functions, the Spirit would have done things to be done by the flesh, and the flesh such as are effected by the Spirit: or else such things as are suited neither to the flesh nor to the Spirit, but confusedly of some third character. Nay more, on this supposition, either the Word underwent death, or the flesh did not die, if so be the Word was converted into flesh; because either the flesh was immortal, or the Word was mortal. Forasmuch, however, as the two substances acted distinctly, each in its own character, there necessarily accrued to them severally their own operations, and their own issues. Learn then, together with Nicodemus, that "that which is born in the flesh is flesh, and that which is born of the Spirit is Spirit."[21] Neither the flesh becomes Spirit, nor the Spirit

flesh. In one Person they no doubt are well able to be co-existent. Of them Jesus consists—man, of the flesh; of the Spirit, God—and the angel designated him as "the Son of God,"[22] in respect of that nature, in which he was Spirit, reserving for the flesh the appellation "Son of Man." In like manner, again, the apostle calls him "the mediator between God and humans,"[23] and so affirmed his participation of both substances. Now, to end the matter, will you, who interpret the Son of God to be flesh, be so good as as to show us what the Son of Man is? Will he then, I want to know, be the Spirit? But you insist upon it that the Father himself is the Spirit, on the ground that "God is a Spirit,"[24] just as if we did not read also that there is "the Spirit of God"; in the same manner as we find that as "the Word was God," so also there is "the Word of God."

---

[21]John 3:6.
[22]Lk 1:35.
[23]1 Tim 2:5.
[24]John 4:24.

---

74. Origen: On First Principles

Of the nearly thousand writings that Origen of Alexandria reputedly produced during his prolific career, none proved more significant for the development of Christian doctrine than his four-volume work, "On First Principles." This represents the first major attempt by a Christian intellectual to produce a systematic theology. It was a brilliant achievement that provided much of the conceptual framework for subsequent theological reflection.

As with his proto-orthodox predecessors, Origen begins by affirming the regula fidei, but he notes that this "rule of faith" leaves many points completely ambiguous. His treatise then takes up some of these critical issues, including such fundamental matters as the nature of God; the relationship of the divine and human natures within Christ; the (sub-

---

Origen: "On First Principles," from *Origen: On First Principles*, ed. G. W. Butterworth. London: SPCK, 1973. Used with permission.

ordinate) relationship of Christ, from eternity past, to God; the role of the Holy Spirit; the nature of the human soul and its preexistence, including the preexistent soul of Jesus; the inspiration of Scripture as the word of God; and, correspondingly, the proper way that it is to be interpreted.

Despite its brilliance, this venture into largely uncharted waters proved hazardous for Origen, or at least for his posthumous reputation. Although he was considered a bastion of orthodoxy in his own day, later, when Christian intellectuals began developing theological systems with increasing nuance, many of Origen's views came to be seen as implausible and, eventually, heretical—especially his notions that human souls preexisted their births and "fell" into human bodies and that, at the end of all things, God would redeem his entire creation, including the Devil himself. Some three centuries later, these views, along with Origen himself, came to be condemned at the Second Council of Constantinople (553 C.E.).

The following selections from "On First Principles" include many of its central theological points and set forth Origen's approach to interpreting Scripture (in which the "literal" meaning is often to be set aside), revealing something of the workings of the mind of this great Christian intellect. (NB: the original Greek text is given whenever it is available; otherwise, the excerpts are of the Latin translation.

Book I

Preface

1 All who believe and are convinced that grace and truth came by Jesus Christ and that Christ is the truth (in accordance with his own saying, "I am the truth"[1]) derive the knowledge which calls people to lead a good and blessed life from no other source but the very words and teaching of Christ. By the words of Christ we do not mean only those which formed his teaching when he was made man and dwelt in the flesh, since even before that Christ the Word of God was in Moses and the prophets. For without the Word of God how could they have prophesied about Christ? In proof of which we should not find it difficult to show from the divine scriptures how that Moses or the prophets were filled with the spirit of Christ in all their words and deeds, were we not anxious to confine the present work within the briefest possible limits. I count it sufficient, therefore, to quote this one testimony of Paul, taken from the epistle which he writes to the Hebrews, where he speaks as follows: "By faith Moses, when he was grown up, refused to be called the son of Pharaoh's

daughter, choosing rather to suffer affliction with the people of God than to enjoy the pleasures of sin for a season, accounting the reproach of Christ greater riches than the treasures of Egypt."[2]

2 Many of those, however, who profess to believe in Christ, hold conflicting opinions not only on small and trivial questions but also on some that are great and important; on the nature, for instance, of God or of the Lord Jesus Christ or of the Holy Spirit, and in addition on the natures of those created beings, the dominions and the holy powers. In view of this it seems necessary first to lay down a definite line and unmistakable rule in regard to each of these, and to postpone the inquiry into other matters until afterwards. For just as there are many among Greeks and barbarians alike who promise us the truth, and yet we gave up seeking for it from all who claimed it for false opinions after we had come to believe that Christ was the Son of God and had become convinced that we must learn the truth from him; in the same

---

[1]John 14:6.
[2]Heb 11:24–25.

way when we find many who think they hold the doctrine of Christ, some of them differing in their beliefs from the Christians of earlier times, and yet the teaching of the church, handed down in unbroken succession from the apostles, is still preserved and continues to exist in the churches up to the present day, we maintain that that only is to be believed as the truth which in no way conflicts with the tradition of the church and the apostles.

3 But the following fact should be understood. The holy apostles, when preaching the faith of Christ, took certain doctrines, those namely which they believed to be necessary ones, and delivered them in the plainest terms to all believers, even to such as appeared to be somewhat dull in the investigation of divine knowledge. The grounds of their statements they left to be investigated by such as should merit the higher gifts of the Spirit and in particular by such as should afterwards receive through the Holy Spirit himself the graces of language, wisdom, and knowledge. There were other doctrines, however, about which the apostles simply said that things were so, keeping silence as to the how or why; their intention undoubtedly being to supply the more diligent of those who came after them, such as should prove to be lovers of wisdom, with an exercise on which to display the fruit of their ability. The people I refer to are those who train themselves to become worthy and capable of receiving wisdom.

4 The kind of doctrines which are believed in plain terms through the apostolic teaching are the following:—

First, that God is one, who created and set in order all things, and who, when nothing existed, caused the universe to be. He is God from the first creation and foundation of the world, the God of all righteous men, of Adam, Abel, Seth, Enos, Enoch, Noah, Shem, Abraham, Isaac, Jacob, of the twelve patriarchs, of Moses and the prophets. This God, in these last days, according to the previous announcements made through his prophets, sent the Lord Jesus Christ, first for the purpose of calling Israel, and secondly, after the unbelief of the people of Israel, of calling the Gentiles also. This just and good God, the Father of our Lord Jesus Christ, himself gave the law, the prophets and the gospels, and he is God both of the apostles and also of the Old and New Testaments.

Then again: Christ Jesus, he who came to earth, was begotten of the Father before every created thing.[3] And after he had ministered to the Father in the foundation of all things, for "all things were made through him,"[3] in these last times he emptied himself and was made man, was made flesh, although he was God, and being made man, he still remained what he was, namely, God. He took to himself a body like our body, differing in this alone, that it was born of a virgin and of the Holy Spirit. And this Jesus Christ was born and suffered in truth and not merely in appearance, and truly died our common death. Moreover he truly rose from the dead, and after the resurrection companied with his disciples and was then taken up into heaven.

Then again, the apostles, delivered this doctrine, that the Holy Spirit is united in honor and dignity with the Father and the Son. In regard to him it is not yet clearly known whether he is to be thought of as begotten or unbegotten, or as being himself also a Son of God or not; but these are matters which we must investigate to the best of our power from holy scripture, inquiring with wisdom and diligence. It is, however, certainly taught with the utmost clearness in the church, that this Spirit inspired each one of the saints, both the prophets and the apostles, and that there was not one Spirit in the people of old and another in those who were inspired at the coming of Christ.

5 Next after this the apostles taught that the soul, having a substance and life of its own, will be rewarded according to its deserts after its departure from this world; for it will either obtain an inheritance of eternal life and blessedness, if its deeds shall warrant this, or it must be given over to eternal fire and torments, if the guilt of its crimes shall so determine. Further, there will be a time for the resurrection of the dead, when this body, which is now "sown in corruption," shall "rise in incorruption," and that which is "sown in dishonor" shall "rise in glory."[4]

---

[3]John 1:3.
[4]1 Cor 15:42–43.

This also is laid down in the church's teaching, that every rational soul is possessed of free will and choice; and also, that it is engaged in a struggle against the devil and his angels and the opposing powers; for these strive to weigh the soul down with sins, whereas we, if we lead a wise and upright life, endeavor to free ourselves from such a burden. There follows from this the conviction that we are not subject to necessity, so as to be compelled by every means, even against our will, to do either good or evil. For if we are possessed of free will, some spiritual powers may very likely be able to urge us on to sin and others to assist us to salvation; we are not, however, compelled by necessity to act either rightly or wrongly, as is thought to be the case by those who say that human events are due to the course and motion of the stars, not only those events which fall outside the sphere of our freedom of will but even those that lie within our own power.

In regard to the soul, whether it takes its rise from the transference of the seed, in such a way that the principle or substance of the soul may be regarded as inherent in the seminal particles of the body itself; or whether it has some other beginning, and whether this beginning is begotten or unbegotten, or at any rate whether it is imparted to the body from without or no; all this is not very clearly defined in the teaching.

6 Further, in regard to the devil and his angels and the opposing spiritual powers, the church teaching lays it down that these beings exist, but what they are or how they exist it has not explained very clearly. Among most Christians, however, the following opinion is held, that this devil was formerly an angel, but became an apostate and persuaded as many angels as he could to fall away with him; and these are even now called his angels.

7 The church teaching also includes the doctrine that this world was made and began to exist at a definite time and that by reason of its corruptible nature it must suffer dissolution. But what existed before this world, or what will exist after it, has not yet been made known openly to the many, for no clear statement on the point is set forth in the church teaching.

8 Then there is the doctrine that the scriptures were composed through the Spirit of God and that they have not only that meaning which is obvious, but also another which is hidden from the majority of readers. For the contents of scripture are the outward forms of certain mysteries and the images of divine things. On this point the entire church is unanimous, that while the whole law is spiritual, the inspired meaning is not recognized by all, but only by those who are gifted with the grace of the Holy Spirit in the word of wisdom and knowledge. . . .

Everyone therefore who is desirous of constructing out of the foregoing a connected body of doctrine must use points like these as elementary and foundation principles, in accordance with the commandment which says, "Enlighten yourselves with the light of knowledge."[5] Thus by clear and cogent arguments he will discover the truth about each particular point and so will produce, as we have said, a single body of doctrine, with the aid of such illustrations and declarations as he shall find in the holy scriptures and of such conclusions as he shall ascertain to follow logically from them when rigidly understood. . . .

Chapter 1

1 . . . God must not be thought to be any kind of body, nor to exist in a body, but to be a simple intellectual existence, admitting in himself of no addition whatever, so that he cannot be believed to have in himself a more or a less, but is Unity, or if I may so say, Oneness throughout, and the mind and fount from which originates all intellectual existence or mind. Now mind does not need physical space in which to move and operate, nor does it need a magnitude discernible by the senses, nor bodily shape or color, nor anything else whatever like these, which are suitable to bodies and matter. Accordingly that simply and wholly mental existence can admit no delay or hesitation in any of its movements or operations; for if it did so, the simplicity of its divine nature would appear to be in some degree limited and impeded by such an addi-

---

[5]Hos 10:12.

tion, and that which is the first principle of all things would be found to be composite and diverse, and would be many and not one; since only the species of deity, if I may so call it, has the privilege of existing apart from all material intermixture.

That mind needs no space in which to move according to its own nature is certain even from the evidence of our own mind. For if this abides in its own proper sphere and nothing occurs from any cause to enfeeble it, it will never be at all retarded by reason of differences of place from acting in conformity with its own movements; nor on the other hand will it gain any increase or accession of speed from the peculiar nature of any place. And if it be objected, for example, that when people are travelling by sea and tossed by the waves, their mind is somewhat less vigorous than it is wont to be on land, we must believe this experience to be due not to the difference of place but to the movement and disturbance of the body with which the mind is joined or intermingled. For it seems almost against nature for the human body to live on the sea, and on this account the body, as if unequal to its task, appears to sustain the mind's movements in irregular and disordered manner, giving feebler assistance to its keen flashes, precisely as happens even with people on land when they are in the grip of a fever; in whose case it is certain that, if the mind fulfils its functions less effectively through the strength of the fever, the cause is to be found not in any defect of locality but in the disease of the body, which renders it disturbed and confused and altogether unable to bestow its customary services on the mind under the well-known and natural conditions. For we people are animals, formed by a union of body and soul, and thus alone did it become possible for us to live on the earth. But God, who is the beginning of all things, must not be regarded as a composite being, lest perchance we find that the elements, out of which everything that is called composite has been composed, are prior to the first principle himself. . . .

Chapter 2

1 First [with respect to Christ] we must know this, that in Christ there is one nature, his deity,

because he is the only-begotten Son of the Father, and another human nature, which in very recent times he took upon him to fulfil the divine purpose. Our first task therefore is to see what the only-begotten Son of God is, seeing he is called by many different names according to the circumstances and beliefs of the different writers. He is called Wisdom, as Solomon said, speaking in the person of Wisdom: "The Lord created me the beginning of his ways for his works. Before he made anything, before the ages he established me. In the beginning before he made the earth, before the springs of waters came forth, before the mountains were settled, before all the hills he begets me."[6] He is also called Firstborn, as the apostle Paul says: "who is the firstborn of all creation."[7] The Firstborn is not, however, by nature a different being from Wisdom, but is one and the same. Finally, the apostle Paul says, "Christ, the power of God and the wisdom of God."[8]

2 Let no one think, however, that when we give him the name "wisdom of God" we mean anything without hypostatic existence, that is, to take an illustration, that we understand him to be not as it were some wise living being, but a certain thing which makes people wise by revealing and imparting itself to the minds of such as are able to receive its influence and intelligence. If then it is once rightly accepted that the only-begotten Son of God is God's wisdom hypostatically existing, I do not think that our mind ought to stray beyond this to the suspicion that this hypostatis or substance could possibly possess bodily characteristics, since everything that is corporeal is distinguished by shape or color or size. And who in his sober senses ever looked for shape or color or measurable size in wisdom, considered solely as wisdom? And can anyone who has learned to regard God with feelings of reverence suppose or believe that God the Father ever existed, even for a single moment, without begetting this wisdom? For he would either say that God could not have begotten wisdom before he did

---

[6]Prov 8:22–25.
[7]Col 1:15.
[8]1 Cor 1:24.

beget her, so that he brought wisdom into being when she had not existed before, or else that he could have begotten her and—what it is profanity even to say about God—that he was unwilling to do so; each of which alternatives, as everyone can see, is absurd and impious, that is, either that God should advance from being unable to being able, or that, while being able, he should act as if he were not and should delay to beget wisdom.

Wherefore we recognise that God was always the Father of his only-begotten Son, who was born indeed of him and draws his being from him, but is yet without any beginning, not only of that kind which can be distinguished by periods of time, but even of that other kind which the mind alone is wont to contemplate in itself and to perceive, if I may so say, with the bare intellect and reason. Wisdom, therefore, must be believed to have been begotten beyond the limits of any beginning that we can speak of or understand. And because in this very subsistence of wisdom there was implicit every capacity and form of the creation that was to be, both of those things that exist in a primary sense and of those which happen in consequence of them, the whole being fashioned and arranged beforehand by the power of foreknowledge, wisdom, speaking through Solomon in regard to these very created things that had been as it were outlined and prefigured in herself, says that she was created as a "beginning of the ways" of God, which means that she contains within herself both the beginnings and causes and species of the whole creation.

3 Now just as we have learned in what sense wisdom is the "beginning of the ways" of God and is said to have been created, in the sense, namely, that she fashions beforehand and contains within herself the species and causes of the entire creation, in the same manner also must wisdom be understood to be the Word of God. For wisdom opens to all other beings, that is, to the whole creation, the meaning of the mysteries and secrets which are contained within the wisdom of God, and so she is called the Word, because she is as it were an interpreter of the mind's secrets. Hence I consider that to be a true saying which is written in the Acts of Paul, "He is the Word, a living being." John, however, uses yet more exalted and

wonderful language in the beginning of his gospel, when by an appropriate declaration he defines the Word to be God; "And the Word was God, and he was in the beginning with God."[9] Let him who assigns a beginning to the Word of God or the wisdom of God beware lest he utters impiety against the unbegotten Father himself, in denying that he was always a Father and that he begat the Word and possessed wisdom in all previous times or ages or whatever else they may be called.

4 . . . Whatever then we have said of the wisdom of God will also fitly apply to and be understood of him in his other titles as the Son of God, the life, the word, the truth, the way, and the resurrection. For all these titles are derived from his works and powers, and in none of them is there the least reason to understand anything corporeal, which might seem to denote either size or shape or color. But whereas the offspring of humans or of the other animals whom we see around us correspond to the seed of those by whom they were begotten, or of the mothers in whose womb they are formed and nourished, drawing from these parents whatever it is that they take and bring into the light of day when they are born, it is impious and shocking to regard God the Father in the begetting of his only-begotten Son and in the Son's subsistence as being similar to any human being or other animal in the act of begetting; but there must be some exceptional process, worthy of God, to which we can find no comparison whatever, not merely in things, but even in thought and imagination, such that by its aid human thought could apprehend how the unbegotten God becomes Father of the only-begotten Son. This is an eternal and everlasting begetting, as brightness is begotten from light. For he does not become Son in an external way through the adoption of the Spirit, but is Son by nature. . . .

10 Let us now look into the saying that wisdom is "an effluence," that is, an emanation, "of the clear glory of the Almighty," and if we first consider what "the glory of the Almighty" is, we shall then understand what its "effluence" is. Now

---

[9]John 1:1–2.

as one cannot be a father apart from having a son, nor a lord apart from holding a possession or a slave, so we cannot even call God almighty if there are none over whom he can exercise his power. Accordingly, to prove that God is almighty we must assume the existence of the universe. For if anyone would have it that certain ages, or periods of time, or whatever he cares to call them, elapsed during which the present creation did not exist, he would undoubtedly prove that in those ages or periods God was not almighty, but that he afterwards became almighty from the time when he began to have creatures over whom he could exercise power. Thus God will apparently have experienced a kind of progress, for there can be no doubt that it is better for him to be almighty than not to be so.

Now how is it anything but absurd that God should at first not possess something that is appropriate to him and then should come to possess it? But if there was no time when he was not almighty, there must always have existed the things in virtue of which he is almighty; and there must always have existed things under his sway, which own him as their ruler.

Chapter 3

We come, therefore, to the investigation in as brief a manner as possible, of the subject of the Holy Spirit. . . .

3 It is proved by many declarations throughout the whole of scripture that the universe was created by God and that there is no substance which has not received its existence from him; which refutes and dismisses the doctrines falsely taught by some, that there is a matter which is co-eternal with God, or that there are unbegotten souls, in whom they would have it that God implanted not so much the principle of existence as the quality and rank of their life. Moreover in that little book composed by Hermas, called "The Shepherd, or the Angel of Repentance," it is thus written: "First of all, believe that God is one, who created and set in order all things; who, when nothing existed before, caused all things to be; who contains all things, but himself is contained

by none."[10] Similar statements are also made in the book of Enoch. But up to the present we have been able to find no passage in the holy scriptures which would warrant us in saying that the Holy Spirit was a being made or created, not even in that manner in which we have shown above that Solomon speaks of wisdom, nor in the manner in which the expressions we have dealt with, such as life, or word, or other titles of the Son of God, are to be understood. The "Spirit of God," therefore, who "moved upon the waters,"[11] as it is written, in the beginning of the creation of the world, I reckon to be none other than the Holy Spirit, so far as I can understand; which indeed I have demonstrated in my exposition of these passages, not, however, according to their literal but according to their spiritual meaning.

4 . . . And my Hebrew master used to say that the two six-winged seraphim in Isaiah who cry one to another and say, Holy, holy, holy is the Lord of hosts,[12] were the only-begotten Son of God and the Holy Spirit. And we ourselves think that the expression in the song of Habakkuk, "In the midst of the two living creatures you shall be known."[13] is spoken of Christ and the Holy Spirit.

For all knowledge of the Father, when the Son reveals him, is made known to us through the Holy Spirit. So that both of these, who in the words of the prophet are called "animals" or "living beings," are the cause of our knowledge of God the Father. For as it is said of the Son that "no one knows the Father but the Son, and he to whom the Son wills to reveal him,"[14] so in the same way does the apostle speak of the Holy Spirit; "God has revealed them to us by his Spirit: for the Spirit searches all things, even the deep things of God."[15]

15 . . . The God and Father, who holds the universe together, is superior to every being that

[10]Herm. *Vis* 5.8.
[11]Gen 1:2.
[12]Isa 6:2–3.
[13]Heb 3:2.
[14]Matt 11:27.
[15]1 Cor 2:10.

exists, for he imparts to each one from his own existence that which each one is; the Son, being less than the Father, is superior to rational creatures alone (for he is second to the Father); the Holy Spirit is still less, and dwells within the saints alone. So that in this way the power of the Father is greater than that of the Son and of the Holy Spirit, and that of the Son is more than that of the Holy Spirit, and in turn the power of the Holy Spirit exceeds that of every other holy being.

Chapter 8

1 . . . . God did not begin to create minds; before the ages minds were all pure, both daemons and souls and angels, offering service to God and keeping his commandments. But the devil, who was one of them, since he possessed free-will, desired to resist God, and God drove him away. With him revolted all the other powers. Some sinned deeply and became daemons, others less and became angels; others still less and became archangels; and thus each in turn received the reward for his individual sin. But there remained some souls who had not sinned so greatly as to become daemons, nor on the other hand so very lightly as to become angels. God therefore made the present world and bound the soul to the body as a punishment. For God is no respecter of persons, that among all these beings who are of one nature (for all the immortal beings are rational) he should make some daemons, some souls and some angels; rather is it clear that God made one a daemon, one a soul and one an angel as a means of punishing each in proportion to its sin. For if this were not so, and souls had no pre-existence, why do we find some new-born babes to be blind, when they have committed no sin, while others are born with no defect at all? But it is clear that certain sins existed before the souls, and as a result of these sins each soul receives a recompense in proportion to its deserts. They are sent forth from God as a punishment, that they must undergo on earth a first judgment. That is why the body is called a frame, because the soul is enclosed within it.

But when they had revolted from their former blessedness they were endowed with bodies in consequence of the fall from their first estate which had taken place in them, and allotted to various ranks. So from being "minds" they have become angels, archangels. . . .

Just as the daemons, sitting by the altars of the Gentiles, used to feed on the steam of the sacrifices, so also the angels, allured by the blood of victims which Israel offered as symbols of spiritual things, and by the smoke of the incense, used to dwell near the altars and to be nourished on food of this sort.

But when they fell away, as the New Testament says, from their unity with God, they were given the rule and lordship over those who had fallen lower still and were also "sent forth to minister to those who are to inherit salvation,"[16] though they themselves had fallen from this salvation and were in need of one to lead them back. . . .

9 . . . . Whole nations of souls are stored away somewhere in a realm of their own, with an existence comparable to our bodily life, but in consequence of the fineness and mobility of their nature they are carried round with the whirl of the universe. There the representations of evil and of virtue are set before them; and so long as a soul continues to abide in the good it has no experience of union with a body. But by some inclination towards evil these souls lose their wings and come into bodies, first of humans; then through their association with the irrational passions, after the allotted span of human life they are changed into beasts; from which they sink to the level of insensate nature. Thus that which is by nature fine and mobile, namely the soul, first becomes heavy and weighed down, and because of its wickedness comes to dwell in a human body; after that, when the faculty of reason is extinguished, it lives the life of an irrational animal; and finally even the gracious gift of sensation is withdrawn and it changes into the insensate life of a plant. From this condition it rises again through the same stages and is restored to its heavenly place. On earth by means of virtue souls grow wings and soar aloft,

---

[16]Heb 1:14.

but when in heaven their wings fall off through evil and they sink down and become earthbound and are mingled with the gross nature of matter.

Book II

Chapter 6

1 Now that these points have been discussed, it is time to resume our inquiry into the incarnation of our Lord and Saviour, how he became man and dwelt among people. . . .

2 . . . . Of all the marvellous and splendid things about him there is one that utterly transcends the limits of human wonder and is beyond the capacity of our weak mortal intelligence to think of or understand, namely, how this mighty power of the divine majesty, the very word of the Father, and the very wisdom of God, in which were created "all things visible and invisible,"[4] can be believed to have existed within the compass of that man who appeared in Judaea; yes, and how the wisdom of God can have entered into a woman's womb and been born as a little child and uttered noises like those of crying children. . . .

When, therefore, we see in him some things so human that they appear in no way to differ from the common frailty of mortals, and some things so divine that they are appropriate to nothing else but the primal and ineffable nature of deity, the human understanding with its narrow limits is baffled, and struck with amazement at so mighty a wonder knows not which way to turn, what to hold to, or whither to betake itself. If it thinks of God, it sees a human; if it thinks of a human, it beholds one returning from the dead with spoils after vanquishing the kingdom of death. For this reason we must pursue our contemplation with all fear and reverence, as we seek to prove how the reality of each nature exists in one and the same person, in such a way that nothing unworthy or unfitting may be thought to reside in that divine and ineffable existence, nor on the other hand may the events of his life be supposed to be the illusions caused by deceptive fantasies. . . .

3 The only-begotten Son of God, therefore, through whom, as the course of our discussion in the previous chapters has shown, all things visible and invisible were made, according to the teaching of scripture both made all things and "loves what he made."[17] For since he is the invisible "image" of the "invisible God,"[18] he granted invisibly to all rational creatures whatsoever a participation in himself, in such a way that each obtained a degree of participation proportionate to the loving affection with which he had clung to him. But whereas, by reason of the faculty of free-will, variety and diversity had taken hold of individual souls, so that one was attached to its author with a warmer and another with a feebler and weaker love, that soul of which Jesus said, "No man takes from me my soul,"[19] clinging to God from the beginning of the creation and ever after in a union inseparable and indissoluble, as being the soul of the wisdom and word of God and of the truth and the true light, and receiving him wholly, and itself entering into his light and splendor, was made with him in a preeminent degree one spirit, just as the apostle promises to them whose duty it is to initiate Jesus, that "the one who is joined to the Lord is one spirit."[20] This soul, then, acting as a medium between God and the flesh (for it was not possible for the nature of God to mingle with a body apart from some medium), there is born, as we said, the God-man, the medium being that existence to whose nature it was not contrary to assume a body. Yet neither, on the other hand, was it contrary to nature for that soul, being as it was a rational existence, to receive God, into whom, as we said above, it had already completely entered by entering into the word and wisdom and truth.

It is therefore right that this soul, either because it was wholly in the Son of God, or because it received the Son of God wholly into itself, should itself be called, along with that flesh which it has taken, the Son of God and the power of God, Christ and the wisdom of God; and on the other hand that

---

[17]Wisd 11:24.
[18]Col 1:15.
[19]John 10:18.
[20]1 Cor 6:17.

the Son of God, "through whom all things were created," should be termed Jesus and the Son of man. Moreover the Son of God is said to have died, in virtue of that nature which could certainly admit of death, while he of whom it is proclaimed that "he shall come in the glory of God the Father with the holy angels" is called the Son of man.[21] And for this reason, throughout the whole of scripture, while the divine nature is spoken of in human terms, the human nature is in its turn adorned with marks that belong to the divine prerogative. For to this more than to anything else can the passage of Scripture be applied, "They shall both be in one flesh, and they are no longer two, but one flesh."[22] For the Word of God is to be thought of as being more "in one flesh" with his soul than a man is with his wife. Moreover what could more appropriately be "one spirit" with God than this soul, which joined itself so firmly in love to God as to be worthy of being called "one spirit" with him?

It was on this account also that the man became Christ, for he obtained this lot by reason of his goodness, as the prophet bears witness when he says, "You have loved righteousness and hated iniquity; wherefore God has anointed you, your God with the oil of gladness above your fellows."[23] It was appropriate that he who had never been separated from the Only-begotten should be called by the name of the Only-begotten and glorified together with him.

As a reward for its love, therefore, it is anointed with the "oil of gladness," that is the soul with the word of God is made Christ; for to be anointed with the oil of gladness means nothing else but to be filled with the Holy Spirit. . . .

5 But if the above argument, that there exists in Christ a rational soul, should seem to anyone to constitute a difficulty, on the ground that in the course of our discussion we have often shown that souls are by their nature capable of good and evil, we shall resolve the difficulty in the following manner. It cannot be doubted that the nature of his soul was the same as that of all souls; otherwise it could not be called a soul, if it were not truly one. But since the ability to choose good or evil is within the immediate reach of all, this soul

which belongs to Christ so chose to love righteousness as to cling to it unchangeably and inseparably in accordance with the immensity of its love; the result being that by firmness of purpose, immensity of affection, and an inextinguishable warmth of love all susceptibility to change or alteration was destroyed, and what formerly depended upon the will was by the influence of long custom changed into nature. Thus we must believe that there did exist in Christ a human and rational soul, and yet not suppose that it had any susceptibility to or possibility of sin.

6 To explain the matter more fully it will not appear absurd if we use an illustration, although on so high and difficult a subject there is but a small supply of suitable examples. However, if we may use this one without offence, the metal iron is susceptible of both cold and heat. Suppose then a lump of iron be placed for some time in a fire. It receives the fire in all its pores and all its veins, and becomes completely changed into fire, provided the fire is never removed from it and itself is not separated from the fire. Are we then to say that this, which is by nature a lump of iron, when placed in the fire and ceaselessly burning can ever admit cold? Certainly not; it is far truer to say of it, what indeed we often detect happening in furnaces, that it has been completely changed into fire, because we can discern nothing else in it except fire. Further, if anyone were to try to touch or handle it, he would feel the power of the fire, not of the iron. In this manner, then, that soul which, like a piece of iron in the fire, was for ever placed in the word, for ever in the wisdom, for ever in God, is God in all its acts and feelings and thoughts; and therefore it cannot be called changeable or alterable, since by being ceaselessly kindled it came to possess unchangeability through its unity with the word of God. And while, indeed, some warmth of the Word of God must be thought to have reached all the saints, in this soul we must believe that the divine fire itself essentially rested, and that it is from this that some warmth has come to all others. . . .

---

[21]Matt 16:27; Mark 8:28; Luke 9:26.
[22]Matt 19:5–6; Gen 2:24.
[23]Ps 45:7.

Book IV

Chapter 1

1 Now in our investigation of these important matters we do not rest satisfied with common opinions and the evidence of things that are seen, but we use in addition, for the manifest proof of our statements, testimonies drawn from the scriptures which we believe to be divine, both from what is called the Old Testament and also from the New, endeavoring to confirm our faith by reason. We have not yet, however, discussed the divine character of the scriptures. Well then, let us deal in a brief manner with a few points concerning them, bringing forward in this connexion the reasons that influence us to regard them as divine writings. And first of all, before we make use of statements from the writings themselves and from the events disclosed in them, let us speak of Moses, the Hebrew lawgiver, and of Jesus Christ, the introducer of the saving doctrines of Christianity.

For although there have been very many lawgivers among both Greeks and barbarians, and teachers who proclaimed doctrines which professed to be the truth, we have no record of a lawgiver who has succeeded in implanting an enthusiasm for the acceptance of his teachings among nations other than his own. A great apparatus of supposed logical proof has been introduced by people who profess that their philosophy is concerned with truth, and yet none of them has succeeded in implanting what he regarded as the truth among different nations or even among any number of persons worth mentioning in a single nation.

Yet it would have been the wish of the lawgivers to put in force the laws which appeared to them to be good among the whole race of mankind, had that been possible; while the teachers would have wished that what they imagined was the truth should be spread everywhere throughout the world. But knowing that they could not summon people of other languages and of many nations to the observance of their laws and the acceptance of their teachings they wholly refrained even from attempting to do this, considering not unwisely how impossible it was that such a result should happen to them. Yet all over Greece and in the barbarian part of our world there are thousands of enthusiasts who have abandoned their ancestral laws and their recognised gods for observance of the laws of Moses and of the teaching contained in the words of Jesus Christ, in spite of the fact that those who submit to the law of Moses are hated by the worshippers of images and that those who accept the word of Jesus Christ are not only hated but in danger of death. . . .

5 And what need is there to speak of the prophecies relating to Christ in the Psalms, in which a certain ode is headed "For the beloved," whose tongue is said to be the "pen of a ready writer" who is "fairer than the children of men" because "grace was poured on his lips"?[24] Now a proof that "grace was poured on his lips" is the fact that although the time he spent in teaching was short—for he taught only about a year and a few months—the world has been filled with this teaching and with the religion that came through him. For there has arisen in his days righteousness and an abundance of peace lasting until the consummation, which is here called the taking away of the moon; and he continues to have dominion from sea to sea and from the rivers to the ends of the earth. And a "sign" has been given to the house of David, for "the virgin" did "conceive and bear a son," and his name is "Emmanuel" which means "God with us."[25]

There has also been fulfilled that which the same prophet says, "God is with us. Know it, you nations, and be overcome; you that are strong, be overcome."[26] For we who have been captured from among the nations have been overcome and conquered by the grace of his word. Moreover the place of his birth is foretold in Micah. "And you, Bethlehem," it says, "land of Judah, are in no way least among the rulers of Judah; for out of you shall come a governor, who shall shepherd my people Israel."[27] And the "seventy weeks" until the coming of Christ the governor were fulfilled

---

[24]Ps 45:1–3.

[25]Isa 7:14; Matt 1:23.

[26]Isa 8:8–9.

[27]Mic 5:2; Matt 2:6.

in accordance with Daniel's prophecy.[28] He, too, has come who according to Job has "subdued the great fish"[29] and who has given to his true disciples authority to "tread on serpents and scorpions and over every power of the enemy," without being in any way harmed by them.[30]

Let anyone also consider how the apostles who were sent by Jesus to preach the gospel sojourned everywhere, and he will see that their daring venture was not merely human and that the command was from God. And if we examine how, when people heard the new teachings and strange words, they welcomed these men, the desire to plot against them being frustrated by some divine power that watched over them, we shall not refuse to believe that they even worked miracles, "God bearing witness with their words, and through signs and wonders and manifold powers."[31]

6 Now when we thus briefly demonstrate the divine nature of Jesus and use the words spoken in prophecy about him, we demonstrate at the same time that the writings which prophesy about him are divinely inspired and that the words which announce his sojourning here and his teaching were spoken with all power and authority and that this is the reason why they have prevailed over the elect people taken from among the nations. And we must add that it was after the advent of Jesus that the inspiration of the prophetic words and the spiritual nature of Moses' law came to light. For before the advent of Christ it was not at all possible to bring forward clear proofs of the divine inspiration of the old scriptures. But the advent of Jesus led those who might have suspected that the law and the prophets were not divine to the clear conviction that they were composed by the aid of heavenly grace.

And he who approaches the prophetic words with care and attention will feel from his very reading a trace of their divine inspiration and will be convinced by his own feelings that the words which are believed by us to be from God are not the compositions of humans. Now the light which was contained within the law of Moses, but was hidden away under a veil, shone forth at the advent of Jesus, when the veil was taken away and there came at once to people's knowledge those

"good things" of which the letter of the law held a "shadow."[32]

Chapter 2

4 The right way, therefore, as it appears to us, of approaching the scriptures and gathering their meaning, is the following, which is extracted from the writings themselves. We find some such rule as this laid down by Solomon in the Proverbs concerning the divine doctrines written therein: "Portray them threefold in counsel and knowledge, that you may answer words of truth to those who question you."[33]

One must therefore portray the meaning of the sacred writings in a threefold way upon one's own soul, so that the simple person may be edified by what we may call the flesh of the scripture, this name being given to the obvious interpretation; while the person who has made some progress may be edified by its soul, as it were; and the person who is perfect and like those mentioned by the apostle: "We speak wisdom among the perfect; yet a wisdom not of this world, nor of the rulers of this world, which are coming to nought; but we speak God's wisdom in a mystery, even the wisdom that has been hidden, which God foreordained before the worlds unto our glory"[34]—this person may be edified by the spiritual law, which has "a shadow of the good things to come."[35] For just as a person consists of body, soul, and spirit, so in the same way does the scripture, which has been prepared by God to be given for a person's salvation.

We therefore read in this light the passage in The Shepherd, a book which is despised by some, where Hermas is bidden to "write two books," and after this to "announce to the presbyters of the Church" what he has learned from the Spirit. This

---

[28]Dan 9:24.
[29]Job 3:8.
[30]Luke 10:19.
[31]Heb 2:4; Acts 5:12.
[32]2 Cor 3:15–16; Heb 10:1.
[33]Prov 22:20–21.
[34]1 Cor 2:6–7.
[35]Heb 10:1.

is the wording: "You shall write two books, and shalt give one to Clement and one to Grapte. And Grapte shall admonish the widows and the orphans. But Clement shall send to the cities without, and you shall announce to the presbyters of the Church."[36]

Now Grapte, who admonishes the widows and orphans, is the bare letter, which admonishes those child souls that are not yet able to enrol God as their Father and are on this account called orphans, and which also admonishes those who while no longer associating with the unlawful bridegroom are in widowhood because they have not yet become worthy of the true one. But Clement, who has already gone beyond the letter, is said to send the sayings "to the cities without," as if to say, to the souls that are outside all bodily and lower thoughts; while the disciple of the Spirit is bidden to announce the message in person, no longer through letters but through living words, to the presbyters or elders of the whole Church of God, to people who have grown grey through wisdom.

5 But since there are certain passages of scripture which, as we shall show in what follows, have no bodily sense at all, there are occasions when we must seek only for the soul and the spirit, as it were, of the passage. And possibly this is the reason why the waterpots which, as we read in the Gospel according to John, are said to be set there "for the purifying of the Jews," contain two or three measures apiece.[37] The language alludes to those who are said by the apostle to be Jews "inwardly,"[38] and it means that these are purified through the word of the scriptures, which contain in some cases "two measures," that is, so to speak, the soul meaning and the spiritual meaning, and in other cases three, since some passages possess, in addition to those before-mentioned, a bodily sense as well, which is capable of edifying the hearers. And six waterpots may reasonably allude to those who are being purified in the world, which was made in six days, a perfect number.

6 That it is possible to derive benefit from the first, and to this extent helpful meaning, is witnessed by the multitudes of sincere and simple believers. But of the kind of explanation which penetrates as it were to the soul an illustration is found in Paul's first epistle to the Corinthians. "For," he says, "it is written; you shall not muzzle the ox that treads out the corn." Then in explanation of this law he adds, "Is it for the oxen that God cares? Or does he say it altogether for our sake? Yes, for our sake it was written, because he that plows ought to plow in hope, and he that threshs, to thresh in hope of partaking."[39] And most of the interpretations adapted to the multitude which are in circulation and which edify those who cannot understand the higher meanings have something of the same character.

But it is a spiritual explanation when one is able to show of what kind of "heavenly things" the Jews "after the flesh" served a copy and a shadow, and of what "good things to come" the law has a "shadow."[40] And, speaking generally, we have, in accordance with the apostolic promise, to seek after "the wisdom in a mystery, even the wisdom that has been hidden, which God foreordained before the worlds unto the glory" of the righteous, "which none of the rulers of this world knew."[41] The same apostle also says somewhere, after mentioning certain narratives from Exodus and Numbers that "these things happened to them figuratively, and they were written for our sake upon whom the ends of the ages are come."[42] He also gives hints to show what these things were figures of, when he says: "For they drank of that spiritual rock that followed them, and that rock was Christ."[43]

In another epistle, when outlining the arrangements of the tabernacle he quotes the words: "You shall make all things according to the figure that was shown you in the mount."[44] Further, in the epistle to the Galatians, speaking in terms of reproach to those who believe that they are reading

---

[36]Hermas *Vis* II.4.3.
[37]John 2:6.
[38]Rom 2:29.
[39]1 Cor 9:9–10.
[40]Heb 8:5; 10:1; Rom 8:5.
[41]1 Cor 2:7–8.
[42]1 Cor 10:11.
[43]1 Cor 10:4.
[44]Heb 8:5.

the law and yet do not understand it, and laying it down that they who do not believe that there are allegories in writings do not understand the law, he says: "Tell me, you that desire to be under the law, do you not hear the law? For it is written, that Abraham had two sons, one by the handmaid and one by the free woman. Now the son by the hand-maid is born after the flesh; but the son by the free woman is born through promise. Which things contain an allegory; for these women are two covenants,"[45] and what follows. Now we must carefully mark each of the words spoken by him. He says, "You that desire to be under the law" (not, "you that are under the law") "do you not hear the law?"—hearing being taken to mean un-derstanding and knowing.

7 This being so, we must outline what seems to us to be the marks of a true understanding of the scriptures. And in the first place we must point out that the aim of the Spirit who, by the provi-dence of God through the Word who was "in the beginning with God,"[46] enlightened the servants of the truth, that is, the prophets and apostles, was pre-eminently concerned with the unspeakable mysteries connected with the affairs of people— and by people I mean at the present moment souls that make use of bodies—his purpose being that the person who is capable of being taught might by searching out and devoting himself to the deep things revealed in the spiritual meaning of the words become partaker of all the doctrines of the Spirit's counsel.

And when we speak of the needs of souls, who cannot otherwise reach perfection except through the rich and wise truth about God, we at-tach of necessity pre-eminent importance to the doctrines concerning God and his only-begotten Son; of what nature the Son is, and in what man-ner he can be the Son of God, and what are the causes of his descending to the level of human flesh and completely assuming humanity; and what, also, is the nature of his activity, and to-wards whom and at what times it is exercised. It was necessary, too, that the doctrines concerning beings akin to humans and the rest of the rational creatures, both those that are nearer the divine and those that have fallen from blessedness, and the

causes of the fall of these latter, should be in-cluded in the accounts of the divine teaching; and the question of the differences between souls and how these differences arose, and what the world is and why it exists, and further, how it comes about that evil is so widespread and so terrible on earth and whether it is not only to be found on earth but also in other places—all this it was nec-essary that we should learn.

8 Now while these and similar subjects were in the mind of the Spirit who enlightened the souls of the holy servants of the truth, there was a sec-ond aim, pursued for the sake of those who were unable to endure the burden of investigating mat-ters of such importance. This was to conceal the doctrine relating to the before-mentioned subjects in words forming a narrative that contained a record dealing with the visible creation, the for-mation of humans, and the successive descendants of the first human beings until the time when they became many; and also in other stories that recorded the acts of righteous people and the sins that these same people occasionally committed, seeing they were but human, and the deeds of wickedness, licentiousness, and greed done by lawless and impious people.

But the most wonderful thing is, that by means of stories of wars and the conquerors and the con-quered certain secret truths are revealed to those who are capable of examining these narratives; and, even more marvellous, through a written sys-tem of law the laws of truth are prophetically in-dicated, all these having been recorded in a series with a power which is truly appropriate to the wisdom of God. For the intention was to make even the outer covering of the spiritual truths, I mean the bodily part of the scriptures, in many re-spects not unprofitable but capable of improving the multitude in so far as they receive it.

9 But if the usefulness of the law and the se-quence and ease of the narrative were at first sight clearly discernible throughout, we should be un-aware that there was anything beyond the obvious meaning for us to understand in the scriptures.

---

[45]Gal 4:21–24.
[46]John 1:2.

Consequently the Word of God has arranged for certain stumbling-blocks, as it were, and hindrances and impossibilities to be inserted in the midst of the law and the history, in order that we may not be completely drawn away by the sheer attractiveness of the language, and so either reject the true doctrines absolutely, on the ground that we learn from the scriptures nothing worthy of God, or else by never moving away from the letter fail to learn anything of the more divine element.

And we must also know this, that because the principal aim was to announce the connexion that exists among spiritual events, those that have already happened and those that are yet to come to pass, whenever the Word found that things which had happened in history could be harmonized with these mystical events he used them, concealing from the multitude their deeper meaning. But wherever in the narrative the accomplishment of some particular deeds, which had been previously recorded for the sake of their more mystical meanings, did not correspond with the sequence of the intellectual truths, the scripture wove into the story something which did not happen, occasionally something which could not happen, and occasionally something which might have happened but in fact did not. Sometimes a few words are inserted which in the bodily sense are not true, and at other times a greater number.

A similar method can be discerned also in the law, where it is often possible to find a precept that is useful for its own sake, and suitable to the time when the law was given. Sometimes, however, the precept does not appear to be useful. At other times even impossibilities are recorded in the law for the sake of the more skilful and inquiring readers, in order that these, by giving themselves to the toil of examining what is written, may gain a sound conviction of the necessity of seeking in such instances a meaning worthy of God.

And not only did the Spirit supervise the writings which were previous to the coming of Christ, but because he is the same Spirit and proceeds from the one God he has dealt in like manner with the gospels and the writings of the apostles. For the history even of these is not everywhere pure, events being woven together in the bodily sense without having actually happened; nor do the law and the commandments contained therein entirely declare what is reasonable.

Chapter 3

1 Now what person of intelligence will believe that the first and the second and the third day and the evening and the morning existed without the sun and moon and stars? And that the first day, if we may so call it, was even without a heaven?[47] And who is so silly as to believe that God, after the manner of a farmer, "planted a paradise eastward in Eden," and set in it a visible and palpable "tree of life," of such a sort that anyone who tasted its fruit with his bodily teeth would gain life; and again that one could partake of "good and evil" by masticating the fruit taken from the tree of that name?[48] And when God is said to "walk in the paradise in the cool of the day" and Adam to hide himself behind a tree,[49] I do not think anyone will doubt that these are figurative expressions which indicate certain mysteries through a semblance of history and not through actual events.

Further, when Cain "goes out from the face of God" it seems clear to thoughtful people that this statement impels the reader to inquire what the "face of God" is and how anyone can "go out" from it.[50] And what more need I say, when those who are not altogether blind can collect thousands of such instances, recorded as actual events, but which did not happen literally?

Even the gospels are full of passages of this kind, as when the devil takes Jesus up into a "high mountain" in order to show him from thence "the kingdoms of the whole world and the glory of them."[51] For what person who does not read such passages carelessly would fail to condemn those

---

[47]Gen 1:5–13.
[48]Gen 2:8–9.
[49]Gen 3:8.
[50]Gen 4:16.
[51]Matt 4:8.

who believe that with the eye of the flesh, which requires a great height to enable us to perceive what is below and at our feet, the kingdoms of the Persians, Scythians, Indians, and Parthians were seen, and the manner in which their rulers are glorified by people? And the careful reader will detect thousands of other passages like this in the gospels, which will convince him that events which did not take place at all are woven into the records of what literally did happen.

2 And to come to the Mosaic legislation, many of the laws, so far as their literal observance is concerned, are clearly irrational, while others are impossible. An example of irrationality is the prohibition to eat vultures, seeing that nobody even in the worst famine was ever driven by want to the extremity of eating these creatures.[52] And in regard to the command that children of eight days old who are uncircumcised "shall be destroyed from their people,"[53] if the law relating to these children were really meant to be carried out according to the letter, the proper course would be to order the death of their fathers or those by whom they were being brought up. But as it is the Scripture says: "Every male that is uncircumcised, who shall not be circumcised on the eighth day, shall be destroyed from among his people."[54]

And if you would like to see some impossibilities that are enacted in the law, let us observe that the goat-stag, which Moses commands us to offer in sacrifice as a clean animal,[55] is a creature that cannot possibly exist; while as to the griffin, which the lawgiver forbids to be eaten,[56] there is no record that it has ever fallen into the hands of a human. Moreover in regard to the celebrated sabbath, a careful reader will see that the command, "You shall sit each one in your dwellings; let none of you go out from his place on the sabbath day,"[57] is an impossible one to observe literally, for no living creature could sit for a whole day and not move from his seat.

Consequently the members of the circumcision and all those who maintain that nothing more than the actual wording is signified make no inquiry whatever into some matters, such as the goat-stag, the griffin, and the vulture, while on

others they babble copiously, bringing forward lifeless traditions, as for instance when they say, in reference to the sabbath, that each man's "place" is two thousand cubits. Others, however, among whom is Dositheus the Samaritan, condemn such an interpretation, and believe that in whatever position a man is found on the Sabbath day he should remain there until evening.

Further, the command "not to carry a burden on the sabbath day"[58] is impossible; and on this account the teachers of the Jews have indulged in endless chatter, asserting that one kind of shoe is a burden, but another is not, and that a sandal with nails is a burden, but one without nails is not, and that what is carried on one shoulder is a burden, but not what is carried on both.

3 If now we approach the gospel in search of similar instances, what can be more irrational than the command: "Salute no one by the way,"[59] which simple people believe that the Savior enjoined upon the apostles? Again, to speak of the right cheek being struck[60] is most incredible, for every striker, unless he suffers from some unnatural defect, strikes the left cheek with his right hand. And it is impossible to accept the precept from the gospel about the "right eye that offends,"[61] for granting the possibility of a person being "offended" through his sense of sight, how can the blame be attributed to the right eye, when there are two eyes that see? And what man, even supposing he accuses himself of "looking on a woman to lust after her" and attributes the blame to his right eye alone, would act rationally if he were to cast this eye away?

Further, the apostle lays down this precept: "Was any called being circumcised? Let him not

---

[52]Lev 11:14.
[53]Gen 17:14.
[54]Gen 17:14.
[55]Deut 14:5.
[56]Lev 11:13; Deut 14:12.
[57]Exod 16:29.
[58]Jer 17:21.
[59]Luke 10:4.
[60]Matt 5:39.
[61]Matt 5:28–29.

become uncircumcised."[62] Now in the first place anyone who wishes can see that these words have no relation to the subject in hand; and how can we help thinking that they have been inserted at random, when we remember that the apostle is here laying down precepts about marriage and purity? In the second place who will maintain that it is wrong for a man to put himself into a condition of uncircumcision, if that were possible, in view of the disgrace which is felt by most people to attach to circumcision?

4 We have mentioned all these instances with the object of showing that the aim of the divine power which bestowed on us the holy scriptures is not that we should accept only what is found in the letter; for occasionally the records taken in a literal sense are not true, but actually absurd and impossible, and even with the history that actually happened and the legislation that is in its literal sense useful there are other matters interwoven.

But someone may suppose that the former statement refers to all the scriptures, and may suspect us of saying that because some of the history did not happen, therefore none of it happened; and because a certain law is irrational or impossible when taken literally, therefore no laws ought to be kept to the letter; or that the records of the Savior's life are not true in a physical sense; or that no law or commandment of his ought to be obeyed. We must assert, therefore, that in regard to some things we are clearly aware that the historical fact is true; as that Abraham was buried in the double cave at Hebron, together with Isaac and Jacob and one wife of each of them;[63] and that Shechem was given as a portion to Joseph;[64] and that Jerusalem is the chief city of Judaea, in which a temple of God was built by Solomon; and thousands of other facts. For the passages which are historically true are far more numerous than those which are composed with purely spiritual meanings.

And again, who would deny that the command which says: "Honor your father and your mother,"[65] is useful quite apart from any spiritual interpretation, and that it ought certainly to be ob-

served, especially when we remember that the apostle Paul has quoted it in the self-same words?[66] And what are we to say of the following: "You shall not kill; you shall not commit adultery; you shall not steal; you shall not bear false witness"?[67]

Once again, in the gospel there are commandments written which need no inquiry whether they are to be kept literally or not, as that which says, "I say unto you, whoever is angry with his brother,"[68] and what follows: and, "I say unto you, swear not at all."[69] Here, too, is an injunction of the apostle of which the literal meaning must be retained: "Admonish the disorderly, encourage the faint-hearted, support the weak, be longsuffering toward all";[70] though in the case of the more earnest readers it is possible to preserve each of the meanings, that is, while not setting aside the commandment in its literal sense, to preserve the depths of the wisdom of God.

5 Nevertheless the exact reader will hesitate in regard to some passages, finding himself unable to decide without considerable investigation whether a particular incident, believed to be history, actually happened or not, and whether the literal meaning of a particular law is to be observed or not. Accordingly he who reads in an exact manner must, in obedience to the Savior's precept which says, "Search the scriptures,"[71] carefully investigate how far the literal meaning is true and how far it is impossible, and to the utmost of his power must trace out from the use of similar expressions the meaning scattered everywhere through the scriptures of that which when taken literally is impossible. . . .

---

[62] 1 Cor 7:18.
[63] Gen 23:2, 9, 19; 25:9, 10, 49:29–32; 50:13.
[64] Gen 48:22.
[65] Exod 20:12.
[66] Eph 6:2–3.
[67] Exod 20:13–16.
[68] Matt 5:22.
[69] Matt 5:34.
[70] 1 Thess 5:14.
[71] John 5:39.

75. Novatian: On the Trinity

Novation was a leading member of the Roman church in the mid-third century. After the persecution of the emperor Decius (251 C.E.), in which many members of the church had compromised their Christian convictions, Novation opposed the Bishop of Rome, Cornelius, by insisting on a rigorist position: the "lapsed" should be required to undergo a long and public period of penance before being admitted back into the church's good graces (see the introduction to Cyprian in Chapter 10). A schism erupted, as Novation and his party were excommunicated from the church only to start their own, with Novation himself elected as a rival pope. He was martyred several years later, during the persecution under the emperor Valerian (258 C.E.).

That the Novatian controversy was over not doctrine but church policy becomes clear upon reading Novatian's own treatise, "On the Trinity," a work that embodies a completely orthodox theology, as can be seen in the following excerpt, which deals with the nature of God.

Chapter 1

The rule of truth requires that we believe, first in God the Father and almighty Lord, the most perfect Creator of all things. He suspended the heavens above in their lofty height, made firm the earth with the heavy mass under it, poured forth the free flowing water of the seas; and he arranged all these, in full abundance and order, with appropriate and suitable appurtenances. In the firmament of heaven he summoned forth the light of the rising sun. He filled the candescent sphere of the moon with its monthly waxings to relieve the darkness. He also illuminated the rays of the stars with varying flashes of twinkling light. He willed that all these things in their lawfully regulated orbits encircle the entire earth's surface to form days, months, years, seasons, signs, and other things useful for humankind. On earth he lifted up the highest mountains to a peak, threw down the valleys into the lowlands, leveled the plains, and created the different kinds of animals for the various

needs of humans. He also hardened the sturdy trees of the forests to serve people's needs, brought forth the fruits of the earth for food, opened the mouths of springs, and poured them into the flowing rivers. After these things, lest he should have failed to provide our eyes with beautiful objects, he clothed all things with the various colors of flowers to delight all those who look upon them. Although the sea was wonderful both in its extent and for its usefulness, yet in it also he fashioned many kinds of living creatures, both small and large, which show the intelligence of the Creator by the variety of his creation. Not content with all this, lest the rushing and the flowing of the waters occupy territory not its own with loss to its human possessor, he enclosed its limits with shores, so that when the roaring waves and the foaming surge would come forth from the sea's bosom, they would return into themselves and would not pass beyond the limits allowed them. They would obey their prescribed laws, in order that people would

Novatian: "On the Trinity," from *Novatian*, ed. Russell J. DeSimone. Fathers of the Church, 67; Washington, D.C.: Catholic University Press of America, 1974. Used with permission.

more readily keep God's laws, seeing that even the elements themselves obey them.

After all these things had been accomplished, he placed man at the head of the world—man made to the image of God, endowed with intelligence, discernment, and prudence so that he could imitate God. Although the primordial elements of his body were earthly, nevertheless the substance was infused by a heavenly and divine breath. When God gave him all these things for his service, he willed that man alone should be free. Nevertheless, lest man's unrestrained freedom prove dangerous, God imposed a command in which he stated that indeed evil was not in the fruit of the tree, but warned that evil would follow if, in the use of his free will, man disregarded the command laid down. On the one hand, man ought to be free lest the image of God serve in unbecoming manner. On the other hand, a law had to be imposed that unrestrained liberty might not break forth even to contempt for its Giver. Hence, man might receive either merited rewards or due punishments as the result of his actions, recognizing these actions as his own doings, because it was in his power to act, through the movement of his mind in the one or the other direction. Whence, indeed, hated mortality comes back upon him. He could have avoided mortality by obedience, but he subjected himself to it by his headlong and perverse determination to be God. Nevertheless, God mercifully mitigated his punishment by cursing not so much man as his labors on earth. The fact that God searches for him does not proceed from any ignorance on the part of God but it manifests man's hope of a future discovery and salvation in Christ. Furthermore, that man was prevented from touching the wood of the tree of life did not spring from the malicious ill-will of envy but from a fear that man, living forever, would always bear about with him for his punishment an abiding guilt, had not Christ previously pardoned his sins.

In the higher regions—those above the very firmament itself, which at present are beyond our sight—he previously called the angels into being, arranged the spiritual powers, set over them the Thrones and Powers, created many other measureless spaces of heavens and mysterious works without limit. Therefore, even this measureless universe seems to be the latest of God's material creations rather than his only work. Even the regions that lie beneath the earth are not without their ruling powers duly appointed and set out. For there is a place to which are taken the souls of the just and the unjust, already aware of the sentence awaiting them at the future judgment. We see, therefore, that the vast works of God, exuberant on all sides, are not shut up within the confines of this world spacious to the utmost as we have said: but we can also contemplate them beneath both the depths and the heights of the world itself. Thus, after having considered the greatness of his works, we can fittingly admire the Maker of such a mighty mass.

Chapter 2

Over all these things is God himself, who contains all things and who leaves nothing devoid of himself; he has left no room for a superior god as some think. Since he himself has enclosed all things in the bosom of his perfect greatness and power, he is always intent on his own work and pervades all things, moves all things, gives life to all things, and observes all things. He binds together the discordant materials of all the elements into such harmony that out of these dissimilar elements, there exists a unique world so compacted by this consolidated harmony that no force can dissolve it, save when he alone who created it orders it to be dissolved in order to grant us greater blessings. We read that he contains all things; therefore nothing could have existed outside of him. For indeed he who has no beginning whatsoever, must necessarily experience no end, unless—far be the thought from us—he began to exist at a certain time and is therefore not above all things. But if he began to exist after something else, he would be inferior to that previously existing thing; hence he would be found to be of lesser power, since designated as subsequent even in time itself. For this reason, therefore, he is always infinite because there is nothing greater than he, ever eternal, because nothing is more ancient than he. In fact, that which is without a beginning can be preceded by nothing, because it lacks time. Therefore he is immortal, for he does not pass away to a consummate end. And since whatever is without a beginning is without a law, he excludes the restriction of time because he feels himself a debtor to no one.

Concerning him, therefore, and concerning those things which are of him and in him, the mind of humans cannot fittingly conceive what they are, how great they are, and of what their nature; nor has human eloquence the power to express his greatness. For all eloquence is certainly dumb and every mind is inadequate to conceive and to utter his greatness. In fact, he is greater than the mind itself, so that his greatness is inconceivable; for if he could be conceived, he would be less than the human mind which could conceive him. He is also greater than all speech, so that he cannot be expressed; for if he could be expressed, he would be less than human speech, which through expressing Him would then comprehend and contain him. Whatever can be thought about him is less than he; whatever can be uttered about him will be less than he when compared with him. When we are silent we can experience him to some extent, but we cannot express him in words as he really is. If, for instance, you should speak of him as light, you would be speaking of a created thing of his, not of him, you would not express what he is. If you should speak of him as power, you would be speaking of and bringing out his might rather than himself. If you should speak of him as majesty, you would be describing his honor rather than him. But why am I making a protracted affair of this matter by running through his attributes one by one? Once and for all I will sum up everything: whatever you might affirm about him would be expressing some possession or power of his rather than God himself. For what can you fittingly say or think about him who is above all speech and thought? There is only one thing that can fittingly be said or thought about him who is above all speech and thought: namely, that—within our power, our grasp, our understanding—there is only one way in which we may mentally conceive what God is—viz., by realizing that he is that Being of whose nature and great-

ness there is no possible understanding, nor even any possibility of thinking. If the keen sight of our eyes grows dim by looking at the sun so that their gaze, overpowered by the bright rays that meet it, cannot look at the orb itself, our mental vision undergoes this very same thing in its every thought of God. The more it endeavors to contemplate God, the more is it blinded by the light of its own thought. In fact, what (to repeat once more) can you worthily say about him, who is more sublime than all sublimity, loftier than all loftiness, more profound than all profundity, brighter than all light, more brilliant than all brilliance, more splendid than all splendor, mightier than all might, more powerful than all power, more beautiful than all beauty, truer than all truth, stronger than all strength, greater than all majesty, more potent than all potency, richer than all riches, and more prudent than all prudence, and kinder than all kindness, better than all goodness, more just than all justice, more clement than all clemency? Every kind of virtue must of necessity be less than he who is the God and Author of them all, so that it can really be said that God is that which is of such a nature that nothing can be compared to him. For he is above everything that can be said of him. he is, so to speak, an intelligent Being who without any beginning or ending in time engenders and fills all things and governs, for the good of all, with supreme and perfect reason, the causes of things naturally linked together.

Chapter 3

We acknowledge, therefore, and know that he is God, the Creator of all things; their Lord, because of his power; their Author, because of creation. "He," I say, "spoke and all things were made; he commanded, and all things came forth."[1] Of him it is written: "You have made all things in wisdom."[2] Moses says of him: "God is in heaven above and on earth below,"[3] and according to Isa-

---

[1]Ps 148:5.
[2]Ps 104:24.
[3]Deut 4:39.

iah, "He has measured the heavens with a span, the earth with the width of the fist, who looks upon the earth and makes it tremble, who holds the orb of the earth and those who live on it as if they were locusts; who weighed the mountains on scales and the groves on a balance, by the exact precision of the divine plan. And he laid out this weight of the earth's mass with precise equipoise, lest the huge ill-balanced mass should easily fall to ruin, if it were not balanced with proportionate weights."[4] It is he who says through the prophet: "I am God, and there is none beside me."[5] He says by means of the same prophet: "I will not give my majesty to another,"[6] so that he might exclude all heathens and heretics with their images, proving that he is not God who is made by the hand of an artificer; nor is he God whom heretical ingenuity, has devised. For he is not God whose existence requires an artificer. Again, he says through the prophet: "Heaven is my throne, earth the footstool under my feet: what sort of home will you build for me, or what is the place of my rest?"[7]—this to make it clear that since the world cannot contain him, much less can a temple enclose him. God says these things for our instruction, not to boast of himself. Nor does he seek from us glory for his own greatness; rather, as a Father, he desires to bestow on us God-fearing wisdom. He desires, moreover, to attract our minds, so cruel, so proud, and so obstinate in their rude ferocity, to gentleness; hence he says: "And upon whom shall my spirit rest but upon him who is humble and peaceful, and trembles at my words?"[8] Thus a person may know, to some extent, how great God is, while he learns to fear him through the spirit given to him. Ever desiring to become more completely known to us and to incite our minds to his worship, he said: "I am the Lord who made the light and created the darkness,"[9] that we may not think that a certain "nature"—I know not what—was the artificer of those alternations whereby the nights and days are regulated; but rather, and with greater truth, we may acknowledge God as their Creator. Since we cannot see him with the sight of our eyes, we learn to know him from the greatness, the power, and the majesty of his works. "For since the creation of the world," says the apostle, "his invisible attributes are clearly seen—his everlasting power also and divinity—being understood through the things that are made."[10] Thus the human mind, learning to know the hidden things from those which are manifest, may consider in spirit the greatness of the Maker from the greatness of his works which it sees with the eyes of the mind. The same apostle says of him: "To the King of the ages, who is immortal, invisible, the one only God, be honor and glory."[11] He who has surpassed the greatness of thought has passed beyond the contemplation of our eyes; for, he says, "from him and through him and in him are all things."[12] All things exist by his command, so that they are "from him"; they are set in order by his word and therefore "through him." Finally, all these things have recourse to his judgment so that, while they long for freedom "in him," after corruption has been done away with, they appear to be recalled "to him."

Chapter 4

The Lord rightly declares that God alone is good, of whose goodness the whole world is witness. He would have not have created it if he were not good. For if "all things were very good,"[13] it logically follows that not only do those things which were created good prove the Creator is good, but they also prove that those things which owe their origin to a good creator cannot be other than good themselves. All evil, therefore, is a departure from God. It is impossible that he who claims for himself the title of perfect Father and Judge would be the instigator or author of any form of evil, precisely because he is the Judge and the Avenger of every

---

[4]Isa 40:12, 22; Ps 104:5, 32.
[5]Isa 45:21–22.
[6]Isa 42:8; 48:11.
[7]Isa 66:1.
[8]Isa 66:2.
[9]Isa 45:6–7.
[10]Rom 1:20.
[11]1 Tim 1:17.
[12]Rom 11:36.
[13]Gen 1:31.

evil deed. A person encounters evil only by his departure from the good God. This very departure is blameworthy in a human, not because it was necessary but because the person himself willed it. Hence it was made clear to us not only what evil was but also from whom evil had taken its origin, lest there should seem to be envy in God.

He is always, therefore, equal to himself; he never changes or transforms himself into other forms, lest through change he should appear to be also mortal. For the modification implied in change from one thing to another involves a share in death of some sort. Therefore there is never any addition of parts or of glory in him, lest anything should seem to have ever been wanting to the perfect one. Nor can there be any question of diminution in him, for that would imply that some degree of mortality is in him. On the contrary, what he is, he always is; who he is he always is; such as he is, he always is. For increase in growth indicates a beginning; whereas any wasting away evidences death and destruction. And therefore he says: "I am God, and have not changed."[14] He always retains his manner of being, because what is not born is not subject to change. For—whatever that being may be that is God—this must always be true of him, that he always is God, preserving himself by his own powers. And therefore he says: "I am who am."[15] That which is has this name because it always preserves its same manner of being. Change takes away the name, "That which is"; for whatever changes at all is shown to be mortal by the very fact that it changes. It ceases to be what it was and consequently begins to be what it was not. Of necessity, then, God always retains his manner of being, because he is always like unto himself, always equal to himself without any loss arising from change. For that which is not born cannot change, since only those things undergo change which are made or which are begotten; whereas things which at one time were not, experience existence by coming into being, and by coming into being they undergo change. On the contrary, things which have neither birth nor maker are exempt from change because they have not a beginning, the cause of change.

And so God is said to be also unique since he has no equal. For God (whatever that Being may be that is God) must necessarily be supreme. Now whatever is supreme must be supreme in such wise that an equal is excluded. Therefore he must be the one and only being with whom nothing can be compared, because he has no equal. As the very nature of things demands, there cannot be two infinities. That alone is infinite which has absolutely neither beginning nor end; for whatever occupies the whole excludes the beginning of another. If the infinite does not contain all that exists (whatever it be), then it will find itself within that which contains it and therefore it will be less than the containing element. Hence it will cease to be God, since it has been brought under the dominion of another whose magnitude will include it because it is the smaller. As a result what contained it would itself claim to be God.

It results from this that God's own name is ineffable because it cannot be conceived. The name of a thing connotes whatever comes under the demands of its nature. For a name is significant of the reality which could be grasped from the name. However, when it is a question of something of such a nature that not even the intellectual powers themselves can form a proper concept, then how will it be expressed fittingly by a single word of designation, for it so exceeds the intellect that it is necessarily beyond the comprehension of any name? When God takes for himself a name or manifests it for certain reasons and on certain occasions, we know that it is not so much the real nature of the name that has been made known to us as a vague symbol appointed for our use, to which people may have recourse and find that they can appeal to God's mercy through it.

God is, therefore, immortal and incorruptible, experiencing neither diminution nor end of any sort. Because he is incorruptible, he is also immortal, and because he is immortal, he is therefore also incorruptible. Both attributes are reciprocally

---

[14]Mal 3:6.
[15]Exod 3:14.

linked together between and in themselves by a mutual relationship. Thus are they brought by the ensuing union to the condition of eternity: immortality proceeding from incorruptibility and incorruptibility coming from immortality.

Chapter 5

If in Scripture we consider instances of his legitimate wrath and descriptions of his anger and learn of the instances recorded of his hatred, we are not to regard these things asserted of him as examples of human vices. Although all these things can corrupt humans, they cannot vitiate the divine power in any way. Passions such as these are rightly said to exist in humans but would wrongly be declared to exist in God. Humans can be corrupted by them because they are capable of corruption; God cannot be corrupted by them because he is not capable of corruption. Therefore they have a power of their own which they can exercise only where they find passible matter, not where they find an impassible substance. The fact also that God is angry does not arise from any vice in him; rather he acts thus for our benefit. He is merciful even when he threatens, because by these threats people are re-

called to the right path. Fear is necessary for those who lack an incentive to good living, so that they who have rejected reason may at least be moved by terror. And so all these instances of anger, hatred, and the like, on God's part, are revealed, as the truth of the matter shows, for our healing and arise from deliberate purpose, neither from vice nor from weakness. Therefore they do not have the power to corrupt God. The different elements of which we are made are wont to arouse in us the discord of anger which corrupts us; but this diversity of elements cannot exist in God either by nature or from vice, because he cannot conceivably be made up of a union of corporeal parts. He is simple, without any corporeal admixture—whatever be the total of the being that only he himself knows—since he is called spirit.[16] Thus those things which are faulty and the cause of corruption in humans, inasmuch as they arise from the corruptibility of his body and matter itself, cannot exercise their power of corruptibility in God. As we have already said, they did indeed spring not from any vice in him but from reason. . . .

_____

[16]John 4:24.

➤┤◄►─○─◄►├◄

76. Dionysius of Rome:
Letter to Dionysius of Alexandria

As an example of the way orthodox theological opinions, when pursued rigorously, could lead to views that themselves were deemed heretical, consider the following letter written by Dionysius of Rome to his namesake, Dionysius of Alexandria (ca. 260 C.E.). The latter had taken a strong stand against patripassianism (supported by a Christian named

_____

Dionysius of Rome: Letter to Dionysius of Alexandria, from *Documents of the Christian Church*, ed. Henry Bettenson, 2d ed. © Oxford University Press, 1963. Reprinted by permission of Oxford University Press.

"Sabellius"), which maintained that Christ, the Son of God, was actually God the Father himself become human; but in voicing his opposition, Dionysius of Alexandria had gone too far in the other direction, in the opinion of his colleague in Rome. This letter warns that Dionysius should not differentiate *too* much between the Father and the Son, since to do so could lead one (a) to maintain that the Son was not eternal but had been created at some point in time, like other creatures, and/or (b) to think that there were three different Gods (Father, Son, and Spirit) instead of one God, as affirmed by orthodox Christians from time immemorial.

Evidently this letter had its effect, as Dionysius of Alexandria later convinced his counterpart in Rome that he was not in fact propounding a view of tritheism.

In this connexion I may naturally proceed to attack those who divide and cut up and destroy that most revered doctrine of the church of God, the Monarchy, reducing it to three powers and separated substances and three deities. For I learn that there are some of you, among the catechists and teachers of the Divine Word, who inculcate this opinion, who are, one might say, diametrically opposed to the views of Sabellius; he blasphemously says that the Son is the Father and the Father the Son, while they in a manner preach three Gods, dividing the sacred Monad into three substances foreign to each other and utterly separate. For the Divine Word must of necessity be united to the God of the Universe, and the Holy Spirit must have his habitation and abode in God; thus it is absolutely necessary that the Divine Triad be summed up and gathered into a unity, brought as it were to an apex, and by that Unity I mean the all sovereign God of the Universe. . . . Equally to be censured are they who hold that the Son is a work, and think that the Lord came into being, whereas the Divine Oracles testify to a generation fitting and becoming to him, but not to any fash-

ioning or making. . . . For if he came to be a Son, there was when he was not; but he was always, if, that is, he is in the Father, as he himself says, and if the Christ is Word and Wisdom and Power, as, you know, the Divine Scriptures say he is, and if these are attributes of God. For if the Son came into being there was when these attributes were not; therefore there was a time when God was without them; which is most absurd. . . . Neither then must we divide into three deities the wonderful and divine Monad: nor hinder the dignity and exceeding majesty of the Lord by describing him as a "work." But we must believe in God the Father all sovereign, and in Jesus Christ his Son and in the Holy Spirit, and hold that the Word is united to the God of the universe. For "I," says he, "and the Father are one,"[1] and "I in the Father and the Father in me."[2] For thus both the Holy Triad and the holy preaching of the Monarchy will be preserved.

---

[1]John 10:30.
[2]John 14:10.